DATE DUE

			PRINTED IN U.S.A.

Children's Literature Review

Guide to Gale Literary Criticism Series

When you need to review criticism of literary works, these are the Gale series to use:

If the author's death date is:

You should turn to:

After Dec. 31, 1959
(or author is still living)

CONTEMPORARY LITERARY CRITICISM

for example: Jorge Luis Borges, Anthony Burgess,
William Faulkner, Mary Gordon,
Ernest Hemingway, Iris Murdoch

1900 through 1959

TWENTIETH-CENTURY LITERARY CRITICISM
for example: Willa Cather, F. Scott Fitzgerald,
Henry James, Mark Twain, Virginia Woolf

1800 through 1899

NINETEENTH-CENTURY LITERATURE CRITICISM
for example: Fyodor Dostoevsky, Nathaniel Hawthorne,
George Sand, William Wordsworth

1400 through 1799

LITERATURE CRITICISM FROM 1400 TO 1800
(excluding Shakespeare)
for example: Anne Bradstreet, Daniel Defoe,
Alexander Pope, François Rabelais,
Jonathan Swift, Phillis Wheatley

SHAKESPEAREAN CRITICISM
Shakespeare's plays and poetry

Antiquity through 1399

CLASSICAL AND MEDIEVAL LITERATURE CRITICISM
for example: Dante, Homer, Plato, Sophocles, Vergil,
the Beowulf Poet

Gale also publishes related criticism series:

BLACK LITERATURE CRITICISM

This three-volume series presents criticisms of works by major black writers of the past two hundred years.

CHILDREN'S LITERATURE REVIEW

This series covers authors of all eras who have written for the preschool through high school audience.

SHORT STORY CRITICISM

This series covers the major short fiction writers of all nationalities and periods of literary history.

POETRY CRITICISM

This series covers poets of all nationalities and periods of literary history.

DRAMA CRITICISM

This series covers playwrights of all nationalities and periods of literary history.

ISSN 0362-4145

volume 29

Children's Literature Review

Excerpts from Reviews,
Criticism, and Commentary
on Books for Children
and Young People

Gerard J. Senick
Editor

Sharon R. Gunton
Associate Editor

Gale Research Inc. • *DETROIT* • *WASHINGTON, D.C.* • *LONDON*

STAFF

Gerard J. Senick, *Editor*

Judy Galens, Sharon R. Gunton, James E. Person, Jr., *Associate Editors*

James A. Edwards, Anna J. Sheets, Brian J. St. Germain, *Assistant Editors*

Jeanne A. Gough, *Permissions & Production Manager*

Linda M. Pugliese, *Production Supervisor*

Paul Lewon, Maureen A. Puhl, Camille Robinson, Jennifer VanSickle, *Editorial Associates*

Donna Craft, Rosita D'Souza, Sheila Walencewicz, *Editorial Assistants*

Sandra C. Davis, *Text Permissions Supervisor*

Maria Franklin, Josephine M. Keene, Michele M. Lonoconus, Denise M. Singleton,
Kimberly F. Smilay, *Permissions Associates*

Brandy C. Merritt, Shalice Shah, *Permissions Assistants*

Margaret A. Chamberlain, *Permissions Supervisor (Pictures)*

Pamela A. Hayes, *Permissions Associate*

Karla Kulkis, Nancy Rattenbury, Keith Reed, *Permissions Assistants*

Maureen Richards, *Research Supervisor*

Robert Lazich, Mary Beth McElmeel, Tamara C. Nott, *Editorial Associates*

Andrea Ghorai, Daniel J. Jankowski, Julie K. Kazmarin, *Editorial Assistants*

Mary Beth Trimper, *Production Director*

Mary Winterhalter, *Production Assistant*

Cynthia Baldwin, *Art Director*

C. J. Jonik, *Keyliner*

Contents

Preface

Children's literature has evolved into both a respected branch of creative writing and a successful industry. Currently, books for young readers are considered the most popular segment of publishing, while criticism of juvenile literature is instrumental in recording the literary or artistic development of the creators of children's books as well as the trends and controversies that result from changing values or attitudes about young people and their literature. Designed to provide a permanent, accessible record of this ongoing scholarship, *Children's Literature Review* (*CLR*) presents parents, teachers, and librarians—those responsible for bringing children and books together—with the opportunity to make informed choices when selecting reading materials for the young. In addition, *CLR* provides researchers of children's literature with easy access to a wide variety of critical information from English-language sources in the field. Users will find balanced overviews of the careers of the authors and illustrators of the books that children and young adults are reading; these entries, which contain excerpts from published criticism in books and periodicals, assist users by sparking ideas for papers and assignments and suggesting supplementary and classroom reading. Ann L. Kalkhoff, president and editor of *Children's Book Review Service Inc.,* writes that "*CLR* has filled a gap in the field of children's books, and it is one series that will never lose its validity or importance."

Scope of the Series

Each volume of *CLR* profiles the careers of a selection of authors and illustrators of books for children from preschool through high school. Author lists in each volume reflect these elements:

- an international scope.

- approximately fifteen authors of all eras.

- a variety of genres covered by children's literature: picture books, fiction, nonfiction, poetry, folklore, and drama.

Although earlier volumes of *CLR* emphasized critical material published after 1960, successive volumes have expanded their coverage to encompass important criticism written before 1960. Since many of the authors included in *CLR* are living and continue to write, their entries are updated periodically. Future volumes will supplement the entries of selected authors covered in earlier volumes as well as include criticism on the works of authors new to the series.

Organization of This Book

An author section consists of the following elements: author heading, author portrait, author introduction, excerpts of criticism (each followed by a bibliographical citation), and illustrations, when available.

- The **author heading** consists of the author's name followed by birth and death dates. The portion of the name outside the parentheses denotes the form under which the author is most frequently published. If the majority of the author's works for children were written under a pseudonym, the pseudonym will be listed in the author heading and the real name given on the first line of the author introduction. Also located at the beginning of the introduction are any other pseudonyms used by the author in writing for children and any name variations, including transliterated forms for authors whose languages use nonroman alphabets. Uncertainty as to a birth or death date is indicated by question marks.

- An **author portrait** is included when available.

- The **author introduction** contains information designed to introduce an author to *CLR* users by presenting an overview of the author's themes and styles, occasional biographical facts that relate to the author's literary career or critical responses to the author's works, and information about major awards and prizes the author has received. Introductions also list a group of representative titles for which the author or illustrator being profiled is best known; this section, which begins with the words "major works include," follows the genre line of the introduction. Where applicable, introductions conclude with references to additional entries in biographical and critical reference series published by Gale Research Inc. These sources include past volumes of *CLR* as well as *Authors & Artists for Young Adults, Classical and Medieval Literature Criticism, Contempo-*

rary Authors, Contemporary Authors Autobiography Series, Contemporary Authors Bibliographical Series, Contemporary Literary Criticism, Dictionary of Literary Biography, Drama Criticism, Nineteenth-Century Literature Criticism, Poetry Criticism, Short Story Criticism, Something about the Author, Something about the Author Autobiography Series, Twentieth-Century Literary Criticism, and *Yesterday's Authors of Books for Children.*

- **Criticism** is located in three sections: **author's commentary** (when available), **general commentary** (when available), and **title commentary** (in which commentary on specific titles appears). Centered headings introduce each section, in which criticism is arranged chronologically. Titles by authors being profiled are highlighted in boldface type within the text for easier access by readers.

The **author's commentary** presents background material written by the author or by an interviewer. This commentary may cover a specific work or several works. Author's commentary on more than one work appears after the author introduction, while commentary on an individual book follows the title entry heading.

The **general commentary** consists of critical excerpts that consider more than one work by the author or illustrator being profiled. General commentary is preceded by the critic's name in boldface type or, in the case of unsigned criticism, by the title of the journal. Occasionally, *CLR* features entries that emphasize general criticism on the overall career of an author or illustrator. When appropriate, a selection of reviews is included to supplement the general commentary.

The **title commentary** begins with title entry headings, which precede the criticism on a title and cite publication information on the work being reviewed. Title headings list the title of the work as it appeared in its first English-language edition. The first English-language publication date of each work is listed in parentheses following the title. Differing U.S. and British titles follow the publication date within the parentheses.

Entries in each title commentary section consist of critical excerpts on the author's individual works, arranged chronologically by publication date. The entries generally contain two to six reviews per title, depending on the stature of the book and the amount of criticism it has generated. The editors select titles that reflect the entire scope of the author's literary contribution, covering each genre and subject. An effort is made to reprint criticism that represents the full range of each title's reception—from the year of its initial publication to current assessments. Thus, the reader is provided with a record of the author's critical history. Publication information (such as publisher names and book prices) and parenthetical numerical references (such as footnotes or page and line references to specific editions of works) have been deleted at the editor's discretion to provide smoother reading of the text.

- Selected excerpts are preceded by **explanatory notes,** which provide information on the critic or work of criticism to enhance the reader's understanding of the excerpt.

- A complete **bibliographical citation** designed to facilitate the location of the original book or article follows each piece of criticism.

- Numerous **illustrations** are featured in *CLR.* For entries on illustrators, an effort has been made to include illustrations that reflect the characteristics discussed in the criticism. Entries on major authors who do not illustrate their own works may also include photographs and other illustrative material pertinent to the authors' careers.

Special Features

Entries on authors who are also illustrators will occasionally feature commentary on selected works illustrated but not written by the author being profiled. These works are strongly associated with the illustrator and have received critical acclaim for their art. By including critical comment on works of this type, the editors wish to provide a more complete representation of the author's total career. Criticism on these works has been chosen to stress artistic, rather than literary, contributions. Title entry headings for works illustrated by the author being profiled are arranged chronologically within the entry by date of publication and include notes identifying the author of the illustrated work. In order to provide easier access for users, all titles illustrated by the subject of the entry will be boldfaced.

CLR also includes entries on prominent illustrators who have contributed to the field of children's literature. These entries are designed to represent the development of the illustrator as an artist rather than as a literary stylist. The illustrator's section is organized like that of an author, with two exceptions: the introduction presents an overview of the illustrator's styles and techniques rather than outlining his or her literary background, and the commentary written by the illustrator on his or her works is called "illustrator's commentary" rather than "author's commentary." Title entry headings are followed by explanatory notes identifying the author of the illustrated work. All titles of books containing illustrations by the artist being profiled as well as individual illustrations from these books are highlighted in boldface type.

Other Features

• The **acknowledgments,** which immediately follow the preface, list the sources from which material has been reprinted in the volume. It does not, however, list every book or periodical consulted for the volume.

• The **cumulative index to authors** lists all of the authors who have appeared in *CLR* with cross-references to the various literary criticism series and the biographical and autobiographical series published by Gale Research Inc. A full listing of the series titles appears on the first page of the indexes of this volume.

• The **cumulative nationality index** lists authors alphabetically under their respective nationalities. Author names are followed by the volume number(s) in which they appear. Authors who have changed citizenship or whose current citizenship is not reflected in biographical sources appear under both their original nationality and that of their current residence.

• The **cumulative title index** lists titles covered in *CLR* followed by the volume and page number where criticism begins.

A Note to the Reader

CLR is one of several critical reference sources in the Literature Criticism Series published by Gale Research Inc. When writing papers, students who quote directly from any volume in the Literature Criticism Series may use the following general forms to footnote reprinted criticism. The first example pertains to material drawn from periodicals, the second to material reprinted from books.

[1] T. S. Eliot, "John Donne," *The Nation and the Athenaeum,* 33 (9 June 1923), 321-32; excerpted and reprinted in *Literature Criticism from 1400 to 1800,* Vol. 10, ed. James E. Person, Jr. (Detroit: Gale Research, 1989), pp. 28-9.

[1] Henry Brooke, *Leslie Brooke and Johnny Crow* (Frederick Warne, 1982); excerpted and reprinted in *Children's Literature Review,* Vol. 20, ed. Gerard J. Senick (Detroit: Gale Research, 1990), p. 47.

Suggestions Are Welcome

In response to various suggestions, several features have been added to *CLR* since the series began, including author entries on retellers of traditional literature as well as those who have been the first to record oral tales and other folklore; entries on prominent illustrators featuring commentary on their styles and techniques; entries on authors whose works are considered controversial; occasional entries devoted to criticism on a single work or a series of works by a major author; sections in author introductions that list major works by the author or illustrator being profiled; explanatory notes that provide information on the critic or work of criticism to enhance the usefulness of the excerpt; more extensive illustrative material, such as holographs of manuscript pages and photographs of people and places pertinent to the authors' careers; a cumulative nationality index for easy access to authors by nationality; and occasional guest essays written specifically for *CLR* by prominent critics on subjects of their choice.

Readers who wish to suggest authors to appear in future volumes, or who have other suggestions, are cordially invited to write the editor.

ACKNOWLEDGMENTS

The editors wish to thank the copyright holders of the excerpted criticism included in this volume, the permissions managers of many book and magazine publishing companies for assisting us in securing reprint rights, and Anthony Bogucki for assistance with copyright research. We are also grateful to the staffs of the Detroit Public Library, the Library of Congress, the University of Detroit Library, Wayne State University Purdy/Kresge Library Complex, and the University of Michigan Libraries for making their resources available to us. Following is a list of the copyright holders who granted us permission to reprint material in this volume of CLR. Every effort has been made to trace copyright, but if omissions have been made, please let us know.

COPYRIGHTED EXCERPTS IN *CLR* VOLUME 29, WERE REPRINTED FROM THE FOLLOWING PERIODICALS:

The ALAN Review, v. 12, Spring, 1985; v. 19, Fall, 1991. Both reprinted by permission of the publisher.—*America,* v. 111, November 21, 1964. All rights reserved. Reprinted with permission of America Press, Inc., 106 West 56th Street, New York, NY 10019.—*Appraisal: Science Books for Young People,* v. 16, Winter, 1983; v. 20, Summer, 1987. Copyright © 1983, 1987 by the Children's Science Book Review Committee. Both reprinted by permission of the publisher.—*Best Sellers,* v. 24, October 15, 1964. Copyright 1964, by the University of Scranton. Reprinted by permission of the publisher./ v. 37, December, 1977; v. 43, June, 1983. Copyright © 1977, 1983 Helen Dwight Reid Educational Foundation. Both reprinted by permission of the publisher.—*Book World—The Washington Post,* May 4, 1969; November 8, 1970. © 1969, 1970 Postrib Corp. Both reprinted by courtesy of the *Chicago Tribune* and *The Washington Post./* May 19, 1974; May 13, 1979; May 10, 1981; July 11, 1982; May 11, 1986; July 20, 1986; August 12, 1990; November 10, 1991; December 1, 1991. © 1974, 1979, 1981, 1982, 1986, 1990, 1991, *The Washington Post.* All reprinted with permission of the publisher.—*Bookbird,* v. XV, September 15, 1977; June 15, 1990. Both reprinted by permission of the publisher.—*Booklist,* v. 72, January 1, 1976; v. 72, June 15, 1976; v. 74, June 1, 1978; v. 75, February 15, 1979; v. 75, May 15, 1979; v. 76, December 1, 1979; v. 76, July 1, 1980; v. 77, November 15, 1980; v. 77, May 1, 1981; v. 77, June 15, 1981; v. 78, December 1, 1981; v. 78, July, 1982; v. 79, November 1, 1982; v. 79, March 1, 1983; v. 79, April 1, 1983; v. 79, June 15, 1983; v. 79, August, 1983; v. 80, October, 1983; v. 80, November 15, 1983; v. 80, February 15, 1984; v. 81, January 15, 1985; v. 82, September 1, 1985; v. 82, October 1, 1985; v. 82, March 15, 1986; v. 82, July, 1986; v. 83, November 1, 1986; v. 83, May 1, 1987; v. 83, June 1, 1987; v. 84, September 1, 1987; v. 84, December, 1987; v. 85, April 1, 1989; v. 85, April 15, 1989; v. 85, May 1, 1989; v. 86, October 15, 1989; v. 86, January 15, 1990; v. 86, May 15, 1990; v. 87, October 1, 1990; v. 87, December 15, 1990; v. 88, September 1, 1991; v. 88, September 15, 1991; v. 88, November 1, 1991. Copyright © 1976, 1978, 1979, 1980, 1981, 1982, 1983, 1984, 1985, 1986, 1987, 1989, 1990, 1991 by the American Library Association. All reprinted by permission of the publisher.—*Books for Keeps,* n. 59, November, 1989; n. 65, November, 1990; n. 69, July, 1991. © School Bookshop Association 1989, 1990, 1991. All reprinted by permission of the publisher.—*Books for Your Children,* v. 24, Summer, 1989; v. 26, Summer, 1991. © *Books for Your Children* 1989, 1991. Both reprinted by permission of the publisher.—*British Book News Children's Books,* December, 1986; September, 1987; December, 1987. © The British Council, 1986, 1987. All reprinted by permission of the publisher.—*Bulletin of the Center for Children's Books,* v. XV, March, 1962; v. 24, May, 1971; v. 25, September, 1971; v. 27, November, 1973; v. 27, May, 1974; v. 28, July-August, 1975; v. 29, November, 1975; v. 30, January, 1977; v. 31, March, 1978; v. 32, November, 1978; v. 29, March, 1979; v. 33, June, 1980; v. 34, November, 1980; v. 34, January, 1981; v. 34, March, 1981; v. 34, April, 1981; v. 35, November, 1981; v. 35, May, 1982; v. 35, July-August, 1982; v. 38, November, 1984; v. 38, June, 1985; v. 39, September, 1985; v. 39, December, 1985; v. 39, May, 1986; v. 40, November, 1986; v. 40, February, 1987; v. 41, April, 1988; v. 42, October, 1988; v. 42, November, 1988; v. 42, May, 1989; v. 43, March, 1990; v. 43, July-August, 1990; v. 44, November, 1990; v. 44, April, 1991; v. 45, October, 1991; v. 45, April, 1992. Copyright © 1962, 1971, 1973, 1974, 1975, 1977, 1978, 1979, 1980, 1981, 1982, 1984, 1985, 1986, 1987, 1988, 1989, 1990, 1991, 1992 by The University of Chicago. All reprinted by permission of The University of Chicago Press.—*Catholic Library World,* v. 36, January, 1965. Reprinted by permission of the publisher.—*Chicago Sunday Tribune Magazine of Books,* November 13, 1955; May 24, 1959; December 11, 1960. All reprinted by courtesy of the *Chicago Tribune.*—*Chicago Tribune,* December 27, 1953. Copyrighted 1953, renewed 1981, Chicago Tribune Company. All rights reserved. Used with permission.—*Children's Book News,* London, v. 3, March-April, 1968; v. 4, July-August, 1969. Copyright © 1968, 1969 by Baker Book Services Ltd. Both reprinted by permission of the publisher.—*Children's Book Review,* v. II, September, 1972; v. IV Spring, 1974; v. VI, October, 1976. © 1972, 1974, 1976 by Five Owls Press Ltd. All rights reserved. All reprinted by permission of the publisher.—*Children's Book Review Service,* v. 12, February, 1984; v. 14, November, 1985; v. 18, December, 1989. Copyright © 1984, 1985, 1989 Children's Book Review Service Inc. All reprinted by permission of the

COPYRIGHTED EXCERPTS IN *CLR,* VOLUME 29, WERE REPRINTED FROM THE FOLLOWING BOOKS:

Children's
Literature
Review

Marc Brown

1946-

American author and illustrator of picture books, fiction, and nonfiction.

Major works include *Arthur's Eyes* (1979), *Why the Tides Ebb and Flow* (written by Joan Chase Bowden, 1979), *The Bionic Bunny Show* (with Laurene Krasny Brown, 1984), *Dinosaurs Divorce: A Guide for Changing Families* (with Laurene Krasny Brown, 1986).

An author-illustrator of humorous and educational books for preschoolers and early elementary students, Brown is best known for the "Arthur Adventure" series, a collection of more than a dozen anthropomorphic tales featuring young Arthur the aardvark. Like much of Brown's other work, which ranges from counting and how-to books to comic-strip style works discussing modern-day problems, the Arthur stories are based on Brown's personal life and cover such topics as self-acceptance, friendship, fear, and leadership amid school and family experiences. The recurrent message of these works is one of triumph and well-being through love and understanding. Brown's heavily lined pen-and-ink and pencil-with-watercolor drawings serve as striking complements to his generally light narratives. His technique is further distinguished by playful visual games and meaningful commentary in the form of pictorial subtexts which help enhance the reader's attention and understanding. Since 1984 Brown has collaborated with his second wife, child psychologist and writer Laurene Krasny Brown, on a number of projects, including *The Bionic Bunny Show* and *Dinosaurs Divorce: A Guide for Changing Families*. The partnership allows him to focus more exclusively on his artwork, which he considers his obvious métier. As he explained in an autobiographical sidelight for *Something about the Author:* "When Laurie and I do a book together we work in our separate studios—she on the text, I on the pictures. But we consult often, contributing ideas to every aspect of the book. Laurie is an expert nonfiction writer, researcher, and organizer. I generally cede all those responsibilities to her, although I suggest particular lines of dialogue or individual episodes."

At the beginning of his career, Brown was an avid student of painting and illustration, an admirer of such notable figures as Georges Seurat, Maurice Sendak, and Marc Chagall, whom Brown honored by altering his given name. Following his graduation from the Cleveland Institute of Art in 1969, he worked first as a textbook illustrator for Houghton Mifflin before undertaking two independent assignments which proved important to his creative development, Isaac Asimov's *What Makes the Sun Shine?* (1970) and Norma Farber's *I Found Them in the Yellow Pages* (1972). In 1976 came his first work as both author and illustrator, *Arthur's Nose,* which Brown views as an artistic breakthrough. Like the other books in Brown's highly successful and continuing series, *Arthur's Nose* con-

cerns the typical childhood fears and frustrations—in this case, an unusually long nose—of a likable, mild-mannered elementary student in the animal world. Other works in the series include *Arthur's Eyes* (1979), *Arthur's Valentine* (1980), *Arthur Goes to Camp* (1982), *Arthur's Baby* (1987), and *Arthur Meets the President* (1991); each reassuringly treats a special event or problem in Arthur's life, the resolution of which facilitates his understanding of himself and others. Other key characters in these books include Arthur's family members, particularly his feisty younger sister, D. W., and Arthur's antagonistic classmate, Francine the ape. From them Brown conceived such spinoffs as *The True Francine* (1981), *D. W. Flips* (1987), and *D. W. All Wet* (1988).

Next to the "Arthur Adventure" books, which many critics describe as comfortably predictable, sensitive, witty, and endearing, Brown's single most applauded work of humor is *The Bionic Bunny Show,* which is both a Superman-spoof and an entertaining guide to how television shows are produced. The first collaboration between Brown and his wife, *Bionic Bunny* was followed by other joint efforts which include *Dinosaurs Divorce, Visiting the Art Museum* (1986), *Dinosaurs Travel: A Guide for Fami-*

1

lies on the Go (1988), and *Dinosaurs to the Rescue!: A Guide to Protecting Our Planet* (1992). Of these practical guides, by far the most serious is *Dinosaurs Divorce*, a thorough, well-regarded discussion aid for families involved in divorce. Here Brown's anthropomorphic drawings, serviceable even in his lightweight Arthur books, are especially appropriate as a means for softening his potentially distressing subject matter.

Aside from the rare charge that some of his artwork demonstrates carelessness or insensitivity, or the more common criticism that his story lines and text are occasionally uninspired, Brown has enjoyed wide approval for his long list of publications for children. Among his numerous awards are the Children's Choice by the Children's Book Council and the International Reading Association for *Arthur's Nose* in 1976, *Arthur's Eyes* in 1980, *Arthur's Valentine* in 1981, and *The True Francine, Arthur's Halloween,* and *Arthur Goes to Camp* in 1982; the *Boston Globe/Horn Book* Honor Award for Illustration for Joan Chase Bowden's *Why the Tides Ebb and Flow* in 1980; and one of the Library of Congress's Book of the Year awards for the illustrations in M. B. Christian's *Swamp Monsters* in 1985.

(See also *Something about the Author,* Vols. 10, 53; and *Contemporary Authors,* Vols. 69-72, rev. ed.)

AUTHOR'S COMMENTARY

I seem to have more ideas for books I would like to do than time to do them. I also love illustrating other people's stories. In the children's-book world you often get stereotyped—just as actors do. I have to credit Walter Lorraine for allowing me to draw people for the first time in *Why the Tides Ebb and Flow.* I had a wonderful time illustrating that book, and everyone was surprised that I could draw people. I feel I am capable of doing many different kinds of things that I haven't made happen for myself—yet.

Usually my story ideas come from something that happens in real life. My sons were eating dinner one night, and they were having mashed potatoes and little peas, or rather *heaving* mashed potatoes and little peas. That prompted me to look for a good book on manners at the library. The ones I found were very stale. I wanted a fun manners book. A friend of mine, Stephen Krensky, and I worked on the book, *Perfect Pigs. Dinosaurs, Beware!* evolved from growing up with a sister who was accident prone. She was the only person I ever knew who got her foot caught in the electric door of a supermarket on the same day that she was hit in the nose by a baseball—watching the game!

Again, I was observing my children at the time, seeing how independent they and their peers had to be at such a young age. Many were latchkey children who had little instruction and information from their parents. I wanted to give these children the information they needed to take care of themselves. I used dinosaurs because I found that the content of the book might be too frightening. Dinosaurs—because they aren't real—seemed ideal, and, of course, children are always interested in them. It also allowed me to use humor. Humor is an important creative element for me. I think children learn better when humor is involved in the teaching process.

If I'm originating the idea and I'm writing the book, I always struggle with the writing. I mean *struggle.* Writing is a necessary chore for me to get through in order to do the pictures and see the whole idea happen. I often create thirty versions of the book before I will show it to anyone. Sometimes I will put the book away for a year before I feel I can even finish it. All this for just a simple picture-book text, thirty-two pages. I don't type or use a word processor. I use pencil and paper. I cut up the paper and move things around with scotch tape and make a long strip of these ideas. I then put them into the proper sequence. Once I have the right sequence I start to think of picture possibilities. But actually I am always conscious of the picture possibilities right from the start, thinking about which words I can replace with pictures.

When I feel that I have a text that's solid, I will show it to my editor, and she usually reacts to it and will point out areas that are weak and strong. I then do thumbnail sketches, then a dummy, and lastly turn these ideas into full-size drawings. More and more, I find myself wanting to make my drawings freer and more effortless. In my Arthur books I am always struggling with a tone of informality so that children can just fall into these books and have fun with them. I want children to enjoy reading them. I feel there is a place for books like that. I hear from people all the time that children come into libraries hunting for more Arthur books; when they find they are all checked out, the children find other books to read. They discover that there is life beyond Arthur, and some very good life at that.

I want the art to feel light. Usually I work over my full-scale sketches on a light table with permanent ink pens that will not run or blur when I go over them with watercolor. When they are dry I go back into the drawings with colored pencil to add more detail and to build texture without making the art look too overworked. Sometimes I have the tendency to overwork things, so I have to start over again, trying to make the drawing freer, livelier, and more spontaneous. I want the drawings to look as if they happen effortlessly, and the watercolors should sparkle.

A very exciting part for me is adding the color. I love moving from the black-and-white world to the color world. I allow myself music when I get to that stage of the process. It's the fun part. By this point I feel as if I have really pulled the words and pictures together; it's working; it's going to be a book.

Children's books are one of the most carefully controlled and highly scrutinized media that reach a child's hands. As the creator, I have to know at which point I am investing too much energy in the preliminary process and when to hold back that enthusiasm and energy for the final product. That is always a struggle in a book because I may be working with an editor who wants to see it all. They can't see what I see in my mind. If I show them everything, I always feel I am beating the final product into the ground. I have this beautiful vision in my mind of the end result, and I am very protective of it. (pp. 567-70)

The limitations of camera, paper, and printing are constantly in my mind as I create my art. I consider materials that I can and can't use to get a certain effect. For instance, certain paints, because of their chemical qualities, don't reproduce well. That's something I've learned to accept over the years. Of course I'd love to spend more money in the production of my books, as every illustrator must.

For me the most satisfying part of the process is how children feel about these books. I never can get used to the fact that the book I create privately actually ends up in someone's hands. They like what I am doing. I never get tired of hearing that. (p. 570)

> *Marc Brown, "The Artist at Work: The Importance of Humor," in* The Horn Book Magazine, *Vol. LXVI, No. 5, September-October, 1990, pp. 563-70.*

TITLE COMMENTARY

Arthur's Nose (1976)

The species is novel but the story an old one: Arthur the aardvark doesn't like his nose, but when Dr. Louise the rhinologist (guess what kind of animal) lets him try on some others for size (chicken . . . fish . . . elephant . . . toucan . . .) he decides not to make a change after all. His friends, who used to laugh at him, now accept him as he is, for "There's a lot more to Arthur than his nose"—but not much that makes him different from a menagerie of other picture book patients.

> *A review of "Arthur's Nose," in* Kirkus Reviews, *Vol. XLIV, No. 3, February 1, 1976, p. 128.*

Marc Brown has illustrated several books but this is the first he has written as well. It's a winner. Arthur the aardvark frets because his nose is (he feels) unattractive and so long it's a nuisance. He suffers more than others when he has a cold; in school, the girl seated in front of Arthur complains that his nose is constantly poking her. Arthur seeks the advice of a plastic surgeon in hopes of getting himself a new, no-nonsense, handsome proboscis. The smart lady doctor (a rhino) gives Arthur pictures of various noses to choose from. Will he be happy with the nose of a goat, a mouse, an alligator, or what? The answer is not really a surprise but the storyteller gives a neat twist to the ending. His bright pictures are in keeping with the text.

> *A review of "Arthur's Nose," in* Publishers Weekly, *Vol. 209, No. 17, April 26, 1976, p. 58.*

One, Two, Three: An Animal Counting Book (1976)

Number books with so many examples can grow monotonous; however, Brown's expertly drawn illustrations avoid this problem by containing numerous surprises for observant children. In the group of four alligators, two have a

His friends thought his nose was funny. But what could he do about it?

From Arthur's Nose, *written and illustrated by Marc Brown.*

jagged series of the number four to represent sharp teeth. The tails of six monkeys form together in the shape of the number six. In addition, every animal has a slightly different playful pose and expression. The author-illustrator has also taken pains to place the animals in sets: for example, the number nine is made up of three groups of threes. A carefully put together and pleasing book.

> *Gemma DeVinney, in a review of "One Two Three: An Animal Counting Book," in* School Library Journal, *Vol. 23, No. 3, November, 1976, p. 43.*

One elephant, 2 gnus, three raccoons, and so on, up to twenty turtles; each picture carries the number, the requisite number of animals, and—on most of the drawings of individual animals—the number again. Each of the three raccoons, for example, has a "3" tucked in its ear. The game element can reinforce memorization of the digits, and the drawings are attractive, but the concept is neither unusual nor unusually well executed.

> *Zena Sutherland, in a review of "One Two Three: An Animal Counting Book," in* Bulletin of the Center for Children's Books, *Vol. 30, No. 5, January, 1977, p. 71.*

It would be easy to write a highly critical review of this book. Like so many others written for very young children, it is very expensive (more than 14¢ per page; at that rate an average novel would cost $35.00). Mathematical purists may be concerned about symbolism: Some of the numerals appear on the pictures of individual animals (like brands of reindeer, for example. This could be misleading, but it isn't and the book serves its purpose). It is a counting book designed to be used by an adult with a small child. Children will enjoy counting the animals, saying the numbers and finding where they appear in the pictures (on alligator teeth for example.) We need not worry that they will remember 18 as 18 hippopotamuses—if that helps them to remember this number, fine. They will learn that it applies to other things elsewhere.

> *Gerald R. Rising, in a review of "One, Two, Three: An Animal Counting Book," in* Science Books & Films, *Vol. XIII, No. 2, September, 1977, p. 94.*

Marc Brown's Full House (1977)

Three mini-sequences, in an uninspired adaptation of the comic strip format. Brown starts with a cat's account of how his fussy former owners got rid of all their pets and settled down with the "perfect" one, a stuffed moose head. The last bit (you can't call it a story) is a sort of reversal of the first, featuring "Frisbee the freeloader's dream" with whom the other animals move in. And, on three double-page house cutaways that fall before, between, and behind the other two numbers, a family of monsters goes about its daily rounds. Brown fills his studio-card-type cartoons with lots of black lines and dashes—which makes for fur on the animals, grain on the wood fence, etc., but can't cover up the pervasive vacuity of the project.

> *A review of "Marc Brown's Full House," in* Kirkus Reviews, *Vol. XLV, No. 22, November 15, 1977, p. 1191.*

The comic book layout—three cutaway views of the Monsters' home and two stories concerning the perfect pet (a stuffed moose head) and Frisbee (a gracious host)—will attract children, but the episodic adventures, though mildly funny, are so short they will leave readers feeling cheated. There are details for browsers to discover, but, despite the busy artwork, **Marc Brown's Full House** is emptier than it at first appears.

> *Carol Chatfield, in a review of "Mark Brown's Full House," in* School Library Journal, *Vol. 24, No. 5, January, 1978, p. 76.*

Lenny and Lola (1978)

Illustrated with Brown's usual heavy hatching, this is the story of trapeze partners Lenny and Lola (like the audience and the other performers, they happen to be dogs), who break up when Lola tries a solo flourish and Lenny objects. Unsuccessful with other partners, Lenny goes solo (a tear in his eye suggests his feelings), but one night as he prepares to do his special "triples" Lola appears on the opposite platform. "They both did triples. The crowd went wild!" Then "the magic happened" and together they fly round the tent, out the door, and up into the stars. There's not much magic in Brown's performance, though the ending does pick up an otherwise ordinary routine.

> *A review of "Lenny and Lola," in* Kirkus Reviews, *Vol. XLVI, No. 8, April 15, 1978, p. 431.*

[The final scene of this book, with its] fantasy break may be too much for some, but it's pulled off with style and a kind of unquestioned continuity from the couple's skill and togetherness, which is magic in itself. The author's pen-and-ink drawings, washed in gold, combine a heavily lined technique with a light touch of humor for an unusual picture book effect. (p. 1550)

> *Betsy Hearne, in a review of "Lenny and Lola," in* Booklist, *Vol. 74, No. 19, June 1, 1978, pp. 1549-50.*

A delightful, if offbeat, circus fantasy? Hardly. The writing is forced (e.g., "They moved like the works of a beautiful clock"; "The trapeze had become a part of him."). The woodcut illustrations are technically well done and expressive, but they are too grounded in realism to complement the fantastic element. No encores, please. (pp. 103-04)

> *Gemma DeVinney, in a review of "Lenny and Lola," in* School Library Journal, *Vol. 25, No. 1, September, 1978, pp. 103-04.*

Moose and Goose (1978)

Moose lives upstairs, making noise and much trouble for Goose who lives downstairs and mainly complains. After suffering not-so-silently Goose accepts Moose's offer to change apartments. This is an adult problem, not a topic for a children's book. The story line, which unfairly makes Goose look silly and Moose a hero, is just as heavy-handed and overbearing as the black-and-white drawings.

> *Anne Boes, in a review of "Moose and Goose," in* School Library Journal, *Vol. 25, No. 5, January, 1979, p. 40.*

A seemingly lighthearted story of the conflict between a tap dancing, party-giving moose and his goose neighbor who wants to sleep, this book nevertheless should not be taken lightly. It contains what may be one of the most offensive recent examples of racial stereotyping, and is either a throwback to the practices of several decades ago or a leap to the forefront of the current resurgence of racism in the arts.

Among the book's anthropomorphic characters are three hip musicians who arrive with their instruments at Moose's party—a hippopotamus with his tuba, a bear lugging a drum, and a baboon with a trombone tucked under his arm. The baboon, his long tail curling out from underneath his coat, sports a well-shaped Afro.

Remember the thirties and forties? Remember Black soldiers fighting the war in Europe, while white soldiers spread rumors that they were actually members of the ape family, hiding hairy tails inside their uniforms? Remember the Hollywood portrayals, now enjoying a second life on television, of Africans as a slightly elevated variety of ape?

We can expect that Black critics will be reminded that this book is intended to be fun. They will be accused of "taking themselves too seriously" and advised of the need to develop "a sense of humor." I doubt that they will heed this advice. *Moose and Goose* is blatantly racist. The only question that remains is whether this 1978 publication is an anachronism or a part of the avant-garde. I fear the latter. (pp. 25-6)

> *Eloise Greenfield, in a review of "Moose and Goose," in* Interracial Books for Children Bulletin, *Vol. 10, Nos. 1 & 2, 1979, pp. 25-6.*

Arthur's Eyes (1979)

Poor eyesight is Arthur's problem. It keeps him from seeing math problems and shooting baskets. It makes him persona non grata with Francine, who asks sarcastically "Are you blind?" The optometrist, Dr. Iris (hurray for non-sexist career people!) intensifies the problem by fitting Arthur with glasses. Myopic Mother thinks her son looks brilliant, and photopic Father believes him handsome, but Arthur's difficulties increase. His classmates call him four-eyes and sissy. Naturally, Arthur pretends to lose his spectacles. That leads to blundering into the girls bathroom, and the ultimate discovery that his male second grade teacher dons corrective prisms for reading. Thus is Arthur saved. He sees well, gets his math problems correct, sinks more baskets than does Francine, and is the model for her donning paneless movie star shades. The satisfactory resolution finds both wearing optics for the class photo. The pictures are large and bright. Brown has endowed his animal characters (Arthur is an ant eater, Francine an ape) with distinctive personalities. The Moose Teacher, with his buck teeth, is quite appealing. The women are ample bosomed and nonthreatening. For children who are comfortable with Waber's Lyle stories, this book will be a good choice.

> *Reva Pitch Margolis, in a review of "Arthur's Eyes," in* School Library Journal, *Vol. 26, No. 1, September, 1979, p. 104.*

Arthur, a myopic animal of uncertain species, discovers that the advantages of wearing glasses definitely outweigh the disadvantages—though this did not seem to be the case at first. Such overt didacticism is not, in my opinion, the best way to improve the image of children who wear spectacles. It is all rather too obvious for my taste, but some of the incidents and the jokey illustrations in this very American story will undoubtedly amuse young readers.

> *Jill Bennett, in a review of "Arthur's Eyes," in* The School Librarian, *Vol. 30, No. 2, June, 1982, p. 119.*

This is Arthur before he got glasses. He looked fine, but he couldn't see very well. Sometimes he got headaches.

From Arthur's Eyes, *written and illustrated by Marc Brown.*

The Cloud over Clarence (1979)

Clarence the klutzy cat bumbles his way through his birthday from the moment he rolls out of bed and onto his turtle to the more embarrassing moment at his party when he serves friend Danny's ice cream scoop on top of Danny's head. Clarence is worried when his friends retreat to whisper, but then they deliver the "best of all his birthday presents"—a note expressing loving concern and urging him to "think about what you are doing." And just-like-that, "from now on he would always think about what he was doing." But any four-year-old knows that it isn't that simple—and that this wistful word of guidance isn't a story.

> *A review of "The Cloud over Clarence," in* Kirkus Reviews, *Voll. XLVII, No. 17, September 1, 1979, p. 997.*

This simple idea is depicted amusingly by the full-page line and wash pictures. Rather than plumping up the theme, they act on an independent track, satisfying curiosities related to the inner workings of this unusual feline world. (How is a tabby's breakfast table set? What party games are preferred by kitties?) Simplicity in text and theme, combined with abundance of engaging supplementary pictures, makes this latest by author/illustrator Marc Brown a pleasant success.

> *Liza Bliss, in a review of "The Cloud over Clar-*

ence," in School Library Journal, *Vol. 26, No. 2, October, 1979, p. 134.*

Why the Tides Ebb and Flow (1979)

[Why the Tides Ebb and Flow *was written by Joan Chase Bowden.*]

A wonderful "just-so" story, with a bonus ending explaining more than the title promises. A stubborn old woman who needs a hut cannot get the Sky Spirit's attention. Then, craftly, she asks him only for a rock, and he "too quickly," grants her request. Forced to take notice when she takes the one in the bottom of the sea, Sky Spirit sends Little Dog, Young Maiden and then Young Man to plug the hole, but each fails. The old woman, however, sees that they will be her family and give her the attention and shelter she needs. She puts back the rock, and Sky Spirit promises that she can have it back, briefly, twice a day. But there is more to the story than an explanation for the draining and filling of the ocean. Its attractiveness rests not only on its rhythmic and idiomatic style, but also on the eye pleasing design and detail of the simple and expressive illustrations. Each double-page spread in charcoal pencil and ink on sepia-toned paper is bordered by a narrow geometric band recalling African folk art. Brown ingeniously overcomes the limits of sepia in conveying the "great, green ocean," while he makes the most of its advantages in suggesting the skin tone of the characters—whose faces viewers return to again and again. Perfectly harmonizing with the text, the pictures underscore its humor and drama, giving it a special ethnic character without diminishing the universality of its appeal.

> *Patricia Dooley, in a review of "Why the Tides Ebb and Flow," in* School Library Journal, *Vol. 26, No. 2, October, 1979, p. 134.*

[This] lyrical text, perfect for reading aloud, is touched with humor and lightly seasoned with onomatopoeic expressions. The elegant illustrations sweep in broad strokes across buff-colored pages, suggesting the strength of the elemental forces against which the defiant old woman wages her battle. The figures have a sculptured appearance, underscoring the story's mythic quality; their faces are marvelously responsive, striking the right balance between the heroic and the humanistic. A stylized geometric border frames the double-page spreads, containing without restraining and providing an effective contrast to the expansive, expressionistic line of the drawings. (p. 652)

> *Mary M. Burns, in a review of "Why the Tides Ebb and Flow," in* The Horn Book Magazine, *Vol. LV, No. 6, December, 1979, pp. 651-52.*

[This] story has an air of melancholy, which is curiously attractive, and there's a cozy quality in the resolution. This is enhanced by a heavy, smoky look in black-and-beige illustrations with blurred lines. Brown makes varying use of space and perspective, which gives a sense of action to the two-tone pictures and prevents them from looking static or dull. The design that borders each page gives the work a trim look.

> *Marilyn Kaye, in a review of "Why the Tides*

Ebb and Flow," in Booklist, *Vol. 76, No. 7, December 1, 1979, p. 553.*

Witches Four (1980)

Told in verse, this lightweight, amusing tale follows four witches through the sky. When their magic hats fall off, four homeless cats use them for houses until the witches return and demand them back. The cats protest, the witches foment a spell, and KERBOOMS—the crones are seen flying happily off in the sky—with four cats tucked beneath their hats. The rhythm breaks from time to time but not enough to detract when read aloud, and youngsters reading alone will find the pace easy to follow. Though the green-faced witches are somewhat garish, the total effect of the colorful illustrations sets a Halloween-time tone. (p. 1605)

> *Barbara Elleman, in a review of "Witches Four," in* Booklist, *Vol. 76, No. 21, July 1, 1980, pp. 1604-05.*

The four witches of the title have smiling green faces, wear spectacles and boots with turned-up toes, eat bat-wing sandwiches and brush their teeth with spider paste. . . . Marc Brown shows a good sense of design and texture in the warm and humorous watercolor and pen-and-ink drawings, but awkward rhyming and a slim plot may limit the book's usefulness with large groups. Norman Bridwell's *The Witch Next Door* (Scholastic, 1971) is more exciting for reading aloud.

> *Jean Hammon Zimmerman, in a review of "Witches Four," in* School Library Journal, *Vol. 27, No. 7, March, 1981, p. 129.*

Splendidly nasty details of their domestic life (frog-eye soap, bat-wing sandwiches) extend the account, in doggerel verse, of the day when the witches lost cats and hats at the same time and had difficulty in persuading the cats to give up new and comfortable shelters. The cheerfully grotesque illustrations are full of humour and offer plenty of enjoyment to the young who follow them, in nicely manipulated colour; the shade of the witches' complexions is especially amusing and suitable in this lively frolic.

> *Margery Fisher, in a review of "Witches Four," in* Growing Point, *Vol. 24, No. 6, March, 1986, p. 4584.*

Arthur's Valentine (1980)

It could happen in any classroom, it would pass as one of many incidents in a story of school days—but Arthur's discomfiture as the recipient of teasingly unsigned valentines doesn't stand alone very well as a picture-book story. . . . It's all very plotty, however compressed, and predicated on third- or fourth-grade relationships, situations, and in-jokes that have no younger equivalents—unlike the universal dilemmas projected in ***Arthur's Nose*** and ***Arthur's Eyes.*** Brown is better than most at projecting whatever's on the mind of his animal school kids, but there remains an inconsistency between the format and the content.

A review of "Arthur's Valentine," in Kirkus Reviews, *Vol. XLVIII, No. 22, November 15, 1980, p. 1459.*

Arthur and his classmates are all animals, although what kinds of animals some of them are is moot. The illustrations are large-scale, bright, and not overly crowded although they have little grace. The story, told in a light style and brightened by the rhymes of the valentines Arthur gets from "Secret Admirer," has a modicum of suspense and some humour: convinced, by the time Valentine's Day arrives, that his loving messages are from the attractive new girl, Sue Ellen, he sends her a special valentine. He's teased by his classmates; his secret admirer sends him a movie ticket and proves to be another girl. Arthur handles the whole business nicely, in an ending with a modest twist.

> *Zena Sutherland, in a review of "Arthur's Valentine," in* Bulletin of the Center for Children's Books, *Vol. 34, No. 5, January, 1981, p. 88.*

One of the book's attractions is the interplay of story and pictures; the text is direct and understated, and the colored cartoonlike illustrations of the anthropomorphized animals express Arthur's state of mind and his friends' reactions. There are visual hints of the plot; but although Arthur does not notice the clues, nor are they mentioned in the text, alert readers will enjoy finding them. Without overemphasizing the young hero's chagrin or pointing a moral, the author-artist resolves the story in a way that is appropriate, unexpected, and funny. Among the relatively few picture books about Valentine's Day, the new one is notable for its unforced, natural storytelling. The endpapers, decorated with candy hearts, set the right tone for what is in between. (pp. 39-40)

> *Holly Willett, in a review of "Arthur's Valentine," in* The Horn Book Magazine, *Vol. LVII, No. 1, February, 1981, pp. 39-40.*

Finger Rhymes (1980)

Brown's witty black-and-white drawings are a real drawing card for this collection of 14 best-loved finger games. There are larger collections (and certainly these rhymes appear many other places), but the book lends itself to an adult-child sharing experience. While the child looks over illustrations for such favorites as "Where Is Thumpkin" and "There Was a Little Turtle" or the lesser-known "Five Little Mice" and "Ten Little Candles," the adult can learn the action from the tiny but clear pictures next to each line. A good addition to any toddler shelf.

> *Judith Goldberger, in a review of "Finger Rhymes," in* Booklist, *Vol. 77, No. 6, November 15, 1980, p. 512.*

Fourteen familiar finger rhymes, one to a page, are accompanied by black-and-white line drawings shaded with gray, old-fashioned in detail but contemporary in style. At the head of each appropriate line of text, directions for finger actions are given in tiny, precise drawings enclosed in boxes. That such clear instructions can be conveyed in such small spaces, without words, is surprising. The visual instructions are integrated with the text and do not interrupt the illustrations—a nice bit of design that allows each page to work as an illustrated poem without reference to hand motions. Most of the rhymes are to be found in other, larger collections; but they appear here in a format decidedly appealing to young children.

> *Dudley B. Carlson, in a review of "Finger Rhymes," in* The Horn Book Magazine, *Vol. LVII, No. 2, April, 1981, p. 180.*

The True Francine (1981)

Some stories make very little sense, yet seem to summon a response from children. A spinoff from **Arthur's Eyes,** et al., **The True Francine** is also so firmly rooted in mass culture that it is written in a kind of shorthand, and with unabashed grammatical sloppiness ("Everyone was worried about which teacher they would get."). The story starts on the first day of school with the arrival of Muffy, a new girl who is a teacher's pet and who is assigned to Mr. Ratburn's class along with Francine and Arthur. Although Francine is messy and athletic and Muffy is a fibber and a pest, we are told that they are best friends. When Muffy copies Francine's test paper, both are called before the teacher. " 'I don't cheat,' " Muffy smiles, and on the strength of this and Francine's silence Mr. Ratburn sets a punishment that will prevent Francine from playing in an important baseball game. Eventually guilt gets to Muffy, and she confesses in the nick of time. The story has a ready-made but unexplained ending of amiability among all (including Mr. Ratburn) as the group sits around an ice-cream parlor table with no hard feelings and no apologies. As with the Arthur stories, it is the illustrations that carry the book. Brown's sense of scale and placement bring a feeling of closeness and fullness to every page, and the colors are bright and dense. If Brown can master narrative as he has mastered illustration, it will be cause for great rejoicing.

> *Mary B. Nickerson, in a review of "The True Francine," in* School Library Journal, *Vol. 27, No. 9, May, 1981, p. 53.*

Brown's brash, rambunctious illustrations may not be to everyone's taste, but their cartoony exuberance fits his story of two friends and classroom cheating. . . . The text catches the tone of grade-school banter, with groaning over teacher and classroom assignments. The lightness stretches even further thanks to the look of Brown's animal children, who keep the theme of honesty from becoming too weighty. (pp. 1192, 1194)

> *Denise M. Wilms, in a review of "The True Francine," in* Booklist, *Vol. 77, No. 17, May 1, 1981, pp. 1192, 1194.*

Your First Garden Book (1981)

The theme of this whimsical but clearly written book is that gardening is fun. Rather than concentrating on making a vegetable garden, as Daddona does in *Hoe, Hoe, Hoe,*

Watch My Garden Grow (Addison, 1980), Brown invites the reader to do more than 20 different gardening projects. The results of some of these projects can happen quickly, which is a boon for impatient beginning gardeners. The cress garden in a dish can yield a crop in about three days and, as it says in the balloon over the cress-sandwich-man's head, "Cress sandwiches taste better because you grow them yourself." Plants are shown to be grown in many different places, indoors and out; a "crack garden," for instance, is made in a crack of pavement. Many bright illustrations of tempera with black outline add to the clarity and the atmosphere of this slightly oversize book. Brown's familiar plump orange cats are seen pinching off the top of the plant started from an avocado seed, or gently transplanting seedlings. Gardening is, to many people, a form of play, and this is a playful, inviting introduction to it.

> *Carolyn K. Jenks, in a review of "Your First Garden Book," in* School Library Journal, *Vol. 28, No. 3, November, 1981, p. 72.*

Over thirty plant projects are presented with an engaging simplicity and clarity, which also mark the large, bright, predominately primary-colored illustrations. More familiar than innovative, the projects are practicable for very young children, employ readily available materials, and involve minimal expense. Indoor activities predominate—for instance, growing bean sprouts and cress, roasting pumpkin seeds, and potato-printing on paper; some of the outdoor ones are developed with city children in mind, such as sidewalk-crack gardens and container gardens for roof tops, fire escapes, and window boxes. Animating and supplementing the typically four-to-seven-step, one-sentence directions are a bevy of beasts, birds, and objects. They communicate—often humorously—through actions, expressions, and comments enclosed in cartoon balloons. Sequential drawings illustrate procedures and plant growth, while cross-sectional views show a flower bud forming inside a bulb and peanuts developing underground. The book is nicely balanced with short- and long-term projects as well as with individual and group activities. With an index, a glossary, and a list of "where to find garden basics."

> *Nancy C. Hammond, in a review of "Your First Garden Book," in* The Horn Book Magazine, *Vol. LVIII, No. 1, February, 1982, p. 62.*

Marc Brown, best known for his **Arthur** books, succeeds beautifully here in presenting gardening to young children ages four to ten. With humor and imagination the basics of gardening indoors and out, for city, suburban and country dwellers are presented in a clear well-organized fashion. Though the book is not cluttered, small and large projects, seasonal activities, ecological information, jokes, and contest ideas are all included, and everything looks easy and fun! My one complaint has to do with the repeated use of the term "bad insects" in the section on insects, when the term "harmful" or "pests" could have been used.

Parents and teachers will enjoy helping youngsters with some of these projects, though many can be done independently by even a very young child.

> *Diane Holzheimer, in a review of "Your First Garden Book," in* Appraisal: Science Books for Young People, *Vol. 16, No. 1, Winter, 1983, p. 15.*

Arthur Goes to Camp (1982)

Arthur is off to Camp Meadowcroak, like it or not, with Buster and Francine and Muffy—and from the moment he hears Francine chortle about bats and snakes in the boys' tent, he's sure "It's going to be just like school: the girls against the boys." Worse, the girls have a solicitous counselor, while the boys draw gruff, tough Rocky—whose disgust when the girls outperform the boys only deepens their shame. As for Arthur, he didn't want to go to camp, and—as he writes in daily, imploring letters—he doesn't want to stay. Then, "really weird things" start to happen: the doing of rival Camp Horsewater. But the annual Meadowcroak-Horsewater Scavenger Hunt turns the trick: boys-and-girls-together get revenge; and runaway Arthur accidentally emerges a hero. The last letter home reads: "Camp is great. I want to come back next year." Not the snappiest in the series but passable-plus: authentic summer-camp travails and a made-to-order setting for faint-hearted Arthur.

> *A Review of "Arthur Goes to Camp," in* Kirkus Reviews, *Vol. L, No. 9, May 1, 1982, p. 551.*

Though some may find the ending a bit of a letdown, Brown agilely weaves familiar camp high jinks (smoke bombs, frogs in bed) and activities (canoeing, plant identification) into his text and brightly colored pictures, and offers young readers an adventure they can easily relate to. Delightful endpapers provide an illustrated map of Camp Meadowcroak, which children will enjoy exploring.

> *Barbara Elleman, in a review of "Arthur Goes to Camp," in* Booklist, *Vol. 78, No. 21, July, 1982, p. 1442.*

All of the characters in this camp story are animals, and the theme is that in union there is strength. . . . This is an amusing variant on the adjustment-to-camp story, it's told in a direct, simple style, and most of the humor lies in the situation and in the illustrations, which are colorful, lively, and peopled by slightly grotesque animal figures.

> *Zena Sutherland, in a review of "Arthur Goes to Camp," in* Bulletin of the Center for Children's Books, *Vol. 35, No. 11, July-August, 1982, p. 202.*

Arthur's Halloween (1982)

Paying no particular heed to the personalities of aardvark Arthur and his school chums, Brown just puts them through some routine Halloween-story paces (Arthur's fright at pesky little sister D. W.'s devil regalia, his recoil at the "horror" food passed around at school) which lead, inevitably, to the local haunted house . . . which turns out, after the undaunted D. W. disappears inside, to harbor a friendly old lady who just can't afford to keep the place in repair. Arthur promises to return to tidy up the yard and, newly emboldened, leads the others home through the cemetery—"a great place. People are just dying to get in." Skippable except for slavish Arthurians.

> *A review of "Arthur's Halloween," in* Kirkus Reviews, *Vol. L, No. 14, July 15, 1982, p. 793.*

Arthur is spooked by Halloween, but won't admit his fears. . . . When his trick-or-treating younger sister enters the purported witch's house, however, his courage never falters. He dauntlessly rushes to her defense. . . . Details of Arthur's home décor form a background that is warm and cheerful. Characters are all comfortingly anthropomorphic. The sky blue pink sunset is delicious. Even though most parents do not let kids go it alone on Halloween, the net result of sharing this book could be a calming of early childhood fears.

> *Leslie Chamberlin, in a review of "Arthur's Halloween," in* School Library Journal, *Vol. 29, No. 1, September, 1982, p. 104.*

Arthur's fears are natural and childlike, and the emotions and reactions of the other children, including the precocious D. W., are amusing and believable. The illustrations—mostly double-page spreads—complement and extend the text. Softer, less garish colors than the ones in some of the previous *Arthur* books are used; and there is more shading and subtle detail—well-suited to the cobwebbed halls of the old house, the cozy kitchen, and the autumn night. (p. 508)

> *Nancy Sheridan, in a review of "Arthur's Halloween," in* The Horn Book Magazine, *Vol. LVIII, No. 5, October, 1982, pp. 507-08.*

Dinosaurs Beware! A Safety Guide (with Stephen Krensky, 1982)

At last, a painless way to teach children safety rules (unless they hurt from laughing so hard!). Broken down by situation—"At Home," "At Night," "In the Car," etc.—these 60 safety tips are illustrated by dinosaurs, usually undergoing the consequences of their ill-advised actions. "Chew well before swallowing" shows a bibbed dino swallowing a fish whole. In the next picture the fish is clearly outlined in the eater's gullet. "Don't play with matches" features a reckless birthday dinosaur lighting his candles, flinging a match aside, and setting his presents on fire. Some pages feature several tips, others one large one, but in all cases the message is clearly stated and the vividly colored pictures will make that message stick in a child's head. Perfect for individual and group discussions about safety matters.

> *Ilene Cooper, in a review of "Dinosaurs Beware! A Safety Guide," in* Booklist, *Vol. 79, No. 5, November 1, 1982, p. 365.*

Dinosaurs Beware! an hilarious strip-cartoon book with a touch of the Raymond Briggs, is a skilfully alluring guide to the prevention of everyday accidents in the home, in the playground or garden, with animals, in the car, at the beach—or through talking with strangers. The ab-

surdly exaggerated illustrations with homely dinosaurs make commonsense advice such as 'Keep a list of important phone numbers handy in case of an emergency', 'Chew well before swallowing', 'Never move an injured animal by yourself', 'Never skate or walk on thin ice', thoroughly memorable. This absolute must, at home and in the classroom, concludes 'Dinosaurs, beware! Wouldn't you rather be safe than sorry?'

> *M. Hobbs, in a review of "Dinosaurs Beware!," in* The Junior Bookshelf, *Vol. 47, No. 4, August, 1983, pp. 158-59.*

An effective method of teaching young children is to use positive statements; these work much better than their negative counterparts. Many of the safety rules in ***Dinosaurs, Beware!*** are stated in the negative and give the book a poor beginning. Turning these statements around would make the book more enjoyable and more effective in presenting the concept of safety. The colorful illustrations will attract the attention of young children, but often the safety measures presented are not pertinent to the age of the child attracted to the pictures. Although the book seems to be most suitable for children in the early elementary grades, it contains some questionable items—a warning to children to wear light-colored clothing when outside at night and a note from a child who has run away. Young children learn a great deal from pictures, even though the text may say something else. This book has many illustrations that show unsafe practices for children, including using a sharp knife alone, riding a bicycle at night, crossing a street alone, and swimming alone. These things have no place in a child's book about safety! This book might be used as a basis for discussion in a group, but only if an adult corrects the misinformation that might be learned by children who read it or look at the illustrations by themselves. There are better books about safety for children than this one.

> *Jane Wolfle, in a review of "Dinosaurs, Beware! A Safety Guide," in* Science Books & Films, *Vol. 19, No. 1, September-October, 1983, p. 29.*

Arthur's April Fool (1983)

This is one of Brown's niftiest outings with Arthur—and one that also, for a change, makes the most of the illustration. The book begins with a wacky page of mug shots: Arthur (aardvark) and best friend Buster (rabbit) trying on assorted April's Fool disguises. It winds up with thuggish (bulldog) Binky Barnes, Arthur's nemesis, as the crestfallen April Fool. And meanwhile Binky, out to make Arthur a laughing-stock from the start, has been laughed off the stage himself at the April's Fool Assembly—for taking flight when Arthur shrewdly proposes to saw him in half. Snappy, good-natured fun and comical pictures that register at 20 feet. (pp. 241-42)

> *A review of "Arthur's April Fool," in* Kirkus Reviews, *Vol. LI, No. 5, March 1, 1983, pp. 241-42.*

One of the better books in this series, ***Arthur's April Fool*** does a nice job of dispelling the bully's mystique for young readers. The entertaining pictures get off to a good start with nine frames that show Arthur and friend Buster trying out some of the magic shop's finer accessories, including arrows through the head and fright wigs. As before, the good-sized illustrations contain plenty of visual witticisms. (pp. 1028-29)

> *Ilene Cooper, in a review of "Arthur's April Fool," in* Booklist, *Vol. 79, No. 5, April 1, 1983, pp. 1028-29.*

How Arthur turns the tables on Binky by means of April Fool's tricks is a clever and satisfying story. The fact that Arthur worries, anticipates and has nightmares not only makes the situation more realistic but also makes his triumph sweeter. An amusing number of tricks and practical jokes fill out both the story and the illustrations, almost distracting readers from the fact that villain Binky seems too easily conquered.

> *Elizabeth Holtze, in a review of "Arthur's April Fool," in* School Library Journal, *Vol. 29, No. 10, August, 1983, p. 49.*

What Do You Call a Dumb Bunny? And Other Rabbit Riddles, Games, Jokes, and Cartoons (1983)

Brown doesn't stint on the extras in this comic cornucopia. The title indicates the wealth of laugh makers in the book, but there are also tiny pictures at the bottom of each page to flip and create a "movie" of capering rabbits; pictures of bunnies to cut out and turn into puppets that can perform the antics described; and hints on making your own rabbit shadow show and puppets. The compiler's black-and-white drawings are tinged with a pleasing pink shade and add to the nonsense in the one-liners and other playful entries. Kids will love the book, although it's easy to believe Brown's acknowledgment, that some of the groaners here have come from his young fans. On the whole, the jokes are really original and funny.

> *A review of "What Do You Call a Dumb Bunny? And Other Rabbit Riddles, Games, Jokes and Cartoons," in* Publishers Weekly, *Vol. 223, No. 16, April 22, 1983, p. 103.*

As joke books go, this is as witty—or witless—as any, depending on your taste. The rabbit theme spawns a number of hare-y takeoffs on familiar joke patterns. There are some "what-do-you-get-when-you-cross" funnies (rabbit plus elephant = elephant who never forgets to eat his carrots); some famous rabbits (Rabbit Hood, Rabbitson Crusoe); plus a few rabbity old chestnuts (What do rabbits get when it rains? Wet). Brown also includes a few real facts on rabbits, plus some tongue twisters, a find-the-rabbit puzzle, and instruction on how to draw your own rabbit. All this unfolds amidst the artist's spoofy, cluttered charcoal-and-ink drawings overlaid with (what else?) pink accents. Frivolous but sure to win its share of jokers.

> *Denise M. Wilms, in a review of "What Do You Call a Dumb Bunny? And Other Rabbit Riddles, Games, Jokes, and Cartoons," in*

Booklist, *Vol. 79, No. 20, June 15, 1983, p. 1335.*

Rabbits, rabbits and more rabbits! Brown has put together a unique collection of rabbit humor, puzzles, facts and other activities. The total effect, in pink, gray, black and white, is charming and engaging to both the eyes and funny bone. Brown has actually put four books together in one binding: in the lower corners of the book are two flip books, each about one square inch in size; across the top inch of the pages, a race between a tortoise and a hare forms yet another story; and the body of the book is found in the remaining space. Each page is packed with illustrations and humor. This book should keep children of any age busy for some time.

> *Paula J. Zsiray, in a review of "What Do You Call a Dumb Bunny? And Other Rabbit Riddles, Games, Jokes, and Cartoons," in* School Library Journal, *Vol. 30, No. 1, September, 1983, p. 102.*

Arthur's Thanksgiving (1983)

Arthur's problems begin when he's made director of his class Thanksgiving play. Most distressing in his inability to find someone to take on the role of the turkey. Despite all Arthur's finagling, he can't persuade anyone that coming onstage decked out in turkey feathers is the first step to stardom. Finally, Arthur must play the role himself, but his most embarrassing moment turns out to promote togetherness and embody the very spirit of Thanksgiving. Readers familiar with Arthur's past adventures will welcome this frankly funny addition to the series. The pictures, as bright and sassy as any in the previous books, are filled with jokes. It will take a second look to see them all, but that will simply double the reader's pleasure.

> *Ilene Cooper, in a review of "Arthur's Thanksgiving," in* Booklist, *Vol. 80, No. 6, November 15, 1983, p. 494.*

Brown is adept at creating characters with a few lines of dialogue and facial expressions. This book has the colorful and humorous illustrations, amusingly realistic situations and believable characterizations that have made **Arthur's Halloween** and the others in the series such fun to view and read.

> *Jean Hammond Zimmerman, in a review of "Arthur's Thanksgiving," in* School Library Journal, *Vol. 30, No. 5, January, 1984, p. 62.*

The Silly Tail Book (1983)

The Silly Tail Book is more foolish than it is silly. It shows some of the different kinds of mammals that have tails and some of the uses that tails have. The cartoonish watercolor and pencil illustrations do help to get the simple idea across but the verse is atrocious and the illustrations are not much better.

> *Craighton Hippenhammer, in a review of "The*

Silly Tail Book," in School Library Journal, *Vol. 30, No. 5, January, 1984, p. 62.*

This is indeed a little silly and not terribly unique, but there are moments of fun, too, as author Brown describes all the animals that have tails and what those tails are good for (swinging on trees, swatting flies, and following wherever you go, to name a few). Though the singsong rhyme gets a little tedious, the bouncy, colorful, cartoon-style pictures should encourage beginning readers to persevere through the mostly one or two lines of text per page.

Ilene Cooper, in a review of "The Silly Tail Book," in Booklist, *Vol. 80, No. 12, February 15, 1984, p. 862.*

Perfect Pigs: An Introduction to Manners (with Stephen Krensky, 1983)

A light-hearted primer of etiquette spells out proper behavior for a variety of situations familiar to a child, whether at home, at school, at a friend's house, or in a public place. Each bit of calm, straightforward advice serves as a caption for a boxed illustration showing—in most cases—young pigs acting in a contrary manner. For instance, while the text intones, "Don't play with your food," a pig constructs an elaborate mashed-potato castle complete with gravy moat. Most of the pages are divided into several rectangles, somewhat similar to a comic-book format, but the varied shapes and the inclusion of full-page illustrations prevent the book from appearing busy. Unifying the collection of helpful suggestions is the commentary provided by a pompous, know-it-all pig, who receives his comeuppance in the end. Although the color is muddy, the illustrations are lively and full of witty detail and show that even pigs can overcome their natural inclinations.

Kate M. Flanagan, in a review of "Perfect Pigs: An Introduction to Manners," in The Horn Book Magazine, *Vol. LX, No. 1, February, 1984, p. 41.*

Handsomely produced is this self-proclaimed introduction to manners. Its pages are full of advice on how to behave around the house, when giving a party or in public places. Its pig/people sometimes enact the rules in the illustrations, but at other times they violate them, confusing readers on the correct behavior. For instance, is sitting on the bed and reading aloud to a sick buddy a good way to "let others know you care about them," a rest-disturbing intrusion or dangerous to your health? The topic covered and the book's antic, comic-strip approach suggest that it is intended for the primary years rather than the kindergarten. Especially with younger and literal-minded audiences, Brown and Krensky fans are advised to use this book with caution, reading it with the children and talking it through as you go.

Joan W. Blos, in a review of "Perfect Pigs: An Introduction to Manners," in School Library Journal, *Vol. 30, No. 6, February, 1984, p. 56.*

Spooky Riddles (1983)

How can one go wrong with the winning combination of spooks and riddles? Marc Brown doesn't. His spooky creatures (skeletons, vampires, mummies, ghosts, witches, bats) all provide the foil for advancing clever solutions to unusually simple riddles. Brown's usual zest for zany situations comes through to provide an entertaining riddle book which is a pleasure to look at as well as to solve. His full-color illustrations shine throughout. Very young readers will adore this book because they can read it by themselves; older children will delight in the riddles and the art.

Catherine Blanton, in a review of "Spooky Riddles," in School Library Journal, *Vol. 30, No. 8, April, 1984, p. 99.*

The Bionic Bunny Show (with Laurene Krasny Brown, 1984)

Wilbur, the star of *The Bionic Bunny* television series, may be a superhero on television but is an ordinary bunny in real life. As an episode involving the Bionic Bunny capturing a pair of bank robbing rats is taped, this picture book introduces the actual workings of a television studio and will help youngsters understand the reality of television heroes. Many different jobs (happily held by both male and female animals) and pieces of equipment are introduced without interrupting the story. A glossary, "Television Words and What They Mean," appears on the last page. The segments of the show are clearly indicated by TV screen shapes against a black background, so children will have no trouble keeping the two plots straight. Colorful, cartoon-like illustrations complement the text, and Wilbur's bumblings will delight youngsters. An entertaining story, this will be a good read-aloud with groups small enough to see the pictures.

Candy Colborn, in a review of "The Bionic Bunny Show," in School Library Journal, *Vol. 30, No. 9, May, 1984, p. 62.*

As announced, "two books in one": a scatty rendering of the production of a single TV program; and the actual episode underway of the Superman-spoof *Bionic Bunny Show.* There's a lot of overlapping, hard-to-distinguish technical business in the behind-the-scenes scenes (a confusion compounded by representing crew-members as different, hard-to-identify animals). There's also a crossfire of spoofery—with Wilbur, who plays the Bionic Bunny, a hapless sort in real life as well as a stumblebum on the set. So the book doesn't quite come across as an unmasking of TV marvels: props apart, only one genuine camera trick is unveiled. But the full-color watercolors are packed with on-the-set detail; the action doesn't let up; and Wilbur's good-humored fluster as the Bionic Bunny (who has trouble opening a kitchen jar) has built-in appeal. (pp. J-28-J-29)

A review of "The Bionic Bunny Show," in Kirkus Reviews, *Juvenile Issue, Vol. LII, Nos. 6-9, May 1, 1984, pp. J-28-J-29.*

What "The Mary Tyler Moore Show" did to television news anchors with the cardboard and pompous Ted Baxter, *The Bionic Bunny Show* does to television superheroes. We see there is less than meets the eye.

The husband and wife team Marc Brown and Laurene Krasny Brown have written and illustrated a very funny book about the making of one episode of "The Bionic Bunny Show." This episode, as it is finally seen on the television screen, is laid out in black-and-white frames across the endpapers of the book, but between the covers, in color illustrations, is the hilarious real story of how the episode was made. It debunks the myth of the effortless superhero by showing us how very much help the Bionic Bunny needs to pull off his heroism. A glossary of television terms at the end defines "teleprompter," "special effects" and more.

We meet the actor rabbit who plays the Bionic Bunny as he arrives for work with a Chevy Chase dive outside the television studio that sends his script scattering. He is late and does not know his lines. An interspecies crew snaps on his costume with built-in muscles, ties on his elevator sneakers and pulls on his bionic ears, "which supposedly let him hear everything."

In the course of making the episode in which the Bionic Bunny, à la Superman, tracks down the dirty rat bank robbers, we see the flat sets amid serpentine television cables, studio lights and video and audio crews.

While the cameras roll, the seemingly invincible Bionic Bunny crashes through a brick wall. When the cameras stop, the actor bunny cries out for a Band-Aid. "If those bricks were real and not rubber you'd need more than a Band-Aid," a cameraman says. . . .

With humor and sarcasm, *The Bionic Bunny Show* shows readers that television's superheroes are not what they seem. They cannot do everything, and they do make mistakes.

The only part of the book that doesn't sit well with me is the last scene. After a hard day at the studio, Daddy comes home to ridicule because as a regular bunny he can't even open a jar of carrots. What he does with all those bionic bucks is support a house, a set of twins, a set of triplets, a singleton and however many are gestating. Can't a bunny get some respect?

> *Carrie Carmichael, in a review of "The Bionic Bunny Show," in* The New York Times Book Review, *July 22, 1984, p. 24.*

Arthur's Christmas   (1984)

Trying to decide on a gift to Santa, Arthur notes that everywhere he goes, Santa seems to be eating. (Readers will ¬ioy feeling superior as *they* note that all the Santas are ¬nt.) Arthur mixes up some dreadful food combina- ¬ his crafty sister gets rid of the food and leaves ¬nsibly from Santa) to thank Arthur. It ends, ¬ lucky to have such a nice little sister?" ¬e lap audience for which this is also ¬ as they have with earlier Arthur ¬rs, the scruffy paintings of ev-

eryday objects, and the light style that unerringly reflects children's attitudes.

> *Zena Sutherland, in a review of "Arthur's Christmas," in* Bulletin of the Center for Children's Books, *Vol. 38, No. 3, November, 1984, p. 41.*

As it must in the life of every series character, Christmas has come to Brown's aardvark Arthur—who looks, as it happens, more human at each installment. What's bothering earnest, considerate Arthur is what-to-give Santa! While little sis D. W., pushy as usual, keeps adding to her want-list, Arthur keeps searching for the perfect gift. Then he sees the department store Santa ordering an elaborate banana split, other Santas (all humans, various races)—whom he takes for one fast-mover—eating "subgum chow goo" and "pickled peppers." So his present for Santa will be impromptu combinations of "Santa's favorite foods"—which D. W., and meek dog Killer, surreptitiously dispose of—lest Santa take flight and Arthur's feelings be hurt. It's a hoary, gimmicky situation—redeemed by Arthur's warm heart and D. W.'s unexpected kind-heartedness. Or, true Christmas spirit, in a trite form.

> *A review of "Arthur's Christmas," in* Kirkus Reviews, *Juvenile Issue, Vol. LII, Nos. 18-21, November 1, 1984, p. J-87.*

There's No Place like Home   (1984)

Beginning readers may delight in discovering the many different places that people, animals and objects call home, but those who have any knowledge of science will immediately realize the inaccuracy in the opening rhyme: "Long ago when / Dinosaurs roamed, / The family cave / Was home sweet home." The accompanying illustration shows a woman, child and unshaven man living in a cave as green dinosaurs run to greet them. Most of the examples are true to life: "A plant likes soil. / That's where it grows. / And glasses are always / At home on a nose." The cartoon illustrations in clear washes with chalk are humorously wrought.

> *Rebecca Jennings, in a review of "There's No Place Like Home," in* School Library Journal, *Vol. 31, No. 9, May, 1985, p. 68.*

Arthur's Tooth   (1985)

Arthur is back again. This time his problem is a loose tooth that won't come out, making him the only one in his class who still has all of his baby teeth. That dubious honor makes him something of an outcast to some members of the group: "Everybody line up for a squirting contest—everybody except Arthur. Babies with baby teeth can't squirt water," taunts Francine. Arthur's complaints about his stubborn tooth net him a trip to the dentist, but the only consolation he gets is "Just wait." That's what Arthur does, but thankfully not for long: Francine bangs into Arthur on the playground and knocks his tooth loose. Brown's ability to zoom in on childhood concerns is in full evidence here. Even though the story is slightly contrived, it has a natural air that's quite convincing; moreover, Arthur and his comrades seem so similar to their real-life counterparts that this latest tale should be readily embraced by Arthur's following.

> *Denise M. Wilms, in a review of "Arthur's Tooth," in* Booklist, *Vol. 82, No. 3, September 1, 1985, p. 55.*

Hand Rhymes (1985)

This beautifully illustrated collection of finger-play rhymes is a perfect choice for parents and their toddlers or nursery school teachers looking for fresh material. Though there are a few familiar verses ("The Church," "Two Little Monkeys"), many of the others will be new to readers. Each rhyme has small boxed diagrams depicting the necessary hand movements, but best of all are the delicately colored scenes that Brown has fashioned as backdrops for the rhymes. These present eclectic but always comfortably childlike displays that are notable for their gentle colors and subtle shadings. A departure from the brassier style Brown has used for his Arthur books, these are a pleasure to see.

> *Denise M. Wilms, in a review of "Hand Rhymes," in* Booklist, *Vol. 82, No. 3, October 1, 1985, p. 218.*

Two-page spreads of palely colored, amusing pictures illustrate this collection of fourteen unfamiliar fingerplays. The instructions, given in tiny squares next to each line, are unclear, complicated and a waste of time. The verses are poor and frequently don't scan. Better material available.

> *Lenore Rosenthal, in a review of "Hand Rhymes," in* Children's Book Review Service, *Vol. 14, No. 3, November, 1985, p. 24.*

Fourteen rhymes culled or adapted from traditional sources and accompanied by miniature pen-and-ink diagrams of hand motions are set into soft watercolor spreads that make this dually useful for reading aloud or remembering in situations where distracting entertainment is desperately called for. The illustrations are consistently engaging while the verses vary. One or two seem artificial, but **"Two Little Monkeys"** is a nursery school standby, and **"The Church"** a perpetual favorite. **"Five Little Babies"** and **"Five Little Goblins"** will prove popular, the first for every day and the second especially in preparation for sometimes frightening visits of trick-or-treaters. A fit companion volume for Brown's earlier *Finger Rhymes.*

> *A review of "Hand Rhymes," in* Bulletin of the Center for Children's Books, *Vol. 39, No. 4, December, 1985, p. 63.*

Visiting the Art Museum (with Laurene Krasny Brown, 1986)

A book that attempts to make a visit to an art museum an enjoyable experience for children and one that will help them begin to appreciate art. In this story, told in dialogue balloons, parents drag their reluctant children to the art museum. They stroll through many galleries, including displays of Egyptian mummies and the arms and armor gallery. Exuberant drawings of the family and other visitors to the museum are highlighted with photographic reproductions of famous paintings and sculptures. This gives the opportunity for the characters to mention some facts about the piece, or to discuss what to look for in the work. There are also some very funny comments from the other visitors in the galleries. The drawings are clever in their direct and indirect references to well-known art. One problem is that some of the blurbs are poorly positioned, making it difficult to follow the sequence of dialogue. Notes at the end of the book describe each piece of reproduced art in greater detail and provide an overview of each period of art, from primitive to the 20th Century. Also included is some practical advice for enjoying an art museum. The first tip, that there is no need to see everything on display in one visit, should have been followed by the family in the story, as the amount of art that they view during their visit may overwhelm some young readers.

> *Lisa Castillo, in a review of "Visiting the Art Museum," in* School Library Journal, *Vol. 33, No. 3, November, 1986, p. 72.*

A family's peregrinations through an art museum are chronicled in the lively, cannily designed pages of a full-color picture book. . . . The author manages to keep separate three strands of verbal expression: as the mother explains the displays and responds to the children's irreverent questions and remarks and the father helpfully reads aloud from a museum booklet, other people are unconcernedly communicating with their own companions. Two kinds of artwork are integrated into the pages. The bustling throngs appear in cleverly executed gallery settings that include Marc Brown's skillful renditions of architectural details and of famous statues, artifacts, and paintings as well as actual reproductions of internationally known works, from the *Discus Thrower* to noted paintings—both representational and abstract—by such masters as Copley, Renoir, Rousseau, and Pollock. . . . Lighthearted but not facetious, the inviting book should quicken the interest of children without trivializing the subject matter.

> *Ethel L. Heins, in a review of "Visiting the Art Museum," in* The Horn Book Magazine, *Vol. LXII, No. 6, November-December, 1986, p. 754.*

Though children and art museums are fairly incompatible, they should, I suppose, occasionally be exposed to each other. Such exposure is the theme of ***Visiting the Art Museum,*** which portrays a family trip to an institution that suggests both the Metropolitan Museum of Art and the Museum of Modern Art in New York City.

In cutesy drawings by Marc Brown, tricked out with reproductions of "real" art, mother, father and kids follow a docent through the galleries (from primitive to 20th-century art). They talk—via comic strip blurbs—in standard Philistine-ese about each work. Pointing to Jackson Pollock's "Portrait and a Dream" (1953), for instance, mother says to child, "This artist paints how he feels."

Child responds, "If he feels that bad he should stop painting and go to bed." Ho, hum.

As Mom, Dad and the docent give out with "facts" about the art ("It says here the Greeks loved sports," says Dad, reading from a pamphlet in front of an athletic classical sculpture. "They held the first Olympics back in 776 B.C."), the children behave as children often do when it's not television—looking a little, but mostly acting up, getting bored, wanting to eat or go to the bathroom. So, rather than being a how-to book, as the title suggests, this is a string of routine adult jokes on how children behave when visiting an art museum.

Scrunched in at the back of the book, along with more information on the art depicted, are mildly useful "tips" on enjoying an art museum, including games to play with the pictures. My own Pavlovian formula for visiting an art museum with a child is simple. Go as often as you like, but never stay more than 15 minutes. Pick out in advance one thing—and one thing only—to look at and to explain. On quitting the place, take her or him or them immediately to an ice-cream store. And—although the Browns have acquitted themselves nicely in two earlier books, **The Bionic Bunny Show**, about how television shows actually work, and recently in **Dinosaurs Divorce: A Guide for Changing Families,** aimed at children of parents who are separating—don't look to this one for too much help at the museum.

> *Grace Glueck, in a review of "Visiting the Art Museum," in* The New York Times Book Review, *December 21, 1986, p. 21.*

Arthur's Teacher Trouble   (1986)

Arthur's not at all happy when he is assigned to Mr. Ratburn's third-grade class. "Make one wrong move . . . and he puts you on death row" warns one kid. Maybe that's why Mr. Ratburn's students study extra hard for the 200-word spelling test that will yield the class' representatives to the all-school spellathon. Arthur and a classmate called the Brain are the winners. In the week before the match, Arthur studies hard and turns out to be the winner—not a bad way to remember third grade. Mr. Ratburn, meanwhile, announces that next year he'll be teaching kindergarten, which is startling bad news for D. W., Arthur's pesky sister. Story is the strength here. Brown manages the school setting with self-assured skill; meanwhile, his full-color pictures—bustling pen, crayon, and wash drawings—create the comfortably busy backdrop that his readers will find familiar. A nice tale for Arthur fans. (pp. 404, 406)

> *Denise M. Wilms, in a review of "Arthur's Teacher Trouble," in* Booklist, *Vol. 83, No. 5, November 1, 1986, pp. 404, 406.*

Arthur and his friends are back, beginning another year of school, and who does Arthur have but Mr. Ratburn, the "strictest teacher in the whole world." This year the students are preparing for the September spellathon, and while Miss Sweetwater's class is making popcorn and Mrs. Fink's class is going to the aquarium, the students in "the

Rat's" class are studying harder than ever for the big event. . . . The outcome is predictable, but the story ends on the same fun-filled child-pleasing note established on page one. As with previous Arthur books, there is a subtle message—this time that perhaps Mr. Ratburn and others of his ilk aren't such bad teachers after all—but this may be too subtle for the intended audience. No matter—Brown's appealing plot and grand illustrations (facial expressions are priceless) assure this book's popularity.

> *Hayden Atwood, in a review of "Arthur's Teacher Trouble," in* School Library Journal, *Vol. 33, No. 5, January, 1987, p. 58.*

I would not have considered this book worth reviewing had it not been for the enthusiasm of every child I read it to or showed it to. . . . Spurred on by their enjoyment I had a good look at the book and decided it was worthy of my attentions!

Marc Brown manages to appeal to English children despite the strong American flavour of his books. He writes about situations they can relate to and sympathise with. In this story Arthur is a reluctant finalist in the school spellathon. His teacher, the unpopular Mr Ratburn, expects a child from his class to win every year. However, even with his cheeky little sister, Div, to contend with, Arthur manages to come out on top. Marc Brown's illustrations are full of amusing detail which my children greatly appreciated. The look on Div's face when she hears that Mr Ratburn will be teaching her next year is wonderful!

> *T. Trafford, in a review of "Arthur's Teacher Trouble," in* Books for Your Children, *Vol. 24, No. 2, Summer, 1989, p. 11.*

Dinosaurs Divorce: A Guide to Changing Families   (with Laurene Krasny Brown, 1986)

A sensible, reassuring look at the changes brought about by divorce and the means for a child to deal with them may help in bringing calm and confidence to distressed children of divorce. The authors are very thorough; they deal with the causes of divorce, living arrangements, remarriage of parents, and stepparents and their families. They always stress the continuing love of both parents for the child. The book offers sensible advice on how to deal with feelings of guilt, depression, difference, and jealousy, parents who cast blame on the other parent, and even parents who do not stay in touch. They point out some good consequences—a calmer lifestyle, no more arguments, twice as much celebration on holidays. The picture-book, almost comic-book, format, the touches of humor, and the distancing effect of the dinosaurs as surrogate humans may make the book accessible to young or extremely anxious children. A thoughtful, useful book.

> *Ann A. Flowers, in a review of "Dinosaurs Divorce: A Guide for Changing Families," in* The Horn Book Magazine, *Vol. LXIII, No. 1, January-February, 1987, p. 42.*

An openly prescriptive text is relieved by its simple, smooth style of delivery in comic-strip format, with ridiculously funny green reptile children expressing their way through the vicissitudes of divorce. After a table of contents and glossary of relevant terms (readers are challenged to find the starred ones in the book) come 11 sections on some reasons why parents divorce, on likely repercussions and reactions, and on ways to deal with visitations, living in two homes, dealing with holidays, and adjusting to new developments such as parent dating, remarriage, and step-siblings. While the child's point of view is always respected and given sympathy, there are also reminders of the trials of single parents and suggestions on ways for children to help out. The cartoons are, for the most part, well designed and funny without poking fun; they extend the book to a wide age range of users, who will benefit from this discriminately light treatment of a serious subject.

> *Betsy Hearne, in a review of "Dinosaurs Divorce: A Guide for Changing Families," in* Bulletin of the Center for Children's Books, *Vol. 40, No. 6, February, 1987, p. 102.*

Dinosaurs seem inappropriate as characters in a book about divorce for children, but the Browns use their lovable, personified dinosaurs skillfully to drive home their points. . . . The information is not original, but it is presented in understandable terms, emphasizing love and understanding: "Remember, divorce is new for your parents too, and they may make some mistakes." The text suggests specific actions in various situations. This is an informative, charming, appealing presentation of a topic often dealt with only in clinical terms with little appeal for the child reader. It is an excellent read-together book and a useful book for children who can read on their own. It will help them deal with the many questions or concerns that they might have when their parents or their friends' parents are in a divorce situation.

> *Sharron McElmeel, in a review of "Dinosaurs Divorce: A Guide for Changing Families," in* Science Books & Films, *Vol. 22, No. 4, March-April, 1987, p. 237.*

D. W. Flips! (1987)

Arthur is one of Brown's most popular characters, so it makes sense to start a series about the animal child's sister, D. W. Smaller in format than the Arthur books and gentler in color, this story describes an excited D. W.'s first visit to her gymnastics class. At first, D. W. is put off at being in the "the baby class," but she discovers that she is not as adept at flipping and flopping as she thought she'd be: her forward rolls are definitely deficient. Determined to improve, D. W. practices at every opportunity, even in the grocery store, where she knocks over a display of grapefruits in the process. Practice makes perfect, however, and at her next class, her somersaults are A-OK. Then comes a surprise—it's time to learn backward rolls! Listeners may find the ending a little abrupt, but they will surely like everything that comes before. The humor is revealed through the pictures, which are filled with acrobatic animal children determined to become future Olga Korbuts and feature expressive-faced D. W. as she persistently

practices her flips. Sharp-eyed readers will see glimpses of Arthur as he observes his sister's progress.

> *Ilene Cooper, in a review of "D. W. Flips," in* Booklist, *Vol. 83, No. 17, May 1, 1987, p. 1364.*

Marc Brown's apparently implausible combinations of human, although sometimes furry, bodies and animal heads work remarkably well as surrogate people, and D. W. is an engaging and sensible heroine. An encouraging look at beginning any sport and a lesson in how to make a moral—"Practice makes perfect"—enjoyable.

> *Ann A. Flowers, in a review of "D. W. Flips!" in* The Horn Book Magazine, *Vol. LXIII, No. 5, September-October, 1987, p. 597.*

Play Rhymes (1987)

Twelve nursery rhymes, each accompanied by a charming illustration—with a difference. Two aspects of the book make it unique. First, Brown precedes each line of the rhyme with simple but clever line sketches that illustrate movements to accompany the verse. While the sketches are probably too small and abstract to be used by very young children, they will be welcomed by those who plan programs and activities for them. Second, the music for six of the rhymes is included, a welcome addition. While most of the rhymes are well-known and frequently included in other collections, there are several less familiar and delightful rhymes that parents, librarians, and teachers of the very young will want to add to their repertoire. The illustrations are full-color pastels with many small details and humorous elements to appeal to children. This is a good choice for program planning or for a rainy afternoon with a favorite child.

> *Constance A. Mellon, in a review of "Play Rhymes," in* School Library Journal, *Vol. 34, No. 2, October, 1987, p. 120.*

[The] presentation of a dozen traditional rhymes set in playfully illustrated double-page spreads offers a rich treasure for family enjoyment or the storyteller's pack. Pretty colors and humorous details mark scenes that are in turn comic, energetic, and cozy; families of teddy bears, rabbits, and humans are often featured with scenes varying in setting from modern to old-fashioned or even historic times. The rhymes include English nursery verses, such as "The Noble Duke of York"; street games—"Teddy Bear, Teddy Bear, Turn Around"; familiar songs, "Do Your Ears Hang Low?," "The Wheels on the Bus," and "I'm a Little Teapot"; and assorted nonsense verse. Intended for participatory use, each rhyme is accompanied by a set of small frames picturing suggested motions; though some are less interesting as action rhymes, all are fine for reading aloud or reciting, and music is provided at the end of the book for the six verses best known as songs. Like the lighthearted lady who "sailed away on a happy summer day, / On the back of a crocodile," readers of many ages will savor the witty rendering of the verses, "wearing a happy smile."

> *Margaret A. Bush, in a review of "Play*

Divorce in your family means many things will change, but one thing that never changes is your parents' love for you.

From Dinosaurs Divorce: A Guide for Changing Families, *written by Laurene Krasny Brown and Marc Brown. Illustrated by Marc Brown and Laurene Krasny Brown.*

Rhymes," in The Horn Book Magazine, *Vol. LXIII, No. 6, November-December, 1987, p. 751.*

Peopled with endearing animals and human characters, luxuriously colored illustrations, twinkling with humor or glowing in the warmth of cozy Victorian decors, surround the text of tried-and-true play rhymes. "The Noble Duke of York," "Wheels on the Bus," and "I'm a Little Teapot" are among the most familiar inclusions, while "Elephant" and "Bears, Bears, Everywhere" are equally enjoyable though not as well known. . . . Brown's well-received **Finger Rhymes** and **Hand Rhymes,** this collection will delight and inspire young audiences.

> *Ellen Mandel, in a review of "Play Rhymes," in* Booklist, *Vol. 84, No. 7, December 1, 1987, p. 627.*

Arthur's Baby **(1987)**

The tale of the beleaguered but always appealing hero, Arthur the aardvark, is a family story of a new sibling, Kate. Arthur's friends each contribute dire predictions as the birth draws closer. " 'Better get some earplugs,' said Binky Barnes, 'or you'll never sleep.' " " 'And you'll probably start talking baby talk,' said Francine. 'Doo doo ga ga boo boo.' " Arthur's mother, sensitive to his trepidation, tries to reassure him by bringing out his own baby pictures, but her plan is snafued by D. W.—ever the brash, pushy, younger sister—in a typical family scene. After the birth D. W., in her usual takeover manner, appropriates Kate as " 'my baby,' " and Arthur remains an onlooker until Kate begins to cry and cry and cry; then it's big brother who comes to the rescue. While the book will appeal to fans of Arthur's school stories, it is younger in feeling and format—less text, more open space, softer colors. A comfortable, satisfying book written with a light touch that will be perfect for the two- to four-year-old who's about to become an older brother or sister.

> *Elizabeth S. Watson, in a review of "Arthur's Baby," in* The Horn Book Magazine, *Vol. LXIII, No. 6, November-December, 1987, p. 721.*

Like its predecessors, **Arthur's Baby** deals reassuringly with a developmental issue. And like those earlier books, the humor lies in the colorful, sunny illustrations (pen, crayon, and wash), as well as the witty banter between siblings. Combined with a simple, direct style, this has sure-fire appeal for the primary grade set, as well as Arthur addicts of all ages. It should also be of special interest to families expecting a new arrival. (p. 71)

> *Julie Corsaro, in a review of "Arthur's Baby," in* School Library Journal, *Vol. 34, No. 4, December, 1987, pp. 70-1.*

D. W. All Wet (1988)

Arthur the aardvark's younger sister returns in true D. W. fashion. She's obstinate, whiney, and totally irresistible—to Arthur and to his fans. Here the family is at the beach, and D. W. is determined to let everyone know how miserable she is. She hates the beach, the water, the sun—everything about the experience, until a wise and loving older brother forcefully coaxes her into the water. Families of rabbits and aardvarks bask in the sun or take shelter under colorful beach umbrellas; children (except D. W.) build castles, swim, or play in the water. All the while, D. W. remains high and dry—until the very end. The book is so expertly conceived that non-readers will be able to follow every moment of D. W.'s day, from unhappiness to delight. Youngsters will predict the ending, but they'll still love seeing her about-face and relate to her fear of the unknown. D. W. and Arthur at the beach—they're sure to make a big splash with the preschool crowd as well as with beginning readers.

> *Trev Jones, in a review of "D. W. All Wet," in* School Library Journal, *Vol. 34, No. 7, March, 1988, p. 158.*

Here's a situation common in the real world and uncommon in children's books: D. W. (of **D. W. Flips**) spends her first day at the beach avoiding the water and asking, "When are we leaving?" Big brother Arthur finally sweeps her up into a piggyback ride (in spite of D. W.'s hands over his eyes, which provide a nice bit of humor) and dumps her in. Fortunately, she loves it. Brown's watercolors have all their usual comic good nature, combined with the lovely lyricism that the beach landscape evokes in so many artists. No matter how many beach books are already in the collection, this is a must.

> *A review of "D. W. All Wet," in* Kirkus Reviews, *Vol. LVI, No. 8, April 15, 1988, p. 615.*

Brown's illustrations depict his now familiar race of properly dressed families who just happen to be part aardvark or donkey or possibly even cat or rabbit. Mild-mannered Arthur is already a comfortable friend from previous books, but now younger sister D. W. brazens her way into a series with the same gentle humor and softly colored pictures. Endpapers with checkerboard squares enclosing mementos of days on the beach—shells, sun glasses, and popsicles—are a nice addition to the unpretentious story of D. W.'s conversion from grouch to water baby.

> *Ethel R. Twichell, in a review of "D. W. All Wet," in* The Horn Book Magazine, *Vol. LXIV, No. 3, May-June, 1988, p. 338.*

Dinosaurs Travel: A Guide for Families on the Go (with Laurie Krasny Brown, 1988)

Having seen their young fans through family upheaval in **Dinosaurs Divorce,** the Browns present a similar guide for vacations.

The format is the same: dinosaurs go through familiar experiences in a series of brightly colored panels in which the reader is directly addressed, while the text cheerfully imparts a variety of data. The occasionally somber information (like enjoinments against talking to strangers) is mitigated by the young dinosaurs' fun riding bikes, skateboards, boats, subways, trains, airplanes, etc. From preparation for a trip and the journey itself (in an escalating series of vehicles) to possible experiences during the vacation and returning home, this is an accurate, reassuring introduction to a common experience. For families planning a trip with nervous young companions, an enjoyable preparation.

> *A review of "Dinosaurs Travel: A Guide for Families on the Go," in* Kirkus Reviews, *Vol. LVI, No. 14, July 15, 1988, p. 1056.*

A variety of tips for young travelers, with journeys that range from the ordinary (a roller skating trip around the block) to the exotic (an airplane ride around the world). The busy dinosaurs who populate the pages offer helpful hints on getting ready, what to pack, means of locomotion (cab, boat, airplane, on foot, etc.); and gentle reassurances about what to expect. The advice is practical and straightforward, but the three or four illustrations on each page are delightfully silly—small dinosaurs riding an elephant, six dinosaurs in a bed while staying with relatives. Advice is current ("only pack a few toys, games, books, and tapes"), and the book is totally child orientated. A perfect introduction to armchair traveling, as well as a soaring success as an opener for primary grade units on transportation.

> *Trev Jones, in a review of "Dinosaurs Travel: A Guide for Families on the Go," in* School Library Journal, *Vol. 35, No. 3, November, 1988, p. 100.*

Party Rhymes (1988)

Following the by-now familiar format of the earlier **Finger Rhymes, Hand Rhymes,** and **Play Rhymes,** and aimed at slightly older children, this collection of 12 standard action songs invites group participation. Included are such chestnuts as "Farmer in the Dell," "A-tisket, A-tasket," "In and Out the Window," and "Fox in a Box," most available elsewhere but not all under one cover. Circled and boxed sketches show some of the movements, but this collection relies more on verbal instructions than the previous books do. All are comprehensible and manageable to small children with adult intervention. The hallmark playfulness of this artist's work is present here, with stylized forms and muted colors in a wide but harmonious palette in the manner of Tomie dePaola. Lots of fun here, with the music, and all verses, appended.

Karen Litton, in a review of "Party Rhymes," in School Library Journal, *Vol. 35, No. 5, January, 1989, p. 69.*

This sunny compilation extends the scheme of Marc Brown's attractive books, **Finger Rhymes, Hand Rhymes,** and **Play Rhymes.** The new volume is half again as long as the others; the rhymes are longer, too, often spilling across two sets of double-page spreads and allowing for a fuller development of the picture scenario which spins story from the verse. Beginning with "The Farmer in the Dell" and working through a dozen familiar selections to "The Muffin Man," these vignettes are filled with humorous touches that invite lingering enjoyment. Comic expression of children and animals, plentiful round and rolling shapes and lines, and the liberal use of soft green tones in a pretty range of colors all add to the reader's pleasure. The customary small drawings showing movements in the games are further expanded with a short paragraph describing more fully the directions for playing the game. Though the well-known songs and rhymes are not particularly associated with parties, a sense of play is conveyed throughout. . . . It is a special pleasure to see a nice series exceed itself, and this book offers wonderful versatility for use as it breathes new life into the traditional games, songs, and dances of the young and not-so-young. (pp. 84-5)

Margaret A. Bush, in a review of "Party Rhymes," in The Horn Book Magazine, *Vol. LXV, No. 1, January-February, 1989, pp. 84-5.*

Arthur's Birthday   (1989)

The popular Arthur returns to celebrate his birthday and finds himself contending with a troubling situation that will be familiar to readers. Excitement reigns when Arthur invites the class to his party, but Muffy is upset—her party is on the same day. At first, it looks as if there will be a standoff, with the boys going to Arthur's house and the girls celebrating at Muffy's. Happily, Arthur has an idea to rectify the dilemma. He sends invitations to the girls and a note to Muffy asking her to come over and pick up a special present. She arrives to find that the kids have joined forces; Arthur's birthday gala is now also a surprise party for Muffy—a happy, if not entirely realistic solution. While some of the drawings do not look as carefully executed as others in the series, for the most part, the illustrations do capture the story's festive air. A welcome addition for Arthur's fans.

Ilene Cooper, in a review of "Arthur's Birthday," in Booklist, *Vol. 85, No. 16, April 15, 1989, p. 1463.*

Brown's familiar watercolors have lots of interesting details—kites caught in trees, a male relative wearing a "Liberated Partner" apron. Arthur's warm, loving family and his diplomatic approach to problem solving strike just the right note—positive and believable. The "Arthur" stories are primary-grade favorites; children will enjoy this latest offering.

Lucy Young Clem, in a review of "Arthur's Birthday," in School Library Journal, *Vol. 35, No. 11, July, 1989, p. 62.*

Baby Time: A Grownup's Handbook to Use with Baby (with Laurie Krasny Brown, 1989)

Brown's ingenious guide offers solid suggestions for parents interested in enriching a child's early development. Designed with parents (or grandparents, babysitters, siblings, etc.) as well as babies in mind, the book's text is limited to brief paragraphs at the top of each page, with the remainder of the space devoted to the gentle, pastel illustrations. Together, text and pictures outline ideas for activities such as bathing, massaging, singing and shopping—all commonplace events that, with a little thought, can serve to stimulate a baby's five senses. Although the Browns haven't come up with anything particularly new or earth-shattering, their efforts have produced an agreeable addition to a parenting bookshelf and a worthy companion volume to the more detailed advice of Spock or Brazelton.

A review of "Baby Time: A Grownup's Handbook to Use with Baby," in Publishers Weekly, *Vol. 236, No. 19, November 10, 1989, p. 59.*

Being a first time mom, **Baby Time** was a joy to read. Probably the most outstanding feature is the remarkable illustrations. The Browns have realistically captured each and every moment of having a little one. The text, though very practical and common sense, will refresh and enlighten readers with valuable pieces of information. This book is so true it is though the Browns have peeked into each of our homes to gather information for their book.

B. C. S., in a review of "Baby Times: A Grownup's Handbook to Use with Baby," in Children's Book Review Service, *Vol. 18, No. 4, December, 1989, p. 46.*

"The more confident you become as a parent, the better nurturing you can provide." Laurie Krasny Brown's advice on handling babies and playing with them to stimulate understanding and growth seems at once obvious and beguiling in its simplicity. Each large page carries a short band of text for the parent, set above softly colored illustrations intended for use with babies. The book is broadly organized around sensory experiences and movement, with several single page units related to each general concept. "Hear," for example, includes as topics sounds to hear, sounds to make, conversation, tone of voice, gestures, reading and rhyming, and music and dance. The numerous pictures, one or several to a page, feature good-natured babies and objects galore. Short lines of hand-lettered text occasionally instruct parents but are usually meant for reading to baby: "Rub-a-dub-dub, / It's fun in the tub" and "The toilet flushes. Whoosh! / Glub glub goes the water." A page summing up physical milestones in whole-body and hand skills precedes a concluding double-page spread featuring a selection of toys and household objects attractive as playthings. A whole sheet of humorous babies, in various stages of dress and undress, makes up the appealing front and back covers, and the book contains a colorful pullout mural intended for recording a baby's first experiences. Filled with conventional wisdom and practical information, the flat oversize volume should lessen the anxieties of new parents and provide enjoyment for babies.

> *Margaret A. Bush, in a review of "Baby Time: A Grownup's Handbook to Use with Baby," in* The Horn Book Magazine, *Vol. LXVI, No. 2, March-April, 1990, p. 223.*

Dinosaurs Alive and Well! A Guide to Good Health
(with Laurie Krasny Brown, 1990)

A liberal mix of humorous dinosaurs and lively text create a unique treatment in health education. A regular dose of the Browns' loveable creatures is sure to become the enticement to a better and more healthful life. The smooth style of writing develops the theme across a broad span of coverage, giving information and advice about nutrition, cleanliness, illness, the value of exercise, and how to handle stress (child oriented!). Frequent exposure to this book will help children realize the ultimate goal—that of staying healthy and feeling good about themselves. An upbeat mood pervades this nonpatronizing treatment of an otherwise "doesn't-everybody-know-that" subject. The exuberant watercolor illustrations make the book a complete success. Teachers will find it invaluable for classroom collections, and librarians should consider multiple copies. There are no others like it!

> *Mary Lou Budd, in a review of "Dinosaurs Alive and Well! A Guide to Good Health," in* School Library Journal, *Vol. 36, No. 4, April, 1990, p. 102.*

Decked out in contemporary garb, the chartreuse-shaded prehistoric creatures who learned to cope with some of life's situations in **Dinosaurs Divorce, Dinosaurs Travel,** and **Dinosaurs Beware!** (on safety) return in the authors' typically zesty format. Here, the Browns address wellness of body and mind, with the dinosaur children learning about nutrition, hygiene, first aid, self-esteem, and constructive ways to deal with stress. The busyness of the line-and- wash-illustrations is balanced by a stable, reassuring text—easy for youngsters to assimilate yet not simplistic. Such advice as "Getting out and exercising can help you shake off tense feelings" is valuable for any age. A particularly effective title and likely to promote good discussion. (pp. 1796-97)

> *Phillis Wilson, in a review of "Dinosaurs Alive and Well! A Guide to Good Health," in* Booklist, *Vol. 86, No. 18, May 15, 1990, pp. 1796-97.*

Advice on topics of great concern to many adults—diet, stress, and exercise—is dispensed in a straightforward manner. Additional suggestions are given about first aid, dressing properly, and building one's self-esteem. Whether or not young people will be attracted to the subject matter is open to debate, but adults seeking an imaginative and palatable way to introduce these ideas to children will find the book a practical and helpful compendium of health and hygiene tips. The almost comic-book format is identical to that of the other books in the series, **Dinosaurs Beware!, Dinosaurs Divorce,** and **Dinosaurs Travel;** a family of green-faced dinosaurs cavorts across the pages, adding the levity necessary to raise this book from the didactic to the delightful. (pp. 345-46)

> *Ellen Fader, in a review of "Dinosaurs Alive and Well! A Guide to Good Health," in* The Horn Book Magazine, *Vol. LXVI, No. 3, May-June, 1990, pp. 345-46.*

Arthur's Pet Business (1990)

In the latest adventure of aardvark Arthur, his parents agree to get him a puppy if he proves himself responsible. Egged on by his smart-mouthed little sister, who wants him to pay back the money he owes her, he starts a business caring for other people's pets in his home—all over his home. There's not much story, but kids will enjoy the family chaos, as a boa constricter, a spoiled yapping dog, frogs, and sundry other clients clamor for Arthur's attention and invade sitting room, bath, and bed. No one will be surprised to learn from the back flap that Brown has a menagerie of his own. He clearly knows that in families there's lots going on all at once, and his text is just the outline for what the ebullient pictures tell.

> *Hazel Rochman, in a review of "Arthur's Pet Business," in* Booklist, *Vol. 87, No. 8, December 15, 1990, p. 860.*

Arthur Meets the President (1991)

This lively story . . . features the popular aardvark winning a "How I Can Help Make America Great" contest. Arthur and his classmates are excited about attending the special ceremony at the White House, but when Arthur learns he has to recite his winning essay on TV "while all America looks on," he is terrified. In the end, when Arthur's notes are blown away by the helicopter's wind, it is his irrepressible sister D. W. who saves the day and underscores Brown's message that "we can all help to make America great by helping others." Brown's attention to visual details provides much of the book's humor, and Arthur fans will delight in deciphering D. W.'s list of ideas about how to run the country. Although the appearance of too many characters makes the text seem needlessly disjointed, Brown's sensitivity to Arthur's frets is right on target. (pp. 71-2)

> *A review of "Arthur Meets the President," in* Publishers Weekly, *Vol. 238, No. 20, May 3, 1991, pp. 71-2.*

In this latest book about Arthur, the aardvark wins an essay contest, and he, his class, and his family are invited to Washington, D.C. to meet the president at a special ceremony. . . . The bright, full-color illustrations are lively, and Brown portrays the emotions and facial expressions of the characters well. While the book is definitely not as strong an entry as others in the series, teachers and parents looking for easy fiction on the presidency and Washington will want this; kids, as always, will want the newest of Arthur's stories.

Marge Loch-Wouters, in a review of "Arthur Meets the President," in School Library Journal, *Vol. 37, No. 7, July, 1991, p. 54.*

Dinosaurs to the Rescue: A Guide to Protecting Our Planet   (with Laurie Krasny Brown, 1992)

The Browns' sensible, cavorting dinosaurs are back again, this time regaling readers with some advice on how they can rescue our ailing Earth. In this latest foray into social issues, the authors present major environmental problems with such practical, easy, and entertaining solutions that children will be enthusiastic from the very beginning. The first page introduces Slobosaurus who is "full of excuses for why he can't use less, use things again, and give something back to the earth." Succeeding pages show the boorish way he reacts by tossing his empty soda can on the ground, wasting water, using electricity unwisely or unnecessarily, etc. Plants, animals, and insects, too, are given a place in this environmental treatment. Each framed watercolor cartoon is bursting with activity showing the busy, happy creatures going about their daily routines with Slobosaurus sulking somewhere in the action. He is finally convinced by the hardworking dinosaur children that his help is indeed needed because . . . "protecting our beautiful planet is a big job. Every one of us can help!" This author/illustrator team knows precisely how to hit the mark for young readers, and their newest venture is no exception.

Mary Lou Budd, in a review of "Dinosaurs to the Rescue: A Guide to Protecting Our Planet," in School Library Journal, *Vol. 38, No. 3, March, 1992, p. 226.*

Peter (Malcolm) Dickinson

1927-

Zambian-born English author of fiction.

Major works include *The Changes* trilogy: *The Weathermonger* (1968), *Heartsease* (1969), and *The Devil's Children* (1970); *Dancing Bear* (1972), *The Blue Hawk* (1976), *Tulku* (1981), *A Box of Nothing* (1985).

A prolific, versatile, and widely praised writer of books for children and young adults, Dickinson is known as an imaginative storyteller whose attention to detail makes his literary fantasy worlds vivid and believable. His penchant for detail extends in particular to mechanical processes; he admits that he is fascinated with how things work, and his stories often include careful description of the workings of such things as submarines and drawbridges. Dickinson is also praised for his storytelling ability; his stories typically have suspenseful plots full of action and excitement. Beneath the surface of his tales, however, lie deeper philosophical, social, and moral questions raised directly or indirectly by the characters and their actions. For this reason, and because of their brilliantly imaginative content, critics have often observed that his works can be appreciated by adults as well as by children. Some critics have faulted his novels for insufficient attention to character development; Dickinson himself has acknowledged, "Place and feel, even of imaginary landscapes, are important to me, nuances of character less so." Many reviewers, however, have praised his characters as realistic and well drawn.

Dickinson worked as an editor and reviewer at *Punch* for seventeen years before launching his career as a writer in 1969 with *The Weathermonger:* the first book of *The Changes* trilogy to appear but the last in the chronology of the series's extended plot. The story, which won immediate critical recognition for Dickinson, is set in an England where most of the population has turned against machines of any kind and returned to a medieval agricultural social structure. Two children whose minds are unaffected by this development attempt to find the cause of the changes. Some critics have found fault with the explanation that Dickinson provides, calling it an implausible way to conclude an otherwise satisfying story. For this reason, some prefer the other two books of the trilogy, which do not address the reason for the changes. The exotic settings of several of Dickinson's stories demonstrate his interest in history and anthropology: *The Dancing Bear* is set in sixth-century Byzantium and tells of a slave's adventures in rescuing his master's daughter from a group of marauding Huns; *The Blue Hawk* has a setting that resembles ancient Egypt and involves a young boy-priest who rescues a hawk from a ritual sacrifice and sets in motion political changes; and *Tulku,* set in China at the time of the Boxer Rebellion of 1900, tells of an American boy's escape to a lamasery in Tibet after the death of his father. *A Box of*

Nothing mixes fantasy with mathematical and scientific concepts, including the big bang theory of the creation of the universe out of "nothing." After young James purchases a box of this same nothing from a shopkeeper in an empty store, his mother throws the box into the local dump, sparking the creation of a nightmarish fantasy world. E. Colwell has called it "a remarkable book which, whether one understands it or not, is a challenge and experience. It can be read at several levels as can all books of genius."

Dickinson is also a popular author of mystery novels for adults. He has received many awards for his children's books, including the *Guardian* Award for *The Blue Hawk* in 1977, Whitbread Awards for *Tulku* in 1979 and *AK* in 1990, and Carnegie Medals for *Tulku* in 1979 and *The City of Gold and Other Stories from the Old Testament* in 1980.

(See also *Contemporary Literary Criticism,* Vols. 12, 35; *Something about the Author,* Vols. 5, 62; *Contemporary Authors New Revision Series,* Vol. 31; and *Dictionary of Literary Biography,* Vol. 87.)

AUTHOR'S COMMENTARY

I prefer not to think, let alone write, coherently about how I do what I do, or why, or even for whom. Part of the reason will be obvious to anyone who has ever had an on day at some sport, say tennis: the moment you start to wonder what you're doing right your game goes to pieces. Another part of the reason is that I might grow to the shape of my theories—one of the pleasures of writing for children is that it is a sufficiently small world for a single writer to be able to explore large districts of it.

The Stevenson of *Treasure Island* is, I suppose, my Socrates and the Kipling of *Rewards and Fairies* my Plato. But though I am aware of working inside a strong tradition I regard myself as a primitive. I have a function, like the village cobbler, and that is to tell stories. Everything else is subservient to that. This doesn't mean that everything else can be left out (though I do know books which are abysmally written, for instance, and yet tell their story well enough to be good books). For example, if a story needs a priestly caste, those priests have to have gods to worship, and a coherent theology, and besides that they must come from a society in which it makes sense to devote a proportion of the men to the priesthood, and an economy that will support the extra mouths, and so on. These needn't be endlessly described, but I must have imagined them as I wrote so that the reader can be subliminally aware of them as he reads. The same applies to vaguer concepts, even to what is normally called the 'idea' of a book. For me, it is there because the story is there, and not the other way round.

If I fight shy of positive notions about my writing, I do have one fairly coherent negative belief. It's about what I'm not doing. I am not whittling rungs for the great ladder that leads up to Lawrence and Proust. I think children read differently from adults, and have a different use for books. (I also think that many adults have never learnt to read the way adults are supposed to, which accounts in part for the decline of the novel.) To me the great ladder tradition is something of a tyranny. So if, for instance, the intricate development and exploration of character plays no great part in my stories, that's because I don't think it is a proper element in the genre. People have to have characters, of course, in the same way that priests have to have theologies; but if I get it right then the person is there in the book, clear and rounded-seeming, and the reader acknowledges her existence and gets on with the story.

Finally, I am strongly against the religion of art, and the priesthood of artists. I am a cobbler. Given good leather I can make a comfortable shoe. (pp. 53-4)

> *John Rowe Townsend, "Peter Dickinson," in his* A Sounding of Storytellers: New and Revised Essays on Contemporary Writers for Children, *J. B. Lippincott, 1979, pp. 41-54.*

GENERAL COMMENTARY

Frank Eyre

Peter Dickinson [is] a comparatively new writer whose stories about 'The Changes', a time when men in England had learned to fear and dread machines, and so destroy them, have been one of the most refreshing discoveries of the last few years. (p. 124)

The first of these three books, *The Weathermonger,* is a straightforward and vividly exciting adventure story. This is a wonderfully imaginative adventure story, of a kind that seemed almost to have ceased to exist, and no one who has read it will be surprised that its author should also have written a series of detective stories (or something like detective stories) which are as unique in their own way as *The Weathermonger* is among children's adventure stories of today. The second book about The Changes, *Heartsease,* is even better, because the story is just as exciting but there are also strongly drawn characters. The girl who is the centre of the story is clearly drawn and the villagers and other adults are only too true to life. This is a story of prejudice and oppression, that paints an all-too-recognisable picture of what English villages could become in a time of such Change. [*The Devil's Children*] is a book which, once the basic situation is accepted, is completely real. There are no gratuitous sensations, no thrills for the sake of thrills, and no easy solutions, but the author leaves us a believable hope. (pp. 124-25)

> *Frank Eyre, "Fiction for Children: 'The Weathermonger,' 'Heartsease,' 'The Devil's Children',"* in his *British Children's Books in the Twentieth Century, revised edition, Longman Books, 1979, pp. 124-25.*

Marcus Crouch

The future has always been a theme which exercises the imagination powerfully. In one of the short novels of which he was a master [H. G.] Wells looked at stages in the progress or decay of the world to the ultimate—or penultimate—vision of a tideless sea and a dead land. Two modern writers have chosen coincidentally to look at a nearer future, but one separated from the present by a huge catastrophe. It is not altogether surprising that Peter Dickinson and John Christopher should have hit upon much the same idea. Both, as sensitive observers must be, were conscious of the shadow of disaster thrown by the H-bomb and by abuse of the environment. In the event Christopher showed, in *Prince in Waiting,* a society rebuilding itself after a natural disaster, while Dickinson saw technological man overreaching himself as the agent of destruction. In the vision of both writers society reverts to its primitive condition. Not paleo- or neolithic. The England of *The Weathermonger* and *Prince in Waiting* (1970) is mediaeval. Dickinson's Englishmen turn on the machines which seemed to threaten their existence and destroy them, replacing the old civilization with a new—or perhaps an older—one based on the village unit and the unassisted work of hands. Christopher's society is a rather more complex one built around city states which are perpetually at war with one another. Technology has been banned too, not as a result of the instinctive revulsion of Dickinson's countrymen but by the deliberate establishment of religious taboos. (pp. 49-50)

John Christopher's stories are distinguished by excellent writing and keen, original and logical thinking. The thought is subordinated to the writing in Peter Dickinson's three stories of England in its second Dark Age. In *The Weathermonger* Dickinson was not content only to paint a brilliantly colourful picture of a country which has developed certain instinctive skills to replace the destroyed machines; he attempted to explain his theme, and the explanation was sadly inadequate. In the two later books he confined himself to a smaller canvas and a shorter span of time, and the stories, freed of specious explanations, took wing magnificently.

Like Christopher, Dickinson is greatly affected by decay. The descriptions of London in the first stages of its decline which occupy the early chapters of *The Devil's Children* are sharply realized and profoundly disturbing; this, one feels, is uncomfortably near a possible reality. *Heartsease,* the most tightly constructed of the three novels, shows England long after the cataclysm. Society has settled down to a Dark Age existence, content for the most part to live under a system of rough and ready justice and petty tyranny. Much of the action takes place in and around a Cotswold village, and this helps to concentrate the impact of the quietly grim story. Topography gives the book its unity. *The Devil's Children* is centred on the character of Nicky, a little lost Londoner who joins a party of Sikh immigrants in their search for a safe haven after the destruction of London. This child, armoured by her determination not to allow herself the soft option of love, is, in her strength and weakness, the most pathetic and the most deeply examined of Dickinson's creations.

Apart from the adventures and the occasional profundities of the character-drawing, much of the interest of Dickinson's achievement comes from his examination of society, whether the embryo manorial system of *The Devil's Children* or its matured counterpart in *Heartsease.* (p. 51)

> *Marcus Crouch, "To the Stars," in his* The Nesbit Tradition: The Children's Novel in England 1945-1970, *Ernest Benn Limited, 1972, pp. 48-56.*

Jay Williams

[*Williams was a prolific author whose most popular books are the science fiction fantasies about Danny Dunn, an inquisitive youngster with a penchant for adventure and trouble. Noted for combining exciting plots with scientific facts in a distinctive fashion in these works, Williams is also the creator of mysteries, historical and realistic fiction, picture books, and nonfiction.*]

A children's book in which Merlin is hooked on morphine? Another in which the hero is a slave who is only with the greatest difficulty dissuaded from slavery? Still another which offers a completely rational explanation for the survival of a kind of dinosaur but then an equally convincing argument for keeping it a secret? My own feeling, on reading these books, was of having discovered an original and audacious explorer at work in the mine field of children's literature where most authors prefer to keep to the safety of well-worn paths.

I had wanted to meet Peter Dickinson ever since *The Weathermonger* appeared in 1969. Like him, I take the writing of children's books very seriously; like him, too, I alternate them with writing crime novels. I enjoy talking shop with a writer whose work I admire, and particularly so with one whose attack, like Dickinson's, is always fresh and unconventional. Writers, however, are notoriously solitary, sluggish and wary, and it was four years before a meeting could be arranged when we found ourselves within a few miles of each other in Gloucestershire. (p. 21)

I asked him about his background, and how he had begun writing. "I was born in Zambia," he said. "My father was a colonial civil servant; he came from a family which lived around here a lot." "Here" was the neighbourhood of Painswick. His mother, he went on to say, was a South African farmer's daughter. Soon after they returned to England his father died, leaving them without much money, "so we had to live in the intermediate world," he said, "of being educated like gentlemen but not being able to keep it up." Dickinson eventually got a scholarship to Eton, "bottom scholar in the worst year on record. I did a short, ludicrous career in the army as a conscript, went to Cambridge, read English, got a research readership but found I was unable to find my way around the university library." Luckily, he didn't have to; he was offered a job on *Punch* and settled down there as editor and writer for the next seventeen years.

For five of those years, one of his jobs was reviewing detective stories. Inevitably, the time came when he got an idea for one himself, and he settled down to write it. His labour was broken into when his boss took three months off to write a book of his own and Dickinson had to take over the magazine. At the end of that time, he said, "I didn't have any creative juice in me any more." The book had grown cold and he put it aside. Then, one night, he dreamed a long incident which became, when he wrote it down, the first chapter of *The Weathermonger.* The children's book went rapidly and unblocked the adult book which, when it appeared, was called *Skin Deep* and won a prize for the best crime novel of its year.

Both books reflect his unorthodox approach. *The Weathermonger* rests on what he himself recognizes is a venerable science-fiction idea, a world in which machines are regarded as evil; he, however, makes it stem from the aberrant dreams of an awakened Merlin, kept doped up by a nervous little chemist. *Skin Deep* supposes a primitive Papuan tribe living in London, and a murder that can be solved partly by a knowledge of anthropology, "which," Dickinson said, "I invented, of course." As he put it, "All my novels are very 'iffy' books. My last published one, *The Green Gene,* was what England would be like if the Scots, the Irish, and the Welsh all had green skins and we could have seen that we had a subject race among us. It's an attempt, among other things, to persuade the English what it really would be like to live in a South African situation. It's a very, very nasty book indeed," he finished, with relish.

I was struck by the phrase, "which I invented, of course," and asked him about his research. He confessed that he researches his books "in mad ways". Speaking of *The Dancing Bear,* a richly textured historical novel, he said, "I made it all up and did my research afterward. I did a history science-fiction. You know how a science-fiction writer knows a bit of science and extrapolates the rest? I know a bit of history and extrapolate the rest." In fact, his knowledge is extremely wide, which allows his guesses to be good. After he had invented a Hunnish raid on Byzantium in the period of Justinian, he discovered that one actually took place almost as he had imagined it. He does, however, sometimes find himself spending an enormous amount of time getting some detail right which may be relatively trivial but which appeals to him. In one of his mysteries there is a bone-meal mill which figures only briefly but for which he wrote thirty letters to find out how it ought to work. To get the nineteenth-century submarine accurate in **Emma Tupper's Diary,** he wrote to a submarine designer at the Admiralty who, intrigued, sent him a seven-page letter of advice and specifications. Having worked out the general framework for the survival of the plesiosaurus in that same book, he engaged in long discussions with a staff member of the Natural History Museum who, although he felt the whole thing to be sheer fantasy, ended by saying that it was far and away the most plausible theory he'd ever come across.

I asked about his reading. As a child, he was one of the few who genuinely liked the *Alice* books, although *The Wind in the Willows* bored him stiff. He read a lot of Henty, and during one period read *Ivanhoe* during every holiday. He admired Doyle's *Sir Nigel* although he saw at once that the scene in which Nigel wears his father's armour for a joust was inaccurate because the boy wouldn't have been able to move his arms inside the sleeves of a suit too big for him. "I like to feel that everything works," he observed. He devoured Shakespeare; once, he says, his mother came into a room and found him putting down a book and saying, "There! That's the comedies, now for the tragedies."

He read a great deal of poetry and could learn it very rapidly. He once memorized one of the choruses from Swinburne's *Atalanta* in the five minutes while waiting for a school lunch. His memory served him well later, and not only as a poet, for when he was on guard duty in the army he could make four hours fly past by reciting to himself from the repertory of poetry he knew. "I've never been happy with what passes for normal fiction," he said. "I have no need for ordinary fiction because I think my own fictions. Nor do I like films. Even as a child I couldn't watch Charlie Chaplin because the formula for the film is, he's made a fool of. I can watch plays because they're much more distant than films are. I enjoy fiction which contains its own distancing, like Jan Austen, Trollope. Dickens with his greater rawness, I can't cope with."

Distance is important. When I said that I sometimes find, in my own books, that I echo situations from my childhood, or even find overtones of speech from books I read when a boy, he replied, "I would rather not do that, and possibly because I am a very cerebral writer. I think that I distance, I transmute things very much in my books. I don't think there's anything in any of my books which has ever happened to me." In **Heartsease,** the second of the books dealing with an England which has rejected machinery, he used the valley below Painswick as the setting

but, he pointed out, "It is there as the drive of the book. It can be perceived that I like this landscape but the element of *me* in it doesn't exist. That's my Wordsworth book," he mused. "A re-creation of those periods when one was sixteen, seventeen, eighteen, when you could—fill the whole valley with your sound. You had the sense of belonging there and being part of it all.

"I think there is a weakness in bookish authors, of which I am one, that one may use turns of phrase which come from other people. I've got no ear for the dialogue of anybody except my own class. And this means that I have to work very hard at trying to construct an acceptable dialogue for others. If one is off form, one uses bits of old Kipling . . . "

We laughed; he has a laugh as rich as Grandma's fruitcake. I pointed out that the dialogue of the lower-middle-class children in **The Gift** seemed to me to come off perfectly. "Yes," he said, "but the children there talked, deliberately on my part, a sort of classless language. I think it's all right but I won't defend myself strongly against anyone who said that a couple of parents like that could obviously not have such 'officer class' children." I said that perhaps because I was an American the shading wasn't apparent to me. "I did my best about it," he went on, "in the sense of reading it carefully to see if I had put in 'officer class' slang, as it were, and consulting my daughters about turns of phrase, but in fact an ear for language is very rare. You ask a child, 'What do you say nowadays when you want to say it's a drag?' and although they'd use the word naturally if they had to, they can't think about it."

On the other hand, although he maintains what might be called a personal distance between himself and his characters, his children's books come out of something very deep within him. He uses water metaphors when speaking of them. "I am by most people's standards a very prolific writer, that is, I expect to write a children's book of my length in about four months and an adult book in about six; that leaves me two months in the year for the wells to fill up again." Or again, "If an adult book goes wrong, you can toil at it and get it right, whereas with a children's book—it's the spring coming out of the hillside again, if the spring dries up there isn't much you can do about it. My children's books come out of me, whereas my adult books are much more intellectual constructs, in which I may draw out of myself, certainly, but which in theory I could do with total detachment, which I don't think I could do with a children's book." And then he said something which touched me sharply. "There are honestly— this is a ridiculous thing to say, but there are passages in my children's books which I find it very difficult to read without a lump in my throat . . . they have this resonance for me which summons up that response." (pp. 22-5)

What he calls his "cerebral" quality appears in the careful accumulation and working out of details, all of which go to reinforce the feeling of truth and reality in his stories. "If you're writing fantasies," he said, "you're like somebody who is trying to lay a carpet where there's a terrifically strong draught coming up between the floor-boards; the carpet keeps billowing up and so you've got to tack it down with detail all the time." His tacks range from minute instructions for how to operate an antique submarine to the explicit way in which a syringe is filled with morphine, from the exact use of a scoop-shovel in a payroll heist to the performance of a trained bear. He clearly enjoys this detail himself and said that he plans it all out "because I want to know". Considering the creatures in *Emma Tupper's Diary,* he began with a kind of ecological systematization: "How could they survive? What was the minimum breeding population which could statistically survive?" When I remarked that he seemed to like machinery, he first made sure that I didn't mean plot machinery, and then said, "Yes, but it needn't be machinery in the purely mechanical sense. Systems would be a better word (although a machine is a system). I like social systems. In *The Devil's Children,* for instance, where you first see the new myths being built up in the court house, and the society beginning to break up and the beliefs just starting . . . "

He used the word "myth" not in its folklore or Frazerian sense, but, so it seemed to me, in a looser way, to express social or cultural patterns. (p. 26)

He is deeply concerned about language. At one point, speaking of the teaching elements which often, even if unconsciously, appear in children's books and which he agreed might appear in his, he said, "What I would like to teach is the use of the English language as it *should be.*" He polishes his work carefully, and embeds in it lapidary phrases: "His mouth lusted for meat, and fish, and bread with a crackling crust . . . " When his American editor wanted to make some cuts in *The Dancing Bear,* Dickinson agreed but insisted that no change be made in the sentence, " . . . even the bushes and thickets looked footloose and peregrine". "Kipling is my hero!" he exclaimed. "The only writer of the same kind as Shakespeare—I don't mean of the same calibre, but using language in the same way, taking absolutely anything for his own purposes . . . every phrase is unmistakably Kipling."

A little later, he said, "I think that a lot of things have changed which you and I haven't taken sufficient account of. The disappearance of the Authorized Version of the Bible from the resonances of people's minds . . . the fact that I've got two literate, grown-up daughters, and I can use a common phrase, 'the fall of the sparrow' and they won't know what it means or where it comes from, or won't recognize a Biblical tone.

"When I write poetry I give it to my wife and I have to say, 'Now let me see your lips move.' My children's books are meant to be read aloud as well. I know that a child reading something for the first time is going to go zzt!—read it straight off and miss an enormous amount. I read my books aloud to my boys (he has two sons, ten and eleven) in manuscript and in proofs partly to catch misprints and transitions in phrasing, but partly because that's the tone in which they're written, the tone of the speaking voice."

We came around to the question which is often raised with writers: Who do you write for? I said that basically I wrote for one child—myself, as a boy. He agreed, but added that

that didn't mean we never thought of other children. "One is conscious of a desire that as many children as possible should read one's books," he said. "However, they are subsumed into the one reader. You think of them as individuals. I'm delighted when a child says to me, 'Oh I couldn't finish that book,' because it carries the individual who's had an individual response. Of course, when somebody has read it and has enjoyed it, that's better still . . . Yes, the drive to write children's books does, I think, tie up with trying to satisfy the one child, by re-creating moments in his existence."

He looked thoughtful, and went on, "My world is a reader going under a bed—he's crept under a bed in order not to be found and is reading with his thumbs in his ears so as not to hear anybody calling for him while he finishes the book."

I asked him if he was talking about himself. "I did that," he admitted. He dropped his voice and said solemnly, "One of the things which has changed the way people read is that now beds are built too low to get under." (pp. 27-8)

Jay Williams, "Very Iffy Books: An Interview with Peter Dickinson," in Signal, *No. 13, January, 1974, pp. 21-9.*

Nigel Grimshaw

Bald summaries may give something of the dramatic quality of the books [of Peter Dickinson] but do not suggest much of their broad but often penetrating power of characterisation nor how, along with a skilful manipulation of a fast-moving sequence of sometimes sensational events, Peter Dickinson manages to convey a sense of the supernatural and the mysterious context of existence. If there is a theme that unites all the books, it is that of a sensitive child's feeling of isolation and of his, or her, attempts to accept and even, possibly, to forgive the world of adults in which he, or she, has to come to live. (pp. 219-20)

There are two qualities of story-telling. If a reader can afford consciously to wonder what next surprise the narrator will contrive, he is not under the supreme spell. With Dickinson, whether it is a race to get the Heartsease down to the sea, or the testing of Silvester in the camp of the barbarians, or a hubristic Rolls Royce journeying among avenging thunderbolts to its dark destination, the fascination for the reader is always more than merely intriguing. Convincingly articulated and exciting as the movement of events is, that alone does not account for the absorbing nature of the narrative. One might also instance the memorable vitality of incidents and still not fully sum up Dickinson's gift. Emma, apparently trapped amid the stench of prowling dinosaurs in an underwater cave, the cracked laughter of a murderous young man riding out to a death he does not know will be his own; even flatly stated like that, such moments are going to have something of a *frisson* about them. *Frissons,* however, are shallow. There is a fullness of imagination about these fictional worlds which gives them solidity and their characters depth.

This imaginative penetration goes beyond fanciful invention or hectic scenes and finds its sharpest stimulation in re-creating the odd variousness of existence. His people, feckless or faithful, are not one-dimensional manifestations of a single attribute, never totally good or evil, ever aware of their own shifting relationships and suggesting more than they seem. The eccentricity of the beautiful Poop Newcombe in *Emma Tupper's Diary* or of Furbelow in *The Weathermonger* throws the ordinariness of those around them into relief, though what is highlighted is neither trivial nor simple. If Nicola Gore in *The Devil's Children* is bravely ordinary, she still has insight into the likeness between herself and the marauding horseman. His aggressive courage is high because he is isolated; since people for him are no more than objects, he is devoid of compassion. It does not need the old lady to indicate this before Nicola is aware that he is what she may become. Margaret in *Heartsease* has more sensitivity than her uncle but he also, on occasions, can feel an unspoken judgement and the need to justify himself. Silvester in *The Dancing Bear* can be conscious of his slave conditioning without being able to free himself from it. In *The Gift* the children endure both the unreliability of their father and his irritating resilience. Beyond that we know the uneasy foundations of that resilience; it can well be simply a pathetic whistling in the dark. Dickinson's people do not discuss themselves but they are nevertheless awake to their own personalities, the effects of changing circumstances and the play and shimmer of relationships.

The world they inhabit is an often cruel one of stupidity and imprisoning fact whose values are those of kindness and the capacity for humane and intelligent action. It is a world, imaginatively complete and recognisable, in which a smithy, a tug, the process of charcoal burning can be seen to work. The language of the Sikhs, elaborate and faintly archaic, has the same authenticity as the Cotswold of the Felphamites. Seneschals, for sufficient reason, talk Latin, if ineptly.

There is catastrophe and suspense enough in Peter Dickinson's writing for his tales to appeal to any age. The sophisticated level of characterisation, however, is probably not completely within the taste and comprehension of every child below, say, the age of ten or eleven. *The Gift,* for instance, or *The Dancing Bear* would seem most suited to children in the upper forms of secondary schools, while the trilogy of the Changes appears to recommend itself to early secondary years. Categorisation, though, can be misleading. There is nothing to disqualify these books from being read by the more literary-minded upper primary child—or indeed by adults. (pp. 222-23)

> *Nigel Grimshaw, "Peter Dickinson's Children's Stories," in* The School Librarian, *Vol. 20, No. 3, September, 1974, pp. 219-23.*

Joanna Hutchison

Peter Dickinson's first three children's books, *The Weathermonger, Heartsease* and *The Devil's Children,* form a trilogy. They are all set in a Britain chronologically of the near future yet also of the past, for the 'Changes' have taken place, causing the country to become an island

> . . . fragmented into a series of rural communities, united by a common hostility to machines

of any sort and by a tendency to try to return to the modes of living and thought that characterized the Dark Ages.

> (*The Weathermonger*)

This basic hypothesis, that Britain has changed in this way, provides the mainspring of the trilogy.

The order of time in the books is in fact the reverse of that in which they were written. *The Weathermonger* takes place six years after the Changes, but in the course of the adventures of the weatherworking Geoffrey and his sister, Sally, Peter Dickinson gives a full and elaborate explanation of the origin and effects of the antimachine madness which afflicts the people until Merlin and Mr Furbelow are dealt with and Britain returns to its own proper time, with people rediscovering such delights as cars, aeroplanes and tin-openers.

The other two books simply ask one to accept the Changes without explanation, and are more successful because of it. *Heartsease* takes place about five years after the Changes, and *The Devil's Children* is set at the very beginning of the Changes, when people are leaving in the thousands for other countries. I think I was fortunate in reading *The Devil's Children* first, for it seems to me that the weakness of the trilogy lies in the cause of the Changes, and in *The Devil's Children* this seems irrelevant, or certainly obtrudes least. Any fantasy asks one to accept a certain hypothesis, to exercise a 'willing suspension of disbelief', and this one agrees to do if the book has an inner consistency and if our credulity is not expected to stretch beyond what we feel to be the probable or likely outcome of the original hypothesis. I feel that this is what *The Weathermonger* does expect of us. I read *Heartsease* to a class of mixed-ability eleven-year-olds. They seemed quite happy to accept a Britain that had reverted to the Dark Ages and was against machines.

They even had their own theories about it—which were almost unanimously that machines were held responsible for destroying Man (perhaps there had been some sort of war or atomic holocaust), and therefore it seemed logical that Man should turn against machines. When I told my class the explanation for the Changes given in *The Weathermonger,* they were both puzzled and derisive to find that it is Merlin, discovered and then held in the drugged sway of Mr Furbelow, who is causing Britain to revert to a more familiar time. It was as if the book had stepped outside its own borders of probability.

I was often niggled by other inconsistencies in *The Weathermonger* and *Heartsease*—inconsistencies which perhaps only strike one when one is reading in a more critical fashion and not when one is being swept along by the excitement of the story. Why is Geoffrey, who is so strongly affected by the Changes that he acquires the powers to become a weathermonger, not affected by the antimachine feeling so that all through the Changes he regularly services his motor boat? Why isn't Mr Furbelow returned to the Dark Ages in the same way as the other people in the book? Why are some people only partially affected by the Changes? Jonathan in *Heartsease* wonders if the immunity is, ' . . . something to do with children's minds. . . . Not being so set in their ways of thinking.' But one would in fact expect memories of machines and their usefulness to be much weaker in their minds, and that those minds should be equally susceptible to an exterior force driving them in a particular direction.

The fact that it is an exterior force is the cause of another weakness of the books—their attitude to machines. I'm not suggesting that the books should have come out wholeheartedly for or against machines. But they do invite one to consider the good and bad effects of machines, although this is done rather vaguely and weakly. Mr Gordon, the evil old sexton in *Heartsease,* and the rabble that he is able to arouse, are against machines not because they see them as something with a power to harm because of what they can *do;* they loathe machines for what they think they *are*—the Devil's work, evil for reasons they cannot clearly justify. Their hatred of machines becomes simply another superstition of the Dark Ages. And yet one seems to be asked to give serious consideration to this superstition:

> They're right about machines somehow—Mr Gordon and his lot, I mean. Machines eat up your mind until you think they're the answer to everything.

So speaks Jonathan. 'Mr Gordon and his lot' aren't half so perceptive. They've turned against machines not because they are *machines* but because they are at variance with the forces that are causing them to revert to the Dark Ages. I sense an uneasiness in the books over this question. In *The Weathermonger* there is obvious admiration for the beauty of the Rolls Royce Silver Ghost but not for 'those little French beetles whining about'. Part of the trouble is that in *The Weathermonger* and *Heartsease* the antimachine feeling is so negative. The world without machines that we are presented with has little in its favour. People are withdrawn, ignorant, superstitious, suspicious of each other: 'Nobody liking or trusting *anybody*—it couldn't have been like that before the Changes. Or in the Dark Ages? Given this, it is difficult to feel more than token regret when Britain is removed from the crazed grip of a morphine addict, even when one reads in the last line of *The Weathermonger,* 'And the English air would soon be reeking with petrol.'

It is in this regard that I feel that *The Devil's Children* is better than the other two books in the trilogy. Machines don't figure so largely, though the attitude towards them comes across very vividly when Nicky is overcome by a sort of madness as one of the Sikhs starts up an abandoned bus. More important, the community life of the Sikhs— farming their land, using their forge, bartering what they have made or repaired with the villagers—presents a kind of positive side to life without machines. I admit much of this comes through the Sikhs themselves. They have a generosity and dignity that the rather mean and ignorant villagers lack. (Partly, it must be owned, because they are not affected mentally by the Changes, not having been a part of Britain in the Dark Ages.) But even the villagers in this book are not so unpleasant as the ordinary people one meets in *The Weathermonger* and *Heartsease.* They are more recognizable as human beings, and when the two communities come together at the end of the book, one

can see a value in their way of life that forms a definite counterbalance to a noisy, industrialized Britain, whose rotting relics are left behind at the beginning of the book.

I have rather ungenerously started by saying what I don't like about the trilogy, but there are many positive elements in the books. Peter Dickinson knows that familiar and concrete objects lend an air of reality to a story that in other ways is fantastic. (pp. 84-91)

Peter Dickinson seems concerned that places in the stories be real places. In *Heartsease,* except for one small change, ' . . . everything is just as you would find it if you went there.' (Preface to the book). The village in *The Devil's Children,* though its name is changed to Felpham, is a real village, its geography accurately rendered in the book. It is characteristic that the car in *The Weathermonger* should be one that anyone can go and see for themselves in the Museum, though the new Museum would make the car rather more difficult to remove now. The author describes mechanical processes in such detail that one feels quite sure they would work in reality—processes such as the mending of the motor boat's cooling system in *The Weathermonger* or the ways in which the various bridges in *Heartsease* operate—though I did sometimes find this a problem when reading the books aloud.

Another of Peter Dickinson's strengths is his ability to pack a story full of exciting incident. A journey often figures in the books, giving opportunity for a wide-ranging and swiftly changing sequence of events. As one might expect from an author who also writes detective fiction, he is a skilful manager of plot and knows how to grip the reader's interest. Despite my criticisms of it, I would acknowledge *The Weathermonger* to be an exciting tale and I know it has been enjoyed by some of my pupils. Feeling as I do that it is not the best of Peter Dickinson's books, I don't particularly encourage them to read it, nor would I choose to read it to a class. I have noticed that *Heartsease* is popular with girls in my classes, who are interested in horses, for they can identify with its heroine and the sympathy she has with her pony. It is a book which I recommend. Apart from the exciting story, there is greater reflection in it, greater self-realization. Margaret, the principal character, has to come to acknowledge the particular strengths of Lucy, whom she has before now dismissed as a lazy and inefficient servant. And there is an interesting contrast between the peculiar virtues and weaknesses of the very different characters of Margaret and her cousin Jonathan.

As I have mentioned, I read *Heartsease* to a class of first-year pupils in the comprehensive school where I work. About two-thirds of them enjoyed it, a few people were indifferent and only two of the class positively disliked it. Those who liked it included a good cross-section of the class—boys and girls and the whole range of ability. (The children are not predominantly middleclass.) I found that on the whole it was a good book for class reading, the volume of incident in the story dividing well into lesson-sized sections. As I mentioned earlier, the detailed narration of mechanical processes wasn't easy to read aloud. One needs considerable time and concentration in order to visualize what the author has in mind. (pp. 91-2)

The other major criticism of the book which the children had was 'too many bridges'. The tug, on its journey along the canal to the Severn Estuary has to pass through bridges which have to be operated by Margaret, travelling ahead on her pony. Although this gives rise to a number of exciting incidents, I would agree with the class that it does seem a rather prolonged process, an effect which is obviously increased when the book is read aloud.

I used *Heartsease* in the way I mentioned at the beginning of this article, as a basis for various pieces of work. Quite a lot of this centred on machines. We tried to imagine what a machine, especially a large and complex one, would have looked like to someone who had never seen one before. It becomes clear that one would probably think in terms of comparison, and most of the class seemed to feel that the machines would probably appear as some sort of monsters. The children wrote descriptions of the machines from this standpoint and illustrated these, producing some splendid amalgamations of animal and machine.We tried to capture in words the sound, smell, movement and power of a machine, trying to explore something of the fascination that they can have. . . . Since I was working with a junior form, I approached the question of the possible benefit or danger to man brought about by machines in a very simple way by making collages with the class of those machines we thought useful and beneficial and those we thought were potentially destructive. (pp. 93-4)

I also did some work on superstition with the class, as I felt this was another strong element in the book, causing the villagers to become embittered and very ready to suspect their neighbours of dealings with evil powers and unleashing bouts of sudden and irrational violence. We examined some popular superstitions and their origins (I found useful here a book called, *Touch Wood: A Book of Everyday Superstitions* and carried out a small survey on whether people still believed in them. In this context we were able to look at the way in which the villagers regard Tim, Lucy's mentally retarded brother, who is threatened with being their next scapegoat, and the way in which people still regard those who are 'odd' or handicapped).

This link between ancient superstition and current prejudice is strong in *The Devil's Children,* whose title indicates the way in which the native Englishmen see the Sikhs, whom we discover to be a warm, friendly, courageous and dignified people. Our sympathies are with them throughout the book.

The element of self-realization that we find in *Heartsease* is developed further in this book. Nicky Gore is a more tangible heroine than Margaret in *Heartsease,* and alongside the story of the Sikhs' journey to Felpham and their coming to terms with the village is Nicky's coming to terms with herself. She tries to keep at bay the loneliness and desolation she feels from being separated from her parents, by refusing to become involved with people again and even when she joins up with the Sikhs, feels she must maintain her independence from them. It is the old Sikh grandmother who makes her acknowledge the barriers she is building within herself and the necessity of putting an end to these through going to find her parents.

This greater complexity of characterization makes *The Devil's Children* the most satisfying of the trilogy for me, though I would have to agree with Peter Dickinson that:

> A children's book which concentrates much on the development of character and much of whose plot hinges on character, is not of as great interest to children as it would be to an adult.

The Devil's Children has its highly exciting moments but the story's beginning does not have such an impact as in the other two books. Many children pick the book up, attracted by its title, but few of them read very much of it despite my encouragement, and for this reason I wouldn't choose to read it to one of my present classes, though I think it could be enjoyable in this context.

Emma Tupper's Diary breaks away from Britain under the Changes and turns to Scotland of the present day. Here again Peter Dickinson brings in his carpet tacks of reality to anchor the fantasy. The submarine in which the children discover animals surviving from prehistoric times is described in loving detail, and its working operations are carefully explained. . . . And like the submarine, the arguments for the existence and survival of the Plesiosaurs are carefully and convincingly worked out. In fact I found the submarine and Plesiosaurs rather easier to accept than the people. Peter Dickinson seems to have a liking for somewhat bizarre and eccentric characters. It is from them that he derives much of his humour both in his children's books and in his adult novels, where I feel they are more successful. When plot depends on character it is important that character can sustain this. Several incidents in the story spring from the constant quarrels of the McAndrew brothers, Andy and Roddy, which I found unconvincing and tedious. Poop Newcombe, a luscious, dumb, blonde kleptomaniac, who keeps an eye on the children while they keep an eye on her, is perhaps typical of the kind of unusual character that Peter Dickinson seems to enjoy creating. She adds to Emma's sense of displacement from her ordinary and stolid surroundings, but like the other McAndrews, her credibility tends to suffer when compared with tangible objects like the submarine. (pp. 94-5)

The journeys in the submarine are exciting, though the story moves rather slowly to the point where the machine is got into working order, and the scene where Emma and Roddy surface in the reeking, nightmarish cave where the creatures live is superbly described and, I think, the highlight of the book.

It is a book which I would encourage children to read on their own rather than use as a class book. I have read to a class some passages that they have enjoyed, but I don't think the work can sustain the level of interest one wants from a class book. It does, of course, raise the popular question of Man's relation to his environment, and if one was working on this subject it could be useful, though in a contributary rather than in a fundamental way.

The Dancing Bear is quite different again. Its setting is the Byzantium of 558 A D, whose atmosphere is colourfully and vividly evoked in all its complexity, vitality, beauty and squalor. I think the illustrations to the book (by David

Smee) are a considerable contribution to this atmosphere. They have a stylized and intricate quality that reflects the Byzantine world of the main character, Silvester, the bear-ward. Byzantium is Silvester's home in a very real sense; it is where he feels he fulfils his purpose and place in the world, as bearkeeper and slave in the house of the noble Lord Celsus, a house whose complex order mirrors that of the city. As well as its complexity and wealth of inci-dent, *The Dancing Bear* has excitement and charm. The journey which forms the central line of the book allows a great variety of setting and never allows one's interest to flag.

I read the book to another first-year mixed-ability class, and we enjoyed it very much. It was certainly a book which I found very enjoyable to read aloud, and a high proportion of the children liked it, including the whole range of ability. Without doubt the element in the book which they enjoyed most was Bubba. She is a superb bear and very real. She never takes on anthropomorphic fea-tures. It is often her very stupidity and lack of understand-ing, her desire for a wrestling match at a most inopportune moment and her dismay when she slides down a bank and then turns it into a new game that make her so engaging and so credible.

The feature of the book that the children did have difficul-ty with was the religious element. One of my pupils wrote, 'I thought the author should make it without people like Holy John.' and I could sympathize with him to a certain extent. Holy John is a very necessary character to the plot but his religious arguments, his asceticism and his trances or epileptic fits, are all rather difficult for a child to under-stand or accept. Despite the author's foreword, I don't think my own class could begin to comprehend the *impor-tance* of religion to the Byzantines. Most of them seemed to find this element in the book, if not confusing, then ir-relevant. I'm afraid that I edited parts of the book, leaving out the more complex religious points or glossing over them. They are by no means a barrier to reading the book in class, however. I found it a very good book for reading in class, but I didn't—and I wouldn't—use it as the basis for a scheme of work. I think it could be too heavy-handed treatment for such a story, and although it is a book of considerable depth—Silvester's journey is not only to dis-cover Ariadne but to discover himself and what it means to be a slave—I feel that the story could be spoilt by la-bouring this.

The Gift returns to the present day. It contains an element of fantasy, but here it is even more securely anchored to the familiar and recognizable. The fantasy concerns the 'Gift', now possessed by fourteen-year-old Davy Price, of being able to receive images from other people's minds, to see the pictures that they are conjuring up in the mind's eye. The history of the Gift is contained in Welsh legend; it was reputedly given by Glyn Dwr to Dafydd of Berwyn, Davy's ancestor, who requested in recompense for battle services, '. . . . a gift such as you have, Glyn Dwr, To see through the sight of the hawk on your hand.' The Gift is given, reluctantly, to the last in the family for twenty gen-erations until, 'by a deed of like daring' the last son will put an end to it.

This legend, contained in a skilfully wrought piece of verse, is delicately and characteristically handled by the author. It isn't made a focal part of the story as in Alan Garner's *Owl Service*, but introduced subtly as an explana-tion for those who choose to believe it. Or one can think like Davy's grandfather that the poem could have been written at some later time to account for the existence of a power which is not so far from known forms of extrasen-sory perception as to stretch our credulity.

The story is chiefly anchored to the familiar through its setting, a world of comparative ordinariness; a housing es-tate, a small Welsh farm, school and a building site. Davy's father is a rather shiftless, optimistic yet invariably unlucky person, unable to keep any job for long. Davy's mother gets fed up with her husband's inability to cope or to provide her with a sufficiently high standard of living and periodically leaves him and the family. During these times, Davy and his brother, Ian, and sister, Penny, stay with his father's mother on the Welsh farm. It is here that Davy discovers that he has the Gift and is warned by his grandmother of its dangers. The mental pictures that are received can easily be misinterpreted and the Gift has usu-ally brought grief to those who had it. It brought about the death of the grandmother's first husband and is at the root of her still-enduring quarrel with Davy's father.

It is a story of suspense, mystery and excitement and also one in which character is drawn with great sympathy and understanding, not only in the case of Wolf, who becomes a figure more pathetic than frightening, but also in the cases of Davy's father, irritating and unstable yet likeable, and his grandmother, with her unforgiving and wounded pride. People are portrayed convincingly with all their weaknesses yet without being judged. Much of this insight into other people is shown through Penny, whose sensitiv-ity to others is a gift too, a gift which the book suggests is of greater value and more reliable than Davy's.

All the boys and girls of twelve to fourteen that I have lent the book to have enjoyed reading it. I think it would inter-est a class as a whole, especially once the plot leading up to the robbery has been reached. (Depending on the atten-tion span of the class, I think it would be worth consider-ing beginning with the chapter entitled 'Wolf' and then going back.) The kind of perception shown by the book could encourage work on personal and family relation-ships, especially the part played by trust in such instances. An examination of other forms of extrasensory perception would probably be interesting and enjoyed by the class, but I feel it might lead one away from the book rather than towards it. (pp. 95-8)

> *Joanna Hutchison, "Peter Dickinson Consid-
> ered, In and Out of the Classroom," in* Chil-
> dren's literature in education, *No. 17, Sum-
> mer, 1975, pp. 84-103.*

Margery Fisher

The first story [*The Weathermonger*] in Peter Dickinson's impressive trilogy is a fantasy-adventure in which the final complicated explanation of the Changes does not really match the spirit of youthful gallantry in which the plot moves forward. Returning to the subject in a second book set at an earlier date, *Heartsease,* Peter Dickinson describes the efforts of two young people to save the life of an American who has come secretly to England to find out why the country has cut itself off from the rest of the world. The village where he is captured is ruled by Davie Gordon, whose sadistic deeds are disguised as righteous witch-hunts. He incites the villagers to stone Otto, who has been found using a tape-recorder, but the children nurse him and eventually take him on an old tug down the canal to the sea. Though this book too has the movement and tension of adventure, character plays a greater part in it. The farmer's son Jonathan and his cousin Margaret are generous young people and their hatred of superstition and intolerance makes a strong point in the story.

The third book, *The Devil's Children,* takes a further step in exploring the Changes as they affect people rather than events. It opens with a scene in London when the Changes, in the early stages, have caused accidents, destruction and panic. Nicky Gore has been separated from her parents in the rush to escape from plague in the city. Desperate and afraid, she travels with a band of Sikhs into Surrey; they are not affected by the Changes but must avoid machines if they are not to be persecuted by their fellow men, and Nicky is able to warn them of danger, for she is strongly affected by the proximity of machinery. The Sikhs settle down to work a neglected farm and though the intolerant head of the village is hostile at first, the two communities come together in opposing a band of looters. Nicky has won a precarious comfort and peace with the Sikhs but the wise old grandmother realizes that the girl has shut herself away from human feeling as a protection, and persuades her at last to go to France and find her parents.

The three stories, originally published singly, were later issued in a single volume, with their order reversed, so that the Changes could be seen as a continuous process from beginning to end. The effect of this was to show up very plainly the different nature of the character-drawing in the three books. With the penetrating analysis of Nicky's feelings put first, followed by the moving contrast between the liberal attitude of Jonathan and Margaret and Davie's bigotry, the characters of Geoffrey the weathermonger and his sister, lightly drawn, seem unequal to the emotional implications of the Changes now that their story is placed as a climax to the whole.

A television adaptation of the three books, made by Ann Home of *Jackanory* in consultation with the author, has partly resolved this difficulty. To make a serial of ten episodes it has been necessary to have one central character throughout. Nicky Gore is seen first as the lonely, lost girl in the Sikh community, then as the 'witch' hounded by Davie Gordon and finally she goes with Jonathan to look for the cause of the Changes. The awakened Merlin, who is described more as an emanation than a person, is shown to be reacting powerfully against Man's misuse of his environment, but the explanation for the Changes is ultimately left to suggestion, a challenge to thought and imagination. The new ending knits the three stories together in a neat and convincing way. However, it is obvious that a theme as demanding as this is best studied, ultimately, at reading

pace, and the omnibus volume seems the best way to see how Peter Dickinson has related an exceptionally provocative and topical idea to a close examination of the behaviour of individuals under exceptional stress. (pp. 114, 16)

> *Margery Fisher, "Who's Who in Children's Books: 'The Weathermonger' and Others," in her* Who's Who in Children's Books: A Treasury of the Familiar Characters of Childhood, *Holt, Rinehart and Winston, 1975, pp. 114, 116.*

John Rowe Townsend

[Peter Dickinson's] books for children have been extremely varied in setting and action. Some could be called, in his own phrase, 'science fiction without the science'; some are fantasy in realistic contemporary settings (or realistic fiction coloured by fantasy, depending on which way you look at it); and there is one full-blooded historical novel, set in sixth-century Byzantium and barbarian lands to the north of it, in which, however, the author admits that he 'had to invent quite a lot'. For all their variety, the books have had much in common: strong professional storytelling, rapid action and adventure, continual invention, a proliferating interest in ideas, and an understanding of how things are done. Behind all this one glimpses an energetic, speculative mind with a leaning towards the exotic. There is no great inwardness in the books, no exploration of character in depth, and one feels that moral problems are touched on lightly as interesting puzzles rather than felt as taxing human dilemmas. Dickinson does not give the impression of wishing he were Tolstoy; rather, he seems to work within well-understood limits. Within these limits he has written one outstandingly fine novel, *The Blue Hawk,* and at least two very good ones, *Heartsease* and *The Dancing Bear.*

His first three books for children were about a time, stated to be 'now or soon', when people in Britain are supposed to have turned against machines and retreated into a new Dark Age of malicious ignorance, superstition and xenophobia: the period of the Changes. The order of the books as originally written was back-to-front. The first, *The Weathermonger,* tells how the time of the Changes ended; the second, *Heartsease,* is set in the middle of the five-year period; the third, *The Devil's Children,* is about the beginning. The three have since appeared the other way round in an omnibus volume, *The Changes.* It is only the situation that links them; they do not have any characters in common.

Though *The Weathermonger* and *Heartsease* were published within a year of each other, there is a striking qualitative difference between them. I cannot think of another case of comparably rapid improvement. *The Weathermonger* bears many of the marks of the first-book-for-children. The main characters, a brother and sister called Geoffrey and Sally, are a resourceful boy and girl with little in their personalities to distinguish them from other children in fiction. Conveniently there are no parents or relatives around. And the mission on which they are sent is one which, outside fiction, one cannot imagine being entrusted to children. Having got a motorboat working, and escaped in it from benighted England, they arrive at a small port in Brittany and instantly meet a French general—France is unaffected by the Changes—who dispatches them to look for the source of the trouble, rumoured to be somewhere on the Welsh borders. 'You will find out the location, the exact location of the disturbance, and then we will send missiles across. We will cauterize the disease.' The children return to England on board a ketch belonging to 'an angry millionaire, who hadn't been willing to lend it until he received a personal telephone call from the President of France'. Fortunately no missiles are needed, because Geoffrey and Sally, in the time-honoured way of fictional children, deal with the entire situation unaided.

And the explanation of the Changes is outrageous. It transpires that a Mr Furbelow, who used to keep a chemist's shop in Abergavenny, has found the sleeping body of Merlin, the wizard of Arthurian legend, and has bound Merlin to himself by getting him hooked on morphine. The powers of the revived but drug-sick magician have radiated outward and affected the population. . . . Merlin now lies sick in his underground chamber, but the children persuade him to renounce the drug, and after suffering withdrawal symptoms which have fearful effects on his surroundings Merlin returns to his long rest and normality is restored. This is, to my mind, an abuse of major legend, as well as being totally unconvincing.

Yet *The Weathermonger* has some very good things in it. There is a splendid dash across a hostile England in a 1900 Rolls Royce Silver Ghost from the Montague Motor Museum at Beaulieu. And although it is not clear why an effect of the Changes should have been to give a few people the power of making the weather they want, the author himself makes brilliantly effective use of this notion. Geoffrey happens to be a weathermonger—hence the title—and the passages in which he conjures weather-changes are at once poetic and meteorologically precise. On its first appearance, *The Weathermonger,* in my view, was praised beyond its true deserts; yet its reception does credit to the reviewers, whose most important task is to recognize new talent, and who certainly did so in this case.

In the other two books of the sequence no more is said about the cause of the Changes. It is simply assumed that they have happened; and, given that assumption, everything else follows. There is no further fantasy element. In *Heartsease,* Margaret and her cousin Jonathan, who are both fourteen and live on a farm, find a 'witch'—actually and American investigator who has been stoned and left for dead. They and Lucy, the house servant, look after him, take him by sledge through a snow-covered countryside to Gloucester docks, hide him on a tug, and later run the gauntlet of the ship-canal to get him safely to sea. In *The Devil's Children* Nicola, aged twelve, is adopted by a group of Sikhs, who are unaffected by the Changes but endangered by the attitudes that result from them, and helps the Sikhs to set up a successful rural community in the face of local hostility. *Heartsease* in particular is a well-shaped, well-told story, with unified action and interest. Jonathan, who knows about engines, and Margaret, who knows about horses, are a complementary pair and make a good team; and though the servant girl Lucy does

not play a big part, there is an intriguing sense that there's a good deal more to Lucy than might appear on the surface. Dickinson has described *Heartsease* as 'a winter book, harsh and claustrophobic'; but there is warmth in its human relationships, and it ends with Margaret riding home on her horse Scrub, on a morning when 'weald and wold were singing with early spring' and 'every breath she took was full of the odour of new growth, a smell as strong as hyacinths'. *The Devil's Children,* though not I think quite so good a novel as *Heartsease,* has a fine robust climax in which the Sikhs live up to their martial reputation and defeat a band of robbers in pitched battle.

A curious feature of these three books is their assumption that ignorance and malice go hand in hand with the rejection of machinery. It is not unreasonable to suppose this, and it is certainly useful for the author's fictional purposes; but it is not a self-evident proposition, except perhaps to those who unthinkingly equate 'modern' with 'good'. Peter Dickinson himself is not one of these. *The Weathermonger* ends with the rueful observation that 'the English air would soon be reeking with petrol'; and in *Heartsease* there is a moment when Margaret says that 'they're right about machines, somehow . . . Machines eat your mind up until you think they're the answer to everything.' But these are isolated remarks: very little to set in the balance against an overwhelming general sense that 'our' side is the side of the machines. As in some other places in his work, Peter Dickinson is aware of an issue and makes his awareness clear, but backs away from any serious dealings with it.

Another three Dickinson books, though without formal links, can conveniently be looked at together. These are the ones that have contemporary settings but also fantasy elements. In *Emma Tupper's Diary,* the young McAndrew cousins with whom fourteen-year-old Emma is staying decide to reactivate the miniature submarine which Grandfather built many years ago, and use it in the loch beside which they live, to hoodwink a television company by simulating a monster. And then Emma and cousin Roddy, submarining unofficially at night, find that truth can be stranger than hoaxes.

The social background here is somewhat aristocratic. The McAndrews live on their own land, surrounded by retainers and clansfolk, and Father is the clan chief: he has 'never had a job, except during wars', but 'he's been everywhere and seen everything and met everyone . . . and whenever an Honours List is published he has to spend several days writing to all his cronies who've become Lords and things'. His son Andy dazzles girls with his 'looks and money and style'. It seems almost indecent in these days when children's books are expected by many to reflect the lives of ordinary people rather than the privileged; but in fact the participants and setting are right for the story, and there is no obvious reason why any social class should be excluded from the literary scene. There is a strong contrast, however, between the McAndrews and the family of Davy Price in *The Gift.* The Prices are much more humble folk: the grandparents on their Welsh hill farm, Mum and Dad in the little house in the new town. Davy's gift, passed down in the family for generations, is that of seeing the pictures formed in other people's minds. It seems to him fairly harmless, though a bit of a nuisance, until the day he finds himself looking into the violent, destructive mentality of a dangerous psychopath. A sequence of events then leads to a situation in which only Davy, still using his gift, can avert a mass slaughter.

At one point in **Annerton Pit,** Dickinson's latest book for children at the time of writing, there is a similar phenomenon to that of Davy's gift. Blind boy Jake and older brother Martin, looking for their missing grandfather, have stumbled on the Green Revolutionaries (militant environmentalists), who are using an abandoned mine on the Northumbrian coast as headquarters for an attempt to hijack a North Sea oil-rig. When all three are imprisoned in the old workings, it is Jake—his blindness no longer a disadvantage—who leads the way out. But in the course of the escape Jake, while alone, encounters a being which appears to inhabit the hill, to feel the workings as a wound, and to defend itself by communicating terror. Jake appears to perceive what the thing perceives and feel as it feels; but the possibility is left open that it exists only in his own mind. And yet at the end, when one of the Green Revolutionary activists blows up the workings, 'Dyingly, the air moved up the shaft as the last compression of the explosion eased itself out of the maze of galleries below. To Jake it sounded like a whispering sigh of content.'

Of these three books, all with contemporary settings yet with touches of the exotic, **Emma Tupper** is the most satisfying. In most ways it is the simplest. It is a variation on the old holiday adventure story: an unusually good one, with a strong storyline, tense moments, a splendid surprise, and a good deal of high-spirited humour and wordplay. The descriptions of the launching and operation of the miniature submarine are a fascinating technical *tour de force*. Emma's diary is deftly handled in such a way as to escape the improbabilities inherent in this kind of first-person narration: namely, an undue literary sophistication and a length so inordinate that the diarist would have had no time for the activities described. Here the diary is merely referred to in italic opening paragraphs at the heads of chapters; and the few words quoted from it are perfectly credible as the work of a fourteen-year-old. The author's way of dealing with the problem set by the discovery of a colony of real-life monsters—a species of plesiosaur—in a cave beneath the loch surface is particularly ingenious. Should the discovery be exploited, or made available only to scientists, or kept secret? The argument is organized in the shape of a family conference, with appeals on points of order, requests to address remarks to the chair, casting votes and the other apparatus of meetings. The result is to dramatize the matter, express character through it, incorporate it into the body of the fiction—and incidentally to demonstrate that discussion of an issue can be included in a children's novel without loss of impetus.

The Gift is less successful. Perhaps it tries to work on two planes at once and doesn't quite succeed on either. At one level, the author has had material for an effective thriller, but he has not been content to write a thriller. His criminal is no mere baddie but is mentally ill, a pathetic creature. Davy's family background is drawn in much more detail

than would be needed for an action story alone—an important part of the matter of the book is the situation of Davy and sister Penny in a home where Dad is always likely to mess things up and Mum might skip off at any time—yet although in plot terms the family problems, the crime theme and Davy's gift are linked together, they do not cohere emotionally. And the effect of the gift on Davy himself is surely underplayed.

Annerton Pit also seems to try to do too much, and raises more issues than it deals with. The morality of violence, when used to advance a cause, is touched on but not seriously examined; the psychological roots of violence likewise. And the mine, or maze, with a monster in it has symbolic and mythological associations of which the author is certainly well aware. But all these strands are thin and wispy, not woven into a fabric. **Annerton Pit** can of course, and by a great many young readers will, be read as a straight adventure story, and it's quite a good one: the escape through the workings of the pit achieves a prolonged and well-sustained tension. Even in this aspect however, as in others, Dickinson's two remaining books, **The Dancing Bear** and **The Blue Hawk,** are stronger and stranger.

The Dancing Bear tells of the sack of a great house in Byzantium, and the journey into Hunnish lands of Silvester, a slave, in search of the abducted daughter of the house. He is accompanied by Holy John, a dirty old domestic saint with a newfound mission to convert the barbarians, and Bubba, the bear of whom Silvester is keeper. It is a vigorous, rich and close-textured story; episodic, as quest stories must be, but fully controlled and shaped. There is always something going on: the book is alive with colourful and humorous incident. (pp. 41-8)

A contrast between civilized and barbarian life runs all through the book. Holy John points out to Silvester near the end of the journey that he has travelled from 'a city of intricate beauties and also of intricate evils' to 'a land of simple beauties and of simple evils'. And Silvester encounters—later to serve and to succeed—the Slav Antoninus, who has established an outpost of order and tradition in a lost imperial province, proclaimed himself Roman, and 'lived his lie until it became true'. Silvester himself belongs to civilization and moreover is a slave, knowing his place and knowing his value 'almost to a coin'. Though intelligent and able, he expects to be told what to do by his superiors, and only when the rescued Lady Ariadne gives him his manumission can he approach her as man to woman. He marries her, but for him at least it is only a modified happy ending, because he is exiled from the empire: he will never again cross the Danube, never return to the Byzantium he has loved. Holy John, combative and intensely opinionated, throws a shrewd oblique light on the nature of sainthood. And Bubba—stupid, affectionate, soppy, irritable—is a triumph of animal characterization; she is presented with a humorous half-anthropomorphism that never contradicts her animal nature or sinks to facetiousness.

Peter Dickinson's brief foreword to **The Dancing Bear** is illuminating. After summarizing the state of affairs in city and empire in 558 A.D., he goes on: 'And still the tides of savage nations flood out of Russia, for gold and cattle and the glory of slaughter.' The choice of words should be noted: tides, savage, flood, gold, cattle, glory, slaughter. They are powerful and evocative, a storyteller's words rather than an academic historian's, and in their context none the worse for that. *The Dancing Bear* is a splendid piece of storytelling.

Nevertheless, *The Blue Hawk* is Peter Dickinson's most impressive novel up to the time of writing. Set in a land that suggests ancient Egypt, at a time that is remote and perhaps hypothetical rather than past or future, it tells of a boy priest Tron, servant of Gdu, the god of hawking and healing. The god speaks in Tron's heart, bids him save a hawk from sacrifice and break a ritual; this causes the death of a king and sets moving a train of events that are to open up a closed land and free powers that have been rigidly bound. There is no lack of the continuous action which characterizes a Dickinson novel. But this is only part of the story. *The Blue Hawk* is about a struggle for power in a closely-controlled, priest-ridden society where everything that happens is governed by ritual, knowledge is transmitted by memorized hymns and nothing can change; yet without change the fields will silt up with salt and the land will die of inanition if it is not killed by savage enemies.

Behind the political struggle lies a further question: do the gods exist, other than as a source of power for priests? One might think not; myth and management are the same thing in this rigid society. Yet Tron *experiences* the presence of the gods; it was a god's speaking to him that set moving the wave of change. Perhaps he is indeed the instrument of higher powers, perhaps what happens had to happen. At the end Tron offers his own explanation, though only 'as a story'. The gods, he suggests, do exist but don't belong in this world; they are immensely powerful but not clever and have been trapped by wise men (as it might be ourselves). Maybe they have wanted to break out and away, and a great ritual in which Tron took part near the end of the book has opened the way for them to go. Yet this may be 'just guesses'; or may be an image for something of which we are unable to grasp the truth. And yet again, when Tron is asked whether he thinks the gods have flown and there are none any more, he says that there must be:

> I've got something in my soul which is there to love and serve the gods. So even if all my supposings are right there must still be the true gods of this world to love and serve . . . Perhaps the true gods are . . . inside us, all round us, like the air we breathe without noticing. The noise these other gods made meant we could never hear them.

There is no need to go further into these perplexities. The author is not laying it on the line, declaring in unambiguous terms what is going on. Tron does not know what the gods are; he can only wait, be ready, be receptive. Within his imaginative framework, Dickinson has left room for the imagination of the reader to move; and the reader, too, can speculate—if he wishes to do so. Alternatively he can just read the story. There is plenty to make him want to turn the page.

There is a great deal of violence in *The Blue Hawk,* with nothing spared: at one point a grisly cairn of priests' heads; at another, mothers hurling their children over a cliff to destruction on the rocks below, before leaping to their own deaths. Dickinson has said he thinks the style of writing and the context make these horrors acceptably distant from the young reader's world, and this comment would presumably also apply to various violent incidents in the other books. There are moments, however, when violence is seen closer up and in a different light, with the apparent implication that it is something to be accepted. Tron watches his hawk make a kill, and

> it struck him for the first time how strange it was that the perfection of the moment had to end in a death. It was as though he were a god who needed the sacrifice of the kingfowl to fulfil his nature. Were the gods indeed like that? No. It was the blue hawk that needed the death, to fulfil *its* nature.

Closer to ourselves, one recalls that Nicky in *The Devil's Children* felt a kinship with the robber who 'laughed like a lover' as he swung his axe; one recalls, too, Jake's reflection at the end of *Annerton Pit* that 'if you mine down through the maze of your own being, perhaps in those deeps you will find the explosive gas of violence, the springs of love'.

These last aspects of violence—questions of the necessity of it, the attraction of it, its association with fulfilment and even with love—are the most difficult and worrying ones in the Dickinson novels. The psychology of violence can be explored in adult fiction but is probably too complex, too demanding in terms of experience and understanding required from the reader, and perhaps too disturbing, to be dealt with in depth in novels for children. In spite of the reference to 'mining down through the maze of your own being', Peter Dickinson does not, I think, attempt such exploration; and he is probably right not to do so (though it may be questioned whether, this being so, the more intimate encounters with violence, as distinct from the 'acceptably distant' variety, might not be better omitted). This may be a point at which Dickinson, like other writers in other respects, comes up against the boundaries of the children's list. Or it may be that he comes up against a personal boundary: that he does not go deeply down into the human heart because that is not the kind of writer he is. The latter hypothesis, if correct, is not a cause for complaint. Writers must do what they can and want to do; and Peter Dickinson can do things in fiction that less fertile and vigorous contemporaries would never have the creative energy to achieve. (pp. 49-52)

> *John Rowe Townsend, "Peter Dickinson," in his* A Sounding of Storytellers: New and Revised Essays on Contemporary Writers for Children, *J. B. Lippincott, 1979, pp. 41-54.*

Sheila A. Egoff

With the imaginative ruminations of scientific surmise taken out of science fiction, writers tended not only to keep their stories earthbound but to cast them in future agricultural or medieval societies, thereby giving their stories a quasi-historical sense. The advantages are obvious.

Although earthbound imaginatively, the writers can convince by plausible, and indeed, accurate details. Such a technique can be seen in Peter Dickinson's trilogy about a weather change in England that caused a revulsion against machines and technology and a reversion to an agricultural society: *The Weathermonger, Heartsease,* and *The Devil's Children.* These are, first of all, solidly based in the topography of England; the setting and the journeys of the children, different in each book, can almost be mapped. Therefore, actual rivers, canals, bridges, and rights of way provide a convincing context for hunts and chases.

All the details, some of them most memorable, are skillfully woven into the plots and do not strain credulity. In *The Weathermonger,* the children, having escaped from England to France, are ordered to return, to try to uncover the secret of the weather change. They need transportation while in England and a Rolls Royce, a "Silver Ghost," which was left carefully covered up, is available to them. Mechanics and fuel are sent with them. The adult mechanics, being more subject to the effects of the changes than the children, have to leave England as soon as the car is in running order. This kind of realistic touch is absent in poorer science fiction, such as Andre Norton's *Star Man's Son* (1952), in which an automobile starts after 200 years of standing idle. Norton valiantly tries to bolster her plot action by noting that the car had a "sealed" engine, but ignoring the fact that any fuel is highly volatile. As opposed to Norton's vagueness in both topography and incident, Dickinson's work is strengthened by precision. Even the shock of the sudden introduction of Merlin into *The Weathermonger* is cushioned by the practicality of the children. They face Merlin's problem not only with the aplomb of Alice in Wonderland, but with some childlike culinary and medicinal knowledge. (pp. 137-38)

> Sheila A. Egoff, "Science Fiction: 'The Wea- thermonger', 'Heartsease', and 'The Devil's Children'," in her Thursday's Child: Trends and Patterns in Contemporary Children's Lit- erature, *American Library Association, 1981, pp. 137-38.*

Michael Dirda

Peter Dickinson possesses the enviable talent of being able to write all kinds of books equally well. His mystery novels—such as *The Glass-Sided Ants' Nest* and *The Poison Oracle*—have won England's equivalent of the Edgar; his most recent novel, *Tefuga,* earned acclaim for its depiction of whites and blacks in Africa; and his children's fiction has been set, with easy mastery, in both the distant past and the near future.

Dickinson first made his mark as a writer for young people in these three newly reissued novels [The *Devil's Children, Heartsease,* and *The Weathermonger*], first published in 1968, '69, and '70, and known collectively as The Changes Trilogy. Sometime around today, or perhaps tomorrow, the entire population of England turns against all machines; indeed, the mere presence of a machine, whether automobile or electric can opener, induces a destructive frenzy, a blend of religious mania and temporary insanity. Soon England has closed in on itself "like an anemone"

and cut off the island from the rest of the world. When Europeans or Americans try to investigate, they are either killed as "witches" or find themselves falling prey to the strange madness; spy planes crash repeatedly because their pilots suddenly lose all understanding of how to fly. As the Changes continue, England grows feudal, rural, simple. Dickinson's young heroines and heroes find themselves caught up in strange times indeed.

In *The Devil's Children*—the first novel in the series, though the last to be written—12-year-old Nicola Gore joins a clan of Sikhs after she is abandoned by her maddened parents. Eventually, the Sikhs—immune to the Changes—must rescue a village held hostage by robbers (who wear armor and carry swords). In the wake of their victory a new community is established, a haven of peacefulness. The tone of this lyrical novel is almost Tolstoyan: the evocation of a life in harmony with nature, the workings of field and forge, an epic battle, and a gentle close. Out of confusion has arisen clarity.

By contrast, *Heartsease* suggests Hawthorne in its depiction of fanaticism, in its evocation of a claustrophobic village ruled by the sinister witch-hunter Davey. At its opening young Margaret and her cousin Jonathan rescue an American "witch" stoned and left for dead; for weeks they—along with an idiot boy and his spiteful sister— nurse the spy back to health. Eventually, though, this resistance group must make a daring run to the sea: they repair the motor on an old boat and brave an embattled countryside before they pass into open water. Where *The Devil's Children* is a book filled with light, hope in reason, and the promise of community, *Heartsease* is set in a wintry landscape of prejudice, desperation and uncertainty, and it ends with its heroine rejecting the world of machines to stay in her pastoral purgatory.

After confusion and claustrophobia, *The Weathermonger* feels carefree, T. H. White out of the *Boy's Own Paper.* Its teen-aged protagonist Geoffrey—gifted with shamanlike powers of weather control—suddenly finds his mind clear of his machine-hatred and escapes with his younger sister Sally to France, though the pair eventually return to England to seek out the source of the Changes. To travel to its center, a forest in Wales, Geoffrey daringly starts up a Rolls Royce Silver Ghost and soon undergoes a series of picaresque and magical adventures on the road: he and Sally fall prey to a charming con man, swindle various yokels, are nearly killed by a mysterious cloud, discover a forbidding castle, and finally meet up with none other than the magician Merlin. Eventually, the two children, in the best E. Nesbit fashion, become the rescuers of their country.

Paradoxically in each of these Luddite books some piece of machinery takes a starring role: a forge, a boat, a car. Dickinson describes their functioning as lovingly as Kipling or a writer for *Popular Mechanics.* Clear and direct in his prose, Dickinson reveals an engineer's appreciation for the exact, so readers young and old may need to look up words like "tilth" or "meniscus." He is moreover a writer who refuses to repeat himself; consider his main characters: Nicola hates machines, Margaret's unsure of them, and Geoffrey quite likes them. Finally Dickinson possesses a quiet but winning sense of humor: It's heartening to see a short, fat Sikh singlehandedly defeat a trio of handsome, teen-aged ruffians.

It's also a pleasure to have these humane and intelligent books back in print. . . .

Michael Dirda, "Merlin and the Machines," in Book World—The Washington Post, *July 20, 1986, p. 11.*

Margery Fisher

As a subject, international politics has been largely untouched or skirted round in junior novels, at least until recent years. During the 1970s two writers [Peter Dickinson and Robert Cormier] challenged this particular omission and in doing so they took the thriller to extreme limits—extreme, especially, in the sense that the subject of terrorism in the context of today might even be considered inadmissible in the genre of the adventure story. Yet there seems good reason for authors to present, in the format of action-stories which young readers can take at a pace suitable for their emotional judgement, certain issues which they will also meet in the more hasty and ephemeral media of newspapers and television reports.

The media can name and even describe individuals concerned in terrorist activities: fiction alone can probe the motives and personal pressures behind an ideological issue. The particularisation of a story can guide the young towards some understanding of large issues. At the same time, these young readers have a right to demand the pleasures associated with adventure-fiction—pace and tension, verisimilitude, atmosphere and an absence of overt moralising.

This is partly a matter of technique. To produce a story and not a sermon an author must organise his material so that his final commitment and the direction of his work do not hamper the story line. Buchan's novels, to take one example, show considerable variation in the success with which this kind of balance is achieved; so do the 'entertainments' of Graham Greene. Peter Dickinson was obviously well aware of the problem when he planned the structure and set the symbolic framework of ***The Seventh Raven,*** which is above all a brilliant piece of narrative. The plot is simple. In a prosperous district of Kensington a committee of men and women, known to the narrator ironically as the Mafia, are organising rehearsals of an ambitious annual opera, to be performed by children but with theme, music and technique addressed to their elders. The libretto is based on the conflict between Elijah and Jezebel; it includes Elijah's exile in the desert and the horrific death of Jezebel. Both words and music emphasise the dilemma of a weak king, 'in a muddle in the middle' between the stern conviction of Elijah that Jehovah's rule must prevail and the fervent support of Jezebel for the cruel rituals of the god Baal, both ideologies implying force, violence and antagonism echoed in the clashing musical motifs allotted to each. In a well-bred, artistically accomplished manner the conductor and committee set themselves to express the conflict through music: philosophy is to be painlessly, even elegantly, expressed in performance.

Reality intrudes, abruptly. To satisfy a government plan for détente with a South American dictatorship about to change leaders, the committee reluctantly agree to include as an extra raven the young son of the Mattean ambassador in London. Terrorists plot to seize young Juan as a hostage, to achieve freedom for political prisoners in Matteo. Failing to snatch the boy before he enters the church for the first dress rehearsal, the four terrorists hold more than a hundred adults and children in siege; a long period of argument and tension ends in a counterattack from outside and, seemingly, the defeat of the terrorists.

A physical victory, certainly, a successful strategic coup in which the terrorists are captured and given over to justice: in terms of right and wrong, no victory but a series of questions posed in verbal argument and never more than tentatively answered. Has music the right to remain abstract and detached or should composer and musician serve a particular ideology? Has anyone the right to stay in the middle? The narrator herself is in the middle in some ways. Doll at seventeen is now too old to perform in the opera which has absorbed her energies for several years but she can act as a useful liaison between the 'Mafia' of parents and their offspring, trying to bring some kind of order into costumes and groups of singers. More dangerously, she becomes the liaison between besiegers and besieged and has to try to reconcile uncomfortable ideas with her comfortable middle-class assumptions.

Through Doll we listen to the arguments of two of the terrorists—Danny the schoolteacher and Chip, who has escaped imprisonment in an Amnesty exchange, and to the informed explanations of international power politics from Mrs Dunnett, a dedicated Communist whose search for justice for the individual seems a hopeless one. We notice that Doll calls the invaders of the church 'bandits' but feels she is unfair to do so. Meanwhile through her eyes we watch in close-up, sharing her mixture of amusement and apprehension, the ingenious efforts to hide Juan, the stolid common sense of the child whose name, Elizabeth Windsor, has inevitably become Queenie and the exhibitionism of a more precocious one, the self-contained nervous tension of Doll's musician mother, the improvisations of the terrorists and the barely concealed aggressiveness of the girl Angel, who represents one extreme of the rebel attitude as Danny's reasoned stance stands for the other. Angel's deliberate pose with a machine-gun, her beaded plaits and military costume, her set expression ('guerilla chic', Doll thinks) come near to melodrama:

> Suddenly she shook her head, like a horse pestered with flies, so that the beads rattled as they whirled and settled. The noise made the children turn, and she did it again for their benefit, a deliberate signal of danger, like the rattle of a snake when the cameraman gets too close.

Yet the final impression left by the book is neither terror nor relief but the sense that questions of great importance have been properly and firmly posed and may perhaps one day be answered. As an event the siege ends with little physical harm and the opera is safely, even splendidly performed: nobody in fact remains untouched by it.

This is one way to make a topical point, alleviating violence with moments of humour, relaxing tension with quirks of personality, making a kaleidoscopic pattern of mood and atmosphere. As a contrast to Peter Dickinson's graceful, assured style Robert Cormier's prose in *After the First Death* is hard, concrete, a style of serious reportage transferred to narrative and retaining some of its formalities. Yet this, too, is a story intended to expose the dangers of ideology through the crisis, mental as well as physical, of individuals. (pp. 149-51)

Peter Dickinson probed deeply into the significances of a tunnel in **Annerton Pit,** luring his readers from the explicit and understandable to the near-mystical. In a topical plot he describes how two boys looking for their over-adventurous grandfather, who had disappeared on one of his ghost-hunting journeys, were involved dangerously with a revolutionary ecological group working from deserted mineworkings in a northern county.

The stretch of mine-galleries is at first a simple hiding-place for the boys after they have rescued the old man from his captors, and for seventeen-year-old Martin it remains a refuge, cold and uncomfortable but unalarming. The reader 'sees' through the eyes of Jake, blind eyes helped by the compensation of acute senses and intuitions beyond his thirteen years. Smells and textures build up the underground world for us and then, gradually and intermittently, intensify the whole picture intellectually as Jake recalls random facts about children in Victorian mines. Recollections of history lessons help him identify aspects of the mines in which he has lost his way but they also sharpen his feelings so that fear becomes urgent and, together with physical pain, it induces an ultimate experience. At first he has an illusion of seeing colours and shapes; then he seems to detect a presence other than his own; finally he senses that the presence is somehow a hidden part of himself. In the simple language of a boy in trouble, believing anything is possible, he asks 'What are you?':

> The answer came strongly, but not in that first impossible blast. There was very little in it Jake could grasp. It was like hearing music, so strange that you can't even recognize that it's music at all. Pressure of rocks. Growth like roots along the shifting pressurelines. Waiting that wasn't waiting, because time wasn't the time Jake knew. A curious caution and wariness, as if the life that was fulfilling its nature in this way was somehow a frontier life. Other lives—not the scurrying crowds of Jake's experience, but few, remote, deeper, safer, known along fine tendrils of contact, all waiting through the time that wasn't time. Not simply waiting. Waiting *for* . . .

The slow, elaborate yet simply planned winding into the inmost possibility of the potent image is here to work on the reader through the sound, the arrangement, the meaning and the mystery of words. The purpose is not to establish a setting but to convert that setting into an experience. The intensity of this moment in a very varied experience for a blind boy goes far beyond the expectation which the average reader would be likely to hold of an adventure in a tunnel. (pp. 327-28)

In the widest sense any adventure story is educational. Whatever the relative importance of action and character, there will be some direction towards an implied statement about human behaviour. The adult reader has the choice of enjoying the action and ignoring a moral or psychological point or of meeting the author halfway and using imagination to appreciate what he implies in the plain course of his narrative. A young reader does not have the same choice—or, at least, the author makes it clear that he *does* intend that reader to profit by his story. The fact that many children ignore this aspect of it does not alter the writer's intention or his duty. Apart from the moral need to make some kind of clear statement about the theme and purpose of his fiction, he has the literary need to integrate his lesson with his narrative, which will be either didactic or truly, broadly educational, according to his presentation of people and events.

Here some distinction must be made between education and information. This may be best pursued by comparing two books for children whose plots and characters are not dissimilar but whose purpose and effect are very different. Patrick O'Brian's *The Road to Samarcand,* published in 1954, is based on an almost formal thesis. A boy in the early teens, orphan son of missionaries, has been given a temporary home on the *Wanderer,* in which his uncle trades in the China Seas, but in time Captain Sullivan realises Derrick must go to England and become a schoolboy again. . . . When the adventure is over, it is evident to the reader that while fear and physical deprivation have to some extent tested Derrick, he has not really changed as a result of this exciting, varied and exacting journey. He has acquired information rather than growing in stature as a result of education.

In my second example, information is secondary in the experience of a boy travelling in the East at the turn of the century and meeting similar hazards. Peter Dickinson's historical adventure *Tulku* was written almost a quarter of a century later than Patrick O'Brian's spanking yarn and though I would not claim that any specific chronological change could be traced here, it does seem to me that the emotional, even philosophical tone of Dickinson's book has something to do with the present-day view of the moral development of the young and the way writers are responding to this in the tone of their fiction. Certainly *Tulku* should serve to show what I mean by education as opposed to instruction.

The central character of the book is a boy of ten, Theodore Tewker, who alone survives a raid of Boxer rebels on the mission station run by his American father. In terms of actual physical danger Theo is as adequately protected by his elders as Derrick was in *The Road to Samarcand.* In place of the ministrations of the traditional Omniscient Uncle figure in that book (a role shared between several characters, in fact, each one focusing his attention on the boy) Peter Dickinson has drawn as Theo's protector the magnificently individual figure of Mrs Jones, a strident Cockney travelling as a flower-collector, a woman of bold integrity who has no intention of subordinating her own journey through life to the needs of a small boy.

Although she acts with tact and delicacy towards Theo

after she has accepted and returned the love of her servant and fellow-traveller, the Chinese poet Lung, she leaves it to the boy to find his own way out of the misery and loss he has suffered and to adjust to the behaviour of his elders. Instead of setting her up as a mother-figure to fill the place of Theo's dead father, Peter Dickinson has made her the means by which the boy gradually comes to look, again and honestly, at the strict, theological education which he has taken for granted. Father would have disliked Mrs Jones for her brazen speech and sexual manners, Theo realises very early in their escape, but he need not necessarily feel the same. . . . (pp. 346-48)

Guilty but delighted at his feeling of freedom, Theo grows into his independence, at first learning to accept Mrs Jones for what she is; then in the Lamasery where they wait for the birth of her child, by divination believed to be the Tulku, the new lama, Theo moves out of received dogma and realises that he is an individual, solely responsible for himself. In keeping with his age and experience, he does not arrive at this vital point in his moral education by reason but through an inrush of feeling, a sharpening of the senses, partly due to the alarming and unfamiliar procedures of the oracle-priest and partly through the influence of the remote community where he has time to grow into his experiences:

> . . . and now, here, he was fiercely conscious of himself as Theodore, of the central numbness flooding with life, the broken roof rebuilt and the cold hearth glowing. He had heard Lama Amchi talk of those moments on the path to enlightenment when the soul seems to leave the body and soar free, and of the agony of its return to clogging flesh. Theodore felt the exact opposite. The return was the ecstasy. He was whole, and body and mind and soul sang at their healing.

The whole course of this travel-adventure is built on the theme of education in the basic sense of the difficult search for identity. Supported as it is on recurring images of plants, growth and gardening, the book is educational but in no way didactic. (pp. 348-49)

Margery Fisher, in her The Bright Face of Danger, *The Horn Book, Inc., 1986, 439 p.*

TITLE COMMENTARY

The Weathermonger (1968)

Five years from now England turned (or will turn) against machinery and destroyed the lot. What a good idea! some adults will say. (Children will take quite a different view.) The drawback to this revolution is that it is a return not to some William Morris art-and-crafty Middle Age but to the Dark Ages. Witches are drowned, inventors stoned. Latin is compulsory in all primary schools. There is a nasty air of hatred abroad.

This is the situation in *The Weathermonger,* a remarkable story which seems at first like an anti-science-fiction novel but which by degrees becomes a fantasy of the Celtic fringe. It all began when Mr. Furbelow, a little chemist from Abergavenny, found Merlin sleeping beneath a rock

in the Black Mountains and, like the fool he certainly was, woke him up. The mighty spirit of Merlin spreads out over England, turning everything to the likeness of the fifth century.

But all this is at the climax of a masterly story. The country is rescued from the past by an assault force composed of one boy, aged sixteen, and his sister, aged eleven. They escape from ceremonial drowning to a France firmly established in midtwentieth century. Here a French general, drawn with just the finest touch of irony, briefs them for their forlorn expedition. This, when it comes, is an admirable piece of narrative. The children's journey through an England living among the ruins of its lost civilization—the parallel with Britain after the departure of the legions is implicit but not laboured—is made in a Silver Ghost 1909 vintage, stolen from Lord Montagu's museum at Beaulieu. In this they travel crosscountry towards the Welsh border until, coming on the Ross motorway within range of the full blast of Merlin's power, their lovely car is destroyed by a thunderbolt. The rest of the journey is made with the help of Maddox—a malevolent doormat of a pony.

This is to give away just a little too much of a very good story. What gives it an individual quality is that, like all the best and only the best fantasies, it is firmly grounded in reality. The reader accepts the huge improbabilities because they are placed in a setting which is consistent and convincing. The author does not attempt to cheat. There are no easy solutions. The children achieve their task not just by luck—although there is an acceptable amount of this—but by courage and resolution, and by Sally's skill in oral Latin.

Above all, this is very good storytelling. The reader—and not only the child reader—is on the edge of his chair with the excitement of the drive across England, and the earthquake in which the nigromancer's dark tower falls, in a night of chaos and terror, is finely described. In face of such convincing writing disbelief is readily suspended.

In the end England returns to rainy skies and the reek of petrol. Was it all worth it? It is an adult's question. Children will be content with a fine tale and a modern world in which to read it.

"The Sleeper Wakes," in The Times Literary Supplement, *No. 3446, March 14, 1968, p. 257.*

"He woke up suddenly, as if from a deep sleep full of recoverable dreams. He was very uncomfortable." The reader either stops here or races through *The Weathermonger* at one sitting—though a "sitting" sounds a more passive experience than it is; the first chapter jolts him out of present time and space into a marvellously unpredictable, incredible story; and since he knows no more than the boy Geoffrey knows, he shares Geoffrey's frightening bewilderment at finding himself, without memory of the past five years, on a rock with an unknown girl in Weymouth Harbour faced by a jeering line of spearmen bent on drowning him. (p. 143)

The children's escape to France, their superbly funny interview with General Turville, their return to England to find the cause of disruption—"not for France or the world or anything, but just to know", makes a fast-moving, very original story. I imagine it will be most enjoyed by the imaginative child, able to read anything and interested in everything. (pp. 143, 145)

> *N. Danischewsky, in a review of "The Weathermonger," in* Children's Book News, *London, Vol. 3, No. 2, March-April, 1968, pp. 143, 145.*

Whatever the faults of our age there is something very encouraging about the emergence of authors of this quality; surely the children who respond to the intense awareness of life manifested by Garner, Mayne, Pearce and now Peter Dickinson will continue to respond more intelligently to both life and literature and will take a livelier interest in the world as a whole? The "better" authors have always appealed primarily to the "better" readers and this situation is unlikely to alter, but for many decades better reading tended to lead the reader to an ivory tower; these new authors are able to blend traditional and topical themes in a way which promises to lead to a keener appreciation of both modern problems and universal concepts. Thus this little book, written sheerly for entertainment and extremely entertaining and readable, includes both some very shrewd comments on war and the military mentality, and a brief but memorable appearance by Merlin which opens up a whole world of possibilities under the reader's feet. The description of the 1909 Rolls Royce Silver Ghost can impress even those usually left cold by cars of any vintage, and the horse Maddox is a considerable creation. Amongst its other achievements, such as originality of plot, ease of writing, feeling for place and credibility of action, the book is one of that most civilized group which prove it is possible to have suspense and drama without making anyone play the villain; even the con-man schoolmaster, even the General, is likable. The plot is too good to give away, but concerns an England of the future where life has mysteriously reverted to Dark Age superstitions. . . . Invigorating stuff, stylistically experimental in a way which should intrigue more than the literary, with a climax which should intrigue *anybody.*

> *A review of "The Weathermonger," in* The Junior Bookshelf, *Vol. 32, No. 3, June, 1968, p. 176.*

Idealism, we recall, is the philosophic doctrine which teaches that the world we know is the product of our ideas about it. At its most extreme, Idealism wonders whether, if we do not think it there, the floor will actually *be* there when we step out of bed. In its commonplace forms it is the doctrine which most people in Britain and the United States learn naturally as they grow up; its limitation is of course that by definition it tends to overvalue the place of ideas in life, and to underplay the significance of material forces, from physical to economical ones. What it obviously permits is the possibility of an ideal world at some remove from the real one. Such a movement of the imagination is presumably possible in any culture, but the habits of Idealist thought enable us to move very much more freely into an imagined world, and having got there, to give it greater significance than the real one.

A radical tradition has long accused Western society of doing this to art. The bourgeoisie, the case goes, has used art as an ideal refuge from an awful reality, and abused it to *justify* that reality. Its critical, reflexive power has been switched off insofar as it has been made merely an escape. Such a charge sticks fairly and squarely to many of the mythic or crypto-Arthurian novels. Dickinson in **The Weathermonger** tries ingeniously to get round it by making the science-fiction into a critical comparison of industrial and pre-industrial society: he does this in a necessarily coarse and caricatured picture of medieval life, bonded by bigotry and cruelty as well as by the slow, wholesome rhythms of rural work deepened and enriched by the return of pre-pesticide butterflies and wild flowers. At the same time he notes not only the convenience of machinery and medicine, but the tolerance and reasonableness of the way of life it brings. Furthermore, he devises an attractive way of giving his two children something to do. They are not the ciphers of so many similar novels; they seek out Merlin in his latter-day castle, and find that he has been discovered in his age-old sleep by a well-meaning, small-minded chemist who sought to bind the magician's power by addicting him in his sleep to morphine. Merlin's terrible and magnificent spirit is distorted by the drug but rules the chemist; he causes England to revert to an Arthurian society, and only when the children explain his plight to him (in Cambridge Project Latin) does he renounce the drug voluntarily, 'Perdurabo, deo volente', and after a hideous withdrawal, unclenches his grip on the country.

It is a rather roughed-out, racy tale, strong and crude. According to the conventions, it presents to children a picture of the power of magic and the beauty and honour of the ancient order. Its narrative fairly strides along. What Dickinson does not give his novel is a means of mitigating the crude Idealism whereby Merlin creates a material forest and castle by imagining it, and Geoffrey, the 16-year-old hero, changes the weather by thinking hard in poetic-meteorological diction. By the same token, he gives his reader (and the novelist's own intelligence) nowhere to live. For all the agreeable detailing of road numbers—the A35, the M5—and place names, the regression of the country to the old order is as placeless as any monastery or castle in Hermann Hesse or Mervyn Peake. The strength of the book lies in its brisk invitation to compare the present outside the novel with the new machineless age inside it. But the writer's cheerful, breezy way with his excellent tale only makes the comparison a casual idea; it is not worked out in any subjective intensity. (pp. 241-42)

> *Fred Inglis, "Rumours of Angels and Spells in the Suburbs," in his* The Promise of Happiness: Value and Meaning in Children's Fiction, *Cambridge University Press, 1981, pp. 232-50.*

Heartsease (1969)

Mr. Dickinson proposes a thought-provoking situation in his story of children living on a Cotswold farm at a time when an extraordinary social revolution has outlawed all machines and the traditions associated with them. While there might be some sense in this, there is less in the extension of the feeling that machines are immoral to the resurrection of suspicions of witchcraft among the less fortunate members of the community who behave oddly or ineffectually. The irrationality of the witch-hunting is as galling as the incidents at Salem to the practical mind. Into the situation falls an American spy sent to discover the source and nature of the 'changes' which have taken place over most of the United Kingdom, and his rescue, and that of the idiot Tim, from the witch-hunters, their concealment on a river tug whose engines are eventually re-started, and the highly dramatic escape down river to the open sea make for an exciting story in which thoughtful young readers may read a significance which is at once frightening and maturing. *Heartsease* should prove to be an outstanding achievement.

> *A review of "Heartsease," in* The Junior Bookshelf, *Vol. 33, No. 3, June, 1969, p. 177.*

Peter Dickinson made a startling debut last year with *The Weathermonger,* surely one of the most original of first novels. Mr. Dickinson showed an England which, not far in the future, had turned against the machine. The situation was highly intriguing: the explanation just a little hard to swallow. *Heartsease* describes an episode in the same period, this time without a solution, and the story is the better for the omission. . . .

Mr. Dickinson's imaginative control is absolute. He makes the reader feel the weight of the spirit of this strange age, so that the children's success in resisting it is the more impressive. Youth, and the retarded mentality of Tim the moron, insulate them a little, but it is still a triumph when they defy the tribal taboos and risk the savage sanctions which their actions evoke.

Heartsease scores very high marks for sheer story-telling, narrative which is packed full of suspense and pace and in which the action springs from the clash of personalities and the stress of circumstance. It is more than a very good yarn. The scene-painting is masterly, discreet and economical and always consistent. Some of the characters are types or ciphers, but Margaret, the central figure, is finely conceived. It is she who straddles the gulf between the old world and the new, and she, not her cousin Jonathan for whom it is home, who returns to the farm after the excitement of flight and the promise of freedom, to an ailing senile aunt and an uncle who beats her for her good and his satisfaction. It is a satisfying, unpredictable ending to a remarkable and moving story. In Mr. Dickinson we have another of those writers, in whom this age is so rich, who push back the boundaries of the children's novel.

> *"After the Machine Age," in* The Times Literary Supplement, *No. 3513, June 26, 1969, p. 687.*

Peter Dickinson's first book for children, *The Weathermonger,* was an original and stimulating fantasy that was highly praised on its publication last year. In this second book, Mr. Dickinson has returned to the situation which he used so effectively in the earlier story: England in the grip of the ideas and superstitions of the Middle Ages. But although the setting is the same the mood is not and the humour and originality which characterised *The Wea-*

thermonger have been replaced in *Heartsease* by a more serious and straightforward attempt to examine life in a society dominated by fear of machines and adherence to ancient superstition.

The story concerns a group of children who rescue an American spy from death by stoning and smuggle him out of the country. It is an exciting story and Mr. Dickinson tells it well but the plot is less interesting than the background and the characterisation of the children themselves is less effective than that of the adults who are their enemies.

There is no weathermongering and no Merlin in *Heartsease* and the book is less a fantasy than a realistic adventure in an alien setting. Children of ten to twelve will enjoy it as such but admirers of *The Weathermonger* will, I think, be disappointed.

> *L. E. Salway, in a review of "Heartsease," in* Children's Book News, *London, Vol. 4, No. 4, July-August, 1969, p. 201.*

Although this story follows on from the author's excellent first book *The Weathermonger,* and will be enjoyed more by those who have read its forerunner, it is complete in itself. . . . The claims on the dust-jacket are not exaggerated. Mr Dickinson is indeed an exciting find, and to mention him with Mayne, Garner and Pearce may well be justified. It may be just a little early for 'Hats off, gentlemen . . . ,' but I shall be astonished if we do not have more very good things from him. All junior and senior schools should acquire both books without delay.

> *Robert Bell, in a review of "Heartsease," in* The School Librarian, *Vol. 17, No. 3, September, 1969, p. 296.*

The Devil's Children (1970)

Some time soon the Changes will take place. The English people will take against the machine age. They will smash every mechanical contrivance in uncontrollable rage. The cities, which live by the machine, will run down and become concrete deserts. In the country, society will revert to the dark ages.

The chronicler of the Changes is Peter Dickinson. In *The Weathermonger* . . . he described the last stage of their history and ventured, perhaps unwisely, on an explanation. *Heartsease* was a story of the society in which the Changes had become accepted as the natural order. Now he turns to the beginning of the story, not to the moment of change but to a country coming agonizingly to grips with its crisis. *The Devil's Children* is the best story-telling of the trio. It may matter to some unsophisticated children that the mystery is not explained, but this, for all its outward violence of action, is not a book for the unsophisticated. The readers who will enjoy it best—and what a pity that the rules of the game will exclude all but a handful of adults from their number—are those who have a sense of history and a sharp appreciation of modern society. Only these super-readers will be competent to test the validity of Peter Dickinson's concept and its resolution.

The time is the future—but only just. Nicky is alone in Shepherd's Bush. The cars and buses stopped weeks ago, and the refugees abandoned their homes and headed for the coast. Those who were left died one by one of the "sickness". Nicky has waited vainly for her parents to come back for her. Now she deliberately cuts her roots and goes out into England. "Nicola Gore was going to look after herself, and not let anyone love her again, ever."

Nicky joins a migrant band of Sikhs, busmen, factory-workers and their families. She becomes their "canary". Their alien culture has made them incompletely sensitive to the Changes, and she is their test of the new normality. The motley train of prams and carts crosses London and makes its way into open country. There are battles with hooligans and robbers, and the Sikh "lions" rediscover their warrior pride. At last, just beyond the "bad wires" of a line of pylons, they settle down, to live in uneasy peace with the nearby feudal village where a herculean stockman dispenses rough justice.

Despite hazards and discomfort there is almost an idyllic quality about this interlude. The Sikhs toil in the fields and make tools and weapons in their forge. Slowly the Devil's Children—the villagers follow immemorial tradition in ascribing anything strange or inexplicable to the Old One—build up a viable economy. Then the harsh world breaks in. The village is raided by a band of knights in armour—bits of drainpipe—and the village baron is slain. In an heroic climax the Sikhs and the robber knights fight it out to the finish.

This is strong stuff and Mr. Dickinson, if he invents no gratuitous horrors, pulls no punches. It is a grim story about grim times. If one accepts his initial premise, then the whole of Mr. Dickinson's narrative follows logically. There is no plausibility, no easy conclusions. The sharpness of his imaginative creation is heightened by the reality of his characters. These are not cardboard; villagers and Sikhs alike bleed when they are hurt. The one full-scale portrait is that of Nicky herself, and this is a most subtle study of a complex human.

> *"Recognizable Futures," in* The Times Literary Supplement, *No. 3555, April 16, 1970, p. 417.*

[*The Devil's Children* is an] outstanding [book] of SF. . . . Peter Dickinson returns to the scene of the future of which he has written before—an England in which machines have been forbidden and all occupations must be undertaken with the tools in use before the industrial revolution. The girl Nicky finds herself totally alone in London, surrounded by areas of pestilence; she attaches herself to a band of travelling Sikhs, and with them settles outside a Hampshire village, in spite of distrust between the two different races. After the necessity to unite against a common enemy has broken down this barrier, Nicky discovers that in her fight for independence she also has built up barriers against the outside world, which she must now learn to break down. The lesson isn't hammered home, and the difficulties of learning to trust what is strange are an integral part of the story.

> *Catherine Storr, in a review of "The Devil's*

Children," in New Statesman, *Vol. 79, No. 2044, May 15, 1970, p. 704.*

The progress of [this] story is a dual one. The journey through Surrey is meticulously plotted and the hillside farm where the Sikhs settle is described so well that you feel you are present at every conference, at the meeting with the giant Barnard, ex-farm worker, who keeps the village under his thumb, and through the terrible days when thugs wearing armour fashioned from beaten tins occupy the place and persecute the inhabitants. Through this action, logically developed and utterly absorbing, runs the parallel journey of Nicky's heart—for this, sentimental though it may sound, is just what it is. Quite rightly the story does not end with the victory over the invaders nor with the village festival (described with sly humour) in which brown people and white celebrate their better understanding; it ends with Nicola's departure to France to look for her parents and to try to become human once more. Using the Changes to illustrate the growing-up of a girl, the author has given them an emotional dimension deeper than that of the earlier books. (pp. 1559-60)

> *Margery Fisher, in a review of "The Devil's Children," in* Growing Point, *Vol. 9, No. 2, July, 1970, pp. 1559-60.*

[*The Devil's Children*] is again concerned with the years when our islanders turned against machines and similar aspects of contemporary civilisation to the point where any attempt to revive the least sophisticated machine produced a neurotic reaction. Here, after the flight from London, the twelve-year-old Nicky Gore, separated from her family, tags along with a group of Sikh immigrants who accept her with reluctance and later protect her with a kind of fury. Consequently, the author is able to stage a conflict which is a medley of the medieval and the Asiatic within a twentieth century environment in which almost all accepted amenities and social services have disappeared. The possibilities which Dickinson implies are sometimes little short of terrifying but the traditional values of sincerity and straight dealing prevail. There is as much excitement as in any adventure story and a great deal more humanity. For readers of *Heartsease* this is an essential sequel.

> *A review of "The Devil's Children," in* The Junior Bookshelf, *Vol. 34, No. 4, August, 1970, p. 222.*

This is Peter Dickinson's third and best story of England under the Changes. A sudden shocking madness, or sanity, has swept the country clean of modern technocracy. Twelve-year-old Nicky finds herself alone and friendless among a people who will tolerate no machines more complex than ploughs, no weapons more sophisticated than longbows, no horsepower but horses. Her adoption of, and by, a stranded band of Sikhs and their common search for sanctuary in a hostile, looted land is a superb adventure story.

As a fantasist for young readers, Dickinson is on the same high level as John Christopher. Nothing is too fantastic to believe if it happens to real people, and Dickinson's people are splendidly real. "You are very practical-minded," one of the Sikhs tells Nicky. "That is how the English ruled India. They would admire the Taj Mahal, but all the time they were thinking about drains." This is Dickinson's own secret. No matter how dizzyingly he soars, he never forgets the drains.

Digby Whitman, in a review of "The Devil's Children," in Book World—The Washington Post, *November 8, 1970, p. 10.*

Emma Tupper's Diary (1971)

[*Emma Tupper's Diary*] is by Peter Dickinson, whose trilogy about a frightening England of the future I admired. This is a different sort of thing altogether and, under its sophisticated surface, it turns out to be an updated *Swallows and Amazons,* with sailing dinghies on an English lake replaced by a Victorian submarine in a Scottish loch. ' "That end's entrophic," said Andy. "This end's oligotrophic. If that's Greek to you, that's because it is Greek." ' I was entertained, but I think a lot of the young will think it very irritating.

Ann Thwaite, "Not as Good as Tolstoy," in New Statesman, *Vol. 81, No. 2085, March 5, 1971, p. 312.*

Peter Dickinson is [a] writer of quality who never quite seems to have fulfilled his imaginative potential. In *Emma Tupper's Diary* (his first book not set in an imagined future) the plot turns on a Victorian submarine and the discovery of a living species of prehistoric reptile which gives him the chance to indulge a bent for slightly over-eccentric detail more usually demonstrated in his detective stories. This can be irritating—indeed it seems laboured at times. . . . He certainly overdoes the conflict between Emma's two cousins Andy and Roddy. In the end it is obsession, as always, which makes for the real writing. Peter Dickinson's obsessive love-hate relationship with the machine age provided the tensions in his earlier books. It does so again here; there is the hate (Emma's terror underwater, inside the submarine, the fears for the fate of the reptiles) and certainly also the love. The greater part of the book describes the resuscitation of the submarine, and no one else could have done this so well. Possibly even he cannot quite get away with it. The technicalities sometimes defeated this non-technical reader, while the actual climax, the discovery of the reptiles, appears almost hurried, perfunctory in comparison. Yet you can forgive anyone anything who has such a gift for communicating the fascination of technical skills.

"Pure Enjoyment," in The Times Literary Supplement, *No. 3605, April 2, 1971, p. 391.*

Extracts from Emma's diary serve as the author's version of Victorian chapter-headings; with their hints of mysterious adventure they whet the appetite for the flashbacks in which the course of the past day or days is traced. This cunning narrative scheme and the peculiarly subtle divulging of the central surprise bring this new book closer to Peter Dickinson's detective stories than to the "Changes" books. Here, it is true, is the same concern for the state of Britain, the same obsession about machines,

that have informed all his children's books; man's effect on his environment provides a firm, if implied, moral for an exceptionally exciting story. Emma Tupper, a thirteen-year-old from Botswana, blessed with common sense and a lively intelligence, is packed off to the Highlands to her cousins the McAndrews, also highly intelligent but hardly sensible. To help family finances Andy, Fiona and Roddy plan to build a "monster" for their private loch and lure a television company to film it. Great-grandfather's submarine is re-floated but a trial trip at night reveals that there really was truth behind the local legend. Tension and surprise are beautifully managed, in regard to human and extra-human affairs. One can only be thankful for an author who conceives his books for the young on the same grand scale as his adult novels and puts into them ebullient humour and stylishness of expression. (pp. 1749-50)

Margery Fisher, in a review of "Emma Tupper's Diary," in Growing Point, *Vol. 10, No. 1, May, 1971, pp. 1749-50.*

A girl spends her summer holiday with hitherto unknown Scottish cousins, and while they are faking a kind of Loch Ness Monster to fool the B.B.C. people they discover a living species of prehistoric beast in their own lake. An interminable amount of technical detail in describing the two-man submarine (almost prehistoric itself) which is to be used for the deception plus the constant bickering of the two boy cousins, could all add up to a pretty tedious narrative. That it does not is due to the fact that the author is a writer of quite extraordinary talent who has already produced two or three winners in the realm of science fiction. True, there are some passages that make for dull reading for the non-technically minded, but press on, there are exciting things to come, working up to a major climax in the loathsome caves and a minor post-climax when Emma nearly drowns herself. Yet what make the book stand out from the general run of holiday adventures are the characters. Emma the visitor and diary-writer, so sensible and intelligent and yet at times absolutely terrified at having to join in the wilder pranks of her cousins, the McAndrews. These consist of Andy and Roddy the boys, each with the most hare-brained ideas and preposterous conversation, each too with a secret fear inside, and their sister Finn, who tries to be neutral but is at the same time touched with the family eccentricity, while living with them is the completely dotty Miss Newcombe, a quite impossible creation and yet curiously endearing in her weaknesses. With their brash or stolid exteriors and their soft centres so typical of much of the human race, they should prove sympathetic to the twelve-year-old reader, unsure of himself and eager to identify with other imperfect spirits. And though there is too much engineering technique for some of us, the author's love for and suspicion of his subject is only too appropriate for this day and age, when our machines will kill us unless we alter our course in time, just as the submarine nearly destroyed Emma. In short, this is a well-written book. Not perhaps the author's best, but far from being a failure. (pp. 178-79)

C. Martin, in a review of "Emma Tupper's Diary," in The Junior Bookshelf, *Vol. 35, No. 3, June, 1971, pp. 178-79.*

The Dancing Bear (1972)

Peter Dickinson, who has already proved his mastery in two very different types of story, now tries his strength in another. *The Dancing Bear* is a magnificent tale of adventure, a penetrating study of history, and a close examination of human and animal relationships. In each it is an outstanding achievement. Silvester's master is killed and his young mistress stolen in a "Trojan-horse" raid by Hunnish commandos, and he is left to suffer the traditional fate of slaves who know more than is good for their future masters. But Silvester escapes from the city in the company of Holy John the household saint and Bubba the dancing bear. This beautifully assorted trio takes the road, threatened more by imperial civil servants than by warring Huns, and after many adventures they find the Lady Ariadne and the Hunnish Khan. Here Holy John goes his own way. He has already selected himself as apostle to the Huns, and it is a good role for the old ascetic who was a soldier in his unregenerate days and knows the language of warriors. Silvester is left to escort his lady, not home, for Byzantium has nothing to offer a usurped heiress and to him only a beastly death, but to a wonderful wish-fulfilment fortress in the wild, where he can play king of the castle for ever. It is a highly satisfactory conclusion.

This is to say nothing of the bear. Bubba's is a fine portrait, for she, although never more than animal, is full of personality. From her first appearance, playing cat-and-mouse with the live crabs which are her supper and weeping because the honey jar she has filched has fallen just out of reach, till at Silvester's betrothal feast she gets drunk and has a "hideous hangover". Bubba gains the reader's unconditional devotion. There are more convenient companions for an odyssey than a slow, moody, thick-headed dancing bear, but none more endearing.

Mr Dickinson is firmly established as one of the most original, versatile and uncommitted of contemporary writers for the young. He confirms and extends this reputation in a novel which tells a great story with restrained eloquence, with deep human understanding, and above all with tolerance. There are no villains in *The Dancing Bear,* not even the Empire, only people following their destinies towards happiness or disaster.

> *"The Language of Warriors," in* The Times Literary Supplement, *No. 3661, April 28, 1972, p. 485.*

The Dancing Bear is an ebullient, whimsical and very circumstantial tale of a journey from sixth century Byzantium made by three improbable companions. . . . The passage of time, the slow progress on the road, are powerfully real and so are the various people met or evaded along the way—the white-faced civil servant who has put Silvester on a proscribed list, the solitary householder in his stone tower reviving the life-style of the extinct Roman Empire, the wounded Hun who is tended by Holy John and who helps to save the lives and the future of boy and girl, as effectively but hardly as amusingly as Bubba the bear, who miraculously does the right tricks at the right moment. This is a glorious mixture of history and fiction, lightly dallying with racial behaviour and ancient geography, ut-

terly compulsive in its ironic, complex, pictorial narrative style. I can imagine the book capturing the time and attention of many boys and girls in the early 'teens.

> *Margery Fisher, in a review of "The Dancing Bear," in* Growing Point, *Vol. II, No. 2, July, 1972, p. 1966.*

Traditionally historical tales like Henty's *The Young Carthaginian* hang historical background rather ponderously around a young hero whose exploits are well-nigh concessionary episodes amid the textbookery. *The Dancing Bear* is a superbly readable and subtly interrelated story with none of this fault. Even the least communicable character, Holy John, is a knowable man, helping not patronising, commenting aptly not mumbling gnomic generalisations, and motived to convert the Huns.

Byzantium is a city continually under threat from the Hun hordes. When events disorientate city-dwelling Ariadne and Silvester, they find they grow into real people: Ariadne ceases to be a puppet in a political power-game, Silvester loses 'the slave look' and comes to see that his destiny *does* lie in his own hands. In keeping with this sensitive approach to character is the solution: no glib happiness is machined, for the quest teaches them to look for true freedom in a most unexpected place.

Silvester is the bear-ward to one of the most vividly drawn bears to appear in children's fiction for many years. Friendly, moody, curious, playful, savage—a real bear not diluted into being cuddly—Bubba is the central link in a set of relationships and adventures which is stretched and strengthened by the most unusual pressures history can provide. Her dancing proves powerful magic to the northern peoples in whose folklore bears cure sick people by dancing *on* them! She rolls down slopes for fun, disturbs beehives for food, and savages a man for revenge: no dilution of Bubba's bear-ness, and so no betrayal of it.

This tastefully decorated panoply of richness [the illustrations are by David Smee] is for twelve up. (pp. 116-17)

> *C. S. Hannabuss, in a review of "The Dancing Bear," in* Children's Book Review, *Vol. II, No. 4, September, 1972, pp. 116-17.*

The author shows how individuals adjust in alien surroundings. He also points to the need of adolescents to establish their own identities: the daughter seems happy to adopt Hun society while the slave, trying to decide whether he is merely a thing, or an individual in his own right, accepts the Roman model for its civilized standards. These are important matters. That he uses them as the backbone in an absorbing tale is a measure of the quality of this writer. (pp. 252-53)

> *Bill Messer, in a review of "The Dancing Bear," in* The School Librarian, *Vol. 20, No. 3, September, 1972, pp. 252-53.*

The Iron Lion (1972)

The Iron Lion is an example of a totally modern "folktale" which, while treating its stock characters with an amused irreverence, does not descend into parody or pastiche, but successfully uses the traditional framework for its own purposes. It's a lighthearted entertainment, the tongue-in-cheek humour nearer to Peter Dickinson's adult fantasies than to his previous books for children. Highly topical too, in that the solution to everyone's problems lies in the accidental discovery of Oil, which valuable commodity finally saves the day for hero, princess, kingdom and lion. The unusual pictures [by Marc Brown], which accompany the text page for page, play an integral part in the success of a sustained and witty joke.

> *"Aladdin's Caves,"* in The Times Literary Supplement, *No. 3742, November 23, 1973, p. 1431.*

Written as a straight folk tale, shortened and illustrated in four colours, this story for young children could have been quite successful. Peter Dickinson has established himself as a writer of adventure stories for older children and this is his first book for the younger age-groups. Unfortunately, whilst the basic ideas of the story are good, based on the traditional Arabian Nights theme, they are developed at far too much length for picture-book treatment. The author also allows his sense of humour to intrude and the witticisms tend to direct attention away from the main story which deals with the perennial folktale idea of who shall marry the Emperor's Daughter. . . .

The whole book is a fair example of a good idea overdeveloped and given the wrong treatment.

> *Edward Hudson, in a review of "The Iron Lion," in* Children's Book Review, *Vol. IV, No. 1, Spring, 1974, p. 10.*

[*The following excerpt is from a review of the 1983 edition of* The Iron Lion *illustrated by Pauline Baynes.*]

Peter Dickinson has never been one to fit neatly into conventional classification. **The Iron Lion** may at first glance look like a picture-book but it is not. Mr. Dickinson has made a superb long-short story out of a number of folk themes, dressing it with great elegance and giving its development just the degree of depth that the form allows. . . .

The story is the age-old one of the princess who makes impossible demands of her suitors. The winner is an outsider, Mustapha, Prince of Goat Mountain. (His father had ruled a much bigger kingdom but, having written a book on the Art of War, he had felt bound to put his theories into practice and had found his realm reduced to Goat Mountain—population: eleven goatherds, thirty thousand goats.) Mr. Dickinson fills in the detail of this promising outline with many characteristic, shrewd and humorous touches. It is a story that could stand up well on its own. Miss Baynes' pictures are a bonus, but what a bonus! Not only has she a loving and scholarly command of eastern motifs; her delicate and refined art has been greatly strengthened in recent years, and here she shows herself the master of action and drama. For her, I think, this book marks a substantial stride forward. For Mr. Dickinson just another small masterpiece to add to his massive achievements.

> *M. Crouch, in a review of "The Iron Lion," in* The Junior Bookshelf, *Vol. 48, No. 2, April, 1984, p. 67.*

The Gift (1973)

Peter Dickinson remains the most fascinating unpredictable of contemporary writers for the young. Each book, while containing the common qualities of unobtrusively excellent writing and sound psychology, turns in a new direction.

The Gift is a novel about the present, but a present deeply involved with the past. It is a present of New Towns, feckless fathers and flighty mums, and of brothers who grow up and away. The Prices are not used to a settled home life. When Dad has an unusually extended spell of foolishness Mum goes off with her Gentleman Friend. She always comes back, sometimes with a black eye, but it is rather disturbing. Davy, at seven, should not have to understand his father so well, father who "always managed to feel that everything was going to be all right". He is perpetually on the brink of a "new rich, carefree life". Mostly his dreams end in the labour exchange, but once he gambles for higher stakes and risks greater hazards.

This is where Davy's gift comes in. For Davy is Welsh, and Davy can see pictures of people's thoughts. Sometimes these are impertinent and embarrassing. Sometimes they are full of terrors. Always, as Granny warns him, they threaten to bring grief.

In the little stone farmhouse in Wales, from which father had escaped long ago, the gift seems at home. It is incongruous in Spenser Mills, the half-built New Town where father has for once got himself a steady job. The Prices revel in the security of a home and a school and Mum returned chastened from one of her "holidays". But here Davy sees pictures in his mind, of violence and crime, and of a formless horror. Father, it appears, is going to get rich quick by working for a wage-snatch gang, and one of the gang is Wolf, strong and retarded, whose thoughts of uncontrolled savagery fill Davy's mind with horrible images.

The hold-up, predicted in detail by Davy's gift, fails. Dad has been persuaded to turn Queen's Evidence, and the family go back to Wales until the publicity dies down. But Wolf follows them. In the chill dark of the farmyard Davy tunes in to his fury and despair and realizes for the first time the misery which underlies the violence. "Poor Wolf", he says aloud, and establishes communication with the deranged mind. In the moment of reconciliation reality, in the shape of Davy's grown-up brother armed with a Welsh Nationalist gun, breaks in and Wolf is doomed. Once again Davy's gift has brought grief, but for the last time, for Davy's courage in facing the danger has freed him from the burden of insight.

"It's a complicated world", says sister Penny in the last words of the story. It is a complicated book too, but a powerful and wise one and marvellously convincing. Mr Dickinson explores his characters and their bitter world with unfailing sureness of touch, not a word too little or too much and all precisely geared to his theme.

"Unquiet Spirits," in The Times Literary Supplement, *No. 3709, April 6, 1973, p. 380.*

Peter Dickinson is [an] interesting writer never afraid of taking on a large theme, although his latest book *The Gift* . . . , is ultimately something of a disappointment. The boy hero, Davy Price, finds he has the ability to read minds, but while this gives him insight into the different worlds people live in, his own personality remains fairly static as the plot around him develops at an alarming rate, bringing in madness, attempted murder, family quarrels and brooding marriages. . . . Most of the other characters also tend to lack conviction, however exciting the story; one can accept the childish adults, but not those oh-so-adult children, with their no-nonsense leadership qualities. (pp. 778-79)

Nicholas Tucker, "Bridging the Gap," in New Statesman, *Vol. 85, No. 2201, May 25, 1973, pp. 778-79.*

Davy Price had the unique ability to see other people's thoughts in his own mind. Through his Welsh grandmother, who confided to him her own poignant story of past guilt and secret shame, Davy learned that the strange gift appeared from time to time in members of his grandfather's family. Past and present, legend and fact are woven into an intricate web of suspense and climax in the psychologically charged confrontation of the boy with a crazed killer whose violent thoughts have been forced into Davy's consciousness. Adult emotions and experiences—the story of the grandmother's illicit love for her husband's best friend, the flighty mother's periodic holidays with her latest bloke, the weak-willed, personable father's disastrous get-rich-quick schemes—are handled subtly and honestly. The author has avoided sensationalism by consistently retaining the perspective of his adolescent protagonist both in dialogue and in narration. Superb touches of humor, contrasting sharply with the gravity of the situations, give depth to the characterizations and balance to the structure without destroying the feeling of thrill and suspense. A novel which can be classified according to many of the currently fashionable categories—social realism, psychological analysis, interest in occult phenomena—but which remains in the memory first and foremost as a masterful example of storytelling. (pp. 141-42)

Mary M. Burns, in a review of "The Gift," in The Horn Book Magazine, *Vol. L, No. 5, October, 1974, pp. 141-42.*

[*The Gift* is a] first-rate novel about second sight. . . . Sometimes entertaining (at church Davy tunes into the sex fantasies of parishioners) and sometimes embarassing (he unintentionally eavesdrops on the millionaire pipedreams of his down-and-out father), the gift becomes a terrifying burden when Davy's mind is flooded with the mad imaginings of a half-wit out to destroy the Prices. From Wolf's distorted visions which are masterfully described as Van Gogh-esque nightmares of swirling shapes and overly bright colors, Davy discovers and helps foil a robbery scheme involving his father. Ironically, through his special relation with Wolf, Davy's numbed emotions are awakened and he comes to a fuller understanding of his own family—the tangled relationships between his selfsuffi-

cient brother and sister; his parents (a pair of middle-aged adolescents who are Dickinson's weakest characters); and his Welsh grandparents who are accorded a passion and depth rarely seen in children's books. A consummate craftsman, Dickinson skillfully mixes folklore and modern suspense to create an affecting story about perception—both the extrasensory and everyday kinds.

Jane Abramson, in a review of "The Gift," in School Library Journal, *Vol. 21, No. 2, October, 1974, p. 118.*

Chance, Luck, and Destiny (1975)

The distinction between the three concepts in the title of this fascinating compendium is enforced by the story of Oedipus, told in sections and, at first, without identification, with the finding of the exposed infant standing for Chance, his adoption by the childless rulers of Corinth for Luck and the final tragedy for Destiny. Between the several parts of the story of Oedipus lie anecdotes, reflections, examples, statistics (including a table of possibilities supposing that Red Riding Hood had answered the wolf differently). A curious mixture of guesswork, reason and off-hand belief characterises this unusual book, which should by no means be confined to young readers. (pp. 2751-52)

Margery Fisher, in a review of "Chance, Luck and Destiny," in Growing Point, *Vol. 14, No. 5, November, 1975, pp. 2751-52.*

This is a curious junk-shop of a book. In different heaps lie scraps of argument; dusty talismans and amulets and luck-bringers, ancient and modern; dice, and packs of playing cards and tarot cards; astrological booklets; pages from popular science manuals portraying frilly dinosaurs, fish who shoot down insects with water bullets, bower-birds building their blue-decked nests; strip-cartoons and other drawings; and various leaves from the Golden Bough.

Read bit by bit, it is not incoherent, but as a book it does not cohere. There is no strong web of dreaming continuity such as reinforces the experience of *Alice's Adventures in Wonderland* and *Through the Looking Glass* where mathematical and philosophical concepts jostle caterpillar and Mock-Turtle, Dormouse and Duchess and chessmen, in a completely acceptable way. And there seems to be no waking reason why all the little lumps of information and discussion should be laid out arbitrarily side by side. What is worse, there is no way of tracing them to their several sources, as any child old enough and patient enough to read about them would surely want to do.

"Is it true?" is the first question likely to be asked, and unfortunately no overall answer could be given. The piece about chance, at the beginning, is clear and well set out, and there are useful expositions of the fallacy of *post hoc propter hoc* reasoning, of what is meant by odds, of "the law of large numbers", of what coincidences may imply, and of the possibility of some pattern emerging in evolution. The stories about eighteenth-century gamblers are authentic. It is a fact that people have believed in the extraordinary fantasies of numerology, in the authenticity of the myth of Oedipus, in the inescapable workings of destiny, in the existence of powerful, malevolent witches, and in thousands of trivial superstitions about wood, iron, salt, ladders, the inadvisability of lighting three cigarettes with one match, and so ceaselessly on. But the pages of spells are purely *folklorique* and the various anecdotes or parables—about the Delphic oracle, about "a West-African wonder worker", about an adventure in some updated Ruritania—owe much to the writer's imagination, while the lists of gothick "devils" owe all. (He should surely have included one traditional example, Titivillus, scourge of small communities, who picked up scraps of gossip for his bulging sack.) The time-lag between the completion and the production of the work probably explains why a now slightly discredited experiment in psychical research has been cited, but does not explain the curious assumption that there is some link between the fact that "there is a level of matter at which events seem to happen without causes" and the argument for the freedom of the will.

It is sad that in its mixture of sense and chaos, its suspension of judgment as well as of disbelief, this book manages to irritate the mind without stimulating thought.

> *Renée Haynes, "Chance Companions," in* The Times Literary Supplement, *No. 3847, December 5, 1975, p. 1459.*

This is a splendid companion-book: it offers the reader so much. As Peter Dickinson understandingly observes at the beginning, it is very hard to read it straight through—one is tempted by delightful illustrations [by Victor Ambrus and David Smee] and eye-catching titles to dip all over the place. Not that it matters, since most of the sections stand on their own, but there is, in fact, a plan of progression, differentiating between Chance, Luck and Destiny, "with Magic to bind them into a ring". A further unity is achieved by serialising the story of Oedipus, from the different angles of the various people concerned in his destiny: the illustrations mark the stages of the story and are recapitulated when the mysterious threads are drawn together into one near the end of the book. Victor Ambrus is chiefly responsible for fiction and historical stories, while David Smee's drawings, both fine and funny, enliven the facts, with the occasional strip cartoon for good measure. There are also photographs and reproductions of old prints, and further variety is achieved by varying the type face to signal lists of facts. The range is enormous: anecdote and legend, short stories by Peter Dickinson to illustrate his points, charts, the psychology of gambling, folk lore, and instructions for fortune-telling by means of cards, Tarot packs, and palmistry. Mr. Dickinson preserves an interesting balance between mystery and belief, and a gentle ridiculing of credulity. Sometimes this is achieved by retailing absurdities with a straight face, sometimes by a sudden jolt, like the note to his convincing list of demons: "It is strange that no authority mentions a fiend who sits on the shoulders of other authorities, whispering to them lists of imaginary fiends . . . " Some readers, however, will object with some justice to the absence of any indication of Mr. Dickinson's authorities for historical incidents, which they might well wish to follow up.

> *M. Hobbs, in a review of "Chance, Luck and*

> *Destiny," in* The Junior Bookshelf, *Vol. 40, No. 1, February, 1976, p. 41.*

The Blue Hawk (1976)

[In *The Blue Hawk,*] Peter Dickinson leaps still further from any actual historical starting-point than he did from Byzantium in *The Dancing Bear.* As in that book, he produces an illusion of authenticity while taking freedom to arrange events and choose characters as it suits him. At the same time, the associations with an exotic past that flock into the mind as we read cannot but add to our enjoyment of this complex, circling narrative.

In a certain kingdom, then, the boy Tron, chosen for the service of the god Gdu, is assisting at the ceremony by which a blue hawk is to be sacrificed to ensure the renewal of the King's soul. That morning the boy has received signs of warning—one of them, the finding of the Goatstone in his breakfast loaf, a guarantee of protection if he should stray from the strict observance of ritual. From many indications Tron knows that he must prevent the sacrifice, though he does not realise that it is planned to disguise a palace plot; when he walks out of the House of O and AA with the drugged hawk he starts a sequence of events which lead ultimately to the defeat of priestly tyranny and the start of a liberal rule in the kingdom. Thus far, a political theme easily related to our own time. But this is also the story of a boy whose coldly organised education left no room for affection and whose alliance with the young King in his fight to escape his enemies brings a real if tentative friendship and, in addition, a warm, rewarding attachment to the hawk which, against all precedent, he has tamed and trained.

This is not the first story of the clash between tyranny and freedom of thought and it will not be the last, but it is certainly one of the most specific and compelling. Quotations from the texts prescribed by the priests for any and every contingency, religious or domestic, texts committed to memory by acolytes like Tron, are inserted naturally in the story and provide evidence of the power of the priesthood beyond what is obvious from their actions, whether honest or conspiratorial; these snatches of chanted words seem to go right to the heart of the matter. The tight quasi-verse structures, as well as the elaborate, concentrated descriptions of ritual, create a strong atmosphere of ancient mystery; the tyranny of O and AA, or rather, of those who purport to interpret Sun and Moon to the people, is in this book a great deal more than a mere matter of statement. Again, Peter Dickinson stresses through their speech the contrast between the inexorably formal priests and the human, freedom-loving King whom they must destroy if they are not to lose their unique status in the kingdom.

The patterns of action and feeling in this book are as various as its style. Harsh, vivid descriptions of conflict; evocations of riverside, mountain gorge, the secret tunnels of the Palace; soldiers' banter, the uncouth mumblings of outland folk, the innocent exchanges between Tron and the shepherd girl Taleel; continual changes of colour, sound and scene contribute to the creation of a world as absolute as if it had really existed. (pp. 2811-12)

Margery Fisher, in a review of "The Blue Hawk," in Growing Point, *Vol. 14, No. 8, March, 1976, pp. 2811-12.*

Peter Dickinson is the critic's joy, as well as the child's. Other writers, including the best, settle into a uniform excellence which is wholly to be admired but which scarcely lends itself to individual appreciation.

Mr Dickinson keeps us guessing. Will the next be about a society without machines, or a school of Loch Ness monsters, or the second sight, or the Byzantine Empire? Probably not, for he has had his say on these matters. **The Blue Hawk** seems to be about Pharaonic Egypt. This is what David Smee's excellent decorations depict, and the impression is reinforced by a quick reading. A little reflection suggests that this is too facile a view. The sacred river Tan whose waters keep the land fertile may seem like the Nile, but she flows south. Other details are equally disconcerting, and they give rise to more fundamental doubts. Are we in the past? The kingdom operates according to rituals whose rigidity suggests a civilization moving towards decay. It is not just that the revolution which is the main theme of the story is overdue. There are hints of a greater, more sophisticated civilization in the remote past. Can it be that we are, in fact, not in the past but the future, and that—flattering thought—the Wise whose memory and relics remain are ourselves?

It is to be hoped that such considerations will not distract readers from the pure and wholehearted enjoyment of this magnificent tale. It is acknowledged that in the children's book the fine art of story-telling has its last manifestation, and—setting aside his political, sociological and psychological concerns—Mr Dickinson is the past-master story-teller of our day.

It is tempting to dwell on the fascinating political and philosophical overtones of the book. They are of the greatest interest, but they are inseparable from the tale of adventure and the study in depth of a most subtle character.

Marcus Crouch, "Ritual or Revolution," in The Times Literary Supplement, *No. 3864, April 2, 1976, p. 375.*

The great reward of writers for the young is that they are expected to tell stories. The readers look for secondary worlds to find themselves in and the critics examine 'How does the author do it?' The virtues of narrative, response and criticism meet in this remarkable novel. . . . Rarely have I read such vividly imagined scenes as that of the dead king's barge floating down the great river and the lifting of an age-old curse. It is a spiritual autobiography, the kind of book written with power and commitment for which no adult outlet exists. I will promote this story with fervour, but only experienced readers could read it, and they usually want something else.

Margaret Meek, in a review of "The Blue Hawk," in The School Librarian, *Vol. 24, No. 2, June, 1976, p. 146.*

Few writers are more adept than Peter Dickinson at the creation of exotic, enclosed communities, and few authors for the young share his ability to tell an exciting story well.

In **The Blue Hawk** both these gifts are brought into full play. The book is set in a kingdom. We are not told where the kingdom lies or, indeed, the historical period in which the story takes place, and, despite surface resemblances to ancient Egypt, the reader is not given—and does not require—a specific location or period for the setting. The story is all, and an exciting one it is, too. . . . Tron's adventures in the service of the king provide enough action and suspense to satisfy the young reader in search of a gripping story. But the book is not merely a remarkable adventure story, it is also a perceptive study in character. And the kingdom itself, with its complex religious and social structure, its ritual, legends and chants, provides a background so compelling and so authentic that it is hard to believe that it does not—did not—exist. **The Blue Hawk** is a remarkable achievement, further proof—if any is needed—that Peter Dickinson is perhaps the most imaginative writer for the young today.

Lance E. Salway, in a review of "The Blue Hawk," in Children's Book Review, *Vol. VI, October, 1976, p. 16.*

Annerton Pit (1977)

This is Peter Dickinson rather below par, with a trendy plot showing the terrible brittleness of the ultra-contemporary. The theme may be eternal—do ends justify means?—but the militant conservationists who blow up motorways and plan to take over an oil rig are a dismally catchpenny collection. Just as Roy Brown's amnesiac drug is called "Compound Y" [in his *The Cage*], so these conspirators are a weak pastiche of newspaper realities. But this matters far less in *The Cage* than in **Annerton Pit** because Peter Dickinson has at hand a far richer and more subtle substructure. The book is masterly in its presentation of the thirteen-year-old Jake, whose consciousness carries the narrative. Jake is blind, and the modulation of experience through heightened senses other than sight, the acceptance of blindness as normality, and the deep rapport with and respect for Jake which are built up, are very impressive indeed. Interpersonal relationships really mean something—especially between Jake and his impetuous but very caring elder brother. Equally, the ghostly terrors of the abandoned coal-mine, Annerton pit itself, and Jake's final encounter with the terrors in his own mind, all evolve, are all integral with the pervasive sightlessness. It is only the slackness of the central incidents, and the unnecessary striving for "excitement" and "significance" which undercut the real potential of the book.

Peter Hunt, "Causes for Concern," in The Times Literary Supplement, *No. 3915, March 25, 1977, p. 359.*

Peter Dickinson's stories have a way of settling around you, so that when thirteen-year-old Jake is disclosed to be blind, the news seems simply to confirm his extraordinary powers of observation. And it is these powers—aptly, the ability to "see" in the dark—that will safeguard Jake and older brother Martin when their ghost-hunting grandfather disappears. Martin has just put his savings into a BMW bike—better that, Jake decides, than the Green

Revolution Defense Fund—and on their half-term holiday the brothers head for Newcastle where Granpa was last inquiring after apparitions to explain away. Oddly, he has always been a presence to Jake—a comforting, "protecting intelligence." But, pursuing the mystery of Annerton coal pit, he stumbles upon a sinister true-life intrigue, and the boys fall in behind him. This has to be a Green Revolution job—as Martin is of course the one to discover—so that the issues shaping up en route can be aired. Like not only being willing to die for a cause but, as GR leader Andrews explains to the anguished Martin, "to kill for it." Or, on Martin's part, to denounce its agents in order, hopefully, to save the cause. But meanwhile the three are trapped in Annerton Pit, and it's the devil's own cave to escape from, with *something* present even rational, home-in-the-dark Jake can't shake. Until, within him, the dark lifts . . . The exorcism of Jake's ghost entails prolonged groping about, literally and figuratively, and the analogy between the pit's terror and political terrorism—both extinguished by a mine detonation—is forced upon the reader. But this intelligent, literate, thoughtful thriller—so intrinsically a blind child's experience—is worth having on any terms. (pp. 788-89)

A review of "Annerton Pit," in Kirkus Reviews, *Vol. XLV, No. 15, August 1, 1977, pp. 788-89.*

In *Annerton Pit* Jake, who is blind, and his elder brother, Martin, buy a second-hand motor cycle and on impulse ride off to search for their grandfather, who had disappeared near Annerton Pit. They find him in the pit's outbuildings, held prisoner because his captors are conservationist protesters, manufacturing bombs there. Of course Jake and Martin are held prisoner, too. So far this is simply quite a good novel about two boys in our familiar world. Jake's blindness, and his composed acceptance of it, is beautifully presented; but—and this is really well conceived—it makes him especially competent and especially sensitive when the two boys escape into the passages of the mine and become separated and lost.

Annerton Pit has been the scene of a disaster. Their grandfather is there because he is a ghost investigator. Jake, in the darkness, finds a presence, great, hurt, brooding, seeking peace, and comes to terms with it. Neither he nor we ever know what it is. Martin has his own problem, for, in saving his brother, he has to decide whether or not to give evidence about the conservationist bombers to the police. The ending is neat, smooth, beautifully judged. This is a remarkable book, not to be missed. (pp. 357-58)

Norman Culpan, in a review of "Annerton Pit," in The School Librarian, *Vol. 25, No. 4, December, 1977, pp. 357-58.*

A powerful, wholly original novel is constructed with enormous skill and written with rare perception and intuition. . . . [In the story of the incarceration of Jake and Martin] and of their attempts to escape from the chill, slimy, terrifying underground labyrinth, the horror of the deliberate, detailed writing approaches that of Poe. But there are also intimations of Dostoevsky, for the greatest impact of the novel is psychological. Martin, who has secretly been an idealistic young supporter of the revolution-

ists, is placed in an agonizing situation; after the rescue by the police he must, ironically, become "the tool of the very system that scarred the green hills, poisoned river and sea, murdered plants and creatures and spun mankind faster and faster towards destruction." Moreover, he realizes miserable, "It's not much of a problem *being* right. It's *doing* right where the trouble begins—doing it and going on doing it while life comes up and hits you with situations where there aren't any rights to do." And left alone in the mine, sightless Jake undergoes a devastating mental experience and suffers the worst trauma of all; physically agile, intellectually keen, and uncannily sensitive, he is the real hero of the book.

Ethel L. Heins, in a review of "Annerton Pit,"
in The Horn Book Magazine, *Vol. LIV, No.*
2, April, 1978, p. 150.

Hepzibah (1978)

Despite some really beautiful illustrations by Sue Porter, *Hepzibah* is a disappointing story. The jokes are not based on any kind of reality or morality and therefore misfire quite dismally. The book is accompanied by a record but since it is one of the soft, floppy variety, it does not stand up to very much wear and tear and my review copy was very nearly unintelligible.

Lesley Lancaster and Naomi Mitchison, "A
Laugh a Minute," in The Times Educational
Supplement, *No. 3308, November 24, 1978, p.*
50.

Peter Dickinson's tendency to obfuscation disqualifies the text of his first picture-book for reading aloud and, indeed, for any reader who is intellectually inactive or who prefers to read pictures rather than words. An extravaganza built round an anarchic small girl who "never goes to bed, but hangs herself up by her feet from a beam in the roof and goes to sleep like that" describes her dealings with the black King of Corumba (who invents ice-cream flavours) and hatmaker Evans with his lazy, window-gazing wife. The story, intricate, sophisticated and bizarre, is supported by pictures [by Sue Porter] so crowded with detail that each looks like a jumble sale organized by inmates of Bedlam. Two brilliant talents combine in a book which has a weird force but which is likely to prove caviare to the general.

Margery Fisher, in a review of "Hepzibah," in
Growing Point, *Vol. 17, No. 6, March, 1979,*
p. 3476.

The appeal of naughty children is perennial, and the publishers are no doubt right in foreseeing a long and productive life for Hepzibah. I must admit that I find her awfulness somewhat contrived. She eats soap. She hangs upside down by her feet instead of going to bed. She keeps a cow in the bath. So what? one might ask. Chacun a son gout. Peter Dickinson, who normally plays in a very different league, has carefully built up Hepzibah's image and provided her with an appropriately zany menage—depicted in all its frightfulness by Sue Porter in fittingly ugly pictures—but one reader at least remains unmoved. It must be added, in fairness, that the book comes at a very low price for colour printing and that a 'single' record is thrown in; the latter is suitably awful, too. (pp. 93-4)

M. Crouch, in a review of "Hepzibah," in The Junior Bookshelf, *Vol. 43, No. 2, April, 1979, pp. 93-4.*

Tulku (1979)

The classic journey-adventures of the past, from Marryat and Scott downwards, have most of them been journeys of body and spirit together: the most stringent and compelling accidents have their full effect when we can see how they have changed the protagonist other than by merely breaking his head. The divagating and dangerous journey taken by Theodore Tewker into Tibet is, to outward appearance, a flight; surviving a Boxer raid on his father's mission in China, the boy attaches himself to chance-met travellers without any particular plan or hope. It is not for many months that he is able to admit that there was a pattern, mysterious and inexplicable, in his journeying. On that first terrible day, as he saw from a ridge the smoking ruins of the settlement, he began to face in the way of a child the testing of his faith, a matter of automatic obedience to his formidable father: he felt and resisted with confusion of mind the influences of Buddhist ritual during the period of isolation in the Lamasery of Dong Pe: safely back in England, he admitted to himself that if "the foundations which Father had given him had been shaken", he had "discovered other foundations beneath, broader and more enduring", not by denying the value of the old Lama's teaching or reacting against his father, but by growing into himself.

It is difficult, for reviewer as for writer, to indicate this kind of growth without smudging the total effect of adventure-narrative, a genre which at its best should achieve the reader's belief in emotional change not through sermonising but through a passionate reality of character, action and place fused together, a veracity of detail so strong that he cannot fail to be drawn into the secondary world. *Tulku* is a most impressive and artfully wrought book. It has the outward trappings of a great adventure—an exotic setting of mountain, plateau and river, expert variations of pace and tension and strong character-drawing. As in *The Dancing Bear,* a journeying child is surrounded by odd, unexpected companions—in this case the young poet Lung (a subtly developed personality) and the raddled, cockney-voiced, superbly wise Mrs. Jones, who refuses to be outfaced by danger and who is equally brave in the face of spiritual challenge. For her unborn child, whether it is or is not to be the Tulku which their rescuer the Lama is seeking, becomes a compelling reason for her to accept a contemplative end to a strongly active and unorthodox life; her change of heart, sympathetically suggested, provides an essential part of the fugue in which Theodore's behaviour provides the subject.

The small but brilliantly conceived group of monastic dwellers and incoming strangers is presented to the reader in dialogue, description and action with precisely chosen detail and with an illusion of reality supported by the set-

ting, the vividly imagined foothills and mountain fastnesses of Tibet as they might have been seventy years ago. Descriptions are at times extremely simple and direct; . . . . At other times statement gives place to images as surprising as they are appropriate. The monastery is aligned on the cliff as if it had grown there but its geometrical shapes make the growth "seem more like that of a crystal, which increases by angles and facets, than that of a plant." The effect of a piece of action is often enhanced in an image that works like a mentally visual shock in the reader. At the beginning of the journey Mrs. Jones, holding bandits at bay with a shot-gun, orders Lung to cut their trouser-belts, as she says, "from . . . belt to arse":

> He darted forward, grabbed up a knife and bent behind the right-hand man, then moved down the line like a gardener performing some rapid piece of pruning on a row of fruit-trees. As he left each man a dramatic change took place, the shabby but serviceable pantaloons tumbling down to ankle-level, leaving some with bare buttocks and some with a twist of loin-cloth.

The humour and the sharpness of activity clash together with musical force. The image is important too for its place in the theme of the book, the idea of the growing points of personality. Plants and gardens run fugally through the narrative. Daisy Jones is a plant-hunter, working alone as she once worked with the lover she generously renounced for his social good: the undescribed yellow lily she finds on the hillside seems to symbolise the love she enjoys with Lung: the book ends on a note of mingled humour and philosophy as the lily bulb she has sent by Theodore to her erstwhile lover is unpacked and pronounced to be dried out but still living. It will grow in the greenhouse just as Theodore, by the owner's help, is to be planted again to grow more sturdily than before. Action, image and feeling come together in a few sentences to demonstrate the incalculable power of the right word in the right place to embody a strong imaginative vision. (pp. 3462-63)

Margery Fisher, in a review of "Tulku," in Growing Point, *Vol. 17, No. 6, March, 1979, pp. 3462-63.*

Tulku is an exciting, beautifully written adventure story which intelligently illuminates, in the course of its narrative, a number of different spiritual perspectives and mystical ideologies. . . .

Obviously, the characters, whose lives and destinies are joined together . . . , could not be more disparate. Nor could their adventures be more compelling. (p. K1)

The best part of this excellent novel takes place in the monastery. Here, Dickinson's extensive knowledge and appreciation of Tibetan temple art and architecture add dimensions to the story, while his clear grasp of the principles of Tibetan Buddhism give it unusual depth. The author is never didactic; though he explains things with great care, the momentum of the story never flags. What is more, his characters never lose their integrity because each one is affected by what happens in the monastery according to his or her level of spiritual development. It is this, even more than the brilliant descriptions and careful explanations, which gives this amazing story its ring of truth. (p. K4)

> *Winifred Rosen, "Quest for the Lama," in* Book World—The Washington Post, *May 13, 1979, pp. K1, K4.*

What a writer! Unlike Alexander, Peter Dickinson does not weep for new worlds to conquer; he goes out and finds them, and if he can't he invents one. Every new book represents a fresh exploration. (p. 165)

A dozen or so contemporary writers might have devised the central idea of this book, and one can readily imagine how each would have developed it. Needless to say Mr. Dickinson's solution is all his own. He produces a miraculous blend of oriental philosophy, high drama and melodramatics. Above all he is an inventory of characters, and of all his work Mrs. Jones is the most deeply imagined and the most consistently developed. Whether as woman of action, and very handy with a gun she is too, or as mystic, Mrs. Jones is always true to her inner nature. She may surprise the reader, but the surprise is always fair; it comes from a consistent individual reacting to changing circumstances. Only a little less subtle is the development of Theodore in coming to terms with the devil-haunted temples of Dong Pe.

As always this is not, in any exclusive sense, a book for children. There are, thank goodness, plenty of children who will meet its demands, but their parents must not on that account be denied a great and formative experience. (p. 166)

> *M. Crouch, in a review of "Tulku," in* The Junior Bookshelf, *Vol. 43, No. 3, June, 1979, pp. 165-66.*

His Reverend father's flock decimated in the Boxer Rebellion, the lone surviving son of a charismatic American missionary and a Chinese convert is picked up in shock by a woman as worldly-wise as he is un-. Mrs. Jones is a peripatetic Cockney botanist of 40, with a freely confessed checkered past and a present—she's Tibet bound with Lung, a 20-ish Chinese scholar-poet, as lover/guide—that defies Theo's efforts to judge not. Threatened on all sides by Mrs. Jones' traitorous former retainers and roadside bandits, Theo follows her lead until they're all taken in by Tibetan monks convinced that Mrs. Jones is carrying their pre-natal *Tulku* (reincarnated spiritual leader). By then you can well believe she's the Tulku's mother-to-be: always in command, at ease with pistol and easel, the force of her personality puts a stamp on the book, and she has a like effect on her traveling companions, tempering Theo and inspiring Lung to the heights and depths of passion. Not *Lost Horizon* territory, Dickinson's polyandrous, flea-infested Tibet is made palpable in prose that is a sensory experience; and readers come to know the characters (including the very British Buddhist, Major Price-Evans) as well as they come to know each other. Thick with detail and containing what amounts to, but never feels like, a crash course in comparative religion, *Tulku* can be tough going; but it's well worth saving for any reader with a reflective bent.

> *Pamela D. Pollack, in a review of "Tulku," in*

School Library Journal, *Vol. 25, No. 9, May, 1979, p. 71.*

[*Tulku* is] a superb adventure novel. . . . Theodore's Christian faith is severely tried by his love for Mrs. Jones and for the lama, neither of whose lives are compatible with his beliefs. But Theodore is strong-minded and full of insight; he eventually comes to have a broader understanding of the meaning of religion. The book may be compared with *Lost Horizon* (Morrow), but *Tulku* is richer and more complex. The only flaw in the masterful story is that Lung, the Chinese lover, is not as fully developed as the other characters, who are unforgettable. The author, always noted for his style and versatility, has achieved a tour de force, a magnificent adventure story with an exotic setting and a philosophical theme.

> *Ann A. Flowers, in a review of "Tulku," in* The Horn Book Magazine, *Vol. LV, No. 4, August, 1979, p. 421.*

The Flight of Dragons (1979)

The evidence that dragons "flew, breathed fire, hoarded gold, laired in a cave and had poisonous blood" all but overwhelms a reluctant believer in this impressive, serio-comic study of those much maligned creatures. With tongue-in-cheek scrupulosity as to scientific probabilities regarding not only their existence but their utility, author Dickinson . . . , assuming the role of investigative reporter, finds support in history and legend, as well as fiction, for his theory that "clearly there is something badly wrong with our assumptions" about the flying pterodactyls whose dietary preference is "young ladies of noble breeding." With a bow to Hobbitland, there is a Dragon Country map, a catalogue of sightings in Britain and sundry dragonisms to amuse and amaze. A grotesquely fantastic bestiary assembled by artist [Wayne] Anderson (60 color plates; 30 drawings) may frighten the children but underscores the storyteller's caution: "Remember. The dragons live. Inside us."

> *A review of "The Flight of Dragons," in* Publishers Weekly, *Vol. 216, No. 4, July 23, 1979, p. 147.*

Any theory arguing the existence of dragons is likely to be written off as a lot of hot air. In this case, the charge would merely affirm the theory, for Dickinson assumes their existence and sets out to prove that your basic dragon was a kind of highly specialized, animate, prehistoric blimp. Is he kidding? I think so. But Wayne Anderson's magnificent leering cover dragon is the only giveaway. Dickinson's deadpan prose exposes the aerodynamic absurdity of the traditionally conceived dragon and replaces it with a strikingly plausible conception of lighter-than-air creatures whose evolution, physiology, and life cycle not only jibe with the laws of nature and the major motifs of dragon lore, but demonstrate convincingly that the complete lack of fossil remains is one of the surest proofs that dragons did exist. Even if this book weren't beautifully conceived, written, and illustrated, the sheer novelty of its approach would make it a work no serious collection on dragons should be without.

John W. Eldridge, in a review of "The Flight of Dragons," in Library Journal, *Vol. 104, No. 18, October 15, 1979, p. 2230.*

With a sure touch of whimsy, [the author] develops his premise logically and seriously, drawing evidence from modern fiction, ancient and oral legends, and factual laws of flight and biological chemistry. He assumes that the dragon's specialization was flight and proceeds to demonstrate how this function evolved, what ensued in the way of behavior, and what finally led to the extinction of these glorious antecedents of dinosaurs. Author and artist indulge engagingly in a lavish flight of fancy of their own.

Mary Silva Cosgrave, in a review of "The Flight of Dragons," in The Horn Book Magazine, *Vol. LV, No. 6, December, 1979, p. 696.*

City of Gold and Other Stories from the Old Testament (1980)

AUTHOR'S COMMENTARY

One of the problems about telling Bible stories is that of context. The Bible has been a living book for so many generations, and it has been seen through so many different visions, adapted to particular ways of thinking by so many minds, that it has almost entirely become its own context. The events in it seem to take place somehow out of time, in a different set of dimensions, a sort of generalized vague, hot landscape called the Holy Land. But for the people who originally told the stories, it was not like that at all. The events had taken place among the very rocks where their goats browsed, and long after the events themselves were past, the context remained the same. Not only could a particular field at Beth-Shemesh be pointed out as the place where the Ark of the Covenant had rested when the Philistines sent it back to Israel, but a particular custom, a particular habit of thought, could be justified and passed on by this story of a deed of Joshua or that of a quarrel between the sons of Jacob. The stories themselves had the substance and actuality almost of tactile objects, so much so that when eventually they were written down and codified by priests who wished to draw from them a particular set of inferences—a whole world view central to the faith—there were still inconvenient elements which didn't fit that picture but had to be left in because their solidity was too great merely to wish away.

And before that writing down, through how many mouths and ears must the stories have threaded almost unaltered? In some cases it is possible to do rough calculations. The crossing of the Red Sea—or at least the definite event which few scholars now doubt gave rise to the story in Exodus—must have taken place very approximately in 1300 B.C. Shortly after that, the Song of Miriam came into existence. All we have of the song now are the words which King James's Bible translates "Sing ye to the Lord, for he hath triumphed gloriously; the horse and his rider hath he thrown into the sea." For something like four hundred years these words were passed on, probably as a central element in an annual ritual of thanksgiving, until they were written down shortly after the time of Solomon in the earliest of the documents which were collated several hundred years later still to make the book of Exodus.

Think of that in terms of our own history. It means that the tradition must have lasted, mouth to mouth, since before the *Mayflower* sailed.

Well, my idea was that if I were to make the imaginative leap and tell these stories as they might have been told during those four hundred years—and tell them not just as stories but as things used for definite purposes in a particular culture and context; if I were to choose here and there among the many, many mouths that might—must—have told them, then I would be able to do something different from other collections of Old Testament stories. Not different for the sake of my own vanity but different for the sake of the stories themselves. (If you want to see how I made out, you'll have to get hold of a copy of *City of Gold* and read it.) (pp. 93-4)

Peter Dickinson, "The Burden of the Past," in Innocence & Experience: Essays & Conversations on Children's Literature, *edited by Barbara Harrison and Gregory Maguire, Lothrop, Lee & Shepard Books, 1987, pp. 91-101.*

It would be nice to say that *City of Gold* is a tour de force and leave it at that. Unfortunately it doesn't, quite, come off. Ambitious and innovative it certainly is. Peter Dickinson is a master storyteller and the Old Testament stories themselves are indestructible. That only leaves the audience, or the writer's relationship to it to go wrong.

Each of the 33 episodes, from the Fall in the garden to the fall of Jerusalem, is, technically, told by a different voice, as part of the oral tradition from which the written Bible grew. One or two are songs, set out as poems. But for the most part we are eavesdropping on the reminiscences of an old priest, or a shepherd, or a persecuted Jew. Most were onlookers, like the veteran soldier who watched Absalom die, or inheritors of a tradition, like the fisherman whose great-grandfather saw the Red Sea overwhelm Pharaoh's army. But some were participants in a larger drama, even if they had only bit-parts, like the boy Elijah raised from the dead, now grown up to be a philosophical sea-pilot.

The trouble is they are not *really* different voices, as the blurb claims. They are not the anonymous Jewish historians of the Authorised version, nor the commonplace people-in-the-desert out of which all that history was built. They are all Peter Dickinson. It is the voice of an author, which is what these stories resist.

Here and there is a total success, as when the David and Goliath story is given as a cautionary tale by a sergeant lecturing his Babylonian recruits on slingshot avoidance. This is as surefooted as David Jones, a little bit of military knowhow that nicely pleats the centuries. But the more serious and lyrical moments often do not find so happy a convention.

The hopping from one register to another makes for bumpy reading; perhaps Peter Dickinson intended us to skip? But there is a a momentum to the stories and, of course, a cycle through the building and destruction of the

City, so that they cannot really be absorbed piecemeal. It is a handsome book, with subtle and dramatic paintings by Michael Foreman, who often comes closer to depicting the invisible than Peter Dickinson does to describing the ineffable. And it is so nearly brilliant, if only with reflected glory.

Mary Hoffman, "Reflected Glory," in The Times Educational Supplement, *No. 3361, November 21, 1980, p. 30.*

The retelling of Bible stories demands a certain flair if respect for the original narrative is not to be reduced to mere repetitiveness. Peter Dickinson has met this need by a creative reconstruction of the oral tradition that preceded the more definitive shaping of the Old Testament text, *City of Gold* comprises thirty-three stories, told as they might once have been told, in an imaginative variety of human situations. Narrators include an Edomite hunter, an Egyptian fisherman, parents speaking to their children and grandchildren, and professional story-tellers. The overall narrative is consecutive, from the stories of Genesis to the fall of Jerusalem, but the presentation is enhanced by moving the location of the story-telling back and forth between widely differing periods. The twelfth plague of Egypt is envisaged as being recounted during the persecution of Antiochus Epiphanes in 168 BC.

The context is less directly relevant, but again enlivens its content when the tale of David and Goliath is placed in the mouth of a sergeant in the Babylonian army, instructing recruits on how not to behave when confronted by a slinger. There is a pervasive humour—where humour is appropriate—and one of the most ingenious vignettes is the description of King Saul's illness as part of a course in an early medical school. The reader is informed of the difficulties of "diagnosis of possession by Rational Demons", and signs and symptoms are outlined in a style that combines the clinical with the anecdotal.

These stories may well be read individually, but taken together they constitute the epic that is the Old Testament: the birth and growth of a nation, then its decline and eventual exile after the destruction of Jerusalem, the City of Gold. The beginning and the end are skilfully and unobtrusively linked by setting the telling of both stories during the Babylonian exile. Each alike suggests a note of hope. The story of the garden of Eden concludes with the longing for a second Adam to undo the foolishness of the first Adam, and the journey into exile is made with the vision of a new Jerusalem yet to come. This is a good drama and it is good theology. Never pious in a pejorative sense, the narrative nevertheless does justice to the faith of the tradition it expresses. Peter Dickinson's skilful handling of his material is well matched by Michael Foreman's excellent illustrations. This is altogether a most impressive and delightful volume.

Elizabeth Moberly, "A New Jerusalem," in The Times Literary Supplement, *No. 4051, November 21, 1980, p. 1325.*

The notes appended to Peter Dickinson's retellings of Old Testament stories emphasise the variety of sources—from early oral tradition ('folk tales, songs, legends, treaties, proverbs and so on') to the work of recorders and scholars determined to keep tradition alive during the Exile and the later collation of around 200 BC. The use of the term 'stories' in the sub-title is apt, for he evokes oral tradition deliberately in his narrative method, but the pieces are linked by a theme at once historical and doctrinal. These 'stories' relate to the history of a nation and a faith: the title *City of Gold* indicates that Jerusalem, the goal for centuries of wandering and dispersal, is the true centre of the book. The last piece, **'The Fall of the City',** is put in the mouth of an exiled Jew speaking to 'an informal class of boys' in Babylon: they are to 'remember Jerusalem, the city you have never seen' so that future generations may rebuild it. The relevance to the present day is part of the broad historical theme.

History takes more than one form in the book. Facts and dates, with comments on the author's interpretation of his sources, are given succinctly in appended notes. Formal history is also served by the order of the pieces, corresponding to that of the Bible; they are grouped in sections which serve to distinguish the legendary and figurative material (Fall and Flood, for example) and the centuries during which a nation was slowly and painfully created, from the intricate, changeable years of Kings and Judges and the final collapse of the Israelite kingdoms. The idea of God, the establishment of monotheism, lies behind each event and its political significance. This is narrative rather than theology, but behind the most rational interpretations (of the crossing of the Red Sea, for example) there is always a fundamental meaning.

A third, indirect historical element comes from the selection of narrators for the various stories. Often these throw unexpected light on them. For instance, the contest of David and Goliath is described by 'a sergeant in the Babylonian army, training recruits in weapon drill' during the Exile, particularly in the proper use of the Shield; Saul's mental state is analysed in a lecture on demonic possession given at a Jewish medical school in Alexandria some two centuries after the King's death; there is an acid undercurrent in the story of Joseph as told by a professional story-teller at a wedding feast in North Canaan, since the guests belong to a district in rivalry with the Southern tribes of the house of Joseph.

With this device, Peter Dickinson reflects the stylistic variety of the Old Testament in his own way. The homely voice of a shepherd suits his retelling, to his son, of the near-sacrifice of Isaac; the death of Absalom is described in practical but feeling tones by a veteran soldier of David's army; a Hebrew entertainer compares notes with a Babylonian rival on the details of the Flood legend; there is a stark relevance in the way a father hiding with his family during the rebellion of Antiochus explains the parallel with the Twelfth Plague of Egypt and the Exodus. Events which often seem puzzling and obscure to the young can be illuminated by a particular approach. Elijah's defeat of the worshippers of Baal, for instance, is described by a priest of one Israelite kingdom to a colleague from another, at a time when beliefs were obscured or forgotten. He speaks with longing of older, simpler times than his own:

I'm sorry, my dear fellow—one gets worked up,

telling these old stories. I can see it all so clearly in my mind's eye; the delegates from the ten tribes gathering clan by clan on Carmel; the King rattling up in his chariot with his runners in front of him; the priests of Baal coming wailing up the track—you know the racket they make on a big occasion with their tambourines and those rattling little drums—four hundred and fifty of them they say Jezebel had sent along; and Elijah standing alone up the slope, like a hawk among starlings; and over it all the glaring sky.

The mystery of belief is carried as well in robust passages like this as in the plangent tones of a father taking his son on his first pilgrimage to Jerusalem, in the secure years of the Temple:

> . . . sometimes, drawing a stillness round myself in the clamour and jostling of the courtyard, it is almost as though my soul were standing, eyes closed, by a great fire, whose heat throbbed out towards me. I do not need even to be there to feel it, because always I carry in my heart the vision of Jerusalem, lying in gold and stillness, along its ridge, which my father gave me on my first pilgrimage.

Continuity, pictorial drama, meaning, human feelings combine in Peter Dickinson's striking text. They combine also in the water-colours and black and white decorations with which Michael Foreman confirms the essential mood of each piece. . . . From this fruitful partnership has come a version which should stir a wide readership to look again at the Old Testament, as history, myth and a record of human thought. (pp. 3802-03)

> *Margery Fisher, in a review of "City of Gold and Other Stories from the Old Testament," in* Growing Point, *Vol. 19, No. 5, January, 1981, pp. 3802-03.*

The trouble with nearly all 'versions' of the Bible, even De la Mare's, is that the modern words, be they never so comprehensible, are infinitely inadequate when compared with A.V. How wise therefore of Peter Dickinson—and what a brilliant brainwave!—to avoid comparisons. His *City of Gold* selects stories from the Old Testament from Eden to the Babylonian Exile, and narrates them in a variety of voices, some contemporary, or nearly contemporary, some looking back from some specified point in remote time. . . . Every reader will identify his own favourite, grim or funny, poetic or spiritual. Folk-tale addicts will note how, in this kind of retelling, the primitive tale out of which the Biblical story evolved shows up clearly, as in the story of Joseph and his brethren, or in that of Samson, which Mr. Dickinson turns into a kind of Border ballad.

We are in Mr. Dickinson's debt already for many and varied experiences. Now he adds to our debt with this remarkable book, a tour de force, brilliantly executed, and a revelation to Bible-readers and others alike. How wise of him to stop where he does, before written history comes to shine a light on the Bible narrative which extinguishes its mysteries. . . .

City of Gold is illustrated by one of the most intelligent

of modern book-artists, Michael Foreman. There is no doubt at all about his vision, or his feeling for atmosphere. . . . [His full-page colour plates] have a curiously old-fashioned air, as if they were done by a disciple of Nielsen or Rackham. The broad frame around each adds to the artifice. Brilliantly drawn, it is true, but not, for the most part, contributing to the mood set by Mr. Dickinson's prose. A most memorable book, nevertheless.

> *M. Crouch, in a review of "City of Gold," in* The Junior Bookshelf, *Vol. 45, No. 1, February, 1981, p. 27.*

A fresh, zestful retelling of thirty-three Old Testament stories. . . . [Dickinson's] storytelling artistry gives a strong sense of immediacy to the past, which reaches beyond the Bible and written sources to the oral lore of the ancients. . . . The tales are told in imaginative settings, their style and manner reflecting the author's literary versatility, his knowledge and understanding of the Bible. His notes on sources, interpretations, theories, and variations add further dimension to a work of distinction.

> *Mary Silva Cosgrove, in a review of "City of Gold and Other Stories from the Old Testament," in* The Horn Book Magazine, *Vol. LVII, No. 5, October, 1981, p. 563.*

How to choose a book of Bible stories? The cry of 'Bible stories are part of our culture so children ought to know them' is familiar enough—and *not* good enough. We need to take account of a crucial question. How can we offer the stories in a way which helps children appreciate their imaginative, creative power and avoids a cosy, preaching literalism? . . .

For me, . . . the best text, particularly for older children, remains the rather under-valued *City of Gold*. . . . Michael Foreman's magical illustrations combine excellently with the off-beat retelling of the major Old Testament stories. What makes this the bench-mark for good quality is the way in which Dickinson creates a sense of a time before the text was set in stone, when it still lived as part of the Jewish storytelling tradition. The book conveys superbly the sense that the stories have been told, re-told, interpreted and re-created. The Red Sea story is told by a peasant fisherman to an Egyptian official some hundred years after the Exodus—in front of a monument to Pharaoh's great victory! Who has the truth?

> *Alan Brine, "Faith in Story," in* Books for Keeps, *No. 69, July, 1991, p. 32.*

The Seventh Raven (1981)

The Seventh Raven is narrated by a seventeen-year-old girl, a participant in a real-life drama which draws her aside from immediate preoccupations and briefly offers her a new and wider perspective—one in which right and wrong are not clearly defined, and the nature of art, commitment and loyalty are called into question. Peter Dickinson has always been fascinated by the motive power of faith, which can work in his view either for good or evil. His new novel contains his most overt discussion of the subject to date.

It is necessary to start with the philosophical basis for this story, because that is the book's raison d'être. It is also necessary to get it out of the way quickly since, in the words of one of the characters, "good messages make bad music". The dialogue between art and commitment, between freedom and liberation, might have been earnest and tedious in the hands of a less able writer. Couched as it is in the language of an articulate teenager, the discussion is never boring, merely a little contrived: messages make the music too good to be true.

Most people, however, don't bother to listen to the music, and most people will find **The Seventh Raven** a very good read. The wit, the pace, the sympathetic characters and the oddballs—Dickinson hallmarks—are all here. The setting for the book is the annual children's opera mounted by a small semi-professional band of Kensington parents known as the Mafia. Doll Jacobs at seventeen, with eight years of playing owls, slaves, whaleribs (Jonah), flames (Burning Fiery Furnace), and numerous wicked women behind her, is too old for the opera and manages to infiltrate the organizing Mafia. Her descriptions of casting a hundred children as priests of Baal, tribesmen, warriors, handmaidens and bulls that can be chopped up on stage, is horribly funny. And all too recognizable to anyone involved in drama and children is the account of the first rehearsal where the composer makes his work come alive for the children only to be sabotaged by the scrapping of Elijah's ravens—the youngest, and loudest, offstage performers.

The pleasure of joint effort, of seeing the work develop, the security of being amongst "our sort"—that is the social/aesthetic elite of Kensington squares, Westminster and St Pauls—these are the qualities that feed Doll's enthusiasm for the opera and inform the early spirit of the book. The intrusion of violence on to a scene of civilized excitement—the day of the dress rehearsal in the church—comes as a hideous shock.

At first it is a game: Mattean (read Chilean) terrorists burst into the church after some gunfire outside and imprison the cast in full costume. They are looking for Elijah's seventh raven, nephew of the future president of Matteo, but Juan is already disguised as a handmaiden. As the children are organized and secrets are kept, the terrorists begin to chat and time passes. Then Juan is discovered by the ruthless girl terrorist and the atmosphere changes: the children are frightened, the adults unsure of the situation and the terrorist jumpy. The edginess continues as the terrorists mount a show trial, choosing as their representative criminal the most vulnerable person in the church: Doll's cellist mother. Council for defence, in the person of the costume-designer, an old-guard socialist no longer so sure of the party card she has carried over the years, asks awkward questions. The trial is brought to a sudden end with a sentence of death and a shot. Immediately police rush in, and a relative normality is restored. Doll has been changed however—by the events themselves, by what has been said on both sides, or possibly by no more than the passage of time. Now she is free to go on.

Peter Dickinson has a splendid creation in his narrator. He has totally absorbed her attitudes to other people, her views and especially her language—part schoolgirl (all beastlies and actuallies), part mature and reflective. His setting, too, and minor characters are bursting with life and humour, and his plot is cunningly set about with surprises and shifts of mood. It has to be said, though, that this is a lesser piece, a work that feels more thought-up than it should. A book that, in the last analysis, lacks that quality of absolute strangeness and wonder that pervades the very best of Peter Dickinson's work.

Sarah Hayes, "As Awareness Grows," in The Times Literary Supplement, *No. 4086, July 24, 1981, p. 842.*

Hats off to the most original writer of this generation! Peter Dickinson follows his second Carnegie Medal with yet another book which resembles its predecessors only in excellence. Never was a writer less set in his ways. (p. 156)

The novel, which is packed full of action, acute observation, humour and social comment, is divided roughly between the opera and the siege. The opera is marvellous. (I wish there could be an accompanying cassette.) Conductor and composer—both are of course world-famous—are drawn with enormous penetration, yet consistently seen through the eyes of a precocious teenager, and the reactions of performers and mafia are presented beautifully. In fact we could have had a grand story with never a sight or smell of a terrorist. Yet, for once, the violent action is an integral part of the whole. Enormous tension builds up as the siege drags on and children and gunmen react to the pressures. The portraits of, for example, Danny, the terrorist who is an actor manqué, and his sidekick Chip are masterly, not a move or an inflection wrong. There are lots here to thrill over, to enjoy all over again at a second reading, and to ponder over in tranquillity. It is a fine example of the Gollancz novel of social relevance, and much more besides: a rattling good read, a portrait gallery of fascinating individuals, a study in depth of one young woman finding herself under stress, an exercise in philosophy and in dramatic criticism, and so on. I could go on. But don't waste time reading reviews; get this outstandingly fine book and let the whole family enjoy its profundities and its high spirits. (p. 157)

M. Crouch, in a review of "The Seventh Raven," in The Junior Bookshelf, *Vol. 45, No. 4, August, 1981, pp. 156-57.*

[Topical] and exciting, the plot [of **The Seventh Raven**] is as fruitful in allowing the author to suggest clashes of character as well as actual conflicts of political interests. . . . Make no mistake, this is not just another look at the currently fashionable topic of terrorism. To start with, the narrative is spoken by Doll, a girl of seventeen who has grown up with the yearly opera and is now a kind of non-acting liaison between producers and cast. Highly intelligent, mildly cynical and politically innocent, Doll gives us her view of the situation—the siege in the church, the behaviour of individuals young and old, the careful deploying of outside forces—as well as her definitions, discerning and impetuous, of the personalities concerned; and all the time we can see how the terrorists, from being a group of four anonymous terrifying invaders, are seen to be individuals with their own strengths and weaknesses.

Magnificent in character-drawing, in the highly pictorial style, brilliant in the way the opera comes through bit by bit and echoes the violence and terror of actual happenings (with Ahab, the 'King in the Middle', as a symbol of Doll and of much more), the book is most telling in the way it implies change, in wild Juan and in Doll's detached, musical mother, in Danny the revolutionary and Mrs. Dunnitt the social-liberal, and most of all in Doll, whose views on life are tested and stretched in a way that she only partly realises. Of all Peter Dickinson's books for the young, this is perhaps the most skilfully devised, with its shifting atmosphere, its glancing wit and its sharp eye for individual speech and behaviour.

> *Margery Fisher, in a review of "The Seventh Raven," in* Growing Point, *Vol. 20, No. 3, September, 1981, p. 3941.*

[The events in **The Seventh Raven**] transcend the merely sensational and become a vehicle for exploring personal and societal values and attitudes, the relationship between liberty and neutrality, and the rights and responsibilities of both the government and the governed. Yet, as in many of the author's previous works, difficult philosophical and moral questions do not take over the story but become an integral part of the pattern, resulting in a dynamic and compelling narrative remarkable for its evocation of mood and creation of character.

Beginning with ordinary details, the book captures the petty, often comic political struggles of community organizations, foreshadowing the larger, more dominant conflict to come. A significant element in both conflicts, ultimately the point of convergence, is the idea of a "middle ground," that undistinguished turf where most folk, unremarkable and unremembered, play out their lives. Introduced initially as an idea in the opera—which is based on the Biblical story of Jezebel, Ahab, and Elijah—the concept is described by the composer as " 'the music you hear whenever people fight for ideas that seem to them so important that the lives of ordinary people don't matter any more . . . the still, sad music of humanity.' "

Then, as the story builds to its climax, the concept is reexamined as a moral issue. The revolutionaries, in a mock trial, claim that neutrality is synonymous with betrayal; therefore, art cannot be neutral. The only legitimate activist among the hostages—Mrs. Dunnitt (a singularly appropriate name)—counters with the statement that there is " 'little liberty . . . in a society which has no middle ground, no areas of neutrality. Art and poetry and music are . . . one sort of freedom.' " The issue is not entirely resolved, however, for the author depicts the ambivalent emotions of those taken hostage and suggests that no one remains unchanged by the experience. But in creating tension, he avoids unnecessarily harrowing his readers—a technique more powerful in its restraint than many a more violent portrayal. With carefully honed phrases and superb imagery Dickinson has created a suspenseful, multidimensional narrative. (pp. 31-2)

> *Mary M. Burns, in a review of "The Seventh Raven," in* The Horn Book Magazine, *Vol. LVIII, No. 1, February, 1982, pp. 31-2.*

Healer (1983)

"Bloody rum thing, the human mind", says Pinkie's irascible, indomitable Grandad. Pinkie is a healer: she stopped the pain in his leg. It is not even a real leg, but a phantom limb, a reminder of Alamein. Grandad is talking to Pinkie's friend, Barry. Barry also knows of Pinkie's powers: she can calm his ferocious migraines. He knows, too, that the human mind is a bloody rum thing. Inside his head, summoned to deal with the migraines but gradually invested with independent life, is a prowling, growling secret creature he calls Bear. Later, when he is relying on Bear's instincts in his attempt to free Pinkie from a cult which manipulates her power, she calls him, naturally, "Bear".

Bear is the right weapon to use against the cult, founded by Pinkie's charismatic stepfather—half charlatan, half prophet. For "Bear wasn't troubled by thoughts. Bear just felt." And in the costly "Harmony Session," Barry attends in the first chapter, the halt and the sick, hoping to draw on Pinkie's power, are "supposed to be feeling, not thinking". Pinkie's guessing about Bear is important, because it cuts across any simplistic opposition of science and mumbo-jumbo. She does have a gift, and her stepfather, Mr Freeman, though he drugs and exploits her, is sincere. In the authentically messy, confused violence at the book's climax, the death of the villain yields, in a vivid explosion of colour, a temporary justification of his arrogance: "The golden beard was soaked with blood. There was a crimson pool in a fold of his cloak near his neck. The tanned face was muddy grey. His lips were blue, but moving, and his gold eyes stared at the sky."

There are links with earlier books by Peter Dickinson: to **The Gift,** in which Davy's ability to see pictures of the thoughts of others is of doubtful value, and to two of his Jimmy Pibble detective novels, **Sleep and His Brother** and **The Seals.** As in **The Seals,** Dickinson has constructed his cult religion of exactly the right mixture of real and fake materials. As with the "cathypnic" children of **Sleep and His Brother,** Pinkie's power is more something missing than something added: Barry notes, "she didn't seem to know how to play".

Barry, not Pinkie, is the book's central consciousness. The adults—Mr Freeman, Pinkie's Grandad—are drawn with bold strokes but little shading, and Pinkie necessarily remains mysterious to the reader as to the other characters, but Barry is splendidly realized. At every turn in **Healer** Dickinson rejects the easy option, and Barry is no idealized saviour. He is a rather gruff, unhappy boy, who impeaches the rest of the world for "conspiracy to conspire". He does not really know how to gauge or use his feelings; his dissociation into the separate personality of Bear is not simply a narrative ploy, but is fundamental to him. At every point he questions his involvement with Pinkie. He is sixteen, she is ten. So before he decides to help her escape, he must confirm that there is nothing sexual in his feeling for her: he knows what the newspapers could make of the story.

In the event the media drop the "sex angle" for "the much less rewarding Guard-dog-slays-health-crank approach" but the fact that the book takes account of such a possible outcome is some indication of Dickinson's seriousness of purpose. *Healer*'s thriller format is never allowed to make life simple; it is used to show ideas in action, to explore, among other things, the responsibilities of care. The book's tensions are not easily or tidily resolved; the tale serves them, not they the tale. The prose is lucid, unshowy and cleverly keeps the reader involved yet detached. *Healer* is not Dickinson at full strength, but it is a reminder, after his weak *The Seventh Raven,* of his adroitness in prodding his readers into engagement with the text, by using the techniques which are employed by lesser writers simply to make the pulse race.

> *Neil Philip, "An Animal Anima," in* The Times Literary Supplement, *No. 4200, September 30, 1983, p. 1049.*

The only thing we may predict about Peter Dickinson is that his next book will always be unpredictable. So it is with *Healer.*

As one of the bigger boys in junior school Barry has had a curious relationship with Pinkie, a very small girl distinguished for most of the time by an inability to solve the most ordinary problems of school life. But Pinkie has one extraordinary power. When Barry has one of his intermittent migraines she can take it away by her touch. When he is sixteen he finds Pinkie again, she is still a small and mainly helpless child, but she has become the heart of the Foundation of Harmony, an organisation devoted to healing. Is she a willing part of a force dedicated to the service of mankind, or the victim of a ruthless racketeer? As the story is by Mr. Dickinson, there is no simple answer.

Nor is Barry a simple instrument of Pinkie's salvation. He too is a complex being in whom 'reality' is in constant conflict with the alter ego he calls Bear. In this confused state he infiltrates the Foundation and plans and carries out a daring rescue plan. There is a tremendous and exciting climax, but no simple happy ending can be contrived. Only Pinkie has learnt to laugh at her dreadful mother, and Barry can perhaps live successfully with Bear as he, in the post-hibernation sunshine, sniffs 'the air of a world made new.'

This is a marvellous book, superficially a story of adventure and chase, but one from which one peels different levels of meaning layer by layer. What it means fundamentally is for each reader to decide for himself; certainly each will find his own satisfaction in the search and his own enlightenment from the final discovery. As always Peter Dickinson writes beautifully, using words with great freshness and delicacy.

> *M. Crouch, in a review of "Healer," in* The Junior Bookshelf, *Vol. 47, No. 5, October, 1983, p. 212.*

[*Healer* is a] dark contemporary fable of power and dualism. . . . Dickinson's novel is balanced on a keen edge, as characters flip from geniuses to charlatans (and back), from victims to heroines, from Barry to Bear. These ambiguities are developed subtly and sparingly—Pinky utters little more than a few sentences throughout the book, yet she is skillfully revealed as a complex little girl. The psy-

chological tensions of the novel are daring, and they are matched by a swift, suspenseful story which culminates in a chase scene to rival *North by Northwest.*

> *Roger Sutton, in a review of "Healer," in* School Library Journal, *Vol. 31, No. 8, April, 1985, p. 96.*

Giant Cold (1984)

Allegory works with key-words, and so which is the key-word of *Giant Cold*—is it cold, or love, or one-ness, or rejuvenation, or venturing, or all of these? Everyone who reads this haunting tale will provide an individual interpretation according to personal preoccupations, associated thoughts, the degree to which verbal rhythms and meanings make their impression. Behind the bare story of a father, mother and child on holiday in a sun-nourished island and a climb to a volcanic mountain lies a mysterious sequence of events. Becoming ant-size after eating a strange fruit, the child makes a magic journey to Apple Island, impelled (as the migrating loobies are impelled) towards the innermost secrets of the dangerous, metamorphosed giant. This is the kind of book one feels obliged to read aloud, for the sound of the prose as it extends the historic-present narrative is as important as the strong visual images it moves along. The rhetoric of the book can be seen in every careful, flowing paragraph. . . . Eloquent, too, the haunting drawings [by Alan E. Colser], finely shaded, which seem to emanate from the words to form a new mystery. Not 'for' any particular age-group or belonging except peripherally to any one literary tradition, this book makes its own demands and establishes its own frontiers.

> *Margery Fisher, in a review of "Giant Cold," in* Growing Point, *Vol. 23, No. 1, May, 1984, p. 4250.*

Whether aimed at older or younger readers Peter Dickinson's novels have always been more than eventful narratives, for all the bustle of their well-constructed plots. Below the surface of his chosen time and setting—the present-in-the-future of *The Changes* trilogy, sixth-century Byzantium, Wales, Loch Ness, down an old mine, ancient Egypt, or Tibet after the Boxer Rebellion—there lie puzzles about dreams, second sight, prophecy and magic. Dickinson's poetic imagination thickens what may seem at first to be no more than a straightforward adventure story with the possibility that things may be other.

Now in *Giant Cold,* a beautifully wrought fable of deceptively open prose mirrored in remarkable hair-line drawings by Alan Cober, he deals with the emotional size of childhood, when feelings are immense, and understanding a spark to make sense of the world. If the reader resists the temptation to rush over the early pages to get into the story, and, instead, accepts the narrator's invitation to "play" the text, then the plot becomes an adventure of both thought and feeling.

The opening is all-important, for there the rules of the game are laid out. The publishers have taken care to leave space round the words:

> On a holiday island, somebody falling asleep—it
>   might be you.
> "Hush, shush," murmurs the sea. . . .
> Voices of parents from the next room.
> *"It's much too far for a child."*
> *"But it's our last day, tomorrow. We mustn't*
>   *waste it."*

The reader and the child protagonist are elided at the end of this argument when the narrator asks "What does it mean, loving someone? How can you get love? Can you keep it?"

Part of the puzzle is who is telling the story. The answer seems to be: the reader, the child protagonist of the story and the storyteller, who appears from time to time to address the reader directly: The reader is in dialogue with the storyteller. He lets "you" hear your parents bickering in a way that shifts the ground of all your certainty. The resulting feeling of coldness invades your dreams, so you set off to find the golden centre "where all the warmth of the island has been sucked to", not at the brisk pace of "what happens next", but in the strange floating dream logic in which to want, to fear, to see and to know are all one. For help you have the hints in the conversation which disturbed you: the island's strange fruit, the looby birds, the volcano, the sunshine and, more deeply hidden, the stories which have been read to you of small people who have overcome giants.

Paraphrasing this story will only do it less than justice. Dreams, as Ursula Le Guin says, must explain themselves. The images of the mind's mountains, the sensation of the "sweet sick stink of the inside of the sailor's tobacco box", the fear of size, space, uncertainty, falling, are locked into the act of reading itself. With great subtlety Dickinson has caught the inner speech of combined thought-and-feeling the necessary oppositions of understanding before these become ideas to be structured into what the world counts as knowledge.

Talk about the mirror stage, the dialoguing imagination or other theories. For me this remarkable book reveals something that the narratologists neglect, notably that childhood is essentially the time when feeling is understanding and understanding is feeling.

> *Margaret Meek, "Mirror Reading," in* The
> Times Literary Supplement, *No. 4233, May
> 18, 1984, p. 558.*

I had to read Peter Dickinson's story three times, and I still would not be sure that I know what he is after. Perhaps that doesn't matter. Who knows what 'Kubla Khan' is about? This strange poetic fantasy, allegory, whatever it is, haunts and nags at the imagination, inviting continued reading and meditation. . . .

With Peter Dickinson the idea and the means for its expression always go hand in hand. It is an essential part of his scheme that the story should be told in the historic present. This is never very easy for the reader, however insistently it brings home the urgency of the theme, and I must admit that the few uncrowded pages of this book were uncommonly tiring to read. I cannot honestly claim to have enjoyed it, but I was hugely disturbed and impressed. Perhaps, coming back to it after an interval, all will be made plain. I don't think I was helped by the illustrations. These are imaginative and finely drawn, but I felt that Alan Cober had not quite got his scale right, and that, in capturing the dream atmosphere, he had to sacrifice clarity and contact with reality. **Giant Cold** will be a book for Dickinson fans—of whom I count myself one—and for those who like allegorical fantasy, but it would be a mistake to consider it primarily, if at all, as a book for young readers.

> *M. Crouch, in a review of "Giant Cold," in*
> The Junior Bookshelf, *Vol. 48, No. 4, August,
> 1984, p. 175.*

A Box of Nothing (1985)

A Box of Nothing starts with a nice combination of the mysterious and the ordinary. Young James hides from his mother in a derelict shop opposite the Council rubbish dump. He thinks of it as the Nothing Shop because it has been empty for years, but there is a man behind the counter. So he asks for some nothing and is solemnly sold a box of it for nought pounds, nought shillings and nuppence. His exasperated mother throws the box on the dump, James gets through the fence to retrieve it—and finds that the heaps of junk have become a vast landscape of mountains and gaseous lakes. It looks as though there will be little scope for the concerns that are often thought proper for children's fiction—no social *Angst*, no warnings against nuclear catastrophe, no studies of first love. But by the end of the book a new universe is coming into being.

Perhaps the project is rather too ambitious; certainly the explanation of what happens makes no pretence of being fully intelligible, but it remains interesting. James has just seen a television programme about life developing out of the debris left by the big bang. Now the dump is slowly coming alive. He meets its personification, an amiable being which has put itself together out of cast-off toys, with a video-game voice and a donkey's head. It calls itself the Burra (*burro*/Borough). The rats and gulls which inhabited the "real" dump have become enormous, and the rats are establishing a kind of civilization, a pitiless, heavily armed and industrialized dictatorship under a monster rat called General Weil. So there are politics in the book as well as science; the Burra ("we are a democratic institution") is composed of different but equal members and it speaks for the dump, and Rat City is centralized government. The allegory is not meant to be taken too precisely but all is not well in this curious world.

Driven by an impulse that baffles them, as it may do the reader, James and the Burra set out in a home-made airship to put things to rights. Assailed by gulls and rats, they survive a variety of adventures, crossing a terrain which gradually ages from fossilized fridges and kitchen cupboards to bits of old carts, flint axes and finally an immense desert of geological waste. The inboard computer busies itself with abstruse calculations, the airship just overtakes an intrepid rat explorer and the two travellers reach the black hole at the centre of it all. Knowing at last what to do, James drops his box of nothing in and the sum is completed. The dump—desert, mountains, airship, Burra and everything—slides roaring into the hole to be the stuff of a new creation. What the rat explorer might have done had he won the race is not stated, but his failure ensures that the new order will incorporate the Burra's values rather than his. He ends up an ordinary rat again, and James finds himself giddily up a tree on the edge of the dump, hearing the roar of Council bulldozers as they clear away the rubbish to make a park.

The end of the book, like the beginning, successfully balances the unfamiliar and the familiar, but the balance is less well maintained in the intervening narrative. Neither the tone nor the scratchy illustrations [by Ian Newsham] fully recognize the element of nightmare that the story inevitably brings with it. Although the dump is animated there are no plants or people—only vast tracts of rottenness turning to dust. Ferocious rats are no fun, and anyone who knows anything about Weil's disease will have difficulty in accepting the General's name as lightly as it is given. But then James doesn't know—and the dream, after all, belongs to him.

> *Dominic Hibberd, "In the Dumps," in* The Times Literary Supplement, *No. 4278, March 29, 1985, p. 347.*

There are not many writers as deft as Peter Dickinson in creating that particularly edgy feeling that the ordinary has already been transformed into the mysterious without our noticing. We sense it almost at once in *A Box of Nothing* when 10-year-old James, late for school because he botched his homework, hides from his mother in the doorway of an abandoned shop. The image of the woman, looking as though she's "fighting her way into a wind, though there wasn't a whisper of one in the long, empty street," is disquieting.

And the feeling of a world out of joint gets worse when James somehow slips into a shop and immediately begins to bargain with a shopkeeper amid the empty, dusty shelves for a box of nothing. Not an ordinary box of nothing, it emerges, but some of the real nonstuff from which the universe originated. James and the shopkeeper are both so much at ease that their playful, punning conversation is hair-raising. But it is not until James's mother impatiently throws the box of nothing into the Borough Dump across the street, and James slips through the fence to recover it, that we again begin to appreciate just how out of whack things are.

The Dump has ceased to function. Not the ordinary Dump, which the local government has promised to clear and make into a park, but the Dump whose task it is to recycle all existing matter through primordial nothingness back into new universes. Yes, *that* Dump. As a consequence, James finds himself in a world whose landscape is formed from fossilized junk and whose dominant inhabitants are gigantic, scavenging gulls and a technological society of rats racing to industrialize. And there is no fence. He can't get back.

James is given shelter almost at once by the Burra, a wonderful, shifting collection of odd parts, spare parts and discards. The Burra speaks with a voice from a video game

and seems to center on an attractive figure shuffled together from odds and ends of toys. All of the members of the Burra are alive enough not to be fossilized, but not so well organized as to be comfortable calling themselves "I."

It is while James is getting to know the Burra and to appreciate the problems of the Dump that the story is most engaging. Mr. Dickinson, . . . is able to enliven questions about the nature of life and personal identity in a way that is whimsical, provocative and even touching.

When James and the Burra decide to try correcting the Dump's problems, however, the story begins to lose its grip. They set off in a balloon, delightfully contrived of some of the Burra members themselves, but their quest seems curiously desultory, not prompted by any clear sense of what is wrong or what might be done about it. It simply seems like a good idea, and James has the notion that it might help him get home.

He does get home, but the manner in which this is accomplished is not so much wonderful and mysterious as murky. On their way home he and the Burra have a number of adventures among the rats and gulls that cast a few flat reflections on human society, but these events, particularly James's experiences as an inmate of a rat concentration camp, are hurried over with impatience, and one is left with a sense of dramatic possibilities that are not pursued, finally, because they don't advance the thematic interests of the quest.

Even the climactic race against a party of rats toward a stalled black hole at the center of the disturbance has, despite careful managing, a certain staginess about it, a merely adrenal urgency. We never know what is at stake in the race or why it is so important that James and the Burra get there first. Some answers to these questions are considered, but they are proposed with such diffidence that they seem makeshift and don't engage the imagination. There are, finally, too many problems of purpose and effect left dangling. It's hard to see how it could be otherwise. But the idea of dramatizing the central mystery of the big-bang theory of creation with a human adventure story is certainly very bold.

> *Brock Cole, "The Right Nonstuff," in* The New York Times Book Review, *May 8, 1985, p. 37.*

Few authors for children have written stories on such a wide variety of themes as Peter Dickinson. This new book has yet another unusual and odd motivation.

A boy buys a Box of Nothing for nothing. His mother throws it over the fence on to a rubbish dump and James sets out to find it again. But the familiar Dump is now an 'iron' sea, surrounded by cliffs of fossilised rubbish and terrorised by abnormally large rats and seagulls. A strange creature, the Burra, composed of unmatching limbs from discarded toys, watches over the Dump. 'Nothing,' says the Burra, 'is totally dead. If all co-operate, there can be a living thing.'

So begins this complex story of the Burra's struggle to restore the Dump to normality, for it has ceased to function. The culmination is the construction of an airship from 'co-operating' rubbish of every kind—a fascinating operation. In this airship the Burra and James journey to the centre of the world, a bottomless hole, 'the original nothing which was there before anything was there'. As everything plunges into this hole, James throws in the Box of Nothing also. There is a gloriously creative explosion. The Box blows itself apart subtracting its nothing from its nothing and dividing it by its nothing and making ! $(0+0+0=!)$ A new universe is born, an ecstatic vision of shining stars and galaxies. The airship disintegrates, the Dump becomes normal and James finds himself perched on the branch of a 'conker' tree. Only in his mind can he see what has happened. 'He thought ideas with numbers and they were beautiful'.

A remarkable book which, whether one understands it or not, is a challenge and experience. It can be read at several levels as can all books of genius. (pp. 138-39)

> *E. Colwell, in a review of "A Box of Nothing," in* The Junior Bookshelf, *Vol. 49, No. 3, June, 1985, pp. 138-39.*

Anyone who knows the work of Peter Dickinson knows that each new book will be fresh and full of surprises. *A box of nothing* is likely to take its place alongside that small batch of highly original works of fantasy. Some of the ideas underlying the story are complex and difficult, though they give a powerful drive to the whole and the book makes a very compelling read. The move from the natural world of Floral Street and the Borough Dump into the slightly terrifying world of a Dump which has 'fossilised' and stopped working is splendidly handled. The Burra, whom ten-year-old James meets, is one of the most original creations in recent children's fiction. Incidents are varied, characters are vividly drawn. The climax is awesome, whether one understands the science behind it or not. This is a very clever book which will intrigue many young readers and listeners.

> *Peter Kennerley, in a review of "A Box of Nothing," in* The School Librarian, *Vol. 33, No. 3, September, 1985, p. 237.*

Mole Hole   (1987)

This is an absolute joy; go out and buy it at once! Any family which doesn't have this for Christmas is deprived of a treat. It needs careful handling, like a pop-up book. The story is that of a gardener trying to get rid of the mole in his lawn, using a variety of wildly over-the-top ideas. Flaps, holes and wheels in the page reveal the mole foiling all his plans and getting the last laugh. Story and pictures [the illustrations are by Jean Claverie] match beautifully, and the humour is zany in a way that children love. The book is expensive, there are very few pages, but it is well worth buying and can be enjoyed for a long time. Recommended unconditionally for the sevens to seventies.

> *Ann G. Hay, in a review of "Mole Hole," in* British Book News Children's Books, *December, 1987, p. 13.*

'Turn the wheel (to line up the two numbers)—then lift the flap—' Having read the instructions and still hesitated about what to do, it became obvious that this is not a 'child only' book. An adult will be required to supervise the operation and ensure enjoyment of the story. The theme itself, how to get rid of moles, is excellent, and one which has always brought forth bizarre remedies. Despite the ingenuity of the enraged owner of the unsightly mole hills, the mole always wins. Provided that this is read on a one-to-one basis, and the turning of the wheel explained, what is revealed under the flaps will certainly amuse. The strange traps are beautifully portrayed on a bright green sward, rapidly being taken over by heaps of brown earth. This is a clever idea for a picture book, but the mechanics might prove too difficult for the youngest, who, quite rightly, will want to explore it on their own. (pp. 97-8)

> *Maisie Roberts, in a review of "Mole Hole," in* The School Librarian, *Vol. 36, No. 3, August, 1988, pp. 97-8.*

Eva   (1988)

Peter Dickinson is the least predictable of all our major writers. All one can be sure of is that each book will be quite unlike the rest except in excellence.

So it is with *Eva.* I am in some difficulty in writing about this extraordinary story because I cannot bring myself to give away the basic surprise from which the whole springs. As this is sprung in Chapter 2 it leaves little to write about. I can say that the action takes place in the future when human technology has developed enormously, far more than human understanding. This is a world run by the media, more specifically by the sinisterly-named 'shaper' (a development of TV which not only gives shape to every concept but also shapes the minds and lives of all who come under its influence). In this world lives Eva, an intelligent and pretty thirteen-year-old. A terrible road accident puts her grievously at hazard, but her life is saved— at a price. That price, and how she and those near to her pay it, is the substance of a story which is shatteringly moving, intellectually demanding, and relentlessly readable.

I will say no more, except to urge parents, teachers and all children mature enough to stand up to its emotional demands to read this most disturbing and important book. They will find it of absorbing interest. In it there is little of comfort, except perhaps the thought that mankind is on the way out and that the world will then come under the control of a species better able to control its greed and treat its resources with respect.

> *M. Crouch, in a review of "Eva," in* The Junior Bookshelf, *Vol. 53, No. 1, February, 1989, p. 26.*

Eva is a bold and remarkable work of science fiction, which imagines both an end and a new beginning to the human story. It is set in a world in which the rapid pace of scientific discovery and experiment is matched only by the decline of the human will to achieve or even to live. Most people simply stay indoors twenty-four hours a day, watching "the shaper". By the end of the book, technocracy is at its last gasp, and the listless population of the world is heading towards aimless self-destruction.

Against this negative but disturbingly plausible scenario, Peter Dickinson plays out a powerful fable of evolution and regeneration.

The novel focuses on the liminal area between mind and instinct to explore mankind's place in and responsibility towards nature. While the mechanics of his story—including Eva's transformation, her leadership of the chimps out of Egypt, and the cautious beginnings of a new culture—are brilliantly realized, their aura of reality is not the point. It is the import of the story which is primary: that if man will not work with nature, nature will work against man.

Eva is one of the better books of a first-rate writer. It is highly provocative, it has tenderness, humour and passion. It involves the reader from the very first page and will not quickly leave the mind.

Neil Philip, "Working with Nature," in The Times Literary Supplement, No. 4483, March 3-9, 1989, p. 232.

Dickinson's story of a young girl named Eva is unusually rewarding and challenging. . . . Ecological indifference, human greed, a deterioration of ethical standards—these are among the themes addressed in this gripping chronicle of a world gone wrong. . . .

[The] horrific revelation [that Eva's mind resides in Kelly—a young female chimpanzee] is made plausible by the author's wise and careful reeling out of events and information. Believability comes to readers as it does to Eva, slowly and with difficulty. Meticulous plot construction covers all the bases and makes the bizarre seem possible: Eva's dad is Director of Primate Zoology, a research center, and Eva grew up among chimps—indeed, she made chimp chatter before she said her first human word; experimentation with neuron memory transfer has already begun on animals (Eva is the first human). The mixed reactions of her mother—the sense of relief that her daughter lives countered by the agony of reality and loss of the Eva she has known—and the gradual emergence of Eva as an integrated being who bridges the interface between chimp body and human mind and finally accepts herself as a whole give the story a psychological complexity that makes it seem real. . . .

Readers will find that Dickinson's portrayal of chimp behavior, habits, and habitats is as sturdy as in any nonfiction book; couched here in fiction, it makes for dynamic reading, indeed. But perhaps even more riveting is the author's probing of such larger issues as animal environments, rights, and freedoms. Pertinent to this futuristic story, these topics are relevant to today's world as well, and the implications won't be missed by perceptive readers.

Dickinson's disturbing and intensely thought-provoking novel, a natural springboard to discussions of moral and ethical issues concerning medical technology and of life itself, is first and foremost a powerful story; one handled with integrity and finesse.

Phillis Wilson, "Focus: 'Eva', by Peter Dickinson," in Booklist, Vol. 85, No. 17, May 1, 1989, p. 1946.

A superb storyteller, Peter Dickinson has used his energetic imagination to add driving force to a variety of first-rate novels. Now he has written an astonishing work of biological science fiction that, in its portrayal of a future time on the brink of a new dark age, seems to be a devastating extension of the theme of his first children's books. . . . The account of [Eva's] mental and physical reconstitution is dramatic, but the reconciliation of her dual nature, of which she is acutely conscious, becomes a stormy, shocking, yet ironically logical process. . . . The differing personalities of chimps and humans are clearly defined, Eva's mother especially adding a credible note of ineffable sadness. It is difficult to imagine a more timely book, and while it succeeds as a daring, often horrifying adventure story, it is also a work of passion and eloquence, and its sobering significance increases in proportion to the reader's maturity. (pp. 487-88)

Ethel L. Heins, in a review of "Eva," in The Horn Book Magazine, Vol. LXV, No. 4, July-August, 1989, pp. 487-88.

Merlin Dreams (1988)

The eerie narrative framework of this enterprising set of latter-day Arthurian tales for children derives from the hallucinating consciousness of Merlin the magician, cast into lonely underground exile, able to register but no longer to control the wisps of dream and fragmentary waking recollection which drift across his mind. The stories here represent the dreams themselves. Motifs or objects established within the linking passages are, in transposed form, at the heart of each adjacent story. From the first such passage, young readers are challenged by writing which can be as taut and tense as the neo-Ossianic mindscape depicted with deftly deployed flecks of alliteration, bleak and artful metaphor—flames as steady as sword-blades, syllables as solid as pebbles—and a vivid word stock, with its froths of spittle, dribbles of leaves, and blotches of rust. Only occasionally do weary vapidities—"the evening air shimmered with departing energies"—slip through the net.

Within the tales, several of the principal characters will soon establish themselves as favourites in the eyes of discriminating young readers—the bizarre but likeable Scipiod, a creature whose provenance appears to include King Kong and Loki, with more than a touch of ET, and even a passing glance at the Abominable Snowman; or the splendidly squalid Sir Tremalin, the Sir Les Patterson of Camelot, unkempt, unshaven, and hung-over. His trenchant, anti-heroic, knee-in-the-groin pragmatism when confronting the apparently daunting Knight Who Rode Invisible suits the demands of his mysterious quest far better than the keep-a-straight-lance ideals of the knightly "noble ninnies" back at the court.

As one would expect in stories whose spells, quests, impossible tasks and violated interdicts mimic many of the characteristics of traditional fairy-tales, several narratives mirror, through human/animal transformations, aspects of those family-drama tensions in traditional tales about which Derek Brewer in particular has written so illuminatingly: the complexities of child-stepmother relations in the excellent **"Sword"** tale (one of the many stories to benefit from Alan Lee's bold and perceptive illustrations); the decay and restoration of confidence within the mind of a monarch father-figure, reduced to the role of a lonely and dishevelled Timon, while his subjects long for his renewed exercise of power and justice; and, not least, the tensions of sibling rivalry encoded within the power-struggles of a community. The prim Sir Hugh is translated from the familiar world of Camelot into a granitic Highland setting in a tale whose snarling spirit and uncomfortable battle with dialect seem closer to Sir Walter Scott, and to the fetches of the Icelandic sagas beloved by Scott, than to Malorian images of English chivalry.

Other tales are leaner in execution—cautionary stories in which, for instance, the self-confident Sly finds himself bested by the unlikely combination of "four Bumpkins, two Hicks, and a Clod". There are poems, too: a wry but puzzling Audenesque dialogue relating to the Vikings, and more notably, a hauntingly elegiac evocation of the decay of myth and of its potential for renewal through the power of imagination. It is an entirely appropriate coda to a book of "fresh born" medieval legend which older children—and many of their parents—will much enjoy.

> *Andrew Wawn, "A Camelot without Comfort," in* The Times Literary Supplement, *No. 4469, November 25-December 1, 1988, p. 1325.*

I don't know when Peter Dickinson first fell under the spell of Merlin. Certainly the old mage, albeit slumbering, is at the heart of his first children's novel, ***The Weathermonger,*** in 1968. In this new, beautifully presented and absorbing book he makes another attempt to exorcise Merlin's spirit. The book is a remarkable experience.

According to one version of the story Merlin was bewitched by Nimue who trapped him in a rock. There he lies, sleeping and dreaming. In his dreams he sees the growth of the Arthurian legend, its moods and fashions reflecting distortedly his memories of the past. Out of this come nine stories, sometimes ironic, sometimes pathetic, sometimes humorous, and all commenting in one way or another on the chivalric ideal and its decay. I particularly liked **'Damsel',** the longest tale in the book dealing, at first conventionally enough, with a young knight called to rescue a damsel in distress. As he travels north through the Arthurian realm his mission changes fundamentally, and he has experiences and faces dangers undreamt of at the Round Table. There are convincing descriptions of physical delight and stress. The ending is sad and satisfactory. But each reader will choose his own favourite: the story of two children, one beautiful, one hideous, of the sciopod, escaped from a travelling circus and finding her destiny among a primitive tribe; of the child seeking justice from a king who has lost his kingdom and, almost, his hope.

Peter Dickinson's writing is as fine as he has ever given us, varied, sensitive, wonderfully evocative. The words are supported by Alan Lee, an artist who is sensitive to every

nuance of the text. The delicacy of his drawing in colour and monochrome never makes us forget the underlying strength of these fine and moving designs, which underline the writer's message without ever coming between reader and author. The book comes from a very successful marriage of text and picture. (pp. 26-7)

> *M. Crouch, in a review of "Merlin Dreams," in* The Junior Bookshelf, *Vol. 53, No. 1, February, 1989, pp. 26-7.*

A short quotation from Malory's *The tale of King Arthur* at the beginning of this book describes what happens when Merlin begins to dote on a damsel named Nenyve. In his first chapter Peter Dickinson gives his own version of the incident: 'They stood on bare moor. No house between horizon—no, not even a path . . . He was not old, but haggard. She was young, still, watchful.' It is the language of a spellbinder, pared down to the bone, clear, strong, confident that the tale is riveting enough to hold the attention without any verbal fireworks. Having imprisoned Merlin, Nenyve, too, seems to have chosen her doom. It is to become like other people, ordinary. Merlin lies forever beneath the rock, but he dreams . . . 'the pool of memory wrinkles as he slides back into sleep.'

The stories that follow are his dreams. They are extraordinarily compelling, rooted in Celtic mythology and based on the Arthurian legends. An errant knight, conspicuously lacking knightly qualities and reluctant to embark on a quest, sets out to subdue a daunting invisible foe and encounters the Green and the Red Knights on his way. Dragons, damsels, hermits, unicorns, kings and queens, all are to be found here. This is one of those rare joys, a book to be read quickly to find out what happens next, then to be savoured again and again. Ideally there should be one copy always available for browsing on the reference shelves of the school library, another on the fiction shelves.

> *Barbara Sherrard-Smith, in a review of "Merlin Dreams," in* The School Librarian, *Vol. 37, No. 1, February, 1989, p. 21.*

AK (1990)

As ever, Peter Dickinson takes his readers by surprise. Each of his stories is totally unlike the others.

Here his scene is a fictional, but almost recognisable, country in Africa. The war is in its last day, and Michael and his guerillas can look forward cautiously to the possibility of building a nation in peace. Side by side with the adults have fought the Warriors, a child army, among whom is Paul, an orphan of the wars. Michael adopts Paul as his son, and arranges for him to be educated with a few other Warriors so that they can play a part in the future. The peace is shortlived. In an armed coup Michael is arrested, and the Warriors' school is destroyed. Paul, Francis (who, though little more than an infant, is marked out for the highest office in a free country) and Jilli, a little girl whose ambition hitherto has been to become a waitress in the Hilton, escape the carnage. Paul has his sights set on rescuing his father and overturning the dictator. His first thought is to rely on his AK, the automatic rifle won in battle. Later he finds better allies among the people. The story moves, at first slowly, then with relentless momentum, to its great climax. Was it all worth the suffering? Michael says 'It will be twenty years before we know . . .' In two epilogues, Peter Dickinson offers alternative answers, one hopeful, the other (more probably) full of bitter irony.

Mr. Dickinson is a superb story-teller, and here at his best. He is also, as befits a Gollancz author, a social critic and an historian. This may be fiction, but it has all the marks of reality. As comment on the sufferings of the Third World the book has much relevance. But it is also a novel, an account of people reacting to the stresses posed by their times and their environment. Paul, the little boy who, instead of playing football as befits his years, overthrows a government, is deeply convincing. He shoulders his burden, but it remains a burden unreasonably great for so small a boy to bear. As a rounded portrait Paul is matched by Jilli, who gives up her Hilton dream in favour of being a Warrior, a delightful, courageous and vulnerable child. All the other parts, including sketches of people glimpsed in passing, are beautifully drawn. Mr. Dickinson's telling avoids heroics, but matches exactly the tempo of the action and captures the noise and smells of a mob on the move. Immensely readable, the story will appeal even to teenage boys not normally attracted to reading. Adults will miss a rewarding experience if they dismiss the book as kids' stuff. (pp. 305-06)

> *M. Crouch, in a review of "AK," in* The Junior Bookshelf, *Vol. 54, No. 6, December, 1990, pp. 305-06.*

Everything about Nagala feels flawlessly authentic: the structure of command and relationship within guerrilla groups, outback village communities and urban gangs (the Deathsingers, the Soccer Boys, the Scorpions). The atmosphere of bush, desert and shanty-town, and the detail of tribal politics, are absorbingly real. There is nothing conventionally exhilarating or romantic about the journey to the city which Paul and Jilli make. Kindness is rarely encountered, instinctive violence is an everyday expectation. The author has delivered in its entirety a wholly credible African country, down to the peculiar variety of condenscension shown by certain European visitors.

But the overwhelming presence of Nagala itself as the anti-hero of the novel is so complete and successful that the importance of its individual characters is inescapably diminished in a short book. Dickinson's principal characters are not often rendered physically vivid, and their deepest thoughts (not least those of the shadowy Michael and Paul himself) tend to be offered in the form of admirable but stereotyped political sentiments. The AK remains an uncomfortable instrument: Paul buries it in the bush, but the author fails in the attempt to bury it as a rather ordinarily sinister symbol of masculine pride and conquest. Some imaginary countries have become part of our own imaginations. The dreadfully real Nagala could never be made as attractive as the unreal terrains explored by Haggard or Hope.

> *Alan Brownjohn, "A Region without Romance," in* The Times Literary Supplement, *No. 4582, January 25, 1991, p. 20.*

The theatre of the war, a bitter simulacrum of so many alignments in Africa in reality, is broad and brilliantly pictured but never in impersonal description; tangled thickets, the close air and perilous footing of marshes, stretches of mountain or desert, all impress through the deeds and feelings of the young survivors addressing themselves to the dangers of corrupt politicians, brutal soldiers, and the treacheries of former comrades. No Dickinson novel ever lacks the sheer excitement of action, of triumph and heroic defeat, of complex loyalties and alliances, but the ending of this superb tale takes it far beyond entertainment. The book ends with a hint of triumph but, equally, more than a hint of danger to come, and there follow two 'twenty years after' sections, one showing a country democratically ruled and increasingly prosperous, the other sardonically, even cynically showing that nothing has really changed, that corruption, betrayal and inter-tribal conflict are still the norm. Beyond the impressive narrative pattern, the striking crowd scenes and incisive character drawing, this is a novel which encapsulates reality unforgettably. (pp. 5515)

> *Margery Fisher, in a review of "AK," in* Growing Point, *Vol. 30, No. 1, May, 1991, p. 5514-15.*

[**AK** is] one of the outstanding teenage novels of the last few years—a dazzling, haunting and daringly constructed novel set in modern Africa. . . . Dickinson offers two alternative endings for both hero and gun, one optimistic, one pessimistic, each in themselves extremely moving. This is a complex book about the labyrinthine politics of modern Africa. Well worth reading by young readers and adults alike. (pp. 20-1)

> *A review of "A.K.," in* Books for Your Children, *Vol. 26, No. 2, Summer, 1991, pp. 20-1.*

Lois Duncan (Steinmetz Arquette)

1934-

(Also writes as Lois Kerry) American author of fiction, nonfiction, short stories; poet, and journalist.

Major works include *Ransom* (1966), *They Never Came Home* (1969), *Summer of Fear* (1976), *Killing Mr. Griffin* (1978), *Chapters: My Growth as a Writer* (1982)

Duncan is best known for her compelling novels of psychological suspense which frequently feature elements of the supernatural and the occult. The hallmark of her plots—explorations of murder, extrasensory perception, astral projection, the appearance of ghosts and witches, and the spread of evil—is an uncomfortable, escalating tension that culminates in an unforeseen climax. Although her style has been labeled lean and nonliterary, Duncan is nonetheless considered a master at her craft, the creator of highly plausible, fast-paced tales which afford the young adult reader a chilling glimpse of the darker sides of humanity. Less regarded are Duncan's forays into poetry, lullabies, fantasies, and family situation books for preteen readers. Duncan is also the author of two works of historical fiction, *Major André: Brave Enemy* (1969) and *Peggy* (1970); numerous magazine articles and short stories for adults; an autobiography of her early life, *Chapters: My Growth as a Writer;* and a factual account of the circumstances surrounding her daughter's unexplained murder, *Who Killed My Daughter?* (1992).

The daughter of renowned photographers Joseph and Lois Steinmetz, Duncan began her writing career at an early age; at 10 she submitted her first story, a fantasy about a little boy, to *Ladies' Home Journal.* By her teen years she was a published writer of romance stories. Her first major work as an adult was *Debutante Hill,* a teenage love story which she refers to in *Something about the Author Autobiography Series* as "sweet and sticky and pap." Duncan distanced herself from such fare with her first suspense novel, a story of counter-espionage entitled *Game of Danger* (1962), but more markedly with her next work in this vein, *Ransom.* A story of five teens who are kidnapped and held for ransom, this novel is noteworthy for the complexity of its main characters, all strikingly different from each other, all differently equipped to face their common, difficult challenge.

Duncan's insight into both the banalities and the specific concerns of teen life lends her novels—which after *Ransom* become increasingly bizarre and terrifying—a high degree of surface realism. In addition, her preference for dialogue over description, and her penchant for devious plot twists, affords her work the same level of intensity as highly polished television drama, an entertainment form with which Duncan believes she must compete. One of her best known works, the story of a young witch's disruption of an Albuquerque family entitled *Summer of Fear,* was in fact adapted to TV as "Stranger in Our House," a movie-of-the-week starring Linda Blair. At least two of

Duncan's young adult novels, *Killing Mr. Griffin* and *Daughters of Eve* (1979), have received criticism for their ostensible promotion of violence. In the former, a group of high-school seniors successfully carry out the murder of an unpopular teacher; in the latter, the members of an all-female social club conspire against the domineering males in their lives. While *Daughters of Eve* is most susceptible to unfavorable reactions, particularly for its ostensibly harmful message to feminist groups, it is important to note that at the core of all Duncan's major works is her belief in the presence of evil, which engenders violence before goodness can triumph.

Ironically, since 1989 and the death of her youngest daughter, Kaitlyn, Duncan has been unable to write the thrillers that have made her a mainstay of the genre. One work that has arisen from her tragedy is *Who Killed My Daughter?,* the eerie but true story of Duncan's search for clues regarding the identity of her daughter's murderer or murderers. Several striking parallels between her novel *Don't Look Behind You* (1989), whose heroine was based on her 18-year-old daughter, and the murder investigation itself, led Duncan to explore psychical research and phenomena in depth and before writing *Who Killed My*

Daughter?, a work which is expected to capture the public's attention for many of the same reasons as has her fiction. Duncan, a five-time runner-up for the Edgar Allan Poe Award, was the recipient of the Dorothy Canfield Fisher Award for *Summer of Fear* in 1978; the Best Novel Award from the National League of American Pen Women for *Stranger with My Face,* in 1982; the Children's Book Award from the National League for *Horses of Dreamland* in 1987; and the 1992 Margaret A. Edwards Award for her contributions to young adult fiction.

(See also *Something about the Author,* Vol. 36; *Something about the Author Autobiography Series,* Vol. 2; *Contemporary Authors New Revision Series,* Vols. 2, 23; *Authors and Artists for Young Adults,* Vol. 4; and *Contemporary Literary Criticism,* Vol. 26.)

AUTHOR'S COMMENTARY

[The following excerpt is from an interview by Roger Sutton.]

[Sutton]: You've been around for a long time. How do you think your work has changed over the years?

Duncan: It's changed tremendously. I started submitting stories to magazines when I was ten, and made my first sale at 13. I wrote for teenage publications, particularly *Seventeen* magazine, all during my teens. I wrote my first young adult novel when I was 20. **Debutante Hill.** Well, the title tells you everything you need to know. I wrote **Debutante Hill** because at that stage of my life the only thing I knew about was gentle adolescence. It was a time when a lot of the threats that are out there for our young people today were not there.

[Sutton:] Do you think the world is a different place now?

Duncan: Yes. I started so long ago that I have worked my way through stages as the world changed and society changed. I found my books changed along with what was happening in my life. When I wrote **Debutante Hill** in 1958, it was returned to me for revisions because I had a 19-year-old take a beer. My editor said that no librarian would ever allow it on the shelf. So I had to change it to a Coca-Cola.

[Sutton:] It wouldn't have been possible to publish **Killing Mr. Griffin** as a "teen novel" in 1958, or even in the 60s.

Duncan: No, and it wouldn't have been possible for me to write it then, either. I didn't know about such things. I was raised in a very loving, gentle home, we had rules and I obeyed them and all my friends obeyed them. I didn't know violence existed; we didn't even have television to let us know that. And the books I was writing at the beginning of my career are bounced off the life I'd lived. As I got older and began facing life's problems and had children of my own and saw the things they were facing, my view of life changed. I was divorced. I'd never known a divorced person my whole life. But I was divorced at, let's see, 27, and had three young children to support. I had not been to college, I'd never held a job, I had to grow up very fast and learn how to handle myself in the rat race. My oldest daughter is now 36, and there was a 16-year differ-

ence between her and her youngest sibling. There were five kids, and they fell into different brackets of change. And, they kept growing! My oldest children were born in a time when drugs were not an issue in high school. But later, drugs had come along, and violence was coming into the schools. The whole world seemed to be changing in that 16 year space between oldest child and youngest. I was so invested in all of them that my view of the world, and my view of what teenagers were faced with, kept changing as well. I think my books got stronger, and they were certainly feeding off different emotions than I had earlier.

[Sutton:] Sometimes I think we're back to the old days. In a lot of the new novels, for instance, no one smokes unless it's the bad guy.

Duncan: Well, I'm for that. (pp. 20–1)

[Sutton:] Would you call yourself a YA writer?

Duncan: As far as the fact that most of my books have been YA novels, yes, I'm a YA novel-writer, but I really run the gamut. Until a couple of months ago, I was a contributing editor for *Woman's Day,* doing a lot of woman's-type nonfiction. I have a number of small children's picture books out; my oldest daughter Robin is a musician and producer of audiocassettes and we've collaborated on a series of musical cassettes for young children. I tried my best to make a mix because I didn't want to be the kind of author who wrote the same book over and over. In between novels I would do a little child's book, or I would do magazine articles for adults, to cleanse the palate.

Probably more than some writers who handled the heavy subject matter, I made a conscious effort to entertain. I was always aware that I was competing with television, and that fiction books today need to utilize many of the elements of television in order to capture and hang on to the reader. Kids are so conditioned to being able to flip that channel if they don't get instant entertainment that I realized that I could lose them early on by starting out in a manner that was difficult for them. I had to pull them into the story quickly and also use a good many television techniques: a lot of dialogue, not too much description, and pace that kept moving along. So I tried to use entertainment techniques to develop a readership who would want to read my books, who wouldn't just drop them and run and turn on the tube.

[Sutton:] What do you think that is, the ability that you have to write a real page-turner? Do you think that's an inherent gift, or do you use conscious techniques?

Duncan: I think it's some of both. I certainly use conscious techniques, but also it seems to be a natural way for me to write.

[Sutton:] Do you know what's going to happen at the end when you start?

Duncan: Yeah, I know how it's going to end. I basically know the major developments that will lead me toward the end. I know about where they're going to happen, and I know that I'm probably going to catch the reader early on, and once I have him caught I will establish my characters and set up my situation. Then I will have things starting to happen and will build towards the end of the book, and the pace will pick up as we near the end. And I know I'm going to need certain suspenseful scenes, certain strong scenes strategically placed to pace the book correctly. I have all that in my mind before I get started. I don't have every detail of the book in my mind, but I have my road map so I know where I'm going to be at different stages of the book, and I know where the destination is.

[Sutton:] Your books—I'm thinking particularly of *Killing Mr. Griffin* as well as some of the supernatural books—have had trouble getting into some schools and public libraries because people don't approve of your subject matter or your way of handling it. Have you heard from people who were troubled by your books in that way?

Duncan: Only secondhand. I don't usually know about the times that they're challenged unless somebody tells me after the fact. So I just have not been very involved in that. It's hard—you invest in one book so thoroughly, and when that one's done, it's done; then you turn to the next book. So it's quite hard for me to go back and re-immerse myself in *Killing Mr. Griffin.* The jump-off point for that book was the psychopathic character Mark, who was based upon my oldest daughter's first real boyfriend. He was a very sick young man, and he was the most charming young man you could ever meet. It wasn't until things got very bad that we discovered he was the kind of guy who would swerve in the road to run over a dog. The personality of that young man stayed in my mind long after my daughter had broken up with him. I couldn't write about him right away, but I started thinking. "These people— they're *there.*" They don't just spring full-grown out of an oyster shell. The Charles Mansons of this world, the Hitlers of this world, they are children, and they grow up, and they go to high school. As young people, they are becoming what they're later going to be. They're very charismatic people, usually, and teenagers are so easily influenced, so easily led by charismatic people, that I started thinking about what could happen with a teenage psychopath of that type in a high school setting and what type of young people he would attract as followers. They would need to have certain weaknesses, they would need to be needy young people, and yet I didn't want them to be bad because I don't think they're all bad, by any means, those who are attracted to such people. So I began building on that concept. Then I thought "What could he make them do?" The book moved from there. Also, I liked the character of Mr. Griffin. Looking at my own children, I realized that some of the demanding teachers that they couldn't stand when they were in school were later, when they grew up, teachers they remembered with great affection and gratitude, because those were the teachers who had made the biggest difference in their lives. I wanted Mr. Griffin to be one of those teachers, symbolic of that kind of teacher—of the ones who aren't appreciated at the time but later are.

[Sutton:] I think that you probably have been characterized as a genre writer; that is, of thrillers, suspense, supernatural stories, which often people don't take as seriously as they do "real books." Is that a distinction that you have felt from people?

Duncan: I never thought about it. It was what I wrote. What I've written isn't all based on metaphysical subject matter, certainly not *Killing Mr. Griffin,* and *Daughters of Eve,* and some of the others. I thought of them as adventures, things that happen to other people. Unfortunately, I now know that's not true.

[Sutton:] I think kids like that mix of safety and scariness that thrillers provide, and that they especially enjoy your books for being firmly based in a teenage world.

Duncan: Kids like reading these things as fiction and having the feeling that everything will eventually come out all right. Kids all think everything will come out all right. They don't think anything bad could really happen to them. They're used to—there again—watching TV, seeing all these awful things happen in a television show, but next week turning on the same program and everybody's starting all over again. When characters get shot down in one show, they then show up in another show. Disaster is unreal. The fact that you have to take care is something they don't take in. I don't know that it's just this generation— maybe more this generation because they're the television generation—but I think all young people have that sense of immortality. Don't you?

[Sutton:] I do. But I think they get a charge out of the possibility that life may not in fact be that way, as long as it's a charge that's safely contained within, as you say, TV or it's in the pages of a book.

Duncan: Well, the only real criticism I've gotten from young readers who write to me is when they say, "Why did you make it end like that? Why didn't you make them get married and live happily ever after? Why did you have so-and-so die? And why is so-and-so going to go to jail? And why couldn't it all have come out like it was meant to?" They think happily ever after is what life ought to be and what life in reality is. I did too—when I was their age.

[Sutton:] One thing I think that all of your teenage novels have in common is that at some level or another they're very scary. Do you think that the world is scary?

Duncan: Yes. I certainly do now. The greatest tragedy of my life has also proven to be the most bizarre experience in my life. I always thought everything I wrote was pure fiction, right out of my head, and when I wrote my recent YA suspense novel—it's called *Don't Look Behind You*—I modeled my heroine April on the personality of my teenage daughter Kait. In my book, April and her family had found out about interstate drug trafficking, and she was chased by hit men in a Camaro. It came out in June of 1989 and in July of 1989 my daughter Kait was chased down and shot to death by a hit man in a Camaro. It was as if these things I'd written about as fiction became hideous reality. . . . The police work was very poor, and the investigative reporter for our local paper began turning up all kinds of information that the police had not discovered. The reporter's name was Mike Gallagher, and my heroine's boyfriend in *Summer of Fear* was named Mike Gallagher. These connections began to pile up to such a degree that I wondered if I was going crazy. I contacted Dr. William Roll, the director of the Psychical Research Foundation. I said, "What's happened? Am I crazy?" And he said, "Not at all." He said that precognition is very much a proven reality, that it's also been proven that people who are creative individuals have much more psychical ability than others. He had a colleague who did research using students from the Juilliard School (for music, drama, and dance in New York City) and found that they scored far above the average on all the various ESP tests. He said that very often, as far as writers go, future events will turn up in their fiction, especially if the situation has to do with violence.

So I have certainly opened my mind to things that I never truly believed in before. And the next book I'm going to do—I have not been able to write a murder mystery—is a collaboration with Dr. Roll. It's a nonfiction book called *The Psychic Connection,* based on psychical phenomena that Dr. Roll explored with the late Dr. J. B. Rhine. This won't be one of those *Ghostbuster* books. It's going to be based totally on Dr. Rhine's research and the research of his colleagues. I think it will be a fascinating book to write. I look forward to doing it both because I think it will be an interesting book for young people and because I can't wait to read all that research.

[Sutton:] Some people looking at the events around your daughter's death might say, "Gee, this sounds like a Lois Duncan book." How is this different from a Lois Duncan book?

Duncan: It isn't, and that's what's so horrifying. If I had written about this experience four years ago as fiction, everybody would say exactly that, it's a Lois Duncan suspense story. It's as if every book I wrote was getting ready to write about this dreadful thing. I started writing *Who Killed My Daughter?* as the events of our investigation unfolded, with no idea what was going to happen next, or what the ending would be. As things happened, I'd just sit at the computer and write another chapter. Then I'd stop until more things happened, and then write the next chap-

ter. It fell onto the page so that I didn't have to change anything. It just came out like a Lois Duncan novel.

[Sutton:] And now you're the Lois Duncan heroine. Aren't you? I mean, you have to solve the murder.

Duncan: I guess. I'd say I'm the protagonist; I don't know if I come out as a heroine. But it's in first person, and I'm solving the murder with the help of my family and psychic detectives and this newspaper investigative reporter and some private investigators. At this point I still owe Delacorte another book on a three-book contract, and they've been very patient letting me work through my situation before having to go back and do that book. I've really had to solve our own murder before I can make up a murder and that's what I hope to be achieving in *Who Killed My Daughter?* My hope is that its publication will bring informants out of the woodwork and we can finally close the door on this nightmare and move on.

[Sutton:] Do you think you could go back to writing mysteries?

Duncan: We'll have to see. (pp. 21-4)

> *Lois Duncan and Roger Sutton, in a conversation in* School Library Journal, *Vol. 38, No. 6, June, 1992, pp. 20-4.*

TITLE COMMENTARY

Debutante Hill (1958)

Older girls, aged 12-16, will love this story of true love emerging triumphant over difficulties. Some will appreciate the high principles that keep Lynn from joining her set in a round of exclusive coming-out parties. Left out of the fun her friends are having, however, she is free to get to know many other fine girls and boys she has been too absorbed to notice. Plot is well worked out; good characterization. Recommended.

> *Ruth M. McEvoy, in a review of "Debutante Hill," in* Junior Libraries, *Vol. 5, No. 2, October 15, 1958, p. 163.*

Lynn Chambers, pretty and popular high school senior, declines to join the Rivertown debutante group because her father thinks the idea undemocratic. Thus cut off from the social life of her normal circle of friends, and lonely for Paul Kingsley, her "steady," who has gone away to college, Lynn finds herself pushed toward a new series of experiences. Some of them are good, some are bad, but from all of them Lynn learns a lot. The end of the winter season finds her a much wiser and happier girl. Miss Duncan writes exceptionally well, and has the happy ability to make a reader care what happens to her characters. A few places are weak in plausibility, notably Paul's involvement in his first date with Brenda. It makes him more of a spineless wonder than the author has prepared us to believe.

> *Silence Buck Bellows, in a review of "Debutante Hill," in* The Christian Science Monitor, *February 5, 1959, p. 11.*

Duncan, with her brother Billy, celebrating her sixth birthday.

A Promise for Joyce (as Lois Kerry, 1959)

A sequel to **Love Song for Joyce** (which told of Joyce Reynold's freshman year at college) and again Joyce has adjustments to make. As a sophomore she feels at home on the campus, but she fails to understand the rigid program of studying that her beloved Jeff, a medical student, feels he must keep. So they quarrel, and Joyce dates a young roué; she gets into a frightening situation, calls Jeff, and they are reunited in a glow of new understanding. Writing and plot are equally patterned and it is difficult to to believe in the cardboard characters.

> *A review of "A Promise for Joyce," in* Bulletin of the Center for Children's Books, *Vol. XIII, No. 1, September, 1959, p. 62.*

The Littlest One in the Family (1960)

Story and drawings are the collaboration of two young mothers [Duncan and illustrator Suzanne K. Larsen] familiar with the disappointment of a child who tries to imitate his elders and is frustrated by his own ineptitudes, until the arrival of a new baby bolsters the small one's ego. Many youngsters will be pleased by the familiarity of the situation.

> *Elizabeth M. Beal, in a review of "The Littlest One in the Family," in* Junior Libraries, *Vol. 6, No. 8, April 15, 1960, p. 51.*

The Middle Sister (1960)

Emphasis on an important phase in the life of a teen-age girl: realization that her own life, talents, and interests are important to her family. Ruth Audrey Porter's gradual flowering from a tall, shy, awkward girl into a self-confident, lovable personality will appeal to most girls. The opportunity to take a leading part in a community theatrical production brings this young senior into the limelight. Good school story with characters well drawn and realistic and a sense of values in family relationships. Recommended.

> *I. Elizabeth Stafford, in a review of "The Middle Sister," in* Junior Libraries, *Vol. 7, No. 1, September 15, 1960, p. 78.*

The story of a girl's discovery that although she could not follow in the footsteps of her older sister, she was a person in her own right with her own beauty, talent, and integrity. The characters are alive and also very pleasant to know, and while the outcome of events is never surprising, the old theme is handled so exceptionally well that interest never lags.

> *Ruth Hill Viguers, in a review of "The Middle Sister," in* The Horn Book Magazine, *Vol. XXXVI, No. 5, October, 1960, p. 408.*

Silly Mother (1962)

A read-aloud book about a mother who made foolish mistakes: put the tablecloth on Michael's bed and set the table with a blanket, put the puppy in the bureau drawer and pajamas in the puppy's basket. Michael worried about her; next day he helped her, and in the evening she baked a cake and played with him, because his help and Daddy's gave Mother extra time. There is some appeal for small children in the exaggerated humor they enjoy, but the message is obtrusive and the rather slight theme is belabored. (pp. 123-24)

> *A review of "Silly Mother," in* Bulletin of the Center for Children's Books, *Vol. XV, No. 7, March, 1962, pp. 123-24.*

Game of Danger (1962)

Mother's frantic voice beckoning Anne and her brother to follow instructions without question sends the teenagers scurrying from the house for the bus terminal at 2 AM with an important letter, some money and orders to visit an old friend of mother's in Maine. Bewildered, Anne and Rob board the bus and wind up in a rented beach cottage when Mrs. Corrigan is no longer at her address. Shocking newspaper headlines proclaiming father a communist and announcing his disappearance add to their disbelief. Father was a respected school teacher at Belleford High and the McQuarters had always led normal lives. Surely this was a nightmare. Could mother's sister in East Berlin have anything to do with their predicament? And what about the secret letter? The pieces of the puzzle take awhile to fit together, but the maneuver is well worth the reader's time. Returning home to a house guarded by FBI agents as well as commies determined to get the letter, Anne and Rob learn of their father's activities as a counter-spy and prove their own bravery in facing the disdain of public opinion as well as a dangerous game with the enemy until the truth is out. This is terse melodrama that involves the reader all the way through.

> *A review of "Game of Danger," in* Virginia Kirkus' Service, *Vol. XXX, No. 13, July 1, 1962, p. 570.*

Giving Away Suzanne (1963)

Along the lines of the author's **Silly Mother** but lacking the humor of the earlier book, this gentle story of an annoying little sister who breaks crayons, etc., and is consequently traded by her big sister for a goldfish, is weighted down by a too sweet approach to the world of siblings. The end is obvious—big sister finds life dull in the company of a goldfish, and demands the return of her sister Suzanne.

> *A review of "Giving Away Suzanne," in* Virginia Kirkus' Service, *Vol. XXXI, No. 17, September 1, 1963, p. 857.*

Older sisters will sympathize completely with Mary Kay's actions, and some will wish they could do likewise. The natural bond of family affection will, however, evoke an understanding smile when "giving away Suzanne" fails to bring the anticipated contentment. Drawings [by Leonard Weisgard], dressed up in lavender, suggest the deceptive innocence of little girls not unaware of their ladylike charms. A book to ameliorate life with a little sister.

Priscilla L. Moulton, in a review of "Giving Away Suzanne," in The Horn Book Magazine, *Vol. XL, No. 1, February, 1964, p. 48.*

Season of the Two-Heart (1964)

When the missionaries encouraged Natachu Weekoty, a young Pueblo Indian girl, to continue her education she enthusiastically accepted their arrangements. Living with a prosperous family in Albuquerque, New Mexico, Martha (as she was called) enrolled as a senior in the public high school and looked after the two small Boynton boys in the evenings. The story delicately handles racial prejudice and the lack of understanding of both the Indian and American cultures. The characters bring out the fact that, if there is an honest effort and a willingness to try, the prejudice will melt into the background and personal worth will come to the forefront. A well-written story with evidence of much research in Indian customs present. Characters are life-like. (pp. 288-89)

A review of "Season of the Two-Heart," in Best Sellers, *Vol. 24, No. 14, October 15, 1964, pp. 288-89.*

Martha Weekoty takes her first step away from her Pueblo Indian environment by attending high school in Albuquerque. Now she can evaluate the loving but lackadaisical ways of the Pueblo. She sizes up the white family with whom she is living—the self-centered girl, the club-conscious mother, the lovable small boys, the kindly father. Above all, she weighs her love for the white boy Alan, who wants to marry her. The author does not provide a pat answer for Martha's dilemma concerning her future, but leaves the reader to ponder things from all angles as Martha will have to do. An absorbing story with serious undertones.

Ethna Sheehan, in a review of "Season of the Two-Heart," in America, *Vol. 111, No. 21, November 21, 1964, p. 670.*

Ransom (1966)

The story concerns a clutch of five teenagers, each with distinct, individual problems. Marianne, the most spirited of the group, still retains her devotion to her irresponsible, uncaring father and refuses to accept her mother's remarriage or her stepfather; Jesse has lived in many parts of the world, is quite sophisticated and cultured for her age but doesn't know much about dealing with other people and is particularly withdrawn around her contemporaries; Dexter is slightly crippled, orphaned, self-conscious and solitary; Glenn is the school leader, handsome and suave, but totally self-interested with no capacity for sympathizing with anyone else; his younger brother Bruce is puppy-dog affectionate and helpful, totally idolatrous of Glenn. They, and to some extent their parents, are drawn together in a complete and cohesive novel when a "substitute" school bus driver kidnaps them and holds them for ran-

som. Each one's reactions are revealed according to personality and the author has credited her characters with a proper amount of maturity. The resolutions of their problems are a little pat and typical of the teenage romance approach, but the unusual and holding story helps give them substance.

A review of "Ransom," in Virginia Kirkus' Service, *Vol. XXXIV, No. 3, February 1, 1966, p. 111.*

[**Ransom**] deserves . . . mention for its portrait of the thoroughly amoral, egocentric Glenn Kirtland, a character unique in children's books, though not in life. Glenn, the high-school wonder boy, is one of five teen-agers kidnapped because they live in wealthy Valley Gardens. The other four have conventional problems: shyness, divorce in the family, physical handicap and lack of self-confidence. As each reacts in his own way to being held captive atop an Arizona mountain, the predictable growth takes place—except in Glenn. It is this consistency of Glenn's personality that sets the book apart and makes it something more than another good mystery.

Dorothy M. Broderick, in a review of "Ransom," in The New York Times Book Review, *June 5, 1966, p. 42.*

The plot is familiar and the resolution is not altogether unpredictable. The appeal of this book—beyond the usual element of suspense one comes to expect of this kind of story—is in the complexities of character among the five teenagers. Herein lies the strength of Lois Duncan.

There is Marianne who is bitter about her parents' divorce and her mother's new husband, who fails to measure up to the idealized image she holds of her father. There are the Kirtland brothers: Glenn, the student body president and football team captain, and Bruce, the frail freshman who is excessively proud of his older brother. There is Jesse, a newcomer whose mother wants her to have a sample of ordinary life that her father's military travels have denied her. Finally, there is Dexter, who lives with an uncle he seldom sees and hides his physical limitations from his peers. The kidnappers are stock characters for the most part, but what teen readers will relish most is the way each of the five principal characters meet the challenge facing them. Needless to say, there are interesting discoveries and some disillusioning revelations. The book ends on a note of irony that would prompt further discussion.

Hugh Agee, in a review of "Ransom," in The ALAN Review, *Vol. 12, No. 3, Spring, 1985, p. 35.*

They Never Came Home (1969)

Effective characterizations, dialogue, and transitions from one set of characters to another can't redeem this melodrama in which a corkscrew plot curls around coincidences and contrivances. Psychopathic 17-year-old Larry Drayfus, owing money to a dope ring, decides to drop out of sight and plans a camping trip to cover his disappearance. He attempts murder twice and concocts an elaborate background for his camping companion, Dan Cotwell, who developed amnesia after Larry shoved him over a cliff. Larry's heroine-sister Joan gets involved with the dope smugglers when she tries to make good her brother's debt, accepts responsibility for their mother whose grief over Larry causes her to have a breakdown, and finally finds a recovered Dan (her own boyfriend) just as Larry, in attempting to kill Dan, has himself fallen to his death from a hotel balcony. An unlikely story from an author whose competence with main elements of fiction promises more and better storytelling to come.

> *Peggy Sullivan, in a review of "They Never Came Home," in* School Library Journal, *Vol. 15, No. 8, April 15, 1969, p. 126.*

Lois Duncan writes well and simply on mature situations. She gives her readers comprehensible, yet not oversensational descriptions of a mother's nervous breakdown; of a plain girl discovering beauty in herself; of a younger brother learning not to live in the reflected glory of an older one; of a mentally deranged boy who has cut himself off from the love his family wanted to give him. **They Never Came Home** is a well-paced action story, with a full quota of heroes and villains, and a series of narrative hooks guaranteed to hold any reader.

> *Richard F. Shepard, in a review of "They Never Came Home," in* The New York Times Book Review, *June 8, 1969, p. 42.*

Although events are stock, and all goes as expected, the author grabs the reader early and sustains interest well. The lean style and extensive use of credible dialogue create a brisk pace and heighten tension. Flashbacks skillfully and judiciously fill in information important for the plot and help in understanding the characters. The two-strand plot structure works well, and the main figures are quite firmly drawn for this genre. Joan is especially so, and, although Frank's determination to accompany her on her trips to Juarez seems improbable, the experience helps him to develop into a steady, sensible youth with a more positive self-image. This problem-adventure story deals with a subject that has received considerable attention in the late twentieth century, but the handling of it here already seems obvious and trite. (p. 656)

> *Alethea K. Helbig and Agnes Regan Perkins, in a review of "They Never Came Home," in their* Dictionary of American Children's Fiction, 1960-1984: Recent Books of Recognized Merit, *Greenwood Press, 1986, pp. 655-56.*

Major André: Brave Enemy   (1969)

John André was the British Army man who negotiated with Benedict Arnold at West Point, missed the boat to camp and was discovered a few miles from his own base in civilian disguise, the incriminating papers concealed in his sock. A romantic figure of his time and in these pages, he was convicted of spying and hanged, both armies noting his courageous posture. His inner thoughts from boyhood on are imputed, a technique which tends to overdramatize a dramatic personality and force each gesture into

significance. And the "spy" episode is quite brief, so readers looking for that kind of excitement will be disappointed to find so much more about his relationships with women. Easy to overlook.

> *A review of "Major André: Brave Enemy," in* Kirkus Reviews, *Vol. XXXVII, No. 12, June 15, 1969, p. 633.*

The story of the infamous treason plot between General Benedict Arnold and Major André is told in this admiring biography of the dashing young British officer-spy. Some detail on Arnold is omitted, and there is a little fictionalization, though no distortion of facts. However, the book is more interesting and smoothly written than the very similar, recent biography by Nathan, *Major John André* (Watts, 1969) which, though listed as an adult title by the publishers, is not too difficult for good junior high school readers; it has more historical detail, but is far from being comprehensive or scholarly. These two books disagree only on the role of Arnold's wife in the plot: Nathan makes her an accessory, Duncan shows her as an instigator; the exact truth of the matter is not known. Duncan's book has a useful index. . . . (pp. 135-36)

> *Muriel Kolb, in a review of "Major André: Brave Enemy," in* School Library Journal, *Vol. 16, No. 7, March, 1970, pp. 135-36.*

Peggy   (1970)

Titillation, exploitation, anything but history: the cattiest first-person portrait of a vixen, Peggy Shippen, the girl who becomes Mrs. Benedict Arnold. The girl who sulks, screams, cries, faints (and reports it all proudly) when Father moves out of Philadelphia: safety? what about the promised birthday ball, the country? live "like common field hands!" so "degrading"—peasant "louts" no men, no gowns, red hands. . . . The girl who wheedles money for new clothes, who pouts when Father won't give up his precious neutrality and return to public office; what will people think of fading tapestries? wear this blue rag again? The girl who marries Arnold after stealing someone else's beau; who masterminds the grand betrayal; who despises the unborn infant sullying her perfect figure, who declares about the baby that its " 'Mama' (she herself) was ready to put a pillow over his head and sit on it and might actually have done so if Major Franks had not been there." Cloaked with spiteful dagger thrashing out in all directions—unconscionable even as fiction.

> *A review of "Peggy," in* Kirkus Reviews, *Vol. XXXVIII, No. 18, September 15, 1970, p. 1047.*

Peggy Shippen, the Philadelphia belle, at eighteen married General Benedict Arnold, who was more than twenty years her senior. She is an intriguing and controversial historical figure, for the exact extent of her influence over Arnold's attempt to betray his command at West Point is, according to at least one source, a disputed issue. The point of view that Peggy was aware of, approved of, and was indeed implicated in Arnold's treachery is the basic assumption underlying this presentation of a pivotal event in

American history. Peggy as narrator of her story from June, 1776, to September, 1780, is revealed as a self-centered yet fascinating, high-spirited girl whose ability to bend men to her desires finds its match in the equally self-serving Benedict Arnold. Arnold's hurt pride combined with Peggy's extravagance and social ambition leads to the dramatic communication to Captain—later Major—André that " 'General Benedict Arnold is ready to offer his services to His Majesty's army' "—a communication which initiates a long period of negotiation with the British forces as to the exact nature of those "services." Chosen as go-between because of his affections for Peggy during the British occupation of Philadelphia in 1778, the unfortunate Major André is presented as a gentlemanly, artistic, and sensitive officer—an obvious contrast to Arnold—unable to see Peggy's feminine wiles as anything but innocent, womanly charm. The conversational tone of the narrative gives a sense of immediacy to a fictionalized biography of a remarkable anti-heroine, whose unswerving devotion to self is reminiscent of two other famous, although fictional, coquettes Becky Sharp and Scarlett O'Hara. (pp. 622-23)

> *Mary M. Burns, in a review of "Peggy," in* The Horn Book Magazine, *Vol. XLVI, No. 6, December, 1970, pp. 622-23.*

Hotel for Dogs   (1971)

"We're going to be living with allergic (to dogs) Aunt Alice and her white rugs, and I'm going to be 'sweet little Elizabeth' (ten) and you're going to be 'darling Bruce' (twelve) and I don't think I can stand it." When a stray canine pads up Aunt Alice's stairs, unbeknownst to all but Liz who badly misses her dachshund, and bears three puppies, Bruce has a brainstorm—the vacant house down the street. Of course there'd be no need for a hotel of this sort if maltreatment weren't so extraordinarily rampant in Elmwood, especially as close to home as next door where spoiled "only kid" Jerry Bates (one of the meanest boys to ever appear in a docile story) holds court . . . and beats his setter. Red Rover thus becomes another secret guest and then comes MacTavish—some family moved and simply left him to fend for himself. Even with the help of a voluntary exile from Jerry's gang and of (demeaningly) two *girls,* things get out of hand what with food bills, the question of exercise, and Liz's inability to temper her enthusiasm. The children have more than the usual amount of tether and their very often underhanded 'goodness' poses problems: first, it doesn't balance all the badness set around them here: and second, happy-ending notwithstanding, it's variously delinquent (and suggestive).

> *A review of "Hotel for Dogs," in* Kirkus Reviews, *Vol. XXXIX, No. 5, March 1, 1971, p. 235.*

Bumbling adults whose gullibility knows no bounds serve as foils for a group of enterprising youngsters who commandeer a vacant house and turn it into a hotel for various stray dogs. The credibility gap widens as the children's parents buy the house—hard wood floors and all—despite the fact that numerous dogs have been cooped up in it for

several months. The plot fluctuates between being predictable and unbelievable, and the characters lack substance in this bit of doggy nonsense.

> *Judith Janc, in a review of "Hotel for Dogs," in* School Library Journal, *Vol. 17, No. 9, May, 1971, p. 64.*

A Gift of Magic   (1971)

Each of the three Garrett children has a distinctive personality and talent. The older sister, Kirby, is determined to be a dancer, and little brother Brendon is a phenomenal pianist, although he has little real interest in music. But this above-average story centers on middle-child Nancy's gift of extrasensory perception and on the responsibilities, problems (in school, with her siblings), and advantages it gives her. It is an understanding high school counselor in love with her divorced mother who convinces Nancy of the values of her gift, and of the need to use it without trying to manage the lives of others (e.g., sister Kirby and her mother, whom Nancy had wanted to stay with her father). Background on extrasensory perception is well woven into the story, and current interest in the occult and psychic phenomena will widen the audience for the book.

> *Peggy Sullivan, in a review of "A Gift of Magic," in* School Library Journal, *Vol. 18, No. 3, November, 1971, p. 122.*

Duncan with her daughters Robin and Kerry in 1956.

I Know What You Did Last Summer (1973)

In the same mail as Julie's acceptance to Smith College comes an anonymous note with the menacing reminder: I KNOW WHAT YOU DID LAST SUMMER. Though the weight on Julie's conscience seems to have left her more apathetic than anguished, the note sends her into a frenzy because what Julie—and her former boyfriend Ray, and his friends Helen and Barry—did was no harmless frolic; in a moment of panic they left the scene of an accident in which they had killed a 10 year-old boy. Even after Barry is lured to an empty athletic field and critically wounded he refuses to release his friends from their vow of secrecy. But both he and Helen (a narcissistic TV weathergirl) are so vacuous that one hardly cares whether they get murdered or not. Still, the madman murderer is cleverly concealed among a bevy of red herrings and as he zeroes in for his revenge this turns into a high velocity chiller with a double identity twist.

> *A review of "I Know What You Did Last Summer," in* Kirkus Reviews, *Vol. XLI, No. 17, September 1, 1973, p. 972.*

[This] story is cold and almost harsh—with not only its central theme but its suggestions of the long-term effects of the Vietnam involvement on a generation of American young. It is a thriller in a low key, relieved only by the muted feelings two of the group have for each other, and the interesting background of American family and social life. It is an absorbing read, well told and well constructed, and pupils of fourteen or more may well find themselves drawn into its steadily increasing drama. (p. 152)

> *David Churchill, in a review of "I Know What You Did Last Summer," in* The School Librarian, *Vol. 30, No. 1, June, 1982, pp. 151-52.*

I felt a certain smoothness in *I know what you did last summer,* a novel in which the characters seem to have been chosen to fit a highly topical plot rather than the other way round. . . . [The] narrative is assured and the 'teenagers caught in a desperate situation are cleverly manipulated so that we see how each one learns painfully the result of a single action. Julie is sixteen, her boyfriend Roy seventeen and their close friends Barry and Helen the same ages when one night, driving home after a party, they collide with a boy on a bicycle. The boy is killed and Barry, who is driving, refuses to stop and swears the others to secrecy. A year later, when the future is opening for the young people, blackmail notes begin to arrive and a strange youth, returned from Vietnam, intrudes into their lives and forces them to look again at the boy's death and their own relationships as they have been affected by it. The sober style of narrative and dialogue offers a frank look at the contemporary scene in one section of American society and the obvious moral is supported by an element of mystery which defers the identity of the blackmailer and adds an edge to the story. Expertly done, but for me there is something missing in this evenly paced, carefully logical tale. (pp. 3927-28)

> *Margery Fisher, in a review of "I Know What You Did Last Summer," in* Growing Point, *Vol. 21, No. 2, July, 1982, pp. 3927-28.*

Down a Dark Hall (1974)

When Kit and the other three high ESP-quotient pupils who have been chosen for Mme. Duret's new boarding school get their first sight of isolated Blackwood manor only one word comes to their minds—evil. But you don't have to be psychic to anticipate some fishy goings on— what with the locked gates, unmailed letters home and those nightly dream visitors who inspire the girls to discover hitherto non-existent artistic talents. When the spirit guides, including Emily Bronte, Schubert and landscapist Thomas Cole, start using the increasingly weary girls as a channel for delivering their posthumous masterpieces to Mme. Duret (who will use them for financial gain) only resolute Kit has the will to resist openly. Stranger still, Mme. Duret's honest and irresistibly handsome son Jules considers the whole undertaking a noble experiment— until he learns the fate of his mother's previous pupils and sees the nasty creations of some dirty-minded deceased artists who have been insinuating their way into the nocturnal dictation sessions. We aren't let in on the unpleasant details, but of course by this time it's too late anyway. . . . Blackwood goes up in flames and Kit is rescued from a fiery death by the ghost of her own departed Dad. The last (especially?) is on the slick side, but Lois Duncan is a practiced medium and manages to summon up the chilling specter without dwelling overmuch on its distinguishing features.

> *A review of "Down a Dark Hall," in* Kirkus Reviews, *Vol. XLII, No. 18, September 15, 1974, p. 1012.*

Two gothic novels, Lois Duncan's ***Down a Dark Hall*** and David Severn's *The Girl in the Grove* are on the whole, more interesting than many that flood the adult market. Perhaps teenagers more credibly embody, than do women in their twenties, the uncertainties and mild hysteria of gothic personality. At any rate, both books are suitably equipped with bright, attractive heroines, brooding mansions and brooding young men, and the requisite ghosts from the past. David Severn's book is crisply written, although its cloying plot and the heroine's inexplicable attachment to a boorish young man will put it high on feminist lists as a book to avoid. By contrast, Lois Duncan's offhand treatment of romance allows her to focus on the intelligence and rationality of her heroine. The result is highly original; a gothic novel that is more a commentary on the dangers of education than on the perils of unrequited love.

> *Gloria Levitas, in a review of "Down a Dark Hall," in* The New York Times Book Review, *November 10, 1974, p. 10.*

Summer of Fear (1976)

Long before she suspects orphaned cousin Julia of being a ringer, Rae is convinced that the new member of the family is a witch—and when the awkward Ozarks teenager promptly turns into a femme fatale to steal Rae's best dress and best boyfriend, all the while making eyes at Rae's dad, she shows herself to be the kind of villainess who'd make any red-blooded girl spitting mad. Rae finds evidence of supernatural doings—a wax doll, a mutilated photograph, the smell of sulphur . . . even the body of the family dog, felled by Julia's curse. But Duncan doesn't rely overmuch on conventional props; her speciality is high-gloss malice and murder (*I Know What You Did Last Summer,* etc.) and Rae, isolated as much by her uncontrollable jealousy as by Julia's plotting, might just convince even those who swore they'd never taste another witch's brew recipe.

> *A review of "Summer of Fear," in* Kirkus Reviews, *Vol. XLIV, No. 12, June 15, 1976, p. 691.*

Miss Duncan has written a most attractive book. The plot centres around an Albuquerque family; brisk, talented, approachable, photographer mother; handsome, amiable, relaxed father; elder brother Peter; younger brother Bobby; and narrator and heroine, Rachel. Rachel is jolly, uncomplicated and happy in every way, with her family, with her girl-friend, and with her next-door-neighbour boy friend. But her mother's sister and brother-in-law are killed in a car crash, and their daughter, Julia, comes to live in Rachel's home. Except for Rachel and Rachel's dog, Trickle, everyone in the family becomes fond of Julia. Rachel's boy friend too falls headlong in love with Julia. Only Rachel finds Julia devious and calculating, and she gradually unmasks her as a witch and a murderess.

The slow revelation of Julia's propensities raises this tale above inconsequential narration. With mounting urgency Rachel tries to convince her family and friends of what is happening, only to find herself dismissed, rejected and punished as jealous and resentful. Real poignancy is evoked as Rachel's love and concern for her family lead her headlong into arousing their disapproval. Miss Duncan has portrayed an innocent and trusting warmth, which makes the family's reluctance to recognize evil understandable and its existence among them the more eerie. The development of the narrative is steady, and tension is maintained admirably. Suitably baffling clues are dropped throughout and pulled together deftly in the final resolution of the mystery. Characters are rounded, believable and, with the exception of the dastardly Julia, lovable.

> *Jennifer Moody, "A Difficult Age," in* The Times Literary Supplement, *No. 4069, March 27, 1981, p. 339.*

[Lois Duncan's *Summer of Fear*] works hard to establish a tense atmosphere of unhappiness and terror, but the author never convinces in the small details on which the larger design depends. The conversations, descriptions, relationships are all too clearly part of fiction, not part of life. . . .

The story is diverting enough, if the reader refrains from wondering why none of Rachel's family have even an inkling of what the real Julia looked like, but it is emotionally dishonest. What should be the emotional core of the book, Rachel's feelings of jealousy towards her usurping cousin, is never confronted; indeed, Rachel's attitude is justified by her discovery of "Julia's" evil nature.

> *Neil Philip, "Stirring up Emotion," in* The Times Educational Supplement, *No. 3381, April 10, 1981, p. 24.*

In this carefully crafted novel, witchcraft and folklore erupt convincingly into everyday life, tension is carefully built up, and a credible level of alternative explanation for the events is maintained. All in all, it is a gripping and persuasive story which should find a steady readership.

> *Dennis Hamley, in a review of "Summer of Fear," in* The School Librarian, *Vol. 29, No. 3, September, 1981, p. 252.*

Killing Mr. Griffin (1978)

Contrary to certain opinion, the new wave of novels for adolescents hasn't explored every sensational topic after all; mainly because the adult author doesn't live in a world as corrosively conformist or as criminally cruel as that of the teenager. Breathy novels about drugs, sexual liberation and sub-proletariat gang warfare let off scot-free the majority of young readers, who are virtually all middle-class, who deny drugs are a problem, and who are amazingly prudish about other people's sex lives.

Lois Duncan breaks some new ground in a novel without sex, drugs or black leather jackets. But the taboo she tampers with is far more potent and pervasive: the unleashed fury of the permissively reared against any assault on their egos and authority. A group of high-school seniors kill an English teacher who dares trouble them with grades, homework and standards.

Before all this is smiled nervously away as a sick fantasy, let's meet the perpetrators, familiar figures all. There's Jeff, the jock, who suspects his teacher, Mr. Griffin, of lying awake nights "trying to think of questions that don't have answers." Jeff is never likely to learn that this is a central point of education.

There's Betsy, "the all-American girl—head cheerleader—homecoming queen" who has eliminated enemies before, without violence, and is in complete possession of a mother who assures her that her cuteness will last.

There's Mark, who would not like me for failing to list him first. He's been crossed even less often than Betsy. There's madness in his eyes, and in his psychiatric history. But his charisma and talent for delegating authority will make him the most familiar figure to young readers. This is a book for people who've learned in the schoolyard where nice guys finish.

The nice guy is David, senior-class president, quietly sincere, thoughtful, fond of a challenge, and political enough to know that Mark's malevolence takes precedence over Robert's Rules of Order. The novel is of two minds about who the central figure is. It's either David, or Susan—"a little creep with glasses"—early conscripted as a decoy in an asexual seduction by The Group. When she receives this brief acceptance, her parents are thrilled.

We've even come far enough from the 1960's to see the victim clearly. Mr. Griffin is a professor who's given up trying to teach the classics to college freshmen who can't pronounce the words. He explains to his wife why he's turned to high-school teaching: "By the time they're in college, it's gone too far. They've had twelve years without disciplined learning, and they don't know how to apply themselves. They haven't learned to study or to pace their work so that projects get completed on time. They fall asleep in lectures because they expect to be entertained, not educated."

Here's a man heading for trouble. But murder? Yes. His students dislike his punctuality, his necktie, his irony. They're triggered by his assignment of homework on a basketball night. They plan to kidnap and terrorize him into a sort of pedagogical impotence, so he'll be like the rest of the faculty. But the book's title has reached the reader before this plan does. And the scheme becomes feasible to the schemers for the most airtight of reasons: They remind one another that legally they are minors. Not only are they untouchable, they're not *guilty*.

You don't stop reading at this point, though you well might. The value of the book lies in the twisted logic of the teen-agers and how easily they can justify anything. But then the plot descends into unadulterated melodrama. One murder leads to another. And a murder attempt at the end is evidently meant to establish the comparative innocence of one character at the expense of the others. The book becomes "an easy read" when it shouldn't. But there's veracity unto the end: the parents are the last to lose their innocence.

Will this book give the impressionable unspeakable ideas? I doubt it. They already have them. The impulse toward crime is surely to be found nearer than a book: the paranoia of the permissively handled and the unlikelihood of punishment for anything. Adolescents have witnessed far more graphic scenes of teacher humiliation and brutalization in their own schools, in terms more immediate than this book.

And besides, who will read it? Teen-agers won't choose to identify with these meticulously unflattering portrayals, though they'll see their friends in them. Parents won't go near the book. Nor will school administrators who spend increasing time, not in dealing with school crimes but in keeping it out of the newspapers. Perhaps it's a book for teachers.

> *Richard Peck, "Teaching Teacher a Lesson,"* in The New York Times Book Review, *April 30, 1978, p. 54.*

Killing Mr. Griffin is a blunt title for a blunt tale in which a central act of violence is used as a point from which to look at a number of adolescents and their victim and to sort out their motives and attitudes. . . . The author is unreserved in the way she explores the consequences of the kidnapping—a crude burial, the intimidation of Susan, a younger and unwilling accomplice, the hasty switching of cars and inevitable discovery, are described with harsh, literal detail of event and talk. For each of the five involved there is some background to make their complicity convincing, but the flawed, desperate derangement in Mark's mind, casting a shadow over the story, really needs fuller

interpretation if the moral (and there is a moral, not merely a social point) is to have its full effect.

> *Margery Fisher, in a review of "Killing Mr. Griffin," in* Growing Point, *Vol. 19, No. 4, November, 1980, p. 3782.*

The most common backdrop setting in young adult literature is that of a high school. Since school is the business—the everyday life—of teenagers, many of the books relate to school just as many adult books somehow relate to jobs and work. However, there is a difference in that adult jobs are extremely varied, but schools are pretty much the same. There may be boarding schools, exclusive day schools, military schools, and religious schools, as well as the "typical" public high school, but a school is still a school with its stairways, restrooms, lockers, cafeteria, classrooms, and parking lot. There are only so many ways to describe such places, which is one of the things that gives a sameness to books for this age group.

But even in school-related stories in which the setting is pretty much a matter of backdrop, it is more important than many readers realize. Because of the length restrictions in books for this age group, setting is usually established quickly and efficiently. It continues to be developed throughout the story and to affect readers' reactions. A good example is Lois Duncan's *Killing Mr. Griffin,* which is about a group of high-school students who want to get even with a demanding teacher who has publicly humiliated them. They kidnap him, planning only to frighten and humble him, but he has a heart condition and dies.

The first line of the book establishes both the setting and the seriousness of the matter: "It was a wild, windy, southwestern spring when the idea of killing Mr. Griffin occurred to them." From here, Duncan goes on to describe the protagonist's walk across a playing field to the school building:

> Susan McConnell leaned into the wind and cupped her hands around the edges of her glasses to keep the blowing red dust from filling her eyes. Tumbleweeds swept past her like small, furry animals, rushing to pile in drifts against the fence that separated the field from the parking lot. The parked cars all had their windows up as though against a rainstorm. In the distance the rugged Sandia Mountains rose in faint outline, almost obscured by the pinkish haze.

> I hate spring, Susan told herself vehemently. I hate dust and wind. I wish we lived somewhere else. Someday—

> It was a word she used often—*someday.*

In less than half a page setting has already served three purposes. First, it has established a troubled mood; second, it has given basic information about where and who is going to be in the story; and, third, it has revealed something about the character of the protagonist. It has let readers know that she is dissatisfied with her life and will therefore be vulnerable to suggestions or opportunities to bring about changes.

Later in the book, setting serves other important purposes.

We are shown Mr. Griffin at home offering to make breakfast for his pregnant wife, and we see a different side of his personality so that we can feel truly sorry about his death. It would have been less credible if Duncan had tried to show us this different side of Mr. Griffin in the school setting where his students also could have seen it. By showing different characters in different settings, authors are able to reveal things to readers in such a way that the readers get the feeling of being in control of the situation because they know more than some of the characters do.

Settings can also act as symbols. They can provide a visible way to describe feelings that are very real even though they cannot be seen. For example, while the other boys are burying Mr. Griffin, David walks back to the two cars:

> He started first for Jeff's car and then, on impulse, opened instead the door of the Chevrolet and climbed in behind the steering wheel. In times past he had sometimes amused himself by contemplating how cars often seemed extensions of the people who owned them. There was Jeff's car, large and loud and flashy, and David's mother's, compact, economical and serviceable. Betsy's mother's Volkswagen was small and fitful, a nervous little automobile, painted bright yellow.
>
> Now, in Brian Griffin's car, he closed his eyes and tried to feel the presence of the man who had driven it, hoping for one last image of warmth and life. It did not come. The car was as cold and devoid of personality as the thing in the grave by the waterfall.

Mr. Griffin's car brings home to David the fact that Mr. Griffin is indeed dead. Sitting in the car he offers a prayer which is half a defense of himself and half a prayer for forgiveness, but hardly a blessing on the grave or the man whose body lies in it.

Even when the setting is a backdrop through most of the book, there may be places where it becomes integral as a part of the plot. This happens in Duncan's book in relation to the secret waterfall up in the mountains. One of the boys had found it with his former girlfriend. They were the only ones who ever went there so it seems an excellent place to take Mr. Griffin, and, when he dies, it also seems to be an excellent place to bury him. But the former girlfriend also remembers the place and just happens to go on a spring picnic with her new boyfriend. The two of them discover the evidence that leads the police to Mr. Griffin's body.

A setting does not really have to exist to play a part in a story. It might be just a dream of one of the characters, as when David and Sue imagine getting out of the whole problem by driving straight west to California and taking a ship to an uninhabited island. At one point, Sue confides that she has always had a dream of living by herself in a forest cabin by a peaceful lake instead of in a noisy, family household located in a dry and windy desert.

Setting may also serve as foreshadowing. For example, the night that everything comes to a climax (which incidentally is a bit overdone and melodramatic for our tastes), readers are prepared for something awful by the description of the weather:

> The wind began in the early afternoon. It rose slowly at first, but increased steadily . . . The Sunday twilight was muted and pink, as the sun's last rays slanted through the thick, red air, and when dark came the wind did not drop but seemed to grow stronger, whining around the corners of houses and stripping the first new leaf buds from trees.

Being able to establish settings so that they accomplish multiple purposes is one of the most important skills a writer can develop. Successful writers use settings not only as parts of plot, but also to make the story live for readers, to help them visualize exactly what is happening, to illuminate character, to symbolize important feelings, and to establish moods. (pp. 64-7)

> *Alleen Pace Nilsen and Kenneth L. Donelson, "Literary Aspects of Young Adult Books," in their* Literature for Today's Young Adults, *second edition, Scott, Foresman and Company, 1985, pp. 34-76.*

Daughters of Eve (1979)

A slick, scary occult novel with a stereotypical "women's libber" (bitter, frustrated, ultimately revealed as mentally disturbed) as the force of evil. Irene Stark, the new faculty advisor of the Daughters of Eve, an exclusive social club for girls at a suburban Michigan high school, encourages the members to become more socially conscious and assertive. Through the sisterhood, Ruth Grange is able to confront being "the only girl trapped in a family of conceited, overindulged boys"; Jane Rheardon finds the support she needs to cope with an abusive wife-beating father; and Ann Whitten is helped to choose between career and marriage. The only doubter is Tammy Carncross, whose ESP (an artifical device) warns her that something is wrong. She is, of course, correct. Ms. Stark has been manipulating the girls and channeling their anger into a vicious hatred of men. When fat Laura Snow is betrayed by the cruel, handsome Grange brothers and tries to commit suicide, the Daughters lure Peter Grange to a deserted spot, attack him, and shave his head. When Fran is denied a place in a science competition (for legitimate reasons), the girls launch a frenzied attack on the science room, destroying expensive equipment. The inevitable denouement is a cold-blooded murder (Jane's father, bashed in the head with an iron skillet). Though some may object to the violence, most YAs will be drawn by the ease with which this popular author builds suspense. But none of the characters are more than stick figures and the implication that sisterhood is not only powerful but downright dangerous is hardly a progressive message.

> *Cyrisse Jaffee, in a review of "Daughters of Eve," in* School Library Journal, *Vol. 26, No. 1, October, 1979, p. 155.*

Daughters of Eve is a savage novel full of troubled, angry characters. At first it appears that the author has identified completely with Irene Stark, adviser to an exclusive

Duncan, at forty-three, graduates from the University of New Mexico with a B.A. in English in 1977.

high-school girls' club called "Daughters of Eve" and is speaking to us all when Irene urges the club's 10 members toward action against male chauvinism.

Soon, however, as Irene's paranoia reveals itself, the reader begins to see that Lois Duncan has instead chosen the Movement only as a setting, and is detached enough to use it with great effectiveness. I was reminded of William Golding's *Lord of the Flies*—the horror of Lois Duncan's novel erupts just as violently at the end. Still, **Daughters of Eve** seems less real than *Lord of the Flies,* for all of that work's phantasmagoria. Perhaps this is because the Golding novel is set on a desert island where anything might happen, whereas **Eve** takes place down the street.

What *is* vivid, though, is the female rage that Lois Duncan portrays—any open-minded reader is bound to recognize much of it—and the story itself is finely constructed and told. Also—how refreshing!—there are no lessons. Instead, this novel enables us to see ourselves as the barely civilized creatures we truly are, and it is strongly even-handed, for it lets us see that women can be as bloodthirsty as men ever were. We haven't had much of that since Madame Defarge.

> *Natalie Babbitt, in a review of "Daughters of Eve," in* The New York Times Book Review, *January 27, 1980, p. 24.*

Daughters of Eve is a suspenseful novel that invalidates legitimate problems by presenting misdirected solutions. The author raises such feminist issues as wife-beating, inequality on the job, unfairness in high school athletics and the sexist dimension of male/female relationships, but the violence of her solutions implies that it may be dangerous to even recognize the issues. (p. 17)

The book implies that the Daughters have gone too far and that Irene's personal bitterness has caused her to misrepresent matters and incited the violence. For example, after the science lab is destroyed, it is revealed that Fran's project was rejected not because she was female but because her experiment violated state rules. The author

clearly places a harsh value judgment on violent solutions, and because she provides no alternative solutions, she leaves the impression that fighting for women's rights leads to uncontrollable anger and senseless destruction.

In addition, the book contains many negative stereotypes. It is antifat in its description of Laura, who is too "ugly" to "get a man" and is loved only by her mother who overlooks her daughter's "weight problem" because she is overweight herself! The club is elitist in that only the "choicest of the choice" can join. An anti-gay reference is made by Ruth's father, who refuses to let his sons do household work because he's afraid they'll turn into "fags."

The book suggests that Irene is an angry woman, not because she is justified, but because she is "empty" (note the symbolism of her last name, *Stark*). The book also implies that Irene is not a complete, or "normal" woman—she has an "unappetizing" appearance, a low voice, a harsh face and a trace of a mustache! The author subtly distorts Irene's potentially strong feminist character into that of a vindictive fanatic who manipulates and co-opts vulnerable young minds to achieve her sick revenge.

In summary, the book's deceptive interpretation of feminism plus its dangerous stereotypes make it a harmful distortion of reality. However, the book could be sensitively used to raise feminist issues as they affect the lives of adolescents. But the issues must be presented as real to women everywhere, and not as obsessions of fanatics like Irene Stark. If the book is used, it must be followed by a discussion of alternate solutions to violence, all the while stressing the validity of oppressed peoples' anger and frustration. Readers must be asked to consider what they would do when all "rational" solutions to their problems don't work. (p. 18)

> *Jan M. Goodman, in a review of "Daughters of Eve," in* Interracial Books for Children Bulletin, *Vol. 11, No. 6, 1980, pp. 17-18.*

Children experience the mother as the first "other," and a sense of self must be molded out of that relationship. Since the mothering person is nearly always a woman, daughters, according to [Nancy Chodorow's *The Reproduction of Mothering: Psychoanalysis and the Sociology of Gender*], tend to experience stronger feelings of identity with their mothers than do sons. To develop as individuals, the first task that children must undertake is to separate psychologically from their mothers—that is, to discover and understand the boundaries between themselves and their mothers. This task is often more difficult for girls, as is illustrated in Lois Duncan's novel **Daughters of Eve:** the developmental task of becoming an individual is made harder for the young women in Duncan's novel because their mothers see them as a reflection of themselves and assume that their daughters will grow into women looking forward to living the same kinds of lives that they lead.

If this were true, then there would be no tension between the two generations of characters in the novel. The mothers could act easily as role models for the young women. However, Duncan is writing about the complex, contemporary American society where a sense of individualism is rewarded; thus, her young protagonists suffer much confusion in separating themselves from their mothers as do many young women in real life American society. . . .

In *Daughters of Eve,* Duncan creates mothers who expect their daughters to live out traditional lives as wives and mothers, sacrificing their individual talents and ambitions for marriage and family. The daughters, however, in their confusion and in their search for individuation become involved with a mother substitute, Irene Stark, who acts as a powerful role model to the young women and consciously sets out to create women who will not repeat their mothers' experiences. Rather, she provides the young women with information about how to choose educational opportunities, about how to become a risk taker, and about how to love and respect oneself—simply how to define the self.

The ability of daughters to redefine self can be evidence of assertiveness and strength. But sometimes young women find that in their efforts to break away from the patterns of their mother's lives, they lose a sense of their own inner core and become more confused about their independence. This is the case for some of the young women protagonists in *Daughters of Eve.* (p. 36)

> *Jeanne Gerlach, "Mother Daughter Relationships in Lois Duncan's 'Daughters of Eve',*" in The ALAN Review, *Vol. 19, No. 1, Fall, 1991, pp. 36-8.*

Stranger with My Face (1981)

There are small things, at first—a face in a mirror, a presence in an empty room, a beckoning figure on treacherous rocks—that portend 17-year-old Laurie's confrontation with the astral projection of her previously unknown, malevolent identical twin. In the beginning, Laurie is puzzled, then alarmed and finally horrified. The twin wishes to usurp her place among her artist mother, writer father and loving brother and sister at the fortress of Cliff House on Brighton Island, their happy home. The jealous twin, Lia, pursues her, prodding her to explore astral projection so that Lia may enter Laurie's body and have the secure home and future Lia always lacked. The element of the supernatural is so gradually and deftly introduced into the story that its presence seems natural and believable and, hence, more menacing. While some of the author's attempts at "symbolism" are a bit obvious, and some of the minor characters are sketchily portrayed, most readers will not mind. They will be completely caught up in this suspenseful, gripping book. The ironic surprise ending is one more asset in a finely crafted story.

> *Holly Sandhuber, in a review of "Stranger with My Face,*" in School Library Journal, *Vol. 28, No. 3, November, 1981, p. 103.*

The peculiar problems of identity in the lives of identical twins, well vouched for in scientific terms, need in fiction skilful character-drawing to achieve credibility. *Stranger with my Face* has the strong dramatic delineation of people and plot which Lois Duncan's previous books (*Killing*

Mr. Griffin, for example) have established as her hallmark. She touches a sensitive nerve as she explores the differences, in circumstance and in temperament, between twin girls, illegitimate offspring of a Navajo woman and a white pedlar. Laurie Stratton at seventeen is given space to develop emotionally by her adoptive parents, an intelligent New England couple with younger children of their own: Lia Abbott has been fostered all her life and has fought for a dominant position in each family in turn by appallingly simple acts of murder. Ostensibly a thriller, the story turns on the process of astral transference. Lia's interference with her more secure sister's life is conducted at a distance, when she enters Laurie's body and offers violence to the boy with whom Laurie is forging a serious relationship. The externals of the book, the domestic manners and *mores* of a middle class Massachusetts family, the chatter and shifting alliances of school, are expertly managed, but the true personalities of the two girls somehow escape in the frenetic, retrospective narrative in which Laurie, a year after her twin has died and freed her from sinister influence, tries to work out for herself exactly how she has been affected. Perhaps the story should be understood as an image for the confusions of adolescence. At any rate, the first-person approach has placed too much of a burden on the narrator, who in tracing (on the author's behalf) the threads of events in her seventeenth year, has hardly had the space and freedom to emerge as a rounded, believable individual.

> *Margery Fisher, in a review of "Stranger with My Face," in* Growing Point, *Vol. 22, No. 1, May, 1983, p. 4069.*

One might categorise Lois Duncan's tale as an exercise in the theory of astral projection but that would dismiss unfairly the depth of feeling and the breadth of events which the author imparts to the story of seventeen-year-old Laurie Stratton who suddenly finds herself, in the course of her vacation, visited by another self. . . . Around the main characters Mrs Duncan draws in firmly the ambience of American teenagers on holiday in an unspoiled environment, the fun of Christmas and the party-going, the talented but mildly eccentric parents, without sentimentality. When Lia turns out to have been a real person, explanations become acceptable through the author's consistent gift of understatement. Certainly the tale is frightening to a degree, but readers who recall *Killing Mr. Griffin* will find Mrs Duncan has retained her grasp on the retailing of tension and suspense.

> *A. R. Williams, in a review of "Stranger with My Face," in* The Junior Bookshelf, *Vol. 47, No. 3, June, 1983, p. 133.*

Chapters: My Growth as a Writer (1982)

This is an autobiography of Lois Duncan, and should be classified strictly as such; by no stretch of the imagination should it be regarded as containing information having to do with the craft of writing. We get tales from her teens and before on love and life; we get the chance to read short rejected poems and stories she wrote before making it to the big time. It reads easily, like one of her novels; she has a good hold on her adolescence and one would swear she is indeed 14 years old. She always wanted to write, and it seems she has never had to invent much in the way of plot for her novels: her life is one long teen novel. It ends at young motherhood and a big sale. More to come? She should hold back.

> *Terry Lawhead, in a review of "Chapters: My Growth as a Writer," in* School Library Journal, *Vol. 28, No. 7, March, 1982, p. 156.*

Lois Duncan began writing and submitting short stories when she was ten, received her first check when she was thirteen, and continued as a magazine writer for many years before she turned to book-length novels. In this entertaining partial biography, she includes many examples of her stories and shows how she used material and people from her real life experiences. It is interesting to see the literary growth over the years; there is little discussion of her novels. Both the stories she includes and the autobiographical material should appeal to her fans; she writes with candor and discernment, in an easy, flowing style.

> *Zena Sutherland, in a review of "Chapters: My Growth as a Writer," in* Bulletin of the Center for Children's Books, *Vol. 35, No. 9, May, 1982, p. 167.*

This semi-autobiographical book by a prize-winning author unfortunately reads too much like her early short stories written for *Seventeen,* than the later novels for which she justifiably received critical acclaim, ***Daughters Of Eve*** and ***The Killing of Mr. Griffin.*** The subject of the book is aptly described by the title and over 160 pages of this 328 page book contain early poems and stories written by the author at age thirteen, etc. These are followed by Duncan's comments on circumstances which precipitated the story in an attempt to describe her development as a writer. The book ends with her last short story and a short chapter which mentions her divorce, remarriage and later novels; a meatier subject which could have more accurately reflected the evolution of a fine author.

Duncan has also written ***How To Write And Sell Your Personal Experiences*** but ***Chapters,*** aimed at a young audience contains too much of the author's creative work and insufficient information about her personal growth. The young reader may enjoy the early poems and stories; I found them tiresome. Buy for your budding writers or for possible use in a young writers' workshop, not because it is by Lois Duncan. (p. 43)

> *Ellen Carter, in a review of "Chapters: My Growth as a Writer," in* Voice of Youth Advocates, *Vol. 5, No. 2, June, 1982, pp. 42-3.*

From Spring to Spring: Poems and Photographs (1982)

Lois Duncan is not as successful with this book of poetry as she has been with her popular young adult novels. Her writing here is pleasant but pedestrian. This is standard rhyming poetry, with the meter tending to be sing-song. The poems, which portray the world from a child's viewpoint, deal with the predictable themes of love, family and the beauty of nature. Each poem has its own page, facing a full-page black-and-white photograph. There is nothing particularly outstanding or original here. The only distinctive aspect of the book is the strong religious element. God is mentioned in most of the poems, which are to some extent interfaith. The collection includes **"Song for Hanukkah,"** and **"Song for an Indian Child,"** where God "goes not by a Christian name but walks among us all the same." There is an old-fashioned, nostalgic quality to the poems. Many are sentimental to the point of being downright corny. Memories of "golden afternoons" with the "gold of heaven upon my hair" will probably appeal more to grandparents than to children. There is none of the "kid appeal" of Silverstein's zany humor or the unique imagery of Eve Merriam. This book may be useful in parochial schools and where "inspirational" poetry is needed, but it will not significantly enhance most juvenile poetry collections.

> *Candy Bettelson, in a review of "From Spring to Spring," in* School Library Journal, *Vol. 29, No. 7, March, 1983, p. 174.*

In 41 religious poems, Duncan happily combines her reverent theme with an irreverently childlike tone and fresh humor. After three stanzas describing a stint in the shower, a soak in the tub, and a dip in the pool, the narrator of **"Mud Song"** concludes, "When God made the world, I / Am glad there was time / To dig holes for puddles / And fill them with slime." Opposite these verses is a black-and-white, full-page candid photo (this one of four kids ecstatically lolling around in a horrendous loblolly of mud) typical of the others accompanying each poem. Some of the pieces, like **"Dream Song,"** spoken by crippled children without sentimentality, are touching; others, like **"Song of Triumph,"** in which a boy begs for and gets his way, are gleeful. Those that are not inventive have a simple, solid base of experience with which readers can identify. **"Horse Song"** and **"Song for Sisters"** treat aging and death in a way children can deal with; **"Song of Frustration"** exactly captures a difficult sibling. And the pictures are a substantial contribution. **"Song for Something Little"** is saved from being too sweet by the unexpected photo of a mouse looking out of a leering, close-to-collapse pumpkin, while **"Song for a Bad Day"** is deepened by the genuine grief of the girl in the picture. With the few previously published selections appearing in little-known sources, this is a worthwhile, accessible poetic cycle, especially for family sharing.

> *Betsy Hearne, in a review of "From Spring to Spring: Poems and Photographs," in* Booklist, *Vol. 79, No. 13, March 1, 1983, p. 904.*

The Terrible Tales of Happy Days School (1983)

Twelve tales involving the most horrid children at a progressive school are told in couplet rhyme form. Each full-page verse description of the child receives an equally full-page pen-and-ink whimsical illustration [by Friso Henstra]. The descriptions are bizarre. The tales are meant to be cautionary, but one wonders at the audience reaction to these ghastly children. A book to be read with care.

> *Jeanette Cohn, in a review of "The Terrible*

Tales of Happy Days School," in Children's Book Review Service, *Vol. 12, No. 7, February, 1984, p. 73.*

Meet the repulsive students of the Happy Days Progressive School. There's Melissa, who refuses to tend her hamsters, choosing to let them wallow in moldy, smelly litter; Art, whose *raison d'être* is stealing and Dan, whose specialty is eavesdropping. Then there's Jerome, whose contempt for bodily hygiene causes vegetation to sprout under his armpits; Nancy, who delights in stoning a puppy tied to a tree; and Hugh, the liar par excellence. All these paragons, and others, get their comeuppance in fitting ways, in a sort of Dantesque *contrappasso* fashion. The liar is kidnapped and his parents refuse to take the ransom note seriously; the thief is accidentally electrocuted; the stone thrower is attacked and killed by her former victim. And so it goes. The poems are written in sing-song rhyming couplets and are more stomach-turning than frightening or funny, and most of Henstra's clumsy black-and-white line drawings add little to the supposed humor or horror. For better "deliciously frightening" verse, turn to *Monster Poems* (Holiday, 1976), edited by Daisy Wallace.

> *Daisy Kouzel, in a review of "The Terrible Tales of Happy Days School," in* School Library Journal, *Vol. 30, No. 6, February, 1984, p. 68.*

The Third Eye (1984; British edition as *The Eyes of Karen Connors*)

After she tells police where a missing boy can be found and later leads them to the spot where another lost child was drowned, 18-year-old Karen Connors realizes with dismay that she has **The Third Eye.** When word leaks out that she is psychic, her new-found "freak" status not only leads to the loss of her boyfriend but to a deluge of requests from frantic parents to help them find their missing children. Although Karen is able to fend off the calls for help, she is unable to control the awful visions which fill her mind. When she unwittingly helps a duo of child-snatchers pull off a mass kidnapping of babies from the child care center where she works, Karen is forced to use her powers again. With the encouragement of a young police officer, she traces the missing babies and helps break up an illegal child adoption ring. Afterward she decides to accept her powers and use them in a positive way. With a plot that unfolds slowly in the beginning, this does not rank among Duncan's best. Karen's inner struggle, however, is vivid and memorable, as is her strained relationship with her parents. While the plotting sometimes fails her, Duncan's natural storytelling ability never does. Even when she is not at her best, she is still an author that teens will read and enjoy.

> *Nancy Palmer, in a review of "The Third Eye," in* School Library Journal, *Vol. 30, No. 9, May, 1984, p. 103.*

At the start of the book, when the child she is minding goes innocently astray, Karen discovers that she has the psychic ability to locate people using her "third eye". A second child disappears and Karen is persuaded to locate her. She does, only to find that the child has drowned; an experience which her powers force her to share. The plot may be a familiar one but Lois Duncan brings a freshness of writing and some chilling descriptions to make it grip. But then, straight out of some American television series a team of baby-nappers is introduced ("You give me a hard time and you're going to lose those pretty white teeth") and from here the book collapses into patness and predictability.

> *Anthony Horowitz, "Parent Problems," in* The Times Literary Supplement, *No. 4273, February 22, 1985, p. 214.*

Locked in Time (1985)

Duncan's **Locked in Time** is the story of a domineering mother, Lisette, and her two teenage children, Gabe and Josie, who have all drunk from the cup of eternal youth. Seventeen-year-old Nore Robbins goes to visit her father, Charles, and her new stepfamily, Lisette, Gabe and Josie, at Lisette's beautiful old estate deep in the Louisiana bayou country. Nore discovers her stepfamily's secret and, in an attempt to expose this knowledge, becomes Lisette's target for death. This page-turner creates a mood of suspense and mystery through the setting—an old Southern mansion, complete with marshes, Spanish moss, deserted slave quarters and ghosts. The characters are well-rounded, and readers will sympathize with teenagers Gabe and Josie's sense of futility at never being able to grow up, make friends, establish relationships, and with Lisette's single-minded determination to protect her children, even though she must kill to do so. A satisfying suspense story.

> *Carolyn Gabbard Fugate, in a review of "Locked in Time," in* School Library Journal, *Vol. 32, No. 3, November, 1985, p. 96.*

Coincidentally I found myself reading this book immediately after Gina Wilson's *Family Feeling . . .* , and thinking at first how neatly it illustrated the difference between the American and the English approach to a similar situation. Nore, in **Locked in Time,** like Alice in *Family Feeling,* has just acquired a step-parent and a new family of two, a boy ripe for romance and an awkward and difficult younger girl. Very soon it became apparent that Lois Duncan was writing a very different book. Not content, like Gina Wilson, to make a story out of familiar personal problems, she gives us a powerful and torrid romantic novel growing out of the steamy heat of Louisiana and the dark rituals of voodoo. Nore's new stepmother, her beauty untouched by age, turns out to be—as Nore puts it—a 'black widow spider', eternally young and keeping herself and her children on the profits of many advantageous and short-lived marriages. Not a nice discovery for a young girl to make, especially as she has become emotionally attracted to her stepbrother, now more than a century old! Happily the lovely Lisette, although immune from the effects of age, is not proof against accident, and all turns out more or less right.

There were times during the reading of this story when I wondered if Lois Duncan was being serious or whether she was engaged in a parody. Some of the more steamy scenes are grossly overwritten. Life in this hot climate is lived at high pressure; here is Gabe, the centenarian stepbrother, at a disco: 'Gabe danced with the grace of a jungle cat, his lithe body surprisingly strong and under perfect control . . . I could see my reflection in the dark twin mirrors of his eyes.' But no; this is no parody. Ms Duncan is being very much in earnest, and she gives her invention all she has got in pace of narrative and vividness of imagination. The reader may not believe a word of it, but I fancy he (more probably she) will not want to put it down before its breathless conclusion.

> M. Crouch, in a review of "Locked in Time," in The Junior Bookshelf, Vol. 50, No. 2, April, 1986, p. 76.

The growing sense of unease is Lois Duncan's hallmark. Though her heroine is a flesh-and-blood creature, and her moody young teenager a recognizable person, Duncan's real interest lies outside characterization. She can play the part of the novelist, but at heart she is a spine-chiller. Her stories are not literary, or particularly stylish or complex: just readable, compelling and very frightening. . . .

Though primarily a writer of the sinister in a tradition begun by Wilkie Collins, Lois Duncan does not duck the problems of the modern world. Both **Locked in Time** and Gina Wilson's novel [*Family Feeling*] have fashionable "problem" themes. It is a pleasure to report that both writers rise above the worthiness of their subject matter to write novels which entertain far more than they instruct.

> Sarah Hayes, "Front-Preservers," in The Times Literary Supplement, No. 4336, May 9, 1986, p. 514.

Horses of Dreamland (1985)

In this distinctive picture book, a sleeping child makes a voyage to the land of dream horses. They come at her call, and she travels with them through the sky. Sleep is not without perils, however: " . . . to each side, lies darkness / Where nightmare creatures dwell." Wolves disturb the peacefulness of the dream; the horses scream in terror, but the child orders the snarling beasts away. She and her companions gallop away toward sunrise. When she awakens, her friends are gone—to a place where they doze and dream of the children who come to them at night. Striking illustrations [by Donna Diamond] set sharp, high-contrast photographic images against pastel backgrounds in the colors of sunrise and sunset. The end effect is one of moonlit unreality, beautifully conveying the elusive quality of a dream. Duncan's verse completes this portrait of a nighttime adventure with unique and appealing imagery. This unusual book is a bedtime story par excellence with special appeal to horse-loving children.

> Lucy Young Clem, in a review of "Horses of Dreamland," in School Library Journal, Vol. 32, No. 6, February, 1986, p. 73.

Many girls have a passionate and romantic love for horses and their dreams are haunted by them. They are not everyday horses which frequent their dreams but wild and free steeds 'whose manes are twined with flowers; their breath as sweet as hay'. Such dream horses know no bounds but can soar into the sky. At dawn they gallop back to their freedom and the dreamer awakes to reality.

The author has used this dreamland fantasy for a number of simple verses and the artist has responded with paintings of a dreamlike quality, misty and magical. For many girls who are passing through this phase, this attractive little book will have an instant appeal.

> E. Colwell, in a review of "Horses of Dreamland," in The Junior Bookshelf, Vol. 50, No. 3, June, 1986, p. 108.

The Twisted Window (1987)

Brad Johnson wants his half sister back, and he thinks Tracy Lloyd is just the person to help him get her. He is right. Alone, angry at her father for leaving her with relatives, and annoyed by her guardians' overprotectiveness, Tracy falls easy prey to Brad's sad tale of a victimizing stepfather who kidnapped his own two-year-old out of spite rather than love. She agrees to help Brad snatch the child back. It isn't until the deed is done and the three are heading across the country that Tracy finds cause to question whether Brad has been telling the truth, and by the time she gets the facts straight, Brad and the child have gone off without her with a rifle in the trunk of their car. Is Brad so insane that he might use it? Duncan fans will need to suspend disbelief more than usual as they read her

Duncan, seated, with her husband Don Arquette and their children.

latest thriller, which handles some serious problems in a manner more trivial than frightening. But with troubled teenagers as protagonists and a good assortment of cinematic complications, readers will inevitably be curious about how the novel will end.

Stephanie Zvirin, in a review of "The Twisted Window," in Booklist, Vol. 84, No. 1, September 1, 1987, p. 54.

This is another Duncan page turner, yet at times the abduction of the small child is so disturbing that one has to stop reading for a few moments. Brad's instability is so obvious to the reader that it is almost hard to believe that Tracy, who is portrayed as a street-wise smart teen, would buy the twisted story, and even more dangerous plan to abduct the small child. When the reader discovers, at the end of the book, what really happened to Brad's baby sister, that reader will not be left with the memory of a satisfying thriller, but with an uneasy feeling and a question: How will Tracy reconcile herself to the nightmare she involved herself in?

Colleen Macklin, in a review of "The Twisted Window," in Voice of Youth Advocates, Vol. 10, No. 4, October, 1987, p. 200.

Like Judy Blume, Lois Duncan understands the teenage world and its passionate concerns with matters as diverse as dress, death, romance, school, self-image, sex and problem parents. But where Blume reflects real life in an affectionate, often humorous way, Duncan suggests that life is neither as prosaic nor as straightforward as it seems at first. Previous novels have shown her mastery of the macabre. *The Twisted Window* has all of the Duncan hallmarks—the build-up of tension; the manipulation of our sympathies; and the dramatic climax—but here the paranormal has been replaced by the abnormal, and the menace is all in the mind. . . .

Tracy's changing perceptions of reality affect her view of those around her: her apparently uncaring aunt and uncle are in fact anxious to comfort their troubled niece; her seemingly selfish father is consumed with guilt that his work as an actor allows him no time with his daughter. Appearances are misleading: a sister is not a sister; a kidnapping masks a death; even Brad's best friend, Jamie, turns out to be a girl.

Brad is the only character who stays the same throughout, as the story snakes its way towards the climax, slipping away from the reader just at the point when it seems to become clear. During the final heart-stopping scene in a remote mountain cabin, a shot is fired, a little girl falls to the ground, and Brad is forced, at last, to admit the truth.

Duncan carefully uses her character's shifting views to unsettle the reader. Apprehension—for the child, for the gullible girl, for the desperate, disturbed boy—becomes fear as the ground slips from beneath our feet. Those who have enjoyed the thrill of the earlier novels need not be alarmed at Duncan's apparent defection from the supernatural: they need only look through the twisted window into the mind of a crazy boy to feel that same excitement. If Lois Duncan is not a particularly stylish writer, she is none the less able to tell a gripping story.

Sarah Hayes, "Fatal Flaws," in The Times Literary Supplement, No. 4426, January 29-February 4, 1988, p. 119.

Wonder Kid Meets the Evil Lunch Snatcher   (1988)

His first day in the new school starts out even worse than fourth-grader Brian Johnson expects it to. He and his sister Sarah are jumped by a sixth-grade bully, Matt, whose gang of lunch-grabbers terrorizes the school. Yet that very incident leads the Johnson children to make some new friends, and together they concoct a scheme to convince Matt of the existence of Wonder Kid, zapper of bullies. Unfortunately, they have to produce Wonder Kid in the flesh but, in doing so, discover their own wondrous capacities. This is sprightly wish fulfillment for any kid: a skinny, lonely nerd whose only refuge is the world of comic book heroes becomes one. The plot has some unlikely moments, but it's fun and all done with stylistic ease and easy-to-read style. (pp. 153-54)

Betsy Hearne, in a review of "Wonder Kid Meets the Evil Lunch Snatcher," in Bulletin of the Center for Children's Books, Vol. 41, No. 8, April, 1988, pp. 153-54.

When Brian and his sister are mugged for their lunches by the school bully and his gang, a fellow comic book fan and his sister help him cook up a plan involving a superhero called Wonder Kid, and the bully soon has his comeuppance. While this plan is set up well through stories in the school newspaper, it seems too easy to convince the bully and his friends of Wonder Kid's powers. Overall, the plot moves smoothly, although Brian sometimes seems to think of himself in adult terms, and the dialogue is not always convincingly child-like. The friendship between the two pairs of siblings grows naturally, and Brian does become better friends with his own sister because of the experience. This is a serviceable book, but not an outstanding choice.

Annette Curtis Klause, in a review of "Wonder Kid Meets the Evil Lunch Snatcher," in School Library Journal, Vol. 35, No. 8, May, 1988, p. 96.

Don't Look behind You   (1989)

April's peaceful, perfect world is shattered when she and her family are forced to assume new identities after her father, working undercover for the FBI, has testified in court against some dangerous drug smugglers. While Duncan seems to be incapable of writing something that is not a page-turner, the suspense here is vitiated by naggings of implausibility that undermine her premise and plot development. The family hides for two weeks in a hotel, never leaving their room. When taken under the wing of the Witness Protection Program, they simply disappear, change their names, move to Florida, get contact lenses for little brother Bram (whose eyes are two different colors), and April's mother gives up her career as a noted author of children's books, all without much of a peep on the part of neighbors, media, or Mrs. Corrigan's editor.

While April keeps learning the lesson that "real life isn't Cinemax," the novel is framed in terms of the world of the paperback romance: for April, the worst thing about the Witness Protection Program is losing her boyfriend; in the end she finds another. Duncan is usually more complex and careful than she is here, but her talent for suspenseful pacing and melodrama remains unparalleled. Author recognition, the fright-night title, and the cover photo of a gloved hand gripping another hand gripping a phone guarantee absolutely no need for booktalks.

> *Roger Sutton, in a review of "Don't Look Behind You," in* Bulletin of the Center for Children's Books, *Vol. 42, No. 9, May, 1989, p. 221.*

Undoubtedly a master of suspense, Duncan has written a spellbinding tale of uniquely contemporary horror. . . . The entire book is fast-paced and enthralling, but the conclusion will have readers on the edge of their chairs. April and her grandmother get involved a high-speed cross-country chase which culminates in the death of a hit man. Although some readers will not be able to imagine having to sever completely all ties with their past, they won't be able to put this book down. ***Don't Look Behind You*** is filled with booktalk potential.

> *Jeanette Larson, in a review of "Don't Look Behind You," in* School Library Journal, *Vol. 35, No. 11, July, 1989, p. 91.*

Songs from Dreamland: Original Lullabies   (1989)

A delicately illustrated collection of 14 original lullabies and a sweetly sung cassette recording of the songs, each of which can stand alone well but which complement each other nicely. Duncan's lullabies represent many of the aspects of lullaby tradition and have some of the qualities of Malvina Reynolds' songs for children. The poems are rhythmic delights, full of the repeated sounds that make lullabies so appealing to small children. They cover a range of moods from gently loving to sprightly. Duncan's choice of words is perfect, using the common subjects of lullabies, but with creative twists. Kay Chorao's pastel pencil drawings are reminiscent of her illustrations for *The Baby's Bedtime Book* (Dutton, 1984) and are filled with clever transitions from the dreaming to the waking state. Fish sewn on the baby's quilt in **"The Sleepy Sun"** are featured alive and active in her dreams, and the boats on a small child's pajamas float gently in his memories of the day's play. While mothers dominate these lullabies, a number of the songs do not reflect the gender of the singer, and Chorao has included several fathers in her pictures, as well as multi-ethnic children. On the cassette, [Robin] Arquette uses a variety of music to accentuate the rhythms and moods of the lullabies; she uses her fine voice for dramatic effect to reproduce the sliding, ironic, and loving moods of the lyrics. A gentle commentary, accompanied by wind and windchime sounds, ties the songs together. These lullabies would work well in home and nursery-school settings, with the tape used to induce naps and bedtimes and the book to let children see and enjoy the words and images of their favorite songs.

> *Barbara Chatton, in a review of "Songs from Dreamland," in* School Library Journal, *Vol. 35, No. 12, August, 1989, p. 135.*

There is interesting diversity in these fourteen original lullabies composed for the young child. Poems about the wind, sun, and stars are interspersed with those about the child's day and the fact that **"Mommy's Tired Tonight."** The music that accompanies each lullaby is also diverse. The book is worthy by itself, as the poems can be read easily and Chorao's soft illustrations will be pleasing to the young child. Though intended for the home market, this book/cassette package is useful in the preschool classroom for calming children and for playing with rhyme.

> *M. Jean Greenlaw, in a review of "Songs from Dreamland," in* The New Advocate, *Vol. 3, No. 1, Winter, 1990, p. 63.*

The Birthday Moon   (1989)

"On your very next birthday / I'll give you a moon / On the end of a string / Like a golden balloon." So begins Duncan's buoyant verse linking balloons, birthdays, and glowing, magical fun. The appealing images shift according to the moon's changing phases: "If your birthday should come / When the moon is not whole, / I will give you a moon / You can use as a bowl." The accompanying pictures [by Susan Davis] are light, airy watercolors that emphasize the poem's whimsical aspects. In aiming to pique the imagination the book succeeds, and the fun isn't just reserved for birthdays. (p. 456)

> *Denise Wilms, in a review of "The Birthday Moon," in* Booklist, *Vol. 86, No. 4, October 15, 1989, pp. 455-56.*

"On your very next birthday / I'll give you the moon / On the end of a string / Like a golden balloon" begins this sprightly exploration in verse of a number of things the moon might be—a ball, a coin, a hammock, a harp. "There are so many things / You can do with a moon!" This rather slight but pleasantly imaginative exercise is appropriately illustrated with playful watercolors of a pretty, toyland-like world. Acceptable but not outstanding.

> *A review of "The Birthday Moon," in* Kirkus Reviews, *Vol. LVII, No. 20, October 15, 1989, p. 1528.*

Lilting, rhythmic verse, coupled with bright, sparkling pastel illustrations combine to explore the many possible uses of the moon if it were given to a child as a birthday present. This gentle, dreamy fantasy depicts the moon as a ball to toss to the stars, a coin to spend at the candy shop, or to buy the sun "if it's ever for sale." If the birthday falls on a night when the moon is "not whole," it can be used as a harp, as a hammock, as a bowl, or as a bow ("so the arrows you shoot will all shimmer and glow.") Deftly conveying the universal theme of birthday wonder and anticipation, this will be a welcome spark for imaginations of all ages and a valuable asset for thematic uses.

> *Mary Lou Budd, in a review of "The Birthday*

Moon," in School Library Journal, *Vol. 35,
No. 16, December, 1989, p. 78.*

James Cross Giblin

1933-

American writer of nonfiction and biographer.

Major works include *Chimney Sweeps: Yesterday and Today* (1982), *Walls: Defenses throughout History* (1984), *The Truth about Santa Claus* (1985), *The Truth about Unicorns* (1991).

The editor of over 300 books for children and young adults, Giblin, since 1980, has become an important author in his own right. Such titles as *The Skyscraper Book* (1981), *Chimney Sweeps: Yesterday and Today, Fireworks, Picnics, and Flags* (1983), and *From Hand to Mouth: Or, How We Invented Knives, Forks, Spoons, and Chopsticks and the Table Manners to Go with Them* (1987) bespeak his penchant for investigating and writing about commonplace subjects whose often colorful histories have been overlooked or forgotten. Giblin enjoys a reputation for bringing to each of his studies the special qualities of an impeccable researcher, a practiced storyteller, and an ardent lover of facts. His audience is composed primarily of students aged eight to twelve, whom he addresses in a conversational tone while gradually conveying a wealth of entertaining information through a series of short, interrelated chapters. Carefully avoiding contrived dialogue to gird his narrative approach, Giblin instead relies on actual quotations from historical figures to enliven his texts. In addition to his nonfiction work for children, Giblin is also the author of two adult works, the one-act play *My Bus Is Always Late* (1954) and an autobiographical how-to book entitled *Writing Books for Young People* (1990).

Following a short career as a would-be playwright, Giblin rose to prominence as an editor in New York during the 1960s and 1970s. It was not until 1977, however, that he tentatively joined the field of children's nonfiction with a small piece for an anthology on the subject of the Flatiron Building, one of New York's earliest skyscrapers. Giblin later expanded his initial research in order to publish *The Skyscraper Book,* a one hundred-year history of notable urban American architecture. For this work, in what has become his trademark fashion, Giblin presented a great variety of ancillary and anecdotal information to firmly place his topic in the realm of living social and technological history. The year before this study appeared, Giblin published *The Scarecrow Book* (1980) his first full-length publication, which was coauthored with Dale Ferguson. *The Scarecrow Book* bears another characteristic of Giblin's work, in that it features an engaging collection of historical and contemporary photos and illustrations to supplement the author's carefully arranged story, which here has as its underlying thesis that such inventions as the scarecrow exist not only for their obvious functionality but for their sociocultural roles, as well.

Giblin's most successful works include *Chimney Sweeps, Walls,* and *The Truth about Santa Claus.* In each he ranges beyond the simple confines of his subject matter to

explain, respectively, child-labor abuse in nineteenth-century England, the nature of war, and the rich fluctuation of customs related to Santa Claus throughout history. Since 1989, Giblin has devoted his full time to writing and has published *The Riddle of the Rosetta Stone: Key to Ancient Egypt* (1990), *The Truth about Unicorns, Edith Wilson: The Woman Who Ran the United States* (1992), and *George Washington: A Picture Book Biography* (1992). This last represents his first attempt at picture books and the streamlined, lyrical style the genre demands. Several of Giblin's works have received recognition and awards, including *The Scarecrow Book, The Skyscraper Book,* and *Chimney Sweeps,* all of which were named "notable children's books" by the American Library Association. *Chimney Sweeps* was also chosen for both the Golden Kite Award by the Society of Children's Book Writers and the American Book Award for children's nonfiction. Other honors include the *Boston Globe/Horn Book* honor book for nonfiction for *The Truth about Santa Claus* and the Golden Kite Award for *Walls.*

(See also *Something about the Author,* Vol. 33; *Something about the Author Autobiography Series,* Vol. 12; *Contem-*

porary Authors, Vol. 106; and *Contemporary Authors New Revision Series,* Vol. 24.)

AUTHOR'S COMMENTARY

People are sometimes startled when I say that a nonfiction writer is a storyteller. Aren't nonfiction books and articles made up entirely of facts? Yes, of course. But the organizing and shaping of those facts into readable, interesting prose requires all the skills of a storyteller.

It begins with the idea. Since a juvenile nonfiction book often takes six months to research and another six months to write, the idea should be one that captures the writer's imagination strongly. Unless the idea has an element of story, of mystery in it, the writer may not be compelled to invest the time and energy needed to develop it.

One Christmas season I happened to see a picture of our plump, jolly Santa Claus in juxtaposition with his tall, thin ancestor, St. Nicholas. My curiosity was aroused: How did two such dissimilar figures become joined? The result was my book, *The Truth About Santa Claus.* Several years later, as I was eating dinner in a restaurant, I found myself wondering when people first began to use spoons, knives, and forks. That, in turn, led me to write *From Hand to Mouth,* which traces the story of our common eating utensils.

There's that word again: story. With each of these book ideas, I was moved to explore the story behind something, whether it was our favorite gift-bringer, or the common, everyday table fork. And it was the lure of the story, and the promise of discovering the key to it, that sustained my interest through the long hours of research.

As I do research, I'm always on the lookout for dramatic or amusing anecdotes that will help to bring the subject to life for young readers. For example, when I was researching *From Hand to Mouth* I was delighted to find the following anecdote, which tells how table knives came to be rounded.

> The design of table knives changed even more noticeably in the 17th century. Now that people throughout Europe were eating with forks, they no longer needed knives with sharp points to spear their food. Consequently, by the end of the century most European table knives were made with rounded ends.

> Some say Cardinal Richelieu, a French religious and political leader, was responsible for this change in knife design. The Cardinal frequently entertained a nobleman who was in the habit of picking his teeth with the point of his knife. Disgusted with the man's behavior, the Cardinal had the points of all his table knives ground down, and others in the French court followed the Cardinal's lead.

As the research begins to take shape, I frequently discover an overall narrative line in the material and build the structure of the book around it. The book *Walls: Defenses Throughout History* began as simply an account of fascinating walls I'd seen, among them Hadrian's Wall and the Great Wall of China. But it grew first into a history of fortifications and then into a demonstration that no defensive wall, from the Great Wall to the Maginot Line, has ever really worked.

From Hand to Mouth assumed a circular pattern. It opens on a scene of ancient people eating with their fingers and ends with people once again relying on their fingers in today's fast-food establishments. In between we get glimpses of all the elaborate table manners that came into being with the use of knives, spoons, forks, and chopsticks.

Neither of these patterns—these narrative lines—was imposed on the books in question. They emerged naturally the deeper I got into the research and the more connections I saw between the various aspects of the topic and the way they had changed over time. When critics talk of an informational book being well-organized, I think what they're really referring to is a sense of inner-connectedness and thematic progression. It's as crucial to the success of a nonfiction book, I feel, as a strong plot is to a novel.

Once the overall direction has been determined, the outline can be divided into chapters. Here pace is terribly important. Often what I originally thought would be one chapter contains too much information and works better if it is divided in two. Ideally, I aim for no more than ten typewritten pages per chapter, and preferably seven or eight. Most of my books for eight-to-twelve-year-olds have run to eight or ten chapters, resulting in final manuscripts of fifty to ninety pages. That length allows room for illustrations and doesn't seem too formidable to today's young readers, who are confronted with so many different media claims on their attention.

Chapter titles provide another way to inject humor and drama into a book and encourage a youngster to continue reading. Sometimes a straightforward, factual title, such as "Walls of World War II" (used in my book *Walls*) works best. But in other cases, a more dramatic approach seems called for, like "Danger from the Sky," the title of the chapter on the effects of atomic radiation in *Milk: The Fight for Purity.* Never miss a chance for humor, either, if it's appropriate to the subject, as in the chapter about European table manners before the introduction of forks in *From Hand to Mouth.* I called it "Don't Put Your Whole Hand in the Pot!"

The opening paragraphs of each chapter should also be as intriguing as you can make them. Try not to begin a chapter with a flat, factual statement, but start instead with an anecdote or scene that will help establish the mood and lead the reader into the main part of the chapter.

For example, the chapter on Hadrian's Wall in *Walls* might have begun with a straight recital of facts: "Hadrian's Wall bears the name of the Roman emperor, Hadrian, who ordered its construction after he visited Rome's northernmost colony, England, in 122 A.D." Instead I decided to save that sentence for later and began the chapter with the following paragraphs:

> The Roman soldier shivers as he gazes out from the top of Hadrian's Wall at the rolling lands of northern England. It is a chilly October morning in 135 A.D., and a ground fog obscures the view.

The soldier leans against the protective five-foot-high parapet on the north side of the wall's flat top, and peers through the mist. Is that a band of roving barbarians out there? He looks more closely. No, it's just the shadow of a hill.

With a sigh of relief, the soldier turns away from the parapet and continues his patrol along the great stone wall. It rises fifteen feet above the surrounding countryside and stretches to a width of almost ten feet. If the soldier were to walk its entire length, he would cover a distance of more than seventy miles.

These paragraphs convey many basic facts about Hadrian's Wall while at the same time dramatizing it in a way that I hoped would be more inviting to young readers. I try to achieve a similar effect with all of my chapter openings but I don't always succeed. If, as is sometimes the case, the material resists a dramatic approach, it's better not to force the issue, but to settle for a more direct opening paragraph. Opportunities for drama are bound to come up later in the chapter.

While most reviewers and librarians today are opposed to the use of invented dialogue in juvenile nonfiction, especially in biographies, a nonfiction writer can almost always enliven the text with well-chosen quotations and extracts from actual conversations. These can be humorous, like the precepts from Erasmus's 16th-century book on manners, titled *On Civility in Children,* that I quoted in *From Hand to Mouth.* Here are a few examples: "Take the first piece of meat or fish that you touch, and don't poke around in the pot for a bigger one." "Don't pick your nose when eating and then reach for more food." "Don't throw bones you have chewed back in the pot. Put them on the table or toss them on the floor."

Or the quotations can be impassioned, like the words of Nathan Straus, the New York philanthropist who led a 20-year battle to make pasteurization compulsory in the United States. In *Milk,* I quoted the following extract from a telegram that Straus sent to the Chicago Board of Aldermen:

The pasteurization ordinance for which you are fighting means lives of babies saved; its defeat means babies killed. Can Chicago hesitate between these alternatives?

(pp. 29-33)

Crucial as the chapter opening is in getting a reader into the chapter; the ending is equally so in summing up its content and pointing the way toward the next chapter. A novelist often plants a dramatic hook or question in the last paragraph of a chapter, and so do many nonfiction writers.

The hook can be designed to pique the reader's curiosity, like this chapter ending in *From Hand to Mouth:* "The Industrial Revolution, which started in England in the late 1700s, would spur the growth of mass production, including the manufacture of table utensils. And the people of a new nation, the United States of America, would develop their own unique way of using those utensils."

Or the hook can generate suspense, like the concluding

paragraph of the chapter on atomic radiation in *Milk:* "People throughout the world aren't likely to forget the alarm they felt in the 1950s and 1960s when they first realized how easily our environment—and one of our most basic foods—can be poisoned. Meanwhile, new threats to milk have made their appearance in the 1970s and 1980s. This time they haven't come from the sky, but from right here on earth."

There's only one thing no climactic chapter hook should ever do: promise something the following chapter doesn't deliver. That isn't playing fair with the reader.

The narrative techniques I've described so far—the overall direction of the book, careful pacing, lively quotations and anecdotes, effective chapter openings and closings—all build, of course, toward the last chapter.

In fiction, this chapter contains the climax of the story and the denouement. So does the concluding chapter in a nonfiction book, although there the climax may not be so obvious. Then come the final paragraphs—the denouement, so to speak—in which, as a summation of everything that has gone before, the ultimate point of the book should emerge.

This "point" can be serious, as in these last lines from *Walls:*

Today, in the atomic age, some leaders and scientists are still seeking the ultimate defensive wall. But perhaps the time has finally come to admit that no such wall is possible. Confronted by nuclear weapons, any nation that wants to feel secure in the future will have to reach some sort of understanding with its enemies. It can't hope to achieve security by building a wall.

Or it can convey a lighter message, like the concluding sentences in *From Hand to Mouth:*

What's likely is that people in both East and West will continue to experiment with one another's table utensils. And who knows? Perhaps in time they will find a common solution to that age-old problem: how to get food as swiftly, gracefully, and neatly as possible from hand to mouth.

Whichever tone seems appropriate, one element in the conclusion will always be the same, and it's as characteristic of the best nonfiction as it is of the finest fiction. This is the sense that in books, as in life, the story never really ends. Especially not in nonfiction aimed at an audience of young readers who, when they grow up, are bound to write new chapters of their own on every conceivable subject. (pp. 34-5)

James Cross Giblin, "A Nonfiction Writer Is a Storyteller," in his Writing Books for Young People, *The Writer, Inc., Publishers, 1990, pp. 29-35.*

GENERAL COMMENTARY

Allen Raymond

Today, when [James Cross Giblin] puts on his business hat, he's Editor-in-Chief and Publisher for Clarion Books, an imprint of Tignor & Fields, a Houghton Mifflin Company.

Or, if he puts on his writing hat, he's the award-winning author of nine nonfiction books for children, beginning with *The Scarecrow Book*. . . . (p. 45)

His books are what he calls "photo essays." That is, they are picture books with the text kept to a bare minimum.

In the October 1988 issue of *School Library Journal* he wrote, "*The Scarecrow Book* was edited by Norma Jean Sawicki. I often bristled when Norma Jean slashed through some of my favorite passages in the early drafts and scrawled in the margins, 'Compress; this rambles too much' or 'Cut; not necessary; the illustration will convey this.'

"But by the time the book reached the final stages of production, I realized she was right. The text hadn't lost anything by being tightened; instead, I could now see that it was stronger than before."

Jim Giblin takes one to two years to research a book, and keeps all of his notes on 4″ x 6″ cards. He enjoys the research, but sometimes says he "has so many cards I get depressed. You can carry on the research too long; it can be an excuse for not writing."

"I want to be thorough, though," he says. "I want my books to have depth."

When he starts to write, and even during the research process, he's "letting my mind go—sort of free association." He's searching for the thread, "the narrative line" as he puts it, which will hold the book together.

For instance, in *Chimney Sweeps: Yesterday and Today,* he writes, "Imagine yourself travelling back in time to a quiet street in London, England, in the year 1800. It is just before dawn, and the chimneys on top of the five-story brick houses are outlined against a pale pink sky.

"Suddenly a loud cry breaks the silence. 'All up!'

"Then the head of a small boy pokes up from the chimney of one of the houses. His face is covered with a knitted cap, with holes for the eyes, nose and mouth. The cap was once navy blue, but now it is black from chimney soot."

Grabs your interest, doesn't it?

That's the way Jim Giblin begins his books, and no matter what the topic—for instance, he's written books on walls, eating utensils—readers are soon caught up in the romance, the history and the mystery surrounding the topic.

"I try to write what I would be interested in reading," he says. Jim Giblin is a storyteller—but his stories are true.

In *The Skyscraper Book* he tells the story about how Major William LeBaron Jenney, a Chicago architect and engineer, first concluded it would be possible to use an iron-and-steel frame in the construction of a tall building.

"According to one story," Giblin writes, "Major Jenney first realized how strong a steel frame could be when he got angry at the squawkings of the family parrot. He slammed a heavy book down on the parrot's steel wire cage, and was surprised when the wires neither bent nor cracked.

"Thus he became the builder of the first skyscraper, the simplest definition of which is 'a modern building of great height constructed on a steel skeleton.' "

It would be easy to believe that Jim Giblin is like that wire cage—hard to crush. He's built a long and distinguished career in book publishing, and that takes talent, lots of it. And, to survive, one must be "uncrushable."

But there seems to be something more to Jim Giblin. As an editor one senses he's sensitive to the trials and tribulations of those with whom he deals—mostly authors. (pp. 45-6)

He's now working on a book for adults, *Writing Books for Young People.* It's a how-to book, and his sensitivity comes through in these closing paragraphs written for would-be authors of children's books:

> Writing books for children . . . is never easy. But few other types of writing are as rewarding, for unlike most adult books, a children's book can have a unique and lasting impact on its impressionable young readers.
>
> . . . the picture book, nonfiction book or novel that you're working on today may be enjoyed by thousands of young readers in a few years' time, and still be alive in their memories 50 years from now.
>
> Consciously or unconsciously, that's one of the goals most children's book authors aim for . . . and many achieve it. I hope you do, too.

What a nice way to end a book. But then, it's to be expected of Jim Giblin, whose own books have already achieved that goal. (p. 46)

> *Allen Raymond, "James Cross Giblin: Storyteller of Nonfiction," in* Teaching/K-8, *Vol. 19, No. 3, November-December, 1988, pp. 44-6.*

TITLE COMMENTARY

The Scarecrow Book (with Dale Ferguson, 1980)

The Giblin-Ferguson collaboration is so lively, literate and mesmerizing that it's hard to believe the book is their first. The text is as full of information about "bird shooers" as the cornucopia of a protected crop. Period and contemporary pictures and photos illustrate the scarecrow's history from the days of ancient Egypt onward and show several intriguing devices (fearful creatures fashioned by Zuñi Indian children during the late 1800s, clappers used by small boys and girls in medieval England, etc.) and imposing figures guarding fields in America and other countries today. Some are rather pitiable creations, a few are quite foreboding and many are unexpectedly funny. Readers will undoubtedly want to make their own variations of the scarecrow depicted in the book's bonus: clear, easily understood directions with drawings guiding the hands through all the steps.

Giblin, age four, with his mother.

A review of "The Scarecrow Book," in Publishers Weekly, *Vol. 218, No. 18, October 31, 1980, p. 85.*

The variety of solutions that diverse cultures have used to solve a common problem is clearly displayed in an exceptionally well-produced book. The authors describe scarecrows and other deterrents to birds that destroy crops (a tape recording of frightened birds; children or old people guarding fields), including modern-day methods as well as methods used 3000 years ago. Facts, myths and legends make up the conversational, well-written text; the clean design on 10″ x 8″ pages facilitates browsing and highlights photos and reproductions that give some idea of the variety of scarecrows around the world. Instructions for making a conventional scarecrow are appended, but the pictures offer more interesting ideas. The book would be helpful to gardners and useful in an art or social studies class.

Sally Holmes Holtze, in a review of "The Scarecrow Book," in School Library Journal, *Vol. 27, No. 3, November, 1980, p. 62.*

Broad margins and large, well-spaced type contribute to the spacious, attractive format of a book that is plentifully illustrated by photographs and reproductions of prints showing scarecrows. The text gives ample historical coverage as well as describing the various kinds of scarecrows that are in use today, and it carefully distinguishes among fact, conjecture, and legend or superstition. Written in a direct, straightforward style and based on solid research, this makes it clear that there have been—and are—all sorts of devices (including human beings) to scare crows away in addition to the most familiar scarecrow, the effigy.

Zena Sutherland, in a review of "The Scarecrow Book," in Bulletin of the Center for Children's Books, *Vol. 34, No. 7, March, 1981, p. 133.*

The Skyscraper Book   (1981)

Giblin offers a balanced, well-researched survey of urban "skyscrapers" from the 1880s to the 1980s. His text focuses on individual buildings, chiefly in Chicago and New York, that are representative of the architecture of their times. With the exception of the Tribune building in Chicago, which is not pictured, all the main examples discussed in the text are to be seen in excellent photographs [by David Anderson and taken from historical archives]. Small, fine-line drawings [by Anthony Kramer] illustrate structural devices and architectural details. While the text is basically a history of architectural styles, Giblin's lively account includes curious facts about financial backers and their motivations, comments on the public reaction to the presence of these huge structures and remarks on the social implications of the skyscrapers. The book will help city children, particularly, to look at their surroundings with new appreciation. (pp. 70-1)

> *Shirley Wilton, in a review of "The Skyscraper Book," in* School Library Journal, *Vol. 28, No. 4, December, 1981, pp. 70-1.*

[Giblin] writes thoughtfully and with infectious enthusiasm about the skyscraper as a barometer of twentieth-century values and aspirations. He neatly braids strands of essential information on building technology with sharp-eyed observations of structural and decorative details, very sound architectural history, and fresh anecdotes about some famous builders, architects, and even some breathless tourists of times past. The illustrations are not worthy of the text, unfortunately. Some needed ones aren't there; photos range from adequate to inarticulately small or distortive; and some of the drawings are confusingly tiny and minimally captioned. Glossary, bibliography, and index.

> *Julia M. Ehresmann, in a review of "The Skyscraper Book," in* Booklist, *Vol. 78, No. 7, December 1, 1981, p. 496.*

Giblin's thoroughly developed text, illustrated with photographs from historic collections as well as the current photography of David Anderson and sketches by Anthony Kramer, merits the attention of readers of all ages. The discussion of the contribution of various schools of architecture to the skyscraper's development is especially interesting. Architects such as Louis Sullivan, Eliel Saarinen, Mies van der Rohe, and Philip Johnson become more than mere names as the story of the 20th century entwines them with their work and introduces the challenges of the next century. Although a book should not be judged by its cover, the black cover of **The Skyscraper Book** could have been made more attractive to readers. Nonetheless, this is an appropriate centennial observance of Chicago's first iron and steel frame, the Home Insurance Company Building designed by Major Jenney, and a salute to the tallest building in the world, now the Sears Tower in Chicago, birthplace of the skyscraper.

> *S. W. Dobyns, in a review of "The Skyscraper Book," in* Science Books & Films, *Vol. 17, No. 5, May-June, 1982, p. 265.*

Chimney Sweeps: Yesterday and Today   (1982)

The reappearance of chimney sweeps, combined with their earlier incarnation as pitiable small boys, makes for an appealing, instructive mix of technological, economic, and social history. After juxtaposing a pair of modern, vacuum-cleaner-equipped sweeps with yesteryear's scrambling, bare-chested lad (emerging jubilantly from the chimney, in Margot Tomes' puckish picture), Giblin explains why and how chimneys were first built, and the need for sweeps arose. In Germany, we learn, sweeping became a regular, regularized profession in the 1400s when twice-yearly cleaning of chimneys was mandated. (On the Continent, mandatory sweeping, and greater respect for sweeps, has been the norm.) But it was in England, in the 1700s—when flues grew smaller and more crooked, and sooty coal replaced cleaner-burning wood—that recourse was had to young boys, "small enough to crawl up the new chimneys and clean out the soot by hand." Giblin reconstructs a climbing boy's day; recounts the efforts of reformers to improve their lot or, best of all, ban child sweeps; chronicles the different history of sweeps in America (where "the boys were usually treated better"—except for the many who were black); and concludes with particulars on sweeps today. (Most do it in their spare time; women as well as men are involved; the pay can be very good.) As narrator, Giblin is commendably relaxed and precise—and there are curiosity-piquing present-day photos, as well as the storybookish illustrations.

> *A review of "Chimney Sweeps: Yesterday and Today," in* Kirkus Reviews, *Vol. L, No. 18, September 15, 1982, p. 1059.*

William Blake wrote about them. So did Charles Dickens, Ben Franklin and generations of English pamphleteers. Benjamin Britten made them the centerpiece of his 1940's stage work *Let's Make an Opera.*

In fact, the black-rocked, black-hatted chimney sweep, as James Giblin points out in this compactly entertaining little history, has always fascinated. Mr. Giblin has blended fact and folklore into a smoothly readable narrative that runs from the first chimneys of the Norman castle builders, through the child-labor abuses of early industrial England, to the revival of sweeps, stoves and chimneys in the energy-conserving 80's.

There are even fascinating sidelights on the black slave sweeps of the antebellum American South, who escaped to ply their trade in the cities of the North. Mr. Giblin has included a sample street cry of a black sweep offering his services to the householders of New York or Hartford.

The book is well laid out for quick and easy reading, the chapters short, the art, unfortunately, a jumble of styles, the pen-and-ink drawings depicting Dickens's day at odds with the photographs of modern freelance sweeps. Margot Tomes's appealing illustrations of the Victorian apprentices—small victims of England's coal age who worked and slept in soot—seem a trifle too well scrubbed for the sooty little wretches dealt with so poignantly in the text.

> *Ann Sperber, in a review of "Chimney Sweeps: Yesterday and Today," in* The New York Times Book Review, *November 21, 1982, p. 43.*

James Giblin explores the history, folklore and romance of the chimney sweep in this introduction to an old and colorful profession. Following the sweep from his European beginnings to his present-day operation in America, the author details changes and developments in practice. He emphasizes the special contribution of the climbing boys, exploited children who were employed to free soot from the increasingly narrow—and dangerous—chimneys of 19th-Century town houses, and discusses the Parliamentary reforms which liberated those children from cruel, enforced labor. Giblin's relaxed, affable manner belies the amount of information he offers in this highly accessible, enjoyable history of the chimney sweep.

> *Amy L. Cohn, in a review of "Chimney Sweeps: Yesterday and Today," in* School Library Journal, *Vol. 29, No. 5, January, 1983, p. 75.*

Fireworks, Picnics, and Flags: The Story of the Fourth of July Symbols (1983)

Giblin has also been praised for [his] books of nonfiction, written with enthusiasm and clarity. The author pays tribute to the late Edna Barth, whose texts on the symbols of other holidays he edited. This was to be her seventh, in collaboration with Arndt, who illustrates the Independence Day doings colorfully here. It is fun and educational to find out about the genesis of the Declaration of Independence and observations in various parts of the country since the first Fourth of July celebration through the splashy Bicentennial. Probably nothing will match the thrills of that day in 1976 with the Tall Ships in the harbors on the eastern seaboard, the gigantic fireworks displays in Washington, D.C., the marvelous concert by the Boston Pops and other spectacular doings. But Giblin includes, as he always does, intriguing descriptions of little-known aspects of inventions, etc., linked to "let freedom ring" that make his book outstanding.

> *A review of "Fireworks, Picnics and Flags," in* Publishers Weekly, *Vol. 223, No. 20, May 20, 1983, p. 236.*

Giblin was the editor of Edna Barth's books on holiday symbols; according to his author's note, he knew that Barth intended to write about the Fourth of July and took on the project himself after her death. The result is consistent in both format and spirit with the well-known Barth series, complete with Arndt's unpretentious two-color drawings. The background that places the holiday in its historical context is not effectively organized: opening with the signing of the Declaration of Independence on July 4, the text shifts back in time to the origins of the American Revolution and the circumstances leading up to the writing and adoption of the Declaration. After this jumpy start, however, Giblin launches into a fascinating discussion of early celebrations, followed by informative chapters about holiday customs (the showing of the flag, fireworks, picnics, patriotic music) and symbols (Uncle Sam, the bald eagle, the Liberty Bell). A list of important events that occurred on July 4 (such as the opening of the first transpacific cable in 1903) is appended along with an index.

> *Karen Stang Hanley, in a review of "Fireworks, Picnics, and Flags," in* Booklist, *Vol. 79, No. 22, August, 1983, p. 1464.*

In a crisp, conversational style enlivened with poignant, homely, or dramatic details, the author discusses important Independence Day traditions by placing each one in a historical context and indicating its evolution into an annual ritual. From the beginning chapters, which focus on the establishment of July 4 as the national holiday, to the appended chronology of noteworthy events which have occurred on that date, the narrative is readable social history, a worthy addition to the earlier holiday books written by the late Edna Barth. The tensions between Britain and the colonies which culminated in the proclamation of independence in 1776 are summarized. Succeeding chapters are devoted to the genesis of national symbols and customs—for example, the flag, fireworks, picnics, parades, patriotic songs, the eagle, and the Liberty Bell—as well as to examples of traditions indigenous to a specific locale, such as the National Fence Painting Contest in Hannibal, Missouri. Concluding sections highlight the Centennial of 1876 and the Bicentennial of 1976. Formality is leavened with frivolity, and splendor balanced with simplicity to indicate that July 4 is also a family celebration. . . . (pp. 461-62)

> *Mary M. Burns, in a review of "Fireworks, Picnics, and Flags," in* The Horn Book Magazine, *Vol. LIX, No. 4, August, 1983, pp. 461-62.*

Walls: Defenses throughout History (1984)

This chronologically arranged book is a fascinating account of the use and development of walls to protect life and culture through the ages. The scope of **Walls** is broad, ranging from Ice-Age man's mammoth-bone walls to the Maginot Line of World War II to the possibility of a wall of satellites in space. In many ways Giblin's study is a military history, and the art of war and its accouterments are explained. A selected assortment of castles and forts is included, and there are explanations of how and why they were constructed, the methods used to siege a castle and a brief description of the people who inhabited these fortresses. There are chapters on Hadrian's Wall and the Great Wall of China, as well as forts in American history. While not a definitive study, **Walls** does offer an additional dimension to material at this level. Well researched, easy to read and amply illustrated with black-and-white photographs, drawings and reproductions, this fine overview of the subject works as supplemental study information and will be enjoyed by history buffs.

> *L. R. Little, in a review of "Walls: Defenses throughout History," in* School Library Journal, *Vol. 31, No. 5, January, 1985, p. 85.*

The topic may sound unpromising, but award-winning nonfiction writer Giblin's survey of defensive walls through history is as intriguing as it is comprehensive. The account begins with a discussion of Stone-Age barriers—probably walls made of mammoth bones—and moves smoothly on to ancient and medieval walled cities; free-standing defensive walls (Hadrian's Wall and the Great Wall of China); castles of Europe, England, and Japan; and walls designed to deflect artillery fire, with a chapter-long look at American forts of the eighteenth and nineteenth centuries. Examinations of World War I trenches, the Maginot Line, the Berlin Wall, and proposals for a satellite "wall" in space extend the study into contemporary times. The volume is exceptionally well focused: different historical periods are represented by detailed descriptions of a few well-chosen structures, and a barrage of technical terminology is introduced with proficient clarity. Throughout, the author traces developments in warfare and weaponry that prompted corollary changes in defensive structures, and his telling wrap-up points out the practical futility of walls in the face of today's nuclear arsenals. Explanatory diagrams and drawings are accompanied by excellently reproduced black-and-white photographs gleaned from a variety of sources; in a few instances, labels or arrows would have been helpful in pointing out distinctive features to the untrained eye. Altogether a stellar piece of architectural and social history, a factual tour de force.

> *Karen Stang Hanley, in a review of "Walls: Defenses throughout History," in* Booklist, *Vol. 81, No. 10, January 15, 1985, p. 715.*

Whether with mammoth bones or with reinforced concrete, people have endeavored to provide protection from the attacks of their enemies. Each massive and often ingenious defense has almost always been met by equally inventive means of assault. In an interesting, well-planned, and thoroughly illustrated history of the subject, the author has chosen vivid examples starting from the most primitive of walls to the highly sophisticated Maginot Line. The brief, clear text gives the historical background and explains the plans and reasoning behind the various fortifications. Reflections on the Great Wall of China, Hadrian's Wall, and the infamous Berlin Wall offer the reader moments of sober thought. Although the author does not necessarily intend the book as anti-war propaganda, the account of money spent, of the years of labor involved, and of the appalling expenditure of lives transmits its own message. (pp. 66-7)

> *Ethel R. Twichell, in a review of "Walls: Defenses throughout History," in* The Horn Book Magazine, *Vol. LXI, No. 1, January-February, 1985, pp. 66-7.*

The Truth about Santa Claus (1985)

Doing his usual good job of research and well-organized presentation, Giblin describes the various truths, legends, and accretions that evolved or (like the Clement Moore poem) were grafted to produce the characteristics of the Santa Claus figure familiar today, sleigh, reindeer octet, red suit, and all. Reproductions of paintings and cartoons, as well as photographs, illustrate both the diverse European legends and the contemporary Santa Claus figure. A bibliography adds to the usefulness of a book that not only gives information about Santa Claus (Kris Kringle, Father Christmas, the Christ-kind, and other gift-bringers as well) but also gives an interesting picture of the ways in which customs arise, fuse, change, are diffused only to change again.

> *Zena Sutherland, in a review of "The Truth about Santa Claus," in* Bulletin of the Center for Children's Books, *Vol. 39, No. 1, September, 1985, p. 8.*

Giblin delves into the magical world of Santa Claus. Beginning with an in-depth account of Nicholas (280 A.D.), he develops numerous chapters from this story—"St. Nicholas, the Gift-Bringer"; "Nicholas the Man"; "Saint Nicholas." The Americanization of Santa Claus is a more familiar story, but Giblin adds plenty of fresh detail. At first glance, it may seem trivial to have such a thorough investigation of Santa Claus, but Giblin has such a flare for historic detail and research that he translates hoards of tales into a singular creation of Santa Claus. Children will benefit unknowingly from the brief lesson on world history and trace Santa's genealogy through the 30 magnificent black-and-white photographs and reproductions. Margot Tomes' cover illustration makes the book an appealing title to display. This one won't stay on the shelves long!

> *Peggy Forehand, in a review of "The Truth about Santa Claus," in* School Library Journal, *Vol. 32, No. 2, October, 1985, p. 192.*

Writing with the same straightforward thoroughness that characterizes **Walls: Defenses Throughout History,** the author explores another subject of interest to many readers: the history of Santa Claus. The original Saint Nicholas—tall, thin Bishop Nicholas of Asia Minor—had no connection whatsoever with Christmas itself. But following his death fifteen hundred years ago, that wise, kind-hearted man became the patron saint of sailors, marriageable maidens, and children, and various legends about him quickly sprouted up. In tracing the evolution of Saint Nicholas as a gift-bringer, the author describes the emergence of such figures as the German Christkindel and the English Father Christmas and discusses the creation of the American Santa Claus. The book also includes objections to the Santa Claus image voiced by those who feel he has become too much a figure of commercialism. As always in Giblin's work, historical details slide naturally into the text, and one finishes the book with the satisfying feeling of having digested a substantial amount of information—but in the most pleasant and interesting way.

> *Karen Jameyson, in a review of "The Truth about Santa Claus," in* The Horn Book Magazine, *Vol. LXI, No. 6, November-December, 1985, p. 719.*

The "truth" about Santa? Debunking the myth of the jolly fat man whose name is virtually synonymous with Christmas seems downright unpatriotic. But Giblin has not set out to debunk, but rather to explain, and the result is a cogent, concise work of non-fiction that reads like a story. It informs *and* entertains.

Author of the acclaimed ***Chimney Sweeps: Yesterday and Today, Walls,*** and ***The Skyscraper Book,*** Giblin has done considerable research into his latest subject. . . .

Giblin's perspective is balanced and objective; there's a wealth of information here, but it's neither overwhelming nor dull. Photos, prints, works of art, and a marvelous jacket by Margot Tomes provide visual counterpoint. Yes,

Giblin as a young editor in 1964.

Virginia, there *is* a Santa Claus, and Giblin has brought him to life.

> *A review of "The Truth about Santa Claus," in* Kirkus Reviews, *Vol. LIII, No. 24, December 15, 1985, p. 1400.*

Milk: The Fight for Purity (1986)

A thorough, competent history of public health hazards connected with milk consumption describes the most common disease-causing bacteria and the surprisingly long-drawn battle to require pasteurization. Although the writing is smooth, it lacks the spark of Giblin's earlier books on chimney sweeps, scarecrows, and Santa Claus, perhaps because the topic is not as light. Still, the facts are well-organized and integrated into historical (and medical) context. Readers will find the book useful for research if not alluring to browse through. With black-and-white photographs, prints, and a solid bibliography.

> *Betsy Hearne, in a review of "Milk: The Fight for Purity," in* Bulletin of the Center for Children's Books, *Vol. 40, No. 3, November, 1986, p. 48.*

Giblin's carefully constructed account of the major causes of contamination of this most basic food product is by no means sensational, but the information the author presents is surprising and thought provoking. He points out that it has been only about 150 years since a real awareness of the consequences of impure milk developed to any extent, and for many of the subsequent years, indifference, ignorance, and greed impeded progress in making milk clean and safe. The focus is on three major areas in the fight against contamination: the nineteenth-century swill-milk dairies run as adjuncts of distilleries in most American cities, the scientific and political battles to enforce the practice of pasteurization, and the recent decades of radioactive infiltration. Set in an attractive format, the substantial text will be challenging reading for the audience most likely to use the book; it incorporates social history, scientific discovery, and technological devices along with a sketch of the long campaign for safe milk waged by New York businessman and philanthropist Nathan Straus. Though the nearly incredible death rate among infants and young children has been radically reduced, the conclusion is cautionary. In recent years occasional cases of contaminated milk supplies have affected large areas and thousands of people, and safeguards must ever be improved and enforced. The book is illustrated with a good selection of photographs and early drawings, but the bibliography of the author's sources does not include materials for further reading by children.

> *Margaret A. Bush, in a review of "Milk: The Fight for Purity," in* The Horn Book Magazine, *Vol. LXIII, No. 2, March-April, 1987, p. 220.*

Milk. How boring! How seemingly sterile, one might say. Judging from this book's title and cover illustration, I had to force myself to open it. But . . . if you really want to know what's behind that glass of cold milk, keep reading. James Giblin has transferred a commonplace glass of milk into an intriguing phenomenon. At the center of the journey towards pasteurization was Mr. Nathan Straus, a New York businessman of the early 20th Century. Mr. Straus's pasteurized milk depots proved the saving grace for thousands of infants, infants whose milk had been laced with chalk, soot, bacteria and a host of other impurities. Bacteria thriving in whiskey swill and fed to dairy cattle had caused outbreaks of tuberculosis, typhoid fever and diptheria. Ironically, some of Straus's most bitter opponents were physicians, milk distributors and health personnel. Although Nathan Strauss succeeded in his battle for pasteurization laws, the struggle for pure milk is far from over. (pp. 38-9)

This is a very readable book—informative, concise and interesting. It isn't everyone that can make a glass of milk intriguing. The curious eight year old and his elders will find **Milk** captivating! (p. 39)

> *James B. Maland, in a review of "Milk: The Fight for Purity," in* Appraisal: Science Books for Young People, *Vol. 20, No. 3, Summer, 1987, pp. 38-9.*

From Hand to Mouth: Or, How We Invented Knives, Forks, Spoons, and Chopsticks and the Table Manners to Go with Them (1987)

Another highly informative and entertaining glimpse of social history from the author of **Chimney Sweeps.**

Tracing "that age-old problem: how to get food as swiftly, gracefully, and neatly as possible from hand to mouth" takes Giblin back to prehistory, where the point of a knife, invented for other purposes, must have served to convey meat too hot to touch to a hungry mouth and so became the first alternative to fingers. By discussing the evolution of materials used for flatware, he reviews human technology. Economics and fashion also shape tools, which in their turn shape manners: the spectacular ruffs worn in 17th-century Holland prompted longer handles and larger bowls for spoons used for soup; Richelieu probably ordered the ends of knives to be rounded to prevent unsightly picking of teeth at the table. Giblin even knows why Americans, unlike Europeans, transfer their forks from hand to hand. The chapter on chopsticks includes usable instructions on how to hold them. Each detail is not only fascinating in itself but illuminates the society from which it comes. Midway, a quote from Erasmus epitomizes the civility of its time; by the 1920's Emily Post had overruled most of his prescriptions—but in the 1980's we are returning to our fingers, which have always been the primary conveyors of food for many around the world.

This microcosmic view of historical change is attractively illustrated with black-and-white photos and reproductions of contemporary pictures, well-chosen to expand the text. Bibliography, index.

> *A review of "From Hand to Mouth," in* Kirkus Reviews, *Vol. LV, No. 18, September 15, 1987, p. 1392.*

With the same fluid anecdotal writing style found in his earlier books, Giblin traces the history of eating utensils and customs from the ancient world to the present. . . . Readers will be especially interested in the information on eating customs and table manners in different eras and cultures. One chapter is devoted to the history of chopsticks, including the differences between Chinese and Japanese uses and easy-to-follow instructions on how to master chopsticks. This title may not have the immediate appeal of some of Giblin's earlier titles, as eating utensils are not as fascinating as skyscrapers, as romantic as chimney sweeps, or as popular as Santa Claus, but like his book on milk, this look at everyday items offers some fascinating and entertaining information. It is a well-organized and spryly written account, generously illustrated with photographs and period reproductions (including a hilarious photo of a 1950s dinner party), of a subject rarely discussed in children's books. Those who pick it up for reports or browsing won't be disappointed.

> *Heide Piehler, in a review of "From Hand to Mouth; or, How We Invented Knives, Forks, Spoons, and Chopsticks & the Table Manners to Go with Them," in* School Library Journal, *Vol. 34, No. 3, November, 1987, p. 108.*

The eating habits and use of utensils of different peoples and cultures throughout history are the subject matter of this ambitious work. Giblin highlights the contrast and tension between East and West with amusing episodes. When forks, first used in the royal courts of the Middle East, were introduced to the people of Venice, a church leader declared, "God in his wisdom has provided man with natural forks—his fingers." And when a Chinese writer first saw Europeans using knives, he said, "What barbarians! They eat with swords." Giblin treats the mores and styles of other cultures from a Western perspective, sometimes linking foreign eating styles to unsanitary habits and infectious disease rather than describing reasons based in religion or culture. The material is illustrated imaginatively with etchings, drawings of banquet scenes and photographs of utensils—ancient Roman and Egyptian knives and spoons through to modern cutlery. One of the most intriguing nonfiction ideas to come along in seasons.

> *A review of "From Hand to Mouth," in* Publishers Weekly, *Vol. 232, No. 22, November 27, 1987, p. 87.*

Let There Be Light: A Book about Windows (1988)

Another splendid slice of social history by the author of **Chimney Sweeps, Milk** and **From Hand to Mouth.**

From caves to mirror-skinned skyscrapers, a period's climate, evolving-technology, and social forces have influenced dwellings and the apertures that let light and air into them and allow people to see out. Ancient homes faced an inner courtyard, avoiding the dangers and odors of the street; in other times, windows were barricaded against vandals. But people have always been glad of spacious windows, from the conservatories of the wealthy to Philip Johnson's all-glass house. Ranging to the far North and the Orient, while concentrating on Europe and North America, Giblin describes both the typical and the unusual, castles and cathedrals as well as domestic architecture, the many materials other than glass (e.g., oiled paper, horn, and thin slices of marble) used for glazing, and a wealth of architectual details and devices. Windows may be a fine art, like stained glass, both medieval and modern; their destruction may be a significant historical event, as in the bombing of Dresden or Hiroshima; yet they will be needed "as long as people have eyes to see, hearts to feel, and a healthy curiosity about the world around them."

A mind-expanding survey that includes a careful bibliography and source notes, arranged by chapter and with books for children noted. Many carefully reproduced, well-chosen photos and works of art, including a color section on stained glass; index.

> *A review of "Let There Be Light: A Book about Windows," in* Kirkus Reviews, *Vol. LVI, No. 16, August 15, 1988, p. 1239.*

Including "curiosity" as well as light and air among the reasons people put holes in their dwellings, Giblin's historical survey of windows covers a good 12,000 years and an equally impressive span of cultures. Details of glass and papermaking are thorough, and there is a smooth blend of technological and architectural developments. As was true of the author's **From Hand to Mouth,** social commentary runs fluently throughout: why Moslems constructed windows that allowed one to see out but not in; the differences between cultures that built windows facing a courtyard and those that built them facing the outside. This is

Holding the American Book Awared (a relief designed by Louise Nevelson) for Chimney Sweeps, *1983.*

as much a history of how people live as it is a history of windows, and Giblin's impeccable research shines through.

Roger Sutton, in a review of "Let There Be Light: A Book about Windows," in Bulletin of the Center for Children's Books, *Vol. 42, No. 3, November, 1988, p. 71.*

In his 1984 book **Walls: Defenses Throughout History,** James Cross Giblin took a brisk walk through geography and time from ancient Jericho to Carcassone and the Maginot Line. On it he saw a progression of walls intended to shelter cities and, sometimes, empires. He observed the fortifications at work and watched the life behind them. Mr. Giblin stitched his accounts of great defenses together by pointing out that no matter how high or thick, they usually failed. Clever men built walls and clever men overcame them. Jericho's tumbled, Fort Sumter was pounded to rubble and the Nazis sidestepped the Maginot on their way to Paris.

Let There Be Light: A Book About Windows is a similar performance. Using windows as a theme, Mr. Giblin takes another walk through geography and time, but this trip is extended. There is more to the story of windows than of old forts. Their history is a metaphor for civilization, and along the way the author comes upon the rise of architecture, politics, religious institutions, national myths, co-

lonialism, the development of manufacture, morality and much more. . . . In short, he has condensed a daunting body of material to provide young readers with a great deal of information about the evolution and technology of windows.

Windows, as Mr. Giblin views them, are principally agents for introducing light and air into a building and, conversely, for allowing the users of a building to see the out-of-doors. But windows do even more than this. They play a paramount role in achieving the look of a building. By electing not to treat this visual aspect, he has deprived his readers of a rich part of the story. Windows add rhythm, cadence and balance to the face of a building. They often create tension—a visual conversation—between themselves and the solid portions of that face, and that tension is important even to a casual viewer. It bears on how that viewer is going to feel about the building. Windows are wonderful, even mysterious, things, but by omitting a review of their responsibilities toward the mood of a facade, Mr. Giblin deprives us of a thick slice of that wonder.

Among the book's strengths is its clear definition of terms. Mr. Giblin introduces "dormer," "casement," "mullion," "transom" and the like by carefully describing their derivation and their functions. He also reminds us of the energy crisis of the 1970's and describes the technical improvements in windows that followed it. But what about the mutilated windows that accompanied it? Reducing window openings in existing buildings became something of a national sport, one that suspended architectural grace and generosity in many schools. Mr. Giblin's book is going to be read in those schools. He had a ripe opportunity to discuss the matter of visual harmony with people who feel its loss.

> *Philip M. Isaacson, in a review of "Let There Be Light," in* The New York Times Book Review, *March 12, 1989, p. 35.*

The Riddle of the Rosetta Stone: Key to Ancient Egypt (1990)

Take most children to an art museum—or let them take you—and they invariably come away especially intrigued by art and artifacts from ancient Egypt. Why? Because of the breathtaking scale of that civilization? Because the Egyptian mystique has many animals as motifs? Whatever, if you have present or potential Egyptophiles nearby, this book well warrants sharing.

This is the story of the Rosetta Stone: its discovery by the Greeks, its 1,400 years of secrecy, its ultimate deciphering, and its current place of distinction at the British Museum.

The black basalt slab—as easy to underestimate as America's Plymouth Rock—is enscripted with three languages including "hieroglyphics," which means "sacred carvings" in Greek. While the ancient Greeks found the stone and tried to comprehend it, it wasn't until Napoleon's occupation of Egypt in the late 1700s that the stone was rediscovered, though not decoded.

It was called the Rosetta Stone after the site near Alexandria where it was unearthed. When Napoleon's army lost Egypt to the British, the Rosetta went as booty to the conquerors. A succession of British scentists studied the stone beginning in the early 1800s, each making slow, steady headway with the hieroglyphics.

Much of the book is devoted to the painstaking methods by which Jean-Francois Champollion gradually made his translation breakthrough. (Fortuitously, Napoleon's scholars had made prints of the stone, which became available to the Frenchman.) Champollion piggybacked on the work of his predecessors, notably British scientist Thomas Young.

This book, in addition to some scrumptious Egyptology, offers the example of the rewards of patience and solid research. It took literally centuries to comprehend the Rosetta Stone. In our time of quick attention spans, when we need a new generation of scentists with a sense of posterity, this book makes for a great adventure.

> *Barbara Hall, in a review of "The Riddle of the Rosetta Stone: Key to Ancient Egypt," in* Book World—The Washington Post, *August 12, 1990, p. 8.*

Most children's books on Egyptian history make mention of the Rosetta Stone, but few (if any) give it the detailed attention of Giblin's book. This isn't a biography of Champollion, nor is it a dictionary of how to read hiero-

glyphs (as is Katan's *Hieroglyphs: The Writing of Ancient Egypt* [McElderry, 1981]). It's actually more of a "biography" of the stone itself. The writing style is a little dry, and somber photos and black-and-white illustrations lack the vivacity to catch a young reader's eye. But both adults and children will find this a solid reference source for reports or for more detailed information than general books on Egyptology provide. (p. 241)

> *Cathryn A. Camper, in a review of "The Riddle of the Rosetta Stone: Key to Ancient Egypt," in* School Library Journal, *Vol. 36, No. 9, September, 1990, pp. 240-41.*

The Rosetta Stone has become a popular emblem of the "Aha!" myth of archaeology; Giblin does a good and patient job of showing just how gradually the stone revealed its secrets. Discovered in 1799, it was more than a century before the stone was completely translated. Giblin shows us the false trails, piecemeal discoveries, and incremental analyses that followed the stone's discovery; along the way he unobtrusively shares lots of interesting information about hieroglyphs, Egyptian history, archaeology, and historiography. Accompanied by a translation of the stone's text, reading list, index, and plenty of photos and well-placed diagrams, this is ready-made for curriculum units on Egypt, but would be just as welcome in language arts classes. Better still, try it out with the kids who like codes. (pp. 59-60)

> *Roger Sutton, in a review of "The Riddle of the Rosetta Stone," in* Bulletin of the Center for Children's Books, *Vol. 44, No. 3, November, 1990, pp. 59-60.*

The Truth about Unicorns (1991)

Giblin's meticulously researched text examines the historical, mythical, religious and physical significance of the unicorn. He describes unicornlike creatures that have existed through the ages, beginning with a "dinosaur unicorn" that lived 120 million years ago. Also documented is the appearance of unicorns in writings by Greeks and Romans, tales from ancient China and the accounts of Marco Polo and other European explorers. An insert of color photos accompanies a detailed interpretation of the renowned Franco-Flemish Unicorn tapestries. Finally, Giblin examines some contemporary "unicorns," from a goat with a transplanted horn featured in the 1985 Ringling Brothers and Barnum & Bailey Circus to the endangered Indian rhino. [Michael] McDermott's carefully rendered, dramatic drawings complement the volume's many intriguing prints and photos. Through somewhat heavy going for the casual reader, this fact- and legend-filled book will be of great interest to youngsters fascinated by the elusive unicorn.

> *A review of "The Truth about Unicorns," in* Publishers Weekly, *Vol. 238, No. 44, October 4, 1991, p. 90.*

As always, whether his books are about windows, walls, table manners, or unicorns, Giblin's perspective is multicultural, his research scholarly, and his style casual and

Autographing books, Chautauqua, New York, 1988.

with photographs, maps and drawings. And all of them are produced with an attention to detail that makes them pleasures to hold and read.

The Truth About Unicorns shows Giblin at his usual best. He starts with the first mention of unicorns in the work of Ctesias (pronounced Tee-See-Us, 5th century B.C.), touches on animals that probably contributed to the legend (the dinosaur Monoclonius, the rhinoceros, narwhal and certain species of goat and antelope); relates the Indian legend of Risharinga, a beautiful young man with a horn in his forehead; tells the story of the Chinese unicorn Ki-Lin; analyzes the famous tapestries "La Dame a la Licorne" (with special color illustrations devoted just to them); and even brings in the notorious genetically altered goat, heralded as a "living unicorn" by the Ringling Brothers and Barnum & Bailey Circus. The whole is illustrated with original drawings by Michael McDermott and well-chosen reproductions of unicorns in art. A splendid book, one that Giblin need have no fear of blowing his own horn about.

> *Michael Dirda, in a review of "The Truth about Unicorns," in* Book World—The Washington Post, *November 10, 1991, p. 8.*

Edith Wilson: The Woman Who Ran the United States (1992)

Giblin's account of Edith Bolling Wilson's life is brisk but never clipped, and it focuses on her role as the president's wife. The subtitle refers to the responsibilities assumed by Edith Wilson after her husband was disabled by a stroke; her critics felt she assumed too much power, while her supporters admired her competence and industry. Giblin is objective in presenting the facts, and restrainedly admiring in his tone. An authorial afterword points out that all the dialogue, which is woven into the text with smooth naturalness, is taken either from the subject's correspondence with her husband or from her autobiography. This is part of a publisher's series that should be useful for both history and her story units.

> *Zena Sutherland, in a review of "Edith Wilson: The Woman Who Ran the United States," in* Bulletin of the Center for Children's Books, *Vol. 45, No. 8, April, 1992, p. 205.*

An informative and readable introduction to the life of an important First Lady. Giblin focuses primarily on the years after she became the wife of President Woodrow Wilson. He makes clear that throughout her lifetime, Edith Bolling Wilson succeeded in overcoming both personal and professional obstacles. Her marriage immediately put her into the country's political limelight and her strength and support for her husband were evident during the tumultous times of World War I and its aftermath. Her role during his illness is clearly explored. . . . For reports or pleasure reading, this simply written, well-organized volume captures this remarkable woman's personality and contributions to society. (pp. 121-22)

> *April L. Judge, in a review of "Edith Wilson: The Woman Who Ran the United States," in*

open, with vivid examples in story and pictures. McDermott's full-page, shaded drawings capture some of the romance and energy of the legendary creatures, though one love scene is pure schmaltz; it's hard to compete with the vigor and mystery of the medieval engravings and woodcuts reprinted here. What will hold everyone enthralled is the splendid color reproductions of the famous Unicorn Tapestries now in the Cloisters Museum in New York, and Giblin talks in some detail about the hunting story of the seven tapestry panels, what they symbolize, and what's known about their history from the sixteenth century through today. He also discusses real animals, such as the rhinoceros, which inspired the legends.

This is a book for whole-language classes on myth, art, and history. It's also for the dreamer who will want to pore over it alone.

> *Hazel Rochman, in a review of "The Truth about Unicorns," in* Booklist, *Vol. 88, No. 5, November 1, 1991, p. 524.*

Giblin does everything right. He picks odd, appealing topics like chimney sweeps, "the truth about Santa Claus," the invention of eating utensils, the decipherment of the Rosetta stone. He writes clear, unadorned prose, never talks down to kids and keeps the pages turning with plenty of anecdotes. Each of his books is intelligently illustrated

School Library Journal, *Vol. 38, No. 5, May, 1992, pp. 121-22.*

Peter Härtling

1933-

German author of fiction and short stories, and poet.

Major works include *Oma* (British edition as *Granny: The Story of Karl, Who Loses His Parents and Goes to Live with His Grandmother,* 1977), *Theo Runs Away* (1978), *Crutches* (1988), *Old John* (1990), *Ben Loves Anna* (1990).

A prominent German writer of juvenile and adult fiction, Härtling is distinguished for the realistic detail and emotional sensitivity of his stories, many of which are based on aspects of his own difficult childhood in World War II-era Germany. He believes, according to a 1977 lecture, that children's books "should not soothe, but disturb and rouse. They should make children curious about people and things, about the unknown in what they know, curious even about what is impossible." Judged by these standards, his works are enormously successful, for the style is uniformly direct, the characters unromanticized, the situational conflicts typically serious, and the outcomes genuinely moving—even, occasionally, profound. Härtling's predominant themes include: human imperfection and impermanence, the bonds between young and old, triumph over adversity, and the nurturing power of love. Although Härtling's works have been labeled inescapably European in tone and setting, the emotional, universal subject matter and vivid characters cross all national boundaries, contributing to their overall success in translation.

Born amid the rise of Nazism in his native land, Härtling lost both his parents during his adolescence. In 1945 his father perished while a prisoner of war in a Soviet camp; the following year, his mother committed suicide, leaving him and his sister to their grandmother's care. Although Härtling acquired some advanced education at a gymnasium in southwest Germany, he did not graduate. Beginning in 1952, he supported himself as a journalist, eventually becoming literary editor of the national daily *Deutsche Zeitung,* coeditor of the monthly journal *Der Monat,* as well as editor-in-chief of the Frankfurt publishing house S. Fischer. Coincident with these endeavors was Härtling's ascension, in adult literature, as a serious lyric poet and novelist, the prolific writer of such notable works as the historical novel *Niembsch oder Der Stillstand,* which earned him his first literary prize upon its publication in 1964.

Härtling's fame as a children's writer, a career only marginally related to his others, began with the publication of *Oma,* the first of his works to be translated into English and also that which perhaps most closely resembles his early life. Oma, which means grandmother in German, is a carefully drawn character, ill-tempered yet kind, hapless yet undaunted. To her has fallen the responsibility of caring for Karl (Kalle in the U.S. edition), her five-year-old grandson whose parents were killed in an automobile accident. The strong emotional bond that develops—though not without difficulty—over several years between the two

is evoked through a series of incidents which arise from their impoverished situation in working-class Munich, the differences in their ages, and Oma's thinly veiled, continuing dislike for Karl's mother. Thoughtful and poignant, *Oma* achieves its unusual depth not so much through a strong story line as through the indelible combination of character and milieu, underscored by Härtling's technique of allowing his elderly protagonist to comment at the end of each chapter on the events that have transpired.

Härtling's other works in translation—*Theo Runs Away, Crutches, Old John,* and, to a lesser degree, *Ben Loves Anna*—all share with *Oma* a concern for ordinary, extremely fallible protagonists who must come to terms with their stations in life and who ultimately embrace the love and aid of others. *Theo Runs Away* and *Crutches,* two stories of troubled boys who encounter unlikely father figures, are generally viewed as the most artistically successful, lending themselves to multilayered readings. However, *Old John,* the story of a 75-year-old eccentric who moves in with his daughter's family, is considered Härtling's most cohesive children's book. Told from the perspective of Jacob, Old John's grandson, this work is distinctive for its blend of humor and penetrating insight into the problems and blessings of life within a three-generation family. Critics agree that *Ben Loves Anna,* which focuses on the developing love between a ten-year-old boy and girl, and the teasing they must endure, is Härtling's least successful work. Here, his detached style is more pronounced than in his previous books, leaving his main characters and their assortment of shared feelings less than adequately portrayed. The work also suffers, according to several reviewers, from an overly Americanized translation in which the setting and other particulars have been awkwardly and needlessly altered.

Härtling's most disturbing, and instructive, book for older children, *Das war der Hirbel* (1973) is yet untranslated. Nominated in 1975 for the German Children's Book Award, *Hirbel* details the plight of a brain-damaged boy in the larger context of a society which is negligent in its treatment of the handicapped. Although less hopeful than any of Härtling's works in translation, *Hirbel* is emblematic of the author's approach to children's fiction in its unsparing honesty and its sympathy for the downtrodden. Härtling's honors include the German Youth Book Prize in 1976 for *Oma* and the Mildred Batchelder Prize for best children's book translation in 1989 for *Crutches,* a novel that also garnered a Best Book for Young Adults nomination.

(See also *Dictionary of Literary Biography,* Vol. 75.)

AUTHOR'S COMMENTARY

[*The following excerpt is from a speech which was originally delivered on the occasion of the 30th anniversary of the "Österreichische Jugendschriftenkommission" in 1977.*]

The number of cases of maltreated children is rapidly increasing—this is what I read while preparing this speech. And the number of children, ladies and gentlemen, is decreasing in most central European countries. It seems as if we are no longer capable of tolerating and encouraging new beginnings, as if we have abandoned our faith in the future.

The younger generation, anxious to maintain its independence and forever changing its attachments, has become the idol of the consumer society. Children and old people on the other hand demand social attention, care, the commitment of others—that is already asking too much of the asocial attitude now in fashion. At most one might put up with the child of today which can be collected or dropped off at leisure. Crisis-conscious adults now lavish affection only on each other. The child is a nuisance to men and women absorbed in their own emancipation that they so often disastrously misinterpret. As a result, doubt is cast on the purpose, the very meaning of the family—often enough abused as the cell of an ideology of regeneration. The family allegedly restricts, stultifies, fails to match up to a changing society. These are egoistic excuses. Why share out one's goods? Why should one commit oneself for at least half one's life? Why adapt oneself to the consequences of a common bond, entered into only on the understanding that it could be revoked? I know that my anger is driving me to exaggerate, but I am thinking of

children and the conditions in which many of them grow up: from the first accepted as troublemakers and thereafter trained to observe the rules of good-conduct. Today's generation of thirty-year-olds, the young fathers and mothers, has only known a world at peace, but a peace which is threatened all the time—rather a lack of peace cushioned by prosperity. Without giving itself time to think this generation followed the slogans of a truly frenzied consumer egoism and advertising inspired the idea that only the young could guarantee progress. It has trusted all these promises, which likewise find their confirmation in pretty pictures. When that which seemed to be tenable for all eternity began to be questioned, some broke away, much to the amazement and the horror of their elders, shocked by the violence, the despair and the brutality of such a rebellion. The parents of these rebels had indeed longed for peace and secured it too, after their own fashion. But they never really declared peace, its necessity and vulnerability; the fear and destruction out of which it arose. Breathlessly they made up for lost time. The fruits of their efforts fell from the outset into the laps of their children. How could they, so entangled in the cultivation of prosperity, make themselves understood? When their children then began to take material possessions for granted, when, with everything at their disposal, they began to speak of "violence against things" and mocked those who understood the reason for their anger, when violence was finally turned against people, when news of wars and guerillas once again filled the newspapers, this mobile society reacted rhetorically with abhorrence, it is true, but in a mercantile sense with great cunning: the miniature apparatus of war was once more on display in the toy shops—tanks and rockets, warships which one could put together oneself; and in books and magazines "brave Hartmann" is summoned from heaven or foot-slogging infantrymen dig in to wait for the eternal enemy. How, I ask myself, are the young supposed to adjust to the deceitfulness of the shrewd business sense of their fathers? Fashions change and children have to suffer for it. Not so long ago there was a second attempt at making our century the century of the child. Many parents eagerly read the works of the great "children's friends" of our time, studied Anna Freud and Piaget, Bernfeld and Rühle. Anti-authoritarian education was more than just a slogan. Great care was taken at home, in the Kindergarten and in the schools. It wasn't in vain, even though dogmatists ruined some efforts prematurely. And now? Now, in the phase of self-discovery of man and woman, the child is hardly mentioned any more. . . .

I admit I am generalizing. But the books I write for children are based on these experiences that I find so sorely irritating. As I said, I write with pleasure as well as with cunning and anger.

Let me explain more precisely some of the themes and their motives I have already touched upon:

Until a few years ago there was a tendency in children's literature to spare children hard reality, to embellish, to harmonize the rigours of life, to make little of misfortune or to turn it into a happy ending. This is the continuation of a tradition that has its origins in the 19th century: children regarded as miniature adults with a trivial capacity for feeling, firmly harnessed to the concept of higher and lower, good and bad, poor and rich.

Following this pattern a Johanna Spyri girl grew into a Courths-Mahler woman. Emotions wither away into platitudes. Whoever gets to know reality through literature such as this is not only led astray but also left defenceless. If someone wants to escape with the help of literature, he should seek a world which rouses his imagination but does not blind him to reality. Great imaginative literature always has utopian elements: saddened by the imperfections of the world, it gives it a new shape. What does reality mean to children? It doesn't spare them in any way, even though the parents may at times think so. Children observe and take in their immediate and more distant surroundings in bits and pieces. Their perspective is different from that of adults. They barely have the capacity to protect themselves or to select. Everything affects them directly and unexplained. To the person attempting to describe reality to children this means, therefore, that he must take serious account of this special angle of vision. He must not shirk the job, but should assemble the bits and pieces into pictures that can be understood. He must present any action that seems to be larger than life in a way that enables the child to grasp it. He must include in his story whatever has been omitted out of false regard for the child. Only in this way can the child reader be taught how to cope with its environment and defend itself, how to agree, to act and react. The proviso is an ability to describe in pictures that can always be understood. Our own concepts of things should be cast into scenes that are thoroughly exciting. The language should therefore not be abstract; nor ever become childish.

In not a few children's books the reader is made ridiculous by their silly diminutive language. A kind of "dwarf philosophy" rumbles in the minds of the authors. In this way children are insulted. Young readers should take sides—naturally not for any party or ideology, but they should be able to distinguish between right and wrong, and, when they read, they should laugh and cry, be angry and gentle, praise and condemn. The likelihood of this happening is strongest if the children transfer their feelings to one or several characters, when they identify themselves. Carried along by the characters to whom they feel drawn and by a language that does not over-simplify what is difficult, they can be led to the borders of our reality, to loneliness, poverty, silent despair.

At the moment love is discussed as if it were a record-making sport. In the illustrated magazines children see photographs of the voluptuous, unblemished products of a sexual technology designed equally to stimulate consumption. In magazines they learn about a smooth-running partnership with no side-effects. Pain, doubt, passion and sadness are excluded. I recently heard a 10-year-old boy remark laconically of a classmate: He is impotent. An appalling capacity of thought crystallizes into one naive phrase. Is this hell, so perfectly fitted out by the thirty and forty-year-olds, where there is both finance management and sexual management, where the cynical principle of "hire and fire" is applied equally to commerce and

to love—is this hell to be the future of our children? This is something we writers should condemn. Instead one should write of warmth, fellowship, and helplessness which hopes for help; of embraces which express happiness or assuage distress. One should try to create with language a space for a child to warm itself and show tenderness without being laughed at. That man is man's worst enemy is not only drummed into children by words and pictures; it is acted out before them. The bloody tracks of torture and death are smeared across the television screen. The thresholds that protect our life have dropped very low indeed. I don't believe that laws which restrict our freedom are of any use here. We, the writers, can unfold life in our stories, its fullness, its hopes, its invulnerability. We can rouse awareness of cruelty and, already in a way preachers of a better reality, we can tell without pathos of examples of brotherliness, of love for one's neighbour and of courage to face life. Through writing we should dismantle the fear a child has of someone else and spell out the power of the "powerless ones" word for word. He who knows nothing of the other has no regard for him and lashes out all the more wildly. Blind fury sees nothing and no-one any more.

There are still two elements missing which link childhood and literature and join them in alliance: unrest and curiosity. No, the books I mean should not soothe, but disturb and rouse. They should make children curious about people and things, about the unknown in what they know, curious even about what is impossible. Books by their challenge can provoke new thoughts. Think further, say more, tell more. Don't stop! Trust your imagination, but don't let it forget reality. Accept closeness and don't run away from it: these are guide lines for writing words to be read by children.

And all this should be done with humour, pleasure, love, opinion and experience, accuracy, passion, reason. And this in a language which does not belittle the emotional. Because freedom, so often and so deceitfully extolled, begins with the first glance, the first gesture, the first time one turns to someone else, the first word, the first thought. Even then it can already be lost. (pp. 2-6)

> *Peter Härtling, "On the Difficulties and Pleasures in Writing for Children," in* Bookbird, *Vol. XV, No. 3, September 15, 1977, pp. 2-6.*

GENERAL COMMENTARY

Tordis Orjasaeter

[*The following excerpt is taken from an essay in which the critic discusses Härtling's book* Das war der Hirbel *(1973) as an example of commendable literature for children about the handicapped. Although* Das war der Hirbel *has never been translated into English, it was nominated for the 1975 German Children's Book Award.*]

Literature, like reality, has different ways of rejecting handicapped human beings. There is the hidden rejection that we find in many well-intended and nice books where healthy young people—when they meet handicapped children—are filled with gratitude for their own good health. (p. 21)

In books from older times we often meet wealthy children who give poor children alms. In books from our own time in western cultures handicapped children have replaced poverty stricken children—you should be kind to handicapped children. We have had a good many books about children who collect money on behalf of mentally handicapped children. And the mentally handicapped are forever happy and trusting and so grateful for everything. There is no room for personal individuality—in spite of the fact that we who have regular and close contact with mentally handicapped people know that they are perhaps more individual, more different from one another than we who are not mentally handicapped.

It seems to me to be very much a hidden sort of rejection when the principle of compensation is often so heavily stressed. Blind people, mostly girls, are automatically, almost by virtue of their blindness, so extraordinarily kind and good and have such a good ear for music. (pp. 21-2)

You could possibly say that such books give a certain amount of information about handicaps, but on the whole they give a false picture.

A third form of rejection is humour at the handicapped person's expense. . . .

I want to mention some other pitfalls, especially since literature about handicapped children now tends to be in. As an author you have to write about what you, in some way or other, have experienced in your own life, your environment, your fantasy, your dreams. You have to know something about handicapped people before you write about them. I do not know how many untrue books I have read about mentally handicapped children. I can give you some typical examples. Many authors use the description ill when they talk about mentally retarded children. But they are not ill, no more than other children are, unless they have measles or have caught a cold or something like that. They are not ill, they are retarded in their mental development. Other authors tell you that you can suddenly be cured of autism if your brother is kind to you, or you stop stuttering if you get a pet, or you start talking even though you have never talked, if you get a friend. Such things may happen, but very rarely. Handicapped children do not become normal, they just become adults as other children do. (p. 22)

What I really dream about is literature where the handicapped child belongs to its environment as naturally as other people belong to theirs. At any rate I dream about that kind of society.

Happily, in literature for children and young people we also have many fine books where the authors show both insight and poetic power. It is obvious that for many of these authors for children and young people it has been important to write about children who feel they are different from others. (pp. 22-3)

The German author Peter Härtling wrote his book ***Das war der Hirbel*** about Hirbel, a brain-damaged boy who was hidden away and forgotten—one of the most serious

children's books I know of and one of the truest, where the account of a brain-damaged child is at the same time a description of a society characterized by wrong values. Hirbel suffers from brain damage which gives him terrible headaches, and as he grows older the pains grow worse. This brain damage prevents him from learning how to read and write and doing what other children do. He is given lots of medicines, which give him stomachaches and cramps. Yet, his brain damage is not the worst thing for Hirbel. An additional handicap is worse: the fact that there is nobody who really cares about him. His mother does not want to have anything to do with him and he has never known his father. He is sent to foster parents who cannot stand him, and he is continually sent from one institution to another. No one understands what a fine little fellow Hirbel really is, and he is clever too. Peter Härtling writes: "Those people were wrong who said that he was foolish and could not learn anything. He learned a great deal. In reality, Hirbel learned what he had to know in order to get along in hospitals and institutions without being scolded or getting into fights too often. That was what Hirbel learned."

Peter Härtling has managed to write about a handicapped child in such a way that the reader, child or adult, is able to understand. Understand that one who is "bad" is one who has a bad time. Understand something about the wrong values of society as it is. ***Das war der Hirbel*** shows that the author knows a lot about his subject matter, and that his loyalty is with Hirbel, without sentimentality. It is an honest book, and therefore we also miss the happy ending which we are accustomed to in children's books. When we leave Hirbel, he is in a hospital and will probably stay there for the rest of his life, probably in isolation—without anyone who really cares about him. "And so he was forgotten" is the last sentence of this book.

In a postscript the author answers some of the questions which probably arise in the reader's mind after reading about Hirbel—about the primary handicap, the brain damage, and the additional handicap, his surroundings, so very wrong for him, and about what is needed to help Hirbel and those many others: "He must be given the chance to live a normal life, otherwise he will not be able to see what life is. We have far too little time to care for them. And then they become ill. It costs a lot of money. And for this money we prefer to build roads, cars, airplanes and houses, and see to it that we—the others—have a comfortable time in every way". (p. 24)

Tordis Orjasaeter, "The Handicapped in Literature," in Bookbird, *No. 2, June 15, 1980, pp. 21-5.*

TITLE COMMENTARY

Oma (1977)

Oma (British edition as *Granny: The Story of Karl, Who Loses His Parents and Goes to Live with His Grandmother,* 1977)

Oma means grandmother in German, and this Oma is a gutsy, convivial old woman who struggles valiantly with the problems of aging and of raising grandson Kalle when his parents are killed in an automobile accident. Living on a tiny pension which she supplements by distributing ads in her Munich working-class neighborhood. Oma must confront the welfare authorities to get an allowance for Kalle. She wins that round, but the 60 years separating Oma and Kalle present other problems: Oma wants to keep too tight a rein; Kalle must accept his grandmother's idiosyncrasies; and both of them must face her eventual death when Oma gets sick and has to stay in the hospital. Some readers may be deterred by the fact that this is set in a different culture, but the dialogue is lively (Oma argues with herself throughout in italicized paragraphs) and those who make Oma's acquaintance will admire her undaunted spirit.

Matilda Kornfeld, in a review of "Oma," in School Library Journal, *Vol. 24, No. 1, September, 1977, p. 129.*

When Kalle is five, his parents die and he goes willingly to live with his grandmother (after all, "She took him seriously")—and we are into one of those small situation-probes that the Germans and Scandinavians do so well, that fare so poorly here. Still, there is hope till nearly the last that some of the fragments will expand or fuse, that five-years' episodes in Kalle's and Oma's shared life will somehow coalesce into a story. First and last they must adjust to one another: Kalle to Oma's strange modesty ("Old people aren't very nice to look at Kalle"), her nips of brandy ("Especially when I'm scared"), her grudge against her daughter-in-law, his mother—which drives Kalle to tears. "He couldn't make himself admit that [Oma] was just as important to him now as his mother used to be." One reason, the Damocles sword: Oma might get sick. But before that inevitability occurs, they prove their joint mettle at the Welfare Office, come to terms over Kalle's passion for playing soccer, divide Oma's prize airplane trip to mutual satisfaction. The talk is direct, uncomplicated, astringent—but it's there, and in Oma's italicized thoughts, that most of the action lies. And their final conversation—after Oma has indeed been hospitalized—is so *reasonable* a stock-taking ("Some orphanages are nice,") even as almost to say, duty's done. Or in Oma's words: "I've explained things to you. And that's important." In this case, though, explanation overbalances emotion.

A review of "Oma," in Kirkus Reviews, *Vol. XLV, No. 22, November 15, 1977, p. 1197.*

Oma means grandmother in German, and this Oma is another one to add to the growing list of good-guy grandmas in children's books. The story bounces along unevenly but manages to make a warm, human statement about ordinary people who love each other. . . .

Far from an exemplary senior citizen, Oma can be mendacious, jealous and often a downright embarrassment to the growing boy. Even though Kalle's mother is dead, Oma cannot overcome her dislike for her former daughter-in-law, and infuriates Kalle by making snide references to her. Oma takes "a drop now and then," wears funny old clothes and talks to herself. These little soliloquies provide the reader with insight into Oma's fears and uncertainties about Kalle, and also her deep love for him.

The book is clumsy in structure, sometimes awkward in translation yet rich in its picture of a loving and doomed relationship. Only 95 pages long, it chronicles the five years that Kalle and Oma live together. Nothing momentous happens—they go on vacation together, handle (or mishandle) the social worker from the welfare department, Kalle joins the soccer team, Oma threatens to pull the ears of any children who hurt him, and the two grow to love one another. When Kalle is nearly 10, Oma suffers a heart attack. She recovers, but the fear of her dying is now out in the open. They talk over options. If she dies, Kalle will probably have to go to an orphanage. Unhappily he asks, "Do you think you're going to die soon, Oma?" "I've made up my mind to live as long as I possibly can. . . . But making up your mind isn't enough, though it helps."

A quiet, unobtrusive book, **Oma** movingly celebrates love even while mourning its impermanence.

Marilyn Sachs, in a review of "Oma," in The New York Times Book Review, *November 20, 1977, p. 30.*

Granny is an unprepossessing title and the illustrations [by Jutta Ash] are fashionably unattractive but in spite of this it is well worth reading and should give its readers or hearers new ideas about their relations with old people. . . .

The story is told in such a matter-of-fact way as to be almost dull. What enlivens the book for the adult reader is the comment at the end of each chapter by Granny herself; a good mixture of bewilderment at modern trends and shrewd good sense. These can be skipped when reading aloud, but in the stories themselves there are real-life problems that worry Karl and will worry most children if they stop to think. Why do the old seem so depressed and helpless when they are herded together in an Old People's Home? Why could Granny never get on with Karl's mother, whom he loved? What will happen when Granny dies? Granny herself has some honest answers and some equally honest admissions when she doesn't know the answer.

Elinor Lyon, "Simple Pleasures," in The Times Literary Supplement, *No. 3949, December 2, 1977, p. 1412.*

The writing is direct and rather bland, with interpolated musings (in italics) by Oma, stressing her viewpoint; in dialogue and exposition her viewpoint is subordinated to that of young Kalle. The two cope with the differences and conflicts imposed by poverty as well as by a situation that has brought striking changes in the lifestyle of each. The book gives a realistic picture of a resilient, courageous older person; while the story line isn't strong, the establishment of milieu and the development of the grandparent-child relationship are.

> *Zena Sutherland, in a review of "Oma," in* Bulletin of the Center for Children's Books, *Vol. 31, No. 7, March, 1978, p. 113.*

Theo Runs Away   (1978)

The book gets off to rather a bad start as Theo has a habit of inventing comic names for things. It may work very well in German, but in English it's not exactly a laugh a minute ("full stop" for teacher, "seat-scraper" for desk). But once things are happening, the story moves easily enough. [In *Theo Runs Away*] we have not a problem child but problem parents—parents so concerned with their own problems that they have no time for their children ("Dad doesn't notice a thing," thought Theo. "Not anything at all! He hasn't the faintest idea what I'm going to do"). So Theo runs away, not once but twice, and finds himself involved in unpleasant and even dangerous situations.

The blurb makes much of Theo's relationship with Pa Snort, the owner of a fairground roundabout, but in fact it is not explored in any depth. Pa's habit of snorting "Humph!" every two minutes makes real communication difficult, but he is a reasonably effective agent for Theo's reconciliation to his lot at the end of a story which has tactfully steered him through the attentions of a pederast, a gang of car thieves and a pair of social workers from the Children's Welfare Office.

> *Ann Thwaite, "Problem Parents," in* The Times Literary Supplement, *No. 3979, July 7, 1978, p. 771.*

Theo has parents who quarrel. His father is drunk much of the time and his mother is unhappy. As a result Theo runs away from home—twice. He has a series of encounters, from the highly suspicious man who picks him up on the motorway and will insist on holding his knee, to a gang of crooks who use him as a courier and Pa Snort who works on a funfair and who befriends the boy. It is Pa Snort who finally enables Theo to face up to the facts and realise that the home he has is much better than none at all. The book is written very sensitively, the author showing an understanding of human nature far greater than is usually seen. And, what is unusual, it is not just one section of the community that "rings a bell" for Peter Hartling, he can understand the downtrodden as well as those who do the treading, those who stick it out and those who run away, those who try to help and who succeed, and those who try to help and only make it worse. Here is a book that children will enjoy on an obvious level and

adults for the greater depths which are there for those who wish to find them.

> *G. L. Hughes, in a review of "Theo Runs Away," in* The Junior Bookshelf, *Vol. 42, No. 4, August, 1978, p. 204.*

Crutches   (1988)

In a novel that parallels some of the author's refugee experiences immediately after WW II, 12-year-old Thomas is befriended by a German veteran who contrives to find life's necessities even though he has only one leg.

Thomas was separated from his mother while they were en route to Vienna to escape the Russian invasion. Adrift, he follows "Crutches" to his home in a construction trailer. Crutches' reluctance to take Tom in is short-lived; he tries conscientiously to find Tom's mother, but—long before he succeeds a year later in the book's last pages—he and Tom establish a mutually supportive, strongly affectionate relationship that makes their ultimate parting hard indeed. They survive the early scavenging days, say good-bye to Crutches' dear friend Bronka (whom he saved during the war) when she emigrates to Palestine, and make a several weeks' train journey back to Germany, where they receive a cool welcome, since they are refugees, but are able to resume a more normal life.

Full of authentic, lively incident and told with a realistic balance between the difficulties of daily life and the compassionate help people give one another, this is a strong addition to the growing list of fiction based on postwar experiences.

> *A review of "Crutches," in* Kirkus Review, *Vol. LVI, No. 1, September 1, 1988, p. 1323.*

The German author, who lost his parents in the war when he was approximately Thomas's age, says his story "is about the struggle to begin again when all seems to be lost." In this translation [by Elizabeth D. Crawford], it has an austere, elliptical style that matches the reluctance of the characters to be openly emotional. But its poignancy mounts; and by the end, when the question of whether Thomas will find his mother alive—leaving Crutches for her—is answered, it achieves an overwhelming power. (p. 82)

> *A review of "Crutches," in* Publishers Weekly, *Vol. 234, No. 18, October 28, 1988, pp. 81-2.*

There are three portraits here: the boy, the man, and the face of war. The author has achieved concentrated strength by particularizing each of these. Though sometimes the context goes unexplained, the incidents are vivid enough to make the story cohesive. When Thomas and Crutches "organize" some piglets from the countryside, for instance, the tension of crossing check-points and the breakdown of the trailer on bombed-out roads speaks for itself. Other elements are somewhat more mysterious—the survival of a beautiful Jewish woman with a luxury apartment in which Crutches and Thomas take shelter until their return to Germany. Most impressive is the characterization of Crutches, an embittered, anti-

Hitlerian ex-soldier who tries to protect his battered heart from further incursions but who cannot resist getting involved. The translator has worked effectively to capture Härtling's trenchant style without becoming choppy, and readers will get involved in spite of the fact that this is less about the dangers of defeat than about its drudgeries.

> *Betsy Hearne, in a review of "Crutches," in*
> Bulletin of the Center for Children's Books,
> *Vol. 42, No. 3, November, 1988, p. 74.*

Books dealing with the aftermath of war are as important as those which treat its immediate horrors, for they remind us that, like a ravaging disease, such conflict leaves the social fabric debilitated or destroyed. **Crutches** is the story of two survivors: one, a thirteen-year-old boy; the other, a thirty-three-year-old man, crippled by the loss of a leg. The author has described events from the boy's perspective, which gives a sense of immediacy to the whole book. . . . Thomas, whose education has taught him the glories of Nazism and hatred of Jews, begins to acquire from Crutches, as he calls his rescuer, a quite different point of view. Details of their journeys together are sobering: the stench and crowded conditions aboard a transport, concerns about one's future when one does not hold the proper official papers, the need to be on guard at all times. Because of its pacing, the book, while re-creating a specific time in history, has the intensity of an adventure story; it is equally remarkable for its development of theme without sacrificing believability or sense of story. When Thomas is finally reunited with his mother, for example, the moment is tinged with sadness, as it means that he will be parted from Crutches. The bittersweet ending is poignant but not manipulative, reaffirming the author's comment that "the human being is also the friend of humankind." (pp. 787-88)

> *Margaret A. Bush, in a review of "Crutches,"
> in* The Horn Book Magazine, *Vol. LXIV, No.
> 6, November-December, 1988, pp. 787-88.*

Old John (1990)

[This novel] is a refreshingly realistic, funny portrait of an idiosyncratic 75-year-old who moves in with his daughter's family.

A family debate sets the tone: Father, didactic but soon betrayed as having more bark than bite, presents the difficulties of inviting Old John to live with them, but is clearly as fond of his wife's father as are his two children. John does provide some awkward moments: he makes friends with the town drunk, wears a scandalously skimpy bathing suit to the town pool, and falls boyishly in love with a lady who likes him—but who draws the line when he wants to live with her. On the other hand, John defends a local girl from her abusive father and (to the kids' delight) smuggles a puppy into the family.

The Schirmers' joys and anxieties as they cope with this lovable but troublesome grandparent—as well as adjust to the changes as he grows older—are universal experiences that gain clarity here in the context of a slightly different culture. After a stroke, Old John gets more unpredictable,

irresponsible, even paranoiac—phenomena that are much more frequently encountered than discussed. An affectionately comic, memorable portrayal of a vibrantly individual old man lucky enough to have a family united in the difficult, loving task of caring for him until the end.

> *A review of "Old John," in* Kirkus Reviews,
> *Vol. LVIII, No. 8, April 15, 1990, p. 577.*

Johannes "Old John" Navratil is a true eccentric, a delightful grandfather, and the very unusual 75-year-old central character of this succinct and well-polished gem of a story. . . . Each character (Old John accumulates a varied assortment of friends) is distinct and rounded, complementing the others and spicing the tale. Härtling deftly sketches simple chapters, each unfolding into the next, with an economy of vocabulary and a storyteller's sense of timing. Even in translation the story crackles with energy and poignancy. A book to be savored, read aloud, and used to entice older but less skillful readers.

> *Katharine Bruner, in a review of "Old John,"
> in* School Library Journal, *Vol. 36, No. 7,
> July, 1990, p. 76.*

As honest as the author's Batchelder Award-winning book, **Crutches** but more cohesive in narration, this recounts the moving in, adjustment, and eventual decline of Laura and Jacob Schirmer's grandfather, Old John. The central focus on an individualistic family renders each member distinctive and yet reserves central place for the group as a whole: "Everything new or out of the ordinary had to be discussed in detail from every angle and usually at top volume as well." This dynamic is especially touching at the point when a decision must be made about whether to bring Old John home from the hospital after a stroke, even if it means living day by day with his dying. Most impressive, however, is the helter-skelter humor that dominates the book, from Old John's idiosyncrasies (including a pair of triangular swimming trunks) to his December romance with a village teacher. The tone is outspoken, the portrayal affectionate, and the viewpoint true to a child's perceptions. (pp. 266-67)

> *Betsy Hearne, in a review of "Old John," in*
> Bulletin of the Center for Children's Books,
> *Vol. 43, No. 11, July-August, 1990, pp. 266-67.*

The author's affection for Old John is evident, and his skillfully drawn portrait of the old man is warm with sympathy and humor. Old John becomes the central character about whom Jacob and his family revolve, first as bemused satellites and later as devoted caretakers after Old John suffers a stroke. His death, when it comes, is a blow to both the family and the reader. While Old John's story may have limited appeal for readers looking for excitement and adventure, the vivid characterization of the gallant old man and the realistic portrayal of his loving but very human family form an unforgettable study of the strains and rewards of living in a three-generational family.

> *Ethel R. Twichell, in a review of "Old John,"
> in* The Horn Book Magazine, *Vol. LXVI, No.
> 4, July-August, 1990, p. 456.*

Ben Loves Anna (1990)

In this German novel, ten-year-old Ben develops the first crush of his life on Anna, a shy girl from Poland. Hartling's gentle story takes them from their first meeting in school, through tentative flirting and teasing, to spending a lot of time together and getting to know each other. This short novel does not attempt very much, and the action stays very close to the surface. Even though the emotional stakes for both Ben and Anna are high, Härtling maintains the detachment of a grown-up watching childish events from the outside, and only hints at the depth of his protagonists' feelings. Worse, this novel is hampered with a graceless, unidiomatic translation [by J. H. Auerbach] which is sure to put off most readers.

> *A review of "Ben Loves Anna," in* Publishers Weekly, *Vol. 238, No. 9, February 15, 1991, p. 90.*

Härtling's **Old John**, set in a German milieu evoked with perfectly selected detail, exquisitely demonstrated that the verities of the human condition transcend their setting. Here, a disastrous decision has been made (presumably by the publisher): a gentle story about a ten-year-old schoolboy's friendship with a Polish refugee in his class is completely undermined by pretending that it takes place in the US, though almost every incident and detail—the characters' names, a teacher's assignment, Ben's gift of flowers to Anna's mother on his first visit, even the way jobs and housing are acquired—seems European, and is certainly not American. Set in Hartling's homeland (Austria), this would be a quiet but pleasingly warmhearted story; as it stands, it's an exasperating travesty.

> *A review of "Ben Loves Anna," in* Kirkus Reviews, *Vol. LIX, No. 6, March 1, 1991, p. 317.*

Although this is translated from the German, the action appears to take place in the U.S., a fact less evident from details of setting than from several low-key references in the book. It is exactly such missing details that render the situation more generic than individualized. The dynamics between the two main characters and among their classmates seem unrooted in any social milieu, which may be an attempt to broaden the book's appeal. Love between a ten-year-old boy and girl is not often enough developed in children's fiction, and Ben and Anna do show authentic reactions to each other and to the inevitable teasing that ensues from their affection. Anna's outsider status as a Polish immigrant adds a sub-theme with which some readers will also empathize. However, both the new-wave black-and-white illustrations [by Ellen Weinstein] and the translation suffer from occasional awkwardness ("He liked when she was confident"), and Härtling does not seem as comfortable fictionally as he was in **Old John**. (pp. 193-94)

> *Betsy Hearne, in a review of "Ben Loves Anna," in* Bulletin of the Center for Children's Books, *Vol. 44, No. 8, April, 1991, pp. 193-94.*

Gene Kemp

1926-

English author of fiction and poetry.

Major works include *The Prime of Tamworth Pig* (1972), *The Turbulent Term of Tyke Tiler* (1977), *Charlie Lewis Plays for Time* (1984), *Tamworth Pig Stories* (1987), and *Room with No Windows* (1989).

A celebrated author of fiction for children and teens, Kemp writes funny and original books noted for their deep and intimate understanding of the feelings and needs of children. Her books are fresh, direct, and replete with everyday details of a child's life at school and home, evidencing recognition of children as people whose interests, ambitions, and ideals are as important as those of adults. According to Kemp, "the actuality of children's lives—the long daydreamings, desultory conversations, desultory play—is very rarely dealt with in children's books." Therefore, her books tend to diverge from traditional themes in children's literature, such as relationships between children and adults, and focus instead on the experiences of children with other children and with their environment. Kemp's books for younger children tell of the magic and innocence of youngsters' experiences, and are marked by a deflating and down-to-earth humor typical of childhood, pleasing to children and adults alike. A former school teacher, Kemp is skilled in developing plots gradually so that young readers may make discoveries of their own. Also characteristic of her works is a relaxed and deceptively simple writing style containing classroom language and humor, making her books further accessible to her audience. In addition, critics praise Kemp for her ability to sustain interest through finely-drawn characterizations and fully developed narratives. Her works for older children and teens are equally entertaining, but they are also more thought-provoking, addressing issues such as the nuclear threat and the spread of AIDS.

Kemp's writing has progressed through various stages, from the light-hearted humor of *The Prime of Tamworth Pig* to the more contemplative *Juniper* (1986). Her early works often demonstrate a sympathetic and loving portrayal of animals, underpinning the strong belief held by many young children that animals, both real and toy, are trustworthy companions who can talk and reason. Her most famous books of this period are the Tamworth Pig stories, which combine domestic warmth and security with adventuresome outdoor scenes, reminiscent of A. A. Milne's Winnie-the-Pooh books. In her Tamworth Pig stories Thomas, a young boy, pursues his adventures in the company of a conservationist pig, Tamworth, whose wisdom and unquestioning acceptance provide refuge for Thomas throughout a succession of minor calamities. "But these calamities are contained in a reassuring framework of secure familiarity," writes critic Gillian Cross. "The day-to-day events of the stories are the homely ones of parties and competitions, conker collecting and school

plays, and the very jokes that are told are of the sort only too well-known in school playgrounds. . . . This comfortable security runs through all the Tamworth Pig books." Even the bad characters Thomas must confront in these books are not threatening: they suffer from minor vices such as vanity and greed, qualities which children encounter on a regular basis and rejoice in seeing overcome. The Tamworth Pig stories are critically acclaimed for their recognition of the fact that childhood is a time of security, but also for their concern with conservation issues such as growing more food, eliminating litter, and saving trees, all of which encourage children to reach out to the wider world of knowledge and experience. Kemp's *The Turbulent Term of Tyke Tiler,* a story involving an unusual and comically touching friendship between the rebellious Tyke and her dim-witted friend, marks another phase in Kemp's writing style because the children are older, the setting is urban, and the story is more realistic than her Tamworth Pig books. Like the Tamworth stories, there is a strong sense of security in *The Turbulent Term of Tyke Tiler* provided by Tyke's teachers, most of whom are understanding, but who (unlike Tamworth Pig) require active cooperation from the children. A recipient of the Children's Rights Workshop Other Award (1977) and the Library Association Carnegie Medal (1978), *The Turbulent Term of Tyke Tiler* is praised by critics for its twist of plot in which an eleven-year-old "hero" turns out to be a heroine, challenging the imagination of children and many accepted ideas about differences between boys and girls. Cross comments, "[Tyke] is a rounded and recognizable portrait of a bright child, totally at ease in the world of childhood, but reaching out confidently to wider spheres. She provides a striking contrast to the oversensitive, alienated heroines (and heroes) of many children's books."

Kemp's later works—*Charlie Lewis Plays for Time, Juniper,* and her two books for teenagers, *No Place Like* (1983) and *I Can't Stand Losing* (1987)—are more serious books, retaining the quality of writing and humor eminent in her earlier works, but demanding more from her young readers in terms of understanding. *Charlie Lewis Plays for Time* and *Juniper* are incisively funny books centering on a child in distress who, because of domestic problems, must assume an adult role. Consequently, the humor in these books is darker than that of the earlier works, significantly affecting their tone and giving them a haunting quality. Kemp's two books for teenagers have adopted a similar formula, combining humor and sympathy with powerful undercurrents concerning the nature of fear. Despite their popularity with teens, they have undergone extensive criticism by reviewers such as Elizabeth J. King, who has suggested that *No Place Like* is lacking in credibility, characterization, and understanding. At the same time, she extols Kemp's books for younger children, claiming, "Gene Kemp manages to make the junior school classroom and all its inhabitants live in a way no other author has, and to do this with verve, wit, and individuality."

(See also *Something about the Author*, Vol. 25; *Contemporary Authors New Revision Series,* Vol. 12; and *Contemporary Authors,* Vols. 69-72.)

AUTHOR'S COMMENTARY

[*The following excerpt is from an interview by Virginia Makins.*]

"Gene Kemp is small and a bit fat, depending on how she is holding her stomach at the time, is short sighted, deaf and has goofy teeth—not a pretty sight" . . . That's how Gene Kemp introduces herself to her readers in the Puffin edition of her runaway bestseller, ***The Turbulent Term of Tyke Tiler.*** She's also a compelling talker, funny, dogmatic in the nicest possible way, apparently happy to go on for hours about both education and writing: "Look, I'm giving you the wrong impression, that my main interest is education", she said we'd talked about schools and teaching for some time. "I did get caught by teaching—but my main interest is writing."

This year she has three books ready to be published. ***No Place Like,*** set in and around a sixth form college and aimed at rather older readers than Tyke, has just appeared. Another book set in Cricklepit Combined school, where Tyke and her successor, Gowie Corby, struggled with the system, will be published in the spring, and a

third book, written from the perspective of an eight year old, will come later.

Clearly, she feels that her writing is now back on course, after a period where she "was taken over by the Establishment, and went wary and careful and produced innocuous books." She is now about to start writing a book for adults.

Gene Kemp's writing career started when she was at home with three children, five animals, and a husband in local Labour politics, with a series of books about one Tamworth Pig: "Nice little books in the conventional style", she says. The head at the primary school where she taught read out bits at assembly: "It was all seemliness and light." Then she wrote ***Tyke Tiler,*** and the head was less pleased: "It's not like the pigs, is it? I liked the pigs. It won't sell well—don't mind about it." *Tyke* was a marvellous picture of life as it's really lived in a mixed urban primary, from the viewpoint of a disruptive fourth year junior.

It had an added twist, only the most perceptive readers, noticing references to washing up and the lack of references to football, realized that—as is revealed at the end of the second last chapter—the terrible Tyke is a girl.

In fact Tyke started, conventionally, as a boy. But Gene Kemp's second daughter started complaining that the younger brother in the Tamworth Pig books had all the best parts, and Gene Kemp went to a lecture by Rosemary Stones on sexism in children's books. She went back and rewrote the book—and got pretty cross when, after it was published, she was accused of jumping on a bandwagon.

Tyke Tiler won the Carnegie Medal and the Other Award (not to mention two Japanese awards and a near miss at becoming the Best Read Book of the Mid West.) By the time it hit the charts, its successor, ***Gowie Corby Plays Chicken,*** had already been written.

In many ways Gowie seemed a less successful imitation of Tyke: "It's a flawed book", says Gene Kemp: "Gowie Corby would never have reformed. He didn't—he's still stalking about Exeter. But it's done its bit, and got into places Tyke didn't—especially in secondary schools." Gowie gets a lot of fan mail.

The new book is aimed at the awkward teenage bracket, and caused her more trouble, partly because "a true book about teenagers would be all about sex, and I didn't want to do that—it's already been overdone." She says it ended up about the nature of fear—"much more important than the nature of sex"—and about going into society.

She hasn't yet shown it to her family—the father and son in the book are closely modelled on her husband, a senior official at the National Union of Railwaymen, and her son and his friends at Exeter College.

Gene Kemp says that she was very lucky in her own education: at her grammar school in Tamworth the teachers all seemed to have first class degrees, and there was nothing they couldn't discuss. "We used to say: 'what's VD' and we'd be off." She went on to Exeter University to read English, and found the work very limited. "I was told to read so many stanzas of *The Faerie Queen*, toddled back home and was gripped. I read it all, then read it all again.

When my tutor heard she said: 'Don't do that, we don't get carried away with things.' That's the attitude I've been fighting for the rest of my life."

She got into teaching by faltering steps. She walked out of a direct grant grammar: "the hypocrisy there was beyond belief", was terrified by violent 15-year-olds in a secondary modern, and finally arrived at St. Sidwell's primary in Exeter. It was a mixed urban primary that was transmogrified, in her 17 years there, from a rigidly streamed place with resources only for teaching the A stream to something very like Cricklepit Combined school.

After Tyke's success, she left teaching to write full time. "I couldn't stand the moralizing and hypocrisy and assemblies. I'd always done a lot of art and craft, but suddenly I was irritated at having to tidy it away.

"I found I didn't want to teach some children, I wanted them on my lap—their emotional needs seemed so much more vital than teaching them about the Black Death. All teachers should retire after 20 years—except for the few who are quite incredibly much teachers."

Her views of education—and particularly English teaching—are clear from her books. She was very involved in the local discussions about English at the time of the Bullock report. It was terrifically exciting. "Then we watched it ossify", she says, and describes the thick documents on language policy she sees in primary schools these days, setting out hierarchies of skills that must be taught.

"Nobody is moving along the right lines. English should be fun—we had riotous fun in English. With enjoyment, it all clicks into place, sooner or later. You have to do the basics—we did a lot of formal work by stealth—but you should do them briefly, like brushing your teeth. And we push children into literary skills too fast."

She complains that "the literary end of the children's book world dismisses me as a teacher hack." "You can't write for children in an ivory tower," she says. "Children's books shouldn't be about relationships with adults. Even relations with much-loved parents are in the background of children's lives, compared with relations with other children.

"The actuality of children's lives—the long daydreamings, desultory conversations, desultory play, is very rarely dealt with in children's books."

Virginia Makins, "Turbulent Terms," in The Times Educational Supplement, *No. 3509, September 30, 1983, p. 41.*

GENERAL COMMENTARY

Gillian Cross

My eight-year-old daughter was so enchanted by *Christmas with Tamworth Pig* that she insisted on reading the whole book aloud to me, to make sure that I shared her pleasure. Being intrigued as well as entertained by this experience, I wished to discover what makes Gene Kemp's books so satisfying for children, and I read the rest of them with growing enthusiasm. To date, there are five of them—the four Tamworth Pig books and *The Turbulent Term of Tyke Tiler.* . . .

The most obviously appealing quality of the Tamworth Pig books is their humour. They relate the adventures of a small boy, Thomas, and his sister, Blossom, who live in a village and who number among their friends not only the children at school, but also the animals of the farm—most notably the wise and learned Tamworth Pig. The stories abound in knockabout farce of the type which appeals to boys like Thomas. The pretensions of such characters as Gwendolyn Twitchie, the schoolteacher's stuck-up daughter, are exploded in the most basic way. Gwendolyn's arrogance, for example, when she is playing the Princess in the school play, is accidentally but satisfyingly rewarded by Thomas's efforts to escape from sitting opposite her at tea.

> Thomas's chair crashed into Lurcher's, which toppled over, taking Lurcher with it. Crash, clatter, clink went the cups and plates: chunk, whoosh, sloosh went the food and drink. They all received it, the royal party, right in their laps, though they weren't at all thankful.
>
> In the centre of it all, mouth wide open, sat Gwendolyn, her yellow curls wreathed in lemon jelly.

Mess and calamity are exaggerated with schoolboy gusto as disasters erupt around Thomas: he breakfasts off a pint of milk and almost a full packet of cereal, reducing the kitchen to chaos; he inadvertently melts his detested Aunt Cynthia's plastic rollers by leaving them on the fireguard. There is a free-handed generosity, not only in the scale of the incidents, but also in their frequency. The author allows no flat stretches during which a child's attention might flag, but squeezes in as much fun as she can at every point. In *The Prime of Tamworth Pig,* for example, at the end of a gloriously rumbustious fight to save Tamworth from the pigsticker called in by Mrs Baggs, an ancient man rides up "on a matching bicycle." He is the reporter from the local paper, and he greets the fact that he is late with resigned mournfulness. " 'I never do get to a happening, when it's happening,' the old man sighed as he remounted his machine and pedalled slowly away." He is never seen again, but his one felicitous appearance rounds off the chapter perfectly.

The succession of minor calamities which befall Thomas mirror the sense which all children must sometimes have—that they can do nothing right. But these calamities are contained in a reassuring framework of secure familiarity. The day-to-day events of the stories are the homely ones of parties and competitions, conker collecting and school plays, and the very jokes that are told are of the sort only too well-known in school playgrounds: "What's yellow, has twenty-two legs and goes crunch, crunch?" "A Chinese football team eating crisps."

This comfortable security runs through all the Tamworth Pig books. It is embodied most obviously in the huge and authoritative figure of Tamworth Pig himself. His massive bulk provides a refuge for Thomas in times of trouble, and although he is sometimes gently critical, he is never rejecting. With the backing of his owner, Farmer Baggs, he is always wise and powerful enough to overcome the attacks of the bad characters.

There are plenty of bad characters: Mrs Baggs and her spotty son, Christopher Robin; Mrs Twitchie and her daughter, Gwendolyn; repulsive Aunt Cynthia. They are sufficiently horrible for the reader to rejoice in Thomas's extravagant abuse of them, but not so powerful as to be threatening. Their vices are the petty ones of vanity, greed, and squeamishness, which children encounter constantly and can rejoice to see overcome. At the same time, these characters are viewed with humanity. Aunt Cynthia can be generous and is loved by Blossom. Mrs Baggs, wandering in a wood, is rescued by Tamworth on Christmas Day. Except for brief incidents, it is always the good characters who are in control.

The books are written in a form that easily holds the attention of younger children. They are full-length books, but they have about them something of the structure of a collection of short stories. Each book has a unifying thread—usually one of Tamworth's ecologically minded campaigns—but almost every chapter also contains its own event, with its own humorous or rueful payoff.

The books are funny and spirited, perfectly attuned to the capacities of their readers. But if they had no more to them than that, they would not be of any special significance. What makes them unusual is their recognition that even young children have feelings and interests as important as those of adults. This can be seen most plainly, perhaps, in all four books, in the characters of Hedgecock and Mr Rab. These two are given autonomous status, speaking and acting for themselves, but they are, in fact, Thomas's soft toys and they embody, between them, the conflict of a child emerging from babyhood into the tougher world of boyhood. There is no pretentious symbolism about this. But one accepts that the two toys, with their opposed, exaggerated characters, both belong quite properly to Thomas. Mr Rab, a pathetic stripy rabbit, is sentimental and incompetent, loving poetry and Blossom. Hedgecock, a feathery creature resembling a hedgehog, is rude and violent, hating sentiment, poetry, and Mr Rab and adoring arithmetic. The subtle way in which the two toys express Thomas's feelings can be seen, for example, in *Tamworth Pig Saves the Trees,* when Thomas is sent to bed in disgrace.

> Mr Rab sang the song he had made up long ago when Thomas was little.
>
> > "Mr Rab has gone to sleep
> > Tucked in his tiny bed,
> > He has curled up his little paws
> > And laid down his sleepy head."
>
> "Ugh, what muck," Hedgecock growled.

Sometimes, these days, Thomas thought himself much too old for Mr Rab's song, but when things went wrong, he still liked to hear it. It felt comforting.

This ambivalence is a basic, realistic part of Thomas's character. He loves to fight his friend, Lurcher, but he still curls up with his old blanket, Num, when he is upset. He abuses and quarrels with his sister, Blossom, but he is sin-

cerely attached to her. His character owes part of its appeal simply to his naughtiness, the chaos he creates, and the way he flies into a temper when he cannot get his own way. But the more subtle presentation of his inconsistencies, through Mr Rab and Hedgecock, rises above the ordinary knockabout humour of children's books and becomes that rare thing, high comedy of character which a child can actually appreciate.

In other ways also, the Tamworth Pig books recognise that childhood should be a time not only of security, but also of reaching out towards the wider world of knowledge and experience. Tamworth, who is so mysteriously learned that he absentmindedly sings *Silent Night* in German and *O Come All Ye Faithful* in Latin, is Thomas's mentor, feeding the childish love of words, for example, when he lists for him the synonymous words for the runt of a litter in *Christmas with Tamworth Pig.* There is a splendid passage in *The Prime of Tamworth Pig* when Tamworth, shut in a shed facing death while horrible little boys torment him by calling him "Fatty," consoles himself by commenting on the poverty of their vocabulary.

> Tamworth spoke quietly to himself. "There are other words they could use. I can think of great, large, immense, enormous, tremendous, vast, huge, Mammoth-like, Gargantuan, Herculean, well-built, portly, ample, abundant, bulky, massive, gigantic, magnificent, leviathan, giant, mighty, corpulent, stout, plump, brawny, whacking, whopping, colossus, hippopotamus, Brobdingnagian pig, to mention a few."

Tamworth, indeed, is the key to the outside world, a pig of wide horizons, beside whom the adults in the books appear merely parochial. It is his campaigns, quixotically taken up and triumphantly concluded, which provide the backbone of each book. Here again, the level is finely judged. The causes are acknowledged as important by most people—growing more food, getting rid of litter, saving trees—but they are also those causes which are familiar to young children, those which are introduced to them at school and on television and which impinge on their everyday lives. In harmony with the uninhibited vigour of the books, Tamworth's success brings him fame, appearances on television, friendship with the Minister for the Environment, and gifts from the Vegetarian Society. His homely authority extends to the outside world. Yet it never ceases to be homely, and one never forgets that he is a pig. (pp. 131-34)

In another way, less obvious but more serious, Tamworth is the authority who illuminates the world. His moral sense never fails. Although he is always piggish and consoling, he nevertheless encourages Thomas to look beyond his own selfish concerns and take a wider view of things. In *Tamworth Pig and the Litter,* for example, Thomas loses his pocket-money to replace a tennis ball of Blossom's. He goes to Tamworth for comfort, and Tamworth's comments, as the two of them lie under a cosy blanket of piglets, are at once funny and philosophical.

> "Huh. I've got to buy her a new ball with my pocket-money," he muttered into the ears, which twitched a little.

"Justice must be done and must be seen to be done, dear boy," Tamworth murmured sleepily.

"Justice ought to be on my side all the time. That's what I think," Thomas replied.

"But that's what everyone thinks, and that's what causes trouble," yawned Tamworth and, like the piglets, fell asleep.

There is even, from time to time, a half humorous awareness that moral problems are not always simple, that interests or beliefs may conflict. Things as prosaic as sausages are filled with struggle for Thomas. He adores them but can never eat them, because he has promised Tamworth never to eat any food made from pigs. The promise is kept, but with more than one longing sideways glance at the sausages which other people are eating with perfectly clear consciences.

Books for young children are vulnerable to the two dangers of soulfulness and triviality, but, in the Tamworth Pig books, Gene Kemp triumphantly avoids both these pitfalls. The books are filled with that down-to-earth, deflating humour so typical of childhood, yet, at the same time, they acknowledge the importance of feelings, ideals, and aspirations. The fact that they do these things while remaining short, funny books which never for a moment lose a child's attention is a monument to Gene Kemp's skill as a writer and her knowledge of childhood.

In her latest book, *The Turbulent Term of Tyke Tiler,* she has moved into a slightly different type of writing. There is the same schoolboy humour—every chapter is headed by a joke of mind-bending corniness—and the same loose structure, with a high point at the end of almost every chapter, but instead of writing about infant school-children in the country, she is writing about urban junior school-children. The children are older, the setting is more prosaic, and the substance of the story is a step nearer everyday reality. Instead of the extravagances of Tamworth's causes, this book deals with the relationship between Tyke Tiler and Danny Price and the attempts of Tyke to avert the dire results of Danny's irresponsible actions. There are no talking animals or moving toys, only people; and those things which are embodied in nonhuman figures in the Tamworth Pig books here form, more subtly, an integral part of the delineation of characters.

Tyke, for example, although older, is as contradictory as Thomas, capable both of fighting furious battles and of reciting passages from *The Idylls of the King* with appreciative gusto. Without a Hedgecock or a Mr Rab to reinforce the dichotomy, however, these elements must be united simply by good character drawing. And they are. One can easily believe, for example, that a tough child like Tyke might be moved by an account of T. H. White's life.

> He went in for keeping a falcon, and he had a dog who died, and he was heartbroken. That night I sat and looked at Crumble [Tyke's dog] and imagined her dying, though it didn't seem likely. But the idea bothered me so I went and bought some chips and shared them with her in case she died soon. At least she'd know I loved her. She isn't supposed to eat chips, Mum says.

The relationship between Tyke and Danny, which lies at the heart of the book, shares this paradoxical quality. Danny, who has a speech impediment, is weak and not very bright, although well-meaning. Tyke is tough and clever. Yet, when they are together, it is Danny who is demanding and obstinate, Tyke who is protective and exploited. When Danny, who is mildly kleptomaniac, steals a ten-pound note from Miss Bonn, one of the teachers, it is Tyke who is caught while trying to return it, and—although blame is eventually attached to the right person—the injustice does not stop there. "You see, Bonfire took Danny home to tea to have a cosy chat with him, and he had icecream and jelly and cakes and sausages, while I was kept in after school, writing lines for Mrs Somers, the old ratbag." When Danny wants a sheep's skull to take to school to put on the Nature Table, it is Tyke who is inveigled into climbing down into the water to get it, arriving home covered in slime, to meet predictable trouble.

All this is very funny and not in the least sentimental, but at the same time it is moving, because Danny really is at a disadvantage. He does need Tyke's help. It is not his intention to evade trouble. Tyke blames the unfairness on Danny's angelic face, but it is fairly easy to see that he is also shielded by the teachers' awareness that he is in need of special care and child guidance.

The fact that most of the teachers are understanding gives the book its basis of security. But it is not that unquestioning acceptance which Tamworth gives Thomas. It requires some cooperation from the child. When Danny is falsely accused of stealing a watch and runs away to hide, Tyke knows that the solution is not to torture the truth out of the real culprits, but to appeal to the Headmaster's insight.

> I knew the answer. I didn't want to do it. Torturing Kneebags would be easier in some ways. Only real life, my real life wasn't like that. I walked slowly back to school, and up to Chief Sir's room and stood looking at the door for a minute before I knocked on it.

It is a mature decision for a child, but it is a realistic one, just as the hazard—disgrace for stealing—is a more realistic one than, say, the "pignapping" of *Tamworth Pig and the Litter.*

Similarly, the wider world impinges on Tyke in a less extravagant, more realistic way than it does on Thomas. There are no television appearances or friendships with the Minister of the Environment in this book. Instead, Tyke's father is standing for the Council, and there are leaflets to deliver and numbers to relay from the polling station. This is exactly the level at which political life sometimes does involve children. Tyke's elder sister, Beryl, sums it up in a rhyme:

> "Posters on the window,
> Stickers on the car.
> Dad's standing for the Council,
> So here we bloody well are."

Or, as Tyke puts it, "Every year our house breaks out in elections like the measles or chicken pox."

But the thing which really distinguishes *The Turbulent*

Term of Tyke Tiler from the Tamworth Pig books, and from almost all other children's books, is that it is a practical joke on the reader. Until the last chapter, the story is told in the first person by Tyke, and it is not until almost the end of the book that the surprise is sprung, when Tyke is sitting astride the roof of the school bell tower, which it is forbidden to climb. Mrs Somers, "the old ratbag," shouts up, "Get down at once, Theodora Tiler, you naughty, disobedient girl!"

I have never known of an unprepared reader, adult or child, who did not assume automatically, from the beginning of the book, that Tyke is a boy. Yet there is no cheating on the author's part, no place where one could say the account is falsified to hide the fact that she is a girl. Indeed, there are even a few hints of the truth. "You a mermaid, eh, Tyke?" giggles Linda Stoatway when Tyke is going home dripping after finding the sheep's skull. "He's always got a match. He gets out of everything," Tyke complains about her brother when she has to do the washing up and he does not. The clues are there, but somehow one fails to pick them up. Only Tyke's references to "my real name, the one I hate" stick in the mind, preparing one for the final revelation.

For an adult, this revelation is a challenge. Tyke, in retrospect, can so obviously be a girl. She is simply a convincing character, well-described, but without any of the distinguishing marks, such as dolls, names, lack of physical confidence, which are often attached to girls by adults. To see this is to realise how limiting are some of our notions of character, not only in literature but in life.

For children also the revelation is a challenge, but not in the same way. There are no weighty conclusions or theories to digest, no heavy moral or sociological statements to absorb. The author never acknowledges in any way that one might have mistaken Tyke for a boy. The challenge for a child is to accept imaginatively that the book has had a heroine instead of a hero. Anyone who doubts that this is a real challenge has only to watch a group of children reading the book. I have seen one boy read Mrs Somers' revealing shout, see the joke, and greet it with a huge bellow of delighted laughter. But I have known other boys who were outraged, and girls who refused to believe that Tyke could possibly be a girl.

Important as this practical joke is, however, it would be a mistake to regard *The Turbulent Term of Tyke Tiler* merely as a gimmicky book. The final, astounding discovery of Tyke's name and sex is only acceptable because her character has been so firmly and realistically established beforehand, independently of the type-casting of gender roles. Tyke, with her toughness, her attachment to Danny, her common sense, and her love of poetry is a rounded and recognizable portrait of a bright child, totally at ease in the world of childhood, but reaching out confidently to wider spheres. She provides a striking contrast to the oversensitive, alienated heroines (and heroes) of many children's books.

It is to qualities like this that one must look, ultimately, for the appeal of Gene Kemp's books. Funny and original as they are, they do not rely on jokes or fashionable tricks.

They are based upon a deep and intimate understanding of the needs and feelings of children and a recognition that, at any age, children are real people. For an adult, they are bracing and encouraging, a reminder that childhood is a time of growth, a different world, but one whose boundaries overlap the adult world. But the books are in no sense written for adults. They are perfectly attuned to the child reader, accepting his ambitions, his weaknesses and his varied ways of reacting to experience, and reflecting these things back with humour and verve. (pp. 135-39)

> *Gillian Cross, "Children Are Real People: The Stories of Gene Kemp," in* Children's literature in education, *Vol. 10, No. 3, Autumn, 1979, pp. 131-40.*

Colin Mills

A weakness of writing in the past has been the inability to catch the 'felt life' of junior school children. Writers seem to have been more responsive to the nuances and emotions of early childhood and adolescence. Gene Kemp shows in her books that young children have feelings, values and lores just as admissible as those of teenagers. In *Charlie Lewis Plays for Time* and *The Well* she weaves ebullient characters, and home and classroom scenes, with ideas and feelings. (p. 313)

> *Colin Mills, " 'But I'm the Reader: Not the Book': Some Trends in Junior Fiction," in* The School Librarian, *Vol. 32, No. 4, December, 1984, pp. 310-16.*

Elizabeth J. King

It is now nearly fifteen years since Gene Kemp's first book was published. . . . During these years her writing has ranged over the whole age range, from her early stories about young Thomas and his friend Tamworth Pig to a teenage novel, a story of a young girl based largely on her own childhood experiences, a collection of short stories, and an anthology of poetry. Much of her writing, though, has been aimed at top juniors, and it is here that she has had her greatest success and her writing seems to have been most sure.

Her first four books all used the same characters to tell of the adventures of Thomas, a small boy constantly in trouble, and Tamworth Pig, a splendid animal, who talked and planned and was a leader in many conservation battles. School, home, the countryside, and animals are all woven into a series of adventures, happenings and escapades with Blossom, Thomas's older sister, and friends (and enemies) all weaving in and out of the stories. They are gentle, amusing tales all underpinning the strong belief of most young children that animals, both real and toy, have lives and characters of their own and can talk and reason, as well as being companions to be both treasured and trusted. Thomas's toy animals, Rabbit and Hedgecock (of indeterminate ancestry) are always the companions of his bedtime, and are also involved in many of his other adventures. They fight with each other, argue and take opposing views of the world, with Rabbit very much into poetry and love and Hedgecock a 'number-crunching' cynic. Together with Num, Thomas's old blanket, they share Thomas's bed and his ideas.

In these stories Gene Kemp is writing in perhaps a more conventional style than she adopted later. Children's literature has always had stories about young children and their animals, real and imaginary, and Gene Kemp is part of a long tradition with these tales. It is possible to see in them, however, the seeds of what was to come later. There is much humour, a lightness of touch, and a deft hand at work with characterisation. The other noticeable thread evident in nearly all her other books is a sympathetic and loving portrayal of animals and their relationships with humans. So in her Tamworth Pig books, Gene Kemp laid the foundations for what was to come later.

Her next venture broke completely new ground and established her as not only a writer of great originality but also as an expert eavesdropper and chronicler of junior school classrooms and their inhabitants. *The Turbulent Term of Tyke Tiler* blew like a fresh wind through the world of children's literature, leaving a crowd of cheering girls and very perplexed boys in its wake. The writing was fresh, direct, very funny and full of everyday details of school and home. For the first time, though not the last, the name of Cricklepit School surfaced, and the sure and masterly touch of someone who understands schools and children very well was evident. The book was full of jokes and throwaway lines, and went at a cracking pace but, perhaps more importantly, the language was very accessible to young readers and had none of the pretentions found in some children's authors' writing. Gene Kemp's children talk and joke using words and expressions heard all over the country, and you know you could walk into any playground or classroom and hear eleven-year-olds talking just like this. The jokes which head each page are the usual excruciating play on words so beloved of this age group, and reading the book nearly ten years after it first appeared, it still seems to possess a vitality and originality unlike anything else. (pp. 309-10)

Gowie Corby Plays Chicken followed on from *Tyke Tiler* and again used Cricklepit School for its setting. This time, though, the hero was a boy: naughty, unhappy, a misfit and a class wrecker. After much tribulation, and with the friendship of a black American girl, Gowie eventually wins through to some sort of settled relationships, but perhaps because it followed the successful and original *Tyke Tiler* this book seemed pale by comparison and not to have quite the verve or characterisation. It was, however, a more difficult theme to sustain, that of the unloved classroom bully forever beating up other children and stealing their belongings. It says much for Gene Kemp's writing skill that she managed to make Gowie a sympathetic character, and to show, through him, how family background can often have a major impact on both behaviour and self-worth.

It was to be five years before another story emerged from Cricklepit School. During those years, Gene Kemp seemed to rely more on what might be thought to be more conventional themes for children's books, and some of the vitality so apparent in her writing in *Tyke Tiler,* and to a lesser extent in *Gowie Corby,* seemed to be missing from much of her work. Instead, her writing took on a more

contemplative style and in these years she produced stories for a wide age range.

Her only anthology, published in 1980, was *Ducks and Dragons,* a collection of poetry aimed at the junior school and containing a wide and catholic selection of verse. Humour, as one would expect from poems chosen by Gene Kemp, is never far away but there are many poems that point up sadness and leave questions and ideas in the minds of those who read them. Gene Kemp knows, as do all good teachers, that children often have more sophisticated tastes than they are given credit for, and through careful choice they can be led to greater understanding.

Dog Days and Cat Naps was a collection of short stories, nearly all told as though by the narrator, and all on the theme of humans and their relationships with animals. Humour plays a large part in many of these, but there are also stories full of pathos, like 'Joe's Cat'. 'Miss Piggy' is a tale of cowardly children and their equally cowardly pets, who all find to their astonishment that they can triumph after all. Many of these stories are ideal for reading aloud and the easy, relaxed style of writing also makes them an obvious choice for children who find reading long and sustained stories too taxing. The first story in this collection, 'The Grey Invader', is a prelude to Gene Kemp's later book on her own childhood, *The Well,* telling as it does of a young girl in a Midlands village during the war. This is a varied collection which will certainly find favour with animal lovers. Again Gene Kemp's skill in characterisation is evident; even in the shortest stories all the characters are rounded and developed.

In *The Clock Tower Ghost,* Gene Kemp returned to the full-length novel, with a story about a family moving into an old tower as custodians of the ancient monument. Amanda Phillips was a trial to her family, her school and often to herself, but it was given to her to release the poor old ghost from his torment. Again the book is full of characters who, although often only minor, come to life as real people with minds, problems and lives of their own. It's a funny book with sympathy evoked even for the ghost who, because of previous bad behaviour, deserved his fate. There are elements in it, particularly the character of Amanda, which are reminiscent of *The Terrible Term of Tyke Tiler.* The same pace and lightness of touch can be seen in much of the writing, although the book as a whole does not have the sheer brilliance so evident in *Tyke.*

With *No Place Like,* Gene Kemp broke new ground again by writing a story aimed at the teenage market. This book deals with the problems of a teenage boy, unsure of himself, not very clever, and still very much caught in the pangs of adolescence. Although a readable and at times amusing story, this is not nearly so sure in terms of understanding and characterisation as the books which deal with younger children. For the first time elements of stereotyping appear, and I find it very difficult to believe in the mother in the story as a real person. So much of the strength of Gene Kemp's previous books was her skill in creating real people that this lack, minor though it is, seems very obvious in this book. It is as though she has created problems before characters, whereas in all her other novels one of her outstanding abilities has been to create characters, and then, through them, work through their problems to a greater understanding. However, this is a very readable story with a serious undercurrent about the nature of fear, and with lots of humour and sympathy towards the teenage mind.

In *The Well*, Gene Kemp returned to the younger age group with a gentle, quiet story about a girl in a small Midlands village before the war, surrounded by a loving family, animals and the serene life of the countryside, and all based very much on her own childhood. Its perceptive look at a young girl growing up, sometimes fighting with her bossy elder brother, and with a hint of the external world waiting to break in, is presented in a low-key, though often humorous, fashion and shows Gene Kemp in a more contemplative and nostalgic vein.

To the joy of many devotees, Gene Kemp returned in 1984 to Cricklepit School with *Charlie Lewis Plays for Time.* This is another riotously funny story of junior school life but with more maturity and subtlety in the writing than was evident before. The touch, though still light and direct, has more depth, and the portrait of Charlie is gradually and carefully revealed so that in the end, the readers feel they have solved the mystery for themselves. The humour, jokes, problem children and problem teachers are all there still but this seems to me to be a book with more substance, which probes deeper and not only gives its readers more but also expects more from them.

With *Jason Bodger and the Priory Ghost,* Gene Kemp stayed with her much-loved and much-understood juniors though not this time at Cricklepit. Jason is the scourge of Class 4Z, but is picked out by Mathilda de Chetwynde from eight centuries earlier, to rescue her from imprisonment in a convent. Jason's dreadful deeds continue to haunt both his parents and his teachers, but Jason himself is in torment, unable to explain to himself or anyone else what is happening to him. The book is written in a marvellous direct, racy style, full of laughs and again with superb characterisation. It is also a source of painless learning about the Middle Ages. The author's skill with time shifts is clever and, as with most of her books, there is a surprising twist at the end.

Juniper, the latest book to be published at the time of writing, is similar in some ways to *Charlie Lewis Plays for Time,* in that it takes as its major theme a child in distress and in the case of this book, a child who not only has to take on an adult role, but also has to cope with an adult who appears to have reverted to childhood. *Juniper* is much more an in-depth study of a character and of the forces which shape our lives, and although Cricklepit School plays a part in the story, it is not the major element. This is a book of complex and deep emotions but because it is written with Gene Kemp's usual pace and touch it holds the attention of the reader and sustains interest. In one sense it is an adventure story, with Juniper and her friend Ranjit being followed by unknown men, with hidden spoils from an old burglary, and a shadowy 'Mr Big' hovering in the background. At times it seems as if there is enough material here for about three books, and perhaps because of this some of the characterisation is less than sure. As always, an animal becomes an important part of the story and Tom, Juniper's ferocious cat, sometimes seems more real than some of the human characters. (pp. 310-12)

What, then, is the charm of Gene Kemp? Her writing often seems deceptively simple but her books usually have finely-drawn characters, lots of humour, and a narrative that keeps you guessing until the end. They can be read with little or no problem by even the most reluctant or hesitant reader, and are a favourite in all junior classrooms. She makes no pretence about hidden meanings, allegorical allusions or complicated language constructions. Her language is that of the classroom, and she uses this to lead the reader on to an understanding of both motive and character. From the very first page, she establishes direct contact between the reader and the writer, and the reader is immediately hooked. Her writing has progressed through various phases, from the more traditional 'small children and talking animals' theme to the wildly funny, fast-moving *Jason Bodger,* and now *Juniper,* a much more serious book, still retaining the quality of writing and interest for readers but demanding more from them in terms of understanding. In between, her originality has shone through in such books as *Tyke Tiler,* and this talent has been developed and advanced in *Charlie Lewis Plays for Time.* Gene Kemp manages to make the junior school classroom and all its inhabitants live in a way no other author has, and to do this with verve, wit and individuality.

Understanding grows gradually in Gene Kemp's books. It is not thrust at readers, but through her great skill in characterisation, it develops slowly and imperceptibly, so that readers feel they are making discoveries all on their own and coming to a greater knowledge of the characters by themselves. A young reader once said to me that you have to give something to a good book. Gene Kemp allows her readers to feel they have achieved just that. (p. 313)

> *Elizabeth J. King, "Children's Writers: 13—Gene Kemp," in* The School Librarian, *Vol. 34, No. 4, December, 1986, pp. 309-13.*

Gerald Mangan

In the latest of her novels featuring Cricklepit Combined School [*Juniper: A Mystery*], Gene Kemp turns her attention to the fraught home-life of one of its more disadvantaged pupils. As an only child with a withered left arm, Juniper Costello is a daydreamer and a bit of a tomboy, whose domestic problems put a strain on her sense of humour. Her father is missing and wanted by the police, her feckless mother is languishing upstairs in bed, and a bully of a landlord is pressing for the rent. The cat is ravenous, the kitchen-shelves are bare, and there is scant comfort in the charity dispensed by a set of condescending relatives, in the form of a Christmas hamper.

Private jokes and romantic fantasy are Juniper's main refuge, and her inner world is inventively drawn; but the outer world is not all hostile. Her teachers provide a friendly ambience in the background, and her young Indian schoolmate Ranjit gives her the sympathy of a fellow outcast. A handsome next-door lodger promises help in a crisis, and his elderly Yorkshire landlady lends a ready ear to her troubles ("Let's get at it—what's botherin' yeouw?"), while serving hot toast in a homely kitchen. Nothing makes up for the emptiness at home, however; and Juniper's mission in life is to get things back to normal.

Foolhardy but resourceful, she sets out to unravel the mystery of her father's absence, and lay the ghost of his criminal reputation. With Ranjit tagging along, sketching compulsively and urging caution, her explorations uncover hidden links between the various sinister elements in the story; and her dream comes into conflict with an increasingly nightmarish reality. It is an engaging adventure in a minor key, darker in tone than the others in the series, and its amiably spiky heroine gives it a distinctive flavour of its own.

Mr Magus Is Waiting for You is a slighter book with less resonance, betraying its television connection in the text as well as on the dust-jacket, but it offers a fresh mixture of some familiar motifs. Two boys and two girls, meeting by chance in the local park one day at the end of the holidays, follow a stray football over a high wall and find themselves in the garden of an enchanted house, where a silky-voiced sorcerer sits upstairs, stroking a monster cat, and quietly awaits their arrival.

The spooky atmosphere accumulates through effective details; a welcome-notice with each of their names on it, and a table groaning with goodies; a conservatory full of stuffed rodents, and mirrors turned to the wall. There is some patent contrivance in the closing-in of the trap around the foursome, and Mr Magus himself is rather a disappointing villain, smelling a little of grease-paint and lacking in specific motives; but Kemp draws her young teenagers with telling strokes. Between the macho boy and the fat boy, the pretty girl and the swot, the mutual antagonisms work together well for the purposes of suspense; and there is a salubrious moral in their varying degrees of resistance to the evil charisma.

Gerald Mangan, "On Not Giving In," in The Times Literary Supplement, *No. 4389, May 15, 1987, p. 529.*

TITLE COMMENTARY

The Prime of Tamworth Pig (1972)

You can hardly call **The Prime of Tamworth Pig** realistic and yet behind its strange happenings lies a sharp picture of a small boy who is sometimes rational and sometimes anarchic. Thomas is running wild in the school term after various illnesses and he makes the most of his freedom, engaging in a campaign to produce more food (or Grow more Grub, as he puts it) with the remarkable Tamworth as his ally and mentor. Thomas's conversation with the pig, and with his stuffed toys Mr. Rab and Hedgecock, might be taken for an extrapolation of his own fancy if it were not for the Orwellian climax of the campaign, when the Minister retires into Tamworth's style for a solemn conference on future agricultural policy. In a calm, literate style the author piles up amusing and nonsensical scenes lavishly; the offbeat humour will go down best, I think, with children of intellectual bent, nine or ten upwards.

Margery Fisher, in a review of "The Prime of Tamworth Pig," in Growing Point, *Vol. 11, No. 2, July, 1972, p. 1963.*

This book has its clichés, notably of human character and situation. Nevertheless it succeeds in that difficult task of making the reader accept a mixture of humans, talking animals and talking toys without question. The animals and toys are individual and funny—particularly Tamworth pig.

A review of "The Prime of Tamworth Pig," in The Times Literary Supplement, *No. 3672, July 14, 1972, p. 805.*

I thought at first 'What a splendid book this is going to be!' The fantasy was pleasingly nonchalant and young Thomas truly alive, coping with rages and unhappiness and playing the tyrant. His two companions, Mr Rab and Hedgecock, are toys, but also projections of two sides of his own nature: this is very well sustained. And Tamworth Pig, guide, philosopher and friend to Thomas and his sister, and wonderfully conceited, is surely a distant relative of Miss Jean Brodie. Yet somehow I was finally a little disappointed. The story is basically episodic. To hold it together, the author uses the Grow More Grub campaign mounted by pig and children, and this, involving by the end television, Parliament, firemen and the police, is the least successful part of the fantasy. The domestic background is admirable, the prose is a pleasure, and the drawings [by Carolyn Dinan] are exactly in the right humour.

Iris Wilcox, in a review of "The Prime of Tamworth Pig," in The School Librarian, *Vol. 20, No. 3, September, 1972, p. 274.*

It is tempting but not wholly accurate to describe Gene Kemp's first book for children as an offshoot of *Animal Farm*. It has, indeed, political and sociological overtones in that the Tamworth Pig, a very fine specimen, takes umbrage at being fed on oddments because of the high price of recognised pig foods, and when Tamworth eventually appears on television one feels that the shadow of Orwell broods over all. Tamworth's campaign for more and better food certainly enlists a great many sympathisers and even elicits an overt response from the Government (even if that does entail the setting up of yet another committee). Tamworth's main premise is that the shortage of food is due simply to inefficiency and we have all felt this often enough to go along with Tamworth. Of course, this is far from being all that the story has to offer. Thomas has interesting friends in Mr. Rab (his toy rabbit?) and Hedgecock, the spiny mathematician, not to mention Blossom, Thomas' sister. The adults who operate rather on the fringe of events are sufficiently interesting in themselves and Gene Kemp contrives a delightful brouhaha at the climax of publicity. Although this is very much a child's book it does suggest parallels from real life which may give it an extra spice of humour for perceptive readers. It should go down well. (pp. 405-06)

A. R. Williams, in a review of "The Prime of Tamworth Pig," in The Junior Bookshelf, *Vol. 36, No. 6, December, 1972, pp. 405-06.*

Tamworth Pig Saves the Trees (1973)

Tamworth Pig Saves the Trees opens with Thomas and his dawn activities: when, after a few pages, he reaches Tamworth and fantasy begins, one has a slight feeling of anticlimax: reality was so good. Tamworth launches himself into a campaign to save the forest from the motorway; he also falls in love with the black pig, Melanie. Always well-written, the book is enjoyable, but perhaps Gene Kemp might curb her imagination and do even better.

> *"First Steps in Cloud-Cuckoo Land," in* The Times Literary Supplement, *No. 3719, June 15, 1973, p. 687.*

Tamworth Pig enters upon his second campaign, a highly topical conservation project, with his customary dictatorial manner; but after he has met Melanie, a beautiful black and white sow, his bounce gives place to lovelorn melancholy, from which uncharacteristic mood he is rescued by the efforts of young Thomas and his articulate toys. Into the main course of the story are inserted one or two peripheral scenes—a village jumble sale, for instance, where Thomas's few minutes in charge of a stall bring disaster. Plenty of fun in this accomplished mixture of reality and fantasy and in Carolyn Dinan's brisk drawings. (pp. 2199-200)

> *Margery Fisher, in a review of "Tamworth Pig Saves the Trees," in* Growing Point, *Vol. 12, No. 2, July, 1973, pp. 2199-200.*

This low-key fantasy / adventure is one in a series about "the most famous pig in Britain" and young friends Thomas and Blossom. In this book Tamworth, President of the Animals' Union and former campaigner for vegetarianism, crusades to prevent a nearby forest from becoming a superhighway. Despite the fact that his usual activist campaign style is inhibited by a romance with a pretty pig named Melanie, the predictable, upbeat ending manages to occur: forest spared and Tamworth and Melanie as the beaming parents of 20 piglets. Action and suspense are minimal, but the story is saved by an engaging cast of characters, two spunky children and a band of idiosyncratic talking animals.

> *Patricia Smith Butcher, in a review of "Tamworth Pig Saves the Trees," in* School Library Journal, *Vol. 27, No. 9, May, 1981, p. 66.*

Tamworth Pig and the Litter (1975)

Off form . . . is Gene Kemp in her third book about Tamworth Pig, **Tamworth Pig and the Litter.** Like the two earlier books, this is a blend of realism and fantasy—a world of talking animals underpinned by everyday domestic detail. . . .

Given that the portrayal of Thomas is as fine as ever, it seems uncivil to carp. But is not the joke wearing a little thin? It may be that the author's highest level of invention went into making Thomas's toys, Hedgecock and Mr Rab. Much of the exhilaration of the earlier books stems from the sparring between these two, and this is what is missing here.

> *Jennifer Chandler, "Idle Repetition," in* The Times Literary Supplement, *No. 3847, December 5, 1975, p. 1446.*

The message of **Tamworth Pig and the Litter,** suggested in the punning title, is not hard to follow in the ingenuous tale of Tamworth's piglets and their adventures, in which Thomas and his sister Blossom willingly join. In his usual orotund style Tamworth directs an anti-litter campaign in the village; the newly christened piglets are kidnapped and recovered; Albert, the most restless of them, wins permission to stay with his parents instead of going to a "good home" (the ambiguity reminds one of [Beatrix Potter's] *Pigling Bland*) on condition that he learns to read. This is a pleasant little frolic but, as so often with sequels, the given character of Tamworth, once novel and witty, has by now become a little laboured.

> *Margery Fisher, in a review of "Tamworth Pig and the Litter," in* Growing Point, *Vol. 14, No. 7, January, 1976, p. 2787.*

Christmas with Tamworth Pig (1977)

[*The following excerpt is from an essay that reviews the books with a Christmas theme published in 1979.*]

Best of the meow, moo, and grunt school of fantasy, but geared for more developed vocabularies, is **Christmas with Tamworth Pig,** fourth in an English series about a professorial porker and his all too human friends. The cultivated swine swears off causes for Christmas, but stretches out his trotters on TV to the down-and-outers of the nation, inviting them to Pig House in a fine imitation of the Statue of Liberty's "Give me your tired, your poor" pitch. Chaos ensues when they *all* come. Prigs and showoffs are the baddies here; goodnatured troublemakers and honest grouches triumph, a satisfactory balance. Everyone gives and receives in appropriate gifts, except for Hedgecock, prickly admirer of Scrooge, who offers no one a thing but is rewarded with an electric pocket calculator enabling him to do sums (e.g., a comparison of snout dimensions) to his miserly heart's content. The slim story begins with Ethelberta Everready, the ever-laying hen, scaling choral heights to the tune of "O come let's kick the door in" for the benefit of a vicar more devoted to murder mysteries than descants. And it ends with Deadly Dench rocking Church Hall with a rousing rendition of "My baby has the slouchin', grouchin' blues." Those with no taste for Anglo eccentricity should stay away, but this is by far the most cheerful book in the whole end-of-a decade bunch.

> *Laura Geringer, in a review of "Christmas with Tamworth Pig," in* School Library Journal, *Vol. 26, No. 2, October, 1979, p. 118.*

Humanising works in two ways for Gene Kemp in her Tamworth tales. The massive benevolent pig is an uncle-figure, a suitable medium for the conservation message conveyed through his thoughtful approach to nature; meanwhile the two toys, Hedgecock and Rob, encapsulate traits that belong to fancy, the prickly texture of the one fitting the Nesbit tradition of a crusty magical being while the other is as soft and sentimental as a toy rabbit might well be, a kind of Fyleman fairy if you like. Living with, manipulating, influenced by these three splendid natural characters, Thomas and his sister Blossom add their quirks of behaviour to the story. In each episode, linked by the theme of Christmas, predictable matters (snow and the search for mistletoe, wrapping presents, carol singing) are enlivened by Hedgecock's Scrooge-like interjections, Mr. Rab's snatches of poetry, Thomas's noisy anarchy and the majestic pig's reproving or instructive orations. The package as always provokes bursts of laughter, more restrained smiles, admiration at the confident placing of an animal on equal terms with humans and a little thought besides for the underlying message. A word of praise too for the way Carolyn Dinan has made each character a distinct personality with a splendid economy of line and design.

> *Margery Fisher, in a review of "Christmas with Tamworth Pig," in* Growing Point, *Vol. 29, No. 6, March, 1991, p. 5492.*

The Turbulent Term of Tyke Tiler (1977)

> "What's blue and cries for help?"
> "A damson in distress."

A similar gem heads each chapter of Gene Kemp's ***The Turbulent Term of Tyke Tiler*** giving rise to the hope that here might be a children's author capable of writing for, rather than at, her readers. The hope is very nearly justified. Gene Kemp is a primary school teacher, whose previous books were the popular "Tamworth Pig" stories. She has an experienced ear for the lore and language of the upper juniors; their toughness, sentimentality, and deep appreciation of really terrible jokes. This understanding is reflected in her likeable story set in a small town primary school making this a good book to read aloud to a class of ten to twelve-year-olds. Writing "at" creeps in, though, with some reflections on selective schooling which seem to be aimed more at the adult reader than at Gene Kemp's proper audience.

> *Rosamund Faith, "Classroom Lore," in* The Times Literary Supplement, *No. 3915, March 25, 1977, p. 361.*

At the beginning of ***The Turbulent Term of Tyke Tiler*** the central character steals an exam paper but not in a Talbot Baines Reed spirit at all; the idea behind Tyke's action is to coach friend Danny Price, so that however mentally lacking he may be, he will not be sent to a special school but will move with his friend to the local comprehensive. At the end of the story Tyke climbs the school roof to ring the bell as a final fling before leaving the Primary, and so paves the way for a revelation which the author has cunningly deferred (and which I am bound to defer too for fear of spoiling the book for readers). The tag "rattling good yarn" must inevitably be applied to a book which has a shaggy dog joke at the head of each chapter and a rapid sequence of events in Tyke's inventive, noisy and disruptive career. Because Tyke is narrator right up to the final chapter there is an edge to the picture of discomfited teachers and exhausted parents; it is a book to be read with delighted smiles by young and old alike. (pp. 3086-87)

> *Margery Fisher, in a review of "The Turbulent Term of Tyke Tiler," in* Growing Point, *Vol. 15, No. 9, April, 1977, pp. 3086-87.*

Tyke Tiler for all its surface realism does seem to me self-conscious, aware of the effects that are laboriously created and incapable of the 'wit' that permeates [Florence Parry Heide's] *The Shrinking of Treehorn.* That 'wit', I'd want to argue, represents a superior, humane intelligence—conscious and 'artful' but without that feeling of 'constructedness' that marks ***Tyke Tiler*** for me. (p. 63)

> *Eric Hadley, "The Scrubbed Pine World of English Children's Fiction," in* The Use of English, *Vol. 31, No. 2, Spring, 1980, pp. 56-65.*

It is rare indeed for a book to win the prestigious Carnegie Medal and also the Other Award given by the Children's Rights Workshop, but this English story has done that, and it's easy to see why. Tyke, who tells the story, is a lively, active, and articulate girl. . . . There are delightfully funny classroom scenes, sharp and quick character depictions of classmates and teachers, and dialogue that captures the quality of children's speech. It's a happy, pithy story; the flavor is British but the concerns and humor are universal.

> *Zena Sutherland, in a review of "The Turbulent Term of Tyke Tiler," in* Bulletin of the Center for Children's Books, *Vol. 33, No. 10, June, 1980, p. 193.*

In a comment on her novel ***Gowie Corby Plays Chicken,*** Gene Kemp wrote, "The book was written out of a concern for children vulnerable in our society; on the one hand over-pressurised and over-assessed, on the other hand neglected and battered. We do not really do very well by them, despite the efforts of Year of the Child. But over and above that, there is a need for laughter, for children, like Jane Austen, dearly love a laugh." Both novels are set in the same environment, Cricklepit Combined School, in the same city. In both Gene Kemp certainly tries to provide her readers with "a laugh" as well as a concerned view about the way in which the working-class world is seen by a child. Humour is a notoriously difficult element for any writer to handle, and some readers will find the "jokes" which the author uses as epigraphs for her chapters not to their taste. It is not until we come to the "Postscript" in the novel that we realise that the story has been told to her class teacher by Tyke Tiler and that: "(she) wanted the jokes put in, because she says there can't be too many jokes." Indeed it is not until we come to the end of the story in Chapter Fourteen that we are told that Theodora Tiler has, understandably and resolutely, insisted on using the name "Tyke" to disguise, in one sense at least, her sex. The illustrations [by Carolyn Dinan] aid the deception.

The information we are given at the end of the novel does make us look at what has gone before in a different light. The danger is that the reader may have become irritated before that point and given the book up. That would be a pity, for this story of a 12-year-old girl from a working-class family shows Gene Kemp's concern about the vulnerability of children and their difficulty in understanding the mores of the adult world. Tyke's concern for her friend, Danny Price, who is not very intelligent and has a speech defect, engages the reader immediately, and that interest is held until the end of Tyke's story. We share her growing awareness of a world in which adults say one thing and do another, and her anger at the authoritarian attitudes of those adults who make little effort to understand the child's point of view. But the novel is also about growing up, about adjusting to those elements in the adult world which she comes to realise do have some importance. This is the serious core of the novel and why, presumably, its author was awarded the Carnegie Medal in 1977. But the book is also genuinely funny and has some exciting incidents which will appeal to Junior School children. Mrs. Kemp set herself a difficult task, and although the working-class homes she describes are far removed from those depicted in other contemporary novels—Tyke's father is an engine driver actively engaged in local politics—she deals successfully and compassionately with those pressures which are so much a part of life even in a cathedral city in a rural setting.

> *Terry Jones, in a review of "The Turbulent Term of Tyke Tiler," in* Children's literature in education, *Vol. 15, No. 3, Autumn, 1984, p. 159.*

Gowie Corby Plays Chicken (1979)

"Corby, you may be a slob, but you've got guts". Thus, in *Gowie Corby Plays Chicken,* speaks the star player of the school football team. But Gene Kemp is not the recipient of the Other Award of the Children's Rights Workshop for nothing, and her hero is not the teacher's pet, but the teacher's pest, the pupil school would most like to do without. In Gowie—with his jailbird deserting father, uninterested working mother, bully brother in reform school and loved brother dead in a motor-cycle accident—she has drawn a swashbuckling portrait of the class baddie. His chief interests, or obsessions, are Count Dracula, deadly diseases, the pet rat Boris Karloff, tormenting his classmates and disrupting lessons. Presumably otherwise destined to follow in the footsteps of one or other male member of his household, Gowie is redeemed by the friendship of American schoolgirl Rosie Lee.

I guess that Mrs Kemp has it in mind to catch the attention of the disaffected youngster and, having caught it, to reform by stealth. For make no mistake, this is a moral tale. Rosie becomes a Nobel Peace Prizewinner, Gowie a happily married father of four. How this happens is not explained, I fear because it is impossible. What a shame, though, that the secret of Rosie's blackness, deliberately concealed until four fifths of the way through the text, should be incautiously revealed in the blurb. And what a shame that hostility to the fuzz should be the bond that finally unites everyone in non-racial euphoria.

> *Jennifer Moody, "Reforming by Stealth," in* The Times Literary Supplement, *No. 4004, December 14, 1979, p. 124.*

Gowie Corby Plays Chicken follows that robust picture of the same town primary school, *The Turbulent Term of*

Tyke Tiler. After Tyke's spectacular gymnastics on the clock tower the school is suffering from an extensive rebuilding programme, and Gowie, an almost professional bad-boy in the top class, makes the most of this, even though he finds an illicit visit to a medieval cellar more alarming than he had expected. Twelve-year-old Gowie is rough in speech and manner, obsessed by horror films and chewing gum, energetic in stealing from smug J. J. and in insulting fat Heather; he evades work where possible and seemingly owes responsibility to nobody except his pets—gerbils, mice and the rat, Boris Karloff. In fact, he has every reason to be an outlaw, for his family background is disadvantaged, to say the least. Too wise to make a direct issue of this, Gene Kemp skilfully implies it through Gowie's own abrupt, sardonic remarks. For Gowie tells the story himself, officially as a piece of reminiscence to his own children, but in a slangy, fast and extremely pictorial historic present. This gives an immediacy and tension to his account of his own destructive behaviour and his friendship with black Rosie, newcomer from America, who brings a trenchant common sense to the classroom. Like the story of Tyke Tiler, this book has a surprise ending which sums up everything the author has been suggesting about this noisy, determinedly anarchic boy. With comedy in plenty to be enjoyed, with a subtle use of classroom, street and home details, this is basically a serious, layered book that carries lightly a real concern for children as they are and as they can be.

> *Margery Fisher, in a review of "Gowie Corby Plays Chicken," in* Growing Point, *Vol. 18, No. 5, January, 1980, p. 3627.*

The great thing about Gene Kemp is that you feel safe with her from the first page. This school is a real school (the same one almost destroyed by Tyke Tiler), the teachers behave like real teachers and the kids behave like real kids, however disturbing to the sensitive adult. My own children responded to the book with involuntary yelps of pleasure.

Gowie hates the sort of book in which the baddie becomes good, but I am sorry to say that this is what happens to him, through the improbable agency of a black American girl who combines some of the qualities of Muhammad Ali and Martin Luther King and later goes on to a Nobel Peace Prize nomination. This shameless bit of cheek is disarming—but surely Rosie Lee is a major flaw in this book?

Never mind. This is the one book in the bunch [of novels for teenagers reviewed here] that would quell the howling mob at ten to four on Friday afternoon, if Miss or Sir could stand the self-exposure. And books like that are really rare.

> *Andrew Davies, "Sweet Sixteen and Never . . . ?" in* The Times Educational Supplement, *No. 3319, January 18, 1980, p. 39.*

[This] is framed by a father's announcement to his children that his old friend Rosie has been nominated for the Nobel Peace Prize, and a closing note in which he ends his reminiscences. In between, the real story, told by Gowie: an unhappy, rebellious boy, he was the bane of his teachers and the butt of his classmates before he met Rosie. Black, bright, and loving, Rosie became Gowie's dear friend and it was through her that he gained courage and self-confidence, even daring to admit that there were some things he wouldn't do. There's one delightful surprise in the closing sequence, and the story is full of lively class-room banter, schoolboy humor, and some truly touching scenes. Gowie and Rosie are memorable characters, and their relationship is a felicitous one; this is a "good read," but there are depth and substance underlying the fun.

> *Zena Sutherland, in a review of "Gowie Corby Plays Chicken," in* Bulletin of the Center for Children's Books, *Vol. 34, No. 3, November, 1980, p. 56.*

Ducks and Dragons: Poems for Children   (1980)

[Ducks and Dragons: Poems for Children *is edited by Gene Kemp.*]

Ducks and Dragons, is a very good attempt at updating a traditional-style children's anthology. It includes some good and available modern poems, but not quite enough. It suffers from the malady from all such anthologies in that it prints too many standards, such as "Jabberwocky", but it also makes some intriguing choices. G. K. Chesterton's "Song of Quoodle" ("And goodness only knowses / the Noselessness of man") and "The Lambton Worm" from Northumberland ("Whisht lads, haud yer gobs / I'll tell yer all an awful story / Whisht lads haud yer gobs / I'll tell ye 'boot the worm") are both certain to entertain.

> *Myra Barrs, "Capture the Echo," in* The Times Educational Supplement, *No. 3326, March 7, 1980, p. 46.*

'Children take to poetry like ducks to water,' the editor asserts—poetry, that is, with strong rhythms and with colour-imagery, which she is sure 'can weave a spell for footballers as well as dreamers.' Her choice falls on plenty of humour but with nothing slack or meretricious, and every piece (previously tried out in the classroom) has some particular quality of verbal dexterity or strong mood. Among the mainly twentieth-century authors are Yeats, Kipling, de la Mare, with Clare, Beddoes and Drayton pointing further back in time. The energetic cover and roughish, descriptive drawings [by Carolyn Dinan] enforce the friendly, approachable tone of a collection for children from eight or so upwards.

> *Margery Fisher, in a review of "Ducks and Dragons," in* Growing Point, *Vol. 19, No. 2, July, 1980, p. 3731.*

I find this a very agreeable anthology of poetry for children. From Chaucer to Roger McGough by way of Shakespeare, Ted Hughes and Michael Rosen the reader moves easily from page to page finding that poetry is fun. It is a great source book for finding poems to copy out alongside one's own efforts. Teachers who like to read poetry to children rather than 'do poems in class' will find this a handy volume to have on their desk. It may not stay there long unless chained down!

> *D. A. Young, in a review of "Ducks and Drag-*

ons," *in* The Junior Bookshelf, *Vol. 44, No. 4, August, 1980, p. 177.*

You may produce all sorts of fancy criteria for anthologies, but in the last analysis a compiler puts in what he likes, and that is what Gene Kemp has done here. When you are a good teacher, as she so clearly is, what you like you make others like too, by sheer infection of enthusiasm. There is some very good stuff here, not all of it familiar, along with a lot which is less good (in purely literary terms), and it has all stood the test of the classroom. Junior-and middle-school teachers will find it useful to keep at hand, and plenty of children will enjoy exploring the poems and Carolyn Dinan's pertinent illustrations.

> *Marcus Crouch, in a review of "Ducks and Dragons," in* The School Librarian, *Vol. 29, No. 1, March, 1981, p. 40.*

Dog Days and Cat Naps   (1980)

[**Dog Days and Cat Naps** is] excellent for reading aloud, though giggles may have to be repressed here and there. Most of the stories have at least one important cat or dog, not to speak of the occasional tortoise; they are fresh and genuine. Several are told by characters in the adventure; this trick works out very well so that we find ourselves at once in their world; they have made the jump into credibility. The school background is real, distinctly mixed ability and pleasantly multi-racial; the girls are well up to (or over) the standards of the boys. But this is done very cunningly—not a hint of propaganda, everything just seems to happen. One of the stories in particular made both me and a collaborator in the O level range laugh like mad; you will probably be able to guess which. I don't happen to have met Gene Kemp's other books, but I shall certainly look out for the next.

> *Naomi Mitchison, "Guard the Young Poets!" in* The Times Educational Supplement, *No. 3361, November 21, 1980, p. 33.*

The members of the dreaded class M13 (Brain Drain, Hag Stevens, Mandy the Boot and the rest) end up as heroes, to their own embarrassment. This witty bit of hyperbole stands out among tales that centre mainly on pet animals or personal friends. The lively, excitable style suits first-person tales of a cowardly cat, a foxhound walked by an anti-hunt family, a May Queen whose vanity is only skin deep and a stone with mysterious properties taken from a Devon tor. Sharp, offhand drawings [by Carolyn Dinan] match the spontaneous, quick-moving, anecdotal manner of this spanking collection.

> *Margery Fisher, in a review of "Dog Days and Cat Naps," in* Growing Point, *Vol. 19, No. 5, January, 1981, p. 3826.*

Teachers and librarians aware of the popularity of **The Turbulent Term of Tyke Tiler** and **Gowie Corbie Plays Chicken** will be delighted with the ten short stories in Gene Kemp's latest book. She understands children: relationships, hierarchies, methods of coping with adults, humour, dialogue; and she communicates strongly and directly with the top-junior to lower-secondary age group.

Children of this age, together with many of their pets, are the main characters in these stories, and in six of them the narrators are participants. The narrative voice is an important feature in the success of all Gene Kemp's writing and the personae of her narrators have much to contribute to the stories they tell. Whether the narrator is adult or child there is a freshness, vitality, and directness in the tone of voice: here are the effective voices of the good storyteller.

> *Peter Kennerley, in a review of "Dog Days and Cat Naps," in* The School Librarian, *Vol. 29, No. 2, June, 1981, p. 137.*

Of the ten verbal sketches in Carnegie Medal winner Gene Kemp's **Dog Days** . . . , six are ostensibly told by the youngsters who play a central role in them. Curiously, each of the six seems to employ precisely Kemp's own elegant variation in attributing quotations, to use Kempian asides ("you remember"), to use elaborate flashback technique, to be adept with similes and to end with something resembling an artful punch line. Even if the sketches were unified rather than rambling, and even if they were not singlemindedly British in tone, diction, reference and locale, the collection would be put down with alacrity by any American youngster conditioned to a focused plot and even minimal differentiation of character. Amusing dinnertable reminiscences of modest escapades and favorite pets don't make, necessarily, a coherent collection to be made permanent within boards. The last story, **"M13 and the Nine Days' Wonder,"** out of keeping with the other minimal sketches, is a rollicking good school yarn that would get a chortle from anyone finding it in *Punch.*

> *Peter Neumeyer, in a review of "Dog Days and Cat Naps," in* School Library Journal, *Vol. 28, No. 1, September, 1981, p. 138.*

The Clock Tower Ghost   (1981)

I have to admit to being disappointed by Gene Kemp's **The Clock Tower Ghost,** but it is perhaps unfair to expect her to pull off another masterpiece like **The Turbulent Term of Tyke Tiler.** Much of the same humour can be found in this new book, in the relationships between children, for example, and particularly in the exploration of *seeming* awfulness which is this writer's great gift. Mandy Phillips, like Tyke Tiler, is a pretty awful child; but it is she who helps the ghost leave the clock tower it has haunted so long. I am not addicted to ghost stories, but this is one of the best I have come across: I at least believed in the ghost. I found it difficult to believe in much else, however.

> *Will Harris, "Rolling in the Aisles," in* The Times Educational Supplement, *No. 3422, January 29, 1982, p. 30.*

Con brio, a cheerfully exaggerated story of an enfante terrible's encounter with a moping ghost is funny and fast if a bit repetitious. The book begins with a description of the arrogant nabob, Mr. Cole, who has built the clock tower a century ago, then moves to the present; the deserted tower is to become a museum and awful Amanda's father

is to be its curator. Spiteful, bad-tempered, and hostile, Mandy alienates the ghost of Cole as quickly as she does her new schoolmates. Her parents, in patient despair, put up with Mandy's assertion that there's a ghost just as they have borne her tantrums and malicious mischief. There's a turn for the better at the end of the story, as Mandy and the ghost make peace, and as she finds for the first time that there are ways to get along with her peers. This isn't quite convincing, even within the parameters of a fantasy, and Mandy is so egregiously awful she's not quite believable either, but the tale has good tempo and humor.

> *Zena Sutherland, in a review of "The Clock Tower Ghost," in* Bulletin of the Center for Children's Books, *Vol. 35, No. 9, May, 1982, p. 173.*

Gene Kemp has a marvellous ability for depicting, accurately and convincingly, the nastiest imaginable children. The heroine, Amanda in **The Clock Tower Ghost,** is one such; a mean, spiteful, greedy, self-centred child, hated by her school contemporaries and tolerated only under sufferance by her family. When the family move to the Clock Tower, where the father is to set up a museum, Amanda is confronted with an equally mean, spiteful, greedy, self-centred ghost. Their ensuing battles of nerve are humorously portrayed. This is a fast-moving, very funny ghost story likely to appeal to children around eight.

> *Judith Elhin, in a review of "The Clock Tower Ghost," in* The Times Literary Supplement, *No. 4249, September 7, 1984, p. 1006.*

No Place Like   (1983)

Pete is a boy who has lived with failure and fear for so long that he has achieved a kind of comfort crouching within himself, inside his scruffy room at home, while his family—boisterous father, eager, reforming mother and calm efficient sister—range about him.

He survives school by day dreaming, is eased (by his mother) into Sixth Form College, where everyone seems cleverer, more capable, more handsome than he, but where gorgeous girls cuddle him, loyal friends hang round him; though now and then two hard men make him really scared.

He survives again, meets the girl of his dreams and wins her, without visible effort. He knocks out the thicko who, together with a clever manipulator, is robbing the neighbourhood. And at last he can bravely tell his Mum and Dad: "I'm thick and wet and you'll have to put up with it."

No Place Like is a wry, teenage romance for a boy in which all ends well. It succeeds through Gene Kemp's tight writing, her well-known comic sense and sure touch with teenagers. The F.E. mob do indeed sound and behave like this.

I'm less sure about the father, boor with a heart of gold who, despite the fact that he is absent during every crisis for the boy, is worshipped by him. The mother, politically naive, is nevertheless the only one trying to make things work. She is rewarded by unrelenting insult and ridicule from the father and condescension from the son. Humiliated to the last page, she grins and bears it. While the father endlessly brays his feelings to the world, she conceals hers. There's an injustice to it all that goes just beyond the jokes in which the book abounds.

> *Robert Leeson, "School Survivors," in* The Times Educational Supplement, *No. 3509, September 30, 1983, p. 46.*

High praise . . . for Gene Kemp's *No Place Like,* a home-and-school teenage novel which is at once brisk, incisive, perceptive, gloriously funny and—dare I say it?—kind. Peter, the narrator, is a smallish, disaster-prone 16-year-old, who just wants not to *do* anything. 'The life of a walled-in hermit would suit me'—throw in a gerbil or two, a few punk records and things. Pushed into Sixth Form College, he at once achieves distinction by nervously smashing the dreaded Principal's specs. A splendid golden Valkyrie tries to take over his social life. He's invited around. He also discovers poetry, discos and some unknown abilities. But school matters seep into home. Mother, 'stuck in CND' and such, and insisting on the innate good in all criminals, takes two smooth young student crooks into the house; they plant their stolen gear in Peter's room. Meanwhile he tries through the term to find again a girl whose worried-looking face he saw on his first day. Good plot line here, especially at the end. Not to be missed.

> *Naomi Lewis, "Teenage Life," in* The Listener, *Vol. 110, No. 2833, November 3, 1983, p. 28.*

Pete is, to put it kindly, unacademic. He has acquired one CSE grade 4 in Metalwork and failed the other seven. A drifter, he is the despair of his father and teachers, while his mother, depicted with refreshing satire, is a do-gooder obsessed with "problems" but too sentimentally blinkered to grasp them. There are moments when she makes one sympathize with Pete though mostly one wants to shake him until his teeth rattle.

> *Geoffrey Trease, "The Loom of Youth," in* The Times Literary Supplement, *No. 4208, November 25, 1983, p. 1313.*

Adults have an important part to play in *No Place Like,* especially an intellectual housewife whose belief in individual liberty leads her to offer house-room to a couple of vicious young thugs. While Mrs. Williams, in the glow of good will, is easily deceived by Oliver and Kenny, her son Pete is confused by the new contacts and relationships which he, as a loner, enters into in his first term at Sixth Form College. Having always retreated into his room at home as into a cocoon, to escape the abrasions of O Levels and other people, he is ill equipped for the outside world. His unexpected popularity with certain of the leading lights of the college is described in the first person and the author has extracted the last possible ounce of humour out of the unconscious revelations and accidental truths uttered by her ingenuous hero.

> *Margery Fisher, in a review of "No Place*

Like," in Growing Point, *Vol. 22, No. 5, January, 1984, p. 4189.*

Charlie Lewis Plays for Time (1984)

[Gene Kemp], narrative-speaking, sewed up the school scene long ago. **Charles Lewis Plays For Time** take us back to Tyke Tiler territory. Readers will recognise the landmarks straightaway—the grin-and-groan jokes, the storyline that's a lot tighter than it looks, the characters who always seem about to sprawl out of the page onto your lap. The eponymous hero here has everything on his side except what matters. Charlie is in full retreat from the fame and fortune of his concert-pianist mother yet, being a lad of talent and resourcefulness, is an expert at covering his tracks. Covert misbehaviour is one source of refuge—not least against a disciplinarian supply-teacher who compounds his many felonies by paying court to Charlie's mum. Another refuge is the Moffat kids next door who are as lively a bunch of Kemp-followers as this gifted writer has ever drawn in her train. What's especially attractive about the book is its *cheerfulness.* This never falters even as Charlie's crisis looms. The resolution of plot and character at the end is happily, and deftly, synchronised. Who needs Tyke Tyler?

> *Chris Powling, "Bullies Out-Bullied," in* The Times Educational Supplement, *No. 3545, June 8, 1984, p. 49.*

Unlike many contemporary children's authors, Gene Kemp writes for children, but with teachers in mind. Her Cricklepit novels, of which this is the third, are successful because she knows what life is like in the top class of a primary school. She knows what will engage children's interest and how to make them laugh or groan at a corny joke. She also knows how to direct one message to children and encode within it ironic signals to be picked up by adults; and her signals are most likely to be picked up by teachers. Some of these signals are professional jokes ("This is a language lesson so there should be no talking AT ALL"): others are serious insights into victimization, protection of the less able and the prospect of life on the dole. There is also a teacherly authority in her books which could in a lesser writer become unbearable. Kemp makes it work because her novels are set firmly in their background and she convincingly portrays the anxieties, the fun and above all, the seriousness of children's lives.

Charlie Lewis tells the story of his last term at his school. He and his friends had looked forward to a triumphantly happy time with their beloved class-teacher; but instead a supply-teacher, Mr Carter, is brought in and makes their lives a misery. Mr Carter is a sharply drawn comic figure, a combination of all the classroom habits which children loathe. He is authoritarian, aggressively sexist and utterly humourless. He scraps the letters written by the children to their absent teacher and makes them copy out his version and he humiliates slow readers by sending them to an infant class for a more suitable book. He is not a caricature, however, and the reader is not allowed to get away with merely hating him. We discover, mostly through Charlie's remarks, that Mr Carter is as confused and upset by the children as they are by him. The head-teacher realizes this and says to one of the children: "No one is going to be victimized in this school because of being different. Not even a teacher."

Through Charlie's narrative, we also learn that his life at home is far from happy. His mother, who has lost the habit of talking to him, intends him to become a pianist like herself. Much of Charlie's time is taken up with the disorderly Moffat family who live next door. Trish Moffat (rather wild with a shameless crush on her class-teacher) dominates the story but her brother Rocket (not very bright, hopelessly accident prone and obsessed with flying) also plays a part: he is one of Kemp's innocent clowns, inspiring exasperation and love. Charlie's vigorously told account of the children's frustrations at school and the darker story of his unhappiness at home converge when he come home and finds Mr Carter and his mother sitting, arm in arm, listening to Mozart. Soon various acts of minor vandalism break out in the school.

Gene Kemp's other more famous narrator, Tyke Tiler, turned out to be a startlingly unreliable witness but I doubt if many readers will be deceived by Charlie Lewis's bland account of how suspicion fell on the innocent Rocket. Under terrible private pressure, the guilty child blurts out the truth. "Charlie", says the all-knowing head-teacher, "I thought you'd never come out with it." The confession is less of a surprise than the similar revelation in *The Turbulent Term of Tyke Tiler,* but it is more psychologically interesting and more genuinely dramatic. *Charlie Lewis Plays for Time* is a good novel—largely because the characters in it come across as thoughtful, kindly, vulnerable and very active people—and it deserves to be as popular with children as its predecessors were.

> *Victor Watson, "Not Even a Teacher," in* The Times Literary Supplement, *No. 4239, June 29, 1984, p. 737.*

Gene Kemp's humour is sharp, eccentric and pervasive, reflected from the characters and reflecting back on them to make their antics and their problems entirely credible. *Charlie Lewis Plays for Time* is built round two contrasted households and the relationships of the younger members at home and at school. Charlie's mother, a concert pianist, presides obsessively over his music lessons and practice: his song-writer father has long ago been driven away by her rarified talents. Charlie escapes being a prig by secretly writing jaunty songs and by relaxing in the company of the Moffats next door, especially with his friend Trish and her twin Rocket, a crazily accident-prone redhead whose hopeless performance in the classroom is matched by a ferocious energy out of school that strikes terror in the hearts of his neighbours. Because of an accident the friendly form-master in this middle school is replaced by a private-school teacher whose finicky bureaucracy appals Charlie and his mates. Their guerilla warfare offers opportunities for shrewd if hyperbolic scenes, ending with a school concert where Charlie's dotty parody of the song Sir has unwisely chosen, Nymphs and Shepherds, brings down the house. Parents and children, teachers and pupils, are viewed with a shrewd, dispassionate eye in some of the ramifications which are so important in the closed communities of home and school. 'Children rule OK?' might serve as sub-title for this sparkling sub-ironic comedy.

> *Margery Fisher, in a review of "Charlie Lewis Plays for Time," in* Growing Point, *Vol. 23, No. 2, July, 1984, p. 4286.*

This is the third of Gene Kemp's school stories. . . . This time the emphasis is on the Moffat family, six of whom are at Cricklepit Combined School. In fact we might be forgiven for believing for most of the book that it is about the delectable Trish, but Miss Kemp's stories are never as simple as they appear, and in this one there are hidden depths. The narrator is Charlie Lewis, the bright boy whose mother is a concert pianist of world class but who is content to leave her only son—at least until he goes to music school—at such an extraordinary primary school and with the Moffats for friends. The Moffats are a joy, but it would be a mother casual to the point of criminality who would willingly let a sensitive boy get within reach of such rumbustious and scruffy company.

Mr. Merchant (Sir) has an accident on holiday and is away for a term. In his place 4M have to endure a supply teacher, Mr. Carter, who is just as awful as Sir is delightful. Now I know that this book is good clean fun, but Miss Kemp is such a good writer that we demand more than this from her. I cannot believe that the Head (Chief Sir) would allow a temporary teacher turn the curriculum upside down. Alone among Miss Kemp's creations Mr. Carter ('Sir Carter') is too much to stomach. But the dialogue is as good as ever. This writer has an unrivalled ear for the rhythms of ordinary speech. Her invention of comic and credible incidents is as good as ever. And among all the fun she unveils, layer by layer, the troubled soul of Charlie Lewis, who disguises his own cry for help while he reports with joyous fluency and great relish the activities of his contemporaries at Cricklepit.

A splendid story, surely destined for much success with children who, while savouring the schoolboy jokes, will not be unaware of the serious intention and the warm understanding of this outstanding writer.

> *M. Crouch, in a review of "Charlie Lewis Plays for Time," in* The Junior Bookshelf, *Vol. 48, No. 4, August, 1984, p. 176.*

The Well (1984)

I suppose that most authors of books for children are driven along by an autobiographical impetus. Gene Kemp, though, in this latest book has gone beyond the implicit and come out, presenting *The Well* as a collection of plain tales from a Midland childhood just before the second world war.

Many of the ingredients have a familiar ring; "our dad appeared and gave us tuppence each, so we ran to the shop. . . ."

"Every day at milking time Farmer Tulley's cows walked up the lane. . . ."

"Inside there were sausages and creamy mash and spotted dick pud with custard."

However, praise be, the book certainly does not stop at that for these stories are a quantum leap beyond the hackneyed. Cosiness is there certainly and the autumnal tint of longing for a distant time but there is also humour, vigour and, above all, deep understanding of the childhood mind reminding me of Arthur Ransome's belief that the good children's writer is still himself a child.

The stories themselves are homely, familiar ones of elder sisters chasing brothers with the yard brush; of forbidding teachers, posh visitors and dad putting on his best suit; of children who are frit and nesh and barmy. What really matters though is Gene Kemp's loving portrayal of a family whose mutual regard and zest for life stands out from the pages as Lichfield's Cathedral triple spires stood on the horizon of the author's childhood world. This is a delightful book: warm sympathic and entirely pleasing to the ear. It is most welcome.

> *Gerald Haigh, "Plain Midlands Tales," in* The Times Educational Supplement, *No. 3569, November 23, 1984, p. 42.*

Gene Kemp's books, especially the Tamworth Pig stories, provide a mixture of realism and fantasy which is so homogeneous that the lively stories tease the reader into wondering where the recognizable, normal world of the child characters ends and where the extraordinary other world with its animate toys and friendly, talking pigs begins. This kind of make-believe world is itself familiar; what is unusual is the entirely unobtrusive blurring of the frontiers, so that we suddenly find ourselves in the world of talking animals, believing in it. In this way, children are compelled to ask questions which may appear naïve (But surely, pigs cannot talk? Is the little boy dreaming this?), but which are important questions about the nature of "reality" and the ways in which stories are told.

In her latest book, **The Well,** Gene Kemp reveals the source of her gift. This is the autobiographical story of Annie Sutton, alias Gene Kemp, when, as a little girl around 1935, she lived in the Midlands—an evocation in which many echoes from earlier works will be heard. It is the portrait of a real childhood rather than a story, so that mysteries are soon explained (a ghostly creature turns out to be a stray cow), although the complexities of adult behaviour and other uncertain matters do mystify the narrator, who remains little Annie throughout the book. (The narrative is in the past tense, which gives it a hint of nostalgia reflected in the pretty illustrations by Gene Kemp's daughter [Chantal Fouracre], set in tiny circles at the start of each chapter as if the past were being observed through a telescope.) Annie's voice is the voice of a little girl whose trouble is, as her brother Tom remarks, that she does not "know what's real and what isn't". In this way, fantasy creeps in.

Although it is cosy and ordinary, Annie's world is dotted with enigmas and terrors. She is (and so, of course, is her tone) sweetly gullible, impulsive, cheerful, intermittently thoughtful, enraged: Annie is not different from other little girls, but clever and sensitive, the youngest of six, all

grown-up girls apart from Tom and Annie, and all living at home except for the eldest, a nanny in a well-to-do family. The book focuses on an Easter holiday: school, although small and pleasant, does not figure prominently. Home—a modest cottage in a village—is warm and busy (and sometimes chaotic) as the loving parents attempt to keep order among their different children. **The Well** is a charming account of a childhood which will bring much to children of about ten, and in which younger ones, to whom it could be read, will find something of themselves.

> *Nicole Irving, "Earlier Echoes," in* The Times Literary Supplement, *No. 4261, November 30, 1984, p. 1376.*

Short episodic chapters form an affectionate recollection of what the book jacket describes as the author's own childhood. . . . Annie's adventures are modest—among them are her apprehension about a late-evening visit to the outhouse and the heady satisfaction of being included in her brother's cricket match. The author spices the nostalgia for a much simpler existence with her own cheerful humor and with a vocabulary which gives an English flavor to the book but should in no way puzzle readers. Annie Sutton just might be a trans-Atlantic cousin of Ramona Quimby, prone to the same innocent instinct for getting into trouble and equally baffled by the mysterious workings of the world.

> *Ethel R. Twichell, in a review of "The Well," in* The Horn Book Magazine, *Vol. LXI, No. 2, March-April, 1985, p. 179.*

Gene Kemp moulds personal memories into an evocation of childhood that children will read. Of course it's been done before; sophisticated readers and knowledgeable adults can see the complexities of family relationships that Annie fails to understand, but the children who read this book will not be sophisticated or adult, and the surprises will be for them as well as for Annie. Her preoccupations are theirs, her worries theirs. A lovely book.

> *Bryan Jenkins, in a review of "The Well," in* The Signal Selection of Children's Books, *1984,* The Thimble Press, 1985, p. 21.

Jason Bodger and the Priory Ghost   (1985)

[Ten to thirteen-year-olds] will delight in Gene Kemp's hilarious **Jason Bodger and the Priory Ghost.** Jason's main preoccupation is making life hellish for a well-meaning student teacher until his attention is distracted by the ghost of a 12th-century lass condemned to spend her life in a nunnery. Her manifestations in a PE lesson (for which the student is being observed by his tutor) and in the food department of Marks & Spencer are two splendid comic setpieces. The structure of the novel in which the fortunes of the two main characters are unravelled in alternate chapters works well and, despite the author's aside that "as you read this book, you won't learn anything useful at all", it is actually very informative. Just occasionally the relentless jokiness seems a little forced but I am certain this will become a cult if not a classic.

> *David Self, "Ghostly Realism," in* The Times

Educational Supplement, *No. 3620, November 15, 1985, p. 51.*

Gene Kemp has an understanding of modern children which enables her to write of them with humour and tolerance. In this book, however, she transports her unhappy hero, Jason Bodger, into the Middle Ages. His abductor is a ghost nun with red hair, almost purple eyes and bony hands, who walks on a wooden beam that isn't there. The reader must make the transition between the present and the past in alternate chapters, not always a smooth passage. The nun had been walled up in a convent eight centuries ago and now needs Jason's help, why is not altogether clear.

The children of Class Four Z are completely convincing, the people of the Middle Ages less so. The author has involved them in a stormy and sensational existence, but in all fairness, she has no intention of teaching her readers anything useful about the past.

Gene Kemp's talent for writing comical stories is enjoyed immensely by children, but in writing of the Middle Ages her humour is less spontaneous and her facetious style does not seem at ease. Does the unexpected twist at the end of the story mean there is to be a sequel?

> *E. Colwell, in a review of "Jason Bodger and the Priory Ghost," in* The Junior Bookshelf, *Vol. 49, No. 6, December, 1985, p. 278.*

Jason Bodger and the Priory Ghost is perhaps the best novel for older children published this year. The plot is excellent, it's never dull and above all it's very funny. Jason Bodger, the terror of his class, becomes inadvertently and hilariously mixed up with the ghost of a mediaeval nun called Matilda. Their respective stories are told simultaneously by Gene Kemp and illustrated by Elaine McGregor Thurney. Both are full of action and excitement and I constantly found myself laughing out loud. (p. 45)

> *Harriet Joll, "Children's Books II: From Twelve On," in* The Spectator, *Vol. 255, No. 8213, December 7, 1985, pp. 44-5.*

[*Jason Bodger and the Priory Ghost* and *Sir Gawain and the Loathly Lady* by Selina Hastings] provide children with views of the Middle Ages which could hardly be more different. The setting of *Sir Gawain and the Loathly Lady* is the court of King Arthur—luxurious, idle and glamorous. The Middle Ages of *Jason Boger and the Priory Ghost* are more in the Monty Python mould—dirty, dangerous, unchivalrous and hilariously primitive. The ladies of King Arthur's court are likened to peacocks in their fine attire. Jason Bodger's heroine has a dog which cleans her teeth by licking them.

Jason Bodger and the Priory Ghost is much more straightforwardly addressed to children. Its aggressively demotic style may even be distasteful to adults. (Aren't characters who say things like "I fought it was but it ain't" just figures of fun?) The book relentlessly disparages grown-ups and is full of a Shandyesque debunking of its own text—cheery footnotes apologize for boring descriptive bits or advise the reader to skip to the next page.

The author proudly tells her readers that they won't learn anything useful from this book. This is of course disingenuous, for the book is a sustained attempt to excite children's curiosity about the period. Several footnotes, with calculated carelessness, tell the reader to "ask some grown-up hanging about", or even, with a chilly whiff of the history textbook, just to "find out". Although the Middle Ages is defined—as so often—negatively, with a long list of what "they" didn't have, the device of alternating chapters set in the twelfth century with those set in the twentieth is very instructive. The narrative is fast, strong and funny, and in between the jokey bloodthirstiness there are episodes of sudden, gripping unpleasantness.

Some children might find *Jason Bodger and the Priory Ghost* patronizing in its direct address to them, and in its thinly veiled didactic aims. But many will side gleefully with its author and obey her injunctions.

> *Heather O'Donoghue, "Middle English Mores," in* The Times Literary Supplement, *No. 4316, December 20, 1985, p. 1460.*

Mr. Magus Is Waiting for You   (1986)

I get a sense of the perfunctory from jolly Gene Kemp's new story **Mr Magus is Waiting for You,** though this may be something to do with the fact that it is the book of the television play; but both the magic and the characters seem thin.

> *Audrey Laski, "Paper Tapestry," in* The Times Educational Supplement, *No. 3683, January 30, 1987, p. 31.*

In an old ruined house, Mr. Magus and his black cat wait for four children to fall into his clutches. He needs their youth and their energy, to renew his so that he can go on living. Jeff, Vince, Charlie and Tracey were fighting the boredom of the long summer holidays by teasing each other and kicking a football about in Millington Park. When the ball goes over the fence the trap is sprung. How they escape the evil machinations of Mr. Magus makes an exciting story. The four youngsters are amusing to listen to and their varied reactions to the alarming things that happen to them make good reading.

> *D. A. Young, in a review of "Mr. Magus Is Waiting for You," in* The Junior Bookshelf, *Vol. 51, No. 1, February, 1987, p. 43.*

Chasing a football that was thrown over a fence, four children find a beautiful, exotic garden. They are drawn into an ancient, eerie house. One of the children smells danger, but the others enjoy the little escapade—until they realize that the old man waiting upstairs wants their youth, their very lives, and they must find a way out of the trap. All four children are clearly sketched, and the plot builds nicely. The story is brief, and while lacking depth, it should hold readers' attention.

> *Craighton Hippenhammer, in a review of "Mr. Magus Is Waiting for You," in* School Library Journal, *Vol. 34, No. 1, September, 1987, p. 180.*

Juniper: A Mystery (1986)

Role reversal, where the *child* is parent to the adult, is more common in society than many suppose—and it's a theme which lies here in the deeper levels of a plot whose surface is fast moving and mysterious. Juniper, with an arm and a half and a depressed tinsel of a mother, takes her handicaps in her stride and runs full tilt through the clever mists of the thriller to its final cliff-hang and unravelling. Refusing token offers of help from as unpleasant a set of better-off relatives as you'll find outside Dickens, Juniper darts about in a stream of consciousness and waking dreams in a panicked attempt to come to terms with an apparently dark and chilling piece of family history. And there is much else in the well woven mystery which is only apparent.

In Juniper herself, Gene Kemp has found a female hero with the will and the resource inner city children need if they're to survive: an up-and-down tough and bright little fighter with a soul: while in old Nancy next door, a survivor from her own hard times, Kemp shows the same sure touch with adult character. In a book rich with recognizable inventions only Ranjit, Juniper's Sikh friend, refuses to be more than stilted dialogue on the page.

Reminiscent of Roy Brown at his best, this is the best of Gene Kemp—a quirky, individual, perceptive and brilliant book; a mystery that both moves and changes the reader.

> *Bernard Ashley, "Tough and Bright Fighter," in* The Times Educational Supplement, *No. 3672, November 14, 1986, p. 41.*

Juniper Cantello has only one and a half arms. Her mother is a beautiful depressive, her father is on the run and she is being followed by mysterious strangers. She is lucky enough to attend Cricklepit Combined School—like Tyke Tyler and Gowie Corby before her—but the cheerfulness of school is insignificant beside the fear and strangeness that surround her home. Even her loyal and patient friend, Ranjit Singh, cannot really share what she goes through.

Nor, unfortunately, can the reader. The story is told from Juniper's point of view and the atmosphere is eerie and powerful, but Gene Kemp has chosen to conceal, until the very end, most of the things Juniper knows about her family situation and about the men pursuing her. As a result, the plot never really gets going and the powerful, and genuinely frightening, denouement fails to convince.

> *Gillian Cross, in a review of "Juniper: A Mystery," in* British Book News Children's Books, *December, 1986, p. 26.*

There is always a serious core to even the most frolicsome of Gene Kemp's stories; here the seriousness is predominant. In her sub-title the author describes the book as 'a mystery'. It is that, certainly, though not one to tax the brain greatly; it is also a study in psychology and a social document. More than these it is great fun as well as genuinely moving.

Juniper is, I think, the most complex of Ms Kemp's heroines. She is, to use the jargon, 'socially disadvantaged', with a father on the run from the police and the fellow criminals whom he shopped and a mother totally demoralized by her troubles; she is moreover physically handicapped, having, as she puts it, 'one point five arms'. In spite of everything Juniper is quite without self-pity and ready to put her one-and-a-bit hands to anything. At Cricklepit School—where we have been before—she plays a full part and is reasonably popular, but her special friend is Ranjit who can draw like Leonardo. With the support of Ranjit and next-door Nancy, who is undemanding and relaxed, Juniper can face most things that fate throws at her, even Mr. Beamish the fat debt-collector and Olga, her horrible and affluent cousin. Ms Kemp handles competently the twin themes of Juniper's school and home life—there is a lovely description of the carol service in Exeter Cathedral—and the only slightly contrived business of father and his nasty mates, newly escaped from prison. The action rises to a frightening climax, and a rather hasty happy ending follows.

As 'mystery' the book is no more than so-so. As a study of a tough, frightened and resolute little girl and as a picture of a complex small society it is outstandingly good. The school scenes, as in the writer's earlier books, are notable for their honesty and total freedom from caricature. Those in the home are equally candid and almost as amusing. It is a poor-spirited child who could not share the adventure and respond to the dogged courage of this most appealing of heroines.

> *M. Crouch, in a review of "Juniper: A Mystery," in* The Junior Bookshelf, *Vol. 50, No. 6, December, 1986, p. 235.*

Gene Kemp's briskly colloquial, almost rackety style will be modified, for some readers at least, by implicit allusions to that most sombre of folk-tales, 'The Juniper Tree'. The thirteen-year-old Juniper has compensated for the disability of a thalidomide arm with a particularly active and determined way with life, necessary because her alcoholic mother seems incapable of dealing either with a persistent debt-collector or with a second husband whose comparative wealth proves to be the result of well-organised burglaries. The plot is melodramatic indeed, with lost loot, gags, bonds and pistols, and there is more than a touch of the most superficial television thrillers in the thieves' patter. Fortunately there is more to the story than the stereotype of a North Country disadvantaged family in the power of crooks, for Juniper's recurrent soliloquies offer a key to her character and indicate clearly how much events challenge and change her when as well as facing danger she has to work out her relations with her absconded father and her dependent mother. Action, dominant in the plot, is subordinate in the end to the complex relationships in an urban family.

> *Margery Fisher, in a review of "Juniper," in* Growing Point, *Vol. 25, No. 6, March, 1987, p. 4758.*

Tamworth Pig Stories (1987)

Tamworth, a huge golden pig, is a faithful friend to everyone, and when he speaks, everyone listens—even the Minister of Agriculture. Tamworth and Thomas are best friends, and if ever a boy needed a wise, older friend it is Thomas. Full of energy, imagination and uncivilized behavior, Thomas is always in trouble. It can be anything from his rude language to fighting with the neighborhood toughs, from accidentally melting Aunt Cynthia's plastic hair curlers to persuading his terrified sister to join him in flying off the roof holding an umbrella. Tamworth rescues him from his worst predicaments and tries to civilize him. And Thomas in turn saves Tamworth from the butcher and helps him with his campaigns to fight world hunger and to save the local woods. Written in a smooth, gently moving style, the book is enlivened with word play and tongue-in-cheek humor. Those familiar with Milne's "Winnie-the-Pooh" stories will see in Thomas' beloved stuffed animals some similarities to Milne's classic animals. The gentle humor, Tamworth's human kindness, and Thomas' misadventures will delight young readers and listeners, but they may have trouble with some of the British terms. The black line drawings in every chapter [by Carolyn Dinan] add interest to the story, and the jacket watercolor of the cast of characters will attract attention. (pp. 72-3)

> *Virginia Golodetz, in a review of "Tamworth Pig Stories," in* School Library Journal, *Vol. 34, No. 6, February, 1988, pp. 72-3.*

Gene Kemp's stories about Tamworth pig seemed like classics 15 years ago and two have now been bound together and re-issued. But Tamworth revisited is not as good as Tamworth remembered. Aggressive Thomas and his pacific sister Blossom seem more like stereotypes now and so do most of the supporting humans. Tamworth himself remains a different order of being—a self-important heroic figure in the tradition of Falstaff. But the subsidiary talking stuffed toy animals want to take us into a different genre and the mixture of all the elements is less than the sum of its parts.

> *Mary Hoffman, "Artless Animals," in* The Times Educational Supplement, *No. 1109, February 5, 1988, p. 57.*

It is good to be reminded of Tamworth, that benign and supremely self-confident porker whose friendship involves a small visitor to the farm in enjoyable adventures. Two articulate toys, Hedgecock and Mr. Rab, are less Milneish than one might suppose and in fact it is an unpleasant bully, son of the farm, who is called, unsuitably, Christopher Robin. There is a touch of Orwell, too in Tamworth's campaign (in **The Prime of Tamworth Pig**) to Grow more Grub (he is naturally, President of the Animals' Union and sponsored by the Vegetarian Times). The second book in this volume, **Tamworth Pig Saves the Trees,** has a strong conservation theme and in both books a blithe and wayward humour prevails, judiciously echoed in small, vivacious drawings which lend extra personality to boy, toys and splendid pig. Now, how about **TP and the Letter** and **Christmas with TP?** (pp. 4946-47)

> *Margery Fisher, in a review of "Tamworth Pig Stories," in* Growing Point, *Vol. 26, No. 6, March, 1988, pp. 4946-47.*

Crocodile Dog   (1987)

Laddie is not the most endearing of dogs: he has a snout like a crocodile, a rat's tail and a set of vicious teeth—but Mary (variously known as Agatha Gripper or The Agg) loves him and Gregory has to put up with him. Inevitably, he causes chaos, disturbing the neighbours, wrecking a football match, causing mayhem in the classroom, only to vindicate himself by rescuing Gregory from a fire.

A volume in the 'Banana Books' series, **Crocodile Dog** is a tempting enough story for fledgling readers. It is nudged along by Foxy Lewis, the school troublemaker, and Miss Elphick, the new teacher who is as zany as they come. It is spiced with exaggeration and juvenile posturing: Laddie has hundreds of teeth and The Agg is nine feet high and knocks out her younger brother with her swinging plait. The illustrations [by Elizabeth Manson-Bahr] underline the humour of the incidents, spotlighting Laddie's unfortunate deficiencies and Gregory's long-suffering companions.

> *G. Bott, in a review of "Crocodile Dog," in* The Junior Bookshelf, *Vol. 52, No. 1, February, 1988, p. 32.*

Crocodile Dog is funnier [than Penelope Lively's *Debbie and the Little Devil*], and moves at a much livelier pace. Gregory, known as Splodge, tells the story of the stray dog brought home by his sister Agg. Despite Dad's objections, the dog stays, thanks to Agg's complete mastery of the family. Crocodile Dog wreaks havoc at home, with the neighbours, and at school. There is a large cast of characters for such a small book, including comic but recognisable teachers and other adults, and a marvellous head, Mrs Parker, who can quell even the dog with a snap of her fingers. Laddie redeems himself conventionally enough, but the real ending is the beginning of Gregory's affection for a dog which used to scare him.

> *Donald Fry, in a review of "Crocodile Dog," in* The School Librarian, *Vol. 36, No. 1, February, 1988, p. 21.*

Ancedotes like this command attention if in limited space they convey some sense of neighbourhood and of personality—as this one does; the brief text wastes no words and is ably reinforced by cartoon pictures which suit a domestic tale slightly shifted away from the predictable everyday.

> *Margery Fisher, in a review of "Crocodile Dog," in* Growing Point, *Vol. 27, No. 1, May, 1988, p. 4979.*

I Can't Stand Losing   (1987)

[In **I Can't Stand Losing,**] the fun is, to my mind, rather laboured at times. The designer of her book-jacket has really given the game away. In this a number of cardboard cutouts are manipulated, stickpuppet fashion, by a disembodied hand. It is indeed difficult to think of the Gates family as real people, even if the many social ills from which they suffer are real enough. Part of the trouble lies in Miss Kemp's method of narrative. The speaker is Patrick, an obnoxious, self-satisfied young oaf through whose conceited eyes we see all the others in his circle, and no one would accept Patrick's judgment in any matter. As Patrick pursues the seduction of the socially superior Lynne and is himself seduced by her predatory mother, this reader's concern steadily waned.

There are some funny moments in this author's familiar vein, and sometimes an almost acceptable face emerges from the caricature. Then suddenly the mood changes, and for the last dozen pages or so we are in a different book altogether, looking at real human problems in a measured way. A pity that at the very end Patrick is allowed to lapse into his old grotesque ways.

I don't doubt that this book will find many appreciative readers, but from this fine writer we look for something more than popular success. She always has something to say, but I feel that she has not said it—or at least not in the most effective way—here.

> *M. Crouch, in a review of "I Can't Stand Losing," in* The Junior Bookshelf, *Vol. 51, No. 4, August, 1987, p. 182.*

Gene Kemp's second novel for teenagers begins with Patrick Gate's mother moving out of her chaotic household to Greenham Common. The effect this has on the family is catastrophic as each member struggles to survive by doing as little as possible in the home, particularly self-centred Patrick. He, indeed, is having some problems with his sex life for he has bedded not only the lovely Lynne but also her sophisticated mother.

The jacket illustration of *I Can't Stand Losing* is an adroit comment on the writing itself, for it shows a set of toy theatre cut-outs being moved around a stage. This is the major fault of the book; Gene Kemp, one of the more idiosyncratic of children's writers, has created a set of characters with whom it is very difficult to sympathize, in particular the obnoxious Patrick. A curious epilogue drags in the spectre of AIDS and suggests that Patrick's behaviour will be different now: somehow I doubt it.

> *Keith Barker, in a review of "I Can't Stand Losing," in* British Book News Children's Books, *September, 1987, p. 33.*

This is the sort of fast-paced, humorous, twisting and turning story Gene Kemp is famous for, but beware! It is narrated by the kind of egotistical, sexist pig who gives unreliable narrators a bad name. 'Moi. Patrick Gates, entrepreneur, future millionaire, nineteen years old (which is a lie) . . .' Patrick (or Rusty) sees himself as God's gift to women and in the course of the story he 'makes it' with several girls and the mother of the girl he views as his classiest catch so far. Meanwhile life at 'Maison Gates', hitherto kept on an even keel by Patrick's mother, is falling apart. Mum leaves home to go to Greenham, his sister has an abortion, his brother is an unemployed drug addict, his father moves in with his brother's girlfriend, his uncle is an alcoholic and is arrested for shoplifting, and one of Patrick's many ex-girlfriends discovers she is pregnant. Sex, sexism, drugs, nuclear weapons, Chernobyl, unemployment, alcoholism, even, in an embarrassing Author's

Footnote, AIDS—they're all here in, quite literally, a farcical way.

I do not object to the grotesque caricaturing of the characters and their follies, or to the use of humour to draw readers into a consideration of social evils, but this kind of comedy depends, as in Jonson, on the readers' / audience's initial connivance with the rogueish central character turning steadily to profound distaste, and I'm not at all sure that the author has created enough space for the teenage reader to distance him / herself from the objectionable narrator; nor am I sure that peace, drugs, AIDS, family break-up, and unemployment are given anything other than a trivialising and reductive airing. (pp. 352-53)

> *Graham Nutbrown, in a review of "I Can't Stand Losing," in* The School Librarian, *Vol. 35, No. 4, November, 1987, pp. 352-53.*

Room with No Windows (1989)

Gene Kemp has a sharp ear for the vernacular, and an almost eerie ability to speak from inside her characters' minds. Whether this works or not will depend to some extent on the reader. A close affinity with the heroine's raw vulnerability over self-presentation will make *The Room With No Windows* an effortless read, a book that will linger in the memory. To a less sympathetic reader, the elliptical introversion of its "speakese" could seem virtually unintelligible.

Superficially, the book is an impressionistic sketch of contrasting lifestyles. Mizpah is the romantically inclined product of a puritanical, pinch-penny, working-class background. On what ought to be the summer holiday of a lifetime, she comes up against a set of lightly vicious upper-class arrivistes, a formula effective ever since Jane Eyre. The friend who invites her, Tass, so confidently attractive to boys and girls alike, is also a betrayer. Harry, her brother, is amasingly seductive; frustratingly distant. And there is worse to come. Although Mizpah doesn't retreat and settle for the boy next door, she doesn't succeed in miraculously converting the group she half admires, half fears. Her future is left hanging in the balance, unresolved. On a deeper level, the book is about self-knowledge: separating from the bosom of the family and coming to grips with the inherent loneliness of the human condition; the painful process of arming oneself with dissimulation in order to keep faith with private truths—everyone's personal "room with no windows".

> *Christina Hardyment, "Public Appearances," in* The Times Educational Supplement, *No. 3806, June 9, 1989, p. 1315.*

Gene Kemp is a prolific and highly regarded writer for younger children: this is her third novel for teenagers. In this case it is a transition which has not been altogether successfully made. The framework of the story is old-fashioned and familiar, but hung with camouflaging contemporary detail, such as a kind of mantra culled from a pop song, which is repeatedly introduced. The heroine-narrator (who is embarrassed by her name, Mizpah, and conceals it from the reader for most of the book) lives with her father and her embittered grandmother, constantly being told by the old lady to put down her book and *do* something.

A dashing and popular school-friend, Tass Burton, disarms the grandmother, and Mizpah is allowed to go on holiday with the Burtons to a romantic Devon farmhouse called Gooseys, complete with windowless room crammed with books. She is dazzled by the whole family, especially Tass's elder brother Harry, and though their sister Nan seems strangely moody and out of step, a bevy of uncles and cousins are satisfactorily fascinating. Caught up with her new friends and her own fluctuating emotions towards Harry, Mizpah puts off writing to her Gran. Shocked and frightened by a turn of events at the farm, she flees for home, to find that her Gran has died. A previously unknown cousin now warmly receives her, and explains Gran's background of frustrated intelligence and ambition.

All of this is readable if not particularly credible. But the book is nudged into disagreeable outrageousness by the device chosen to galvanize Mizpah into flight. Hidden by a wall of books in the "room without windows", she overhears Nan discussing her drug addiction with one of the uncles, Nick, before they begin to make love. The realities of incest and drug addiction are not contemplated for a second. A final, tidying chapter refers to Tass's Dad "horse-whipping Uncle Nick", and her Mum "taking Nan under her wing", all described among Famous Five shouts of "Come on, you two, I'm starving!"

Mary Sullivan, "Difficult Desires," in The Times Literary Supplement, No. 4509, September 1-7, 1989, p. 957.

Gene Kemp made her reputation with penetrating and very funny portraits of real people in a recognisable world. She is still as penetrating, perhaps not quite so funny, much more subtle in her investigation of young people struggling to come to terms with a bewildering and sometimes threatening society.

The Room With No Windows is not an easy book to read, partly because of its use of the historic present (always a difficult technical device to handle), partly because it is not until almost the end that one discovers the significance of the italicised passages which divide the chapters. Reading calls for dogged persistence for the first thirty or so pages. The rewards are great.

The narrator—her name withheld for good reasons until the last few pages—lives with a harsh and unloving Gran and a colourless Dad. She has a poor time at home and school until the arrival of Tass Burton, a girl of style and force. Tass even manages to get round Gran, and so the narrator is allowed to go on holiday with the Burtons to Goosey Farm on darkest Dartmoor. There she succumbs to the charms of Tass' brother Harry, a smooth talker but in other ways clearly unsound. Her refuge is the little 'room with no windows' that leads off her bedroom. Here she can escape into another world through the books piled high on all sides. This is 'the heart of Goosey'. Here too the world collapses around her and sends her running back to the improbable haven of Gran. By now we know

what all those italics are about, and a happy tale of boys and girls having holiday fun has turned very sour indeed. By the close our little unworldly heroine has accepted her name and her fate, and 'it's all as it ever was'. Any right-minded reader will rejoice with her in the happiness she has salvaged from disaster.

Serious as the book's theme is—and it is very serious indeed—the story will be remembered as much for its fun, its many quirky characters, its picture of a varied, wayward, mostly happy society in which an immature observer can somehow find a place. We know that she will make a good vet or 'an explorer, an actress, writer, who knows?'

M. Crouch, in a review of "The Room with No Windows," in The Junior Bookshelf, Vol. 53, No. 5, October, 1989, p. 240.

Just Ferret (1990)

Cricklepit Combined school has long been a strong setting for Gene Kemp's difficult but credible characters. She has an excellent eye and ear for the behaviour of primary school pupils. This time, Owen Hardacre, nicknamed Ferret, arrives at Cricklepit mid-term and mid-year. Whichever school he's at, and he's been to quite a few, Ferret feels an outsider because of his failure to cope with even the rudiments of reading and writing. Labelled as stupid by teachers and children alike, with no way of showing that he is not, he plays truant, fights and disrupts classes in attempts to escape their contempt.

Ferret's dyslexia (as it is diagnosed by kind Mr Merchant) is eventually tackled at Cricklepit with miraculous results but not before he has been through all kinds of crises. Gene Kemp describes clearly and painfully what it feels like for Ferret to be trapped in his illiteracy and his experiences will reassure others with reading difficulties. At the same time she tells an excellent story of bullying at school; of the wrecking of a beautiful site by exploitative developers; and of friendships: Beany, too ill to fight the bullies but a powerful ally, and Minty, whose mother's own writing helps Ferret see the point of it all.

Julia Eccleshare, "Reading Trap," in The Times Educational Supplement, No. 3842, February 16, 1990, p. 68.

Owen Hardacre, known as "Ferret", is new to Class 4F at Cricklepit Combined School. Nothing is easy. His dad, a struggling painter, has dragged him through many places and schools, since Ferret's mother abandoned him when he was six. He can't read, and is thought to be dyslexic. Though Ferret finds friends in a girl called Minty, and a freakishly tall, frail boy called Beany, Class 4F is controlled by the hateful bully, Magnus, and his sidekicks, Striker and Ceefax. We may conclude what we like about the class teacher. She has blonde curls and cold blue eyes, and is a monster. She regards Magnus as a thoroughly dependable pupil, whereas in fact he takes money from younger children, and has organized and then robbed a fund for the headmaster's leaving present. Her idea of compassionate help with Ferret's reading problem is to force his fingers over words written on the blackboard.

Eventually her colleagues say to her, "I told you, but you wouldn't listen." Her name is Mrs Flint.

Just Ferret tells how Ferret and his friends expose Magnus as the ringleader in the vandalism, bullying and thefts that have been going on; and how Ferret, with the help of a kindly teacher, begins to learn to read. It is an ambitious book, though not entirely consistent or credible. Set out as part of a reading project taped by the teacher, Mr Merchant, Ferret's first-person narrative wavers from the likely to the unlikely, within a few sentences: "I'll not bore you wi' the getting here" on one page, "he indicated with much mitt-waving that I sit down and listen" on the next; and pepperings of "fab" and "brill" don't resolve this discrepancy.

In view of the lifelike situations and difficulties Gene Kemp seeks to portray, approval and disapproval are awarded to characters in too simple a pattern. Minty's mother is a black poet, whose chaotic entrance to the school, shouting Tennyson aloud and crying "Alleluia!", indicates to the admiring headmaster that she has sold a poem to the *Observer.* Ferret's dad turns up trumps, and goes round to sort out Magnus's night-club-manager father. *He* turns out to be Greasy Reynolds, playground bully of the previous generation, and in no time at all is thinking of sending Magnus to boarding-school.

In the closing pages there is an odd, unbalancing addition to the narrative. Ferret discovers a pregnant girl hiding out in a tumbledown empty house, where he has a bolt-hole for himself. He cares for her until she is taken to hospital in labour. This is a short book, with lots of drawings [by Jon Davis], and fairly babyish riddles, jokes and "Knock-knocks" at the beginning of each chapter. The strange inclusion of the characterless, featureless girl, whose predicament cannot, in this book, be convincingly tackled, seems an uneasy makeweight, as does the concluding excerpt from Minty's diary, not previously mentioned, and in which everyting is sorted out and tidied up. Magnus's friends get treatment for their glue-sniffing; Minty's mum rather fancies Ferret's dad, and also offers a home to Ferret's protégée and the new baby.

> Mary Sullivan, "Sorting Things Out," in The Times Literary Supplement, *No. 4545, May 11-17, 1990, p. 509.*

A notable change in the subject-matter of children's books in the last 20 years has been the gradual introduction of stories about life in state schools, some, like the Grange Hill series, stimulated by television programmes. In several cases a whole series is set in the same school. One of the best of these is Gene Kemp's Cricklepit Combined School, famous for **The Turbulent Term of Tyke Tiler.** The most recent addition to this series is **Just Ferret,** a laconic first-person account of the struggles of an outsider to fit in at a new school. . . . This is the first children's book I have come across which deals with the common problem of dyslexia, and it does so coolly, without sentiment and with hope. It is also a study in friendship, and spice is added by the extremely robust war against the school bullies. (p. 34)

> *Juliet Townsend, "The Happiest Daze of Their*

Lives," *in* The Spectator, *Vol. 264, No. 8447, June 2, 1990, pp. 33-4.*

This is the fifth of Gene Kemp's stories about Cricklepit Combined School and will undoubtedly continue the successful line. The story is well told, it is humorous, and moves along at Gene Kemp's usual snappy pace. However, one always has reservations about some of the subject-matter. The dust-jacket calls it 'gritty realism', but one could argue that there is a fair chunk of gratuitous sensationalism. Do we really need a drunken violent father, organised bullying, child extortion rackets, extensive lying, terminal illness, enforced glue sniffing, gambling, random violence, and a teenage unmarried mother giving birth in a shed—all in one book?

> *Robin Barlow, in a review of "Just Ferret," in* The School Librarian, *Vol. 38, No. 3, August, 1990, p. 118.*

Matty's Midnight Monster   (1991)

Gene Kemp has written a picture book story with the problem of children's night fears in mind. Do children *need* these experiences? Do they subconsciously find satisfaction in them?

Matty is fascinated by Granny's storybook about a monster. She asks for it again and again and at last takes it home with her for a night. In the middle of the night the monster comes out of the book, growing bigger and bigger until it even threatens to attack her toys and to bite off her Teddy's head. This is too much! In spite of her terror, Matty orders the monster back into the book—and it obeys her. Next day she returns the book to Granny and never asks to see it again.

Supposedly the author is suggesting that when the child faces up to her fears, she will overcome them, although the reader notices that Matty did not risk opening the dreaded book again.

It is a moot point whether it is advisable to protect a child from such a frightening experience in the first place, or encourage him or her to meet it. The decision must always be made for the individual child.

Pastel illustrations [by D. Timms] and a suitably fearsome monster make the book interesting. (pp. 205-06)

> *E. Colwell, in a review of "Matty's Midnight Monster," in* The Junior Bookshelf, *Vol. 55, No. 5, October, 1991, pp. 205-06.*

M. E. Kerr

1927-

(Pseudonym of Marijane Meaker; has also written under pseudonyms of M. J. Meaker, Vin Packer, Mary James, and Ann Aldrich). American novelist, autobiographer, and nonfiction writer.

Major works include *Dinky Hocker Shoots Smack!* (1972), *Is That You, Miss Blue?* (1975), *Gentlehands* (1978), *Little Little* (1981), *Me Me Me Me Me: Not a Novel* (1983), *Fell* (1987).

A distinguished author of "problem novels" for adolescents, Kerr is acclaimed for her efforts to discuss serious topics and thereby to provoke young people's concerns over a complex and unfair world. Writing in comic and romantic modes, her novels face realistic teenage situations involving drug abuse, racism, troublesome family relationships, and feelings of worthlessness and despair. Although some criticize her works as superficial and trendy, most praise them as relevant and credible depictions of adolescent life. Each of her novels, critics maintain, explains and investigates humanity's ability to give and receive love in the different types of social relations that love creates. Demonstrating how emotional attachments are influenced by people's expectations of one another, Kerr's books examine love's consequences, poignantly describing the pain and conflict which adolescents inevitably experience as they mature and define themselves as independent persons. She is also careful to realistically portray adult characters as fallible human beings with their own needs and problems, something which young people, Kerr contends, must learn to understand and accept. While her works are generally serious, they are not without comic elements as revealed in her phraseology, word choices, and use of metaphors to create vivid pictures and develop characterization. Kerr's ability to uncover life's incongruities and exaggerate them to the point of ridiculousness has led critics to assert that humor, as well as romance, is a hallmark of her popular and highly respected writings for young adults.

Acclaimed as a fresh, perceptive, and often funny treatment of the serious problem of teenage obesity, Kerr's first novel, *Dinky Hocker Shoots Smack!,* is based on her work experience as a creative writing teacher at Manhattan's Central High. The story concerns a frustrated, overweight high school girl whose mother is so absorbed in her own work with drug addicts that she fails to notice her daughter's own problems. In subsequent works such as *If I Love You Am I Trapped Forever?* (1973), *Love is a Missing Person* (1975), and *I'll Love You When You're More Like Me* (1977), Kerr ponders love's complexity and the importance of commitment in relationships. Spirituality figures prominently in two novels, *Is That You, Miss Blue?,* the story of a religiously fervent boarding school teacher who suffers a mental breakdown as a result of students' and parents' ridicule and isolation, and *What I Really Think*

of You (1981), which explores how two teenagers, Opal Ringer and Jesse Pegler, come to terms with their own spirituality and the social, economic, and religious difficulties of being ministers' kids. While most of her novels are told by a single narrator, two teenage dwarves, Little La Belle and Sydney Cinnamon, wittingly describe how they fell in love despite their parents' opposition in *Little Little.* Acknowledged as a story of courage and tolerance, *Little Little* helps readers to understand that all people, regardless of handicap, have basically the same needs and problems. In 1978, Kerr composed *Gentlehands,* a touching story of the romance between a wealthy young beauty and a lower-class boy whose love for his grandfather is shattered by the revelation that the latter was formerly a brutal Nazi concentration camp guard. Inspired by her brother's difficult readjustment to peacetime following military service in World War II and Vietnam, *Gentlehands* is considered an important and useful introduction to the Nazi period and its aftermath. In 1983, Kerr published her autobiography, *Me Me Me Me Me: Not a Novel,* in which she relates childhood and adolescent experiences which have shaped many of her novels. Regarding her own work, Kerr has written, "I would like my readers to laugh, but also to think; to be introspective, but also to reach out . . . and I hope I can give them characters and situations which will inspire these reactions."

(See also *Contemporary Literary Criticism,* Vols. 12, 35; *Something about the Author Autobiography Series,* Vol. 1, and *Authors & Artists for Young Adults,* Vol. 2.)

AUTHOR'S COMMENTARY

[*The following excerpt is from an interview by Jim Roginski. In the first portion of the interview, Kerr discusses her early experiences as a writer. Commenting on her nonfiction book on suicide,* Sudden Endings *(1964), she notes that readers take interest in the problems of famous people. This fact, she states, adds dramatic force to the plot of* Little Little, *where the protagonist, who is a dwarf, comes from "one of the finest families in town."*]

[M. E. Kerr]: [*Little Little*] was one of the hardest books I've written because I wanted it to be funny. When you're writing about handicapped people it's hard for you as an outsider to have the inside humor without being either patronizing or cruel. Finding the right voice is hard.

[Jim Roginski]: What was so "fascinating" about doing a story about a dwarf? Was it somehow based on a personal experience?

M. K.: Yes. . . . When I was a kid, the golden boy in our town—he had everything, he had money, brains, and a good family—went to Harvard and brought his wife back, a stranger in the town. They were the Scott and Zelda Fitzgerald of this upstate town. Then they had a child who was a dwarf, though they didn't know it until she was two years old.

It ruined and changed their lives. With all their privilege they couldn't protect her from the outside. People are very cruel about dwarfs in particular because they are little, so they're assumed to be benign.

When I was doing research on this and mentioned it to people, they all laughed. There is a tendency to laugh because they're little people. But they're often people in terrible pain and some of them don't live long.

This little girl in my hometown had a tragic life. A lot of it was funny and a lot of it was awful. As the family tried to get her to meet other dwarfs when she was in her teens, they invited all these dwarfs to our town. This was a town with a prison in it and a Japanese steel plant trying very hard to woo new industry in. So industrial heads would get on the bus and come to town and on the bus would be the prisoners, the dwarfs, and the Japanese. Then the town tried to get the people not to have the dwarfs come to town. It was hard.

Then the dwarfs became militant and wanted urinals and telephone booths down to their size. The mother became obsessed trying to find a perfectly formed dwarf for her daughter. Her daughter was perfectly formed so her mother didn't want one of the more crippled ones and she didn't want someone she felt looked bizarre to be her daughter's suitor. And, there were a lot of dwarfs lying about their age because they were a wealthy family. A lot of these

young male dwarfs who were twenty-six were saying they were sixteen.

I watched all this and it never went out of my head. I never forgot it because it seemed like such a strange thing to have happened to this privileged, beautiful family, suddenly confronted by problems like everyone else.

I tried several times to write it as an adult book and it didn't work. Then I tried it as a young adult book and for a long time it didn't work, either.

I found I was following my idea of dwarfs in fairy tales and dwarfs on television. Finally I got the voice for it and the story started to come. That took two years and that's longer than most young adult books take me.

J. R.: What do you mean by you couldn't find the "voice"?

M. K.: For a long time the girl in the book didn't talk right and the dwarf who was the "roach" in the book, who wasn't perfectly formed and was her suitor, talked strangely. They didn't seem to have a natural voice. I couldn't find their attitude.

I suppose when you're trying to find a voice, you're trying to find an attitude, how these people feel about life. Until I got a sassy voice—a voice very similar to my own when I was a kid—I couldn't write it. She seemed self-pitying or sad or melancholy; she had no strength. I wanted somebody who was a survivor, that was going to be okay and you felt that. It took me awhile to get that attitude.

I suddenly realized it could have happened to me. I was that smartmouth. I would have been angry. I would have found the humor in it. I would have liked the ones who weren't perfectly formed, and I wouldn't have liked my mother's suggestions at finding the ones who were.

Life is the same whether you're handicapped or not. We're all handicapped in some way. I never liked the nice boys. My mother would fix up these great dates for me when I was young. I always liked the tough outside guys who didn't fit in and weren't from good families.

When I finally found she had a voice very much like mine, I could write it.

J. R.: Another book of yours, **Gentlehands,** created a furor when it was published. Talk about that one.

M. K.: It was very much inspired by my older brother who was a World War Two pilot and never got over it. Then he became a mercenary and then he went to Vietnam with the C.I.A.'s Air America. They were provocateurs. While we are very close, our philosophies have never been close.

He's a charming guy with a great sense of humor. He seems so kind, so all-American. In the back of my head I think he was there somewhere when I wrote **Gentlehands.**

I was interested in the idea that as Pogo used to say, "the enemy is us." I was interested that the Nazis, our great enemies in World War Two, were probably not a great deal different from some of us in Vietnam. We know the soldiers as family men and the enemy knows them in quite a different way. I got caught up in the idea of what is evil.

I wanted to provoke the idea of what if you meet a nice guy, a really nice man, and what if you find out that in his past he wasn't such a nice man? How would you feel? How would you feel about him in your family? That was how it started.

J. R.: You managed to not only provoke the idea, but a whole lot of people as well!

M. K.: There's been a lot of flak about that book. I think Jews hated it because they felt "Trenker," the Nazi, was the nicest guy in the book. I wanted to provoke some questions. I sure did!

J. R.: Despite the controversy, the book has become an important one in the studies of Holocaust literature.

M. K.: I never knew there was a branch called Holocaust literature. You get into it if you write anything to do with the subject.

Of course I wasn't aware of that. When the first bad review came through on **Gentlehands** from a Jewish organization, I was shocked that they didn't appreciate I was trying to provoke some questions about good and bad. I guess because I never had anybody say "De Lucca," the Nazi, was a bad person, people got upset.

J. R.: What about reactions from young adults?

M. K.: Once I saw how kids reacted to it, I realized they very well might have misunderstood what I was saying. They thought I was saying let bygones be bygones, let's get on with our lives. I wasn't.

There was one school where they were putting on trials of De Lucca. The kids let him go! I was quite shocked.

Interestingly enough, too, it bothers people that De Lucca has yellow glasses, which I never thought about. I just thought readers would get a better visual picture of him, that's all. You can't please anybody when it comes to anything to do with religion or the Holocaust.

J. R.: And that brings us to **What I Really Think of You.**

M. K.: Religion is a far more sensitive subject than anything else. It's seldom dealt with in young adult books and I think it's one of the touchiest subjects there is. Harper & Row was very nervous about the book and how it was going to be received.

Except for the East, television preachers all around the country are liked a lot. People aren't so cynical about them.

People felt I was laughing at the preachers, making fun of them. The Little church was a charismatic church and people asked what I was saying. I got a lot of letters about that one from disgruntled people who felt I was making fun of religion. The poor preacher who was head of the charismatic church spoke with bad grammar and colloquial talk. People thought I made him look dumb. They didn't like that. They thought I suggested I thought he was ignorant. They overlooked the fact that what he said wasn't and his attitudes weren't for what he was. I tried to answer it that way.

Someone even wrote an article that was published in *Voice*

of Youth Advocates about religion and how I handled it. The writer was angry at me for making fun of it. I pointed out in a letter that in **Little Little** the only sensible person was the grandfather, who was a preacher. He was the one who took her to the convention for the dwarfs and he was the one that explained how people looked at them. He was the voice of reason. She didn't pick up on him.

J. R.: Read carefully enough, all your books have a subtle moral to them. Is this intentional?

M. K.: Yes, I think.

When I was a kid I used to play two games. One was "Spy" and one was "Preacher." I would get on a box and preach. I called myself Meaker the Great and I would give lectures on a soapbox.

I think those games are both sides of me. There's a side to me that likes to tell little morality tales, which is also why I'm happier in the young adult field. Adults are bored with bleeding hearts. Kids see and feel prejudice up close in high school.

For the first time maybe they find out their family isn't what they thought it was. Or maybe they're outsiders because they're Jews or Catholics or Italians or Polish or anything. It's the first time it hits them. It's the first time they start looking around at their environment and questioning. They're ready to read about it, to try and find out more and to think about it. Adults have blocked a lot of their youth out. They don't want to remember it. Adults want to escape into murders or spies or long historical novels.

So the preacher in me likes this field, telling little morality tales, to tell a little story that has a point to it that I want to make.

The spy, of course, is what a writer is: someone secretly watching and gathering information!

J. R.: Do you think the young adult reader picks up on the morality in your books?

M. K.: I think anybody who reads me carefully, sees it. They know that ultimately in the book there is a lesson, something about prejudice or something about people who are different. I think most people understand that's part of what I write about.

Kids, I think, just want a good story and that's what I want to give them. A good story to me is a story with that kind of point. I give them that. (pp. 164-67)

J. R.: Has your writing style changed much in the course of shifting from writing for adults to writing for young adult books?

M. K.: It's a constant learning process for me. As a writer grows, the style changes, too.

For instance, starting with **Night Kites,** I tried to simplify my style. I became aware that kids get very confused when you have too many subplots and I decided to try writing more directly, without so many subplots, becoming more accessible. It was an interesting challenge.

It's a way also of keeping yourself from being bored, trying new things. Then, too, when I entered the young adult field I found that boys don't like books about girls, but that girls don't mind reading about boys and girls, too. Boys only like to read about boys. They don't like books with "love" in the title and they don't like mush. So I began to write a lot of books through the eyes of a boy for that reason because I was interested in wooing the male audience.

J. R.: Have you made any other changes in your techniques for the young adult audience?

M. K.: Vocabulary. It's nothing I used to think much about.

In *Night Kites* I did use the word "autonomous" and I did have a character question what it meant. My generation was trained to look words up. Today's kids don't seem to anymore. Also, kids don't use big words when they talk, so in vocabulary I have to be careful which words I use. When a kid is talking, he isn't necessarily going to say, "I want to be autonomous."

I also can't assume a kid understands prejudice. If I were writing the voice of the bigot in an adult book, I would assume my audience would know that anybody who used the word "nigger" or "kike" or some word like that was a bigot. In a young adult book, I would be sure that some other character pointed it out. I wouldn't let that go by. I think when you're writing about prejudice for young adults, you have to point out things you don't have to for adults.

J. R.: Characterize yourself as a writer.

M. K.: I see myself as a storyteller. That's what I am. There are people who love words and know how to put them beautifully together, almost poetically, a writer like Alice Hoffman. I'm not that kind of writer. She's able to create a beautiful way to tell a good story. I think I can tell a good story but I don't have her talent and the almost poetic love of words that she has. I think of her as an artist.

I think I'm a writer; I do what I want to do. Joyce Carol Oates, in quoting James Joyce, said, "Other people may have more talent perhaps, but I am willing to work." That's being a writer. Say no more. (pp. 168-69)

J. R.: You write very commanding themes. Where do the ideas come from?

M. K.: I learn an awful lot from librarians and teachers when I visit schools. Interesting things like, don't use "love" in the title!

Every time I go someplace people give me ideas. Every time I go someplace I'm told suicide is a big problem. I don't want to write a book about it.

That's not what I want to do, write a book that's suggested to me. But it does put me in touch with what teachers and librarians feel is going on with their kids. That's very valuable to me.

For myself, I usually just get an idea. The only time I wrote about what people might call a theme was *Night Kites,* because I was very distressed by a neighbor who died of AIDS. He and his family had to deal with the facts

of his life. There was no way to hide what he was dying of. It really struck me and touched me and I thought I really want to do a book about this subject.

Usually, the kind of kids I notice and want to write about are tied into something. For example, with *What I Really Think of You* came from a time when I went by a religious bookstore. I'd heard a piano player over an outside speaker. It was really good so I went inside to learn the name. It was Jimmy Swaggart. While I was in the store there was a little girl answering the phone. Her mother was saying to her, "You answer the phone by saying, Thank You, Jesus!" The girl didn't want to do it. She was embarrassed by it. I saw her again at one of her father's park meetings on a Saturday morning and she had to hand out literature. She was a pretty little girl, but shabby and unhappy looking. Then I went down to the church and watched the family. That started me with *What I Really Think of You.*

Another time, I went to a football game and there was a very cute girl, who looked like a cheerleader. She was carrying a little brown baby in her blanket. She was with a tall, lanky black guy. Where I live, the black guys are good in sports, the old stereotype, and the white girls date them. It never works the other way around, that the black girls are dated by the white boys. It's always the black boys dating white girls. I noticed this and I was standing next to my dentist's wife who said, "That's not the only problem." She said the real problem is the anger of the black girls in coping with white girls dating black boys. That started the wheels turning for *Love Is a Missing Person.*

Him She Loves? came from a long time ago when I dated a Jewish boy and his mother said, "Her he loves?" I was a shiksa, and she was very much against me. There was a lot of humor in her. A lot of that book was remembered back when I was dating that boy. I picked up a lot of Yiddish expressions, a lot of the humor from them, and the agony of trying to date a Jewish guy is in the book. I was bad news in that family!

J. R.: You obviously draw most of your material from real life.

M. K.: Yes, mine and others!

Miss Blue is directly from my own boarding school experiences. *If I Love You, Am I Trapped Forever?* came directly from a kid who was a Jewish refugee. We called him "Hopeless" in high school; I called him "Doomed" in the book. The book was about the violent reaction of having a Jew in town. My father wouldn't even say "Jew," he'd say "a person of the Jewish persuasion."

J. R.: What brought you to writing for young adults anyway?

M. K.: *Pigman* by Paul Zindel is one of the reasons I started writing for young adults. That combined with Louise Fitzhugh, who kept saying to me, "Get in the field, you're always writing about kids." Then I read *Pigman* and thought, "This is a great book." I didn't care if it was a young adult or adult, or what it was, I loved it and that really started me off.

The interesting thing I discovered was there were so many

stories I couldn't have told to an adult audience, that I just stayed with it. Idea after idea kept cooking so I stayed with it.

When I discovered the young adult field it seemed like a miracle that I could tell all those stories about myself as a kid, or stories about kids. Also, the themes are the same whether they're set in 1944 or today. The theme of acceptance, rejection, outsiders, that hasn't changed. (pp. 170-72)

> *M. E. Kerr and Jim Roginski, in an interview in* Behind the Covers, Vol. II *by Jim Roginski, Libraries Unlimited, Inc., 1989, pp. 161-76.*

GENERAL COMMENTARY

Mary Kingsbury

> I'm not going to describe in detail the very personal things that take place. . . . I'm not writing this book for a bunch of voyeurs. . . . It's a story about people and how their minds work. . . . What's fascinating about people is, no one thinks or acts the same way. I am writing about the why of people.

Alan Bennett's apologia in *If I Love You, Am I Trapped Forever?* describes M. E. Kerr's purpose in each of her five novels. If, as Irene Hunt suggests, the strain of excellence to be looked for in an outstanding book is the author's ability to clarify "some problem of the human family, some aspect of human behavior, some quality of the human heart or mind or conscience" and the author's "sensitivity to the problem he has perceived, the credibility and grace with which he has recorded what he has perceived," the novels of M. E. Kerr can be judged as among the most outstanding being published today. For in each of them and with varying degrees of "credibility and grace," she attempts to clarify the why of people. Her willingness to confront serious issues coupled with her artistic abilities lifts her novels above the myriad problem-novels that have little to recommend them but their topicality. Not that Kerr's novels fail to reflect the age in which they are written. They do reflect the 1970s, but they also offer the reader much more than a commentary on contemporary problems. They introduce themes that will continue to puzzle mankind in the future just as they have troubled him in the past.

Discovering the themes and patterns in a writer's total work becomes the principal objective of a reader attempting a critical appreciation of that author's literary contribution. Reading all the novels brings the realization that a common theme appears in each of them, a theme that makes one of the strongest comments on the human condition in literature for young people today. The author is concerned with love, its presence and, more commonly, its absence in the lives of her characters. Virginia Woolf noted in *The Common Reader* that writers are disappointing if they are concerned with the body but not with the spirit. Kerr gave early assurance that she was not going to fall into that trap. The why of people can, in most instances, be explained in terms of who or what they love and whether they receive the love they need from others.

The spiritual element that Virginia Woolf found wanting in much of modern fiction is not lacking in the novels of M. E. Kerr.

A theme in all her novels becomes the title of her latest—*Love Is A Missing Person.* In her first book, *Dinky Hocker Shoots Smack!,* Dinky fails to get the love and attention she needs from her parents until she makes an extraordinary effort to communicate her feelings. As Tucker explains to Mr. Hocker, Dinky's bizarre act is "about things amounting to a lot more than people think they amount to . . . it's about having your feelings shoved aside." Alan Bennett, the narrator of Kerr's second novel, *If I Love You, Am I Trapped Forever?* decides that "the world would be much better off if they could boil down this 'love' business to one meaning." His girl friend and the older woman with whom he is infatuated both demonstrate that love does not mean being trapped forever and that his father's abandonment of his mother was not as unique as Alan had always thought. Love is, at times, "too hard" and not always reciprocated.

The theme of love is less well defined in Kerr's third and least successful novel, *The Son of Someone Famous.* Adam, called "A. J." by his father, has allowed his identity to be defined by his father's. The book raises the problem all adolescents must solve to achieve maturity. An individual can never become a person in his own right if he is always living up to the expectations of those who love him. At what stage of development does self-love strengthen a young person so he can take control of his own identity? "Being the son of someone famous . . . [is] just a part of being me," Adam concludes. "But not the biggest part. I know that now." Adam tells his friend Brenda Belle that " '[l]ife isn't fair, or even, or equal.' " The novel suggests that neither is love. A. J.'s father tells him, " 'I should have loved your mother more. She loved me with a passion, A. J.' " In fact, the boy's mother had been killed in a car accident when she was running off with another man. That marriage does not necessarily assure everlasting love is a minor theme in all of Kerr's novels.

Is That You, Miss Blue? is a tightly constructed novel that makes a harsh but truthful statement about man's inhumanity to his fellows. The book strips away the veneer of righteousness that adorns many who are, in fact, inwardly honeycombed with hypocrisy. Miss Blue's open display of love for Christ leads to her dismissal from the ostensibly Christian boarding school. The ultimate irony is that in a school dedicated to religious principles and practices, a teacher is dismissed for being too fervent in her convictions. Miss Blue loves too much, and her ways of expressing love are unacceptable to those in authority. By saying that the school is a microcosm of the world, Kerr implies that the injustices perpetrated there are only smaller versions of the injustices in the larger world.

Suzy Slade, the narrator of M. E. Kerr's latest book, feels alienated from her mother and unwanted by her father. For her, love is a missing person. Gwen Spring's former sweetheart has been missing from her life for twenty-five years, yet she continues to love him. Suzy's sister, Chicago, falls in love and literally becomes a missing person. The author, as in all her books, is preoccupied with love, the varied relationships it engenders, and man's inability to give and to receive the love that might be expected in such relationships. For most of her characters, in fact, love is a missing person.

In addition to this common theme, the novels share a pattern of elements and literary devices. Each introduces at least one contemporary issue such as mental illness, drug addiction, anti-Semitism, alcoholism, and racism. Each portrays the development of adolescent sexuality, and several offer insight into adult sexuality as well. Adolescents in all the books begin to view their parents more realistically and with greater understanding. Sharply drawn minor characters abound in all the books; frequent use is made of irony, humor, and quotations from literary sources.

The world Kerr creates is more than an adolescent world, for it includes adult characters who are far different from the unsympathetic ones usually portrayed in much realistic fiction. Moreover, she displays great skill in conveying the complexities of the parent-child relationship. Describing Tucker and his mother in *Dinky Hocker*, Kerr juxtaposes the astringent and the tender qualities that make up much of life's relationships. Recall Mrs. Woolf's caustic comment when the usually solemn Tucker laughs. " 'Oh, don't tell me you're going to choke up some youthful laughter, Tucker!' " Then recall the moving scene in which Tucker finds his mother "hunched over some work, crying, at the kitchen table just as dawn was breaking."

In *If I Love You, Am I Trapped Forever?*, Alan compares his father's behavior with that of Mrs. Stein. "The only time I ever thought of my father was when I contrasted his running off with Catherine Stein's staying. His weakness; her strength." Alan begins to acquire wisdom with heartbreaking force when Mrs. Stein runs off with the football coach. The book ends with Alan's protest that her actions have nothing to do with his life. It is a tribute to the author's skill that the reader knows better. (pp. 288-91)

Flan Brown, the narrator of *Is That You, Miss Blue?* rejects any contact with her mother who she thinks has run off with a younger man. Her father's opinions are the ones she quotes and respects. By the book's end, however, she has come to realize that one of her former boyfriends may have been right when he called her father a quack and that she has been wrong in her rejection of her mother. In *Love Is A Missing Person*, Suzy Slade also begins to see her father in a different perspective. "I'd never questioned his behavior in my whole life. . . . Now I just wondered about him, not as Daddy, and not as the man in *Who's Who*. . . . But Barry Slade, the individual. Did I even like him anymore?"

Suzy's ponderings point up an obvious strength in the Kerr novels, one that sets them apart from the many contemporary novels nearly devoid of well-developed adult characters. A reader of the majority of books written for young adults learns what motivates the adolescent characters but seldom learns what makes the adult characters act as they do. The adult characters are so fully realized, however, that readers acquire some idea of the pressures on

adults in American society. The books offer a series of "possible futures" for their readers, a veritable gallery of "there but for the grace of God" vignettes. Flan Brown speculates, for example, about what changed the popular "Nesty" into the shunned Miss Blue. "Could it happen to anyone? To me? And what would it take to make it happen?"

A roster of memorable characters appear in these books, characters as varied as Dinky Hocker, Doomed Stein, Jingle Bell, Chuck from Vermont, Agnes Thatcher, and Gwen Spring. Contrasting characters are adeptly portrayed—Mrs. Hocker and Mrs. Woolf, Mr. Woolf and Jingle Bell, Alan and Doomed, Sophie and Leah, Brenda Belle's mother and her aunt Faith, Ape and Billy Etinger, Gwen Spring and Mrs. Slade; and there are also excellent brief descriptions of some of life's losers, as Alan Bennett would label them. Tucker sees an old man in the library who smells of salami and another old man giving out balloons on the corner; Brenda Belle thinks of the science teacher who has never been young; and Suzy Slade winces as the town drunk slams his head into the stadium wall.

The only flaw in Kerr's depiction of her characters is that they never elicit from the reader a complete sense of identification. The adolescent narrators, for example, are not as memorable as several of the adult characters, possibly because the young people act as observers of the actions of more colorful characters. This is not to say that the reader cannot identify with Kerr's adolescent characters. Tucker's fears about his social acceptability, Flan's feeling of guilt about Miss Blue, and Suzy Slade's disillusionment with her father and ambiguous feelings about her mother can be shared. But rarely, if ever, does a character totally capture both the interest and the emotions of the reader. Her characterizations appeal more to the head than to the heart, but they are, nevertheless, fascinating.

Consider Evelyn Slade in *Love Is A Missing Person*. To dismiss her as "the alcoholic mother" is to miss one of the most complex characters in recent fiction. She relies on her bottle of I. W. Harper whenever she is under pressure: "That was Mother's courage." In the solarium, decorated with yellow and white wicker furniture, she wears a dress from her yellow and white solarium collection. This is a woman who refuses to join an exclusive club because it does not admit Jews and who says that "bravery isn't tested during big moments but in little, everyday ones, in the way one faces people and faces up to problems with them." In the furor over the stolen painting, she tells Suzy to go to her job at the library. " 'In a crisis . . . you do the same as you do every day, as far as possible. That's what holds things together. Routine is fiber, and in a crisis, fiber binds.' " Yet this wise woman later makes a fool of herself trying to get back a husband she doesn't really want; she is an adult who combines a high degree of perceptiveness with a goodly share of human foibles.

Contrast the elegant Evelyn Slade with Suzy's friend, Gwen Spring, a throwback to the 1940s in her saddle shoes and white socks, a memorial to unrequited love. When Susie says she wishes she could write something as beautiful as "Wild Nights," Miss Spring tells her to " '[w]ish instead that you could *feel* anything so beautiful as that poem.' " Another time she tells Suzy that life isn't answers, but questions. She admits that she has wasted herself in a " 'futile fantasy. I grew wrinkles from dreaming. Wrinkles should come from living, not imagining that you are.' "

Evelyn Slade and Gwen Spring are examples of a literary device evident in all of M. E. Kerr's novels, a device used in other books, such as Ruth Sawyer's *Roller Skates* and Louise Fitzhugh's *Harriet the Spy*. These characters, like Uncle Earle and Ole Golly, present a range of views on life and the human dilemma through their own statements or quotations from others. In her bitterness, Dinky says that " '[t]he meek don't inherit the earth. . . . [t]he meek inherit the shaft' " and that " '[l]ife isn't anything to get nervous about; it's something to get furious at.' " Alan's grandfather warns him about his status as the town's golden boy: " '[G]ood looks don't last, and Cayuta, New York, isn't the world.' " His mother tells him that people can't always control their lives and that things can change a winner into a loser overnight. A. J.'s famous father gives him a formula for conversational success. " '[N]ever discuss manifest knowledge. . . . If you can't be original, be silent.' " At another point, he recalls his father's telling him that the Chinese word for crisis is composed of two characters, one representing danger and the other opportunity. When Brenda Belle insists that there must be a right way to look at things, her aunt replies that there isn't one way, " '[t]he right way is what you grow to learn is right for you.' " Flan Brown remembers her father's advice to " '[t]reat yourself to grand-scale dreams backed up by well-organized planning, and you can't fail!' " Later her mother tells her, " 'You're going to meet a very old person one day. And when you do, you're going to have only her to answer to.' " Quotations from a variety of sources ranging from the Bible, Shakespeare, and Dostoevsky to Tennessee Williams, Norman Mailer, and the Beatles are integrated into Kerr's books in a number of ways—as part of an English class activity, in a letter, or in notes on bulletin boards. No other contemporary writer exposes young readers to so much material for reflection.

Another discernible pattern is formed by the balancing of two opposing sets of values—P. John's conservative views offset by the liberal views of his father and the Hockers, the views on atheism of Cardmaker and Flan's father countered by Flan's own ponderings, the two views of life represented by Brenda Belle's mother and her aunt, the contrasting life styles of Tucker's father and his Uncle Jingle. M. E. Kerr offers her readers a choice. One takes from these books a genuine sense of the ambiguity of life and the difficulty, if not the impossibility, of pinning down definite answers. " 'Life isn't answers. . . . It's questions.' " Nor is there an answer that fits all people. " 'The right way is what you grow to learn is right for you.' " Young people, in reading these novels, have the opportunity to think about their responsibility for defining the old people they will become. Always there is the sense, however, that we cannot control our lives entirely—that, as Alan's mother cautioned, our lives are influenced by other people and by circumstances over which we have little or no control. Can fiction become more realistic than that? (pp. 291-94)

Matthew Arnold's definition of literature as a " 'criticism of life' " points up the seriousness of the literary endeavor. For Arnold it was not enough that a work of literature provide diversion. Nor, seemingly, is it enough for Irene Hunt with her criterion that an outstanding book must provide a perceptive commentary on the human condition. Judged by these standards, the novels of M. E. Kerr stand out from the general run of contemporary books. With style, wit, and compassion she describes adolescents coming to the realization that those they love will, more often than not, fail to live up to their expectations. Her concern with themes that have universal significance, her ability to create a variety of characters, her sensitivity to the sufferings of others, her humor and, finally, her use of irony all contribute to the power of her books. She has a clever style that never offends by being too clever. Moreover, she is subtle; where others are heavy-handed, she is light, sharp, and deft—using a rapier but never a sledge hammer.

Having published five books in four years, Kerr demonstrates the capability for sustained effort that is necessary to achieve a lasting place in literature. Time alone will determine the longevity of these novels, but it is worth noting that the last two are the best of the five. Short of writing a masterpiece, an author can establish a claim to fame by producing a number of superior books. M. E. Kerr is well on her way to that goal. (p. 295)

> *Mary Kingsbury, "The Why of People: The Novels of M. E. Kerr," in* The Horn Book Magazine, *Vol. LIII, No. 3, June, 1977, pp. 288-95.*

Patricia Runk Sweeney

"Inside of every fat person, there's a thin one wildly signaling to be let out," P. John Knight reminds his fat girlfriend Susan ("Dinky") Hocker in M. E. Kerr's first novel, ***Dinky Hocker Shoots Smack!*** [The imprisonment of one's true self in a shell of one's own making is a pervasive theme in this novel and its five successors. Though each of her novels tells a different story, the same concern for self-realization—a concern shared, we may assume, by every adolescent who reads these books—dominates both plot and subplot. And overall the message is an optimistic one: many of her characters do succeed in releasing the person shut up inside them, as Susan is shut up inside "Dinky," or Priscilla inside "Chicago" (in ***Love is a Missing Person***). And even for some of the apparent failures, there is hope. At least they have become aware of the possibility of change and they have gained insight into their own identity.

Of course, not all change is for the better. Kerr's characters have free will, and they must ultimately decide whether they are really "grabbing the reins" and "stretching" toward the ideal or simply toward something different. But often they can only find out by trial and error. Revolt for its own sake may not seem much better than passivity, but some of Kerr's characters must "act out" before they understand what they are really disturbed about. When Carolyn Cardmaker, for example, starts an atheists' club in ***Is That You, Miss Blue?*** she is rebelling not against religion but against a world that hypocritically exalts religion while allowing most of its clergymen (including her father) to live on the edge of indigence. Since her quarrel is really with society, she returns, in the last pages of the novel, to her church and her family. But she is more aware, at the end, of the "system" that has beaten her down. . . . Progress, Kerr shows us, cannot always be measured in a straight line.

While the title *Dinky Hocker Shoots Smack!* suggests that it is a book about drug addiction, it is a phrase used primarily for its shock value. Like all Kerr's work, it deals with the many different forms of escapism to which we are all subject at one time or another—obesity, alcoholism, psychosomatic disorders—and with the prejudices and hypocrisies we often adopt. Drug addiction is just a particularly dramatic example, a metaphor used to bring Kerr's readers face to face with their own dependencies. And in every instance, in her work, the recourse is the same: one must take charge of one's own life.

All the novels follow the same basic structure: two plots centering around two characters, one ordinary and afraid to diverge from the norm (Tucker, Alan Bennett, Brenda Belle Blossom, Flanders Brown, Suzy Slade, Wally Witherspoon), the other in some way extraordinary and trying to reach a truce with the rest of the world (Dinky, Duncan Stein, Adam Blessing, Agnes Thatcher, Chicago [Priscilla] Slade, Sabra St. Amour). The two plots often split off into one involving a romantic relationship and the other involving relationships between parents and children. With the exception of *Dinky Hocker,* all are written in the first person, and two, *The Son of Someone Famous* and *I'll Love You When You're More Like Me,* employ a variation of that technique, the double first person. The two alternating voices produce a more complex point of view and help to create dramatic irony.

Certain motifs are repeatedly used in Kerr's work to express the state of mind of her characters. Food is one; clothing is another. A third and particularly interesting one is her use of names. Many of Kerr's characters have strange names or nicknames, and explanations about their genesis appear frequently. The characters' names express the way they feel about themselves, illuminate their relationships with their parents, and allow them to adopt and reject various *personae*. Like P. John, children drop names to rebel against their parents, and re-assume them when they've reconciled. Mrs. Hocker attempts to wield power over her daughter by calling her "Dinky." Mothers' maiden names keep coming up, perhaps to remind children how unfair it is for women to lose a part of their identity by the simple act of marrying. It is one symbolic example of how, "if I love you, I am trapped forever." Characters also use their mothers' maiden names as alternative identities for themselves; having other available names gives them some psychic room to grow. The name changing expresses Kerr's overall theme: the struggle to define and articulate who one is, and it also makes the point that identities are always shifting. What is important is that characters feel the freedom to fiddle with what may seem unchangeable, to recognize that they are never really "stuck" unless they choose to be.

But one cannot change unless the alternatives are more

appealing than what one has, and unless the action is really getting at the heart of the problem. . . . [Ideologies] are generally suspect in Kerr's books. Emotion is a much more effective motivator. In *Dinky Hocker* especially, Kerr shows that ideological allegiances often create smokescreens which, under the right circumstances, can easily be put aside. What can't be put aside and what must guide change are the strong feelings characters have for one another. Chicago Slade [in *Love Is a Missing Person*] tells her sister Suzy that love can make a "missing person" of you, a "shed skin" of your old, false self.

Love also helps Kerr's characters to understand the needs and choices of those around them. Thus Chicago's love for a brilliant but poor black student, Roger Coe, makes her tolerant of her father's infatuation with a nineteen year old former cocktail waitress. And the romances in Kerr's books often demand this kind of tolerance, for they are frequently unconventional. She encourages the notion of "chemistry," of following one's instincts. (pp. 37-40)

Perhaps the notion of chemistry and the celebration of the unconventional are important to Kerr because they involve a surrendering of the staid and sensible—the ostensibly easy but often stifling way—and an embracing by each character of something fresh and different, not only in their loved ones but ultimately in themselves. Such risk-taking relationships also make characters feel special, loved not for their *persona,* their conventional role, but for the real person inside themselves. At the risk of oversimplifying, I can say that all Kerr's protagonists are looking for this kind of love—love for the hidden, needy person inside of them. And what they also seek is a love that lets them be. The ideal relationship in a Kerr novel involves each character recognizing the other's strengths and weaknesses, feeling committed because of, or in spite of, those qualities, and being willing to let the other fly free. (p. 40)

Kerr with her dog.

While this ideal is most dramatically demonstrated in the romantic aspects of the novels, relationships between parents and children also demand acceptance and a letting go. The problems between parents and children in Kerr's works often stem exactly from the unwillingness of parents to recognize this. The parents find it difficult either to let their children make their own mistakes or to let them solve their own problems. For Kerr makes the subtle point that parents often take solace in their children's problems and the resulting dependencies, so that they frequently create "double binds" for them, urging them to change at the same time that they are covertly pressuring them to maintain old, destructive habits. . . . While both [Dinky's mother and P. John's father in **Dinky Hocker**] claim to be concerned about their children's obesity, they are ambivalent about letting them do something about it. If a rebirth is to occur, the parents want to assist at it themselves. At least then, if they lose their fat children, they can take credit for the metamorphoses. What the children are asking for, though, is something more difficult. They are asking to be loved for what they are. *That* will help them to change.

In her later novels, Kerr's characters deal with situations of increasing complexity and gravity. She shifts focus a bit, moving from the need for change to the point at which her characters must accept who they are and then direct themselves back to the community. Charlie Gilhooley, for example, in *I'll Love You When You're More Like Me,* must cope with being a homosexual in a small town. He can't choose not to be a homosexual, but he must decide whether he wants to move to New York or San Francisco where he would feel more a part of a community, or deal with the community he now has. . . . While the concerns are not far from those of the earlier works—what does one owe to one's loved ones and what does one owe to oneself—in these later works Kerr is going one step further, stating not only that one has to help oneself, but also that one ultimately has responsibilities toward others.

Kerr's humanist ethic is perhaps best exemplified in the "Death-Cell Prayer of Mary, Queen of Scots" that hangs in the room of the saintly, martyr-like, eccentric Miss Blue. It reads:

> Keep us, oh God, from all smallness. Let us be large in thought, in word, and in deed. . . . May we put away all pretense, and meet each other with pity and without prejudice. . . . Teach us to put into action our better impulse and to walk unafraid. Grant that we may realize that the little things of life are those which create our differences, and that in the big things of life, we are as one under God. And, O Lord, let us never forget to be kind. Amen.

Progressively, the novels, like the prayers, tell us to see and embrace our differences, to take responsibility for ourselves, and then, recognizing our common humanity, to move back toward those around us.

In showing her readers so many patterns of discovery, revolt, and return, M. E. Kerr is providing them with hope and a wonderful relish for the variety in human nature. Wondering why, with her impressive gifts, she did not choose to write for adults, the answer I came up with is that she likes young people better. She is sympathetic to adults, depicting their struggles throughout her books, revealing them not only as bumblers and seekers, but as occasional finders as well. But her strongest sympathies and her greatest hope seem to be with young people. While they are often foolish, they come closer to Mary Queen of Scots' ideal: however squelched and trampled by life, they have the potential to grow up and out—into something not only bigger but better. (pp. 40-2)

> *Patricia Runk Sweeney, "Self-Discovery and -Rediscovery in the Novels of M. E. Kerr," in* The Lion and the Unicorn, *Vol. 2, No. 2, Fall, 1978, pp. 37-43.*

Marilyn Kaye

From the type of adolescent or junior novel which began to appear in the mid 1960s, certain patterns have emerged in structure and characterization. Among the character elements found in these novels are the troubled, alienated teen-age narrator, parents who are somewhat weak in terms of their ability to guide and counsel, and often an eccentric or unusual adult with whom the adolescent develops some sort of unique relationship. In terms of structure, the story tends to open with the adolescent reflecting on some recent situation which is bothering him, and which has somehow disrupted his life.

A series of incidents and meetings occur which either provokes or aggravates the original situation, or creates an environment for new or refined definitions of the situation. Eventually there is a climactic moment in which some sort of hostile, desperate, or highly emotional act of some sort is committed—usually by the protagonist, occasionally by some one else with the protagonist observing and reacting. Toward the end there is a semi-reconciliation, with the parties involved making movements toward a semblance of resolution. There is an open ending, with the original situation still existent, but with optimistic overtones suggesting that the situation will eventually be under control, if not actually resolved.

The novels of M. E. Kerr embody many of the formulaic elements found in the contemporary adolescent novel. Her adolescent protagonists are confused and apprehensive. They are symbols of a high-strung age where life has become a series of crises, and the objective is to survive rather than to succeed. (p. 226)

Kerr emphasizes the alienation of her protagonists by making most of them 'only' children. The 'only' status of the adolescents makes them more vulnerable to the needs and attitudes of the parents. Flanders Brown, in **Is That You, Miss Blue?,** feels torn by her parents' recent divorce, and compelled to take sides. Although she takes no responsibility for the divorce, she is the only common link between them now and represents the single product of an unsuccessful relationship. The 'only' child in this type of situation has no one to talk to, since pride forbids the discussion of a family member with anyone outside the family.

Kerr takes pains to stress the conventionality of her protagonists; it is important that her main characters be perceived by the reader as ordinary and having a basically normal emotional make-up. The characters describe themselves as being 'average' and non-eccentric. . . . By making her characters ordinary people, without unusual talents, Kerr provides an avenue of identification for her readers. These novels are works designed as communications directed to a specific audience. If the work is to be recognized by the audience, the protagonist has to be portrayed as one of them.

Since Kerr's works deal heavily with emotional reactions, it is important that she maintain the essentially sound emotional make-up of her protagonists so that their reactions may be perceived as normal. In order to emphasize the normalcy of these protagonists, Kerr occasionally offers contrasts in order to show readers a direct comparison between the ordinary protagonist and an extraordinary, or somehow abnormal, peer. In *Dinky Hocker Shoots Smack,* Dinky has a visiting cousin, a diagnosed schizophrenic who talks in rhymes; in *Is That You, Miss Blue?,* Flanders has a deaf classmate who throws screaming tantrums when her garbled words are misunderstood. Alan Bennett, in *If I Love You . . . ,* has a classmate who's a hypochondriac. These are characters with medically confirmed emotional or physical problems. By contrasting their problems with those of the protagonists, Kerr affirms the elemental normalcy of the protagonists, despite their intense emotional reactions.

While few of Kerr's parents are portrayed in a positive light, it is interesting to note that in the majority of her novels the fathers are weaker in temperament than the mothers. Often, there is the suggestion that the father, irresponsible and selfish, is at the root of the adolescent's troubles. . . . Kerr's portrayals of fathers become another method of emphasizing the insecure world of the adolescent. No longer the wise, sane, tower of strength in the traditional model of the American family structure, the father has relinquished his role as head of the family, leaving the family without a figurehead. The suggestion that there has been a breakdown in the traditional, supportive nuclear family accentuates the solitary position of the adolescent, who is forced to make decisions without guidance.

In several novels, the only adult with whom the adolescent can relate in any way is an unusual or strange person, someone who, intentionally or not, has removed him/herself from the society of other adults. In *Love Is a Missing Person,* Suzy Slade is attracted to a middle-aged librarian who dresses in fashions of the 1940s, and talks about her love affair of thirty years earlier. Other adults regard her as bizarre. A strange schoolteacher in *Is That You, Miss Blue?* who claims to receive personal visits from Jesus has the loyalty of her students when they discover that she is to be fired because of her religious fanaticism. In *If I Love You . . . ,* the mysterious and unhappy mother of a classmate captures Alan Bennett's attention and affection. These adults have all in some way left the social order—they have either been rejected by or have intentionally removed themselves from the normal adult world as the adolescent sees it. Their unusual circumstances or behavior has set them apart and alienated them from adult society, just as the adolescent feels alienated

and rejected by parents, and ignored by adults in general. The adolescent recognizes the strangeness of this particular adult, and feels sympathy and compassion.

The majority of Kerr's novels are narrated in the first person. As mentioned earlier, they are designed as communications between the protagonist and the reader. In each of the first-person novels, the protagonists introduce themselves and describe their families, their friends, and their situations. They all acknowledge the reader, who is addressed as 'you'; this sets up an immediate one-to-one relationship and establishes sympathy firmly with the protagonist.

The novels usually begin with a recent change in the protagonists' lives. In *Dinky Hocker Shoots Smack,* Tucker's father has lost his job. The recent divorce in *Is That You, Miss Blue?* has resulted in Flanders being sent away to boarding school. In *Love Is a Missing Person,* the protagonist's sister has left the divorced father she has been living with and comes back to live with the protagonist and her mother. . . . By beginning each novel with a change, Kerr sets up a predicament which is as unfamiliar and new to the protagonist as it is to the reader. Reader and character are sharing the novelty of a new situation.

An uncomfortable family relationship is usually established at the beginning of the novel. Flanders Brown resents her mother for having an affair which Flanders believes initiated her parents' subsequent divorce. Suzy Slade feels unwanted by her father who chose her sister to live with him after her parents' divorce. Adam Blessing feels ignored and unwanted by his famous father. Because Alan Bennett's father deserted Alan's mother, the boy feels hostility towards the man, whom he has never met. Dinky Hocker resents her parents' preoccupation with their work. This immediate awareness of family difficulties sets up an atmosphere of tension.

In accordance with the elements of the formula presented earlier in this paper, a series of incidents and meetings occur which in some way affect the original situation and relationship. A major reason for Kerr's success in operating the basic formula is the clever manner in which the climactic moment is developed. By concentrating on indirect and symbolic reactions, rather than direct confrontations, the climactic act becomes a message that carries implications which are more powerful and more meaningful than a verbal argument could have been. Two examples will illustrate this. In *Is That You, Miss Blue?,* Flanders and her friends steal a valuable painting from their school in order to give it to a teacher who has been unjustly fired. Together, they are making a statement, reacting to what they see as the unfairness of a social order which allows an unsympathetic person (the headmistress) the power to make a defenseless person (the teacher) unhappy. The adolescents identify with that defenseless person, as they too are subject to and affected by adult whims and perceived injustice. Their vandalism is a cry against the society of people who make them unhappy. In *Dinky Hocker Shoots Smack,* Dinky paints the words of the title on the walls outside the building where her mother is receiving a community award for her drug rehabilitation work. Dinky's act is a cry for attention; she asks, must I be a drug addict in order to merit your concern? The author appears to be saying that the fashionable, contemporary concern for the obvious and apparent problems of youth and society has distracted attention from the implicit, common, emotional needs and problems of youth.

The formulaic element to which Kerr invariably adheres in her novels is the open, unresolved but basically optimistic ending. Tentative movements toward reconciliations are made. The protagonist acknowledges the beginning of an understanding. The adult begins to recognize the needs of the adolescent. In essence, Kerr's endings are beginnings for the characters involved. The implication is that the adolescents have survived these particular crises, and have gained some knowledge in the process. The ending of **The Son of Someone Famous** contains the expectant tone typical of Kerr's novels. Adam Blessing is preparing for a reunion with his father, with whom the overtures of a relationship have begun. Adam says: "We'll travel light—I like that. I'm not ready for anything heavy. I want to start out slow and easy while I get used to a few things . . . like being the son of someone famous. That's just a part of being me. But not the biggest part. I know that now". . . . This type of reflective conclusion is ideally suited to the contemporary adolescent novel; each novel constitutes an experience, one of many which the typical adolescent might have, and with each experience comes a little more wisdom, a little more maturity. The emphasis is on the idea that the protagonist will continue to grow, and that the experiences will continue to happen. Therefore, there can be no real resolution in the novel, since few experiences in life are neatly resolved.

Kerr's most recent novel, **Gentlehands,** is a strange and disturbing work; as it poses special problems, it is mentioned separately here. The book deals with an adolescent boy's relationships: a romantic involvement with a wealthy, snobbish girl, and a warm relationship with his adored grandfather. The grandfather, who is portrayed as a sensitive and cultured gentleman, is discovered by a journalist to be a former Nazi SS officer noted for his brutality in the concentration camps. As the journalist is about to reveal the grandfather's identity, the grandfather flees the town, leaving the boy stunned and bewildered.

The work includes several of the character elements one has come to expect from Kerr: the troubled adolescent, weak parents who cannot communicate with their son, and the grandfather who certainly qualifies as an "unusual" adult. The structure of the story also tends to follow the basic pattern of her earlier works, particularly in regard to the unresolved ending. But Kerr falls short this time, and it is the characterization of the grandfather which prevents the novel from being a distinctive work. While Kerr's other "unusual" adults were capable of being understood without any real development of their personalities, the "eccentric" aspect of the grandfather is overwhelming. His past requires some explanation, some further discussion of the nature of this man and his perverse history. His situation distracts attention from the protagonist and leaves the novel without a focus. Kerr has attempted to incorporate a complex and horrifying element into her formula, and the incorporation becomes in-

trusive; her sensitive exploration of identity and relationships becomes buried under its impact.

In her other novels, however, Kerr has been remarkably successful in manipulating the formulaic elements within each work. By concentrating on individual feelings and reactions to a situation, rather than on the situation itself, Kerr avoids being labelled as a "problem" novel writer. She adapts the adolescent pattern to suit her purpose, which varies from novel to novel. For Kerr, the adolescent formula operates as a framework within which she creates unique and distinctive stories. (pp. 227-32)

> *Marilyn Kaye, "Recurring Patterns in the Novels of M. E. Kerr," in* Children's Literature: Annual of the Modern Language Association Seminar on Children's Literature and The Children's Literature Association, *Vol. 7, 1978, pp. 226-32.*

Kathy Piehl

[M. E. Kerr] uses religion as an important component of her books for young adults much more frequently than writers of "mainstream" novels usually do. Three of her nine books—**Is That You, Miss Blue?, Little Little,** and **What I Really Think Of You**—have religion as a major theme. Some of the other six novels also contain references to religion.

Kerr's essential message about religion is that it has little effect on people or society. In fact, Christianity merely reinforces the values of the rich and successful. The business of religion and the business of business are much the same. Both depend on superficial showmanship to attain their goal: money. Religious people distrust those who become too emotionally involved with their beliefs. Instead they accept and support the status quo.

The parallel between organized religion and other businesses is most apparent in **Little Little.** All the major characters are dwarfs, and three of the four are involved in selling something. Sydney Cinnamon, one of the narrators, makes his living as The Roach, the representative of Palmer Pest Company. . . . His female counterpart in the world of advertising is Eloise Ficklin, who stars as Dora, the Dancing Lettuce Leaf, in television commercials for Melody Mayonnaise.

While these two have earned fame and money as a result of their commercial endeavors, the dwarf who has gained the most wealth has been in the business of TV religion. Little Lion's appearances on "The Powerful Hour" have gained him the adoration of "the Faithful" and "a white Mercedes convertible, a ten-room house on the Palisades . . . and a fiancee shorter than he was and prettier than a picture."

Sydney first met Little Lion the summer he was 14 and Little Lion was 17. They worked at Leprechaun Village, and Little Lion, then Knox Lionel, entertained his fellow employees by imitating TV evangelists. A "combination philospher and con man," he posed as preacher Opportunity Knox. "He could cry like Jimmy Swaggart. He could fret like Rex Humbard. He could beam like Robert Schuller and shake a pointed finger like Billy Graham," Sydney tells us. In his move from imitating the TV evangelists to joining their ranks, Little Lion apparently experienced no religious conversion, just the awakening of knowledge that his skills could get him ahead. He drinks double screwdrivers and tries to make love to Dancing Dora in the kitchen during his fiancée's birthday party. The parallels between Sydney's and Dora's selling of roach powder and mayonnaise and Little Lion's selling of religion are obvious.

The relationship between religion and business is discussed openly in *What I Think Of You* when Bud Pegler accuses his TV evangelist father of "turning into big business."

> "It *is* big business," my father'd
> answer.
> Bud would mutter, "Then count
> me out."
> "Should the Lord's work be some
> two-bit operation?" My father.

The most valuable marketing tool in religion as with many products is television. Television has led to Little Lion's success just as it did for Sydney Cinnamon and Eloise Ficklin. His message is marketed in the same way advertisers sell roach powder. Guy Pegler devotes much of his energy to thinking up promotional ideas for his show like the "Charge it to the Lord" campaign for which viewers will get a gold charge plate charm if they send a donation.

These gimmicks point out the superficial nature of televised religion. Because appearance is crucial on television, the TV preachers in Kerr's world are constantly trying to improve their looks. (pp. 307-08)

The fame accompanying such television exposure makes changes in [Guy Pegler's] life and that of his family members. His son Jesse remembers when his father was Brother Pegler, an evangelist who preached in tents. Instead of spending time on clothing selection, he bought ties at a drugstore. His wife wore the same flower-print dress Sunday after Sunday, and Jesse wore his brother's hand-me-downs. Guy was a teetotaler, but now he drinks martinis and hobnobs with the "born again" rich who have seen his program.

His family pays the price of success. He and his wife Rhoda rarely leave the house because they are afraid they will be mobbed. . . . Guy's TV stardom makes his sons cynical about his preaching. Jesse wonders, "When did you change your mind about being a preacher, or did you always think you ought to be a TV star?" Even Guy admits, "This TV business is like a bottomless pit, Jesse. It was a lot simpler in the old days. We just passed the plate." But then without looking back at the old life any longer, he returns to the house for his pre-dinner martini. TV has lifted him out of the tent into the limelight.

In the same book Opal Ringer and her family represent the kind of life the Peglers lived in pre-television days. Opal's Daddy is the preacher at the Helping Hand Tabernacle, a Pentecostal congregation in the same town where Pegler's successful television operation has its headquarters. The Hand loses members and dollars to the television

preachers. When Rev. Ringer visits one of his poor parishoners, he finds the largest thing in the shack besides the bed is a color TV set, turned to Guy Pegler's show. The man tells him that he has sent money to Oral Roberts, Rex Humbard, and Guy Pegler to pray for his healing, but he is still dying. . . .

As the book ends the Ringers are enjoying success of their own—as a result of television. The cameras at The Hand to record the return of Guy Pegler by his kidnapper recorded Opal's singing in tongues instead. . . .

People now pack The Hand to hear Opal sing in tongues. The Hand has a security system to regulate the crowds and a computer to tally the offerings. The Peglers have more companions in the clique of wealthy preachers, thanks to television.

Guy Pegler closely resembles one of the television preachers mentioned in *I'll Love You When Your're More Like Me:* Robert Schuller. Sabra St. Amou's mother tunes him in every week. (p. 308)

Sabra often watches too, which makes sense since she is the quintessential television personality. A soap opera star whose life on camera is more real to her than her life off stage, she always thinks about her show and can't communicate with other teenagers. When she accompanies Wally Witherspoon to a party, she launches into lines from the soap opera.

TV exposure ensures public recognition, but more important, it brings money. The split between rich and poor is a recurring theme in Kerr's books, and the gap occurs as much in religious groups as anywhere else.

Carolyn Cardmaker is the daughter of a pastor who is stuck in poor small parishes because he refused to play ecclesiastical politics. She lacks warm clothes, has to dye the one fancy dress she owns before each dance to make it "new," and attends the Episcopal boarding school on a scholarship. In despair she decides to become an atheist because those who claim to represent Christ are a bunch of phonies.

> Jesus was poor and he didn't own anything and he didn't even have a title, but look at the ones representing him today. Except for my father! They're all hustling to get rich parishes with the big houses and long black cars, and they want to be the Right Reverend this and the Holiness that . . . They all look down on my father because he's not chic or rich or all the rest of the crap they consider important. Well, I've had them and any God who lets them represent him!

> (pp. 308-09)

[The] Ringers accept leftover food and hand-me-down clothes from the rich, and Opal tries to avoid envying those who have more money than she does. Her father tells his listeners that they will be better off being "have-nots" when The Rapture arrives, but Opal is not convinced. She believes in The Rapture, in which those who are alive at the time of Jesus' return to earth will be caught up to meet him in the sky. But she doesn't like being poor while she waits. "The real truth was deep inside me. I would rather be a have, which was why The Rapture sometimes scared the living daylights out of me," she tells us.

Although the Rapture scares Opal, most people are detached about their religious beliefs and resist emotional involvement. (p. 309)

The religion that Opal's family practices is definitely emotional with people swaying, speaking in tongues, offering miraculous cures for disease. In fact, the intensity of their emotion is so great that Kerr seems to draw a parallel between religious fervor and sexual arousal. What is especially interesting about her use of this comparison is that although sex is referred to in Kerr's books, there are no explicit descriptions of sexual encounters. In fact, none of the major characters gets much farther than kissing. The most erotic passages occur not in description of sex but in the account of Opal's religious fervor. Opal's ideas of religion are closely connected to her fantasies about handsome Bud Pegler. She would sit hugging her pillow tight or wake up from fevered dreams. "When I did get to sleep, I saw the speck turn into me again, and felt the glow, and in the dream I told myself it wasn't a dream, that it was really real, then woke up sweating, a little of the glow left," she recalls.

Just before she sings in tongues for the first time, Bud arrives and stands beside her, and the two of them sway together in the midst of the singing congregation. Opal's rhythmic description of the experience seems to describe sexual excitation and climax:

> . . . Bud's body swaying beside my own, everyone moving back and forth, music lifting us up, swaying back and forth. I was going up so high. I was on a climb. I was reaching so high that suddenly Bud's hand reached high to grab mine, holding mine but not able to keep me down until I fell.

Afterwards, when Bud drove her home, she remembers, "I thought of me thinking of everyone going two by two past my window, thought of myself with nothing on but my panties, those hot nights back in my room, like the speck not knowing about the glow."

We are not really surprised that Opal and Bud become involved sexually, "seen the Devil's face, sweet nights when we slip," as Opal puts it. What is interesting is that Kerr employs her usual restraint about that relationship while describing religious ecstasy so fully.

Before Opal spoke in tongues and became involved with Bud, she was often embarrassed when high school kids visited The Hand or her father drove around town in a rusty van blasting out recorded hymns.

> I'll never forget the time Mr. Westminster brought the whole Central High social history class to The Hand. See how the Holy Rollers roll, I guess . . . I wish I was six foot under. I felt like I was walking around in front of all of you in my underwear . . . You'd pretend you were coughing behind your hands, and a couple of you couldn't even fake it, just got to giggling.

Similarly the girls at Charles School react with laughter when Miss Blue mentions the religious visions she had. France Shipp and some of the other popular girls pretend to have a real interest in her account of how Jesus had visited her, but in fact, they are making fun of her. Flanders Brown remembers that when Miss Blue left to pray "our table burst into laughter. I laughed too, partly because I thought it was funny, and partly because I was relieved to have Miss Blue out of France Shipp's cool hands."

Eventually the headmistress at the Episcopal school dismisses Miss Blue because of her visions. One of the students concludes, "She's obviously ill if she's imagining that she was in the presence of Jesus." Flanders points out that the disciples and saints suffered from the same "delusion," that Miss Blue is a good teacher, and that all the faculty suffer from some kind of passion. But Miss Blue is embarrassing in a way the others are not, and she is dismissed just before Christmas. No faculty members defend her, and Carolyn Cardmaker is expelled for questioning the headmistress about "what kind of a religious school was it that believed communication with Jesus Christ was a sign of mental instability?" Clearly, getting too emotional about religion can draw the laughter and antagonism of others.

Religion's capacity to arouse strong feelings is also demonstrated in Kerr's books by adolescents' rebellion *against* religion. The most formal rejection comes when Carolyn Cardmaker forms an atheist club even though her father is a pastor. She rejects institutional religion because "The really religious ones like Miss Blue get pushed around by the money-making rabble like APE (the head mistress)!"

When Bud Pegler leaves home in disgust at his father's constant money raising for his TV show, he is participating in a cycle. His father went through the same process as a young man. Mrs. Pegler tries to explain to Jesse why it seems that his father loves Bud more even though Jesse has been cooperative and obedient. "Bud's familiar. He's going through what your father went through, what my father went through. The anger, the doubting, everything you go through when the Lord is testing you." At the end Bud returns, joins his father on TV, and makes plans for the Winning Rally's foreign tour. Jesse has entered his own period of doubt and won't attend church. His mother is confident that he too will complete the cycle. " 'One day,' my mother says, 'your name will be up there with theirs.' "

Carolyn Cardmaker also relents and goes to her father's church on New Year's Eve to make peace with him and to "take God back" as she phrases it. She too has completed her cycle of rebellion against religious belief.

The end of rebellion often signals a return to accepting the way things are, and many people never question their religious beliefs at all. Those who are comfortable with their religion tend to support the status quo and to respect authority of any kind, no matter how horrible it might be.

The extreme example of this is Grandpa Trenker in *Gentlehands.* He had been responsible for sending hundreds of Jews to their deaths at Auschwitz, and Kerr implies that this sense of "duty" to perform the commands of government resulted in part from his strict religious upbringing. An article about his life summarized his background this way:

> Frank Trenker was born into a very strict Roman Catholic family. His father was a bigoted and fanatic man who took a religious oath at the time of his son's birth, dedicating Frank Trenker to God and the priesthood. He directed his entire youthful education toward the goal of making him a priest, forcing him to do penance over the slightest misdeed. When Frank Trenker broke with the church, he joined the NSDAP. He exchanged Catholic dogma for Nazi ideology.

Buddy's mother, the daughter of Gentlehands, also attends Mass regularly. Although she is horrified by her father's actions and denounces them, she does not see any parallel between her support of the U.S. government's activities in Vietnam and Gentlehands' obedience to German authorities. (pp. 309-10)

The tie between religion and unthinking support of government, even when such support involves violence also comes out when Wally Witherspoon looks around the house of his friend Charlie.

> There was a yellow vinyl recliner with a magazine pocket stuffed with old copies of *Gun World.* There was a machine-made sampler framed on the wall that said: RELIGION SHOULD BE OUR STEERING WHEEL, NOT OUR SPARE TIRE. There were two miniature American flags crossed under a picture of Charlie's father as a sailor in World War II, . . . there was a glass gun case with a padlock on the door.

Religious people support not only government policy but also social policy, particularly the treatment of minorities. Again Grandpa Trenker is the extreme case with his brutality toward Jews, but other people in **Gentlehands** make derogatory remarks about Jews. Three of Kerr's four books set in Seaville, Long Island, mention the Hadefield Club, a private club that accepts members by invitation only. Suzy Slade, the narrator in *Love is a Missing Person,* recalls that her family refused to join because

> My mother calls the Hadefield the Hatefilled. The reason the Slades never joined is because up until five years ago the Hatefilled would not allow Jews, and my mother would not belong to a club so bigoted. When Jews were finally admitted, it was arranged by a quota system which permitted only a few, all carefully screened and handpicked by the board of directors. My mother says it's just tokenism, that it's the same old Hatefilled.

However, Rev. Pegler enjoys going to the Hadefield and apparently never considers their membership practices. . . . The fact that prejudice often stems from religious intolerance is underscored by the fact that the type of prejudice mentioned most often in Kerr's books is against Jews.

Although Kerr never states explicitly how religion *should* affect people's lives, she does include a prayer that seems to summarize her thoughts. Written by Mary, Queen of

Scots, in her death cell, the prayer is printed on the picture Miss Blue takes with her when she leaves Charles School.

> Keep us, oh God, from all smallness. Let us be large in thought, in word, and in deed. Let us have done with complaint, and leave off all self-seeking. May we put away all pretense, and meet each other with pity and without prejudice. May we never be hasty in judgment of others. Make us always generous. Let us take time to be calm and gentle . . . Grant that we may realize that the little things of life are those which create our differences, and that in the big things of life, we are as one under God. And, O Lord, let us never forget to be kind. Amen.

Most of the Christians in Kerr's books come nowhere near these standards of behavior. Only for a few people does religion make a difference, and they are usually considered weird. Of all the characters in Kerr's novels, only three seem to have religious beliefs that strongly affect their lives. Two, Opal Ringer and Miss Blue, have been discussed extensively already. The third is Rev. Cardmaker.

When his daughter Carolyn rebels against religion, she does so mainly because of the way those in power have treated her father. Because he has the courage to point out things that are wrong, his supervisor plans to transfer him to an even poorer parish. But he doesn't share Carolyn's hatred. Despite the drafty house he lives in and the franks and beans his family eats for supper, he seems happy. "He was a thin, tall man with very dark blue eyes and a perpetual little tip to his lips, as though he was always on the verge of telling a funny story." Even his daughter's religious rebellion brings understanding, not rebuke. Rev. Cardmaker is definitely a misfit in a world of slick TV preachers who hustle for dollars.

According to Kerr's books, most Christians, including the clergy, conform more to society's norms than to the ideals in Mary Queen of Scots' prayer. Good looks, success, and money make people worthwhile. Christians control their emotions and support the status quo. Kerr admits that "while I came from a religious background (with one aunt who was a Roman Catholic nun) and attended an Episcopal boarding school, I always seemed to have a quarrel with organized religion." Her books for young adults express that argument through the actions of her characters. (pp. 310, 363)

> *Kathy Piehl, "The Business of Religion in M. E. Kerr's Novels," in* Voice of Youth Advocates, *Vol. 7, No. 6, February, 1985, pp. 307-10, 363.*

Alleen Pace Nilsen and Kenneth L. Donelson

M. E. Kerr is one of the few popular Young Adult writers who has consistently included elements of religion in her books. For example, *Is That You, Miss Blue?* is the ironic story of a very religious teacher who is asked to resign her job in a church sponsored school because her faith makes the other teachers and some of the students uncomfortable. *Little Little* features a young dwarf who under his slogan of "scheme" has become a successful evangelist preacher. And *What I Really Think of You* is a different sort of love story between the son of a rich evangelist and the daughter of a struggling pentecostal preacher. In her autobiographical *Me, Me, Me, Me, Me,* Kerr wrote:

> While I came from a religious background (with one aunt who was a Roman Catholic nun) and attended an Episcopal boarding school, I always seemed to have a quarrel with organized religion.
>
> I suppose the reason was simply that I always had a quarrel with authority of any kind.
>
> Religion still fascinates me, whether it's a book by Paul Tillich, a local church service, a seder I'm invited to by Jewish friends, a talk with a Moonie on the street, a Billy Graham appearance, or one of the Sunday-morning TV preachers. I don't yet "believe"—and some of what I see I love or hate, but I'm rarely indifferent, which leaves me more involved than not.

Kerr's ambivalent feelings come out in her writing. For example in *Little Little,* which is narrated by a misshapen dwarf named Sidney Cinnamon, Sidney tells about a time when he and some of the other handicapped kids who lived at Miss Lakes (commonly referred to as *Mistakes*) went to hear a tent preacher:

> The evangelist was asking people to testify as to what the Lord had done for them. People began getting up and shouting out they'd been changed or transformed overnight. Then there was a lull in the proceedings . . . then Wheels' voice (Wheels has no legs). He raised himself as high as he could on his board, and he yelled, "You was asking what the Lord done for me! So I'll tell you! He just blamed near ruint me!"

Kerr's *What I Really Think of You* was simultaneously criticized for "copping out" with a "spiritual" ending and for "taking cheap shots at religion." What some people interpreted as "cheap shots" were incidents and comments that other readers responded to as "healthy skepticism" about the connections between religion and money. In the spiritual ending, Opal Ringer, the P.K. (preacher's kid), finds herself speaking in tongues and enjoying a celebrity status when television cameras roll into her father's church to film her. Throughout the rest of the book she was terribly embarrassed at the "strangeness" of her family. She hated being a "have-not" living among "haves," and she was humiliated when some of the affluent kids from her high school came to her father's shabby little church acting as if they were on a field trip.

The real power of the book is its portrayal of Opal's ambivalent feelings. One of our graduate students grew up in a family much like Opal's. She has a brother who is now a famous—and as she's quick to add very wealthy—evangelist. She swears by the authenticity of Kerr's presentation of the preacher's family and the girl's feelings, at least in the first nine-tenths of the book. She was less pleased with the ending, but she couldn't honestly tell whether her reaction was due to a literary disappointment in that Kerr failed to make the conclusion ring true or whether she felt uncomfortable simply because Opal's early life closely resembled her own and reading the book gave her such a strong feeling of "What if?" that she couldn't be objective about it. She wanted Opal's choice to be the same as her own. (pp. 432-34)

Alleen Pace Nilsen and Kenneth L. Donelson, "Religious Themes in Young Adult Books," in their Literature for Today's Young Adults, *second edition, Scott, Foresman and Company, 1985, pp. 428-34.*

Alleen Pace Nilsen

At the Fifth International Conference on Humor held in Cork, Ireland, Lawrence Mintz, professor of American studies at the University of Maryland and coeditor of *Studies in American Humor,* analyzed the structure of typical situation comedies appearing on American television. He said that the premise of most sitcoms is that change is bad while the status quo is good.

Each show opens with a scene of normality, followed by the development of a problem. Actions taken by the characters, who attempt to solve the problem, only make it worse. But finally, when the situation appears totally hopeless, someone or something comes in from the outside to rescue the characters. Things return to normal and the show closes with a scene depicting the characters in a very similar position to the one they were in at the beginning.

In the situation comedy, the family is never really threatened. The problems are always the result of bad communication. The inherent, wish-fulfilling premise is that if people are honest and communicate with each other, then their problems will disappear and everything will be back to normal. Some sitcoms will titillate and tantalize viewers by mentioning a serious issue, but then the writers skirt that issue by making a joke. When people laugh, they are not so frightened. The overall effect and the reason for the appeal of the situation comedy is that it lulls viewers into a false sense of security.

Because Kerr says that her goal is to lure young people away from television and point them toward books instead, it is appropriate to compare what Kerr does in her books to what Lawrence Mintz says situation comedies do. Like the sitcoms, Kerr recommends honest communication to solve problems, and like the sitcoms she makes her readers laugh when a topic is uncomfortably serious. However, she does not bring up a serious issue only to skirt away from it with a joke. For example, her readers are well aware that Little Little's dwarfism is a real problem that is not going to go away no matter how honestly her family communicates or how cleverly Kerr makes jokes about it. (pp. 127-28)

A second difference is that Kerr's protagonists do not circle around to end up at the same place they began. Early in the stories, they are preoccupied with themselves, but as the plots progress their views are enlarged and tempered by their experiences and interactions with other characters. Each book ends with the protagonist having arrived at a new level of maturity. For example, *What I Really Think of You* begins with Opal lamenting the hostility and the differences between herself and the "haves" who attend Seaville High. It ends with her expressing love for these same people: "When the Rapture comes, I want you all along, somehow, someway, every last one of you, ascending with me." (p. 128)

The only one of Kerr's books that comes close to having the circular ending is *I'll Love You When You're More Like Me,* in which Wally Witherspoon resumes his courtship of Lauralei Rabinowitz. But even here Kerr is careful to point out one significant difference. Wally is no longer going to be an undertaker. He has managed to make that break with his father's expectations, an achievement not to be underestimated.

The third difference is that Kerr's characters solve their problems or adjust to them through their own actions. This may be as wish-fulfilling as the sitcoms, but at least the underlying premise is one of competence. Kerr's characters set an example of self-motivation. They take action instead of waiting passively to be rescued by the fates.

After reading an M. E. Kerr book and after watching a situation comedy, young adults may feel an equivalent sense of pleasure and security. But if Mintz's theory is correct, the feeling of security engendered by watching a situation comedy comes from the illusion that someone or something will always come along in time to save the protagonists from real danger. In contrast, readers of Kerr's books gain a feeling of security from identifying with the success of the characters, who use their own wits and strengths to solve their problems and/or adjust to those things that cannot be changed.

These three differences between situation comedies and Kerr's books are more than cosmetic. They are what make young readers active participants who vicariously become problem solvers rather than casual observers looking for a few hours of entertainment. And because of this, it is appropriate to borrow what E. B. White said at the end of *Charlotte's Web* when he paid tribute to the spider who saved Wilbur's life. Like Charlotte, M. E. Kerr is in a class by herself. Not often does someone come along who is a true teacher and a good writer. M. E. Kerr is both. (p. 129)

Alleen Pace Nilsen, in her Presenting M. E. Kerr, *Twayne Publishers, 1986, 142 p.*

Jennifer FitzGerald

The pressure to conform and the trauma of not fitting in are among the most pervasively experienced dynamics of adolescence. Adolescents plug in very early to a hierarchy of values determined by peer pressure (a trend much exploited by advertisers); the cost of being different is exclusion and alienation.

The existence of a social norm inevitably produces outsiders, since the norm itself is defined not by means of inherent characteristics but by virtue of opposition: to be inside is to be not outside. But the imposition of such norms is much more rigid among adolescents, as they begin to internalize the values of their culture, to match their experience and environment to the standards of their peer group. Since no one exactly matches the stereotype, the lack of fit, experienced by all to relative degrees, produces turmoil and a greater urgency to force oneself into the mold.

Such struggles, the classic problem of children and young

adults, pervade adolescent fiction—especially that of the last 20 or 30 years. The new writing for adolescents has also begun to address the questions of class, race, and gender norms. This sensitivity, however, is often only skin deep, gestures rather than challenges, comparable to the classic case of the poor orphan in a Victorian novel who is excluded from the security of belonging; as the plot reveals his or her true identity, the orphan is welcomed into the magic circle of a cozy, respectable, middle-class family. The rigid parameters of inside/outside are not removed; all that has happened is that one individual has been rescued from the fate of the excluded ones. Well-intentioned attempts at social responsibility are often merely formulaic, as if it were enough to mention injustice to gain the credit for having done something about it. Judy Blume may take a peek at race relations in *Iggie's House* (1970) or at peer victimization in *Blubber* (1974; both Bradbury), but in a superficial, trivializing manner that leaves social attitudes untouched—in particular, the middle-class, competitive, individualistic ethos which so virulently fuels the problems that she ostensibly addresses. The thousands of Blume fans who revel in the strictly limited problems which are allowed access onto her pages are being indulged—either by the lure of security, of belonging to the privileged elite, or by the fantasy (all that is available to large numbers of them) of what it would be like to be able to take such belonging for granted.

To avoid failure of this kind without indulging in undue gloom and misery demands skill and judgment, and also profound understanding. Preeminent among authors with these qualities at their fingertips are Betsy Byars and M. E. Kerr, who combine unstinted awareness with a remarkable rollicking sense of humor, dispelling despair and self-pity without ignoring pain. (p. 46)

M. E. Kerr's favorite characters are freakish; in their "normal" environments they stand out. But in *Little Little,* Kerr confronts the problems of difference or conformity, accommodation or exclusion, with startling frankness and concomitant hilarity. Belle La Belle (known as Little Little) and Sydney Cinnamon are 17-year-old dwarves. The former is "p.f." (perfectly formed) while the latter has a hump. Her parents, the stereotypical golden couple who represent success in the town, still cannot accept the shattering of their dream with their daughter's difference. Sydney, an orphan brought up in an institution, who works as the Roach, protagonist of a TV ad for a brand of insecticide, represents for the La Belle parents the worst of monstrosity and commercial exploitability. Their efforts to muster the right sort of friends for Little Little introduce a whole army of dwarves, euphemistically known as TADs (The American Diminutives) to the town—all p.f.s, of course. Even among TADs, distinctions operate, revealing their true function as exclusionary devices: the glamorous Eloise, being four foot one, informs Little Little: "I'm not really one of you." Alternatively, ignoring difference and how it is socially interpreted is just as insidious: Sydney's housemother at the orphanage insists that her charges (all handicapped and known among themselves as Mistakes) should "*not* dwell" on their "differences from other people! . . . We will emphasize our similarities, *not* our dissimilarities! It does no good to wallow in it!" One of the Mistakes labels normals "Sara Lees" (Similar and Regular and Like Everyone Else), and refuses to read books about them, since "there was always a ring of untruth about them."

By drawing the reader into the dwarves' perspective, Kerr throws into relief the vast assumptions and complacencies, as well as the imaginative limitations, of the Sara Lees, of the taken-for-granted imposed norm. While Little Little's parents are trying to provide her with as good a life as possible, they refuse to alter their implicit support of the norm, always insisting that she has to accept "the real world." Little Little responds on *her* terms: "The real world isn't very real to me, anyway. . . . What's so real about a world where you can't reach the handles of doors?" By the end of the novel, the reader prefers Sydney's explicit (almost sadistic) exploitation as a freak by his manager to the layers of hypocrisy, of desperate truth-avoidance disguised as patronizing charity which is the most that Little Little's parents, absorbed in their own pain rather than in her reality, are capable of offering her. In this brilliant comedy, the protagonists' comments satirize the unobtrusive bullying which is called normal or real life.

Kerr's finger is evidently on the pulse of teenage needs and fears, giving her, in her most recent *Night Kites,* an especially deft perspective on Erick Rudd's overwhelming emotions: his first experience of sexual passion, bound up with guilt and peer ostracism, since he has fallen in love with his best friend's girlfriend. The usual tensions of family life are skillfully conveyed as parental expectations clash with filial exasperation. When the real crisis comes, these problems don't fade into insignificance but instead indicate the pressure points from which cracks will spread. Pete, ten years older than his brother Erick, has AIDS, and the family has to cope at one fell swoop with his hitherto unsuspected (by them) homosexuality, with the fatality of his disease, and with blanket hysterical community ostracism inflicted on them all.

In this maelstrom of pain and fear, guilt and love, no emotion is clearcut: the survival mechanism of one jars on another; lovers and family members vie for claims of intimacy; family bonds themselves are strained (the grandparents refuse to spend Christmas in the AIDS-stricken household); hurt and anger are repressed ("My problem with it [Pete's homosexuality] isn't a priority right now," says his mother), to erupt traumatically later. This is an analysis not only of an urgent and topical subject, but also an exploration of the real manifestations of crisis: the stresses created on the periphery of the trauma which carry the weight of what cannot be assimilated in itself. Within the structure of the novel, Erick learns, through keeping his own overpowering emotional conflicts from an already burdened family, what it has been like for his brother to lead a closet sexual and emotional life, and what the consequences of such repression must be. He also gets to know before he dies the big brother whom he always admired, the "Night Kite" not afraid to be different or alone. Although there is, inevitably, less humor in this novel, its confrontation with the interwoven versions of

difference, ultimately the difference of death, brooks no avoidance of the other issue, sexual orientation.

In a recent article in the *New York Review of Books,* Oliver Sacks reviewed a new book recounting 250 years of hereditary deafness in Martha's Vineyard. So many there were born deaf that the whole community spoke in sign language, without making distinctions between the handicapped and the whole. Instead of the deaf being defined outside of the norm, the norm was itself expanded to include them. One of the hearing survivors of the integrated deaf-and-hearing population was sketching signs in her sleep: dreaming in sign. Here the limitations and exclusions of our everyday life style reveal their arbitrary injustice.

Although norm and difference are built into our culture as fundamental means of perception and definition, it is not impossible to give them a shake, to loosen the boundaries, or at least to begin challenging the criteria establishing belonging and exclusion. For children, in particular, such questioning must be beneficial: at a time when personal experience reinforces both the need to conform and the pain of insufficient or impossible fit, books which acknowledge difference and question the assumptions according to which such differences are defined encourage them to expand their values—not least their valuing of themselves. (p. 47)

> *Jennifer FitzGerald, "Challenging the Pressure to Conform: Byars and Kerr," in* School Library Journal, *Vol. 33, No. 1, September, 1986, pp. 46-7.*

TITLE COMMENTARY

Dinky Hocker Shoots Smack! (1972)

Dinky Hocker doesn't shoot smack, but M. E. Kerr's funny/sad first novel shoots straight from the hip. A caustic, compulsive overeater, Dinky is the neglected offspring of do-gooding Helen Hocker who runs an encounter group for Brooklyn Heights smackheads. (Her pet ex-junkie, Marcus, punctuates his fond reminiscences of addict days with disclaimers of " '. . . don't get me wrong, my head was messed up then.' ") Normal narrator Tucker Woolf worries about his armpits and lack of "pizazz" and courts Dinky's cousin, Natalia Line, who speaks in rhyme like Rubin's Lisa (*Lisa and David;* Macmillan, 1961). P. John Knight, an adolescent Agnew, is reacting against his father whose sympathies seem reserved for migrant workers. P. John recognizes Dinky's thin inner self and the deprecating quality of her nickname but is blacklisted by her abrasively liberal mother. P. John is sent to a progressive school in Maine where he discovers labor organizing and miraculously mellows. Meanwhile, deprived of P. John, Dinky declines as her girth expands. The writing's on the wall (the title legend inscribed by Dinky in Day-Glo paint) on the night Helen Hocker wins the community's Good Samaritan Award. Dinky's desperate gesture finally grabs her parents' attention; *chutzpah* pays off and proves Dinky's dictum that " 'The meek inherit the shaft.' " Devastatingly funny but stingingly serious about the necessity of direct, outspoken action, the book perfectly presents a wry world view: " 'Life isn't something to get nervous about; it's something to get furious at.' " The characters are sympathetic and engaging, and the whole is a totally affecting literary experience.

Pamela D. Pollack, in a review of "Dinky Hocker Shoots Smack!" in School Library Journal, *Vol. 19, No. 4, December, 1972, p. 67.*

The pages rush by in this superb first novel by M. E. Kerr, who has an ear for catching the sound of real people talking and a heart for finding the center of real people's problems.

Tucker's problem is friendlessness. His family has moved to Brooklyn Heights; his father has lost his job; his mother has to go back to work. Even the cat has to be given away. Which is how Tucker meets Dinky, who adopts the cat, and Natalia, with whom Tucker falls in love. When Tucker invites Natalia to a dance, he gets Dinky a date with P. John. From that night, the four of them begin to help each other in ways their parents can't or won't. . . .

The most difficult problems are Dinky's—whose addiction to food makes her life a nightmare. Her flippant humor about her fat hides a painful sensitivity, until the night of her shocking explosion, when at last some people understand you don't have to be a public loser to have private troubles.

The problems to be coped with are real, contemporary in a contemporary world. The writer is sensitive not only to the dialogue, but to the themes of today's preoccupations. You get the feeling it could all be happening next door.

This is a brilliantly funny book that will make you cry. It is full of wit and wisdom and an astonishing immediacy that comes from spare, honest writing. Many writers try to characterize the peculiar poignancy and the terrible hi-

Kerr, age ten, in her Girl Scout uniform.

larity of adolescence. Few succeed as well as M. E. Kerr in this timely, compelling and entertaining novel.

Dale Carlson, "Smack," in The New York Times Book Review, *Part I, February 11, 1973, p. 8.*

For something truly original one must turn to **Dinky Hocker shoots smack!,** a book as racy as its title and (surely a rarity) a book that scrutinises young people and the pitfalls that lie round them shrewdly, humorously, incisively, with none of the nervous sentimentality that makes so much 'teenage fiction tedious. . . . The fact that Dinky and her friends are analysed with wit and irony does not destroy the real feeling that lies behind the story. The author's succinct narrative and crackling dialogue make a fine medium for the organic development of her characters. For the full horror of parental blindness it would be hard to beat her description of Christmas gift-giving with the Hockers, and the perceptive view of boy and girl love between Tucker and Natalie, both trammelled by difficulties of circumstance and temperament, is as good as anything I have read in this genre. Only too often a reviewer has to decide that a book of this kind will satisfy either adolescents or their elders: this one should certainly satisfy both.

Margery Fisher, in a review of "Dinky Hocker Shoots Smack!" in Growing Point, *Vol. 12, No. 5, November, 1973, p. 2263.*

If I Love You, Am I Trapped Forever? (1973)

This is another of those contemporary, breezy-on-the-outside accounts of smashed relationships and emerging adolescent sensitivity. But instead of the on-target observations of, say **Dinky Hocker Shoots Smack** Kerr gives us here some unfocused tittle-tattle that is unlikely to recall (let alone illuminate) anyone's high school scene. Readers are not only asked to believe in Alan, the narrator (self described as "*the* most popular boy at Cayuta High. Very handsome. Very cool. Dynamite") whose friendliness to newcomer Duncan Stein takes the form of citing famous athletes "of the Jewish persuasion," but also the intellectual senior girl, preoccupied with psychoanalytic jargon, who practices cheers as well. Then comes Stein himself: an aloof, skinny, half-bald outsider Alan calls "Doomed" whose personal newspaper *Remote* "salutes" Dante's Beatrice, Heloise, and the like, and runs ads for soulful one-date relationships; whose romantic poses start all the girls wearing anemones on their sweaters; and who finally steals Alan's beautiful girlfriend Leah (the title question is from her note to Alan). Besides the loss of his girl Alan experiences a disastrous weekend in New York with the father he had never met and a brief platonic affair with Doomed's mother before she runs off with the slobby alcoholic football coach, leaving Alan sobbing as the story ends. So nothing lasts forever—but this isn't even for now. (pp. 123-24)

A review of "If I Love You, Am I Trapped Forever?" in Kirkus Reviews, *Vol. XLI, No. 3, February 1, 1973, pp. 123-24.*

Despite its pretentious title, self-conscious, first-person style, and some caricatures, this is an interesting, entertaining novel. Alan Bennett—a handsome, popular, Protestant jock going steady with a beautiful cheerleader—anticipates a glorious senior year in high school. Then ugly, Jewish, unathletic Duncan Stein transfers in and unexpectedly *becomes* in, as do his passion for poetry and belief in unrequited love. Going steady—and Alan—are suddenly out. Social disaster is compounded by family tension: Alan's father, who'd deserted his mother while she was pregnant, decides he now wants to get to know his son. The boy's ideas of love and loyalty are turned upside down. He finds he really likes the woman who led to his father ditching his mother. He can't decide if love is the warmth of going steady or the excitement of a brief encounter, a comfortable feeling for a contemporary or admiration for someone older. Can love be distinguished from human weakness or need? Is a strong person one who pulls out of an unsatisfying marriage or who works to make it better? When is parental love selfish? At the end of the story, Duncan falls in love with Alan's former steady; having now experienced rather than intellectualized love, Duncan decides he wants to go steady too. Ephemeral love as a school fad dies, but Alan retains his new-found awareness of its power and appeal. The turnabout's a bit too pat but still acceptable and, fortunately for readers, there are more questions than answers.

> *Diane Gersoni-Stavn, in a review of "If I Love You, Am I Trapped Forever?" in* School Library Journal, *Vol. 19, No. 8, April, 1973, p. 75.*

Had M. E. Kerr restrained her literary and academic impulses, *If I Love You, Am I Trapped Forever?* would have been a first-rate young adult novel. Her book is like a Möbius strip onto which are stapled bits of World Lit, Pop-Psych, letters, classified ads, writing style tips and news items. It poses the eternal rhetorical question: "What Is Love?" yet supplies only the basis for a one-dimensional reply.

At the start, Alan Bennett is a football-playing manipulative 16-year-old. He is going steady with a luscious chick named Leah and lives with his divorced mother and his crusty grandfather in Cayuta, N. Y. It appears that everything—or almost everything—would have worked out all right except for the Steins. Papa Stein is the world's most handsome, most gifted psychologist (but his wife leaves him—so he must have been Too Cold). Young Duncan Stein is tall and nearsighted and balding and hideously overcerebral (but he gets Leah—so he must have been Too Hot). Then there is Mama Stein who, though an ex-columnist for the old Trib, is somehow unwrinkled and not above making seductive remarks while dancing with 16-year-olds.

Sandwiched in between his relationship with Leah and his crush on Catherine Stein is a weekend Alan spends with his father who had run off with a woman he despises as he despises himself. This is a shattering encounter for Alan that forces him to probe deeper into the meaning of "Love." However, judging from what kids fantasize about parents from an early age onward, the effect of this meeting on a 16-year-old boy (presumably aware of similar genetic matter existing in his own chromosomes) should have been more profound than making him become impossibly vague with his girlfriend. Thus, the boy's involvement with an older woman upon his return home is not as unconnected as the book would like us to believe. Alan—unlike Sonny in *The Last Picture Show* or Ben in *The Graduate*—does not attempt to have a physical relationship with Mrs. Stein. He has no opportunity, therefore, of resolving his emotional turmoil: indeed, putting emotions into action is something Alan seems no longer capable of accomplishing.

At the very end, Alan's breaking down and weeping when he hears that his "ideal" has run off with a man he deems unworthy does not portend a happy heterosexual future. Alan's decision to become a writer suggests that while love may come in as many varieties as there are people, those who are emotionally castrated are those who understand Romance the best.

> *Carolyn Balducci, "Family Affairs: Love among the Generations," in* The New York Times Book Review, *September 16, 1973, p. 8.*

The Son of Someone Famous (1974)

Brenda Belle Blossom! What a name for a fifteen-year-old who refers to herself as a flat-chested tomboy. Brenda Belle is astounded when a new boy in town seems interested; Adam Blessing, who has come to stay with his grandfather, is easy to talk to and ready to form a defensive alliance. (Brenda Belle calls it going steady.) Adam is the son of a celebrity and doesn't want anyone in town to know it; when his loving ex-stepmother visits him, she—being an actress—is recognized; but Adam keeps his secret. He and Brenda have drifted into relationships with others by the time he leaves town, and she knows but wouldn't betray a friend. The chapters are written alternately by the two ("From the journal of A." and "Notes for a Novel by B.B.B."), a device that functions smoothly in a lively, convincing story that has strong characterization, excellent dialogue, and a novel, convincing story line. The author is particularly deft in depiction of the relationships between adult and juvenile characters, in striking a contemporary note, and in drawing the shifts and balances within the adolescent community so that they are wry and touching without being either cute or sentimental.

> *Zena Sutherland, in a review of "The Son of Someone Famous," in* Bulletin of the Center for Children's Books, *Vol. 27, No. 9, May, 1974, p. 146.*

M. E. Kerr's *The Son of Someone Famous,* fumbles his way through the kind of psychological hangup another sort of children's author might have handled with deadly seriousness. . . . What Kerr has really caught onto here is the sheer, heady delight of discovering that one is old enough to be let in on the secret goings on of adults, and Adam's glamorous connections allow Brenda Belle to indulge her curiosity outrageously. Kerr is, after all, only making the familiar point about learning to accept others and ourselves, faults and all. But she is wise enough to realize that life is more than an extended problem-solving session and adroit enough to entertain the universal passion for gossip and our sense of the ridiculous simultaneously.

Joyce Alpern, "Growing Pains," in Book World—The Washington Post, *May 19, 1974, p. 5.*

Vermont is the backdrop against which two bright, brittle teenagers, both misfits in their disparate social orders, gain insight into themselves and their families. . . . A blending of sophistication and innocence develops the characters as credible teenagers, despite the soap-opera banalities of the plot. Unfortunately, the whole is less than the sum of its parts, for characters and situations are not as fully integrated as in **Dinky Hocker Shoots Smack!;** although the dialogue and description are superb, the incidents seem patched together from speculation about a life style sensed but not experienced. (pp. 384-85)

Mary M. Burns, in a review of "The Son of Someone Famous," in The Horn Book Magazine, *Vol. L, No. 4, August, 1974, pp. 384-85.*

Is That You, Miss Blue? (1975)

"Hilarious and sad and crazy and unbelievable"—that's how Flanders, the 15-year-old narrator, describes the "little world" she has been living in for three months, and the description is totally apt for the novel as well. M. E. Kerr has used the familiar microcosm of boarding school to make several points which apply at large, and to make them with so much grace, charm and poignancy that one closes the book with the feeling, "this is the way life really is." And the way life really is, as even the youngest of us find out soon enough, is unjust and unkind in direct proportion to one's vulnerability.

Miss Blue, of the title, is a religious mystic who teaches at Charles School (as in Dickens: the dorms have superbly fitting names like Bleak House and Dombey and Son). Her greatest transgression of what is considered "allowable" behavior is her belief in Christ in a milieu theoretically and officially Episcopal. Solitary, excruciatingly shy (except when teaching science, which she does with fascinating ardor), Miss Blue is an object of intense ridicule. The cross she bears, both figuratively and literally, is enormous—"a bigger cross than you'll ever see anybody wear" warns an old student to a new. "She calls Him her buddy . . . it's Ding-A-Ling City."

What we witness is Miss Blue going crazy (she not only talks to Jesus, but He apparently drops by her room to chat: "Behold, I stand at the door and knock"). What we actually see is the school driving her crazy; in the course of it, our "agnostic" narrator has her first genuine religious insight: "Were His disciples ill? What about all the saints?"

Flanders is not converted—that is not the point of the story, which is about women and men, girls and boys, children and parents, and what passes between them in "Ding-A-Ling City." What she is protesting is the type of

exile reserved for those who march to the beat of a different drummer—and are accordingly drummed out.

"Who doesn't have a passion? All the faculty do," observes Flanders. Miss Mitchell and Miss Able are lesbians who communicate through hymns ("I look to thee in ev'ry need . . . "); Miss Sparrow is in love with the married minister; Miss Balfour, like Narcissus, addresses her every gesture to whatever mirror is in view; and the headmistress has a passion for arbitrary discipline.

As for the students, they fall into four categories of affliction: Number Ones are Bright and Pitiful—the scholarships; Numbers Twos, On the Ladder—the social climbers; Number Threes are In the Way—"most Number Threes are more of a Three than they ever know"; Number Fours are Out of the Ordinary—"there was a dwarf in the class of 1957. . . . The current semester's Number Four is beautiful but deaf, yet because her father is "so rich he's gross," she's invited to join the prestigious E. L. A. secret society—referred to by the dissidents as Extra Lucky Asses. The dissidents form an anti-coalition of their own, an atheists' club, devoted to "major acts of unfaith" on behalf of the underdog. At the final Inquisition, the atheists' valiant but futile loyalty to religious Miss Blue represents their finest hour.

"Is that you, Miss Blue?" is a question that haunts Flanders long after she has left Charles School. "In my daydreams she suddenly appears . . . on a city park bench in a circle of sun on a cold afternoon." "Is that you, Miss Blue?" is a question that haunts the reader too, but by then it's too late to ask it.

Alix Nelson, in a review of "Is That You, Miss Blue?" in The New York Times Book Review, *April 13, 1975, p. 8.*

This is a sophisticated book, one that demands understanding from its readers and can, at the same time, lead them toward understanding. There are some acid portraits: the arrogant head of the school, the lesbian teachers who bicker with each other, and some scheming classmates, but they are shrewd and convincing portraits, and the book evokes with remarkable conviction the closed world of a private girls' school.

Zena Sutherland, in a review of "Is That You, Miss Blue?" in Bulletin of the Center for Children's Books, *Vol. 28, No. 11, July-August, 1975, p. 179.*

Much of the novel's power is derived from its delineation of character while consistently maintaining the young narrator's perspective. As seen through Flanders' eyes, the conflicting personalities are Dickensian types, skillfully limned but exaggerated. And the author achieves a balance between pathos and humor in documenting Miss Blue's disintegration. In a spare, wryly funny, genuinely moving book, M. E. Kerr surpasses all of her previous achievements.

Mary M. Burns, in a review of "Is That You, Miss Blue?" in The Horn Book Magazine, *Vol. LI, No. 4, August, 1975, p. 365.*

Love Is a Missing Person (1975)

Librarian Miss Spring who wears '40's outfits (from dickey to bobby sox) and makes no secret of her continued devotion to the lover who ditched her then, during World War II . . . rich, unsettled Daddy who divorces mother and marries a shallow chorus girl named Enid . . . spoiled older sister Chicago, who roars home from Daddy's duplex (he sort of jilted her for Enid) with a new motorcycle and a head full of resentment and radical theory . . . competent Nan, a fellow library page, who is embittered when her sports hero, straight A boyfriend Roger, black like her, takes up with Chicago. . . . It is their problems which concern fifteen-year-old narrator Suzy, who doesn't yet have much of a life of her own, and it's true as she observes that love does seem to make missing persons of them all. Kerr's sympathy with the oddballs and her powers of caustic observation are evident here, as is her way with characters. (In her hands, it's the most bizarre caricatures who have the keenest vitality.) Still, even though Kerr is the sharpest yet, her kid glove treatment of the black characters and her liberal's wish-fulfilling ending (wherein Roger and Chicago run off together) do recall those other white writers (Fitzhugh, Konigsburg, Neville among them) who first impressed us all with their hipness to contemporary middle class kids but who—perhaps unwilling to recognize that those characters' limiting insulation is also their own—become self-conscious when they try to incorporate black experience. (pp. 717-18)

> *A review of "Love Is a Missing Person," in* Kirkus Reviews, *Vol. XLIII, No. 13, July 1, 1975, pp. 717-18.*

Affluence, poverty, class barriers, divorce, alcohol, unfulfilled love, miscegenation, racism, sex (adult and adolescent), lack of rapport between parent and child, hostility between spouses—these are among the social quarries mined by M. E. Kerr in her fifth novel, *Love Is a Missing Person.*

As in Kerr's fourth book, *Is That You, Miss Blue?,* a Salingeresque aura hovers about the proceedings: the tone is wry, the milieu is upper middle-class, the narrator is bright, young, self-conscious, painfully observant, the characters, regardless of age or status, are dogged by loneliness and failed expectations, and there is a pervading realization that each person sustains his or her own illusions at the expense of someone else's.

But in this latest effort something seems to have misfired. Although the writing is intelligent, warm and witty in the way one has come to expect of the author, the book's questionable sociology is built on such slender stilts that it buckles and creaks with each new twist of the plot, and the action itself—if not the characters—fails to give credibility much of a foothold.

> *Alix Nelson, in a review of "Love Is a Missing Person," in* The New York Times Book Review, *October 19, 1975, p. 10.*

This is one of Kerr's best, honest and poignant and perceptive. She gives no easy answers to the intricate problems in the lives of her characters, offers no lulling conclusions. The characterization and the dialogue are convincing and

trenchant; while the ending is (as it was in *Is That You, Miss Blue?*) left open (Chicago and Roger disappear, Nan is hostile, Daddy ambivalent) it is the right ending, but what is left is not bitterness, it is an aching compassion.

> *Zena Sutherland, in a review of "Love Is a Missing Person," in* Bulletin of the Center for Children's Books, *Vol. 29, No. 3, November, 1975, p. 48.*

I'll Love You When You're More Like Me (1977)

From *Dinky Hocker . . .* on, Kerr's projection of contemporary craziness and mixed-up kids has been about the sharpest in juvenile fiction, and her talent for combining the representative and the bizarre has never been so evident as in this inspired cast which seems to write its own story. Wally Witherspoon, chief among them, appears destined (though reluctant) to become a funeral director like his father and to marry narrow-vistaed Harriet Hren, who has all sorts of plans for the viewing rooms, and who bugs him for "the ring" though they still have a year of high school. You know it can't be, even before he meets Sabra St. Amour, teenage star of daytime TV. In any case Sabra, who relates only to her mother (and *that's* another tangled story) and to her own packaged image, never does succeed in his "ordinary" world. Then there is Wally's buddy Charlie, who has just decided to come out of the closet—a revelation that surprises no one in town, though he's shown no signs of acting on his inclinations. (Charlie ends up replacing Wally as Mr. Witherspoon's trainee, which *is* a surprise.) As usual, too, there are all sorts of vividly caricatured adults, many of them giving good, bad, and singularly applicable advice—but here the advice that seems most apt comes straight from Sabra's soap opera. Even the wise words she quotes from her shrink are not from her real shrink, who is the silent kind, but from the one on TV. Kerr plays games with them all—but there is method in it.

> *A review of "I'll Love You When You're More Like Me," in* Kirkus Reviews, *Vol. XLV, No. 13, July 1, 1977, p. 673.*

Kerr thinks funny, sees funny, hears funny, and writes funny, but the concerns of her characters are real enough to most teenagers—how to break free from parental guidance and misguidance. . . .

If Charlie's homosexuality and Mrs. St. Amour's amours make this seem a problematic selection for libraries, the novel is easily defensible. It is superb serio-comic writing (the dialogue sizzles but without frying the characters into caricatures) and it touches on nothing outside the ken or the conversation of young teens. (pp. 124-25)

> *Lillian N. Gerhardt, in a review of "I'll Love You When You're More Like Me," in* School Library Journal, *Vol. 24, No. 2, October, 1977, pp. 124-25.*

From the title, this novel by M. E. Kerr, a celebrated author of children's books, sounds like just another "story with a message." Well, it is. The message, simply stated, is that "you have to step out of line to give the world something special." Unfortunately, the story used to portray this sound moral is trite, not unlike a half-dozen recent movies, and it is hardly inspiring.

Sabra St. Amour, a famous soap-opera queen, meets Wallace Witherspoon, Jr., the son of a mortician, while she is vacationing in his resort home town. Different as they are, these teenagers share a common problem: dominating parents who seek only self-centered ends at the expense of their children's freedom. At least this is the point of view of the teenagers in the story—the only point of view presented.

Sabra's mother, the typical pushy stage parent, uses the girl's ulcer as an excuse to keep Sabra out of her starring role despite the fact that she loves acting both onstage and off. Wally's father, who runs a funeral home, expects Wally to take over the business despite Wally's aversion to the idea and his embarrassment at being the son of a mortician. These and all of the parents in the novel appear disgustingly conventional, selfish, and ridiculous as they go about the business of providing for their families. Only our actress, the reluctant mortician, and their homosexual friend, Charlie, come to understand the necessity of defying convention and tradition in order to make a mark on the world.

Ms. Kerr is obviously trying sympathetically to depict a very disconcerting event in many a teenager's life—the realization that he is ashamed of his parents and wants to be anything but like them. I think, however, that such a subtle problem warrants more than the glib, avant-garde dialogue and facile solutions offered in *I'll Love You*. And I believe that the young adult audience to whom this book is addressed deserves better heroes than Sabra and Wally.

> *Janet P. Benestad, in a review of "I'll Love You When You're More Like Me," in* Best Sellers, *Vol. 37, No. 9, December, 1977, p. 294.*

Gentlehands (1978)

The 16-year-old hero of this remarkable novel for young people—and he is a hero, in the only ways he can be—is William Raymond "Buddy" Boyle. His father is a policeman in an unfashionable Long Island village in the Hamptons; he works as a soda jerk for bicycle and clothes money; he dates occasional town girls whose idea of flirting is "to put Wind Song behind their ears and sit there"; he is charged with the care of his demoniac younger brother, Streaker; his parents are not just lower-middle class but resentfully snobbish about it; and he is in love with Skye Pennington, who summers with her parents near Montauk and possesses wealth and beauty in amounts F. Scott Fitzgerald might have hesitated to describe.

Buddy is tall and handsome, which explains Skye's interest in him, but he's diffident and hopeless in the presence of her sophistication. Her pool cabana is bigger than his house. Her father's garage holds six cars, including the Rolls and the Jensen. She and her friends speak the careless argot of the rich. When he hitchhikes to her house, the butler tries to steer him to the tradesmen's entrance,

but Buddy perseveres and manages to hold his own with native wit and good humor.

Overcoming this social and financial gulf is the lesser of Buddy's problems. The larger one concerns his grandfather, and it is insuperable.

His grandfather, the mysterious and wealthy Frank Trenker, alienated from Buddy's mother, welcomes visits from his gauche grandson, and impresses even Skye with his charm, his wisdom, his kindness, his easy and tasteful use of wealth and his nice sense of civilization. Buddy, not entirely free of snobbery himself, is delighted to have at least one presentable relative to show off to Skye. Frank Trenker—multilingual, an opera buff, a man who cooks for and feeds the wild animals near his large house—is certainly presentable. Without making an issue of it, Trenker begins to steer and shape Buddy's mind and his future.

A summer guest of the Penningtons is Nick De Lucca, an investigative reporter whose young cousin was among the Roman Jews murdered at Auschwitz in 1943 by an SS officer known as Gentlehands. (The ironic nickname arose from his custom of taunting Italian prisoners with a recording of Mario's aria from "Tosca," "O dolci mani," before sending them to their deaths.) De Lucca's anti-Nazi research has led him to Frank Trenker, whom he accuses in a detailed newspaper article of being the infamous Gentlehands.

Buddy refuses to believe it. Skye refuses to believe it. The reader—this reader, anyway—refuses to believe it. That lovely man who introduces Buddy to Renaissance art and puffs on a Turkish meerschaum and tells him that a gentleman never points "at anything but French pastries"—that man simply cannot be a Nazi murderer.

De Lucca's documentation is flawless, however. Trenker is—was—Gentlehands. Before he can be questioned by the Immigration and Naturalization Service he disappears, leaving a note for Buddy: "I live in the present between two unfathomable clouds, what was and what will be."

Buddy is the last person to accept the incomprehensible fact of his grandfather's identity, but at the end, on a final visit to Trenker's empty, vandalized house, he accepts the truth, as he must.

The incriminating newspaper article is filled with horrible detail—strong stuff for young people; strong stuff for anyone. But Nazism, that ghastly pit of the human soul, was real, and a young generation of Americans knows of it only vaguely, if at all. There are muted connections in the book between the airy, thoughtless anti-Semitism of Skye and her crowd and the bloody nightmare of Auschwitz that haunts this pocket of the modern world.

Miss Kerr's book is important and useful as an introduction to the grotesque character of the Nazi period, as well as to the paradoxes that exist in the heart of man. Her ear for youthful American speech is superb; her understanding of youthful feelings, and youth's occasional lack of them, is sure. If she fails to explain thoroughly the alarming enigma of Frank Trenker's double life, it is only because there is, finally, no explanation possible.

Richard Bradford, "The Nazi Legacy: Undoing History," in The New York Times Book Review, April 30, 1978, p. 30.

The author has magnificently depicted the clash of values, emphasizing the two families' contrasting lifestyles and prejudices; Buddy's inarticulate father and his uneducated mother are particularly well portrayed. The boy's grief and confusion are understandable and his attempt to accept responsibility, as taught him by his grandfather, is admirable, but the book is seriously flawed by the abrupt and unbelievable transition of Grandpa Trenker from hero to villain. (p. 285)

Ann A. Flowers, in a review of "Gentlehands," in The Horn Book Magazine, Vol. LIV, No. 3, June, 1978, pp. 284-85.

[What] does it all mean? It's hard to tell in this slick little tale in which the Holocaust and Nazi exterminators become cheap devices to move the plot forward. Whatever the author's intention, I was infuriated by this book, which seems to give equal weight to the questions of morality raised by the Holocaust and to an unrealistic teenage romance. It's also hard to tell what the author intends with her anti-Semitic jokes and anti-gay remarks and her stereotypic portrayal of Nick De Lucca who—to further complicate the plot—is apparently gay. The book's glorification of conspicuous consumption and of a very spoiled and bratty young woman were the last straws! The author's "amusing" and witty style and her trendy subject matter no doubt are responsible for her popularity with young readers; it's a great pity that her writings are so devoid of a moral heart.

Ruth Charnes, in a review of "Gentlehands," in Interracial Books for Children Bulletin, Vol. 9, No. 8, 1978, p. 18.

With considerable courage and aplomb the author describes the emotional and actual problems that face the sixteen-year-old son of a police sergeant in a small seaboard town in New York State, as he tries to sort out his feelings for rich Skye Pennington, a summer visitor, and for his own grandfather, whose urbane manner has grown over a disgraceful past as an officer of Auschwitz. The difficulties and dangers of change, personal and social, are explored in a story distinguished by apt domestic detail, an unerring sense of class temperament and behaviour and highly effective dialogue underpinning character.

Margery Fisher, in a review of "Gentlehands," in Growing Point, Vol. 17, No. 6, March, 1979, p. 3486.

[*Gentlehands*] assumes the burden of dealing with a brutality of . . . [great] magnitude—that of Nazi torture and extermination of Jews during the second world war. Kerr has always been conscious in her novels of the ways in which people undermine and attempt to control one another. In **Dinky Hocker Shoots Smack,** for example, a mother is seen causing deep unhappiness in her own child while purporting to help, and in some way feeding off the disadvantaged youth of the community. This book is a bold advance from that perspective; Kerr reveals not just manipulations and subtle abuses but atrocities of an enormity almost too terrible to fathom. And in some ways she does it well. Her treatment is strong and honest, supported by direct accounts of torture written into newspaper articles. And yet the issue seems peripheral, as if Kerr had not written a novel shaped by this issue but rather that the issue had found its way into the standard Kerr novel where, instead of a gentle eccentric like Miss Blue, we find Frank Trenker, alias "Gentlehands," an ex-Nazi torturer living a life of ease in Montauk, New York. And his primary function in the novel seems to be to provide a learning experience for its sixteen year old hero Buddy Boyle.

The story takes place in Seaville, New York, a Long Island resort town. Buddy Boyle, a year-round resident whose father is on the local police force, has a summer romance with "Skye Pennington," the beautiful daughter of a rich oil man who owns "Beauregard," the lavish Pennington summer estate. In an effort to impress Skye, Buddy takes her to see his grandfather, Trenker, and during the course of the novel, Trenker's identity is discovered.

In its broadest outlines the book is about culture and morality, about the displacement of morality by aestheticism, and Frank Trenker is a monstrous and furtive representative of an effete, depraved culture. The Penningtons stand somewhere near him on Kerr's moral continuum, with Buddy Boyle's family, hostile to the culture and money that moves in on them each summer and demeans their status, balanced against them. Kerr shows that no one is pure here, and her work is suggestive in interesting ways. But she relies too heavily on stereotypes. Adolescents can handle more complexity than she brings to her subject.

The book has the usual markings of the young adult novel. The first person narrator, Buddy, tells the story in an unpoetic, colloquial voice full of verbal tics that give the book the same stylistically impoverished quality that Scoppetone's novel has. The voice may work in Kerr's comic novels where the slang and hyperbole reflect the simple intensity of an adolescent's perspective, but in the more somber atmosphere of this work, it is simply a limitation. Buddy's descriptions, for example, rely heavily on the adjective "this," as in, "he lives in this huge house"; "he's this very tall, thin, very undaunted character"; or "my grandfather had this opera going on the stereo." . . . The activities that take place at Beauregard border on parody. Skye's friends, for example, one more conceited and casually bigoted than the next, play a game called "Whose is it" in which each contributes some personal article and then the group tries to guess to whom it belongs. Buddy's contribution is his sweater:

> I saw my new red sweater in the pile, and didn't think anything about it until the girl named Rachel picked it up and said, "The label says Made in Korea." Then she rolled her eyes to the heavens and said, "Now, *really,* how tacky can you get? And it's Orlon!"

Skye later makes up to Buddy for this humiliation by buying him a sweater made of cashmere. And he is so pathetically bound up with her that he appreciates it.

No doubt this kind of thing does go on among the idle rich. Yet Kerr undermines her portrait by relying on the caricature in every instance. She does, however, succeed in making her contempt for the values of these people obvious, showing them clearly capable of evil, while at the same time allowing us to feel sympathy for Buddy's attraction to them. . . . The more he sees of Skye, the more his relationship with his parents develops a brinksmanship quality, wherein they make demands on his time and he breaks promises, generally compromising himself in all sorts of small ways to satisfy Skye's whimsical needs. (pp. 135-37)

Because Trenker abandoned Buddy's mother when she was a child, Buddy has met his grandfather only a few times in his life. He renews the relationship when he meets Skye because he remembered Trenker as a cultured man and considered the house in Montauk a more suitable place to bring Skye than his own home. (p. 138)

[Trenker] is obviously pleased with Buddy's desire to establish a relationship with him and he welcomes Buddy into his home. He understands Buddy's attraction to Skye—"the lorelei" he calls her, encouraging Buddy to become all he can so that he will feel up to her. But he is, from the start, a distasteful character. When Buddy confesses some pecadillo that has been nagging at his conscience, Trenker does not hesitate, for instance, to tell him, "Once you know something is wrong, you're responsible, whether you see it, or hear about it, and most particularly when you're a part of it." While we might consider such a remark a sign of remorse, Trenker still has no trouble living with the trappings of his past. The name Gentlehands, for example, was given to him by the Italian prisoners he tortured because, while he tortured them, he would play the aria from *Tosca* "O dolci mani," O gentlehands. Thirty years later he is still listening to it. And when, through the investigations of a reporter, the token Italian Jew at one of the Pennington's parties, his identity is revealed, he runs, leaving Buddy an evasive, self-pitying letter of explanation. . . . (pp. 138-39)

In the novel's final pages, Buddy returns to Trenker's empty, ransacked house where the neighbors have taken out their anger on the property. As he is wandering through, he hears a noise. It is only a wounded raccoon whom Trenker had been nursing, but Buddy, in a furtive instant of sadness and recognition, whispers, "Gentlehands?" It is one of the book's most affecting moments. There are no resolutions. Buddy has lost the one person who took him seriously, he must acknowledge his grandfather's crimes, and he is alone.

Kerr's achievement in this novel, then is that she has illuminated a painful historical issue, sparing us no detail and yet avoiding sensationalism. The novel's weakness is that it depends so much on exaggeration and stereotype—the inarticulate cop, the morally degenerate rich—with little middle ground to indicate that life is more complex than that. Several of my students have remarked that **Gentlehands** is *The Great Gatsby* for teenagers, and this seems an apt comparison. But the wasted landscape of Fitzgerald's novel carries its symbolic weight more gracefully. (p. 139)

> *Geraldine DeLuca, "Taking True Risks: Con-*

troversial Issues in New Young Adult Novels," in The Lion and the Unicorn, *Vol. 3, No. 2, Winter, 1979-80, pp. 125-48.*

Little Little   (1981)

Teenage Little Little La Belle—dwarf daughter of the town of La Belle's leading family—has led a hothouse life with her pushy mother, forcibly overprotective father and jock sister. Sydney Cinnamon, a hunchback dwarf abandoned at birth, is a selfmade local celebrity appearing as the Roach, symbol of Palmer Pest Control. P.P.C.'s upcoming merger with the Japanese-owned Twinkle Traps factory, based in La Belle, brings the two together. Hired by Twinkle's Mr. Hiroyuki, Sydney's the surprise entertainment at Little Little's exclusive—"perfectly formed[s]" only—coming-out party. Also on the guest list is the elder La Belle's hoped-for son-in-law, TV preacher Little Lion—none other than huckster Knox Lionel, a.k.a. Opportunity Knox, Sydney's pragmatic mentor ("make sure your little ass goes first class") from their "Leprechaun Village" days. It takes a satirist of no small rank to poke pointed fun at the boosterism and pecking order of a TAD (The American Diminutives) convention without missing its members' painful vulnerability and isolation in an outsize world. This Kerr manages with only one misstep. But if the factory owner's son Mock Hiroyuki ("Riddre Riddre") skates too close to the kind of Asian caricature once favored by Jerry Lewis, the rest is bizarrely real and refreshingly funny.

> *Pamela D. Pollack, in a review of "Little Little," in* School Library Journal, *Vol. 27, No. 6, February, 1981, p. 76.*

In a very funny and very witty story, Kerr takes some caustic pokes at some of the aspects of our society, including snobbery, parent-child relations, show business and promotion, evangelistic entrepreneurs, and the treatment of those who differ from the majority. This is also a love story, and it is told in alternate chapters by Little Little [and by Sydney Cinnamon]. . . . Kerr's characters are strong and independent, her plot is novel, and her writing style vigorous, especially notable for dialogue. Hilarious yet provocative, the book elicits laughter, but the reader never laughs at the diminutive people—one laughs with them at the foibles of others. (pp. 153-54)

> *Zena Sutherland, in a review of "Little Little," in* Bulletin of the Center for Children's Books, *Vol. 34, No. 8, April, 1981, pp. 153-54.*

"Don't say 'dwarf,' " Little Little's mother tells her. "Call yourself a little person or a midget or a diminutive. Anything but 'dwarf.' "

Little Little La Belle has long blond hair and neatly tanned arms. Her white cotton dresses are made to order. She drives around town, smoking cigarettes, in her custom blue Volvo and everybody knows she's one of the two best writers in the senior class at La Belle High. But Little Little faces facts. She is 3 feet 3 inches tall. She calls herself a dwarf.

M. E. Kerr has written well and often before about the

sweet miseries of first love and coming of age. In this book, her eighth novel for young adults, those familiar problems come from a new perspective—less than four feet off the ground. It is the place of children, a place where phone booths and water fountains are beyond reach and back yard swimming pools seem as vast as the sea. It is the place of circus freaks, a place where strangers feel free to stare and point and pinch your cheek. It is an especially hard place to be when you're 17-going-on-18 years old.

Kerr's two narrators, Little Little and a young male dwarf named Sydney Cinnamon, have other obstacles to face as well. There is Little Little's family life—her eccentric, tomboy sister, her tippling mother, her overprotective father. There are Sydney's physical defects—his hunchback, his bad legs, his crooked tooth. He is definitely not "p.f." (perfectly formed) and therefore definitely not the kind of dwarf that Little Little's mother has in mind for her daughter.

What Mama La Belle does have in mind is marriage, and her candidate for son-in-law is the famous red-haired midget evangelist, Little Lion. Little Lion wears snazzy white suits, drives a Mercedes convertible and is about as p.f. as can be. He and Sydney vie for Little Little's little heart and some fairly silly stuff ensues—spiked drinks, giraffes delivered by taxi, and a host of hallelujahs from Little Lion. The turning point comes at a dwarf banquet in honor of Little Little's 18th birthday and it involves a gooey white cake and a pint-sized vamp who calls herself Dora the Dancing Lettuce Leaf. It's cartoon material, it's a Little Rascals extravaganza, and none of it matters much. Because the real story this book has to tell lies in the characters of Sydney and Little Little and in the way they cope with their affliction.

M. E. Kerr writes mostly about likeable outcasts—wry and bookish kids who will never be part of the parade but who see it all the better from the sidelines. Sydney and Little Little are no exception. They may be small, but their eyesight's keen. And from where they stand, any passing parade looks about like the next—big and boring, plodding and wholesome as a herd of cattle. What the dwarfs would like to see are different things, freakish things, things that are like themselves somehow. When they visit the library they choose books about dwarfs. When they go to the movies they prefer monster shows. And when Sydney Cinnamon takes a job, he dresses up as a cockroach and appears in commercials for an exterminating company.

"I decided to be something people don't like instinctively and make them like it," he explains to Little Little. "Something bizarre like me. If I'd have been something besides a roach, I'd have been an alligator or a snake. Something people look at and go 'Yeck!' just because of how it looks and not for any other reason. If I'd been a vegetable, I'd have been a piece of slimy okra."

This is a story about courage and tolerance and growing up without growing bigger. Kerr does not preach nor ask for pity. She details the everyday complexities of the dwarfs' lives—big dogs, booster chairs, unwieldy forks and spoons. She shows just how they eat and drive and

kiss. It's disquieting to consider that this is almost side show stuff, that a part of this book will appeal to the gawker, the cheek-pincher in us all. But, at the end, of course, a side show is always a sham, a place of actors and optical illusion. M. E. Kerr doesn't stoop to tricks. Her dwarfs are real and sharp as nuggets. They are small and steady as bookends. They are dwarfs who simply call themselves dwarfs.

> *Suzanne Freeman, "Growing Up in a Small World," in* Book World—The Washington Post, *May 10, 1981, p. 15.*

In several previous books, M. E. Kerr has shown an interest in the underlying passions of individuals, usually secondary characters, with physical or emotional idiosyncrasies. In *Little Little* these characters take center stage as Miss Kerr investigates the relationship between three dwarfs. . . .

Sydney and Little Little share the narration in alternating chapters, a device Miss Kerr has employed before and which is nicely conducive to a tale of romance. And while this *is* essentially a love story, the author gently weaves into the plot the general anguish and specific problems intrinsically bound to a minority world. But the pain, however verbalized or demonstrated, remains implicit. The work goes beyond an account of "what it's like to be a dwarf"; it remains a reality-based story of individuals.

Despite the first-person narrative, M. E. Kerr distances the reader from the work through limited character revelation, and her restraint discourages familiarity. In this way, she prevents the novel from becoming a shallow plea for tolerance. All these characters require is respect.

There is, of course, as in all of Miss Kerr's work, humor and an element of the absurd. Both Sydney's and Knox's occupations lend themselves to a controlled satire. Less restrained, however, is the author's portrayal of Little Little's parents; a well-meaning but rather stupid father, and a fluttering, silly mother who writes inane verse for the local newspaper and checks out other dwarfs to ascertain if they're "p.f."—perfectly formed. In their persistent efforts to uncover euphemisms for everything from their daughter's condition to bodily functions, they move dangerously close to becoming caricatures.

There are other occasional problems. Every now and then one of the protagonists will toss out a vague, poorly disguised throwaway line that is riddled with portent and screams of significance. But for the most part, the author's tone throughout the work blends a matter-of-fact nonchalance with a wry, mildly sardonic humor that is poignant without being sentimental. In the end, the reader is presented with a set of engaging personalities, an unusual perspective, and an entertaining, tender romance that offers both technical strength and a lowkey emotional tug.

> *Marilyn Kaye, in a review of "Little Little," in* The New York Times Book Review, *May 17, 1981, p. 38.*

A humorous look at society and its mores through the eyes of some memorable "little people" is provided in this whimsical tale. . . .

Although satirical, the book is also informative. Little Little's Grandfather claims that Tom Thumb could have been famous without being a dwarf if he had used his intelligence "instead of letting someone exploit him!" When Little Little asks what "exploit" means, he replies: "It means to utilize for profit. This Barnum fellow made a lot of money satisfying the public's curiosity about what someone different looks like. He turned Tom Thumb into a sideshow!"

The leading characters are well-rounded and clearly defined. Readers learn that all people have the same needs, problems and abilities—small persons simply have some special needs which must be met. The dialogue is fast-paced and witty. Although sensationalism is depicted, this is clearly done to educate. Stereotypes are skillfully shown to be just that—stereotypes. This book is recommended for young adults who can understand the satire.

> *Rosemary Kasper, in a review of "Little Little," in* Interracial Books for Children Bulletin, *Vol. 13, Nos. 4 & 5, 1982, p. 15.*

What I Really Think of You (1982)

This surprisingly unspectacular novel concerns two PKs, or preachers' kids. Opal Ringer's father, poor and ungrammatical, preaches of the coming Rapture at his Helping Hand Tabernacle—where people fall in the aisles, "slain with the spirit"; Opal's fat mother is likely to burst out in tongues; and Opal herself, tormented at school for her family's religion, shrinks with shame when the kids from the higher-class high school drop in to observe. Jesse Pegler is one from the other school, and not too sure what or if he believes; but his father is also a Pentacostal preacher—a successful one who does his preaching on TV and devotes much energy to "bottom-line Christianity." There is some resentment on the Ringers' part, especially when a high school girl sheds her crutch at the Hand (that her lameness was faked is her own secret) and Guy Pegler reaps the fame and profit. ("Daddy says Guy Pegler stole our miracle," is how Opal puts it.) Still, Opal is thrilled when Jesse, pressed by the girl he really wants, invites Opal to a big dance. Then on the day of the dance Opal's religious older brother kidnaps the famous Guy Pegler and the date is off—but, that very night, Opal finds happiness with Jesse's religious older brother and a sudden gift of tongues that makes her a successful attraction at the Hand thereafter. And so triumphs the outcast and ridiculed Opal, not with rancor but with love for her former tormentors. Where the freak world of dwarves—including an evangelical preacher dwarf—gave an edge to Kerr's contemporary satire in **Little, Little,** Kerr is less biting, and less on her own edge, in this encounter with the varieties of evangelical religious experience. Simple Opal Ringer, with her vision of blinding light, is a long way from Kerr's sharp, sophisticated, contemporary heroines from Dinky Hocker to Little Little; and though championing Opal may be more deeply defiant, neither Kerr's heart nor her wit seems to be in this ironic vindication. (pp. 349-50)

> *A review of "What I Really Think of You," in*

Kirkus Reviews, *Vol. L, No. 6, March 15, 1982, pp. 349-50.*

M. E. Kerr, whose **Little Little** was published to critical acclaim last year, likes aberrations. Her earlier novel for young people concerned dwarfs. This time she delves into the world of fundamentalist preachers and their long-suffering children. . . .

[Opal and Jesse] are oppressed by the piety and the exhibitionism of their parents, and Opal is at times downright ashamed of hers.

The impetus of the novel, however, is not pathos but farce, and it is Opal who gives the most entertaining reports of life in a home where "Honk If You Love Jesus" bumper stickers adorn the family car. She has the sympathy to love her parents, even when they embarrass her, yet the wit to classify their foibles.

Kerr makes fundamentalism funny through most of the novel. But, alas, she changes her tone near the end, and expects us to accept Opal's reconciliation with something she has so often made quite ridiculous. In a way it seems a desperately contrived case of plotting, and it simply doesn't work. We want more of the Opal who has a keen eye for tackiness but loves its perpetrators just the same.

> *Alice Digilio, in a review of "What I Really Think of You," in* Book World—The Washington Post, *July 11, 1982, p. 11.*

With the rise in popularity of televised religion and of evangelical Christianity, it should come as no surprise that this phenomenon should make its appearance in a young adult novel. The topic lends itself to a range of treatments, from moral directive to satiric indictment. And it should come as no surprise to her readers that M. E. Kerr has avoided the didactic traps that are inherent in the subject.

In her latest account of a fragile boy-girl relationship, Miss Kerr neatly places an incipient romance against the backdrop of evangelism and allows that subject to permeate—but not overwhelm—her story. (pp. 49-50)

With admirable sincerity Miss Kerr explores the tentative relationship between Opal and Jesse and the surrounding tensions that are grounded in class conflict and the inevitable comparisons between the fervor of unabashed, "down-home" faith and the razzmatazz of media-hyped religion, equally fervent but with a polished commercial veneer.

Opal's narrative has a haunting quality that suggests underlying passion. Jesse's remarks are less powerful, but his sense of inadequacy reflects a common adolescent concern.

The novel has its problems. The sudden reappearance of Bud toward the end and his subsequent involvement with Opal has the ring of a slightly contrived denouement, and some peculiarly undeveloped characters drift through the story without adding much.

Despite its shortcomings, the work has integrity. It's hard to believe that a novelist could indulge in such concepts as being "slain in the spirit," waiting for "The Rapture," faith healing and speaking in tongues without either proselytizing or mocking them—but glory be, M. E. Kerr has done it. (p. 50)

Marilyn Kaye, in a review of "What I Really Think of You," in The New York Times Book Review, *September 12, 1982, pp. 49-50.*

Me Me Me Me Me: Not a Novel (1983)

When Marijane Meaker, who writes under the name of M. E. Kerr, was growing up in a small upstate New York town, her mother missed no opportunity to warn her that "there isn't a female comedian alive who's happy." Fortunately, she never paid her mother the slightest attention. She went right on being funny and, after establishing her career as a writer with a series of suspense novels under the pseudonym Vin Packer, she proceeded, as M. E. Kerr, to produce nine highly successful young adult novels about the heartbreaking comedy of American adolescence.

Now, in this autobiographical memoir, Miss Kerr unveils a deliciously wicked sense of humor, reminiscent in style, and occasionally in content, of Jessica Mitford's work. While still in high school in the early 1940's, Miss Kerr tells us, she contrived to pep up a deadly dull romance with the local funeral director's son by helping another couple to elope in the cutaway station wagon that normally carried floral tributes to grave-sites. Shipped off to a highly proper girls' boarding school in Virginia, she showed her rebellious nature by writing to Earl Browder, head of the American Communist Party, informing him that "many of the girls were interested in joining," thus calling down on the school post office a flood of what the headmistress called "tawdry" mail.

And later, when the sorority system at the University of Missouri provided a worthy target for her rebellious instincts, she began dating a Hungarian refugee who lectured her on the capitalist decadence of "boogie voogie" and got her to join the Communist Party for real—an experience that quickly left her disillusioned.

These reminiscences are primarily addressed to fans of Miss Kerr's novels who will no doubt enjoy meeting the real-life models for many of her offbeat characters. (One is hardly surprised to learn that the truth is often more bizarre than fiction, but in this case it is usually more poignant as well since Miss Kerr freely admits that some of these individuals were the victims of her unstoppable writer's drive to know everyone's secrets.)

As for the rest of you, don't let the regrettable title put you off; this book offers a satisfying if brief encounter with a humorist whose delight in poking fun at the trappings of authority is unmarred by either self-hatred or pettiness toward others.

Joyce Milton, in a review of "Me Me Me Me Me," in The New York Times Book Review, *May 22, 1983, p. 39.*

Do the events and persons about which authors write reflect realities of their own lives, or are they the result of their vivid imaginations? M. E. Kerr has been writing popular novels for young adults for many years and has been asked this question frequently by her readers. Her answer to the many letters she has received on the subject is this book.

Me Me . . . begins with a shy 15 year old girl named Marijane Meaker . . . growing up in New York state in the late 1930's, and follows her life up to the year 1951 when her first story was published.

Marijane Meaker is a very complex character. She becomes a rebellious teenager who confronts facets of her life her way, whenever she does not understand. Among her problems are her family, her religion, small town mores, and her culture as a whole. She rebels against the "hardline" approach of her father and never seems to understand her mother. She seems to have trouble with anyone who happens to be an authority figure. From her first day at dance class to her troubles at boarding school and through university, life is a struggle. She battles. She hurts. She grows. She matures. This *is* the story of Marijane and her friends and foes who influenced her formative years.

The author's style and technique are very effective. She presents these autobiographical chapters in such a way that the reader enters into stories without realizing it. Then, at the end of each chapter, she follows up each story by explaining which of the characters and escapades have influenced various characters in each of her books.

M. E. Kerr has answered in good measure the questions put to her by her readers. She has written a fascinating, yet timeless look at herself and others, which will not only delight her fans, but will no doubt increase their number.

Paul A. Caron, in a review of "Me Me Me Me Me: Not a Novel," in Best Sellers, *Vol. 43, No. 3, June, 1983, p. 110.*

Spurred by readers' questions, the author of a string of witty, trenchant contemporary novels delves into her past and writes "what really happened to me when I was a kid, as I remember it." Without resorting to dull chronologies or nostalgic platitudes, the author, as did Jean Fritz in *Homesick,* describes with drama, humor, and perception a youth less exotic but no less entertaining and compelling. . . .

An inveterate writer, M. E. Kerr wrote stories for years that returned "like boomerangs, with printed rejection slips attached." The roots of her writing glimmer in her father's journal entries and in her mother's gossip. Periodic troublemaker and clown and perennial rebel, Marijane Meaker . . . confesses to being the "smartmouth" tomboys populating many of her novels. And she is quite as entertaining as they are. Incisive, witty, and immediate, the book is vintage M. E. Kerr.

Nancy C. Hammond, in a review of "Me Me Me Me Me—Not a Novel," in The Horn Book Magazine, *Vol. LIX, No. 4, August, 1983, p. 462.*

Him *She Loves?* (1984)

If this were Kerr's first novel, or a story by almost anyone

Kerr, at left, on the "Mary Margaret McBride Show," ABC Radio, 1951.

else, it would be hailed as a true original, bittersweet, brilliantly comic. While 17-year-old Henry Schiller's tale of woe deserves such praise, it is not in a class with the author's **Dinky Hocker Shoots Smack! Gentlehands, Is That You, Miss Blue?** or her other superb creations. Henry, new in a Long Island town, has the bad luck to fall in love with gorgeous Valerie Kissenwiser. Her father, Al Kiss, is a famous comic and violently opposed to a Teutonic suitor for his darling Valley. In nightclubs and on TV, Henry becomes the butt of Al's gags, patter in which he calls the youth "Heinrich," complains of his "sauerkraut breath" and winds up his act with the question, "*Him* she loves?" It's up to Henry to convince Al that Valerie has chosen the right lover, a *mensch,* not a *nebbish,* and the way he does that is the story's turning point. But here the reader may ask, "*This* he does?" The resolution hints that Kerr had used all the genuine gems in her imagination before the crisis and had only paste substitutes for the finale.

> *A review of " 'Him' She Loves?" in* Publishers Weekly, *Vol. 225, No. 8, February 24, 1984, p. 140.*

"My daughter," says famous comedian Al Kiss on national TV, is dating "a young German storm trooper with ears so big he could pick up cable TV." Furthermore, "Heinrich . . . goes in an elevator, pushes the buttons, and looks for gum. . . . . . . *Him* she loves?" Imagine the humiliation, then, of 17-year-old narrator Henry Schiller—the jug-eared, not-very-bright lad of German descent who is indeed madly in love with Al Kiss' gorgeous daughter Valerie. It's one thing for Al to throw Henry out of the Kissenwiser's Long Island home, to forbid Valerie to date him—which Al does when he catches the couple in Valerie's bedroom. But to humiliate "Heinrich" almost weekly, coast-to-coast?! It's enough to make a lesser kid slink off into hiding—especially considering the fact that Henry has other pressures to deal with, too: helping out at the German-style restaurant just opened by his widowed mother and boorish older brothers; or getting through his junior year at a new high-school (Valerie's a senior there), required to impersonate a pregnant woman in "Health and Human Relations" class. Still, Henry vows to fight for Valerie. He meets her in secret for tasteful (implied) sexual interludes; he follows her obsessively, with lighthearted echoes of Scott Spencer's *Endless Love* in Henry's slightly *cautious* grandstanding. (" 'I don't care if we die!' I said, a little concerned about her driving.")

Furthermore, to change Al Kiss' attitude, Henry concocts an offbeat PR campaign that transforms Al's career. And if this media-blitz isn't entirely convincing, it sets up Kerr's niftiest shift here: the growing camaraderie between bigot Al ("He's Boche, honeybunch") and fatherless Henry—in parallel with Valerie's rather shrill withdrawal. ("Since Daddy went to work on you, you've become a lousy lover, too, Henry Schiller!") Kerr, an old-hand with turned-around stereotypes, doesn't turn them around quite enough here: some Jewish (and possibly some German-American) readers may be offended. But her double-edged satire is a rare commodity, her supporting cast is a droll-yet-credible assortment, and Al's cruel Heinrich routines—with reactions from Heinrich and family—become laugh-out-loud gems of comic embarrassment.

> *A review of " 'Him' She Loves?" in* Kirkus Reviews, *Juvenile Issue, Vol. LII, Nos. 6-9, May 1, 1984, p. J-48.*

You want funny? Henry Schiller falls big for a Jewish princess, Valerie Kissenwiser, and who should she be but the daughter of Al Kiss, a TV comedian. So what's funny? Well, the gags are hilarious and the dialogue is choice—brittle and witty. The humor overcomes the predictable love story plot. . . . The characters: Valerie and her sister are wisecracking come-on queens, there's a health teacher you love to hate, and Henry has these antic inspirations to keep the book rolling. Offstage, Al Kiss is complex enough to make you almost forgive his ghastly jokes. (pp. 84-5)

> *Kay Webb O'Connell, in a review of " 'Him' She Loves?" in* School Library Journal, *Vol. 30, No. 10, August, 1984, pp. 84-5.*

I Stay Near You: One Story in Three (1985)

Kerr fans will applaud the arrival of *I Stay Near You.* Against the familiar backdrop of Cayuta, New York, a saga of three generations unfolds. In the 1940s, teenage Mildred Cone metamorphoses from a gawky loner and a daughter of a launderer into a Cinderella who captures the heart of dashing Powell Storm, son of the local millionaire. World War II claims Powell as a hero and leaves an unwed Mildred with a baby and a Storm family ring bearing the title's Basque inscription. In the 1960s, Mildred's son, Vincent, a singer and guitarist, pursues Joanna, who steals his heart and the family ring before jilting him. Finally, in the 1980s, Vincent's son, P. S., describes his relationship with his elusive rock star, drug abusing father and the discoveries he's made about his family. The family ring is returned to Grandmother Mildred for safe-keeping. Kerr's characters are vital and distinct. Fate plays a decisive role in each of their lives and in the development of plot. Although a few improbabilities exist, and the linking device of the ring is not essential, the three-part story is well-constructed and poignant. The narrative technique for two sections is effectively different: friend Laura remembers Mildred in Part One, and P. S. recalls his past and Laura's whereabouts in Part Three. Only Part Two, focusing on Vincent, is delivered anonymously and inex-

plicably in third person without mention of Laura. These minor technical criticisms cannot overshadow Kerr's skill as a storyteller. Different eras, conflicting life styles, and contrasting social backgrounds are interwoven into a tale that should captivate adolescent readers.

> *Gerry Larson, in a review of "I Stay Near You," in* School Library Journal, *Vol. 31, No. 8, April, 1985, p. 98.*

Kerr's venture into a different story form succeeds in many ways. The multigenerational approach offers a wonderful opportunity to examine teenagers and the adults they might become. Her characters are as strong or stronger than ever. Proud, vulnerable Mildred's transformation to an embittered middle-aged housewife is heart-wrenching, and Vincent as the burnt-out rocker is unforgettable. However their stories just don't hang together. The promise of a thematic tie-in represented by the ring is not fulfilled. Characters give the ring little significance, and readers are hard-pressed to do more. The first story, which readers of *Me Me Me Me Me* will recognize in tone if not in detail, is effective storytelling. The others are too sketchy or too implausible to work. Still, the powerful characterizations and fascinating ideas will make this one well worth reading.

> *Christy Tyson, in a review of "I Stay Near You," in* Voice of Youth Advocates, *Vol. 8, No. 2, June, 1985, p. 132.*

The author returns to Cayuta, New York, for the setting of a skillfully worked family chronicle encompassing three generations. . . . The three stories are linked by the author's use of irony and her persistent theme of love, both faithful and betrayed, as well as by the continuity of the characters through the years. They are shown mercilessly yet poignantly as the victims of circumstances and of their own weaknesses. Although there are occasional flashes of wry humor, one notes the absence of M. E. Kerr's astringent wit; indeed the book, especially the final part, is overcast by a mood of contemporary melancholy acceptance. (pp. 565-66)

> *Ethel L. Heins, in a review of "I Stay Near You: 1 Story in 3," in* The Horn Book Magazine, *Vol. LXI, No. 5, September-October, 1985, pp. 565-66.*

Night Kites (1986)

The Rudds' family life in an affluent Long Island community is the prototypical good life, American style. Dad stays in New York City during the week to run his prosperous brokerage firm, Mom stays at home and works at good causes and son Erick spends his days with high school, his all-American girlfriend Dill, and lifelong best friend Jack, a good-natured jock who has fallen deeply in love with his flamboyant, glitzy classmate Nicki.

The only clouds on the horizon of Erick's senior year are frustration at his inability to persuade Dill to let him neck with her before they are married (after college, of course), low scholastic aptitude scores and unrelenting pressure from his father to go for a master's degree in business and not end up like his older brother Pete, a Manhattan prep school teacher who writes science fiction on the side. Pete is a failure in his father's eyes, despite the fact, announced during a surprise visit by Pete, that his uncompleted novel has been optioned for a screenplay.

Later, as Erick and Pete are discussing their frustration with their father, Erick tells Pete that he, Dill, Jack and Nicki want to attend a Bruce Springsteen concert in the city, and Pete offers his apartment so that Erick and Jack can try to score with their girls, something else Dad is also always urging Erick to do before settling down to marriage and career.

The concert is a great success, but the rest of the plans fall through when Erick's father seeks him out in Manhattan to announce that Pete's recent bout with "dysentery" is much more serious than that, for Pete has been hospitalized with AIDS. Erick is shocked at the news, but even more shocked by the realization that his adored brother is homosexual. The family confers and, led by Dad, agrees to keep Pete's disease a secret from friends and other relatives.

Things are further complicated for Erick when Nicki begins to make a play for him and their relationship soon reaches a sexual stage. Inevitably, Jack and Dill find out, and Erick and Nicki are shunned by their classmates for the betrayal. Guilt-ridden, struggling to cope with his brother's condition and desperately trying to keep Nicki a secret from his already overburdened family, Erick longs for "the old familiar routines of senior year, being tight with one girl and one crowd, and having a long history with both, instead of it being all new."

As Pete's illness worsens and the family realizes that he will soon die, Erick comes to terms with the imminent loss of his brother and finds solace in Nicki. But Nicki finds out about Pete, confronts Erick with her fear that he may have given her AIDS and refuses to see him again. Finally, Erick discovers Nicki with another classmate; devastated, he goes home to Pete and as they talk of Pete's approaching death, Erick realizes that Pete has come to terms with it, as Erick will sooner or later have to come to terms with the loss of Nicki.

In less sure hands, this moving and understated examination of the angst of first love and first sex, of the effects of a catastrophic illness on one family, especially an illness like AIDS with its undercurrents of irresponsibility on the part of its victims, could have been just another problem novel. M. E. Kerr, the author of **Dinky Hocker Shoots Smack!** however, has managed to transcend that young adult genre, and has, with sensitivity and delicacy, described an issue that may face many more families if predictions about AIDS come true. This is a fine story, beautifully told, with characters that ring true. Mrs. Kerr has simply never been better in her long and lauded career; she too is a "night kite," unafraid to soar into the darkness of the human predicament.

> *Audrey B. Eaglen, in a review of "Night Kites," in* The New York Times Book Review, *April 13, 1986, p. 30.*

Although there is too much camaraderie and sexual joy going on to make this a sad book, the struggle the characters have just liking each other is sad indeed. With Jack's opening assertion that "I really care about Nicki," suspicions arise.

Perhaps it is only in plays and movies that characters adequately show their ragged affections in highly-charged talk. Here, though the dialogue races, the characters act, and the scenes unfold, the conflicts are never quite ignited. It isn't talk we miss, but contemplation. Even with plenty of cause for remorse and guilt, the characters don't have time.

Kerr is a light-footed writer with a keen sense for the things that grate on young men, but are the clichés in her book her own or are they Erick's? Can a high school boy be forgiven for saying, "Count on Mom's heart. Count on Dad's head," as if it were a fresh, revealing statement? Can an author? (pp. 17, 22)

> *Mary Lou Burket, "Teen-Agers and Troubled Times," in* Book World—The Washington Post, *May 11, 1986, pp. 17, 22.*

In her most recent compelling and disturbing novel, M. E. Kerr examines how Pete's illness affects Erick, his family, and his relationship with his girl friend, a Madonna clone and generally unsympathetic character. In the process of examining this difficult subject, the author explores love, betrayal, first sexual encounters, tragedy, and heartbreak—as only teenagers can experience them. M. E. Kerr is undoubtedly at her best as a writer when she is being satirical or humorous, as in **Little Little.** Her more serious, darker books, such as **Night Kites** and **Gentlehands,** never mesh into quite as satisfying wholes as the others because even with serious topics she cannot help being sarcastic. But they are still important books; for, like Robert Cormier and Richard Peck, M. E. Kerr is one of the few young adult writers who can take a subject that affects teenagers' lives, can say something important to young readers about it, and can craft what is first and foremost a good story, without preaching and without histrionics. Consequently, **Night Kites** is an important part of the Kerr canon and an important contribution to the literature for young adults.

> *Anita Silvey, in a review of "Night Kites," in* The Horn Book Magazine, *Vol. LXII, No. 5, September-October, 1986, p. 597.*

Fell (1987)

Not since **Gentlehands** has Kerr so poignantly combined a story of romance, mystery, and wit with serious implications of class conflict and personal betrayal. The book (the first in a projected series) begins in Kerr's favorite resort setting of Seaville, New York, and Fell (like Buddy in **Gentlehands**) is a policeman's son involved with the rich crowd on the hill, including a girl whose "Daddy" disapproves of Fell's blue-collar background. (Fell knows his chances would be better if he were "heir to a fortune and descended from William the Conqueror.") Quieter and a little wiser than Buddy, Fell is sensitive, funny, sexy, and a gourmet cook. He nurtures his family: his recently widowed mother, who works in the fancy clothing store Dressed to Kill and is over her limit on every charge card in her purse, and his five-year-old sister, Jazzy, whose rags-to-riches games with her paper doll reflect the conventional dreams that Kerr both understands and disturbs. When Fell is paid $20,000 to impersonate a rich neighbor's son at an elite prep school, it's like a dream come true, especially when he's chosen for the snob secret society that runs the school like the "Master Race." Written with a light touch and a nod to Cormier, Fell's unaffected first-person narrative shows how the school embodies the world of privilege with its power politics, prejudice, lunacy, and ritualized tyranny. The suspenseful plot flashes with sudden bitterness and violence that reaches back to the Japanese-American internment camps in World War II. Layers of deceit and trickery are revealed with comedy and complexity, and underlying it all is the ache of unfulfilled dreams. (pp. 1515-16)

> *Hazel Rochman, in a review of "Fell," in* Booklist, *Vol. 83, No. 19, June 1, 1987, pp. 1515-16.*

Once again Kerr returns to Seaville, New York and the theme of the haves vs. the havenots. This time it is 17 year old John Fell who is on the outside looking in, first through his romance with Helen J. "Keats" Keating whose family lives ". . . at the top of a hill in a palatial home. Adieu, they had named it, and it looked down on Seaville as surely as they did." Then he literally runs into Woodrow Pingree, neighbor of the Keatings, who offers Fell a most interesting proposition. It seems his son must attend the exclusive Gardner School in order to come into his inheritance and to maintain the family tradition—and the young Pingree does *not* want to go! The solution: send Fell in his place—a free education with a $20,000 bonus at the end. Fell accepts and finds that the deal includes much more than he'd planned on, including membership in the secret campus organization called the Seven.

Kerr manages an almost perfect balance of dry wit and suspense, with Fell standing squarely as a likable, well-balanced hero in a world more than slightly off-kilter. While the first half of the novel, set in Seaville, is Kerr at her subtle, satirical best, part two seems a bit flat in comparison. Occurrences at the school seem rushed, and neither the characters nor the school environment come completely alive. However by this point readers will be hooked and will gladly hang in there to see all revealed—almost. The twist ending promises a sequel which will hopefully allow for a longer stay at a school that may well be the most darkly intriguing since Conroy's *The Lords of Discipline.*

> *Christy Tyson, in a review of "Fell," in* Voice of Youth Advocates, *Vol. 10, No. 4, October, 1987, p. 202.*

If you have ever wondered what books to use when fans of Betsy Byars have grown older, this could well fit the bill. It is full of humour and human insight. We are treated to the same taut, compact prose style, well written and with plenty of depth and innuendo. The text even benefits from a second reading. . . .

Although at first I found it hard to suspend disbelief over the proposal to 'trade places'. I must admit to being completely engrossed. There are several discrepancies in the thriller elements of the story which don't ring true, but all is revealed in the exciting denouement. Standard stuff, but *Fell* will appeal to a wide range of both sexes and I look forward to more in the series.

> *Graham Case, in a review of "Fell," in* The School Librarian, *Vol. 38, No. 1, February, 1990, p. 29.*

Fell Back   (1989)

In a sequel to the popularly acclaimed *Fell,* narrator-hero John Fell emulates his detective dad in tracking down the reasons for the sudden death of Lambert, fellow member of the exclusive prep-school club Sevens.

There are several sure-fire ingredients here: a couple of gorgeous girls, at least one of whose misplaced affection shows promise of being transferred to Fell; a complex network of multipurpose characters, including an overprotective father and a mysterious half-brother who both prove to be part of a drug network—plus the mother of the deceased, who is also another key character's shrink; a suspenseful conclusion with a satisfying collection of surprising revelations; even Fell's continuing culinary prowess. Kerr, always a pro, draws her characters with finesse and keeps the story moving. But there are some problems here—notably, the message that the endowed luxury in which the privileged Sevens live is ultimately corrupting is likely to be outweighed for many readers by the Sevens' beguiling, unlikely life-style. And for those unfamiliar with *Fell,* the many references to his previous amours add little.

Still, engrossing, good-quality entertainment that ends, like *Fell,* with a teaser for a sequel. (pp. 1404-05)

> *A review of "Fell Back," in* Kirkus Reviews, *Vol. LVII, No. 17, September 15, 1989, pp. 1404-05.*

What was so captivating about *Fell* was its crackling narrative and the fact that one could never tell in which direction the story was heading. Disappointingly, the spark that ignited that book seems to have fizzled out, and *Fell Back,* although entertaining, is just another mystery story starring a budding junior detective.

> *A review of "Fell Back," in* Publishers Weekly, *Vol. 236, No. 13, September 29, 1989, p. 70.*

Those who enjoyed meeting Fell in his 1987 debut will be glad to see that he's coping nicely with prep school and that, despite being betrayed by the beautiful, rich Keats and the beautiful, deceitful Delia, he has enough hope left to fall for the beautiful, rich *and* deceitful Nina. And there are enough offbeat characters to please Kerr fans. (Lasher's psychiatrist mother with her chemical imbalance theory for adolescent suicide is enough to make most readers pause to appreciate their own mothers.) However this one is oddly flat, especially compared to its predecessor. Fell, with his flair for cooking and his tolerance for the flaws in others and himself, made for a unique and appealing hero, and his reaction to the prince-and-the-pauper scenario he faced was fascinating. However *Fell Back* offers too many characters insufficiently developed, a prep school campus that never really comes alive, too little humor for a Fell sequel and too much introspection from a too-passive central character for a mystery. And when Fell stumbles across his second major crime ring in less than a year it becomes just too much. Not a bad book, especially for fans of the first, but it could have been so much more. Like the first, this one ends with a cliff-hanger, a hint that something awful has happened to [Fell's best friend] Dib—and that Fell will be back to tell us all about it. Let's hope he does so with a bit more of the style he showed in the first, and with more of the control we've come to expect from this author. (p. 278)

> *Christy Tyson, in a review of "Fell Back," in* Voice of Youth Advocates, *Vol. 12, No. 5, December, 1989, pp. 277-78.*

Shoebag (as Mary James, 1990)

[A] delightful fantasy about a cockroach who suddenly turns into a boy, leading to a clever reversal of Kafka's "Metamorphosis" and an amusing satirical view of human foibles.

Like all his tribe, Shoebag was named for the site of his birth. At first, he is horrified when he discovers his new form; he's fond of his parents (Drainboard and Under the Toaster), and has a natural aversion to people—whom roaches convincingly describe as dirty and who regularly try to exterminate his family. However, Shoebag adapts: adopted by the Biddle family, in whose house he was born, he makes friends with the other misfits at school—including one Gregor Samsa, with whom he has a curious affinity. Meanwhile, he keeps in touch with his real family, protecting them as best he can from spider and cat. Ultimately, he even makes friends with self-centered little "Pretty Soft" Biddle, a child star who is virtually imprisoned by her premature career of making toilet-paper commercials. Then Gregor—who, yes, was also a cockroach—makes the big decision to stay human, and he passes on his ability to return to roachdom to Shoebag, who goes back at last to his loving family.

A highly original story crammed with clever detail, action, insight, and humor, all combined with impeccable logic and begging to be shared—with class, family, or any available audience.

> *A review of "Shoebag," in* Kirkus Reviews, *Vol. LVIII, No. 4, February 15, 1990, p. 264.*

The publisher invites us to identify the pseudonymous "Mary James," "a popular young-adult author"; our marker is on M. E. Kerr for this book filled with *Little Little*-like repartee. Shoebag is a young cockroach who one day wakes up to find himself turning into a boy. . . . The daffy premise is never convincing but always appealing, spiked with barbed observations on the family lives of both cockroaches and humans. Most of the humor is carried in the conversations, which sometimes fall into a he-said-she-

said rhythm that overstates the jokes. But for all its cleverness, this has a Dale Carnegie stick-up-for-yourself theme that gives heart to the wit.

> *Robert Strang, in a review of "Shoebag," in* Bulletin of the Center for Children's Books, *Vol. 43, No. 7, March, 1990, p. 164.*

Mary James gets away with a crazy idea by playing it deadpan, and she carries it off with panache. After all, is it more improbable that a cockroach should become a boy than that a little girl should earn $150 a time advertising toilet rolls? There is drama and human (and cockroach) interest in a story told briskly, without a wasted word or notion. 'Mary James', we are told, is a pseudonym. The author is clearly a highly professional and accomplished writer, whose book will delight as much as it will fascinate.

> *M. Crouch, in a review of "Shoebag," in* The Junior Bookshelf, *Vol. 55, No. 3, June, 1991, p. 114.*

Fell Down (1991)

Acclaimed YA author M. E. Kerr . . . told *Booklist* that for a writer the great thing about a sequel is that you don't have to create a whole new cast. "You know your characters as well as you know your friends," she said. "It's like going home." *Fell Down* represents Kerr's third trip home in a series that begins with *Fell* and continues in *Fell Back*. Kerr is already planning *Fell in Love* and *Fell Away*. "And I suppose the end will have to be *Fell Apart*," she said.

Fell Back was a disappointment, but *Fell Down* is a brilliant mystery, one that will have genre fans fitting the pieces together for days. Still, just because it's a sequel, you keep wondering if you're meant to be confused or if you're missing something that went on in the previous books. In fact, what will hold most readers—even those who haven't read the other books—is not so much the detective work as the witty dialogue, the endearing character of Fell, and the immediacy of his world. Kerr's the most acute social observer in YA fiction ("What did he do for a living?" Lenny asked him. "What I'm going to do, probably. Inherit.") In *Fell Down,* she mixes the weary worldliness of *The Great Gatsby* with the bizarre revelations of "Twin Peaks." There's a strangeness uncovered beneath the surface, a nervy sense of dislocation in family, community, and individual personality.

Fell is down. He's dropped out of the fancy prep school he entered under false presences in *Fell,* but its secrets haunt him. He feels guilty about the death of his best friend in a drunken driving accident, and that draws him back to the place and the world of privilege, and into a mystery of kidnapping, murder, disguise, and obsession that stretches back a generation. His first-person narrative voice is both comic and blue. Though he's no longer corrupted by the rich as he was in *Fell Back,* he has not lost his sharp eye for the phony in style and substance. He knows only too well about those who shop and those who long to join them.

Alternating with Fell's story, interrupting him, is a very

different narrative that begins in the early 1960s. It's about two young loners at the school—one wealthy, one on scholarship—who bond so tightly that they almost become each other. This other narrative is all pretense: brash, self-conscious, sour, outrageous; gradually we realize that it's a ventriloquist telling his story in the voice of his alter ego, his dummy. But who's in control? Which is which? Is the voice male or female? As the two stories come together, and Fell tries to unravel not only who killed whom, but also who is who, the parallels and doubles and coverups in plot, character, and language are dazzlingly clever. Impersonation is everywhere. Even the brand names hold clues.

Kerr told *Booklist* that she'd always been fascinated by doppelgangers and doubles. Before her YA novels, she wrote suspense stories for adults. "They were Whydunnits, not Whodunnits," she said. "I wasn't interested in the detective story, but in probing character. I love the suspense novels of writers like Ruth Rendell."

In *Fell Down,* ventriloquism becomes a metaphor for shifting identity in a mystery that makes you ask questions about love, gender, and power. No wonder Fell decides to go back to school: "In a world so full of cunning and concealment, I needed all the help I could get."

And on the last page, his old love returns. Or is it her sister? To be continued.

> *Hazel Rochman, "To Be Continued: 'Fell Down' and Other Sequels," in* Booklist, *Vol. 88, No. 2, September 15, 1991, p. 135.*

The telling of *Fell Down* is distinctly different from the earlier books: in alternating chapters, the two stories—past and present—are told by Fell and "The Mouth," whose identity is not revealed until the end. This device is jarring at first, but it eventually serves up an intriguing

read as the events merge to create a satisfying whole. There is sure to be another book about Fell around the corner, for he returns to the newly coed Gardner School and Sevens House to find April, the sister of the love-of-his-life, Delia. A must purchase for libraries in which the other two books about Fell are popular. (p. 146)

> *Laura McCutcheon, in a review of "Fell Down," in* School Library Journal, *Vol. 37, No. 10, October, 1991, pp. 145-46.*

The interwining of . . . two stories allows Kerr to revisit the connections between generations begun in *I Stay Near You* but with even greater effect. She again uses different voices and times to develop parallel story lines, and readers will respond as strongly to the voices from the past as they do to Fell's. However the problems that marred the effectiveness in the first two books become almost insurmountable in this third volume. Too much happens coincidentally and far too quickly to Fell and to Lenny and Nels. Plots are left unresolved, and "mood" endings just won't do for mystery readers or for that matter any who read primarily for story. Kerr's mastery at character development is superb, and few can top her for style that can convey both wit and heartache. (Fell to Keats on his previous girlfriend: "Do you know what an oxymoron is? . . . think of cold fire, or hot snow, or over Delia.") It's exciting to read a young adult novel that assumes its readers can think as well as feel. Young adults deserve writing of this caliber. But they also deserve a story completely and credibly told. *Fell Down,* even more than its prequels, promises much but fails to deliver. (p. 314)

> *Christy Tyson, in a review of "Fell Down," in* Voice of Youth Advocates, *Vol. 14, No. 5, December, 1991, pp. 313-14.*

Beverly Naidoo

1943-

South African-born English writer of fiction, nonfiction, and short stories; and editor.

Major works include *Journey to Jo'burg: A South African Story* (1984), *Free as I Know* (editor, 1987), *Chain of Fire* (1989).

An outspoken critic of apartheid, Naidoo has published several groundbreaking works intended to educate a broad spectrum of age groups on the effects of racism within South African society. She was born in Johannesburg to a privileged family, "brought up," she relates, with the usual conceptions most white South Africans have [and] completely taking for granted the services of our cook-cum-nanny. . . . We knew her as 'Mary,' I don't know her real name. What I do recall, with the vivid intensity of one of those seminal childhood experiences, was how when I was perhaps eight or nine, Mary received a telegram and collapsed. The telegram said that two of her three young daughters had died. It was diphtheria—something for which I, as a white child, had been vaccinated." Reflecting on this childhood memory as an adult, Naidoo experienced a profound change of values. Since the mid-1960s she has lived in England and taught primary and secondary school. It is her interest in children, especially, that stimulated her to become an activist writer.

During the 1980s, Naidoo's research work for the Education Group of the British Defence and Aid Fund for Southern Africa—an activist organization designed to assist political victims of apartheid and to raise world consciousness—contributed to the group's realization that an enormous lack of suitable teaching materials on the subject of apartheid necessitated swift corrective action. At the Education Group's suggestion that a work of informed and helpful fiction be commissioned, Naidoo volunteered her services. The result was *Journey to Jo'burg: A South African Story*. Although generally considered deficient as literature by reviewers, the long, simply written story found widespread approval and garnered several awards. Tackling the nonfiction side of the educational problem as well, Naidoo followed *Journey* with *Censoring Reality: An Examination of Books on South Africa* in 1985. This work represents the culmination of research into the then-current nonfiction portrayals of South African society targeted for British middle-grade students. Both *Journey to Jo'burg* and *Censoring Reality* expose the evils of racial hatred and public ignorance, and both were placed on the South African government's list of banned books.

Naidoo's guiding principle for the *Journey to Jo'burg* narrative, which incorporates elements of her own experience, was that the text be immediately understandable and instructive for younger readers; she imagined herself telling the story to her own children, ages ten and six at the time. Perhaps because of this, the critical response to the largely polemical work was varied. The most telling as-

sessment was that of Carla Hayden and Helen Kay Reseroka, who claimed Naidoo's work "fails to make the hideous features of apartheid relatable for children by not providing any memorable imagery, scenes, or characters." Nonetheless, numerous readers found in Naledi, the young black heroine of the story, a strong symbol of the black South African's struggle against oppression. In addition, the black-and-white drawings of Eric Velasquez were praised for their striking evocation of the story's underlying emotional depth.

Naidoo's sequel to *Journey, Chain of Fire,* was published in 1989. In this work Naledi has advanced from 13 to 15 years of age and Naidoo's fictional format has likewise advanced from that of a children's narrative to that of a young adult novel. Although the plot of *Journey* was considered weak due to Naidoo's overt agenda, *Chain of Fire* has been uniformly lauded for its strong development of the characters Naledi and Tiro, her young brother, and the challenges they face as they unite with other demonstrators to save their village and themselves from almost certain destruction under the government's "homeland" policy. The final message of this stark, horrific tale is the resiliency and determination of black South Africans in the face of adversity.

Free As I Know, an anthology of poems, short stories, and various literary extracts edited and introduced by Naidoo, is her other well-known contribution to the rapidly expanding field of multicultural education. Her honors include the Other Award from *Children's Book Bulletin* in 1985; the Children's Book Award from the Child Study Book Committee at Bank Street College of Education in 1986; one of the Child Study Association of America's Children's Book of the Year awards in 1987; and the Parents' Choice Honor Book for Paperback Literature from the Parents' Choice Foundation in 1988; all were given for *Journey to Jo'burg.*

(See also *Something about the Author,* Vol. 63.)

Journey to Jo'burg: A South African Story (1984)

AUTHOR'S COMMENTARY

[*The following excerpt is from Naidoo's acceptance speech for the Award of the Child Study Children's Book Committee at Bank Street College of Education, originally delivered in March 1987.*]

I've always regarded *Journey to Jo'burg* as a sort of window for my readers—to direct their focus onto the drama of children living under apartheid. That is why my initial tribute is to my subject matter: To those young people in South Africa who are struggling to take control of their lives and to reshape their future. They face a cruel, corrupt, relentless power . . . , but somehow they keep picking up the pieces.

I wanted to chart a journey of two such children, on what for them is initially a simply-motivated mission, to find their mother and so save their sister's life. It is their determination, particularly that of Naledi, the older sister, which sees them through. And the journey becomes a learning process, as the nightmare complexities of apartheid in the wider society are revealed to them. By the end of the journey, Naledi has begun to realize the wider dimensions of their own particular problems. She hasn't got solutions, but she has many questions—political questions. Black schoolchildren in South Africa are probably amongst the most politically-conscious children in the world.

My second tribute is to the people with whom I worked on the British Defence and Aid Fund for Southern Africa's Education Group. This fund generally is concerned not only with providing legal and other help for political victims of apartheid legislation and their families, but with keeping the conscience of the world alive. Apart from the Fund's Director, Ethel de Keyser, we are mainly working teachers who started off in a small way in 1981 with an art project for 9- to 11-year-olds, who were asked to submit drawings about children living under apartheid. It became clear that there was a great lack of material on South Africa which was directly accessible to the children. There was the straight informational material, but what we needed was fiction that could stir their imaginations and touch their emotions. Not only were we seriously lacking resources for children, but the research I was carrying out with a local anti-apartheid group revealed that any child referring to school and public library shelves for factual material would be finding and reading books which either omitted or largely distorted the reality of apartheid.

Thus the Education Group decided to find someone who could write a work of fiction which would convey some of that reality. I think, much to the surprise of the others, I volunteered! I was given three months to come up with something. I wrote the text simply, quite deliberately. As I wrote I could hear myself telling [the story] to my own children, aged 6 and 10 at the time. Both had been born in England, and it seemed important to be able to explain, at their level, what was happening in South Africa. For years, in my teaching, I had seen children struggling with the printed word, and I wanted this story to be accessible to as wide a readership as possible. In addition, my children were living in a society in which racist ideas have flourished. I hoped that empathizing with Naledi on her psychological as well as physical journey would encourage all children to explore and help strengthen their responses to the injustice of racism.

Today, it is almost exactly two years since the initial launching of *Journey to Jo'burg* at the Africa Centre in London, alongside my work *Censoring Reality,* which was the result of the research into how South Africa was being presented to British children in non-fiction books. Incidentally, I learned from a recent *South African Weekly Mail* that the latter has just joined *Journey to Jo'burg* on the regime's list of banned books. From one perspective, the notion is, of course, quite ludicrous. To know their own oppression, the majority of South Africans don't need their own lives—nor the lies told about those lives—interpreted for them. People's hearts are already like red-hot coals. As one black 16-year-old put it:

> They can detain me forever. That's no problem at all. Because I am going to live as other people. Because one thing I know is being locked in jail is not far different from being outside. We are all handcuffed, inside . . . and outside the jail.

I was brought up with the usual conceptions most white South Africans have, completely taking for granted the services of our cook-cum-nanny, whose own three children lived more than 300 kilometres away, cared for by . . . I don't know. She provided much of my actual mothering. We knew her as 'Mary,' I don't know her real name. What I do recall, with the vivid intensity of one of those seminal childhood experiences, was how when I was perhaps eight or nine, Mary received a telegram and collapsed. The telegram said that two of her three young daughters had died. It was diphtheria—something for which I, as a white child, had been vaccinated.

It was only years later that I began to realize the meaning of that scene. I must have continued to spout with the arrogance of white youth the customary rationalizations—that Mary, and those who followed her, were lucky because we gave them jobs, sent presents to their children at Christmas, and so on. I still feel intensely angry about the racist deceptions and distortions of reality which the adult society passed on to me as a child.

Most of our children are exposed to a wide range of [media] images, many of which reflect a violent world. Some of these come from South Africa. I believe we owe it to our children here to help them understand what that struggle against an evil system—from which both Britain and America have profited—is about. How can we hope for peace if we refuse to acknowledge that, and deny our children access to the knowledge? We must listen clearly to the voices of young people in South Africa. As one declared:

> One day they—the government—will do what we want. . . . We are prepared to die any moment. We are prepared to be detained any moment. As long as the government does not want to respond, we are prepared to do anything.

> *Beverley Naidoo, "The Story behind 'Journey to Jo'burg," in* School Library Journal, *Vol. 33, No. 9, May, 1987, p. 43.*

GENERAL COMMENTARY

Gillian Klein

A recurring question from teachers is "How young can we start?"—start introducing children to the realities of the world, including political realities; start inculcating a healthy scepticism to the apparent infallability of the printed word. Beverley Naidoo feels that it's never too young to start, but that it has to be done appropriately. She seems to have got it right in her two new publications [*Journey to Jo'burg* and *Censoring Reality*].

Her subject is apartheid in South Africa. To achieve clarity where there is much complexity, she has developed her picture for two different audiences. It is essentially the same picture: a total condemnation of apartheid, an informed knowledge of the political structures that enforce it and an understanding of some of the ways that it affects people's—especially Black South Africans'—lives.

For children, she has written *Journey to Jo'burg*, which is so simple and straightforward that it makes accessible even to quite young children the difficult and the profound. In 66 pages, she tells the story of Naledi and her younger brother who set off to fetch their mother home from Johannesburg. Their baby sister is dangerously ill and their grandmother has no money for hospital or doctors (Lesson One: there is no free medical care for Black people in the "Homelands"). Their mother works as a domestic servant in the plush suburbs of Johannesburg, sole support of the family since her husband was killed in a mine. The children are not permitted to spend the night in her room in the back yard, so are taken to Soweto, the Black "township". There they witness a police raid for pass-books and learn at first hand about the school student uprising in 1976. These experiences help Naledi to come to terms with her next experience, in the Homelands hospital to which her mother takes the ailing baby—an experience which even this post-Sharpville emigrant found distressing to read. The uncompromising realism carries

through to the open-ended conclusion of the book and the photographs of living conditions for Black South Africans.

Teachers using *Journey to Jo'burg* would be advised to read Beverley Naidoo's complimentary publication, *Censoring Reality: An Examination of Books on South Africa.* Aimed at teachers and librarians, it could certainly be used also to develop analytical and evaluative skills in pupils. It invites us to look at the resources currently used in schools and libraries, through the eyes of an imaginary 12-year-old seeking information for her classroom topic on South Africa. Thirty typical and widely used books are considered in terms of what picture they will build up for this British child of South Africa. We are left with no doubt that it will be misleading and inaccurate, and an endorsement of racism.

A chapter is devoted to each of the following issues: bias by commission, bias by omission, the information selected for encyclopaedias about South Africa, the question of providing "balanced" information, books which focus on apartheid, publications emanating from the South African Department of Information, a brief account of shifts in attitudes to racism in books about South Africa and an eighth chapter of recommendations for teachers, librarians and publishers. The conclusion urges us to combat a *laissez faire* attitude to the books examined.

Ms Naidoo makes her points clearly and cumulatively. Praise is due also to those who took part in the original research in numerous school and library collections, the South West Herts Anti-Apartheid Group, and to the splendid photographic material which contrasts so starkly with such quotes from the texts as: "all South Africans benefit from high quality welfare services" (for "all" read "white"). The layout and presentation is a *tour de force* of semiotics, punching home the messages of the author. And the central message is that, regardless of the age of the children handling the books, "with racism we have to choose—either to be for it or against it".

> *Gillan Klein, in a review of "Journey of Jo'burg," and "Censoring Reality: An Examination of Books on South Africa," in* The Times Educational Supplement, *No. 3591, April 26, 1985, p. 26.*

TITLE COMMENTARY

Journey to Jo'burg (1984)

With their baby sister dying of disease and malnutrition in their impoverished rural South African village, Naledi and her younger brother Tiro decide to fetch their mother from Johannesburg, where she works as a domestic servant to support them. Bewildered by the crowds and restrictions in the city, the children board a "white" bus and are caught up in a brutal police raid where blacks without passes are arrested. Naledi and Tiro find the great house where their mother works but are not allowed to stay with her. They spend the night in Soweto, where they are inspired by the story of the 1976 children's uprising as well as the present militancy. The white mistress reluctantly allows their mother a few days' leave, and the three take the baby to a distant clinic, where she recovers. However, they are told she must have fresh vegetables—which they cannot afford. This is not great fiction: story and characters are thinly disguised mechanisms for describing the brutal social conditions and the need for change. But the facts are totally authentic. For children eager for information about a country much in the news, this South African writer frankly depicts the harsh reality in a welcome change from the happy, tribal-native stereotype.

> *Hazel Rochman, in a review of "Journey to Jo'burg: A South African Story," in* Booklist, *Vol. 82, No. 14, March 15, 1986, p. 1086.*

Naidoo's writing style is adequate, and all her characters are believable; most powerful in the book are those things that happen to the children or what they learn about the cruelty of apartheid, through experiences and information supplied in chilling detail. Powerful as expose, yes, but overwhelming the story so that the narrative is dwarfed by the horrors suffered by black South Africans and is thereby weakened.

> *Zena Sutherland, in a review of "Journey to Jo'burg: A South African Story," in* Bulletin of the Center for Children's Books, *Vol. 39, No. 9, May, 1986, p. 175.*

Through Grace, a young woman they meet, the children learn of those who have come and gone before in the struggle against apartheid; the injustice and heartache of it; the indirect way in which it caused their father's death. Overwhelmed by the events of the three days, Naledi ponders her new awareness, as will readers who have shared those thoughts and experiences with her. [Illustrator Eric] Velasquez' soft black-and-white portraits extend the feeling of family closeness and warmth, all the while showing the anger and fear, the harshness and hostility of the characters and situations. Plain and simple, yet evocative and haunting, they correspond perfectly with each chapter. A short story with a wealth to share, this well-written piece has no equal. Believable characters are natural in their love, fear and hope. The quiet bonds through which blacks extend themselves to help each other, despite dangerous risks, is an unspoken comment on survival.

> *JoAnn Butler Henry, in a review of "Journey to Jo'burg: A South African Story," in* School Library Journal, *Vol. 32, No. 10, August, 1986, p. 96.*

The South African situation has unique elements that make it particularly relevant and potentially enthralling in literature for young people of any culture. Black children, under fourteen years old, are fighting, suffering, and dying throughout South Africa. The nation is engaged in a desperate battle for human rights in which these children are not only active participants, but are even, in some instances, leading the political struggle. If they are not protesting in the urban townships of Soweto or Port Elizabeth, young people are struggling in the rural areas of Qwaqwa or Zululand. The acute political awareness of all South African children, black and non-black, was noted by Robert Coles, who had, in interviewing them, "never

heard . . . such a shrewd and knowing appraisal of a nation by 'mere children'."

The subject of South Africa is currently being presented in greater, though still comparatively small, numbers of books for children than ever before. Yet, the "we need something on this subject" mentality may prevail once again in a hurried production of a body of fiction about South Africa that is lacking in quality. This is not to deny the responsibility of publishers and authors to keep abreast of current events and provide children timely information on it. However, as we witness the beginning of the treatment of South Africa as a "hot" issue in children's books, we should give renewed consideration to the importance of retaining the main elements of notable fiction in the presentation.

Literary merit and veracity, not only of factual events but also of culture and character, are the basic components which can raise the literature regarding South Africa out of the mire of expediency into the realm of living fiction. Much of what is excellent and poor in the treatment of South Africa in children's literature is evident in two recent novels, *Journey to Jo'burg* by Beverley Naidoo and *Waiting for the Rain* by Sheila Gordon (1987). To analyze these books is to invite further dialogue regarding the need to present the situation in books that also tell good stories.

Journey to Jo'Burg, written for a middle grade level audience, relates the experiences of a sister, Naledi and her younger brother, Tiro, who travel alone to Johannesburg from a rural South African village. The major portion of the book is an account of a three day trip to alert their mother of a younger sister's illness. This basic plot has one of the most appealing aspects in fiction for a juvenile audience—the long trek, unescorted and unendorsed, that most surely promises to bring with it unexpected and harrowing incidents along the way. However, *Journey* is riddled with artificial plot devices and weak characters that do not sustain suspense or excitement much less the reader's barest interest.

Naidoo introduces numerous incidents, designed to show the forces of apartheid, without regard to their likelihood in real life. These incidents appear to have little impact on the main characters, and consequently the readers as well. The basic premise of the book, the creation of the need to walk to Johannesburg, is not culturally, or even realistically, plausible. From the outset the decision to walk to Jo'Burg, a distance of over 300 miles, rather than risk the grandmother's wrath for borrowing money to send a telegram stretches one's credulity. In fact, borrowing money for such desperate conditions of serious illness is common in South Africa, and so is sending a telegram. The artificial need does, however, create a vehicle to justify the children's subsequent trip and plot developments. How long will it take to travel to Jo'Burg? Will the sister die before Naledi and Tiro return with their mother?

The author, despite the plot's inherent weakness, could have turned the story into a mythlike trek of action and adventure. Yet "adventure" is what is solely missing. During the journey the children experience few incidents capable of creating dramatic tension. For instance, a hitched ride in the back of a truck produces only this: "Tiro began to learn farther out over the side to feel the wind on his face. Naledi called, 'Sit back or you'll fall!' but her brother took no notice. Suddenly the truck went over a bump and Tiro jerked forward. Naledi grabbed him just in time. 'Didn't I tell you?' she shouted over the noise of the lorry. A little shaken, Tiro mumbled 'Sorry' and settled back properly against the orange sacks. Together they watched the road stretching far out behind them."

One of the children's sparse experiences also gives us the most ludicrous plot manipulation in the story. The police are vaguely introduced by Naledi in Tiro's recollection of a popular children's song about the pass book law enforcement. The police later raid a train station where the children are being transported with the help of a new found adult guardian angel, Grace. In the ensuing rush and confusion of the crowded train, the children have been separated from their guardian. Yet they stop, in the middle of this predicament, throwing further caution and fear aside, to rush to a township consisting of hundreds of rows of identical houses. Once there, these rural lost children search for, and find, the son of a complete stranger from the raid whom they urge to take his father's pass. Of course, Grace is conveniently present at the station when they return.

The minor characters are used as mere mouth pieces for the author. Grace, the temporary guardian, is a voice of "new" thinking, in contrast to the children's mother, who is submissive and beaten. The portrayal of women in general is that of pawns with not much sense. They are incapable of action and they lack presence. What type of women are these, one the children's grandmother and the other an aunt younger than Naledi's mother, who cannot between them take a sick child to a hospital, and fail to detect the anxiety Naledi is experiencing? Hospital care was within reach. If Naledi's mother could walk back from the hospital so could her aunt or grandmother who is described as being rather fit and hardy. What prevented them from taking her? The need to have the children take a journey perhaps? The characterization of these women ignores the fundamental strength of neighborly support and the network of kinship prevalent in rural settings in South Africa.

The most lamentable flaw in the author's treatment of the characters is the limited development of Naledi. Instead of a spunky heroine, we are given an unfulfilled promise. There is also a curious lack of planning for a long journey by a thirteen year old girl who is described as being intelligent. It is unlikely Naledi could get to that age, with a background in rural life and "long travel to school," and blithely disregard obstacles like food and money. She is not particularly interested in how long the journey might take, nor does she exhibit any apparent sense of possible danger. Her awareness of the 1976 Soweto massacre is related in an entire chapter—in a slim volume—which is designed only to cram in facts regarding the uprising. In reality, most children of Naledi's age in South Africa are aware of the uprising, described as follows by a thirteen year old in *Two Dogs and Freedom: Children of South Africa Speak Out*: "In Soweto there are a lot of boycotts, chil-

dren boycott because they say they want freedom . . . they say they want equal rights between whites and blacks . . . They say when they are boycotting . . . all children must be in the struggle."

At the end of the story, Naledi reflects on how her experiences during the journey led to her decision to interact with the older students when school begins. In the space of a few days, the effects of apartheid, which had obviously lain dormant in her consciousness, had become clear to her. Despite this revelation, there is no sense that she has had any deeper internal conflicts, struggles, or even pain caused by the policies of apartheid. We are not allowed to care about or even gain any level of understanding of the character. Naledi never becomes real.

The character of Naledi's brother, Tiro, fares even worse—in fact he is almost non-existent. We are left to wonder again. What were Tiro's feelings? Were they significantly different from Naledi's? What type of relationship did they have? How did the political and cultural (e.g. male/female acculturation) situations affect their relationship? Did they join together against weak and helpless adults? The author chooses to ignore the inherent sibling interaction. This is a curious omission in a story of a journey about children with no adult supervision, few resources, and little food. Both of the children appear devoid of any deeper thoughts during their journey. What were their thoughts about their sister or their grandmother discovering their absence? On reaching their mother's place of work, the children show no reaction to the opulence except to open their eyes wide at the size of the workplace. These real questions, which one would naturally think of, are just a few of the elements in the story that are left to the reader's imagination in an unsatisfactory manner.

Journey to Jo'Burg does not allow the characters to develop, and as such be human. They are stick figures who move woodenly through a series of lackluster incidents. This charade denies the characters' individuality, which is the essence of humanness. It also leads us to the crux of the matter in South Africa—a denial of humanness, an inability and refusal to acknowledge blacks as feeling, thinking beings. *Journey,* ironically, makes the same mistake. The author also misses many opportunities for taking advantage of the potential for the natural drama and suspense of the "trek". Instead, Naledi's and Tiro's journey is dull and generally without incident and tension. One cannot help but compare the dramatic excitement and in depth character development in *Homecoming* by Cynthia Voight (Atheneum, 1983). It is the story of another set of children on an unescorted trek, yet Voight's thirteen year old heroine leads her siblings, and captures the reader's heart, with vitality and ingenuity.

The concern regarding *Journey to Jo'Burg* as a presentation of the situation in South Africa should not be focused solely on questionable cultural inaccuracies or passages. Attention must be given to the production of mediocre literature merely to have something timely about a topic, even one as important as South Africa. This book's agenda, to demonstrate what apartheid is about, could possibly have been accomplished more thoroughly in a non-fiction format (although good literary style is an important component in that genre as well). As a story, **Journey to Jo'Burg** takes us on a short and unsatisfying ride.

In direct contrast, *Waiting for the Rain* demonstrates that books about issues can be good stories. As in **Journey**, the author categorically presents the realities of the South African situation in a story about children. Gordon, however, lifts the aspects of apartheid to an even more universal level through the skillful deployment of structure, logical plot, and character development. The story becomes a classic tale of conflict with sure appeal for children—the dilemma of close friends from different backgrounds who are caught up in forces beyond their control. The novel's action is subsequently constructed around the elements of dual forces—conflict and resolution, black and white, before and after. (pp. 57-8)

Although many of the same disturbing elements of the South African issue are treated and included in both novels, there is a striking and significant difference between them. *Waiting for the Rain* makes the reader feel the effects of apartheid through strong identification with and caring for the main characters. We are part of the struggle and conflict. The novel, in its veracity, has frequent correlative aspects to the autobiographical *Kaffir Boy* by Mark Mathabane, a riveting narrative of the hardships of life under apartheid. **Journey** is a weak presentation that dampens the impact of the issues. It fails to make the hideous features of apartheid relatable for children by not providing any memorable imagery, scenes, or characters. The reader is left with a pedestrian story that evokes no emotion and which ultimately does not contain any lasting message or communication.

Another relevant question is whether or not these books serve African children. Would they see a reflection of themselves and be able to identify with the characters? Could the characters, because of honesty in their portrayal, speak to all children regardless of race and culture? We bring our individual perceptual frameworks, particularly regarding cutural status and experiences, to the writing, reading and analysis of any work of literature. It is possible to create and relate to an honest and compelling story about a group or culture of which one is not a member. However, this is not a racial issue, but rather a commitment to truth. Literature written from experience, personal or gleaned from someone who has lived it, allows a certain universality to emerge. The universal aspects of any issue, combined with the effective use of the elements of fiction, can help the reader make a personal connection to the setting and feelings of the characters. That individual connection between the story and reader is what ideally makes an "issue" come alive and turns the statistics into flesh and blood.

We join Mary Q. Steele in the hope that books for children will be "more often written by people who wanted to write a book—not people who importuned an audience. What I hope for is books written out of the heart, out of the strange generosity of the heart of the writer who is determined to speak and let who wishes hear." The South African situation is ultimately a political and moral issue closely akin to Nazism. Apartheid is a word that has become associated with deprivation and cruelty. As a result,

its presence in children's literature must undoubtedly raise questions beyond literary merit alone. These concerns, however, should not overshadow the need to consider the effects of poor literary style in the presentation of this issue in fiction for children. How can children learn about South Africa through literature if we cannot sustain their interest? Good intentions, as we have seen, unfortunately do not make good books. (p. 59)

Carla Hayden and Helen Kay Raseroka, "The Good and the Bad: Two Novels of South Africa," in Children's Literature Association Quarterly, *Vol. 13, No. 2, Summer, 1988, pp. 57-60.*

Free As I Know (1987)

[Free As I Know *was edited by Beverley Naidoo.*]

Free As I Know contains 18 poems, short stories or extracts. The principles behind the selection are threefold: the idea of the seminal experience whereby young people gain insight into themselves and society; the concentration on perspectives that may be passed over in a white monocultural society and the desire to include "stimulating literature of an international character". The pieces are arranged chronologically and range from extracts from *Tell Freedom,* an autobiography set in South Africa in the Twenties, through *Basketball Game* depicting America in the Fifties, to England in the Seventies and Eighties and even the future in an extract from Robert Swindell's *Brother in the Land.*

Each piece is preceded by a paragraph of introduction or explanation and for each there is a follow-on section at the back of the book where can be found ideas for oral work and a variety of written assignments. These sections, though addressed to students, are rather densely written and the editor was wise to suggest that the teacher "preview" them before tackling the text. There are also suggestions for extended study on such issues as "Generations", "Racism" and "Autobiography". The book ends with a full reading list of both fiction and non-fiction.

The collection represents a real attempt, as the national criteria for English literature put it, to "extend the scope of . . . English literature in recognition that awareness of the richness of cultural diversity is one of the rewards of the study of literature". As such it is a welcome addition to any English department library. I would guess however, that most departments will want to buy some of the titles on (and off) the background reading list, to have available some of the sources from which the extracts are taken and to discuss and prepare their own way into the issues raised. As it stands the collection is uneven in quality; many of the extracts are barely long enough for the reader to become engaged with the characters, or familiar with the setting, while the range of times and places depicted is rather breathtakingly wide.

Bill Deller, "Breadth of Vision," in The Times Educational Supplement, *No. 3751, May 20, 1988, p. B21.*

Naidoo with a student in London.

Chain of Fire   (1989)

Beverley Naidoo's first book, **Journey to Jo'burg,** was the story of two black children's journey from their native village to search for their mother, far away in Johannesburg, when the family was struck by illness. It was a protest against the South African economic system which divides families and forces the able-bodied and the breadwinners into compulsory exile from dependent loved ones. In the sequel, **Chain of Fire,** the village itself is under threat. Fifteen year-old Naledi, her family and her fellow villagers face eviction and enforced removal to the so-called "homeland" of Bophuthatswana.

The story is like the slow-motion closing of a trap. Beverley Naidoo's flat, terse, unrelenting narrative gains power from its very lack of embellishment, there is scarcely a single detail which is not implicit comment on the callous process of racial engineering. As the impersonal, bureaucratic cruelties of expulsion take hold, the villagers' resistance is worn down by a succession of calculated blows, psychological as well as physical. Routines of permanence are as much damaged by the bulldozing of the church as by disconnection of the water supply. The villagers, old and young, respond with determined resilience but to no avail. But for the young like Naledi, a local defeat is finally a spur to action in a wider national comradeship of resistance.

As a novel of protest, this is the book's "propagandist" outcome. But its chief strength lies in the moving representation of family and village life. From first to last we see things from the black perspective. The villagers are not by choice "activists". They are people at home, attached to a long-established way of life which differs from its white equivalents only in the terrible impoverishment of permitted standards. This powerful indictment of the "homeland" policy will help young readers to penetrate beyond political argument to human realities.

> *Peter Hollindale, "Bound to Protest," in* The Times Educational Supplement, *No. 3793, March 10, 1989, p. B15.*

This is an outstanding novel. It is set in modern-day South Africa and concerns the lives of Naledi and her family, Tswana-speaking blacks who are to be forced off the land where they have lived for generations, to be resettled in the 'homeland' of Bophuthatswana. The outlook for the family is bleak and the book chronicles the development of Naledi, her brother and their friends from ordinary schoolchildren in the village to vigorous opponents of the resettlement. In particular the character of Naledi is strong and she exemplifies the qualities of intellect, bravery and gentleness. Practically the only white people the family come into contact with are the police, the army and the odd official. The authorities are portrayed as being at best cynical and at worst evil.

One of the many points the book tries to make about South Africa is that although the forces of evil are upon the black community, its spirit is indomitable. The higher the white community raises the stakes for its survival, the more determined the blacks will become. This is an extraordinary and thought-provoking novel of the highest calibre. It is aimed at a teenage and adult readership and would be an excellent book to be used in conjunction with, say, a modern studies course. The real impact of the novel derives from the fact that it has the true feel of an authentic account of what is happening in present-day South Africa.

> *Maureen A. Porter, in a review of "Chain of Fire," in* The School Librarian, *Vol. 37, No. 2, May, 1989, p. 75.*

Like *Journey to Jo'burg,* to which it is a sequel, this is less a novel than a powerful dramatization of the injustices of apartheid. . . .

Characterization is minimal here, and personal lives are in abeyance; parents are powerless to comfort their children, while Naledi's budding friendship with Dikobe's son may never have a chance to blossom. Instead, hearts—like molten iron—are forged by the fire of apartheid's vicious cruelty into links of friendship that will become chains of political power. Stark, honest, unleavened by the poignant human detail that made the stories in Rochman's *Somehow Tenderness Survives* (1988) so memorable: a compelling picture of the results of South Africa's racist policies.

> *A review of "Chain of Fire," in* Kirkus Reviews, *Vol. LVIII, No. 6, March 15, 1990, p. 428.*

As Naledi and the others have matured, politically, since the first book, so Naidoo has matured markedly as a writer. She demonstrates an insight into her characters and their condition—particularly the role of the young in initiating and sustaining rebellion that was far less evident in *Journey. . . . Chain of Fire* flows effortlessly, with power and grace, as it succeeds in making a foreign culture immediate and real. Truly it is the grimmer tale, but one that, in light of its own truth as well as of recent events, readers might look at with a trace more hope. (pp. 108, 113)

> *Marcia Hupp, in a review of "Chain of Fire," in* School Library Journal, *Vol. 36, No. 5, May, 1990, pp. 108, 113.*

Christopher Pike

?-

(Pseudonym of Kevin McFadden) American author of fiction.

Major works include *Slumber Party* (1985), *Chainletter* (1986), *Weekend* (1986), *Remember Me* (1989), *Die Softly* (1991).

Recognized by critic Adrian Jackson as the "junior Stephen King," Pike is considered a master of young adult mystery and suspense fiction whose novels are noted for their grisly horror, interesting teen protagonists, and graphically violent themes. In these controversial novels, involving murder, the supernatural, and sometimes space aliens and the occult, the adult characters are treated with detachment so that primary focus may be upon Pike's teen protagonists, each of which is drawn into a series of violent and terrifying events touching on his or her greatest fears. The exorbitant energy, the complexity, and the "extreme" nature of these characters serve to intensify the fast-paced action of Pike's novels, providing for interesting reading and appealing to teens and critics alike. Commentators have asserted that Pike's popularity among young adults is due largely to his treatment of teen issues and concerns such as alienation, humiliation, unrequited love, and substance abuse. "Pike doesn't talk down to kids," writes critic Pat MacDonald, "he treats them as individuals." In addition, his characters differ from the traditional mystery sleuths found in young adult fiction in that they are realistically, deeply affected by the people and events surrounding them: their observations are essential to the plot and their motives, which generally involve revenge, are viewed by young adults as important. Pike's teen protagonists are also appealing to young adults because while their problems appear to be average, their solutions are atypical, often violating acceptable social norms and involving excessive violence.

Pike, who adopted his name from a character on the "Star Trek" television series, started his career as a writer of adult mystery novels, but after his book proposals were turned down by publishers he began writing teen thrillers. His first three novels, *Slumber Party* (1985), *Chainletter* (1986), and *Weekend* (1986), became bestsellers, winning Pike immediate fame among young adults. Noted for their fully developed characterizations, these and Pike's other works contain a quality of depth lacking in many mysteries for teens, thus distinguishing Pike from his contemporaries. Sue Tait and Christy Tyson wrote of Pike's characters, that "they are forced to recognize . . . that criminal and victim are connected to each other and to the crime in a way that reaches far beyond the mystery's solution." In Pike's *Remember Me* (1989), the main action involves a teenage ghost who, knowing that she did not take her own life, is determined to find her murderer; however, the novel's primary focus appears to be the subject of life after death, a theme which has evoked a favorable response from teens claiming that they had contemplated suicide prior to reading this book. Pike's novels have also been the subject of extensive controversy for their treatment of sex and sexual fantasies, violence, profanity, and also for their complete disregard of morality and social values, all of which contribute to an innovative style characteristic of contemporary high-gloss horror films. Moreover, several critics believe that the overall complexity of Pike's novels render them too complicated for young readers, while others claim that his plots are too far-fetched. Although Pike's novels may be considered contrived by some, commentators agree that their fast-paced action is appealing, making them difficult to put down. With over one half million books in print, Pike, according to a 1991 report by Pocket Books, is "the best-selling single title author in the young adult market today."

(See also *Something about the Author,* Vol. 68.)

GENERAL COMMENTARY

Kit Alderdice

A quick look at the covers of Christopher Pike's new novels *Last Act* and *Spellbound* reveals how much this YA mystery/thriller writer's fortunes have changed since his first book was published in 1984. On the covers of the new titles . . . , his name appears in large letters that rival the type size of each book's title, a ploy usually reserved for adult trade book jackets. Not so long ago, Pike's name was barely a footnote on covers that featured high-concept, eyecatching titles. . . .

For Pat MacDonald, senior editor of Archway paperbacks and Minstrel Books at Pocket, the renewed interest in their editions of the Nancy Drew and Hardy Boys series indicated a resurgent popularity of the mystery genre. The strong showing of Pike's mystery/thrillers on B. Dalton's list piqued her interest in the writer. She also wanted to expand Archway's readership and attract older teens.

"Pike doesn't talk down to kids; he treats them as individuals," MacDonald says. "He writes commercial stories that teens really want to read." But despite the commercial angles, she insists that her main reason for acquiring Pike's works is that "he's a terrific read—there's not much out there that is. And every book he does has its own identity."

Archway's next titles from Pike will be *Gimme a Kiss* in July, and the Final Friends trilogy, to be released this fall. Pike believes that this trilogy, about a group of teenagers in their senior year of high school, will give him a chance to develop characterizations in new ways. The trilogy's narrative is shared by two main characters, one male and the other female; in the past, he has used an exclusively female point of view. "I romanticize a lot about females," he says, "because they seem more complex, and because in horror novels, it's easier for the girl to seem scared." The presence of a male narrator may well encourage more of the crossover in the market for these books; although the audience for mass market fiction is largely made up of teenage girls, Pike's novels are, according to MacDonald, selling to teenage boys as well. . . .

When *Slumber Party* first came out in 1984, followed by the release of *Weekend,* Pike recalls, "I was so ignorant of publishing that I just assumed that they would do well. I didn't know how difficult it was to break out of the group and become a name."

> *Kit Alderdice, "Archway Launches Christopher Pike Novels in Multi-Book Contract," in* Publishers Weekly, *Vol. 233, No. 17, April 29, 1988, p. 49.*

Sue Tait and Christy Tyson

Christopher Pike, author of such popular teen mysteries as *Chain letter* and *Weekend,* gets better with each new novel. Pike has always had a handle on the well-turned plot, although his 1988 entries offer even more complex twists presented with an even surer hand. It's his characters, though, that have really assumed full dimension. Pike's young people are deeply affected by the events that ensnare them. They are more than puzzle-solving sleuths. They are forced to recognize . . . that criminal and victim are connected to each other and to the crime in a way that reaches far beyond the mystery's solution.

Traces from the past are the source of immediate danger for Melanie Martin in *Last Act.* Slow to fit in at her high school, Melanie takes Susan's advice to try out for the school play and finds out that the part she wins involves an on-stage murder that turns out to be the real thing. Melanie, as the only newcomer, realizes that the motive and proof of her innocence can only be found in events from the past, events that all the other cast members were involved in but refuse to discuss.

Spellbound relies more on the supernatural when Karen Holly's body is found mauled by what seems to be a huge bear. The most likely suspect is Jason, Karen's date the night after her death. Now, though seven weeks later, Jason . . . has begun seeing Cindy, and she just can't believe what everyone says, that Jason knows much more than he's telling. As in *Last Act,* it is the relationship between characters that makes it work. Cindy's connection with her brother Alex is believable and touching, as is his romantic interest in new transfer student Joni. These are people who are really involved with each other, and when they are in danger the reader can't help but feel it too. Again, Pike's clear portraits of teens provide the hook that is missing in many mysteries written for young adults. . . .

[*Gimme a Kiss*] is Pike's best yet. Here it is his painfully clear recreation of how deeply humiliation can cut, that provides the premise. Someone, probably cheerleader Patty, has stolen a page from Jane Retton's diary and handed out copies all over school. The page is Jane's fairly specific description of her "first time" with boyfriend Kirk. But (and this is a crucial "but" to Jane if to no one

else) it never happened! It was Jane's fantasy, and no one will believe her, especially when Kirk remains smugly silent. Her employer tells her to learn from her mistakes. Her advisor offers her birth control. Even her best friends tell her, "It doesn't matter what we believe. We're still your friends." Jane wants revenge on Patty, obviously, but also on Kirk for letting her down. She devises a plot to fake her own drowning and implicate Kirk and Patty, but the scheme backfires with deadly results. Less experienced readers may find Pike's use of flashbacks a bit confusing. (When the story begins foul play has already occurred and the investigating detective's interviews are interspersed with more straightforward narrative.) However, it's worth the extra effort as this technique adds real punch to the conclusion.

Pike's latest work is a three-part series begun with *Final Friends Book 1: The Party.* This format offers him even greater scope to explore the connections between past and present events and between old friends and newcomers that characterized his latest books. (p. 53)

> *Sue Tait and Christy Tyson, "Paperbacks for Young Adults," in* Emergency Librarian, *Vol. 16, No. 3, January-February, 1989, pp. 53-4.*

Adrian Jackson

Whodunnits or rather whosedoingits. There's a veneer of sophistication about these two, almost grown-up, horror books, junior Stephen King with Enid Blyton's device of the marginal adults. These kids can play at being adults—the American setting seems to allow supplies of money and cars to keep the illusion going—and there's much reference to sexuality and 'making it'. *Spellbound* is about a nice English girl who's really a vulture and there are some violent deaths and a good bit of twisting of plot. *Chain Letter* sticks to something like normality. The gang of kids share a guilty secret which the writer of the chain letter seems to know as she forces them to commit more and more serious tasks or be punished. Excitement of plot with a few demands on logic and thought.

> *Adrian Jackson, in a review of "Spellbound" and "Chain Letter," in* Books for Keeps, *No. 59, November, 1989, p. 13.*

Linda Newbery

Suspend disbelief firmly for *Remember Me:* it's told from the beyond-the-grave perspective of a girl who died at a party and wants to know why. She and a dead friend—who knows how things work on the astral plane—float about, eavesdrop on people's conversations and get into their dreams. If that sounds ridiculous, it isn't . . . most of the time. The glossy packaging is clearly aimed at young horror fans, but there's no gratuitous violence.

The earlier . . . book by the same author, *Slumber Party,* is decidedly tacky. Six girls—who apparently detest each other in their rivalry for gorgeous guys—get together for a skiing holiday in an isolated lodge and weird things start to happen. It's crude, stilted, sexist, violent and unconvincing.

> *Linda Newbery, in a review of "Remember*

Me" and "Slumber Party," in Books for Keeps, No. 65, November, 1990, p. 12.

Amy Gamerman

[Christopher] Pike is one of the unsung, un-Pulitzered celebrities of today's literary scene, one of a handful of writers who churn out wildly popular spooky tales and murder mysteries tailored for teenagers.

Teen thrillers are the biggest thing to happen to the young-adult book market since Nancy Drew drove on the scene in her blue roadster.

Teen thrillers make regular appearances on the weekly best-seller lists circulated by trade bookstores.

Head for the young-adult section of any chain bookstore and you'll see them: rows of luridly jacketed paperbacks with titles such as *The Cheerleader* ("She would do *anything* to be popular"), *Blind Date* ("It wasn't a date. It was a nightmare"), and *Final Exam* ("If you fail . . . you'll just die"). No teen-related stone is left unturned. *Prom Dress,* reads the jagged orange title on one Lael Littke book, over an eerily glowing white gown. "It's a dress to die for . . . "

These books aren't Newbery Award contenders, but even librarians find them hard to dismiss. "Well, my personal philosophy is, if they're reading anything at all that's wonderful," said Molly Kinney, a librarian with the Miami-Dade Public Library system, who reviews young adult thrillers for School Library Journal. "They're also a way to get involved with something . . . evil without ever acting on it."

Certainly they don't get much more evil than Christopher Pike, who is hailed as the Stephen King of teen fiction. Mr. Pike's novels feature an assortment of stalkers, psychos and killer co-eds that would make Nancy Drew's pageboy flip stand on end. Take Alexa, the homicidal cheerleader and cocaine fiend of *Die Softly:*.

"She just knelt right in front of me, kind of like a sacrifice," Alexa says, describing how she offed her ex-best friend Lisa. "I brought the bat down on her head quickly. The wood cracked—so did her skull . . . The blood gushed over her blond hair. It was much darker than I thought it would be."

If Mr. Pike's novels are gorier than most, they also boast some of the more inventively sexy plots. In *Die Softly*, an amateur photographer sets up a camera in the girls' showers to get shots of naked cheerleaders, only to end up with photos of a murder. In *Remember Me,* a vapid high school co-ed returns from the dead to find out who pushed her off a balcony at a party—taking time out to spy on her boyfriend with his new squeeze.

"Teenagers are very fascinated by the subject of life after death," Mr. Pike said. "I got very beautiful letters from kids who say they were going to kill themselves before they read that book."

Despite his apparent hot line to the teen-psyche, Mr. Pike never set out to write for young adults. A college dropout, he spent years writing science fiction that no one would publish. Then his agent suggested he try his hand at a teen thriller. *Slumber Party*—about a group of girls stalked by a killer on a ski weekend—came out in 1985, and he hasn't stopped writing thrillers since.

"They kept offering me more money." Mr. Pike explained. "But I enjoy it . . . teenage characters are so extreme."

Nightmare-prone readers may find Mr. Pike's characters a little too extreme: The evil Alexa kills the photographer hero of **"Die Softly"** by forcing him to snort a lethal amount of cocaine.

Amy Gamerman, "Gnarlatious Novels: Lurid Thrillers for the Teen Set," in The Wall Street Journal, May 28, 1991, p. A20.

Tom Engelhardt

[In] *See You Later* and *Fall Into Darkness* Christopher Pike pioneers entirely new territory. His books might be described as novelizations of horror films that haven't yet been made. In these books of muted torture, adults exist only as distant figures of desertion; ET—the extraterrestrial teenager—does not call home, and junior-grade psychos reign supreme. If sex never proceeds beyond The Kiss, no mutilation is too terrible for the human face. ("The swollen black cheeks. The twisted purple mouth. The pink slit throat. It was a pity . . . that Ann could no longer close her own eyes and look away from what was left of her body.")

See You Later grabs and shakes its readers. Mark Forum, teenage creator of computer games, lives alone in L.A. and falls in love with Becky, who works in a mall bookstore, but Becky is in love with Ray, a jock, who in a future of nuclear destruction is actually Frederick, a crazed general and psychotic killer, but never mind because Becky is actually Kara ("I'm from the future, Mark. I've come back for you"), who returns to try to split up her younger self and Ray, using Mark, who is actually Vincent, who accompanies Kara back from that future incinerated by Frederick, né Ray, before being saved by the Illumni, which are strange light forms. Quoting *The Wizard of Oz* ("Remember the part at the end . . . Dorothy closes her eyes and repeats, 'There's no place like home . . . ' "), Mark, Kara, and Vincent re-create themselves in the present as an upscale suburban "family," while hearts impaled on knives are left throbbing on kitchen tables and faces are mashed and bodies mangled by brand-name cars. (p. 61)

Tom Engelhardt, "Reading May Be Harmful to Your Kids: In the Nadirland of Today's Children's Books," in Harper's, Vol. 282, No. 1693, June, 1991, pp. 55-62.

TITLE COMMENTARY

Slumber Party (1985)

Six teenage girls in a luxurious winter vacation home experience a series of bizarre and violent incidents during a blizzard that makes communication and travel difficult. Old secrets weigh heavily on the group. Lara has explained to newcomer Celeste that Nell's facial scars were caused by a tragic fire during the group's last slumber party, but she is unable to talk about the death that also occurred. For a while, Lara is pleasantly distracted by handsome Percy, but tension returns when Dana disappears. Where she was last seen, only melted snow, ash, and bone remain. New horrors multiply as the plot races to a surprising and violent end. The easy vocabulary will appeal to reluctant readers, and the light cursing won't bother most students. In spite of simplistic characterization and some incredulous plot elements, a mood of mystery and terror prevails. While critically mature readers may question the idea that parents would stage a mock funeral because a disfigured child doesn't fit the image that they wish to project, this and other elements of sensationalism will appeal to non-critical readers.

> *Cindy Darling Codell, in a review of "Slumber Party," in* School Library Journal, *Vol. 33, No. 4, December, 1986, p. 121.*

Weekend (1986)

Any teen who liked **Slumber Party,** the author's first suspense novel, will undoubtedly be drawn to **Weekend**—and will not be disappointed. **Weekend** is a gripping page-turner that will keep readers guessing until the end.

Several months after Shani's wealthy best-friend Robin is poisoned at a drunken party given by a mutual friend and left with permanently damaged kidneys, every teen-ager who was at the party is invited to spend a weekend at Robin's family's beach house in Mexico. The weekend of pleasure, however, soon turns into a horribly real cat-and-mouse game as someone causes accidents, cuts the phone wires, and eventually isolates the kids in the remote house. Does someone know who tried to poison Robin? Is the poisoner preparing to strike again? Is someone looking for revenge?

Pike's strength is in characterization, and in his ability to write a true young-adult suspenser. No watered-down adult mystery, this honestly engrossing novel about teens on the brink of adulthood is perfect fare for the reader who's past Nancy Drew but not yet ready for Agatha Christie. Parents may object to the heavy drinking scene (although the scene is realistic), to Shani's sexual fantasy, and to the unbelievably offhand attitude of the few adults in the book. However, as Grade B fiction goes, **Weekend** rates a solid B+.

> *A review of "Weekend," in* Kirkus Reviews, *Vol. LIV, No. 5, March 1, 1986, p. 392.*

The author's intentions are not clear to me. It starts off appropriately suspenseful with momentum building as zippy exchanges among envious adolescents heading toward doomsday move the story along. Then the tone changes abruptly with heavy handed contrivances that do not scare but bring on chuckles. I could not decide if the author was spoofing the genre or intending to terrify the reader. It's something to read at the beach.

> *JoEllen Broom, in a review of "Weekend," in* Voice of Youth Advocates, *Vol. 9, Nos. 3 & 4, August-October, 1986, p. 150.*

Chain Letter (1986)

Following the success of **Slumber Party** and **Weekend,** Pike's latest thriller is instantly engaging, as a chain letter forces seven teenagers into bizarre and dangerous activities. A year earlier, they were involved in a car accident in which a man was killed—but they covered up the crime. Now, "Your Caretaker," the author of the letter, threatens to expose them, and assigns each of them a task. If it's fulfilled, they will be left alone. If it's not, the consequences are terrifying. One teen who defies the Caretaker disappears, leaving behind a blood-soaked bed; another is burned in a fire that consumes his home. But just as the reader thinks the teens will confess to their original crime, the author finds a convenient, though unconvincing, way to get them off the hook. Pike's story begins promisingly but leads into implausible motives and a feeble resolution. There are also formulas that crop up from his earlier books: teenagers thought to be dead reappear; alcohol figures heavily in all the plots; people with handicaps or terminal illnesses go "over the edge." Despite these drawbacks, Pike handles suspense well, and has a good ear for dialogue.

> *A review of "Chain Letter," in* Publishers Weekly, *Vol. 229, No. 17, April 25, 1986, p. 83.*

Drinking and driving don't mix as Tony finds out when he inadvertently hits a pedestrian on a deserted roadway. Because each of his passengers feels some amount of culpability for the tragedy—they were all goofing around—the seven agree to bury the victim and keep the incident quiet. A year later, however, their irresponsible actions return to haunt them via a bizarre chain letter, whose writer knows not only the dark details of their secret but also enough about each of them to make the punishments he exacts frightening indeed. Teenage characters in the grasp of a mad avenger—that's a formula that is bound to draw readers. But while Pike escalates the suspense with finesse, his plot is light on credibility, and he completely skirts the moral issues that underpin his story.

> *Stephanie Zvirin, in a review of "Chain Letter," in* Booklist, *Vol. 82, No. 21, July, 1986, p. 1606.*

Last Act; Spellbound (1988)

Lonely Melanie, **Last Act**'s heroine, has won a big part in the school play and believes she will have a chance to make friends with the kids in her new high school. But when it seems that someone has put a real bullet into the gun Melanie fires in the course of the play, she is accused of murder. Once she is bailed out of jail, Melanie resolves to find the real murderer; her investigation reveals an elaborate, revengeful scheme, masterminded by one of her new-found friends. In **Spellbound,** Pike takes on the supernatural. Some people think that Cindy's boyfriend Jason killed his old girlfriend Karen up on top of the mountain. But Jason claims that Karen was attacked by a grizzly bear. A few months later, Cindy's pal Ray is killed in a similar manner. When an African exchange student shares his shamanic knowledge with Cindy, she is convinced that a strange and dangerous force is at loose in her home town and goes forth to confront it. Though both novels' plots are well constructed, some readers may find them a bit far-fetched. Nevertheless, the combination of likable characters, lively writing and lots of action will keep the pages turning.

> *A review of "Last Act" and "Spellbound," in* Publishers Weekly, *Vol. 233, No. 17, April 29, 1988, p. 80.*

The grisly summer murder of a high school cheerleader casts a pall over a Wyoming town and suspicion on her boyfriend who all too quickly finds a new love. . . .

[**Spellbound,** a] well told tale of horror, sparkles with lively dialogue, moody and highly evocative settings in high places with high adventure, daring, and romance among chaste teens being chased by Evil. A fun, frightening frolic indeed.

> *JoEllen Broome, in a review of "Spellbound," in* Voice of Youth Advocates, *Vol. 11, No. 3, August, 1988, p. 135.*

The first half of [**Last Act**] resembles a soap opera in its portrayal of the interrelationships between the in-crowd at the local high school. The story becomes more suspenseful after the murder occurs, and the story begins to revolve around Melanie's attempts to exonerate herself by finding the real murderer. The novel is marred, however, by inconsistent characters and improbable plot developments. At times, it sounds uncomfortably like a morality play. Nevertheless, these flaws are unlikely to deter young adult readers who enjoy light mysteries with a dash of romance thrown in.

> *Ruth Sadasivan, in a review of "Last Act," in* School Library Journal, *Vol. 35, No. 3, November, 1988, pp. 130-31.*

Gimme a Kiss (1988)

When a very private entry from Jane's diary is copied and circulated around the high school, Jane thinks she knows who is responsible. She sets to work on an elaborate but essentially harmless scheme of revenge only to learn that she is a pawn in someone else's murderous (and, by book's end, less than logically motivated) vendetta. Jane must think quickly if she is to avoid being the killer's next victim. While weak-stomached readers may find the last third of this novel a bit hard to take, horror fans will appreciate both the intricate plot and the vivid descriptions of high school life gone berserk.

> *A review of "Gimme a Kiss," in* Publishers Weekly, *Vol. 233, No. 25, June 24, 1988, p. 115.*

Gimme a Kiss should have a wide audience among teens, even those who read only when they must. The story moves at a brisk pace, alternating between a police detective's interrogation of a teenage girl, Alice, and the recent past, which concerns itself mostly with Alice's friend,

Jane. The interrogation has to do with deaths and a disappearance at a senior class boat party. Switch to the past.

Alice's friend, Jane, has been humiliated by a classmate and wants revenge. She devises a scheme, which will take place at the boat party, where it will appear that she has been pushed into the water to drown by the hated classmate. According to the plan, Jane is supposed to hide in the beachhouse, but the house is set on fire, a charred body is identified as Jane's, but is it?

This is a real page turner, and while the reader may have to suspend disbelief at the end, it will not stop anyone from wanting to find out who the real villain is. The book will appeal to younger as well as older teens and is suitable for good or poor readers. I recommend it highly.

> *Madeleine Schulps, in a review of "Gimme a Kiss," in* Kliatt Young Adult Paperback Book Guide, *Vol. XXII, No. 6, September, 1988, p. 16.*

It's important to take an occasional look at what teenagers are reading despite adult intervention, and this shocker by a popular author is a good example. Jane Retton is driven to revenge when a copy of a page from her diary is circulated through school. The entry—detailing a sexual encounter between Jane and her boyfriend—is fictitious wishful thinking on Jane's part, but when Kirk tells everyone it's true, Jane decides to fake her own death at the hands of Kirk and Patty, this trampy cheerleader whom Jane suspects of copying her diary. The plot is wildly implausible, with piled on catastrophe, and the comically lurid denouement reveals what *really* triggered two murders and a fire: Kirk gave Jane's friend Alice herpes (with a kiss). As Alice says, "When you're our age, there's nothing worse than being humiliated." Stringing together all the good parts of everybody's favorite problem novels, this makes no apologies for its straightforward lowmindedness, and readers will probably appreciate the opportunity to revel in their most paranoid fantasies without having to swallow redeeming social value at the same time. The closest this gets to a moral is when Jane, while waiting to chloroform Alice (*"Sweet dreams, bitch"*), reflects that "had she been a little less worried about her goddamn reputation she would still have a boyfriend and a best friend." Well, maybe so.

> *Roger Sutton, in a review of "Gimme a Kiss," in* Bulletin of the Center for Children's Books, *Vol. 42, No. 2, October, 1988, p. 50.*

The Party (1988)

New opportunities for friendship, love and rivalry are created when two high schools merge in this first book of the Final Friends trilogy. Sweet-tempered Alice throws a huge party to break the ice between the two groups of students. The fun ends, however, when Alice is found dead, an apparent suicide—her best friends suspect foul play. By the novel's end, over a dozen relatively unobjectionable teenagers have been introduced: at least one of them is a twisted murderer whose identity and motives will only be revealed in the trilogy's final volume. In fact, this book elaborately sets up all the action but goes no further; the real plot supposedly will be found in the future episodes. A number of the characters are similar to those found in the author's earlier thrillers, but readers who enjoy Pike's characteristic blend of romance, murder and mayhem will have to look forward to the leisurely unraveling of a complex plot filled with red herrings.

A review of "The Party," in Publishers Weekly, *Vol. 234, No. 9, August 26, 1988, p. 91.*

Remember Me (1989)

Shari is dead, and she knows that she didn't kill herself. So rather than merging with the cosmos as other spirits do, she lingers near the world of the living, determined to find her murderer. Fortunately for Shari, she is not alone in the hereafter. She finds a kindred spirit in Peter, the ghost of a boy she went to high school with. The ethereal duo discover Shari's killer in time to prevent another murder. But their techniques are not typical: rather, they solve the mystery by spying on old friends, attempting to communicate through a Ouija board, entering people's dreams and confronting the darker aspects of their own souls. The novel's central mystery, though somewhat contrived, moves along briskly. Plenty of action combined with several creepy seance scenes keep the pages turning. However, although the novel makes it clear that both Peter and Shari would rather be alive, some may question the prudence of presenting young readers with such a seductive vision of life after death.

A review of "Remember Me," in Publishers Weekly, *Vol. 235, No. 17, April 28, 1989, p. 82.*

Shari Cooper, the teenage narrator of this mystery novel, is a ghost, lingering in the world of the living to find out who killed her and why. There is a fair amount of suspense early on as Shari eavesdrops on various conversations among her friends, the police, and her family. The real focus of the story, however, is on Shari's experiences as a dead person. Ideas about life after death abound here. Some are legitimate, but simplistically presented. Others are just plain silly, playing on traditional beliefs about ghosts. One particularly ludicrous scene has Shari flying through the air like Supergirl. As the story progresses, Shari begins to fear that she may have committed suicide, and she takes to wandering in and out of people's dreams. Ultimately she discovers the murderer's identity, and learns that she plans to kill again. It's all very muddled and unclear. The sensational cover art and publisher's summary may draw teens to this novel, but they deserve better. For good mysteries tinged with the supernatural, Barbara Michaels is still the best bet.

Bruce Anne Shook, in a review of "Remember Me," in School Library Journal, *Vol. 36, No. 1, January, 1990, p. 121.*

Scavenger Hunt (1989)

The end of their school career is less than a week away for

the senior class in Express, a town of 20,000 located in the inland desert area of southern California. A secretive club on campus has organized a scavenger hunt for the senior class, dividing the class into teams of three or four, each competing for a promised wonderful prize. Carl and three of his friends are a team; and Traci, who secretly admires Carl, has also formed a team. The scavenger hunt turns into a nightmare for these two teams as they uncover unnatural past events and human sacrifice in an underground chamber, and discover some of their team members are not human after all.

This book may not appeal to every teenage reader but readers looking for a horror book should love it. The book has blood (even black blood), people coming back from the dead, dangerous creatures from the past, and a haunted underground chamber. There is little character development. All the principle characters in the book are teenagers; parents, teachers and other adults are only briefly mentioned. The book, however, is action packed as the characters progress in the scavenger hunt which starts on the school campus and ends violently in an isolated church far from town and school. Much of the story line is unbelievable but readers won't care. Suspense is the "name of the game" and the book will be impossible to put down.

Joyce Hamilton, in a review of "Scavenger Hunt," in Voice of Youth Advocates, *Vol. 12, No. 6, February, 1990, p. 346.*

Once again Pike gives readers a roller-coaster ride. . . . The plot and mood move along consistently drawing readers in and sustaining an uneasy feeling throughout. Parts of the book are very suspenseful, while others give readers a chance to catch their breath. Scant characterization at the beginning is so well done that readers will be compelled to keep reading to find out more. A skillfully woven ending clears up any questions about the characters. This quick read will appeal to teens seeking some distractions from the ordinary, and to those who are interested in the creepy, gory, gruesome, bizarre, and macabre genre.

Molly Kinney, in a review of "Scavenger Hunt," in School Library Journal, *Vol. 36, No. 8, August, 1990, p. 164.*

See You Later (1990)

When Mark, 18, meets Becky, he's sure it's love. But Becky is involved with Ray, 20, and isn't interested in a new relationship. Then Mark befriends Kara and Vincent, a young couple new to the area. Kara soon embarks on a mission to turn Becky against Ray, thus paving the way for Mark, who's puzzled by Kara's determination. He eventually learns that Kara *is* Becky, some 40 years into the future. She's been given the chance to travel back in time and rectify her past in order to prevent World War III. The plot is amazingly convoluted: the story is even more confusing than it sounds. Too many disparate elements are thrown in: romance, computer programming, time travel, murder, space stations, maniacal military leadership and intergalactic aliens. Pike's writing shows a definite comedic flair, but nothing can compensate for this muddled maze of a novel.

> A review of "See You Later," in Publishers Weekly, *Vol. 237, No. 26, June 29, 1990, p. 104.*

This is a convoluted tale of beings from the future returning to the present in order to intervene in their own past lives. If you think that sentence is confusing, you should try Pike's plot. However, he makes it somewhat easier by having the characters teenagers whom YA readers will quickly understand. The main character is a young man with a heart defect who is a creative designer of video games. He falls in love with a young woman who works in a record store. He meets two young people who drive expensive cars and seem amazingly familiar and easy to know. Yes indeed, these two people may or may not be another form of himself and his girlfriend returned to Earth from a future time. YA readers who already love Pike's novels will probably be willing to stick with the twists and turns of this story. Good luck to them!

> A review of "See You Later," in Kliatt Young Adult Paperback Book Guide, *Vol. XXIV, No. 6, September, 1990, p. 22.*

Pike adds a new twist to the paperback teenage suspense for which he is known. . . . There's little of the cleverness of science play of Sleator's back-from-the-future gem, *Strange Attractors,* and Pike's story bogs down with too many explanations. Even Mark admits, "the logic got awfully sticky." But it's still an intriguing scenario, with romance, drama, and even a chase scene or two to keep less-demanding readers plugging along till the end.

> Stephanie Zvirin, in a review of "See You Later," in Booklist, *Vol. 87, No. 3, October 1, 1990, p. 327.*

Witch (1990)

In this hokey, meandering novel, Julia is a girl gifted with a healing touch and the power to glimpse the future. When she sees a vision of her best friend's boyfriend, Jim, shot and bleeding to death, she does her best to keep him out of danger. But then another friend is shot while witnessing a gas station holdup, and Julia and Jim set out to wreak revenge on the gunman. Meanwhile, Julia's best friend discovers that the gunman just happens to be the deranged former boyfriend of Kary, the recently deceased half-sister Julia never knew. Julia's mother—also a healer—had died in an attempt to save Kary's life. In another part of town, a carload of good witches is hot on Julia's trail, determined to keep her from abusing her powers. Typically, Pike's writing is peppy enough to animate his most tangled plots; here, however, his style becomes choppy and unconvincing—unable to sustain the coincidence-riddled story. In addition, the text is littered with sexist one-liners which, along with a humorless running "joke," are as irritating as they are offensive. (pp. 66-7)

> A review of "Witch," in Publishers Weekly, *Vol. 237, No. 47, November 23, 1990, pp. 66-7.*

The plot has lots of loose ends and the dialogue contains many inappropriate asides (usually sexual innuendos). These are distracting and unrealistic. (For example: On the way to the scene of the holdup, Amy asks Randy what's so special about her. He replies, "I figure you'll be easy to get into the sack.") Somehow, any attempt at seriousness after this is suspect. Pike fans will want this book, but it is seriously flawed.

> Rita M. Fontinha, in a review of "Witch," in Kliatt Young Adult Paperback Book Guide, *Vol. XXV, No. 1, January, 1991, p. 12.*

Bury Me Deep (1991)

Another story from a writer who, for good or ill, manages to evoke visions of television right on the printed page. Here, he's got a winning combination of murder, ghosts, and scuba-diving thrills—winning, at least, for teens who read for adventure rather than character. Awakening from a nap on a plane en route to Hawaii, Jean Fiscal finds Mike, a strange, pale young man, sitting next to her. The two speak briefly; suddenly, Mike lapses into convulsions and dies a gruesome death. Determined to make the most of her vacation in spite of the tragedy, Jean decides to join friends for scuba lessons conducted by a pair of handsome tourboat owners, who, it turns out, once gave lessons to unfortunate Mike! The plot thickens—into a rather lumpy brew, with Pike's usual sprinkling of graphic deaths and nightmare sequences. The pacing is quick, however, and there's some downright fascinating stuff (maybe a bit more than some may want to know) about diving that helps readers mark time until tough, smart Jean smokes out the insane bad guy.

> Stephanie Zvirin, in a review of "Bury Me Deep," in Booklist, *Vol. 88, No. 1, September 1, 1991, p. 46.*

Die Softly (1991)

This tightly plotted mystery places baser human instincts under a penetrating microscope and turns the pages—fast. Pike's cast of teen characters mirrors the adult world yet acts independently, with little reference to it. Photographing the cheerleaders for the yearbook is as close as skinny Herb will ever get to his fantasy, the beautiful Alexa. Hiding his camera in their locker room showers, Herb gets far more than a sexy photograph. Before he develops the film, cheerleader Lisa dies in a fiery car crash. But Herb's photo shows Lisa naked in the shower being approached by a fully clothed Alexa holding a baseball bat. As he tries to unravel what happened without revealing his own deception, Herb becomes entangled in a teen underworld of drugs and abuse.

In this dark, taut tale there is no escape for anyone. Although he is uncompromising, Pike angles his lens with sardonic humor. His knack for portraying characters' personal quirks paints them vividly. He demonstrates that drug addiction can become a deadly psychosis, and in the process he packs a strong wallop in this page-turning thriller.

*Cathi Dunn MacRae, in a review of "Die Soft-
ly," in* Wilson Library Bulletin, *Vol. 66, No.
2, October, 1991, p. 101.*

Leo Politi

1908-

American author and illustrator of fiction.

Major works include *Pedro, the Angel of Olvera Street* (1946), *Juanita* (1948), *Song of the Swallows* (1949), *Moy Moy* (1960), *Mieko* (1969).

As an author and illustrator of multicultural books for children, Politi is respected for his efforts to develop an appreciation of differing ethnic groups and regional variations within American culture. He was born in the United States, and at age seven he emigrated with his parents to northern Italy, a journey which served, many years later, as the basis for his 1951 book, *Little Leo*. Sixteen years later he left Italy to return to America; and on the return voyage to California, he sailed through the Panama Canal and was impressed by the beauty of Central America. This experience inspired the desire "to study and learn more of Latin America and its people, their customs and their great civilization." Eventually settling on Olvera Street in the Mexican section of Los Angeles, Politi began work as a street artist, drawing pictures of nature, small children, and the warmth and happiness of family life—simple, earthy things which have characterized his work ever since.

Politi's professional career in America began in the early 1940s when he was hired as an illustrator of children's books by Charles Scribner's Sons. His first work was *Little Pancho,* the story of a small Mexican boy, his dog, and their adventures in the Central American jungle. Several assignments as an illustrator of books about Latin American countries followed. In 1946, at the suggestion of his publisher, he wrote and illustrated *Pedro, the Angel of Olvera Street,* a story about the famous Mexican Christmas celebration, "Las Posadas." Politi continued to show his enjoyment of the warmth and color of Southern California's Mexican heritage in *Juanita,* which describes a young girl's joy in partaking of the customary blessing of animals at Eastertime. In 1950 *Song of the Swallows,* with its vibrant watercolor drawings, won the Caldecott Award for best illustrated book of the year. For this book, Politi traveled to the Mission of San Juan Capistrano where he chronicled the legend of the swallows' annual return to the mission on the Feast of Saint Joseph, combining it with a story of the friendship between a young Mexican boy named Juan and Julian, an aged bellringer. Most of Politi's works are embellished with the lyrics of traditional Spanish, Mexican, or Italian folk music that was brought to California by early settlers, and with simple Spanish or Italian phrases. In addition to Mexican and Italian cultures, Politi has shown great interest in the Asian-American community culture. His 1961 story, *Moy Moy,* describes the Chinese-American celebration of the New Year, for which he was awarded the Southern California Council on Literature for Children and Young People Award; his picture book *Mieko* depicts the Japanese sum-

mer festival held during Nisei week in California's Little Tokyo. While some critics have censured Politi for his stereotypical depiction of minority Americans in regards to dress, occupation, and lifestyle, others commend him for his effort to break down negative prejudices that exist for peoples with different cultural backgrounds. Politi, for his part, considers the content of his books "sound and constructive to [children's] growth": statements against the false, materialistic values he often finds in children's literature. A 1965 recipient of the Regina Medal from the Catholic Library Association for "continued distinguished contribution to children's literature," Politi uses his sense of humor and love for children to enhance his stories. As he has stated, "I love children—all children! I think each of them is like a miracle."

(See also *Something about the Author,* Vols. 1, 47; *Contemporary Authors New Revision Series,* Vol. 13; and *Contemporary Authors,* Vols. 19-20, revised edition.)

AUTHOR'S COMMENTARY

[*The following excerpt is from Politi's acceptance speech for the Caldecott Medal, which he delivered at the Con-*

ference of the American Library Association on July 18, 1950.]

In [*Pedro, the Angel of Olvera Street, Juanita,* and *Song of the Swallows*] and in a new one coming out this fall—*A Boat for Peppe*—I have tried to bring out interesting customs and some of the traditions of California life; customs and traditions which I believe give color and charm to the past and are a part of the life of the state today.

Though these books are regional, I have tried to give them a quality of universality in the hope that children in other parts of the country might also enjoy them. The scene of the first two books is Olvera Street. I wish you might all see this quaint little street in Los Angeles, particularly during the Christmas and Easter festivals.

On the street I drew pictures and sold them and passed many happy years. I knew and loved the children of the street, and they and their elders took part in my books. When Pedro was not singing with his Grandfather, I remember the many times he came to watch me draw, and when I gave him some paper and pencil stubs he was so pleased because he liked to draw too. In the book, *Pedro, the Angel of Olvera Street,* because of his angelic voice, I had Pedro lead "Las Posadas." The impact and beauty of this Christmas festival can better be felt if one can hear the music and lovely hymns sung at this time.

Then I remember the happy young couple with the little daughter they kept so neat and clean. They were the inspiration for the Gonzales family in *Juanita,* the book with the blessing of the animals at Easter time. This beautiful ceremony as well as the Christmas one are suggestive and could be imitated in some way by children in other parts of the country.

In *Song of the Swallows,* I have embodied the charming and poetic happening of the swallows that leave the Mission of San Juan Capistrano for a period of the year and fly thousands of miles away to return punctually every spring to the same lovely mission. This is in fact one of the little miracles with which life is filled.

I should like to tell how I compose a book. I compose a book very much as if I were making a piece of sculpture. First I put down the bulk. When I feel the bulk has body and the right proportions, I begin to work on the detail. I work with the pictures and the text at the same time and make one supplement the other.

A quality I like is rhythm. The rhythm one can feel as he looks at the soft hills after sundown. There are peace and serenity and a rhythmical undulating movement in the lines of the hills. With the flow of pictures and words from page to page throughout the book, I try to convey this same rhythmical movement. I should like to tell of some other things I try to bring out in these books.

My love for people, animals, birds and flowers. My love for the simple, warm and earthy things, from the humblest house to a little tree to the tiniest seashell; for the things made by hands, the sewing of a dress, the painting of a picture; and for the singing of songs and the movements of the body in dancing—all those arts which are instinctive

forms of expression. We take pride in these natural forms and they give us æsthetic and spiritual pleasure.

Today, unfortunately, this folk art is somehow lost and confused in a complex age of overabundance of material things and doubtful values. In schools everywhere I see teachers and librarians trying to keep these folk arts and the finer and sounder things alive, but they are faced with great odds from the outside world by the maddening output of tempting things for the children to see, hear, read; things which confuse and paralyze to a great extent their natural and creative growth. Some day, somehow, I believe that the work of these unknown but great teachers will emerge to shape and temper this modern age to values more æsthetic and spiritual.

Writers, artists and publishers will help, I believe, by thinking less of making books outwardly so attractive that they will sell millions of copies, and thinking more of making books which children will enjoy and which will at the same time be sound and constructive to their growth.

To the best of my knowledge this is the only type of book I care to write and illustrate. (pp. 269-71)

> Leo Politi, "Acceptance of the Caldecott Medal," in The Horn Book Magazine, *Vol. XXVI, No. 4, July-August, 1950, pp. 269-71.*

GENERAL COMMENTARY

Rosemary Livsey

Although I have known Leo Politi only over a period of a few years when his interest in books and children has brought him into our children's library, I count him my friend even as the children do. . . . These children, not unlike those he knew as a child, are the ones among whom he lives now on the great hill in the midst of Los Angeles. Mexican, Italian and Oriental—they are the children of whom he thinks and whom he sees when he makes his books for all children.

"From a playground we watch the children play," he writes. "Some are light, others dark . . . but they are all beautiful, all of them have a live force animating their little bodies. All of them run, play, laugh and cry, and yet if outwardly they look different, they have within the same emotions of life. Each enjoys living; all will later be in the arms of the mothers who love them, live for them and raise them to be good and kind. If we can only understand this force that makes them live . . . the same love between mother and child, the same desire that you and I have to live; the love . . . aspirations . . . dreams like your mother with you, my mother with me, . . . then no dogmas, no prejudices, no fears can stand barriers between man and man."

Leo Politi was born in California in the sun-warmed valley of Fresno. His mother and father had come to this country from Italy. . . . In Fresno they lived in a ranch house and his father bought and sold horses. (pp. 97-8)

When Leo was seven the family returned to his mother's childhood home, the little town of Broni, in the province of Pavia near Milan in northern Italy. He remembers the excitement of the journey—the train, the big cities, the long days on the ocean and the drive from Milan to his grandparents' home in an open wagon through white and glistening snow.

Clearest of all is his memory of the Indian chief costume, complete to the feathers, which his mother bought for him. It made an impression on the children he met in New York City. When they learned that he had just come from the West they wanted to know if California was filled with cowboys, Indians and bandits such as they had seen in the movies. Little Leo did not want to disillusion them, so he obligingly said California was just like that. He even made up exciting stories of his own for them in which he and his father were the heroes!

The Indian costume made an even greater impression on the children in the Italian village when Leo appeared for his first day at school. They could not conceal their wonder and admiration for *il piccolo americano* and followed him everywhere. He became the center of so much attraction that the teacher had to ask his mother not to let him wear the Indian suit to school.

He spent happy days playing, studying and drawing everything that he saw, on scraps of paper, in his books, wherever he could find space. (pp. 98-9)

[In the year his family lived in London,] Leo went often to St. Martin's Lane to watch the artists draw on the sidewalks. He was fascinated by "the deftness of their lines and the speed with which the colored chalk pictures appeared on the pavements."

It was not long before the family returned to Italy.

At the age of fourteen, encouraged by his mother's enthusiastic belief in his ability to draw, Leo entered a competition for a scholarship to the National Art Institute at Monza near Milan. Among the students who competed from all over the country, he was the one chosen from northern Italy. For six years he lived and studied at the Art Institute which was housed in the Royal Palace, formerly the residence of King Umberto the First—a beautiful old building set in a great park with gardens, trees and even a zoo. Much of the students' time was spent out of doors sketching animals, flowers and the countryside. Here, too, Leo studied sculpture, architecture and design, which have played such an important part in the composition of his later work. At twenty-one he was graduated with credits that allowed him to teach art in Italy but he did not attempt or think of teaching, for he was eager to create for himself.

With a school friend he worked at textile and tapestry designing and did his first book illustrations. He is amused when he thinks of these now. "It was not my job," he says, "but my friend was too busy, so, instead of him, I did the pictures for a textbook to be used in schools for deaf and dumb children. It was a government book. It did not bear my name, nor did I ever see it in print."

After fourteen years Leo returned to the United States, sailing through the Panama Canal on his way to California. He was enchanted with the Central American coun-

tries and with Mexico which he visited later. The gentleness and beauty of the Latin Americans filled him with a desire to learn more of these people for whom he felt great admiration and kinship.

It was natural, therefore, that when he and Helen Fontes were married, they should make their first home in that colorful section of Los Angeles, Olvera Street. There the Mexican craftsmen's little shops still continue near the Plaza and the Mission Church in the midst of the great city. There the religious festivals of the people still take place. Leo Politi knows all the families who have shops on Olvera Street, he has watched their children of yesterday grow up and knows their children today.

Life was not easy for the young artist and his wife who lived simply and worked endlessly. "What were you doing then?" we asked him; he spread his arms in a broad expansiveness. "Everything." That "everything" included painting murals for the green room of the State College theater in Fresno; night sketching of the sightseers as they wandered up and down Olvera Street; carving beautiful wooden figures, primitive and simple in feeling; and working at his drawing board night after night to earn a living.

His real entrance into the field of book illustration came as a result of work for Rob Wagner's *Script,* a magazine that is a part of the Los Angeles tradition. Pancho, the little Mexican boy, was familiar to us long before he became a part of the book, **Little Pancho,** for we had watched for him and for the other Mexican children appearing under the signature *Leo* as spots and covers in *Script.*

"That Pancho, he was very bad," says Leo. "I had always drawn him for fun, and one night I started to draw him running and he ran all over the page and right into his own story. In one night I had completed the idea. It was not good drawing—too heavy—but Pancho made my first book and brought me to my first publisher, the Viking Press, and to Miss Massee, who was very kind to me."

Leo Politi enters with naïve sympathy into the mood of the books he illustrates. The childlike quality of wonder and reverence which he gives to the humble, industrious family in Ruth Sawyer's **The Least One** and the mocking pomp of military splendor in the background of Helen Garrett's **Angelo the Naughty One** give distinction and personality to each of these books. Always his strong sense of composition and design give rhythmic beauty both to his panoramas and his simplest drawings. However, it is to the books which he has both written and illustrated himself that one turns to find Leo Politi's full strength.

It was Alice Dalgliesh, juvenile editor for Charles Scribner's Sons, who gave him the incentive to do **Pedro, the Angel of Olvera Street.** To her, as to other of his chosen friends, he had sent as a holiday greeting a drawing of one of the Mexican children with angel's wings for Christmas. Why not do an entire Christmas book, with angels, Mexican children and Olvera Street? The idea did not come to fulfillment immediately, but once started it was inevitable, for "the best time of all the year for Olvera Street is Christmas time. Then the Street looks so gay, all decorated for the Christmas procession called La Posada. . . . The Posada is a procession which, like a Christmas play, tells the

Politi demonstrating his drawing technique to a group of children in Los Angeles.

story of the journey of the Holy Mother Mary and Joseph to Bethlehem. It tells how they sought shelter (*posada*) from the dark night and at last found refuge in the humble stable where the Christ Child was born." The story of Pedro who sang like an angel and walked at the head of the procession is dedicated to the children of Olvera Street.

Two years later, in 1948, Leo Politi repeated his success with an even more childlike and appealing story of the children of Olvera Street celebrating the blessing of the animals on the day before Easter. ***Juanita,*** with its fresh springlike quality, is the endearing story of the little daughter of Antonio and Maria Gonzales whose "*puesto* was more than a booth where they made and sold wares. To them it was also a little home filled with dear and pleasant memories, for in here they had watched Juanita grow up to this day." When Juanita was four years old, she took her birthday dove and walked with all the people and their animals through the Street to the patio of the old church where the kindly Padre blessed each pet saying, "Bless, O Lord, these animals so all will be well with them." Never do church bells ring out their songs more gladly than in a Politi church tower. Never are children in or out of a book happier.

To the children, living near Olvera Street and knowing the Easter blessing of the animals, this book was of themselves. To our great delight a group of small children drew their own pictures for the story of Juanita, leaving out no pet of their own, remembering the high city buildings and

the pushing traffic bordering Olvera Street and the little church across the Plaza.

These pictures were especially appealing to Leo Politi, who feels strongly that children should be encouraged to draw, unhampered by outside influence or adult interference. Because children are direct and sincere with the object or impression they want to convey, he feels their drawings are filled with fresh imagination and delight. Instinctively they are well composed in color and design. He tells with amused pride of his little son, Paul, now in kindergarten, who loves to draw and paint with his father. . . . Suzanne, the baby, is too young to paint. Both children, though perhaps unconsciously on the part of their father, appear in many of his drawings.

Myron Nutting, art editor of *Script,* writes of Leo Politi: "The most striking quality of his work is a gentleness that comes only to those who have known and seen the bitterness of life and can still accept it. Like the youngsters who said that 'a friend is one who knows all about you, but still likes you,' Politi knows about life but still loves it. He meets it with a sort of Franciscan faith and good cheer. It does not occur to him to propagandize or try to reform. A spirit of kindness pervades his work, and God knows this would be a different world if that spirit were more pervasive. His little world is full of it, and makes any arguments as to its limitations futile. . . . He is eager, he is searching, in an unforced and unpretentious way." (pp. 101-07)

Along with the simplicity and goodness inherent in all of Leo Politi's work, there is a conviction and a vigor. It can best be expressed in words he himself used while turning the pages of one of his books: "I am proud of this page. It tells what I feel of a family counting its happiness in little things. I would like my children and all children to seek security less in material things, and more in the spiritual and the aesthetic; to know what it means to enjoy working with their hands; to be reasonable in what they want, and generous in what they have to give."

It is for this simple sincerity that he is to each of us "my friend, Leo." (p. 107)

> Rosemary Livsey, "Leo Politi, Friend of All," in The Horn Book Magazine, *Vol. XXV, No. 2, March-April, 1949, pp. 96-108.*

Alice Dalgliesh

[A well known author of children's books, Dalgliesh was Politi's editor at Charles Scribner's Sons. He illustrated her nonfiction title The Columbus Story *(1955).]*

Leo Politi has been awarded the Caldecott medal for his distinctive work in picture books. There is something, however, beside the fact that he is a fine artist. I am sure that Leo's picture-book children have a great deal to do with the friends his books have made all over the country. They are regional books—with the setting of his native California—but his children are not regional and only a few picture-book children stay with one as Leo Politi's do. A librarian wrote me that one little girl returns to the library again and again to see if her friend Juan is still welcoming the swallows.

The children are very real to me, as they must be to others. Their personal lives and their relationships with adults are always warm-hearted and true. First came Pedro, the little red-winged "angel" of Olvera Street, with his much-loved grandfather, then Juanita, with her pink dress, her dove, and her devoted parents. (True to childhood, the pink dress hangs by her bed as she sleeps.) Then Juan of Capistrano, with his friendship for the swallows and for the old bell-ringer in *Song of the Swallows.* And in the fall there will be Peppe, son of a Sicilian fisherman in Monterey, with Nina his little sister and his old fisherman friend Geramia.

Besides being beautiful books, these are friendly books with a real understanding of children. Undoubtedly part of this is due to the children who are Helen and Leo Politi's own, seven-year-old Paul and four-year-old Suzanne, and pictures and text are tried out in every detail with them. . . .

Our association as artist and editor has been a delightful one. Leo is one of the most co-operative and least temperamental artists it has been my privilege to work with. (p. 649)

Leo Politi was born in Fresno, California, of Italian parents, and the family returned to Italy when he was seven. He grew up in Italy, won a scholarship at fifteen, and studied art for six years in Milan. He was twenty-two when he returned to California. The fact that he speaks both English and Italian, results in a particularly charming use of words, his own way of saying things, that must not be edited. Who else would say that Juanita and her family spent the rest of the day of the Blessing of the Animals "in happy quietude?" He has his own way of seeing things, too, of eliminating the dross, the commercial, the nonessential, and he places his children in the freshness and unsophistication of a child's world. Crowds welcome the swallows at Capistrano, but in *Song of the Swallows* it is only the children and Julian, the bell-ringer who see them come. Monterey is a modern city now, but in *Peppe* we see only the heart of the town, the old buildings that have survived the years, the fishing boats and Peppe's home.

Leo began to draw Mexican children when he lived near Olvera Street in the Mexican section of Los Angeles, and Mexican children and adults have predominated in his books and in his paintings. (His popularity as an illustrator should not obscure the fact that he is also a painter of ability and has had several shows.) He takes his work very seriously. "You have to," he says, "when you think of all the thousands who will look at each page of your book. I love making books. A painting may possibly be seen by only a few; a book goes to so many."

Wherever he goes, Leo's complete sincerity and natural charm makes friends for him. His work, we know, will not stand still, but will continue to grow, and in accepting the medal he said that he took it "as a challenge to better work." His forthcoming book holds to the high standard set by the books he has written and those he has illustrated. Peppe is Sicilian-American, and, as Leo is Italian-American, there is great sympathy between them. You will, I believe, like Peppe. I see in him something of Leo's

dark-haired son Paul. There is in this book, again, the indefinable spiritual quality that is in the other three books, a quality of which many have spoken. To an editor who sees constantly the work of would-be illustrators with the hardness of commercialism, the brittle touch of Hollywood, this is something for which to be very grateful. As Della McGregor of the St. Paul Public Libraries wrote us when *Juanita* was published, "It is many a long day since I have read a story which so naturally and graciously presents fine family relationships and spiritual concepts within the understanding of little children." (p. 651)

Alice Dalgliesh, "Leo Politi," in Library Journal, *Vol. 75, April 15, 1950, pp. 649, 651.*

Gladys English

Ever since the days of the Padres, California has had her own faithful chroniclers. None among them has blended the old and the new with a more magical touch than has Leo Politi in three already beloved California stories for children, *Pedro, the Angel of Olvera Street, Juanita* and the *Song of the Swallows.* A sense of reverence for the past and for California's rich endowment from Spanish and Mexican forebears fills each of these books with warmth and color. Reading the stories over again, and enjoying their gay pictures, one is struck anew with the freshness of Leo's approach to age-old customs and beliefs. (p. 272)

Leo disclaims any musical ability, yet from an air he hummed over and over again, a musical friend composed the melody for Juanita's lullaby. Excepting that and one other song, "Good Morning, Mr. Swallow," which was composed for the children of Santa Barbara by a Franciscan nun, all the music in the three books is traditional early Californian, brought here by the first Spanish and Mexican settlers. It has been simplified by Leo for the children to sing. That for *La Posada* is a masterpiece of beauty. The words for the different songs have been rewritten to evoke the mood of the stories, though they still retain a sense of the past. (p. 274)

"How can one live without God?" asks Leo. And God is manifest in his books, as the people of Olvera Street celebrate His two great feasts of the year, the Nativity and the Resurrection. His presence is also felt in the *Song of the Swallows,* when the swallows find sanctuary in the mission ruins, and when at the end of the summer old Julian bestows God's blessing on their departure and Juan prays for their safe return.

Leo Politi believes "that the beautiful things in life are those of the spirit." These values are expressed in his California stories with a simplicity that children understand. Soaring music, gaiety of spirit, family devotion, religious festivals, love for all God's creatures, are presented with supreme art in these seemingly artless stories. Pedro's red wings, his music box; Juanita's pink birthday dress, her white dove; Juan's little garden with the swallows nesting in it; all are symbols of happy childhood.

Leo has for many years lived and worked in Olvera Street. The people there are his friends, he has shared their joys and sorrows. He, too, well knows the meaning of poverty. He has participated often in *La Posada* and the Blessing of the Animals. So it was to be expected that when Alice Dalgliesh asked him for a Christmas story and then an Easter one from Olvera Street, Pedro and Juanita came alive. And the "Swallows" book is a loving memento to the swallows of Leo's own boyhood in Italy.

There is abundant promise of future books that will present other aspects of life in California. The Caldecott Medal awarded to Leo this spring for illustrations in his *Song of the Swallows* is at the same time a tribute to his other books and pictures for children and will serve as a lodestar for further creative work.

The little Christmas angel winging his way from Olvera Street to Alice Dalgliesh was indeed a joyous messenger for those who delight in children's books that have in them beauty and profound spiritual truth. (pp. 274-75)

> *Gladys English, "Leo Politi," in* The Horn Book Magazine, *Vol. XXVI, No. 4, July-August, 1950, pp. 272-75.*

Elaine Templin

With the sure touch of a master artisan, Leo Politi has blended the old and the new in his stories which depict early California history. With warmth and color he has described the age old customs and beliefs brought to these shores by the Spanish, Mexicans, Italians, and Portuguese who adopted California as their home in the New World. In the simple, childlike atmosphere of these stories, Mr. Politi conveys to his readers a respect for the cultures and traditions of other lands and other peoples, and helps to keep alive for future generations of Americans the great wealth of tradition and folklore brought to America by immigrants of bygone days. (p. 323)

[His] love of life—people, animals, birds, flowers—overflows into everything he draws or writes.

Shortly after his graduation from the [National Art Institute at Monza, Italy], Leo returned to America alone via the Panama Canal. During this voyage he became so fascinated by the warm beauty of the Central American countries that he determined to become better acquainted with Latin American people, their customs, and their great civilizations. Therefore, his recognition today as one of our finest interpreters of Latin America for children would seem unremarkable if it were not for the fact that Mexico is the only country that he has visited "south of the border." Perhaps one clue to such an accomplishment lies in Olvera Street, the colorful, quaint little street where Mr. Politi lived and worked when he first returned to America from Italy. In those days Olvera Street was admirably suited to the life of an artist, for it still retained much of its ancient Mexican culture and traditions in spite of its location near the heart of Los Angeles. (p. 325)

It was not until 1938, the year he married Helen Fontes, that Leo Politi made his real entry into the field of book illustration. In that year Viking Press brought out a slim volume entitled *Little Pancho*, in reality an outgrowth of the illustrations which had appeared from time to time in the Los Angeles magazine, *Script*. As is so often the case with 'first' books, *Little Pancho* met with slight success and soon was forgotten. Nevertheless, this unimportant

little volume proved to be the turning point in Mr. Politi's career as an artist, for Miss [May] Massee at Viking was impressed by its illustrations. Therefore, she arranged for him to illustrate *The Least One,* Ruth Sawyer's story of a humble, industrious Mexican family and a quite small burro. These illustrations reached the book market in 1941 and were the first of his work to gain critical recognition.

One cannot fail to be impressed with the vitality and the strong sense of composition and design which lend both beauty and rhythm to his illustrations for *The Least One.* His strokes are bold and angular, his pictures full of action, his characters individualized, and, interestingly enough, portrayed with oversized hands and feet—a characteristic of primitive art. In fact, those early illustrations are strongly reminiscent of the native art of Mexico.

Three years later, in 1944, Leo Politi mocked the pomp of military splendor in the background of Helen Garrett's *Angelo the Naughty One.* In these illustrations one sees indications of the softer, more rounded style that was to characterize his later work. To each of these books his illustrations give distinction and personality. (pp. 325-26)

[Alice Dalgliesh's suggestion that he do a book for her company] was enthusiastically received by Mr. Politi, for it concerned a subject close to his heart. He had participated often in the Christmas procession called *La Posada,* and he had watched excited children celebrate Christmas Eve with the breaking of the *piñata.* Indeed, "the best time of all the year for Olvera Street is Christmas time. Then the street looks so gay."

And so, in 1946, *Pedro the Angel of Olvera Street* was born. . . . (p. 326)

Two years later [Politi] completed *Juanita,* the gentle story of the four-year-old daughter of Antonio and Maria Gonzalez. Filled with love and kindliness, *Juanita* proved to be a more appealing, more childlike story of Olvera Street than *Pedro* had been. In this story we see Juanita put on her "lovely new rose-colored dress trimmed with lace," take her little white birthday dove, and participate for the first time in "The Blessing of the Animals . . . a ceremony which takes place every year on the day before Easter Sunday. On this day the animals are blessed so all will go well with them during the year."

We see, too, the close and loving ties which bind this little family together. (pp. 326-27)

The soft, muted, rosy-toned illustrations for *Juanita,* runner-up for the Caldecott Medal in 1949, lend a spiritual quality to this work. According to Mr. Politi, it was Ugo Lovetté, his teacher at the Institute, who developed within him this capacity for sensitive portrayal.

The feeling for rhythm in nature, which pervades all of Mr. Politi's work, also reflects the teachings of Signor Lovetté who encouraged his students to see birds and animals and flowers not as objects to be sketched but as living things, possessing a grace, rhythm, and flow of movement that are but outward manifestations of their inner life. We see this rhythm in his work everywhere—in the repetitive roundness of the soft brown hills, in the billowing cloud masses, in the sweeping flight of birds.

Mission San Juan Capistrano, which is renowned for its swallows was chosen by Leo Politi as the setting for his next book, *Song of the Swallows.* Capistrano, seventh in a chain of twenty-one missions established in Alta California for the purpose of Christianizing and civilizing the Indians, proved an auspicious choice since Mr. Politi's interest in swallows dates back to his boyhood days in Italy where he watched a pair nest each spring under the roof beams of his grandfather's house.

Thus in the quiet, peaceful gardens, against the crumbling adobe arches of the old Mission, through the friendship of the boy Juan and the old gardener, Julian, he has told of the mysterious regularity with which the swallows sweep in from the sea each March 19—St. Joseph's Day—to "build their small mud houses against the beams of the roof." (pp. 327-28)

Since Mr. Politi long has been impressed by their joyousness and their elegance in flight, one senses that he affirms his own feeling for swallows in the discussion which Julian has with Juan:

> Just try to picture, Juan, the hundreds and thousands of miles they travel, high up in the air, looking down over strange and beautiful lands.
>
> I believe that, of all the creatures, God has given them the most freedom and happiness.

Skillfully and with disarming simplicity, Mr. Politi has woven together with the story of the swallows the equally charming story of the Mission and of Father Junipero Serra and his band of faithful followers who were building Mission San Juan Capistrano at the same time that George Washington and his weary men were fighting for the freedom of the thirteen American colonies. . . .

Winner of the Caldecott Medal in 1950, *Song of the Swallows* is a worthwhile contribution to a literary field too often ignored by authors of picture-story books. Here Leo Politi succeeds in chronicling historical events in such a manner that even young readers are able to understand and enjoy them. The strength and tenderness portrayed in the muted illustrations as well as the reverent atmosphere of the text combine to make this a picture book of distinction. (p. 328)

[*The Mission Bell*] presents an illustrated historical account of Father Serra's journey "from Old Mexico to California by order of the King of Spain." In some detail it tells of the hardships encountered by Father Serra, his soldiers, and priests during the establishment of the missions; the making of friends with the Indians; and the turning of "the California wilderness into a green and fertile land." It tells, too, of 'The King's Highway,' which with a few changes is still the route of one of California's principal north-south arterial highways. . . . (pp. 328-29)

Mr. Politi's graphic illustrations for *The Mission Bell* demonstrate once again his skillfulness in choosing and using color as a subtle communicative media. There are, for example, the hot golden browns and the greyed greens depicting the empty desert "scorched by the heat of the sun." There are, too, the stark greys of "the steep mountain passes" and of the Franciscan habits worn by Father Serra and his men.

In this book, perhaps more than in his earlier ones, Leo Politi makes known his own deep abiding faith in God and in the power of love. Through Father Serra he says:

> we must always keep in mind, that it is through hard work, pain and sacrifice that God dispenses his richest reward.
>
> . . . . we will succeed in our task, no matter how great the obstacles are, for love can conquer all obstacles.

A Boat for Peppe is the first of Leo Politi's books to have an Italian atmosphere. Published in 1950, it pictures a colony of Sicilian sardine fishermen who live in Monterey, California. On the bustling, busy wharfs, against the large and picturesque fishing fleet, through the friendship of the boy Peppe and the old fisherman Geramia, he has told of the communal closeness of this fishing colony, of the joy felt each morning when the boats return after their all-night fishing expeditions, and of the general concern when one boat fails to return during a storm.

In addition, he has vividly portrayed the ancient, traditional, old-country custom of blessing the fishing fleet—a ceremonial which is still important to the California fishermen who came to these shores from Portugal, Italy, and Sicily. (p. 329)

One senses that Leo's father, and his own happy childhood, served as the prototype for Peppe and his family as he writes: "Peppe's father . . . likes to play with Peppe and Nina and he likes to sing. . . . His warm and clear voice filled the air with happiness."

Leo Politi's most recent work was the illustrating of Alice Dalgliesh's *The Columbus Story.* The pictures are large and bold, full of action, and unhampered by detail. They display an abandon, a freedom in the use of color, and an easy flowing style not discernible in his earlier work. They are, in fact, as refreshing as a breeze blowing in from the sea. Of course, these diversifications in style may have been adopted by Mr. Politi simply as a means of interpreting *The Columbus Story,* but they may on the other hand be an indication that he is reaching upward and outward toward a new artistic style. In either case, they portend a successful future for this gifted author-illustrator.

Leo Politi's work has the sturdy quality of peasant living. It shows the influence of people who work with their hands and who respect others for so doing, of people who live simple lives and have close and loving family ties, of people who have an abiding faith in God. These are the characteristics that are inherited by the Juans, Pedros, Peppes, and Juanitas who people his books.

In addition, the work of Leo Politi reflects a deep sensitivity to the wonders and beauties of nature. He may wrap his special word magic around the coming of spring at Capistrano: "Soon the blossoming trees bent gently over the garden walks. They made lovely patterns against the sky and filled the clear air with fragrance", or he may tell of the beauty of a seashell on the beach of Monterey: "How beautiful the world is . . . even the littlest things such as seashells can be so pretty in shape and color, and so precious." Indeed, the smallest bits of natural beauty are captured by the eye and the pen of this writer, and each is preserved for the reader—as fresh and new and shiny as it was on the day the writer first experienced it.

Each of Mr. Politi's first four books contains music, which for the most part is traditional Spanish, Mexican, or Italian folk music brought to California by early settlers. In most cases he has simplified the tunes to make them easier for young children to sing and has rewritten the lyrics, adapting them to the flow of each story.

Though he disclaims any musical ability, Leo Politi is known to have composed two of the songs—**"Juanita's Lullaby"** and **"Peppe's Seashore Song"**—by humming the melody over and over again to a musical friend who made the necessary notations. (pp. 329-30)

Mr. Politi's stories are enhanced further by the inclusion of simple Spanish or Italian phrases. Unobtrusively and with a disarming casualness, he has woven into the text such expressions as Peppe's "Conta, Papa? Sing, Father?" or Juan's "Buenas tardes, Julian. Good evening, Julian." By allowing his characters to speak occasionally in their mother tongue, Leo Politi has created a more realistic atmosphere and has added rhythmic beauty to each story text.

Leo Politi's working philosophy is expressed in the statement of what he wants for his own children, Paul and Suzanne. He says he would like them:

> and all children to seek security less in material things, and more in the spiritual and the aesthetic; to know what it means to enjoy working with their hands; to be reasonable in what they want, and generous in what they have to give.

With such convictions it is not surprising that the books of Leo Politi speak of peace and serenity, and have within them beauty and profound spiritual truth. Such a man has much to offer the children of America and the world. Thus it is hoped that good books will continue to come from the pen and brush of this talented author-illustrator—books that may present other aspects of historic California to young people everywhere. (pp. 330-31)

> *Elaine Templin, "Leo Politi: Children's Historian," in* Elementary English, *Vol. XXXIII, No. 6, October, 1956, pp. 323-31.*

May Hill Arbuthnot

Leo Politi is an artist whose pictures are deceptively simple, almost primitive. Both his figures and his landscapes are stylized, but the total composition makes a beautiful design. His children are colorful and appealing whether it is **Little Leo,** capering gaily with his friends through Italian streets, or the lovely procession of children and pets in **Juanita,** or the delightful little Chinese **Moy Moy.** This generation needs the gentleness and decorative grace of Leo Politi's pictures. (p. 67)

Leo Politi's beautiful picture-stories are simple in theme and plot, frequently centered on the activities of small children living in a homogeneous racial group in the midst of one of our big cities. . . . A tender understanding of children is reflected in every book and every picture Leo Politi has made, and his smiling skipping children are a delight. (p. 431)

> *May Hill Arbuthnot, "The Artist and the Child's Books: Leo Politi" and "Here and Now: Leo Politi," in her* Children and Books, *third edition, Scott, Foresman and Company, 1964, pp. 67, 431.*

Sam Leaton Sebesta and William J. Iverson

Books from [the category of early childhood fiction of other times and places] can open exciting new worlds hitherto unknown to the young child. The northern regions of the Old World, for example, are beautifully shown in the stone lithographs of Ingri and Edgar Parin d'Aulaire in the simple stories of *Ola, Children of the Northern Lights,* and *Nils.* Such books give evidence that well-executed picture books with substance retain their appeal over many decades. To some extent this is also true of the regional and ethnic picture books of Leo Politi, including his still popular **Song of the Swallows** and **Emmet.** Although the narratives in Politi's books are rather unexciting and too obviously didactic, his highly elaborate color mixes and compositions give the books distinction. (p. 271)

> *Sam Leaton Sebesta and William J. Iverson, "Realistic Fiction," in their* Literature for Thursday's Child, *Science Research Associates, Inc., 1975, pp. 243-306.*

Barbara Bader

Pedro is small and intimate and dear, with little of the obvious portent and pageantry that hobble the later books; but Politi as an interpreter of Mexican-American life has never the zest that he has in **Little Leo** remembering his own early life. Never mind that it's forty years since he went to his parents' native Italy in the garb of an Indian chief—there's fun on the transcontinental train where one little Indian, our little Leo, waves from the back platform; in New York where everyone looks at them (Mama's big hat? Papa's mustache? *my Indian costume!*); on the ship—except for Mama, who's seasick; in San Mateo, where nothing has changed, where Grandma has ravioli ready and makes cookies shaped like fruit and animals, and where the children tag behind Leo in his Indian suit, so absorbed that he is asked not to wear it to school.

They beg for Indian suits like his, and soon the quiet of San Mateo is no more; Mario and Gino, Ugo, Giovanni, Luigi and tiny Orlando are Indians too, whooping through the square and up and down the hill, bright specks against golden tints bleached by time and sun. One thinks back to Edgar d'Aulaire's vision of the prairies, to Bemelmans, nourished on Fenimore Cooper and Karl May, providing himself with pistols and ammunition before he leaves for America; and ahead, to village squares packed with cars and hung with Coca-Cola signs. With **Little Leo,** published in 1951, we have bridged World War II and the past has, in a sense, caught up with the future; among books to be taken seriously, there won't be any more *Mikis* [referring to *Miki* by Maud and Miska Petersham]. (p. 59)

> *Barbara Bader, "Politi and the Persistence of Things Foreign," in her* American Picturebooks from Noah's Ark to the Beast Within, *Macmillan Publishing Co., Inc., 1976, pp. 58-9.*

Patricia Cianciolo

The art of the naive is a layman's art which combines the influences of the collective mentality present in the folk art and in the original. The naive painter represents the essence of things and appearance out of his own experience. Filled with his private visions and concepts, he tackles even the most difficult themes and achieves an integrity and depth of expression which distinguishes his style from all others. All this, he attempts despite the inner conflict and tension that most certainly must result between his technical ignorance and his version of inner truth, between intellectual simplicity and visual invention. Wherever a genuine naivete is found in a drawing or painting the creator of that work must have a tendency toward self-sufficiency and childlike isolation. He must stand removed from artistic tradition so that he will not attempt a particular line of stylistic development or stand in opposition to one. Yet, his art often does bear some of the folklorist regional stamp. . . . (pp. 47-8)

The naive artist like the child tends to present only the clearly outlined aspects of his visual world, the clearly gentle and violent aspects of his world. The "hallmarks" of naive art are perhaps its trusting openness to discovery, its vitality and awkward spontaneity, its candidness and intensity. A naive painting radiates an infectious love for life. The art of the naive is a preperspective art, characterized by the almost exclusive adherence to frontal posture or profile. There is a disregard for anatomy and perspective that suggests a less developed level of consciousness and/or lack of skill in expressing a consciousness, if indeed it exists. His style is that of simplification and only those details that comprise the essence of the reality or the experience are included in his drawings or paintings. (p. 48)

[A] naive artist is Caldecott Medal winner Leo Politi. The viewer of his illustrations, be they the illustrations in his earlier books like *Pedro, The Angel of Olvera Street* and *Song of the Swallows* or those in his latest book *The Nicest Gift,* gets a glimpse at the "wonderment of life" almost as through the eyes of innocence. His love for life and all living things is quite apparent in his illustrations. Like [Jan] Balet there is present in Politi's work a refreshing simplicity in the reality that is portrayed. The figures are lacking in anatomy and the scenes are not done in perspective; the colors are vivid and there is a vitality and a zest in the action. (pp. 48-9)

[Leo Politi's] medium is primarily tempera. One would probably conclude, after having examined the illustrations in *Pedro, the Angel of Olvera Street, St. Francis and the Animals,* and his most recent creation *The Nicest Gift,* that his illustrations are composed with a quiet deliberation. It seems that his style is quite stabilized as is the medium he uses in his work. His illustrations are deceptively simple. In fact, there is a naive look about many of his pictures. Particularly noticeable are the stylized lumbering figures and the oversized, stiff hands and feet, qualities so characteristic of the naive artist. Politi does not include much detail in his work. Indeed, his illustrations are characterized by an economy of detail. Nonetheless, there is considerable action depicted in his paintings, and there is enough suggestion for the child's imagination to expand. He includes enough of detail and attention to human features to give an adequate picture of people in their environment. Politi uses an assortment of tone and color in his pictures. Even when limited to two colors, he manages to produce considerable diversity in shades. His use of color to denote mood and time of day is skillful. He uses black and white or dark colors for evening scenes, for happy moods he uses brighter shades, and for sadness he uses the darker shades. (pp. 69-70)

> *Patricia Cianciolo, "Styles of Art in Children's Books" and "The Artist's Media and Techniques," in her* Illustrations in Children's Books, *second edition, Wm. C. Brown Company Publishers, 1976, pp. 28-57, 58-93.*

Lyn Ellen Lacy

[In 1950, Leo Politi received the Caldecott Medal] for *Song of the Swallows.* Politi himself had twice before received Honor Book awards, for *Pedro, the Angel of Olvera Street* in 1947 and *Juanita* in 1949. Over many years he would continue to contribute illustrations that repeat similar artistic elements for characterization or plot. Typically, small Latin American children involved in traditional activities gave color and charm to customs of the past, and simple images were lovingly rendered of animals, birds, and flowers as the earthy things of life. Little Juan and his experiences with old Julian at California's Mission San Juan Capistrano in *Swallows* is an excellent example. *Swallows* is an illustrated storybook with overlong text for a picture book, but the soft, warm earth tones in Politi's illustrations provide lasting impressions of a boy, an old man, and an even older mission where twice each year occurs the miracle of the swallows. (p. 102)

> *Lyn Ellen Lacy, "Color: 'Drummer Hoff' and 'The Rooster Crows',' in* Art and Design in Children's Picture Books, *American Library Association, 1986, pp. 64-103.*

TITLE COMMENTARY

The Least One   **(1941)**

[The Least One *was written by Ruth Sawyer.*]

A symphony in Mexican reds, browns and warm grays, this tale of the smallest burro in Vicente's pack train of three, strikes the regional note as soon as you look at it. The music of the story—the character of a Mexican Indian, kind, determined, religious with a special blend of naive faith and realistic shrewdness—sounds through an experience in which the miraculous is taken for granted.

Vicente's son Paco loves best the littlest burro, a creature that for all its politeness has its pride. Paco dreads the moment when burro and papacito come to a deadlock—as they do. Vicente loses his temper and curses the animal: may he become a wooden burro, standing still all the rest of his life! As no bird is flying over to carry the curse away, Vicente is horrified to find that it has worked. He keeps still and hopes the affair will blow over.

But Paco, hearing that the local photographer is growing rich by posing patrons on a modern horse, follows the trail and finds Chiquitito. At last accident lends him the wooden burro to take to church, where livestock is brought to be blessed by St. Francis. Paco comes too late, camps in the darkness outside, sees the loving saint in a dream and is awakened by a soft nose on his cheek. The least one is ransomed. This tenderness is tightened with humor: the treatment is that of a story teller convinced against his will—a manner likely to convince in reporting miracles. The pictures have the same subsatiric quality: they see the funny side.

M. L. Becker, "North, South, East and West," in New York Herald Tribune Books, November 2, 1941, p. 11.

It is good to realize in a year when far too many books have been published before text or illustrations were ready that authors and publishers are still willing to wait for the right artist for a given book.

Ruth Sawyer's story of Mexican life, **The Least One,** has waited three years for such illustrations as those of Leo Politi, and the result is [a] book for which I predict a long life. In its characterization, incident and atmosphere this story of a little Mexican boy and his pet burro and of his faith in San Francisco is itself so graphic as to have presented a challenge to a less perceptive artist. Mr. Politi has met it with a wit and tenderness and a true sense of background which will add to the pleasure of the reader of any age. (p. 456)

Anne Carroll Moore, "The Three Owls' Notebook: 'The Least One'," in The Horn Book Magazine, Vol. XVII, No. 6, November-December, 1941, pp. 456-58.

Angelo, the Naughty One (1944)

[Angelo, the Naughty One *was written by Helen Garrett.*]

There was Maria Rosa, the eldest one, who was going to marry a soldier, and Gloria, the rough one, and Juanita, the sweet one, and Louise, the bright one, in this nice Mexican family, and Angelo was the naughty one because he would never, save under strongest compulsion, take a bath. He was afraid of water; whenever it touched even his face he yelled till the remotest neighbor knew that Angelo, the naughty one, was being washed.

The climax came when all the family was being dressed for the wedding. They called loudly for Angelo—the big picture of their doing so is delightful. Even the bride, all dressed up, called for Angelo, the naughty one, but he was running away to be a soldier. Soldiers, he believed, never

took baths. Oh, didn't they? He ran right into the soldier who was going to marry his sister. This hero, with the aid of several of his men, promptly gave Angelo the bath of his life and clad him in a new white suit. Surviving the ordeal, Angelo was so proud of his own appearance at the wedding that he now submits to water without a yelp.

If you know a very little boy, say four or so, who is allergic to water, these gay, affectionate, colored pictures are indicated; a little girl of this age who likes water will love the funny, merry tale and the gay processions and parties shown in its illustrations.

May Lamberton Becker, in a review of "Angelo the Naughty One," in New York Herald Tribune Weekly Book Review, October 8, 1944, p. 5.

Pedro, the Angel of Olvera Street (1946)

Leo Politi's smiles—by which I mean those which identify to readers young and old the faces of tiny Mexicans as those of Politi people—have really a personality all their own. The smile at once possesses you and the face comes along with it. In this enchanting little Christmas book, however, the smiles, though distinctive, are more subdued because the most beautiful picture of the lot is the one in which Olvera Street, Los Angeles, where Pedro lives, is conducting the annual procession in search of a home for the Blessed Jesus. Manuel is a street musician and his grandson, Pedro, comes along to sing—some say, like an angel. You see the children running in every direction in and around the booths and shops, and through the open windows sandal makers, blacksmiths and the like at work at their crafts. Then Christmas approaches. The street, decorated with many-colored streamers; a magnificent Piñata in the shape of a peacock is hung on a rope in the center of the square. Then the procession starts and Pedro is chosen to be the little angel to lead it, singing as he goes

We weary pilgrims come to your door
Shelter in your puesto we beg, we implore.

And for nine nights comes the reply "No posada." Then on the tenth the doors are flung wide and the celebration begins. To round it off nicely, when the Piñata, a large earthenware bowl at which the children, blind-folded one by one, strike in an effort to break it, it is Pedro in his little red wings who performs this feat and gets the music box he so wants.

The colors are soft, bright and rich, and the many little figures are most engaging.

"Witch, Doll, Cats and Angels," in New York Herald Tribune Weekly Book Review, November 10, 1946, p. 10.

Leo Politi has written his own text for **Pedro, The Angel of Olvera Street,** and it is in keeping with his lovely pictures of life on a street in the heart of Los Angeles. With great tenderness he pictures little Pedro with his old grandfather and as a red-winged angel marching at the head of the Posada—the colorful Mexican Christmas procession—bearing a lighted candle and singing "like an

From Pedro, the Angel of Olvera Street, *written and illustrated by Leo Politi.*

angel." The songs, with music, belonging to the celebration are included. The subdued colors in which the book is printed are in harmony with this true Christmas story which the artist had himself experienced when he lived on Olvera Street.

> *Anne Carroll Moore, in a review of "Pedro, the Angel of Olvera Street," in* The Horn Book Magazine, *Vol. XXII, No. 6, November-December, 1946, p. 456.*

In text and pictures Leo Politi has captured both the reverence and the gayety of [the] traditional ceremony, but one wishes that his description had been strengthened by something a little sturdier than the very thin thread of story. However, the book, which includes words and music of two carols, will be useful in planning an out-of-the-ordinary Christmas pageant.

> *Ellen L. Buell, in a review of "Pedro, the Angel of Olvera Street," in* The New York Times Book Review, *December 22, 1946, p. 11.*

Despite the argument of some critics that the story is stereotyped, [**Pedro, the Angel of Olvera Street**] continues to delight adults and children alike. The story focuses on Pedro's involvement in the *posadas* and the Calle Olvera in Los Angeles. Politi does a fine job blending the flavor and history of Mexican American culture and in the process offers the reader some culturally enriching informa-

tion. Enjoyable for reading aloud, **Pedro** can also be used to discuss the early history of California's first major settlement in the City of the Angels.

> *Daniel Flores Duran, "Mexican American Resources: 'Pedro, the Angel of Olvera Street',"* in his Latino Materials: A Multimedia Guide for Children and Young Adults, *Neal Schuman, Publishers, 1979, p. 74.*

Juanita (1948)

On Olvera Street in old Los Angeles all its tiny shops for tourist trade have names as pretty as they are. The one named Juanita is named for the daughter of Antonio and Maria Gomez. On her fourth birthday Juanita receives from Mamacita a rosy dress trimmed with lace and from Papacita a white dove that becomes her constant companion. On Easter she will walk with her dove to the Old Mission church for the Blessing of the Animals. The children in Leo Politi's pictures always look like angels, whatever they are doing, and this time they are acting like them— across the fair pages, in soft, warm colors, winds the procession of little folk bringing their pets to the church. . . . [It] is all so gentle and innocent the book would be a delicious Easter present.

> *May Lamberton Becker, in a review of "Juanita," in* New York Herald Tribune Weekly Book Review, *March 21, 1948, p. 6.*

[Juanita's birthday] party and the charming old Easter custom are described in felicitous prose, lightly sprinkled with Spanish words which children can easily understand from the context. The pictures are in many subtly combined colors and are full of details which bring to life this colorful neighborhood.

> *Ellen Lewis Buell, in a review of "Juanita," in* The New York Times Book Review, *March 28, 1948, p. 33.*

On the day before Easter there is a blessing of the animals in Olvera Street in old Los Angeles. Leo Politi has never made lovelier pictures than those in this book that show this enchanting procession of children with their pets winding along Olvera Street. . . . Here they all are in soft, bright colors, sedate and serious, bringing their pets to be blessed by the padre of Olvera Street. The songs that they sing are here, with the music, even to the lullaby that Juanita's mother hums when the long, happy day is over. This is a picture book that can be given a place of honor on the spring list.

> *Mary Gould Davis, in a review of "Juanita," in* The Saturday Review of Literature, *Vol. XXXI, No. 15, April 10, 1948, p. 34.*

[**Juanita**] is a large-sized picture book in soft colors which is refreshingly childlike in its treatment of children, animals, birds and flowers. Sincerity, tenderness, humor, and a true sense of rhythm mark the pages depicting the colorful parade. . . .

Juanita is four years old, and the inclusion of the music for the Mexican birthday song *Las Mañanitas, La Paloma*

(The Dove Song) and the Lullaby sung by her mother add to its charm as a book for the birthday of a four- or five-year-old who may already be familiar with Mr. Politi's *Pedro* or *Angelo, The Naughty One,* one of the most popular picture books of recent years.

Anne Carroll Moore, in a review of "Juanita,"
in The Horn Book Magazine, *Vol. XXIV, No. 3, May-June, 1948, p. 173.*

AUTHOR'S COMMENTARY

Song of the Swallows (1949)

It happens that doing a book about the swallows at San Juan Capistrano was suggested to me by my editor at Charles Scribner's Sons. When she asked if I would like to make such a book, I was very enthusiastic because I like that Mission so well. The fact that the swallows return punctually every spring is to me such a sweet and poetic happening. But I have been interested in swallows ever since I was a boy in Italy, when two swallows came to nest every spring under the roof beams of my grandfather's house. I remember all the joy they brought. I used to like to watch them and was impressed by their elegance in flight.

When I first went to the Mission of Capistrano to sketch and gather notes for my story, I learned of an old gardener by the name of Julian, who had died recently. I was told that Julian had lived in the Mission all his life, that he was a good gardener, kind and beloved by everyone there. He was also the bell ringer, and it is said that no one ever rang the Mission Bells so well and with so much feeling as he did. I wished I could have met Julian because I felt that he, more than anyone else, knew the story of the Mission and the swallows.

As days went by, in the peace and quietude of the gardens, in the lovely arches of the old Mission walls, in the strong plants with fragrant flowers, in the gay twittering of the hundreds of birds flying all about, in the happy children playing in the school grounds, I felt the spirit of Julian. It was as if I had actually met him.

One day I watched a small, lively boy coming from school. He was full of wonder as he went through the gardens. Then I saw him run down the narrow winding street to his little house. It was an old adobe house built in the days of early California with lots of greens and flowers all around. I named him Juan.

I could picture the hundreds of boys and girls like Juan who on their way to and from school stopped to talk with Julian, watched him ring the bells, and listened to him tell stories of the flowers, of the birds, and of the Mission of San Juan Capistrano.

Through the friendship of Julian and Juan, I have tried to tell the story, and with the drawings and songs I have also tried to convey a general picture of this old and quaint little town. (pp. 64-5)

Leo Politi, "In Italy, Too, I Watched the Swallows Nesting," in Writing Books for Boys and

From Song of the Swallows, *written and illustrated by Leo Politi.*

Girls, *edited by Helen Ferris, Doubleday & Company, Inc., 1952, pp. 63-5.*

This picture book, in the format and with the coloring of Leo Politi's *Juanita,* tells for little children the legend of the swallows at Father Junipero Serra's mission in Capistrano, California. The time is today, and old Julian is lovingly tending the garden that has bloomed within the mission walls for nearly 200 years. He tells little Juan the story of the swallows, and Juan watches them fly back on Saint Joseph's Day. There are three double-page paintings of the mission, and a full-page picture of Juan's little garden and of the children's welcome to the swallows. Two songs are given in full, with the music. It is a lovely book for an Easter gift, with its color and music and its reverent atmosphere.

Mary Gould Davis, in a review of "Song of the Swallows," in The Saturday Review of Literature, *Vol. XXXII, No. 15, April 9, 1949, p. 36.*

As in previous books, Leo Politi transforms a southern California tradition or legend into a fragile story of tenderness and beauty for modern children. Using water colors in lovely pastel shades and disarmingly simple prose, he tells a charming story of friendship between little Juan and the old gardener at San Juan Capistrano Mission and their delight at the swallows' return on St. Joseph's Day. For reading aloud to ages 5-7. Eight- to ten-year-olds can master it themselves.

> *Claire Nolte, in a review of "Song of the Swallows," in* Library Journal, *Vol. 74, April 15, 1949, p. 667.*

The swallows always appeared at the old Mission of Capistrano on St. Joseph's Day and Juan who lived nearby wondered how they could tell that from all others. This tender poetic story of the coming of springtime is touched by the kindliness of the good Fathers of the Mission as a little boy knew it. Lovely pictures in soft colors bring out the charm of the southern California landscape and the melody of the swallow song adds to the feeling of spring. (pp. 209-10)

> *Alice M. Jordan, in a review of "Song of the Swallows," in* The Horn Book Magazine, *Vol. XXV, No. 3, May-June, 1949, pp. 209-10.*

This is a remarkable book. It is a very gentle telling of a simple story. Juan, a small boy who lives in Capistrano sees the departure of the swallows in the fall, and builds his own garden so that in the spring some of the swallows will make their nests near his home. The text has a calm beauty that puts it a good distance above even the cleverest (in the contrived cleverness peculiar to these books) of other children's stories.

But the pictures are what make this a really fine book. The author has illustrated it in a magnificently appropriate manner.

> *A review of "Song of the Swallows," in* The Commonweal, *Vol. LI, No. 6, November 18, 1949, p. 189.*

Another beautiful book from [this] author-illustrator. . . . Again there is a great deal of charm and poetic sense of people and nature that text and pictures combine to convey. . . . A simple story, which sensitive, beauty loving children will enjoy. And—as before—the exquisite pictures in muted tones are in key with the text.

> *A review of "Song of the Swallows," in* Virginia Kirkus' Bookshop Service, *Vol. XIX, No. 19, October 1, 1951, p. 578.*

A Boat for Peppe (1950)

[Leo Politi] here portrays the life of the Sicilian fishermen of Monterey as seen through the eyes of a small boy. Peppe watches the fishing fleet sail out in the evening and wakes to see it returning at dawn. He remembers the time his father was almost lost in a big storm and so he is especially grateful to Saint Rosalia, patron saint of the fishermen. It is on Saint Rosalia's Day, a great festival in Monterey, that Peppe achieves his fondest wish, a tiny boat of his own which is blessed when the fishing boats are blessed.

This is the most satisfying of Mr. Politi's books. There is more substance in the text than in the earlier stories, and his beautifully designed pictures are the finest he has done.

> *Ellen Lewis Buell, "In Monterey," in* The

New York Times Book Review, *September 24, 1950, p. 30.*

Here is the coast of California where a group of Sicilian fishermen have lived for many, many years. In the same rich color printing as in his previous books Leo Politi shows us the little fishing village, the boats tossed about in a storm, the kindly people celebrating the name day of their patron saint, Saint Rosalia. . . . The storm that almost drowns Peppe's father gives drama to the story, but its value lies in the warm, happy relationship of the fishermen and their families and in the lovely drawings.

> *A review of "A Boat for Peppe," in* The Saturday Review of Literature, *Vol. XXXIII, No. 45, November 11, 1950, p. 37.*

The winner of the last Caldecott Medal again offers what may be called a children's travel book of California. . . . Now we go, with the small boy Peppe, to the Sicilian fishing village at Monterey. The slight plot of his wanting a boat and getting a toy boat is not important. There is sufficient story interest in Peppe's share in the life of this fascinating place.

In colorful, explicit pictures, we look down from the cliff to the bay and the fishing boats, look up at the town from the shore, mess around the wharf when a boat comes in, wait through a storm for father, share the procession for Saint Rosalia, and see the bishop bless the boats.

The delightful text gives us a happy feeling about Peppe and his family, and introduces two songs very pleasant for younger boys to know who love the sea.

For its text, color work, and lively sense of an unusual place, this is one of Mr. Politi's best books.

> *Louise S. Bechtel, in a review of "A Boat for Peppe," in* New York Herald Tribune Book Review, *November 12, 1950, p. 8.*

Little Leo (1951)

The author's solid, friendly illustrations tinted in luscious off-colors help tell the story of little Leo, who returned with his American family to a small village in Italy and brought in a touch of the American Wild West. All through the wonderful trip from California to New York by train, from New York to Italy by boat, and to San Matteo, his parents' village, by horse and buggy, Leo wore his beloved Indian suit and the sparkling head dress with feathers. Soon every boy in San Matteo wanted one too, and after the mothers had done some clever snipping and stitching, San Matteo was full of lively little Indians. The American nineties setting is not obtrusive and the Indian suit is a timeless attraction. Enchanting glimpses of life in a small Italian village.

> *A review of "Little Leo," in* Virginia Kirkus' Bookshop Service, *Vol. XIX, No. 19, October 1, 1951, p. 578.*

In this new picture book Leo Politi tells a true story of his own childhood. We see him first in California, where his father bought for him a new Indian suit. Then the whole family go to visit the grandparents in Italy, and Leo wears the Indian suit all along the way. In San Mateo all the little Italian boys envy Leo his Indian costume, so he teaches the mothers to make them for everyone—complete with dyed chicken feathers.

All this gives Leo Politi a wonderful background for his drawings. There is the double-page spread of the home in California; there is one of New York as the family passes through on their way to Italy; loveliest of all is the one of the little Italian village of San Mateo. Here the details are fascinating. There is dramatic contrast between the typical Italian village with its narrow, cobbled streets and stone houses and the procession of small boys in American Indian suits, led by little Leo.

The joyous, childlike atmosphere in this picture book should do a great deal to make American and Italian boys and girls feel mutually friendly.

> *A review of "Little Leo," in* The Saturday Review of Literature, *Vol. XXXIV, No. 45, November 10, 1951, p. 54.*

The soft colors, lovely double-page pictures of the Italian village, interiors and the children are things of beauty and joy. The best Politi book yet.

> *Phyllis Fenner, "Indians to Italy," in* The New York Times Book Review, *November 11, 1951, p. 40.*

From Little Leo, *written and illustrated by Leo Politi.*

[There] is no better example of two cultures mingling happily than in Leo Politi's ***Little Leo.*** The hero travels to Italy and there inducts Italian children into the joys of playing Indians, complete with feathers, war dances, and whoops. Five-year-old togetherness!

> *May Hill Arbuthnot, "Informational Books: 'Little Leo'," in her* Children's Reading in the Home, *Scott, Foresman and Company, 1969, p. 298.*

The Mission Bell   (1953)

We have had several good biographies of Father Junipero Serra for older boys and girls. Now Mr. Politi makes one that is both a handsome color picture book and a story for boys and girls of about seven to ten. It is welcome for the clarity of the story, longer than those in his other popular California books, and fine to read aloud. Father Serra becomes a very real, a lovable hero, both as a courageous pioneer and as a gentle missionary to the Indians. The big bell becomes a happy symbol. We hear briefly of the Royal Road, and the building of other missions. His death as an old man is beautifully handled for children.

The book opens longways, ten by eight inches, giving Mr. Politi room for some of those bird's-eye panoramas he does so well. Here are the dusky mountains and cactus, the Indian villages, the making of adobe bricks. The first mission is shown on a double-page spread, with the village about it, a picture full of clear detail which children of this age will love to pore over and tell about themselves. Loveliest of all pages is that of the arrival of the ship, with its wonderful spaces and colors, and the little welcoming figures on the shore. Alternate pages show details and action in two soft colors and in a pleasant variety of pattern. It will please Mr. Politi's admirers, besides its special audiences of Californians and Catholics.

> *A review of "The Mission Bell," in* New York Herald Tribune Book Review, *November 15, 1953, p. 14.*

The story of the exploration and development of California, begun because of Father Junipero Serra's dream of converting and civilizing the native Indians, is one of courage, faith in God and stubborn resistance to trial. These qualities have been high-lighted to a remarkable degree in this pictured story by Leo Politi. We feel the tranquil gentleness of Father Serra—his tender, compassionate love for the Indians, his unconcern for his own health and safety. Mr. Politi's beautiful pictures capture the quiet, restful simplicity of his story, reflecting it again and again in soft, rich colors.

> *Jeanne Massey, "Serra's Dream," in* The New York Times Book Review, *Part II, November 15, 1953, p. 36.*

The name of Father Junipero Serra has been held in reverence ever since long years ago he traveled on foot from Old Mexico to found missions up and down the coast of California. The story of the long hard journey, made by friars and Spanish soldiers across deserts and thru mountain passes; of Indians, fearful and friendly, met along the way;

of the building of the missions is told anew in this lovely picture book for readers a little older than those who enjoy the author's other books. Father Serra's gentle faith and love for all living beings pervade both story and illustrations.

> *Polly Goodwin, "Father Junipero Serra," in* Chicago Tribune, *December 27, 1953, p. 9.*

The Columbus Story (1955)

[The Columbus Story *was written by Alice Dalgliesh.*]

[**The Columbus Story**] includes those facts which are most impressive to the child who is hearing the story for the first time. [Alice Dalgliesh's] account of the first imagination-shaking voyage is dramatic, told with that repetition of phrases which is very pleasing to young children. For the illustrations Mr. Politi has used deep, almost somber tones, lighting them with flashes of brilliant color. The compositions are bold and the whole effect is one of great vigor, well suited to the subject.

> *Ellen Lewis Bull, "Admiral of the Ocean Sea," in* The New York Times Book Review, *October 9, 1955, p. 34.*

The Columbus Story is completely charming, with perhaps greater appeal for the very young child [than *Colum-*

From The Columbus Story, *written by Alice Dalgliesh. Illustrated by Leo Politi.*

bus by Ingri and Edgar Parin d'Aulaire], emphasizing as it does the adventurous aspect of Columbus' life and minimizing its darker side. Written simply but with a keen eye for the drama of events, it makes a fine book for reading aloud. And children will love the vivid, colorful pictures. Perhaps the most exciting is the double page spread of the three famous little ships at sea, a scene so alive one can almost feel the spray as the bows cut the waves.

> *A review of "The Columbus Story," in* Chicago Sunday Tribune Magazine of Books, *November 13, 1955, p. 14.*

Alice Dalgliesh is writing for very young children, a really "first" telling of the great discovery, to read aloud to ages five to eight. Never has she written with more insight into the imagination of this age, nor with more vivid delightful choice of facts and scenes that will interest them. Plenty of research lies behind the disarming simplicity of her story. . . . Mr. Politi's handsome bold pictures have the same simplicity, and suggest the high points of the tale as a small child might imagine them. It is a happy combination of author and artist feeling deeply about their material and able to transfer fact and emotion to the level of younger children. We could ask for more pictures, but in this book they only suggest; the fine text predominates.

> *Louise S. Bechtel, in a review of "The Columbus Story," in* New York Herald Tribune Book Review, *November 13, 1955, p. 3.*

[**The Columbus Story**] becomes a real picture book as interpreted by Leo Politi to whom the explorer has been a hero from childhood and who imparts to his drawings a boy's feeling of sailing with the boy as Miss Dalgliesh writes about him in a way to make him come alive as boy and man.

> *Anne Carroll Moore, in a review of "The Columbus Story," in* The Horn Book Magazine, *Vol. XXXI, No. 6, December, 1955, p. 444.*

The Butterflies Come (1957)

Handsome patterns, earthy ore-like colors and a decorative style which is childlike yet artful, add extra dimensions of distinction to the author's illustrations of this charming nature story about two children, Lucia and Stephen, who observe with wonder the seasonal migration of the Monarch butterflies returning to Monterey, California. This is a lyric little tale appropriate for children all over America, since the Monarch butterfly is found in all parts of our nation. Especially suitable for the summer reading bookshelf and for classroom use in primary Nature study and seasonal observation.

> *A review of "The Butterflies Come," in* Virginia Kirkus' Service, *Vol. XXV, No. 16, August 15, 1957, p. 582.*

There is a quiet loveliness about the story and in the muted colors of the illustrations. In some instances the size of the butterflies is out of proportion and may give small children a false impression. Otherwise, it will be a welcome addition to the picture-book shelves of all libraries.

Elsie T. Dobbins, in a review of "The Butterflies Come," in Junior Libraries, *Vol. 82, No. 18, October 15, 1957, p. 142.*

This is another of Leo Politi's "little miracles." It tells the story of the annual migration of the Monarch butterflies to the Monterey peninsula in California. . . . This is a book of gentle country scenes, and flashing color, interwoven with an essence of childlike wonder which only Politi can give to his children.

Rosemary E. Livesy, in a review of "The Butterflies Come," in The Saturday Review, *New York, Vol. XL, No. 46, November 16, 1957, p. 5.*

For centuries in the fall of the year golden clouds of monarch butterflies swarm down from Canada to the Monterey peninsula in California and cling to the butterfly trees all winter, until they fly away in the spring. Leo Politi tells the younger children of this in a deep yellow picture book. Within this inviting cover, both lovely and sturdy, the children can read of little Stephen and Lucia who live in Monterey and love the woodland animals, squirrel, skunk and deer. In late fall they are taken to see the butterflies clinging like dead clusters of leaves to the butterfly trees and rising, when startled, to flutter their wings which show all golden, orange in flight. Stephen and Lucia also take part in the Butterfly Festival with a parade of children in butterfly or flower costumes. Beautiful pictures by this gifted artist will certainly quicken his readers' interest: the title page, the double spreads showing dark woods brightened by the brilliant swarms, and other effective sketches, not the least of which are the white pages with just the text and the butterflies.

Margaret S. Libbey, in a review of "The Butterflies Come," in New York Herald Tribune Book Review, *November 17, 1957, p. 5.*

Saint Francis and the Animals (1959)

Leo Politi retells seven stories, including the famous sermon to the birds. These are very brief—a couple seem no more than fragments of tales—but the whole adds up to an illuminating introduction to the saint. The simplicity and reverence of the text are reflected in the subtly toned pictures, done in Mr. Politi's usual felicitous style.

Ellen Lewis Buell, "Man of Assisi," in The New York Times Book Review, *April 12, 1959, p. 42.*

We turn to [*St. Francis and The Animals*] with a delight [*How St. Francis Tamed the Wolf* by Elizabeth Rose and *The Apprentice and the Prize* by Janice Holland] do not arouse. Here is the living influence of the great Saint. Here Leo Politi has been inspired to keep in words and pictures, for six- to nine-year-olds, the simplicity and the depth of feeling of the "Fioretti." Bound in a gray cloth with a homespun look, suggestive of the robes of the famous "gray friars," the cover imprinted in brown, this picture book gives six brief anecdotes, including the story of the wolf of Gubbio. For each incident there are, either in full color or in browns and grays, some of the loveliest pictures

this artist has done. The old hill town of Assisi is shown beautifully, its cobbled streets, tile-roofed houses, its children and its deep blue sky and the gray hills beyond with their sentinel cypresses as well as the little birds, the lamb, the little brother hare, as they yearn toward Francis, while he, gentle and humble, posing not at all, simply looks down at them, showing with his hands his tender affection, and that something that Henry James calls "elementary nature itself like the sun and air." Neither in Elizabeth Orton Jones' pictures for the *Song of the Sun* nor in Valenti Angelo's for Clyde Robert Bulla's *Song of St. Francis* nor in H. B. Beatty's *St. Francis and the Wolf* do we feel such genuine understanding and affection. This spirit will surely communicate itself to the children, and it is one that any faith can accept.

Margaret Sherwood Libby, in a review of "St. Francis and the Animals," in New York Herald Tribune Book Review, *May 10, 1959, p. 4.*

It was inevitable that Saint Francis should one day be the subject of a book by Italian-born Leo Politi, for the artist's own love for children and animals, revealed in his picture books, has long endeared him to young readers. And what a beautiful book he now gives us. Simply and reverently, he tells seven stories which illustrate the saint's tenderness for birds and animals and show how they were drawn to him in return. And he illustrates them with some of his finest work. Pictures in full color and in brown and gray make the saint and his animal friends come alive against the lovely background of Assisi and the Italian countryside. A book for the whole family to cherish.

Polly Goodwin, in a review of "St. Francis and the Animals," in Chicago Sunday Tribune Magazine of Books, *May 24, 1959, p. 10.*

Moy Moy (1960)

Set in Los Angeles' Chinatown, this is the story of a little Chinese-American girl and her role in the celebration of the Chinese New Year. Moy Moy draws the reader into the color and excitement of the dragon parade, the exchange of gifts, and the music of the splendid traditional celebration. Leo Politi captures the mood of the event with beautifully decorative color illustrations which the reader will ponder over for the wealth of detail they contain. A superlatively tasteful Christmas gift selection.

A review of "Moy Moy," in Virginia Kirkus' Service, *Vol. XXVIII, No. 20, October 15, 1960, p. 903.*

Moy Moy [depicts] a Chinese-American community in Los Angeles. Done with obvious affection, this spectacularly illustrated book is one of Mr. Politi's best.

George A. Woods, in a review of "Moy Moy," in The New York Times Book Review, *Part II, November 13, 1960, p. 58.*

[*Moy Moy*] is the engaging story of Moy Moy, a small girl living on Chanking street in Los Angeles. She and her three older brothers look forward with high anticipation to the Chinese New Year celebrations—the first for Moy Moy—and pictures glowing with color reveal them to be marvelous, indeed. It is thru Moy Moy's enchanted eyes that we witness the festivities in which boys perform an amusing lion dance, hundreds of men, holding up a huge dragon, parade thru the streets, and fireworks go off in the public square. The wealth of detail in the illustrations is bound to keep young lookers happy for days.

> *Polly Goodwin, in a review of "Moy Moy," in* Chicago Sunday Tribune Magazine of Books, *December 11, 1960, p. 9.*

All Things Bright and Beautiful: A Hymn   (1962)

An illustrated hymn complete with music in praise of the beauties of nature bestowed by the Creator is an attractive gift item, especially for Christmas. There are no specific religious allusions—and the luminous pastel chalk pictures of children reveling in the outdoors are quite unusual in their glowing quality.

> *A review of "All Things Bright and Beautiful,"* in Virginia Kirkus' Service, *Vol. XXX, No. 19, October 1, 1962, p. 971.*

Rosa   (1963)

Richly applied earth colors and sober greens lit with sudden bursts of pinks and purples, oranges and blues—just to open **Rosa** is to be instantaneously carried back into the special Latin-American world this author-artist's books are opening up for the 4-8's. Huge double-spread pictures have a Gauguin air about them. They are full of tiny scenes that tell more about everyday in Mexico than many words—over there a boy is being fitted with a new sombrero, in the far corner children are buying ice-cream cones from a strange little cart with a striped top, and down here a man is driving a string of laden donkeys. The story is the charming one of little Rosa who wanted a doll for Christmas, but got something better, far better.

> *Pamela Marsh, in a review of "Rosa," in* The Christian Science Monitor, *November 14, 1963, p. 43.*

This very slight story with an overworked plot is more than compensated for by the author's colorful pictures of life in the village of San Felipe. Others in soft brown tones are equally effective. . . .

> *Patricia H. Allen, in a review of "Rosa," in* School Library Journal, *Vol. 10, No. 4, December, 1963, p. 42.*

A thoroughly Mexican atmosphere fills these sun-drenched paintings of children, adobe houses, dry cactus country, an *escuela,* and the rest of the village. . . . Slight and quiet in story; of interest particularly for its typically Politi pictures, half of them in rich, lovely colors.

> *Virginia Haviland, in a review of "Rosa," in* The Horn Book Magazine, *Vol. XL, No. 1, February, 1964, p. 50.*

From Juanita, *written and illustrated by Leo Politi.*

Lito and the Clown   (1964)

A little boy, his lost kitten and a carnival day in Mexico provide a simple and satisfying story for a master hand to illustrate. As the boy and his mother wander through the carnival crowds and stop to look at the attractions, the reader is introduced to the traditional features of a Mexican fun fair. Lito is never quite caught up in its pleasures because of the kitten who had been chased away by a dog, but a clown on stilts dramatically rescues her at the day's end. The eye-filling illustrations are drawn after the fashion of Mexican folk art in bold, carnival colors.

> *A review of "Lito and the Clown," in* Virginia Kirkus' Service, *Vol. XXXII, No. 19, October 1, 1964, p. 1008.*

The quantity of quality may have slipped, but there is still enough splendor on the publishers' shelves to make finding the right book happily bewildering. There is still far from a shortage of illustrations as masterful as Leo Politi's for his **Lito and the Clown.** Mr. Politi . . . has a marvelous way with atmosphere. Earth colors, cool greeny-yellows offsetting startling pinks and vivid greens drench his illustrations with a south-of-the-border feeling. He is one of those illustrators who delight the 4-8's with big detailed paintings meant for fingers and eyes to explore.

> *Pamela Marsh, in a review of "Lito and the*

Clown," in The Christian Science Monitor, *November 5, 1964, p. 2B.*

With his usual charm and grace Leo Politi creates another heartwarming story in ***Lito and the Clown***. A kitten is lost but the carnival clown on stilts proves to be a friend indeed to the sad little boy who lost the cat. The illustrations are the inimitable drawings that only Mr. Politi can create. Full page spreads and double page spreads create old world scenes for the modern child.

> *Sister Marie Pius, S.S.J., in a review of "Lito and the Clown," in* Catholic Library World, *Vol. 36, No. 5, January, 1965, p. 338.*

Piccolo's Prank   (1965)

Piccolo was a Bunker Hill (Los Angeles) monkey who lived and worked with an organ grinder. He showed a great dramatic flair when he did his act, but whenever he got loose, he would crawl under the nearest car to be a mechanic. He caused a neighborhood uproar, though, when he scampered below the Angel's Flight cable car during a stop. The simple but holding story is splendidly illustrated with a Gauguinesque use of color and perspective, and details that can be searched after for hours.

> *A review of "Piccolo's Prank," in* Virginia Kirkus' Service, *Vol. XXXIII, No. 18, September 15, 1965, p. 979.*

In Los Angeles there is a section known as Bunker Hill, where there are old Victorian "gingerbread" houses. It is reached by a cable car, and the little, steep railroad is called "Angel's Flight." Hearing that the old houses were to be demolished, Leo Politi was indignant and went out to make paintings of them. He also made this book, to which he added the story of an Italian organ grinder and Piccolo, his monkey. It has quite a plot, and children will like Piccolo. New York children will enjoy seeing what an organ grinder was like before Fiorello La Guardia banished all street organs with or without performing monkeys. It is too bad that, in keeping with the rest of the book, the title page was not more restrained.

> *Alice Dalgliesh, in a review of "Piccolo's Prank," in* Saturday Review, *Vol. XLVIII, No. 42, September 16, 1965, p. 59.*

Piccolo's Prank . . . is a slight story about Luigi the organgrinder and his monkey Piccolo. Written chiefly as an excuse to record a part of Los Angeles (Bunker Hill) soon to be demolished, it does that well, does less well as narrative.

> *Barbara Novak Doherty, in a review of "Piccolo's Prank," in* The New York Times Book Review, *November 7, 1965, p. 62.*

Mieko   (1969)

Satisfaction long postponed puts a strain on a picture book, and here the first postponement leads only to a second, indefinite deferment: Mieko, too young to be queen of the Ondo Parade the first time, is told, after she's pre-

pared and practiced all year, that she is still much too young to be considered. She had wanted to surprise her parents—"to live up to her name (Mieko = beautiful graceful girl) and to make them proud of her." Their assurance that they *are* proud of her "every day" may hearten Mieko (who is being consoled at the close) but it's a wan way to end a long, festive story. For although the colors are vivid to the point of being livid, the pageantry, and, to a lesser extent, the import of Japanese customs do come across.

> *A review of "Mieko," in* Kirkus Reviews, *Vol. XXXVII, No. 7, April 1, 1969, p. 370.*

Leo Politi's story of ***Mieko*** is a gentle, totally feminine one of a little American-Japanese girl who wanted so badly to be queen of the Ondo parade. His butterfly colored paintings are as graceful as ever Mieko could hope to be, but there is nothing wishy-washy about any phase of this masterly author-illustrator's work.

> *Pamela Marsh, "Come Back, Little Jabberwocky," in* The Christian Science Monitor, *May 1, 1969, p. B3.*

[***Mieko*** is] an enchantingly drawn picture story of Little Tokyo in Los Angeles. Little Mieko, in her second year of dancing in the Ondo Parade of Nisei Week, dreams of being chosen queen. She is too young, of course, but her devoted parents assure her that winning could not make them love her more. There is much of Japanese custom in the story and its richly colored scenes, and a winning child in graceful Mieko.

> *Virginia Haviland, "Catching Essences with Pictures and Words," in* Book World—The Washington Post, *May 4, 1969, p. 6.*

This is a gentle, not-too-sweet story in which Mr. Politi exhibits his skill at integrating unusual background material. . . . The theme of filial respect for parents is dominant but not overwhelming; Politi's illustrations are typically colorful, gay, and warm; and many Japanese customs are straightforwardly related and unobtrusively explained.

> *Ginger Brauer, in a review of "Mieko," in* School Library Journal, *Vol. 16, No. 7, March, 1970, p. 132.*

Emmet   (1971)

The theme of the mischievous animal that misbehaves, then receives approbation because he does a good deed, is not highly original, but it is pleasantly handled here in a simple story with lively pictures in color, many of the pages in subdued tones. . . . Slight but satisfying.

> *Zena Sutherland, in a review of "Emmet," in* Bulletin of the Center for Children's Books, *Vol. 25, No. 1, September, 1971, p. 14.*

Although he is only a mutt, Emmet is the most thoroughly charming of Mr. Winkel's collection of stray dogs. He has boundless energy and enough expression to find his way into any child's heart. Mr. Winkel's biggest problem is that Emmet is a troublemaker: he chases cats, takes stuffed toys from children, and repeatedly sneaks into the grocery store. One day, however, a potential disaster is averted by ever-alert Emmet: in true heroic fashion he foils a burglar/arsonist, and the townspeople love him for it. Politi's beautifully colored pictures are a delight to see; the text is good for telling; and the book as a whole might even be used to motivate reluctant readers.

> *Josette A. Boissé, in a review of "Emmet," in* School Library Journal, *Vol. 18, No. 1, September, 1971, p. 153.*

The Nicest Gift   (1973)

Leo Politi's depiction of a Chicano Christmas in *The Nicest Gift* is warmed over rather than heart warming: the flea-bitten boy loves dog/boy loses dog plot is given yet another airing. Blanco, Carlitos' white dog, backs away from a *payaso* wagon (toy clown that does somersaults) admired by his master and gets lost in the crowded market. Nary a cactus plant is left unturned by the bereft boy and his father, but the cur, who has meanwhile incurred such mild indignities as a dusty coat and trod on paw, is not found. The dog wanders into church where, at services the next morning, he is discovered and limps down the aisle toward a happy reunion. Politi's animated paintings of the Los Angeles Barrio in glowing shades of pink, orange, and yellow and fresh blues and greens plus the sure-fire combination of Christmas and missing canine are the stuff that sales are made of; however, the story, unlike the Mexican delicacies it describes, lacks spice. (p. 96)

> *Pamela D. Pollack, "No Cause for Celebration: Christmas Books 1973," in* School Library Journal, *Vol. 20, No. 2, October, 1973, pp. 95-7.*

A Christmas story that gives, both in the text and the illustrations, a colorful picture of the Barrio of East Los Angeles, a neighborhood pictured as "quaint and picturesque," with no hint of deprivation or segregation but a warm appreciation of family and community life. The story line is not strong or imaginative, but—given the perennial appeal of a child's love for his pet and the seasonal appeal of a Christmas ending—is durable enough to sustain interest, and the pictures have a colorful, busy attractiveness. Carlitos and his mother are in a toy store when his dog, frightened by a toy, runs off; Carlitos hunts for his dog sadly and in vain until—on Christmas morning—the little dog appears in church "stirring near the Nativity scene," a too-pat ending.

> *Zena Sutherland, in a review of "The Nicest Gift," in* Bulletin of the Center for Children's Books, *Vol. 27, No. 3, November, 1973, p. 49.*

[*The Nicest Gift*] is dedicated "to the boys and girls of East Los Angeles."

The lad Carlitos lives in the Barrio area, where many people speak Spanish and follow Mexican customs. Bright detailed drawings, mostly in line and watercolor, depict the life and townscapes of the Barrio. . . .

Speckled with Spanish terms and their translations, this big picture-story book is a genuine aid to interracial understanding.

> *Neil Millar, "Adrift in a Box of Biscuits and Other Animal Stories," in* The Christian Science Monitor, *November 7, 1973, p. B2.*

Perhaps the complete banality of Leo Politi's book *The Nicest Gift* is well suggested by its treacly title. Politi fails as both writer and illustrator. The setting of the book is in the barrio of East Los Angeles and never did a ghetto shine with such luster and greening of many plants and happy peasants. The book in general has an ingratiating tone of "sharing cultures" with cute translations of Spanish words for the gringo, obvious in the opening lines:

> On the outskirts of Los Angeles, in the neighborhood known as the Barrio, Carlitos lives with his father and mother. His dog Blanco lives there too. *Blanco* means "white" and Blanco is a white dog.

Later we learn that the children there "like to play *caballito.* Caballito means little horse."

Such fawning and social white-washing is unworthy of a winner of the Caldecott award and certainly of a writer who himself lives in a great city where the reading proficiency of ghetto children is in the range of 3%. Surely he should possess a greater social conscience than to indulge in the saccharine portrayal of his neighbors and his city. The book (almost majestically) misses the point of the special quality and problems of Los Angeles and is an anachronism in a day when children's books such as *Sounder* do confront racial realities head on. (pp. 217-18)

> *William Anderson, in a review of "The Nicest Gift," in* Children's Literature: Annual of the Modern Language Association Seminar on Children's Literature and The Children's Literature Association, *Vol. 3, 1974, pp. 217-18.*

Three Stalks of Corn   (1976)

Angelica Corrales lives in the old part of Pico Rivera, California, with her grandmother, an excellent cook who tells Angelica corn legends as she makes tortillas; gives the little girl her prized collection of corn husk dolls; and makes such delicacies for the fiesta that the school principal asks her to teach a class in Mexican cooking. Artist Politi's sentimental primitivism is less cloying here than in many of his picture books, and if Mrs. Corrales' early explanations to Angelica sound more like a travelogue than a kitchen conversation, her cooking class is just what it should be. There's no story at all but, with recipes for *enchilada* and *tacos fillings* (only) appended, this could make a sustaining social studies supplement. (A pity, though, that Grandmother's personal tortilla lesson doesn't come with it.)

> *A review of "Three Stalks of Corn," in* Kirkus Reviews, *Vol. XLIV, No. 8, April 15, 1976, p. 465.*

This easygoing story depends on a gentle exposition of Angelica's activities with her grandmother to provide a look at Chicano culture. . . . The illustrations are Politi's best—page-filling spreads, rich with earthy color, rhythmic line work, light and dark patterns, and zesty detail. At the end are recipes for tacos and enchiladas.

> *Denise M. Wilms, in a review of "Three Stalks of Corn," in* The Booklist, *Vol. 72, No. 20, June 15, 1976, p. 1468.*

An easily identifiable Politi book with the familiar bright, colorful, and busy pictures. Unfortunately, the illustrations are far more entertaining than the text: Politi is so intent on explaining the importance of corn in the Mexican culture that the slight story of Angelica and her grandmother comes across as didactic and disjointed. Furthermore, none of the beauty and symbolic meaning of corn to the Mexicans is conveyed. At most, readers will come away knowing how to prepare enchiladas and tacos—the recipes are on the last page.

> *Norma Feld, in a review of "Three Stalks of Corn," in* School Library Journal, *Vol. 23, No. 1, September, 1976, p. 104.*

Mr. Fong's Toy Shop   (1978)

All the children in Los Angeles' Chinatown are welcome in Mr. Fong's toy shop, where he shows them how to make traditional Chinese toys and tells them the legends associated with the mid-autumn Moon Festival. This year he also shows them how to make shadow puppets, and when the time for the festival arrives they cap the celebration—featuring special food, song and dance, and a Lantern Parade—with a performance that makes Mr. Fong proud. Just so, the thank-you poem they write for him makes him happy when he finds it on his way home. Politi doesn't single out any one child or cook up any problem

or uncertainty to give this the appearance of having a plot; clearly, the narrative is only a vehicle for the ethnic lore and customs—yet he doesn't give any exact instructions for making the shadow puppets or performing the other activities either. Still, there is so much good feeling and fun for everyone involved in Politi's celebration that, like his ***Three Stalks of Corn,*** it might motivate an early-grade social studies class to stage a festival of its own.

> *A review of "Mr. Fong's Toy Shop," in* Kirkus Reviews, *Vol. XLVI, No. 13, July 1, 1978, p. 688.*

Shadow puppetry is the subject of a somewhat staid description of how a toy-shop owner and a group of children in the Chinese quarter of Los Angeles prepare a play for the midautumn Moon Festival. . . . The black-and-white pictures are sharply delineated, as effective as the artist's soft-color work in his earlier picture books.

> *Virginia Haviland, in a review of "Mr. Fong's Toy Shop," in* The Horn Book Magazine, *Vol. LV, No. 5, October, 1978, p. 509.*

Black and white drawings have interesting textural variation but are less effective, on those pages that are visually dense, than Politi's work is in color. The story is adequately told but rather stiffly, with a weak story line and no characterization save for the depiction of Mr. Fong as a kindly man who enjoys children.

> *Zena Sutherland, in a review of "Mr. Fong's Toy Shop," in* Bulletin of the Center for Children's Books, *Vol. 32, No. 3, November, 1978, p. 50.*

William Sleator

1945–

American author of fiction, nonfiction, and picture books.

Major works include *Blackbriar* (1972), *House of Stairs* (1974), *Into the Dream* (1979), *The Green Futures of Tycho* (1981), *Interstellar Pig* (1984), *Singularity* (1985), *The Duplicate* (1988).

An imaginative and distinctive author for children and young adults, Sleator has received both popular and critical acclaim for his works, in particular his suspenseful plot development, believable protagonists, and skillful blending of the realistic and the bizarre. In his fiction Sleator explores a variety of genres—fantasy, supernatural, science fiction—elements of which are introduced into a recognizable social structure. Many of the unusual occurrences in his works are based on scientific knowledge; Sleator describes science as a useful field for his style of magical realism because it is both "the ultimate reality" and "as peculiar as anything I could dream up." Several critics assert that, despite occasional inaccuracies in his depiction of scientific phenomena, Sleator's stories are compelling and entertaining. In addition to a highly suspenseful plot and darkly humorous tone, Sleator is also praised for crafting realistic and endearing protagonists. His stories depict teenagers who are often reluctant, even unlikely heroes; they unintentionally become entangled in a conflict—with space aliens, with the CIA, with their siblings—which usually must be resolved through a journey, both physical and emotional. As Suzanne Rahn has suggested, the journey generally results in "the discovery of what was there all along—the beauty of the night sky, a brother's affection, the untapped potential in oneself."

Sleator began his career as an author for children through his work with artist and illustrator Blair Lent, an experience which the writer describes as "having the greatest effect on my career." The collaboration between the two men resulted in *The Angry Moon,* a picture book which retells a Tlingit Indian legend. Elements of magic and fantasy, depicted in this story, have remained an essential part of Sleator's writing throughout his career. *Blackbriar,* his first work for young adults, incorporates mystery and suspense into a tale about a haunted house in an isolated area of the English countryside. Some critics consider his next novel his most powerful work; *The House of Stairs* involves a group of teenagers who are trapped in a huge room containing a maze of staircases. They eventually realize that they are part of a mind-control experiment in which food is dispensed only after the subjects exhibit hostile behavior toward one another. Despite the assertion that it lacks subtlety, most reviewers concur that *The House of Stairs* is a compelling and suspenseful study of human behavior. In his later works Sleator explores such concepts as ESP and telekinesis (*Into the Dream*), black holes (*Singularity*), and time travel (*The Green Futures of Tycho*). In each work, regardless of the scientific proper-

ties depicted in its plot, Sleator focuses primarily on the personal relationships and emotional development of the characters. In both *Singularity* and *The Green Futures of Tycho,* he examines sibling rivalry; through their encounters with scientific phenomena and each other, the characters of these stories are able to clarify misconceptions and achieve reconciliation with their siblings. Sleator comments further on family relationships in *Interstellar Pig,* the story of sixteen-year-old Barney who drearily contemplates a boring summer at the beach with his insensitive parents. He is encouraged, however, when a fascinating trio of strangers moves in next door and invites Barney to join them in a board game called "Interstellar Pig." Barney eventually realizes that the strangers are actually hostile aliens adopting human disguises, and the board game is actually a life-or-death struggle for planetary survival. Sleator received a fellowship at the Bread Loaf Writers' Conference in 1969, in addition to garnering several awards throughout his career. *The Angry Moon* was designated a Caldecott Honor Book in 1971 and was also nominated for an American Book Award for best paperback picture book of 1981. Sleator also received a CRABbery Award for *Into the Dream* in 1980.

(See also *Something about the Author,* Vol. 3.)

GENERAL COMMENTARY

Ashley Darlington Grayson

[The following excerpt is from a review of the paperback editions of Singularity *and* Blackbriar.*]*

Both of these novels suffer the structural and stylistic problems of the author's previous title ***Interstellar Pig,*** but they continue the Sleator tradition of good cover copy. The concepts of the books fit the jackets perfectly.

Singularity is the better book and even ranks as an excellent YA novel. In the best tradition of Heinlein, Sleator blends teenage twin brothers, one plucky girl, and a time warp. After an "old dark house" beginning, the story focuses on the twins' investigation of a shed behind their late uncle's farmhouse. Insects and small animals seem to die inside if the door is closed. The suspense is well handled although the cover blurb gives away the fact that time is distorted inside. The tension between the brothers is what makes the book work. Both boys deduce from their observations but only one has the courage to apply his knowledge. Using the "twin paradox" to escape his tormentor, he earns the reader's respect for his commitment and willingness to sacrifice for his self-imposed goal.

As a science fiction novel, the book fails in the end because the technical problem postulated by the scientific premise simply disappears for no reason other than the hero's personal ordeal is concluded. Implied in this evaporation of the threat is the reality that the things that frighten us as children lose their power when we grow up. If you can ignore the plot problem, this is a nifty tale of an admirable young man taking control of his own life.

In ***Blackbriar*** the author is apparently trying to write a novel like *The Wicker Man,* or one of Dennis Wheatley's occult thrillers. The results are disappointing. Danny, at 15, has passed his O-Levels, the point at which most British lads will enter the work force, but he remains under the thumb of his guardian, a middle-aged woman named Philippa. Unfortunately for the reader, this woman natters constantly: at Danny, to her cat and about virtually nothing. So much of the book is used up by her static that Danny never gets to do anything. This is the book's first problem: it is dominated by an adult.

The two move into an old house in the English countryside and discover that none of the townspeople want to associate with them once they learn where the Londoners have settled. Blackbriar has a dark past and is shunned by the villagers. There are strange doings in the woods and weird people come and go both in and around Danny and Philippa's house, but the mystery remains so unformulated that we never develop a feeling of what is at stake. Danny never deduces anything, but eventually overhears tantalizing bits of local history. Even then he does nothing. He does meet a plucky girl, but the pair never develop any personal electricity; Danny and Lark interact only to advance the muddy mystery plot. This failure of the teen hero to establish meaningful relationships with other teens

is the book's second problem. Danny fails to earn any reader respect because he is thick as a post. He's standing around when he overhears clues. He's standing around when a virtually innocent bystander is kidnapped. He triumphs over the evil because he just happens to have a bit of stronger magic in his pocket. Finally, he stands around while the authorities arrive to clean up.

The story probably looked great as a concept but got out of control in manuscript. A year on the shelf and a complete rewrite would have helped. (pp. 41-2)

> *Ashley Darlington Grayson, "Two by Sleator,"*
> in Fantasy Review, *Vol. 9, No. 11, December, 1986, pp. 41-2.*

Margaret L. Daggett

Recently, I found my students were reading books I didn't know, dogeared paperbacks with covers picturing strange, unearthly creatures, humans frozen in fright, menacing technology, and assorted other bizarre things. I also learned that some of these were by William Sleator. Knowing little about Sleator's fiction, I set out to read and find out why students enjoyed these books. I'm glad I did, for now I can recommend Sleator to other students, and teachers.

Sleator first published ***Blackbriar,*** a novel whose eeriness comes from satanic worship and was written after an experience in England which Sleator called "bizarre." But other of his novels are built on equally unnerving subjects like the time travel in ***Green Futures of Tycho*** and ***Singularity,*** and intergalactic fight for survival in ***Interstellar Pig,*** environmental reconditioning in ***House of Stairs,*** and supernatural transference of talent in ***Fingers.***

These subjects take readers into dream-like fantasies of scientific fact to play out what might be the logical results. Do they frighten readers? What is so satisfying about reading the all too menacing possibilities of science and technology and the supernatural? How does Sleator win his audience? What does he give his readers?

There are several good reasons why Sleator's novels are worth reading, demanding as they often are.

First, understanding the role of the supernatural in our history gives insights into the supernatural's continual fascination for young people. Primitive people felt powerless before the forces of nature, and attempting to understand nature, they ascribed power to superhumans—the gods. As these people began to understand some of nature's laws, they grew less dependent on the gods and more in control of their own destinies.

This development can be seen in a microcosm as children grow up. They are at first powerless since they don't understand all the "laws" of life, but as they grow up and learn more about the causes and effects of life, they grow less dependent on adults and more capable of creating their own destinies.

Growing up and mastering the world is a basic appeal of YA books, but the supernatural adventure story allows readers to identify with a protagonist who's gone one step farther. This hero has seen through the facade of adult worries and goals. This hero reaches for a greater understanding of life and power over life. This hero wants to add to humanity's understanding of nature's laws, thereby making humanity even greater.

In *Interstellar Pig,* Barney's parents desire for a tan takes them to the beach even though Barney's skin burns so easily that he must spend the vacation inside. His parents are concerned about social status and important friends. While his parents are sailing, Barney is pulled into a game of incredible strategies played with beings from other galaxies. He is, of course, the only youngster of any species involved. He barely survives the game, but in doing so he saves our planet through his logic and masterful ability to use whatever resources are at hand. As the aliens race through hyperspace to continue the game, they berate Barney. He has become a symbol of humanity's superiority because he won by choosing not to continue. Young readers identify with him, seeing his parents as involved with trivia while Barney is forced to deal by himself with problems of great importance. What a feeling of mastery to vicariously outwit aliens who have so many technological advances. Barney is a vote of confidence in the future, for his generation will be more capable than his father's. But Barney is no superhuman. He even remembers to sweep up the mess created by the dead cells of the aliens he fought in his home.

Sleator's novels let YAs test themselves to determine vicariously what sorts of controls they might exercise if they were faced with an impossible situation.

Imagine a room so large that without light, the bottom and top and sides cannot be seen. The room is filled with staircases without rails. The stairs turn sharply from small landings to connect over the void by narrow bridges. The stairs go up, down, across, and nowhere. Within this *House of Stairs,* Sleator leaves five teenage, orphaned strangers who must learn to survive. Readers cannot help but see that Sleator's fictional world has much in common with their daily worlds. Can anyone be trusted? How can we survive in a world that seems to go everywhere, and nowhere?

The instinct to survive is strong and primitive among the five young people. To eat, they learn to cooperate in a strange dance to activate a machine which capriciously feeds them, but the machine begins to reshape their personalities by rewarding cruelties to one another with food. And the environment is void of any other stimulus than the need to eat. So the taunting, scheming, abusive treatment they receive reminds readers of their hungering for attention and affection.

Lola and Peter become aware of the reconditioning pattern and choose to starve rather than become cruel to the others. Just before it's too late, all five are removed from the room, and they learn that they have been part of a laboratory experiment. Sleator has involved readers in a story that has just enough reality to be possible and frightening. And readers will learn something about themselves and what they can take—or will allow themselves to do.

Perhaps the greatest appeal of Sleator's novels is the human and believable motivation of his characters. That's especially true in the relationships between siblings in *Green Futures of Tycho, Singularity,* and *Fingers.*

The youngest of four children and the one with the least direction in life, Tycho is disorganized and picked on. When he discovers that time travel is possible with his silver egg, he uses it to frustrate and taunt and frighten his siblings. But it is his love for his family that ultimately makes him reject the ugly, vile, but powerful future that lies ahead, and he risks death to destroy the egg.

In *Singularity,* Sleator explores the brooding rivalry between sixteen-year-old twins. Visiting their late uncle's farm, Barry and Harry discover a time warp and a singularity (the opposite of a black hole, a singularity sends alien things to earth). Barry has been the dominant brother, rejecting and ridiculing Harry. But Harry suddenly sees how he can use the singularity to age a year over night and become Barry's older, bigger, and more mature brother.

Sleator brilliantly handles Harry's sudden change. Initially there is Barry's grief, for his twin is now dead, or so it seems. What should have been Harry's triumph now makes him wonder. Perhaps Barry had not wanted to get rid of Harry. Finally, a new and better relationship comes out of the confusion, and both brothers recognize that they had both been "mistaken about a lot of things and had never known it until now."

The possibility (or certainty?) of supernatural powers is combined with sibling rivalry in *Fingers.* Once a child prodigy at the piano, Humphrey has become a proficient but mechanical performer. To boost his waning audience appeal, his parents hit upon a plan. His older brother, Sam, will compose music, attribute it to dictation from the legendary Laszlo Magyar, and trick Humphrey into believing the music had come during a trance. The media love the mystery, and the music is a success, but then mysterious and unexplainable things begin to happen, and Sam wonders if he isn't haunted.

In the midst of all the spectral goings-on and a good deal of humor, Sam and Humphrey learn about themselves and about each other. Manipulated by their parents, they have been jealous of each other, but the musical fraud brings them together to see their interdependence and caring for each other. Out of all that happens, they find the strength to break loose from parental control.

Sleator succeeds with adolescents because he blends enough scientific realities with supernatural possibilities to tantalize the mind and imagination. Readers feel refreshed after the intellectual and emotional challenges in Sleator's novels. His adventures are set within a recognizable or believable social structure. He sets us in a reality and helps us stretch our imaginations. (pp. 93-4)

> Margaret L. Daggett, "Recommended: William Sleator," in English Journal, Vol. 76, No. 3, March, 1987, pp. 93-4.

Bryan Jenkins

[*The following excerpt is from a review of* The Boy Who Reversed Himself *and* House of Stairs.]

Scientific ideas used in a way suggesting that the American author is poking fun at the stereotyping of SF. *House of Stairs* presents a Kafka-esque scene: five children, confined in a mysterious construction of stairs to nowhere, must learn to respond to stimuli of light and sound for their food. The idea of conditioning, and the symbolism of the stairs, make for an intriguing story—spoilt by a final chapter of explanation: better to be left with an ambiguous ending. *The Boy Who Reversed Himself* is more skilfully constructed and equally imaginative. The author supposes that the universe holds worlds in any number of dimensions. Laura and Peter are caught in the fourth dimension—a dream-like world, with everything backwards, which is absolutely convincing in its grotesqueness. Sleator cleverly lets the humour of the children's situation emerge while the terror of their horrendous adventures keeps us reading.

> *Bryan Jenkins, in a review of "The Boy Who Reversed Himself" and "House of Stairs", in* The Signal Selection of Children's Books, 1988, *The Thimble Press, 1989, p. 43.*

TITLE COMMENTARY

The Angry Moon (1970)

It's not every day that your reviewer gets the chance to use the adjective *strong* about a picture book, but then books like *The Angry Moon* appear only once in a blue moon. Blair Lent, who has already created many strong (and beautiful) books, tops himself with this one, perhaps because William Sleator gave him such a strong story to illustrate. This is a Tlingit Indian legend of a girl who is spirited away because she laughed at the moon, and of a boy who rescues her. There's real plot here. There is terror here and a villain and a hero and magic. This is a rare one.

> *A review of "The Angry Moon," in* Publishers Weekly, *Vol. 198, No. 21, November 23, 1970, p. 39.*

A highly successful adaptation and visualization of a Tlingit Indian tale. Lapowinsa is spirited away for daring to laugh at the Moon's face. Her friend, Lupan, makes use of a ladder of arrows to climb to the sky country and, with the magical aids provided by an old grandmother there, rescues Lapowinsa. A somewhat more difficult version of this story ("The Arrow Chain") may be found in *The Man in the Moon: Sky Tales from Many Lands* (Holt, 1969) by Alta Jablow and Carl Withers. However, Blair Lent's richly colored paintings, derived from Tlingit Indian designs, and the simple way the tale is told here, make this version a natural for story hour.

> *Ann D. Schweibish, in a review of "The Angry Moon," in* School Library Journal, *Vol. 17, No. 6, February, 1971, p. 50.*

An adaptation of a legend of the Tlingit Indians of Alaska, the writing simple and staccato; the illustrations combine colorful, sometimes misty backgrounds and details of costumes or totems that are based on Tlingit designs . . . An attractive book and an interesting legend useful for story-telling, but rather stilted when read aloud.

> *Zena Sutherland, in a review of "The Angry Moon," in* Bulletin of the Center for Children's Books, *Vol. 24, No. 9, May, 1971, p. 145.*

Blackbriar (1972)

Blackbriar is perfectly eerie—the isolated country cottage has a secret passageway, an unsavory past (it was used as a pesthouse during the 17th century plague), an eccentric neighbor (Lord Harleigh who's overheard plotting with the village librarian), and even a resident ghost with the delightful name of Mary Peachy. Philippa and her Siamese cat Islington both seem distinctly unnerved by the murky ambience, but her young ward Danny Chilton finds the promise of adventure analeptic (Could it be that Mary Peachy's spirit has a benevolent effect on him, or was it just that first kiss shared with mettlesome Lark Hovington down among the 17th century skeletons?). In any event, when the night of the full moon comes, and the bonfires are burning on the tumuli, and the naked silhouettes are dancing, and Philippa and Islington have been kidnapped, Danny is ready to act. Bolt the cellar door; watch your cat closely for personality changes, and follow him—vicariously.

> *A review of "Blackbriar," in* Kirkus Reviews, *Vol. XV, No. 8, April 15, 1972, p. 486.*

The background of the story is English in only a general sort of way, and the language wisely avoids leaning too much on British phraseology; the effectiveness of the story, however, lies in its characterization and in its narrative skill. Combined with Danny's growing awareness of himself as an individual are his adventures in discovering the various secrets of the house; and the suspense and the mystery are powerfully suggested in the severely ominous black-and-white illustrations [by Blair Lent].

> *Paul Heins, in a review of "Blackbriar," in* The Horn Book Magazine, *Vol. XLVIII, No. 4, August, 1972, p. 378.*

Run (1973)

Sleator did so well with the medieval haunted house *Blackbriar* that it's a shame to see him fumble in an attempt to inject some contemporary relevance into a well paced suspense melodrama. Fifteen year-old Lillian, scared by the prospect of spending a few days alone in her family's isolated summer house, manages to convince two young cyclists who are caught in a rainstorm to stay overnight. While one of the boys, Mark, frets about moving on and Lillian and Jerry enjoy cooking lunch and tasting a bottle of wine snitched from the cellar, evidence that the house is being watched begins to accumulate—a missing radio, a mysterious shape in the bushes, a midnight intruder who apologizes for scaring Lillian. So far, so good. But when the trio does surprise the stranger in the act of stealing an electric saw, the thief returns and launches into a remorseful confession—he's "not a real criminal at all," just an addict trying to support a 150 dollar a day habit. Without denying that addicts are victims, this particular junkie's irregular method of operation (why does he steal one item at a time, and how does he dispose of them?) and his immediate rapport with the three young people seems farfetched ("you're beautiful," he tells them, when he learns that they haven't reported their suspicions to the police). And his death minutes later at the hands of a suburban lynch mob turns the thief into a martyr, the neighboring property owners into hysterical murderers, and leaves the children filled with regret that they didn't call the kindly police chief at the first sign of trouble. In the rush towards a dramatic ending, somehow an innocuous message about irrational fears and sympathy for the underdog turn into a liberal guilt fantasy, and Sleator's inability to give speech or substance to non-middle class characters—whether junkie or cop—becomes painfully obvious. (pp. 397-98)

> *A review of "Run," in* Kirkus Reviews, *Vol. XLI, No. 7, April 1, 1973, pp. 397-98.*

Heavy-handed symbolism underscores the action: the plight of the herring, attacked by gulls and humans in their upstream spawning run, parallels that of vulnerable individuals who are hounded by respectable society. The three teenage characters (with the possible exception of Mark, whose surliness could be a cover-up for his sensitivity) are unappealing and seem much younger than their given ages. The story's suspenseful beginning deteriorates into a series of encounters between adversaries, the only purpose of which is to drive home the theme of the strong victimizing the weak. Engaging neither readers' sympathy nor interest, this is a disappointment after Sleator's excellent *Blackbriar.*

> *Linda R. Silver, in a review of "Run," in* School Library Journal, *Vol. 20, No. 3, November, 1973, p. 55.*

House of Stairs (1974)

Forceful sci fi based on Skinnerian precepts that will have readers hanging by the skin of their teeth. Deprived of freedom, dignity, and comfort and with no idea why they're there, five 16-year-old orphans are interned in a labyrinth of interlocking staircases and intermittently fed from a machine with a flashing light. Peter is drawn into a dream world and becomes insensible to the surroundings; Oliver, whose surface charm is chipped away by shrewd, belligerent Lola, controls submissive Abigail with alternate cuddles and cuffs; Blossom, well-born and obese, victimizes the captives with her vindicativeness. Lola surmises that the food is a pay off for inflicting pain and tries to involve the others in a hunger strike. This attempt to beat the system is nipped in the bud by Blossom, but Lola's rebellion is unexpectedly abetted by the now all but comatose Peter whom she rouses and reconditions. Saved from starvation by the scientists who secretly set it all up, Lola and Peter are sent to a camp for misfits while the three who turned savage are deemed successes. The post-Watergate propagandizing (the President was in on the experiment which was supposed to turn out operatives who would "follow unquestioningly any order given to them" and not get caught) will not be too obvious for teens, nor

will they be put off by the graphic violence and animalistic acts in what is primarily an intensely suspenseful page-turner par excellence.

> *Pamela D. Pollack, in a review of "House of Stairs," in* School Library Journal, *Vol. 20, No. 7, March, 1974, p. 120.*

A riveting suspense novel with an anti-behaviorist message that works, despite the lack of subtlety or originality, because it emerges only slowly from the chilling events . . . *House of Stairs* is really more a scenario than a novel and as a scenario it has its vulnerable links—for example, Lola's instinctive use of positive reinforcement to strengthen Peter's resolve and her assertion to the doctor later that rewards work better than punishments begs the moral/political question of mind control *per se.* But Sleator does a masterly job of differentiating and developing his five human subjects, compelling readers to share in the process of their enlightenment, and communicating his ominous conjecture.

> *A review of "House of Stairs," in* Kirkus Reviews, *Vol. XLII, No. 8, April 15, 1974, p. 434.*

[*House of Stairs*] is an extremely interesting, uncomfortable novel . . . Mr. Sleator is saying some deep things here about privacy and courage and the rights of the individual; he's not a bit simplistic either. One small criticism—that his children seem more like 12 or 13 than 16—is offset by the sheer power and readability of his unusual and haunting story.

> *A review of "House of Stairs," in* Publishers Weekly, *Vol. 205, No. 18, May 6, 1974, p. 68.*

How far one fights for one's own survival is the theme of William Sleator's Kafka-like novel, *House of Stairs.* In a bare, white, antiseptic environment, filled only with stairs—like an Escher print come alive—five teenagers, all sixteen years old, and all without homes or families, are subjected to a terrifying experiment for control of their minds. What will they do to get food? Played out in this narrow setting—a closed society not unlike a barbaric school situation—and in a brief time span, the story is one of the most brutal in science fiction, all the more sickeningly compelling because of its finely controlled, stark writing. (p. 142)

> *Sheila A. Egoff, "Science Fiction," in her* Thursday's Child: Trends and Patterns in Contemporary Children's Literature, *American Library Association, 1981, pp. 130-58.*

Among the Dolls (1975)

The antique dollhouse Vicky's parents buy for her tenth birthday—instead of the hoped-for ten-speed bike—distresses her even more when she finds herself inside it, the prisoner and intended slave of the contentious doll family whose nasty dispositions she herself has programmed in her unhappy play sessions. Escape is effected (with the help of a new baby doll she had added to the family) when Vicky discovers that her captives too have a dollhouse—a miniature replica of her own home and family through which they manipulate the humans. An ingenious, teasing little twist on behavior control, with just enough psychological furnishing to materialize the spooky fascination of old dollhouses.

> *A review of "Among the Dolls," in* Kirkus Reviews, *Vol. XLIII, No. 20, October 15, 1975, p. 1186.*

The author of the brilliant and bone-chilling *House of Stairs* tells another macabre story. Its mood is enhanced immeasurably by the artistry of [illustrator Trina Schart] Hyman. . . . This a real cliff-hanger, utterly convincing, but not recommended for timid boys or girls.

> *A review of "Among the Dolls," in* Publishers Weekly, *Vol. 208, No. 16, October 20, 1975, p. 74.*

A fast-paced, chilling fantasy of three telescoped worlds that affect each other in a vicious cycle. . . . The only confusion in Sleator's calculations seems to be that Vicky's afternoon-to-dawn absence goes unnoticed by her parents. Otherwise, the plot is airtight, the suspense clutching, the doll personalities real, and the implications scary.

> *Brad Hooper, in a review of "Among the Dolls," in* The Booklist, *Vol. 72, No. 9, January 1, 1976, p. 628.*

The fantasy is adequately resolved and the role-reversal and world-within-a-world concept are presented with enough suspense and sense of horror to be satisfyingly chilling, but the world of the dollhouse has a bleak emptiness that is not quite convincing, nor is the manipulation of parental attitudes by the dolls.

> *Zena Sutherland, in a review of "Among the Dolls," in* Bulletin of the Center for Children's Books, *Vol. 29, No. 7, March, 1976, p. 118.*

Into the Dream (1979)

An overpowering sense of terror builds each night as Paul experiences a recurring dream in which a small figure in white dashes toward a floating object aglow in a field. To his amazement, he discovers that classmate Francine Gill is not only partner to the same nightmare but shares his extrasensory perceptions (derived from contact with a UFO). Realizing they are nocturnal witnesses to an impending disaster, the two use clues from their dreams, along with some detective work, to find the small figure in white. Their search leads them to four-year-old Noah, a young boy whose telepathic and psychokinetic abilities have made him the kidnap-target of men who plan to exploit his talents. Aided by Noah's dog, Cookie, perpetrator of the dreams, the three out-race the strangers. Paul and Noah take refuge in a ferris wheel only to discover they are now playing out in reality the terrifying elements of the dream. Working together through their special talents, they are able to reach safety and ensure Noah's future security. Tightly woven suspense and an ingenious, totally involving plot line (excepting the dog's ability to predict the future and instill the dreams in Paul and Fran-

cine's heads, which nudges disbelief) make this a thriller of top-notch quality.

> *Barbara Elleman, in a review of "Into the Dream," in* Booklist, *Vol. 75, No. 2, February 15, 1979, p. 936.*

"Maybe we should call the police," Paul suggests. "And tell them what? That we're getting messages from a dog?" says Francine. Paul and Francine are seventh-grade classmates thrown together because they're both experiencing the same terrifying recurrent dream. It turns out too that they can communicate without words. But how so? Well, they trace their common experience to a Nevada motel-stay with divorcing mothers four years earlier, when a pregnant woman, there with her pregnant dog, encountered a flying saucer in the motel parking lot. Now the two offspring have even stronger ESP than Paul and Francine; Noah, the human child, also has psychokinetic powers, and Cookie, the dog, can see the future. That's why the two strange men are following all the children. They want Noah for their own ends (CIA skulduggery) and Paul and Francine must save him. They do, after the obligatory chase—through an amusement park, no less—that ends with Paul and Noah on a broken Ferris-wheel seat which Noah, to save them from crashing, sends floating off into the air and then gently down for a landing. "I expect that from now on you'll be dealing with scientists and doctors instead of secret agents," says the TV newsman who happened to be on the spot with cameras. Far-fetched, but fast-paced—kids with a taste for psi-fi fantasy won't stop to look down. (pp. 263-64)

> *A review of "Into the Dream," in* Kirkus Reviews, *Vol. XLVII, March 1, 1979, pp. 263-64.*

Once, Said Darlene (1979)

"Darlene liked to make up stories." But the ones she tells here are mostly just descriptions of her plucky behavior in unlikely places: on a boat in the jungle, hitting snakes with her umbrella; in a tent in the desert, crushing bugs; on a ship in a storm, hitting a pirate with her telescope; and in a castle, where she lived as a princess with magic animals. The other kids get fed up with Darlene for making up such stories, but when one little boy believes her, they're both rewarded—by being transported back to Darlene's sure-enough magic castle. "I made up too many stories. So the magician said I had to go away. I had to go to your world. I had to tell the truth. And I could only come back when one person believed me." The message is clearly pro-fantasy, but Sleator's sentences are thumpingly prosaic—and his concocted surprise ending rings no truer than Darlene's stories.

> *A review of "Once, Said Darlene," in* Kirkus Reviews, *Vol. XLVII, No. 5, March 1, 1979, p. 262.*

At age five or so, Darlene has had a checkered past, according to her. She relates endless stories about when she was a princess, living in a glittering palace and entertained often by a magician. Darlene always ends by saying sadly that she can't tell what happened then. The neighborhood kids get fed up with the girl's whoppers and declare she can't play with them any more unless she confesses to lying. But one boy, Peter, believes Darlene and is amazed to find himself transported to the palace of Princess Darlene where he finds out what happened because of the magician. A [Dutton] Fat Cat book for beginners, this should hold their attention and help them read better. Sleator's "whopper" is a beauty, full of merry suspense. Each incident is enhanced by [illustrator Steven] Kellogg's charming pictures of real, appealing children and the contrasting scenes in fantasy land.

> *Jean F. Mercier, in a review of "Once, Said Darlene," in* Publishers Weekly, *Vol. 215, No. 11, March 12, 1979, p. 77.*

Sleator brings new light to the beginning-to-read bookshelf with a wholly original tale of a girl who tells too many stories. At first, her friends are intrigued by Darlene's fantastic fables of desert safaris and talking animals, but their interest turns to suspicion and then to anger as Darlene insists her stories are true. Finally, all but Peter chorus " . . . we will not be your friends," and strange, sad Darlene seems even sadder. But the next instant finds Peter transported to a magical land where he discovers Princess Darlene, reunited with her talking beasts. "I made up too many stories," she tells Peter. "The bad magician . . . said . . . I had to go to your world . . . [until] one person believed me." For readers, the story may well begin here, but they will have to speculate for themselves on what happens after Peter and Darlene fly up to her castle in the sky. Meanwhile, Sleator's language is full of color, the story is artfully constructed, and Kellogg's pictures brimful of his best humor and imagination.

> *Judith Goldberger, in a review of "Once, Said Darlene," in* Booklist, *Vol. 75, No. 18, May 15, 1979, p. 1445.*

The Green Futures of Tycho (1981)

An 11 year old digging a garden unearths an egg-shaped time-travel device planted by aliens during Earth's Paleozoic Era. Tycho Tithonus is the beleagured youngest in a contemporary family like Cresswell's Bagthorpes (Macmillan)—except devoid of their eccentric charm. Tyrannized by his prying, competitive siblings—all named for the famous personages they're meant to emulate—Tycho uses the egg to escape into the future. His first shock is finding out "the future" isn't fixed; more shocking still, his alternate destinies grow increasingly sinister. In one, he's a sleazy, pathetic purveyor of "Lunar Entertainments"; in the next he's used his knowledge of the future for fraudulent ends and engineered his siblings' ruin; in the last he's a deranged puppet of the aliens, holding his whole family in thrall. A suspenseful confrontation with this monstrous future self, who's been manipulating the past all along, undoes the damage in the present and buries the aliens' device back in the primordial ooze. Sleator's expert blend of future and horror fiction is unusually stark, dark and intriguing; and the breakneck pace he sets never falters.

> *Pamela D. Pollack, in a review of "The Green Futures of Tycho," in* School Library Journal, *Vol. 27, No. 8, April, 1981, p. 133.*

Sleator manipulates the family conflicts and their nightmare transformations expertly—building the ideas through the page-turning action, weaving in subtle variations on the dominant theme, and turning to his own nimble advantage those built-in paradoxes of the time-travel concept which often weaken similar stories.

> *A review of "The Green Futures of Tycho," in* Kirkus Reviews, *Vol. XLIX, No. 12, June 15, 1981, p. 740.*

The development of the story involving the youngest child of a gifted and cultivated but somewhat eccentric family receives its impetus from a concept drawn from science fiction, and the combination of logic and horror gives the telling a Poe-like quality. In the long run, however, the moral significance of the boy's experiences breaks through the aura of fantasy that encases the narrative, and the author has cogently shown how Tycho's realization of the monstrous possibilities of evil ultimately leads to his rejection of it.

> *Paul Heins, in a review of "The Green Futures of Tycho," in* The Horn Book Magazine, *Vol. LVII, No. 4, August, 1981, p. 426.*

[*The Green Futures of Tycho* is] a new variant of an old science fiction concept, and it will probably appeal to sf buffs, but it is not as successful as some of Sleator's other fanciful writing, in part because it is structurally repetitive, in part because the bitter nastiness of the children seems overdrawn and without provocation.

> *Zena Sutherland, in a review of "The Green Futures of Tycho," in* Bulletin of the Center for Children's Books, *Vol. 35, No. 3, November, 1981, p. 58.*

That's Silly (1981)

For Tom, pretending is the spice of life; it's especially useful when you're in a fix. His practical friend Rachel says, "That's silly"; but when Rachel finds a doll's head that turns out to have real magic in it, both friends end up wiser. A wild adventure later, complete with a harrowing hot-air-balloon ride, the two children know the value—and the limitations—of pretending. And it makes them all the more ready for their next escapade, foreshadowed by Rachel's discovery of a doll's hand on the ground. The subject is close to children's hearts, the plot has substance, and characters are convincing.

> *Judith Goldberger, in a review of "That's Silly," in* Booklist, *Vol. 77, No. 20, June 15, 1981, p. 1350.*

The power of pretending—or is it magic?—is ingeniously but mechanically developed in the interplay between Tony, who likes to pretend, and pragmatic Rachel, who scoffs at his make-believe. She scoffs when Tom finds a doll's head and pretends it's magic, but then by wishing on it the children land inside Rachel's scary picture and then go flying on a scarier balloon ride. Rachel says that this proves the doll's head is actually magic; but when "pretending" they know how to operate it brings the balloon down safely in Rachel's back yard, she concedes that sometimes pretending can help you. Sleator's teasing questions and magic/pretending distinction take this a step beyond the usual confrontation between magic *or* pretending and skepticism. However, without the imagined life that wins assent for magic, pretending, or realistic fiction, it might strike children as an arid sort of distinction. (pp. 738-39)

> *A review of "That's Silly," in* Kirkus Reviews, *Vol. XLIX, No. 12, June 15, 1981, pp. 738-39.*

The conflation of pretend and magic here is confusing, and the attempt at an easy-reading fantasy/adventure emerges as flat and unimaginative. . . . A wish-granting token is of enduring allure, but this is a pretty poor vehicle for carrying it anywhere.

> *Nancy Palmer, in a review of "That's Silly," in* School Library Journal, *Vol. 28, No. 6, February, 1982, p. 71.*

Fingers (1983)

Mood changes quickly in Sleator's downright bizarre tale, which begins with a music box hoax and ends up with a creepy foray into the paranormal. To help keep Humphrey, his younger stepbrother (and family meal ticket), from fading into musical oblivion, 18-year-old Sam agrees to use his composing talents to fool his sibling and concert audiences into believing nineteenth-century pianist Laszlo Magyar's ghostly presence is filtering new compositions across Humphrey's keyboard and through his none-too-agile adolescent mind. The gimmick seems to work amazingly well, too—that is, until a strange old man who obviously knows some of what's going on shows up, and Sam discovers that pieces of Magyar's unsettling personal past are surfacing as part of the pianist's musical "reincarnation." None of Sleator's characters are particularly winning types. Humphrey is a dolt, and the boys' greedy parents are the villains with Sam, the novel's narrator, running close behind. Ultimately though, that really doesn't matter because Sleator's plot is so cleverly offbeat—weird coincidences, fore-shadowings, and all—and its suspense so well managed.

> *Stephanie Zvirin, in a review of "Fingers," in* Booklist, *Vol. 80, No. 3, October, 1983, p. 234.*

Fingers is a fast-moving mystery with supernatural elements. . . . Sam is a well-rounded and sympathetic narrator who is convincing both in his lifelong jealousy of Humphrey and in his growing realization that he nonetheless cares for his brother and wants to protect him from exploitation. The characterization of [their mother] Bridget is sometimes too exaggerated to be credible, but the book is highly suspenseful, with effective touches of horror and should please young adult mystery fans.

> *Anita C. Wilson, in a review of "Fingers," in* School Library Journal, *Vol. 30, No. 2, October, 1983, p. 173.*

Sam's mother concocts an impossible scheme to rescue younger son Humphrey's musical career, and the unlikely plan seems to work in this loony, unstrained narrative. Humphrey wakes up believing he has become the medium for deceased gypsy pianist/composer Laszlo Magyar; his family describes his strange behavior the night before and a new score is in his hand. What's more, even music specialists in the audience of his otherwise lackluster concert acknowledge both the Magyar style in the piece and Humphrey's higher artistry in the playing. Suddenly, he's in demand, playing Milan, Geneva, Vienna. In truth, though, his family is tricking him: Sam actually writes the compositions and their mother drugs Humphrey with Seconal so he won't remember the night before. But then weird things happen that also happened to Magyar, and a strange old man appears at the end of each performance, correcting the composition. Sleator has his own choice parody here as Sam takes his inspiration from hotel radiator noises and reads in a biography of Magyar hilarious gypsy anecdotes. But their situation rests on harsher realities and includes some sad truths of family life. Jealousy and other feelings force San to spill the beans to increasingly uppity Humphrey—who really suffers from the news—yet that stage mother still wants the show to go on. Sam tells it all with such brisk good humor that though the parents are manipulative the story is not. Even readers unfamiliar with music terms and room service menus can follow the notes and savor the gypsy in these souls.

> *A review of "Fingers," in* Kirkus Reviews, *Vol. LI, No. 21, November 1, 1983, p. J-208.*

The plot is a "Lady or the Tiger"-esque web of spiritualism, possession and/or ESP. Although the reader understands *why* the characters are as they are, they aren't very likable, with the possible exception of the mysterious old man, and it's hard to be very concerned about any of them. The plot gives no sense of understanding of *why* things are happening as they are, and as the book ends, you are still unsure what the mechanism for Sam's compositions is, making it hard to determine whether ***Fingers*** was intended to be SF or horror.

The plot's clever with enough twists to keep the reader interested, but lacks any real distinction.

> *Richard W. Miller, "Undistinguished Mix of Occult and SF," in* Fantasy Review, *Vol. 7, No. 7, August, 1984, p. 51.*

Interstellar Pig (1984)

Sleator's science fiction story is compelling on first reading—but stellar on the second. . . . It's a frightening, fascinating story with a real twist at the end. It could have been hokey or absurd, but Barney's low-key personality and understated wit keep the story from collapsing during his battles with outer space beings that read like something out of *Star Wars*. He's such a nice, bright kid that readers will believe that what he's describing is really happening. Sleator leaves clues for readers that things are not as they seem—the people, the nature of intelligence and even the rules of the game itself. The ending offers enough answers for a satisfying story but raises enough questions to keep readers thinking—and wondering—well past the last page.

Trev Jones, in a review of "Interstellar Pig," in School Library Journal, *Vol. 31, No. 1, September, 1984, p. 134.*

During the last moments of climactic struggle in William Sleator's exciting time-space fantasy *Interstellar Pig,* Barney, the 16-year-old hero, realizes that unless he can free himself from the membranous skin that surrounds him, he will remain a lichen forever. Even on escaping that gruesome fate, he still has no certainty that his merely human intelligence has successfully fathomed what the superior mental powers of his deadly enemies—Zulma, the spider lady, Jrib, the fish-man, and Moyna, the gasbreathing flying octopus—have not: the inner secret of the all-powerful Piggy.

Barney is a shy, insecure teen-ager whose excessive sensitivity to sunburn has made a seaside vacation with his parents even more boring. Things seem to look up with the arrival of Zena, Manny and Joe, for the glamorous, youthful strangers with god-like bodies and already perfect tans seem friendly and fun-loving. As his attraction toward the exotic neighbors deepens, so does Barney's sense of their strangeness—the suddenness of their movements, their oddly skewed use of English, their frantic interest in the old captain's house Barney's family has rented and, above all, their obsessive absorption in a board game called "Interstellar Pig."

Barney is unexpectedly initiated into this intricate and cut-throat game, in which creatures from fantastic planets vie for possession of The Piggy, a card named for its face-like pink symbol. There are a bewildering number of variables, but most perplexing of all is the finality of the self-destructing ending; when time runs out, all the losers and their planets perish.

Uneasy curiosity leads Barney to a buried object sought by the strange neighbors that links their arrival to a bizarre murder more than a century ago aboard a Yankee trading vessel. Chillingly, it appears to be a three-dimensional replica of The Piggy. Now involuntarily a permanent member of the game, Barney discovers the extent of its terror. Like The Piggy, the game exists off the board, in the real world. Zena, Manny and Joe are human disguises for Zulma, Moyna and Jrib, vicious aliens motivated by fear of the game's ending and ready to kill Barney for The Piggy. Alone and in the dark, he must literally play his cards right for survival.

All this adds up to a riveting adventure that should satisfy readers in the 12- to 14-year range, especially any who happen to be hooked on strategy games. Eery menace penetrates the humdrum normality of the summer holiday scene in a convincing evolution from unsettling situation to waking nightmare. Best of all are the descriptions of the game, both on and off the board. Its players are terrifyingly vivid, with a marvelous correspondence between their human disguises and their unmasked alien natures.

The suspense of *Interstellar Pig* is coupled with a highflying sense of humor that exploits the paradoxes of time-space travel and the baroque violence of the strategy game.

My only reservations concern the story's human characters and its ending. Would a boy as old as 16 be hanging around in Barney's position? And isn't there a gratuitously strong disdain in Barney's characterization of his colorless, stereotypically middle-aged parents? The ending, Barney's arrival at a hypothesis that calls The Piggy's bluff, is logically clever but anticlimactic, though the idea that the solution has been reached through Barney's human inability to accept the concept of a game of ultimate destruction is thematically appealing.

William Sleator is the author of nearly a dozen books for children of various ages. *Interstellar Pig* adds another good one to the list.

Rosalie Byard, in a review of "Interstellar Pig," in The New York Times Book Review, *September 23, 1984, p. 47.*

"Compelling on first reading—stellar on the second!" is amazing praise for a book weak on characterization and plot. Perhaps it is more the general blandness of young adult books than poor taste that led the *School Library Journal* and others to rave about this novel. The author does convey enthusiasm for the story to the reader, but not without stumbling.

Our first-person narrator, young Barney, unfolds the sequence of events that occur while he and his parents vacation in a secluded old house somewhere on the east coast. The beautiful trio who rent the house next door have sinister intentions toward Barney's family's summer rental, especially his room, where a sailor went mad around the turn of the century. Fascinated by the curvacious young woman and her two male companions, Barney joins them in a role-playing board game know as Interstellar Pig. Of course, it isn't a game; the neighbors are aliens and Barney ends up playing to determine the fate of the earth. The problem is that Barney, as narrator of his own novel, reports these events like a radio sportscaster. Since everyone else in the book is either an alien or under the spell of the aliens, Barney never gets to interact with any real people and real characterization cannot occur. His stereotypical parents never utter a non-cliched word. Neither can real suspense develop, since Barney must live to tell the tale and everyone else is a token.

The best thrill of the book is watching Barney deduce what we readers already know. Too bad he never surprises us by noticing something we missed. Over half the book is spent in "the tease," the setting up for the live game. At the height of the physical conflict, Barney discovers some hidden aspects of the game that look promising but never come off as they should.

Despite its flaws, the novel is a lot more worthy than YA novels like *Sweet Valley High #1,998.* The author is clever in his blend of bankable elements (for example: interesting stuff only happens when your parents are out of the house) and he has captured the SF technique of using characters as game pieces to advance an idea-plot.

Ashley D. Grayson, "Alien Game No Fun," in

Fantasy Review, Vol. 9, No. 4, April, 1986, p. 31.

This remarkable story is first a test of stamina, then a reward for perseverance.

Barney is an unprepossessing teenager who has gone to spend the summer by the sea with Mom and Dad. (He tells the story.) He becomes fascinated with the three bright young people in the next holiday house, and is pleased when they let him join in the board game that they play. This is highly complicated and, one would have said, beyond Barney's intelligence. It is concerned with the struggle of creatures from a variety of other worlds for the possession of the Piggy which, it appears, will protect the holder from the annihilation which will overtake the other players. All this is in some way tied up with the Captain who once lived in Barney's house and his unfortunate brother. More I will not say on this matter; the book is all too full of relevant detail and, besides, the surprises must not be anticipated. Let it suffice to say that there is a breathless and fairly unpleasant climax, after which the Piggy and those who have survived go into space, leaving Barney to (literally) clean up the mess.

Difficult as it is to get into the mood of the book, it is surprisingly readable, and the curious details of the game get right into the reader's system. Where the book may fail is in appealing to the reader's sympathy. It is difficult to care in the least about Barney's fate, and without that involvement the story loses some of its point. Mr. Sleator is a very clever writer, but the book leans rather too much on cleverness and not enough on humanity.

M. Crouch, in a review of "Interstellar Pig," in The Junior Bookshelf, *Vol. 51, No. 3, June, 1987, p. 137.*

Singularity (1985)

More wonderful weirdness from the author of **Interstellar Pig** and **The Green Futures of Tycho.** Harry and Barry Krasner of Boston are 16-year-old identical twins; Barry is domineering, boastful, and hates being a twin; Harry (the narrator) is timid, thoughtful, and—despite everything—devoted to Barry. So, when the Krasner family inherits an old house in Illinois from a virtually forgotten great-uncle, Barry immediately comes up with a plan for the twins to spend two weeks checking out this new acquisition. Harry, as usual, passively agrees. And soon the boys are prowling around Uncle Ambrose's creepy manse, viewing his enormous collection of odd animal-skeletons ("Hey! This thing has *six legs!*"), and finding the key to the strange "playhouse" out in the back yard. Could any of these discoveries be connected to nasty local rumors—involving disappearing animals—about the late Uncle Ambrose? They could indeed—especially when freshly shaved Barry gets locked in the playhouse for a few seconds . . . and emerges with five-o'clock shadow, sure that a whole day has passed!! The explanation? "Time goes faster in there," of course. . . . But *why* does time go faster inside the playhouse? Because the star-rock beneath the playhouse is a "singularity" (a.k.a. black hole); furthermore, on the other side of the rock is another universe;

and, from time to time, matter from this other universe (bizarre creatures, mundane garbage) is thrown into *our* universe—via the plumbing pipes in the playhouse. Wisely, however, Sleator doesn't allow whimsical sci-fi speculation to overwhelm this shrewdly balanced novel. Instead, the focus remains on the Barry/Harry tension—which escalates when Barry threatens to lock himself in the playhouse long enough to age a year (and escape twinship)! But, asserting himself for once, it's *Harry* who secretly, as Barry sleeps, undertakes the playhouse ordeal: while only a couple of hours pass outside, Harry survives the boredom and panic of a year inside the playhouse—watching the approach of a scary creature from that other universe, reading *Moby Dick, Anna Karenina,* and *The Way of All Flesh.* ("There was a certain satisfaction in the knowledge that I was doing a significant amount of the rest of life's homework.") A casual yet crafty interplay of fantasy and sibling psychology: disturbing, funny, and occasionally even touching.

J. L. G., in a review of "Singularity," in Kirkus Reviews, *Vol. LIII, Nos. 1-5, March 1, 1985, p. J-19.*

The surprise ending leaves some questions unanswered, but readers will appreciate both the tantalizing glimpse into another universe from an author who specializes in the extraterrestrial and the satisfying transformation of Harry into a self-confident young man. No subtle characterizations occur, but the book has a title with a fine double *entendre* and is an unusual, suspenseful yarn told by a master storyteller. (p. 321)

Ann A. Flowers, in a review of "Singularity," in The Horn Book Magazine, *Vol. LXI, No. 3, May-June, 1985, pp. 320-21.*

As he has in his earlier books, Sleator here conveys a sense of impending doom and builds it into both the realistic and the fantastic elements of a story in which those elements are brilliantly fused. . . . A riveting story.

Zena Sutherland, in a review of "Singularity," in Bulletin of the Center for Children's Books, *Vol. 38, No. 10, June, 1985, p. 195.*

Sleator again proves his singular talent for writing astonishing science fiction novels, although this new novel is not of the same caliber as **Interstellar Pig** . . . Sleator is remarkably able to explain the scientific complexities of his plot without impeding the narrative flow, and the story remains gripping through its stunning climax. Although the brothers are one-dimensional characters whose problems are resolved only through external forces, the quick pace and the chilling mystery will keep readers from putting this one down.

David Gale, in a review of "Singularity," in School Library Journal, *Vol. 31, No. 10, August, 1985, p. 82.*

The Boy Who Reversed Himself (1986)

Suppose there were other spatial dimensions, beyond the three that we know—how would we see them? What would they be like? Here, Sleator paints an eerie, fascinating picture.

Trading on the affections of her uncanny neighbor Omar, Laura persuades him to take her to the Fourth Dimension, a dangerous, surreal territory. Later, she in turn takes a young man there, whom she's trying to impress; they are captured by eight-limbed, three-eyed creatures—who toy with them the way thoughtless children toy with bugs—then rescued by Omar and a network of interdimensional guardians. Inconsistencies (knots either stay tied or don't, depending on where you are in the book), sloppy thinking (Laura makes 4-D food eatable by slicing it thinly), poor verbal descriptions and gratuitous sexism (guess the sex of the weird, powerful Fifth-Dimensional character who asks, "AMMMMMMM IIIIII PPPPPPRETTTTY?") mar an otherwise exciting adventure.

Similar in some respects, but much inferior to [Madeleine L'Engle's] *A Wrinkle in Time.*

> *A review of "The Boy Who Reversed Himself,"*
> *in* Kirkus Reviews, *Vol. LIV, No. 19, October*
> *1, 1986, p. 1520.*

[**The Boy Who Reversed Himself** is] a cerebral science-fiction thriller, cunningly constructed to keep the reader involved until the last pages, which are set sometime in the future. The tale is narrated in the first person by Laura as if it were a journal which must then be destroyed so that its contents will never be revealed—particularly to a publisher—a device calculated to raise the question "What if ?" As in **Interstellar Pig** Sleator demonstrates remarkable originality and ingenuity in postulating a theory and in developing it into a story.

> *Mary M. Burns, in a review of "The Boy Who*
> *Reversed Himself," in* The Horn Book Maga-
> *zine, Vol. LXIII, No. 1, January-February,*
> *1987, p. 62.*

Sleator has definitely broken new ground here. He has managed to create a fascinating tale in which almost two-thirds of the action takes place in a world that can only be perceived in fragments by the central characters and by the reader. He does offer explanations of the fourth dimension through analogies, but many average readers (including this one) will remain confused. However Sleator's brighter fans who liked **Singularity** (or Diana Wynne Jones' *The Homeward Bounders*) will feel right at home in this bizarre world and will enjoy learning how it operates along with the characters. Although Sleator uses a darker approach in this novel, those who loved the offbeat humor of **Interstellar Pig** and **Fingers** will find enough here to keep them satisfied (What other writer would explore the hallucinogenic properties of reversed ketchup?) Though not always a pleasant story to read, due mostly to the distasteful nature of the central characters, Sleator's tight construction and effective resolution make this a powerful tale for more sophisticated readers. Jeff Ayers, a Sleator fan and former YAAC member, responded, "Finally! A Sleator book with a really knockout ending! I've liked all his books, but the conclusions are usually weak. This is his best yet!"

> *Christy Tyson and Jeff Ayers, in a review of*

> *"The Boy Who Reversed Himself," in* Voice of
> Youth Advocates, *Vol. 10, No. 2, June, 1987,*
> *p. 93.*

The Duplicate (1988)

One day at the beach, David discovers a strange machine and takes it home, suspecting that it has the power to duplicate living creatures. A carbon copy is just what David thinks he needs: a replica of himself could go to his grandmother's, leaving the real David free to keep his long anticipated date with Angela. But when the duplicate ends up spending the evening with Angela, David realizes that life with his double could be very complicated indeed. And when his double reduplicates himself, David realizes his life may be in danger. What follows are his harrowing attempts to outwit his doubles. Spine-tingling writing and a well-thought-out plot combine to make a believable novel from the chilling premise; Sleator's mastery of suspense will leaves readers breathless.

> *A review of "The Duplicate," in* Publishers
> Weekly, *Vol. 223, No. 6, February 12, 1988,*
> *p. 88.*

When David observes a seagull inexplicably made into two gulls by a machine (labeled "Spee-Dee-Dupe") that he has found on the beach, it occurs to him that this may be a solution to his immediate problem: how to go simultaneously to his grandmother's birthday dinner *and* on his first date with Angela. Sure enough, the machine creates a duplicate David—who also claims to be the original. Sleator's premise is that the boys will do anything to keep their duality secret (they don't want to spend the rest of their lives as freaks), so they begin to negotiate elaborate plans to take turns at meals, school, and meetings with Angela. Enemies from the start (the duplicate seems to get the best of every bargain, including getting that first date), their enmity becomes more intense even as they cooperate in their increasingly difficult deception; suspense builds as David realizes that the duplicate is not identical to him but, rather, has a mad, vicious side that will dominate as he progresses to a speedy and inevitable end.

There is a satisfying amount of action as David wages clandestine and finally overt war in an abandoned building, with Angela finally becoming an ally; and the question of whether David will be driven to kill before he is killed is mildly harrowing. Though Sleator's characters, especially Angela, lack dimension, his plot is developed with a terrifying logic that should keep the pages turning.

> *A review of "The Duplicate," in* Kirkus Re-
> views, *Vol. LVI, No. 6, March 15, 1988, p.*
> *459.*

Sleator has done it again, writing an intense thriller, with horror building gradually, in which science fiction is blended skillfully with reality. Yet the gadget that sets up the story never becomes the story—the focus is always on David. At the moment of duplication, the copy is exact, with even identical memories. As time goes along, subtle differences emerge. It is to Sleator's credit that he manages to create three closely similar, yet distinct, personalities.

In this way, he avoids potential confusion when all three are together. Sure to satisfy Sleator's many fans and to win him some new ones. (pp. 113-14)

> *Susan M. Harding, in a review of "The Duplicate," in* School Library Journal, *Vol. 34, No. 8, April, 1988, pp. 113-14.*

Sleator comes through again with his usual tight plotting and believable characters. Even Duplicate B, who really has no redeeming qualities, is fully fleshed out and interesting—and less slimy than some of Sleator's baddies from previous books. Sleator somehow manages to make the impossible seem credible, and will keep readers involved right through the gripping climax to the last page. This book will capture those readers who like science fiction as well as those who just like a good story. A BBYA nominee.

> *Ann Welton, in a review of "The Duplicate," in* Voice of Youth Advocates, *Vol. 11, No. 6, December, 1988, p. 248.*

Strange Attractors   (1989)

Sleator incorporates the new theories about chaos and its generation into this dark, complex SF story.

Max awakes one morning to discover that he's lost a day. Furthermore, a brilliant scientist named Sylvan and his glamorous daughter, Eve, are after him to return something he doesn't remember taking. Even more confusing, Max meets a second, less colorful Sylvan and Eve who also want something from him. From various hints and clues, Max assembles an explanation: the missing instrument is a "phaser," a handheld time machine. Using it to change the past inevitably results in a bifurcation of time lines and a chaotic, lawless universe—as the first Sylvan and Eve have ruthlessly proven in their own time line. Now refugees, they must eliminate the other pair before they can settle here. Amid a welter of treachery, half-truths, second thoughts, and brisk zipping through time, Max foils the bad guys and ends up working in the lab with the more cautious Sylvan, while building his own phaser on the sly. To Max, Eve and the phaser are like drugs; though he knows both are deadly (she has matter-of-factly killed her unstable father), he just can't keep his hands off either.

Max may initially enlist reader sympathy, but he's a sneaky, vacillating character, unable to resist his baser urges. Like *The Boy Who Reversed Himself,* the story here is less memorable than the science behind it.

> *A review of "Strange Attractors," in* Kirkus Reviews, *Vol. LVII, No. 22, November 15, 1989, p. 1678.*

In the scientific world's currently popular chaos theory, "strange attractors" are mathematical things that drag systems into chaos. In Sleator's richly imagined fictional treatment of this theory, the strange attractors are people from a parallel universe: a brilliant scientist, Sylvan, and his beautiful daughter, Eve, whose reckless manipulation of time travel has plunged their timeline into chaos. Their search for a stable timeline brings them to our world,

where they must destroy their doppelgängers, the "real" Sylvan and Eve, or drag this world into chaos, too. Max, a teenage science student, is forced to become their unwilling ally or be destroyed himself. Sleator's marriage of chaos theory and the convention of time travel is an ingenious literary conceit beautifully executed and—in the scenes of time travel and of a future world in chaos—brilliantly imagined. To an exciting plot Sleator has added subtexts involving troubling considerations of morality and sexual tension, for despite himself Max finds Sylvan and Eve strangely . . . *attractive* while being simultaneously repelled by the moral corruption which the power of time travel has visited on them. The equation of chaos with immorality and the difficulty of Max's moral choice add a rewarding dimension to one of Sleator's strangest and most attractive novels.

> *Michael Cart, in a review of "Strange Attractors," in* School Library Journal, *Vol. 35, No. 16, December, 1989, p. 120.*

The publication of a new William Sleator science fiction adventure is always a welcome event for the author's legion of teen fans . . .

Sleator's talent for fascinating scientific manipulation is fully in evidence and exceptionally well conceived here—from Max's timeslip journeys and his worries about sending the future into chaos to his first-hand view of chaos itself—an awful place where technology is turned on its head and there are no rules and no safe, quiet havens. Less successful are Sleator's characters, who, though adequately individualized, obviously lack the loving, imaginative attention to detail Sleator has given to the scientific milieu. Still, along with the clever science, Sleator turns in some good suspense as Max plays hide-and-seek with his pursuers and struggles between the lure of illicit excitement and the mundane acceptance of the honorable. His final choice, a compromise of sorts, seems exactly right.

> *Stephanie Zvirin, in a review of "Strange Attractors," in* Booklist, *Vol. 86, No. 10, January 15, 1990, p. 991.*

The Spirit House   (1991)

Sleator here steps away from his usual science-fiction slant to write an eerie evil-spirit story that is both scary and convincing. Julie is relieved that Bia, a Thai exchange student who has come to live with her family, is not the earnest and bookish student he appeared to be in his letters, but she soon becomes suspicious that Bia is *not* the same boy they were expecting. At first charming, Bia becomes manipulative and secretive—and scared of the "spirit house" Julie's younger brother Dominic builds in the backyard to make Bia feel at home. Bia believes, as, increasingly, does Julie, that the house is inhabited by a vengeful spirit named *Phii-Gaseu:* "Look like lady head . . . lady head with no body and entrail coming from neck. Very bad spirit." The evil atmosphere is enhanced by the possibility that Bia and Julie may be imagining *Phii-Gaseu*'s revenge; all of the events in the story are entirely possible, if unremittingly frightening. A stormy climax is appropriately theatrical, and, just as Julie (and the reader) decides that the spirit has been successfully propitiated, there's a nervy twist in the last sentence. Title, author, and alluringly menacing cover art guarantee that this won't be a shelf-sitter.

Roger Sutton, in a review of "The Spirit House," in Bulletin of the Center for Children's Books, *Vol. 45, No. 2, October, 1991, p. 50.*

What happens if you make a deal with a spirit and neglect to leave something? Inevitably Julie finds out, and those who think it's something good have never read a novel by the wickedly imaginative Sleator before. The premise is clever and the characterization of Bia is convincing. However, the thematic confrontation of Western logic and Eastern superstition seems heavy-handed, while the book as a whole is sketchy and underdeveloped, more like a detailed outline than a fully realized novel. The climax is a shocker, though, and strongly suggests that a sequel is in the works—this one to be set in Thailand, perhaps?

Michael Cart, in a review of "The Spirit House," in School Library Journal, *Vol. 37, No. 12, December, 1991, p. 136.*

William Sleator's novel **The Spirit House** is full of interesting facts about an alien culture, . . . that of contemporary Thailand. . . .

William Sleator has obviously made a study of traditional Thai beliefs, and his portrayal of the young Thai student—down to the accent—is extremely accurate. A little cheating does occur, however, when the young student seems to equate the power of the famous shrine to the Four-faced Brahma of the Erawan in Bangkok to that of the spirit guardian of the spirit house that young Dominic has built. Folk-beliefs in Thailand are highly syncretistic, drawing on animism and Hinduism as well as Buddhism, the religion of over 95 percent of its population. But the fact is that the Erawan shrine is of Hindu origin and dedicated to the god Brahma, while spirit houses are of animistic origin and their spirits are considered to belong to an entirely different plane. It's doubtful whether a devoutly superstitious character like Bia would get the two confused, though it is not, of course, impossible.

Nevertheless, **The Spirit House** is so engaging, and its characters so believable, that one can readily forgive a few theological *faux pas.* It's a book that provides no easy answers—it's determinedly ambiguous about whether its action is super-naturally generated or just coincidence—and the ending packs a satisfying punch.

S. P. Somtow, "Something Weird in the Neighborhood," in Book World—The Washington Post, *December 1, 1991, p. 25.*

The problem with this book is that, in order to set the mood of common, everyday life throughout the story so that the ending will be more of a shocker, the situations are trivialized to such an extent that the whole thing is just too tame. It isn't really the end of the world if your friends are nasty to you, and zits on the face are hardly the embodiment of evil. Or has it been too long since I was in school? Not nearly as well done as my favorite Sleator, **House of Stairs,** but it will probably be read and enjoyed by his many fans. It shouldn't be classified as SF because everything that happens can be explained by rational means except the last line, and it ends so abruptly that readers have to fill in their own theories of what happened, some of which could be very down to earth.

Diane G. Yates, in a review of "The Spirit House," in Voice of Youth Advocates, *Vol. 14, No. 6, February, 1992, p. 376.*

Camille Yarbrough

1938-

American author of fiction.

Major works include *Cornrows* (1979), *The Shimmershine Queens* (1989).

A writer of stories for late elementary and middle graders which instill pride in African-American heritage, Yarbrough is praised for depicting family elders as valuable sources of information on culture and tradition and for promoting the building of self-esteem through education. With a background as an accomplished actress, dancer, and singer, she also uses her stories to encourage creative self-expression in children. Yarbrough works in the tradition of the griot, a class of traditional West African musician-storytellers who preserve and teach tribal history and values. She describes the griot as an "oral historian, preacher, teacher, social catalyst who uses song, rhyme, dance, and mime to illuminate and perpetuate, to revitalize and redirect the culture which he or she serves."

In *Cornrows,* a young girl and her brother are entertained by their Mother and Great-Grammaw who tell stories of life in Africa while braiding their hair. Their mother also sings them a song about famous African-American activists and artists including Martin Luther King Jr., Rosa Parks, Langston Hughes, and Aretha Franklin, and tells the children about the African origin and significance of the "cornrow" style of hair braiding. Critics have noted Yarbrough's use of dialect—"used but not overused," according to Allene Stuart Phy—and that the story is narrated in verse by the young Sister, reflecting her continuance of the oral storytelling tradition demonstrated to her by her elders. This theme of children learning from a family elder recurs in *The Shimmershine Queens,* in which 10-year-old Angie receives guidance and support from her 90-year-old Cousin Seatta. The story involves the problems faced by Angie in her daily life: her parents are separated, her mother needs her help in caring for her siblings, and she is ridiculed by other black children in school because she has a dark complexion and distinctly African features. She is given the lead role in the school play but faces additional ridicule as a result. Her visiting Cousin Seatta encourages her to "shimmershine"—to take pride in her features, talents, and abilities, and in the cultural heritage of her ancestors as well. The book has been praised for its realistic and sensitive depiction of such inner-city problems as violence, classroom disruptions, scorn for academic achievement, and intra-racial prejudice. *Publishers Weekly* has called it "a remarkable story about self-esteem and achievement, bringing to light the negative images of sexism and racism that face black girls who strive for success in schools." Like *Cornrows,* dialogue in *The Shimmershine Queens* is written in dialect, and the story is interspersed with African proverbs and customs. Yarbrough is also a songwriter and poet, and in

1975 was honored as "Griot of the Year" by the Griot Society of New York.

(See also *Contemporary Authors,* Vols. 105, 129.)

TITLE COMMENTARY

Cornrows (1979)

We've been really blessed in the Black Community because many of our writers and illustrators have done such important, serious books for our youngest (they are for us old ones, too!). These books have illuminated many important cultural behaviors and have become "cultural mirrors" for us and our children. The books have also become a creative vehicle for sharing with all children and adults information about us and *our own* descriptive perceptions about our African American family and community life. Then, boogity-boogity, here comes a brand new children's author, steppin out there with still another important picture book for us all. The publishers are to be applauded for indicating that this story-within-a-story is for all ages.

Cornrows, written by brand-new children's author Camille Yarbrough, is in part a skillfully written African

American Praise Poem in the African Praise Tradition. And for those of us who've not yet learned what that means, **Cornrows** will provide an introduction. The story and the song (which go hand-in-hand in our tradition) tell children how our culture and many of our traditions were preserved, despite the enslavement of our people. Ms. Yarbrough uses the Oral Tradition form, in which the major story is told by the family elders who convey to children the history and values of the group. Sister, the young girl-child in **Cornrows,** is already a story-teller-in-training, 'cause she tells/presents the reader the whole story. Camille Yarbrough is a poet, griot and a storyteller who has crafted a special, rhythmic and moving story for you and yours.

And let me tell you, the illustrations by Carole Byard dignify and give all due respect to the story! You will give all due respect to Ms. Byard when you see the way in which she portrays figures of respect like Rosa Parks, Harry Belafonte, Langston Hughes, Paul Robeson and others. It is clear that she did some serious, careful research. Her understanding and feeling for the story and for the traditions and history of her people have made the artwork compelling, descriptive and full of detail. The illustrations can be a vehicle for resourceful parents and teachers to "teach on." However, first read it, just read it. Hum some of it, too. Then hope that Yarbrough and Byard do another soul-inspiring book.

> *Geraldine L. Wilson, in a review of "Cornrows," in* Interracial Books for Children Bulletin, *Vol. 10, No. 8, 1979, p. 19.*

A warm slice-of-life from a Black two-parent extended family living in the city provides a thin frame within which to review Afro-heritage. Before Daddy, a handsome, virile head of the household, comes home in the evening, Mother and Great-Grammaw tell a younger sister and brother marvelous stories of ancestral life in Africa and sing a litany to Black-American activists—King, DuBois, Tubman, and Rosa Parks—and artists—Wright, Hughes, Robeson, Belafonte, and Aretha Franklin. Great-Grammaw also has memories of life back in Alabama and explains the origin and significance of the popular Cornrows hair style. Dialect is used but not overused.

> *Allene Stuart Phy, in a review of "Cornrows," in* School Library Journal, *Vol. 26, No. 4, December, 1979, p. 89.*

Using the cornrows hairstyle as an occasion for a paean to black culture, African and American, is a fine idea; but Yarbrough's execution lacks the humble virtues of the hairdo. First, though, comes the question of an audience: though the publishers set an eight-to-twelve age level and readers would have to be that old to pick up on even a reasonable proportion of the 22 names Yarbrough spins off toward the end (. . . DuBois, Garvey, Nzinga, Baldwin, Mary Bethune . . .), the book has a standard picture-book format and the framing story is told at a five-to-eight-year-old level: While Great-Grammaw does Mama's and the children's hair in cornrows, narrator Shirley Ann (or Sister) and her little brother Mike (or Brother, or Me Too) ask questions and Mama tells them all about the heritage the cornrows represent. The rhymed lines that Yar-

brough puts into Mama's and Great-Grammaw's mouths can be stiff and unconvincing ("I delight in telling you, my child— / Yes, you please me when you ask it— . . . ") and their later, chanting evocation can be too stagily poetical (" . . . where they flickered on the pyre . . . ") or muddily abstract. This is at its worst in a long passage about the people of Africa "working through" a spirit "to give life meanin. An to give praise," and about symbols "taking form" as sculptured ware, ritual masquerade, or braided hair. Where the mood and the message are counted more important than such reservations, [Carole] Byard's drawings will be found in conformity with both. But perhaps the words would work best in a dramatic or choral presentation at a school program.

> *A review of "Cornrows," in* Kirkus Reviews, *Vol. XLVIII, No. 4, February 15, 1980, pp. 213-14.*

Some books are so important they should be mentioned and celebrated every year. **Cornrows** is such a book. Originally published in 1979, it weaves together a rich tapestry of many different aspects of Black culture and heritage. Cornrows are the intricate braiding patterns in which Blacks (and now whites) often style their hair: "Great-Grammaw said the braids got that name because our old folks down south planted rows of corn in the fields. And the rows in the cornfields looked like the rows of braids that they fixed in their hair," explains young Sister. But it turns out that the history of these braided hairstyles goes even further back, back to Africa: "You could tell the clan, the village, by the style of the hair they wore," Mama says. A girl and boy learn about their special Black heritage from the stories and songs their Mama and Great-Grammaw offer them afternoons and evenings. A proud story, it should be read by all ages and all ethnic groups.

> *Ann Martin-Leff, in a review of "Cornrows," in* New Directions for Women, *Vol. 13, No. 3, May-June, 1984, p. 16.*

The Shimmershine Queens (1989)

[*The following excerpt is from an advance review of* The Shimmershine Queens.]

This is a remarkable story about self-esteem and achievement, bringing to light the negative images of sexism and racism that face black girls who strive for success in school. Angie, 10, gets the lead in the school play and faces all manner of repercussions: it will take her away from home, where she is needed; she is worried about speaking on stage; there are kids at school who constantly put her down and the play opens her up to more of that. The title, derived from Cousin Seatta's philosophy of life, is termed, "the get up gift . . . when you do sumpum good and you feel warm and shiny all over your body." It's a process that encompasses dreaming, creating and making changes in one's life through positive action. Angie's character may appear too "goody-goody" at times but the overall effect is essentially strong and meaningful. With African traditions and proverbs interspersed throughout the text, this book, by the author of **Cornrows,** reflects the anxieties, pressures and problems as well as the joys, compassion and love in families. It's a value-building, timely book, realistic in its presentation of the needs and aspirations of minority youth.

> *A review of "The Shimmershine Queens," in* Publishers Weekly, *Vol. 234, No. 24, December 9, 1988, p. 66.*

Angie learns to take pride in her African appearance and heritage.

Though ten-year-old Angie has always been shy and has been made to feel ashamed of her dark skin and African features, she knows that she can dance and has her secret dreams. Elderly Cousin Seatta, visiting New York, knows that Angie is gifted and encourages her to let herself "shimmershine"—take glory in learning and strength in the history of her people. Soon after, a new drama-and-dance teacher arrives; and through Angie's determination not to be intimidated by the tough kids in her class and through the teacher's ability to interest them in dramatizing a black American folk tale, the whole class is enriched.

Much in Angie's situation rings sadly true: her father has left the family but is in communication with them; her mother is depressed and relies heavily on Angie for childcare. But some threads are not gathered up (e.g., what became of the boys with bats who chased members of the cast on the day of the performance?), and Yarbrough often relies on stock phrases to express moods—every time characters are angry, they "space out" their words. Still, the messages here are worth repeating, and the plot moves well.

> *A review of "The Shimmershine Queens," in* Kirkus Reviews, *Vol. LVII, No. 1, January 1, 1989, p. 56.*

Yarbrough sensitively tackles the issue of color distinctions among blacks. Black dialect is used in dialogue throughout, and Angie's characterization, more so than that of some other characters, is consistent. (The appearance at the very end of Angie's father seems a bit contrived, although very welcome.) The vital part in which an arts program can play in a curriculum as well as in a young person's development is effectively demonstrated. Angie is a dreamer and wants a better life for her family, and perhaps this shimmershine feeling that she gets at the end will enable her to fulfill these dreams.

> *Jeanette Lambert, in a review of "The Shimmershine Queens," in* School Library Journal, *Vol. 35, No. 6, February, 1989, p. 83.*

Yarbrough offers a vivid depiction of the troubles facing students in some inner-city schools. Sensitive intraracial prejudices and the inverted values that make scholastic achievement something to scorn are portrayed in several riveting scenes of student disruption. This story carries a clear message about the dire need for students to respect themselves, each other, and education. The dialogue (rendered in black English) rings true, and the characterizations have depth—even the troublemakers have unexpected dimension. A brave book.

> *Denise Wilms, in a review of "The Shimmershine Queens," in* Booklist, *Vol. 85, No. 15, April 1, 1989, p. 1393.*

CUMULATIVE INDEX TO AUTHORS

This index lists all author entries in *Children's Literature Review* and includes cross-references to them in other Gale sources. References in the index are identified as follows:

AAYA: *Authors & Artists for Young Adults* Volumes 1-8
CA: *Contemporary Authors* (original series), Volumes 1-136
CAAS: *Contemporary Authors Autobiography Series,* Volumes 1-15
CABS: *Contemporary Authors Bibliographical Series,* Volumes 1-3
CANR: *Contemporary Authors New Revision Series,* Volumes 1-37
CAP: *Contemporary Authors Permanent Series,* Volumes 1-2
CA-R: *Contemporary Authors* (first revision), Volumes 1-44
CDALB: *Concise Dictionary of American Literary Biography,* Volumes 1-6
CLC: *Contemporary Literary Criticism,* Volumes 1-72
CLR: *Children's Literature Review,* Volumes 1-29
CMLC: *Classical and Medieval Literature Criticism,* Volumes 1-9
DC: *Drama Criticism,* Volumes 1-2
DLB: *Dictionary of Literary Biography,* Volumes 1-114
DLB-DS: *Dictionary of Literary Biography Documentary Series,* Volumes 1-9
DLB-Y: *Dictionary of Literary Biography Yearbook,* Volumes 1980-1990
LC: *Literature Criticism from 1400 to 1800,* Volumes 1-20
NCLC: *Nineteenth-Century Literature Criticism,* Volumes 1-36
PC: *Poetry Criticism,* Volumes 1-5
SAAS: *Something about the Author Autobiography Series,* Volumes 1-14
SATA: *Something about the Author,* Volumes 1-68
SSC: *Short Story Criticism,* Volumes 1-10
TCLC: *Twentieth-Century Literary Criticism,* Volumes 1-45
YABC: *Yesterday's Authors of Books for Children,* Volumes 1-2

CUMULATIVE INDEX TO NATIONALITIES

Nationality Index

CUMULATIVE INDEX TO TITLES

Title Index

Title Index

Title Index

Title Index

Title Index

Title Index

ISBN 0-8103-5702-X

90000

9 780810 357020